Contemporary British and Irish Film Directors

A Wallflower Critical Guide

First published in Great Britain in 2001 by
Wallflower Press
5 Pond Street, Hampstead, London NW3 2PN
www.wallflowerpress.co.uk

A catalogue record for this book is available from the British Library

ISBN 1-903364-22-1 hbk
ISBN 1-903364-21-3 pbk

Book Design by Rob Bowden Design

Printed in Great Britain by Biddles Limited, Guildford and King's Lynn

Contemporary British and Irish Film Directors

A Wallflower Critical Guide

Edited by Yoram Allon, Del Cullen and
Hannah Patterson

wallflower

LONDON and NEW YORK

Contents

Editors' Preface

Contemporary British and Irish Film Directors: A Wallflower Critical Guide is the second in a four-volume series of reference books. The first focuses on North American Directors, the third on Continental European Directors and the fourth on World Cinema Directors.

The entries that make up this volume cover both well-established and emerging directors who are currently, or have been recently, working in Britain and Ireland. Each of the entries include brief biographical notes, a comprehensive feature filmography, and engages with the film-makers' main body of work, highlighting their prominent themes, concerns and stylistics.

Certain inclusion criteria have had to be employed. We have tried to cover a large majority of film-makers who have had fiction feature films generally released for theatrical exhibition in the last twenty years or so. In some cases, film-makers who have had animation films or documentaries released have been included, but we have not been able to extend the present *Critical Guide* to cover all film-makers of non-feature-length or non-fiction films. This is not to give artistic or industrial priority to the fiction feature film but is purely a reflection of organisational constraints – we hope to cover animation, documentary and shorts in subsequent editions.

Furthermore, certain issues exist with regard to the inclusion of film-makers who are not native to Britain or Ireland. Our understanding of a 'British' or 'Irish' film director is someone making feature films within the British or Irish film industries, mainstream and independent. Thus directors such as Stanley Kubrick, James Ivory and Joseph Losey are all included here although they may not be British or Irish by birth. Some directors will appear in more than one volume in the series because a substantial body of their work has been produced in different countries.

Each of the entries has been specially commissioned from a wide-ranging mix of film critics and journalists, established academics and postgraduate students of film. Every volume of the *Critical Guide* series will be revised and updated to incorporate the directors' latest works and also to include new entries on emerging film-makers. Where discrepancies exist, the dates of film releases have been taken from the International Movie Database, and details on works that are stated as currently in production may be subject to change.

The views of each contributor are not necessarily those of the Editors. However, we would welcome amendments and suggestions should there be any factual inaccuracies present in the book. Furthermore, we welcome contributions on new and emerging directors and so feel free to contact us. Please send all comments and queries to CGCD@wallflowerpress.co.uk.

Finally, the Editors would like to thank all the contributors to this volume, and to everyone involved in the commissioning, research, editing and production of this unique reference resource, especially John Atkinson, Julia Bell, Hannah Ransley, Ian Haydn Smith, Peter Taylor, Sharon Tay and Lysandra Woods. A special mention should also go to Howard Seal for conceiving the original idea.

We hope you find these essays both helpful and stimulating.

Yoram Allon
Del Cullen
Hannah Patterson

19 November 2001

List of Contributors

AA	Anthony Antoniou	AL	Andrew Losowsky
RA	Richard Armstrong	EMa	Evan Maloney
JA	Jonathan Aronoff	DMJ	David Martin-Jones
PB	Paul Bamford	IM	Ian Mason
RB	Ruth Barton	CM	Carolina Matos
OB	Oliver Berry	BM	Ben McCann
MB	Mark Bould	SM	Scott McGee
DB	David Brown	JM	Jay Morong
LB	Laura Bushell	HO	Harvey O'Brien
BC	Bob Carroll	HP	Hannah Patterson
SCh	Sandi Chaitram	SP	Sean Patterson
SC	Steve Chibnall	BP	Barbara Pederzini
RCh	Robert Chilcott	JP	Jim Penn
JC	James Clarke	HPe	Hugh Perry
IC	Ian Cooper	KP	Keith Perry
JD	Jaqueline Downs	BPr	Becci Pritchard
FF	Fidelma Farley	HR	Hannah Ransley
BF	Ben Felsenburg	PR	Pauline Reay
MF	Martin Flanagan	MR	Matthew Reynolds
FG	Frankie Good	JR	John Rivers
SH	Stuart Hanson	SR	Sandy Robertson
THa	Todd Harbour	RS	Robert Shail
DH	Douglas Hildebrand	ES	Emily Shaw
AHo	Ann Hopkins	KS	K.J. Shepherdson
KHo	Keith Hopper	RHS	Richard Harland Smith
TH	Tanya Horeck	IHS	Ian Haydn Smith
CH	Chris Howard	MS	Martha Snowdon
DHo	Dawn Howat	MSt	Martin Stollery
NI	Natalie Ivemy	ESu	Emily Sumner
NJ	Neil Jackson	AS	Andrew Syder
DJ	Deborah Jermyn	ST	Sharon Tay
PJ	Peter Jones	RT	Roger O. Thornhill
SK	Sabrina Krinsky	TT	Tony Todd
TK	Tanya Krzywinska	JW	Jerry White
SL	Samantha Lay	JWo	Jason Wood
PLe	Paul Lesch		

Contributors' Profile

Anthony Antoniou is a freelance film writer with a special interest in classic and contemporary American narrative cinema. He lives and works in London, UK.

Richard Armstrong is a freelance film writer, Associate Tutor with the BFI, and Content Manager for a video and DVD distributor.

Jonathon Aronoff is a doctoral student at the University of Chicago, with a special interest in the theory and history of montage, historical representations in film and science fiction.

Paul Bamford is a freelance film critic with a special interest in contemporary Hollywood cinema. He lives in Chesterfield, UK.

Ruth Barton is a Government of Ireland Research Council for Humanities and Social Sciences Post-doctoral Research Fellow at the Centre for Film Studies, University College Dublin. Her special area of interest is Irish cinema.

Oliver Berry is a writer and film critic whose interests include 1960s and 1970s cinema, comedy in film and Alfred Hitchcock. He lives in London and Cornwall, UK.

Mark Bould is Senior Lecturer in Film and Media Studies at Buckinghamshire Chilterns University College, with special interests in Marxism, science fiction and American film. He is currently researching the films of John Sayles.

David Michael Brown is a freelance film critic and Production Manager at Visual Imagination. He is currently researching *Faster Pussycat. Kill! Kill!* and lives in London, UK.

Laura Bushell is a postgraduate student at Birkbeck College, University of London.

Bob Carroll is a film writer with special interests in James Bond movies, Sergio Leone, Tim Burton and Alfred Hitchcock. He lives in Edinburgh, UK.

Sandi Chaitram is a freelance film journalist with a special interest in independent films and digital film-making. She lives in London, UK.

Steve Chibnall is Head of Film Studies and Co-ordinator of the British Cinema and Television Research Group at De Montfort University, UK. He has published books on British crime cinema, crime journalism, British horror cinema, and the film directors J. Lee Thompson and Peter Walker.

Robert Chilcott studied Film at the London College of Printing. He lives and works in London, UK.

James Clarke studied Film and Literature at the University of Warwick. He currently lives in South London, working as a writer and film-maker. He has recently been researching the films of Steven Spielberg.

Ian Cooper is a film-maker and Lecturer of contemporary cinema and media at Birkbeck College, University of London, with a special interest in the horror film and American independent cinema.

Jacqueline Downs is Head of Film and Media at South Thames College, with special interests in American independent cinema, 1960s British cinema and melodrama.

Fidelma Farley is Lecturer in Film Studies at the University of Aberdeen, with special interests in gender and Irish and Scottish cinema.

Ben Felsenburg is a freelance news and arts journalist, specialising in film and dance criticism. He is currently working as Arts Editor at the Performance Channel.

Martin Flanagan has recently completed a doctoral thesis applying Bakhtinian theory to Hollywood films. He teaches Film at the University of Sheffield.

Frankie Good is a freelance writer with a special interest in women film directors in Australasian and American cinema. She lives in London, UK.

Stuart Hanson is Lecturer in Media and Film Studies at the University of Birmingham, with special interests in the development of multiplexes and post-war British cinema.

Todd Harbour is founder and moderator of *Mobius' Home Video Forum* and a freelance film and DVD critic with interests in genre, independent and world cinema. He lives in Austin, Texas.

Douglas Hildebrand recently completed his MA in Film Studies at Concordia University, Montreal. His interests include film genre, authorship and critical reception.

Ann Hopkins is a freelance film writer.

Keith Hopper is Junior Research Fellow at St Cross College, Oxford. He is currently editing a series of books on Irish literature and film.

Tanya Horeck recently completed a doctorate at the University of Sussex. Her thesis centred on representations of rape in contemporary literature and cinema.

Christopher Howard holds an MA in Film and Television from the University of Warwick and is currently researching East Asian and Japanese cinema.

Dawn Howat is a writer and freelancer in film production. She lives in Toronto, Canada.

Natalie Ivemy is a journalist with a degree in Media and Sports Science and an interest in British social realist film. She lives in London, UK.

Neil Jackson is a doctoral student at the University of Westminster, with research interests in screen violence, contemporary Hollywood cinema and film genres.

Deborah Jermyn is Senior Lecturer in Film Studies at Southampton Institute, with special interests in feminism and film, Hollywood cinema and melodrama. She is currently researching the films of Kathryn Bigelow.

Peter Jones teaches in the Division of Cultural Studies, University of Southampton. He has written on popular culture, modern art and architecture for a variety of publications.

Sabrina Krinsky is a freelance film critic with special interests in women directors and contemporary French cinema. She lives and works in Paris, France.

Tanya Krzywinska is Lecturer in Film Studies at Brunel University, with a special interest in science fiction, occult fictions and representations of sex in the cinema.

Samantha Lay is Lecturer in Media and Film at West Herts College and a doctoral student at Goldsmiths College, with a special interest in British cinema and society.

Paul Lesch teaches film at Miami John E. Dolibois European Center in Luxembourg, with special interests in Alfred Hitchcock, censorship, animation, and the relationship between film and society. He also directs historical documentaries.

Andrew Losowsky is a freelance writer, editor and photographer. He lives in London, UK.

Evan Maloney is a film critic who has also written for theatre and television. He lives in London, UK.

David Martin-Jones is a research student at Glasgow University. His main interests include narrative time in cinema and the philosophy of Gilles Deleuze, representations of city spaces, and British cinema.

Ian Mason is Film Programmer at the Hyde Park Picture House in Leeds, and also acts as Programme Co-ordinator for the Leeds International Film Festival.

Carolina Matos is a freelance journalist and film critic with an MA in Film and Television Studies from Warwick University. She has interests in Brazilian film, mutli-culturalism and television theory.

Ben McCann is writing a doctoral thesis on set design and spatial configurations in 1930s French cinema at the University of Bristol. His interests also include Japanese cinema, the politics and poetics of cinematic space and watching old Jack Lemmon films.

Scott McGee holds an MA in Film Studies from Emory University. He works as a staff member with the Turner Classic Movies cable network in Atlanta, Georgia.

Jay Morong is a freelance writer and graduate student at Boston University, with special interests in 1970s American film, cinema's relationship to theatre and television, and philosophy of film.

Harvey O'Brien is a Government of Ireland Research Council for Humanities and Social Sciences Post-doctoral Research Fellow working out of University College Dublin.

Hannah Patterson is Series Editor of the *Critical Guides to Contemporary Film Directors* and Assistant Editor at Wallflower Press. She is also a freelance film writer currently researching the films of Terrence Malick.

Sean Patterson is an actor and freelance photographer. He lives in London, UK.

Barbara Pederzini is a graduate from the University of Warwick, with a special interest in studies of spectatorship and new media. She lives in Italy.

Jim Penn holds an MA in Film and Television Studies from the University of Warwick. He is currently working in the television industry.

Hugh Perry is a journalist based in London, with interests in popular culture, particularly contemporary American cinema.

Keith Perry is a freelance writer with a special interest in psychology and film. He lives in London, UK.

Becci Pritchard is an undergraduate Drama student at the University of Bristol with a particular interest in gender, sexuality and genre.

Hannah Ransley is an editor and freelance film critic with special interests in British cinema and the avant-garde. She lives in London, UK.

Pauline Reay is Lecturer in Film and Media Studies at West Herts College, with a special interest in American independent cinema.

Matthew Reynolds is a graduate student at the University of Rochester currently undertaking a critical evaluation of the Hollywood Redevelopment Project.

John Rivers is a film graduate and marketing executive. He lives in Bristol, UK.

Sandy Robertson is a film and music journalist, with a special interest in old horror movies, 'lost' film, cuts and censorship. He lives in London, UK.

Robert Shail teaches Film Studies at the Open University and the University of Exeter where he is completing his PhD on representations of masculinity in British cinema of the 1960s.

Emily Shaw holds an MA in Film and Television Studies from the University of Warwick, where her research focused on masculinity and contemporary British cinema. Having provided educational opportunities for disadvantaged film-makers, she is now training to be a barrister specialising in media law.

K.J. Shepherdson is Senior Lecturer in the Radio, Film and Television Department at Canterbury Christ Church University College. Research interests include the work of Tony Garnett and the relevance of realism to critical analysis and television production.

Richard Harland Smith is a playwright, screenwriter and film critic. He lives in New York City.

Ian Haydn Smith is a freelance film critic and postgraduate student at the University of Westminster, with a special interest in contemporary Canadian cinema. He is currently researching the films of Ang Lee.

Martha Snowdon is a postgraduate student of film at the University of Southampton, with special interests in structures of audience identification and European film.

Martin Stollery is Senior Lecturer in Film Studies at Southampton Institute, with special interests in British film history, Arab cinema and representations of the non-Western world.

Emily Sumner is a freelance production designer and writer with special interests in underground and independent cinema. She lives in London, UK.

Andrew Syder is a doctoral student at the University of Southern California in Los Angeles, with special interests in psychotronic cinema, phenomenology and the relationship between film and society.

Sharon Tay is a doctoral student at the University of East Anglia. She is researching the applicability of Deleuze to feminist film theory and the horror film.

Roger O. Thornhill is a freelance film writer. He lives in London, UK.

Tony Todd is Senior Lecturer in Visual and Cultural Theory at the London Institute. He is currently working on his doctorate on David Lynch at Southampton University.

Jerry White is a doctoral student in Comparative Literature at the University of Alberta, with research interests in Irish and Quebecois cinema.

Jason Wood is a documentary film-maker and freelance film-writer currently researching the films of Steven Soderbergh. He lives in London, UK.

Introduction: Can a film have a soul?
by Mike Hodges

I am prompted to ask this question because of something I recently read in the *New York Times* in an article on film noir by one of their critics, A.O. Scott. He writes: "Too often ... style is a substitute for soul. But there is an English tradition of merging the two." Whilst I had always recognised this in some directors from these islands (youthful memories bring Carol Reed, John Boulting and Ken Hughes to mind), I had never before thought of film in such spiritual terms. Probably because the physical and emotional process of making them (which is what I do for a *living*) is far from spiritual: it is the antithesis of it. Film financiers are not too interested in a film's soul. For most of them spirituality means sentimentality, false and ruthless sentimentality. There's tons of money in sentimentality: that's why I call it ruthless.

While interviewing John McNaughton, an honest *un*sentimental film-maker (see Wallflower's companion guide, *Contemporary North American Directors*), for a television documentary earlier this year, he said something that struck a familiar chord: "You find in commercial film-making that often when you have a story with a heart, with a core, and you bring it into a meeting, they [the financiers] are onto it like heat-seeking missiles. Let's cut out its heart first and then we'll talk." Of course, the heart is something tangible, easy to locate. While the soul is intangible, impossible to locate, subversive. Mr McNaughton used the word *heart*; maybe he was reluctant to use *soul* because the word carries such awesome religious connotations? *That* soul has to be fought over, saved and defended, won or lost, and ends up either in heaven, hell, or limbo. As indeed can a film.

Whilst no mass-market industry is remotely interested in intangibles like the soul, many pretend to be. They are quick learners. Advertisers have adopted the same strategy as preachers and politicians to occupy our souls. They have slyly colonised the high ground vacated by these discredited dogmatists. They have replaced the spiritual icons with brand logos: almost every moral niche is now occupied by a brand image. The redemption, the revolution, is complete. All aspects of our daily lives are finally at the service of the selling machine, and that includes the cinema.

My latest film has recently finished its run in the UK. Every day FilmFour faxed me the box-office returns, and I was able to observe the emerging patterns. Two facts became apparent. First, there are no single-screen cinemas left in London where a film can sit for as long as there is an audience. That was the traditional way for intelligent films to make money while expending little on advertising. Word of mouth is cheap; films could sometimes play for years in one cinema. Most capital cities still have these venues, but not London. The second fact was more disturbing. When such a film leaves the capital it seems to plough into a cultural wilderness. The figures for cities such as Bath, Bristol, Manchester, Glasgow, Edinburgh, Ipswich, Norwich and Newcastle suggest (and they were confirmed by FilmFour as typical) that the audience out there for other than mainstream films is miniscule. I found that difficult to accept. I know there's a sophisticated, bright audience in all of those cities, yet there were the figures in black and white. It wasn't always thus, as this guide shows: there are over 300 directors listed in it. It is a clear reminder that we once had a thriving, vital industry that was our own, with a well-supported network of cinemas and audiences who identified with its films. Apparently not so now.

But how can any national cinema possibly survive without grass roots? Although some good films are made in Britain and Ireland, they often never see the light of a projector. Is it the fault of the distributors or the audiences? Market forces, like water, take the line of least resistance. Speaking personally, my last two films were destined for cinema's eternal darkness – although the latest of them, *Croupier*, miraculously escaped that fate. In short, it seems as if our national cinema circuit is now geared almost exclusively for American blockbusters. If this is so, why did it happen?

Every winter, spring, summer and autumn an American mail order company sends me a catalogue of their preppy clothes. They arrive with the certainty of the seasons. I don't know why they keep sending them; I've never bought any of their wares. However, I do derive great amusement from the romantic locations and the pretentious themes of each collection of clothes. The male models, chiselled and hunky, the females, rangy, all with unoccupied eyes, are ridiculously posed in places unintentionally hilarious. As a result, I can recognise the clothes at a hundred paces. One Sunday I went south of the Thames, close to the Tate Modern, for lunch. The bank is lined with smart restaurants; my companion and I chose one. It was a sunny day and the area was buzzing. Slowly it dawned on me as I watched my fellow diners and waterside boulevardiers that the scenes unfolding before me were from those very catalogues. Whilst I may have found them amusing, others patently did not. Those glossy pages matched *their* dreams in every detail. The conformity was deeply alarming.

That evening I was introducing one of my films and fielding questions from the audience. One young man asked why British producers were only interested in formulaic scripts. The answer was so obvious I batted the question back to the audience, interested to know what they thought. Another earnest young man said it was because we [the British] had lost our sense of identity. Did his comment illuminate my lunchtime experience? I am not sure. Clothes do not maketh the man – but they sure are relevant. For years I have watched the veneer on contemporary people (hair, nails, teeth, shoes, stockings, suits, tan, etc) move closer and closer to the sheen on contemporary cars. What is underneath I keep wondering. An engine? It *is* called power dressing.

When the first thing someone says about a film is that it looks good, I die a little. I genuinely do not know what that means. On investigation, the look usually turns out to be the glossy unreality of television and cinema advertising. For me, the influence of commercials on the cinema has been disastrous. On one thing we can certainly agree – the commercial has no soul. If a cinema film can have a soul – and let us admit it can – then it certainly doesn't matter what that film looks like. Perhaps the current obsession with a film's veneer is hiding something? A void maybe? A spiritual malaise? Keep it fast; keep it sleek; whatever you do keep boredom at bay. "Why has pleasure in slowness disappeared?" asks Milan Kundera. Why indeed? Boredom, slowness, seems to terrify us.

Not long ago, I met a novice director who posited that making a film, any film, was the new rock face for young people. It was at a party, my hearing is faulty, and I have often wondered if he actually said coal face. Surely not? But he did say any film. Does this mean the status of being a director, any director, is now more important than the film itself? Maybe it has always been so? What was it that drove me on, all those years ago, to become a film-maker? Altruism, a desire to change the world? Or access to beautiful women, money, power? In the beginning, the likelihood of my becoming a director was so improbable, and in reality the process so slow, it is hard to remember. It seemed so accidental. It was. It always is. All I do recall is that long before I got to work in it, the cinema had a profound effect on my soul. Whilst I enjoyed it as entertainment, I was always seeking something more substantial – and it always provided it. In those days Bergman, Fellini, Ray, Kurasawa, Kubrick, Antonioni, Buñuel, Bresson, Lean, Powell, Reed, Wilder and many more great directors were trusted by the financiers to bring in good films on a regular basis. I suspect only a few of these masters would get employment now.

Back to Mr Scott of the *New York Times* and his discussion of contemporary British and Irish cinema, which continues: "These films always seem to arrive, for American audiences at least, out of nowhere." If only he appreciated the irony of that nowhere. There is no longer any film industry to speak of here. The one we had was crushed long ago (with considerable help from our totally incompetent executives) by American competition. They colonised our distribution outlets and eventually choked indigenous filmmaking almost to death. Now, our great technicians are often just hired hands, employed when it is cheaper to make the product here, just like in a Third World country. And many of our directors live and work in America. With this in mind, Mr Scott's nowhere takes on a hollow resonance. A nowhere land? "He's a real No-where Man, Sitting in his No-where Land, Making all his no-where plans for nobody." Could the young man who said we had lost our sense of identity be right? There is no denying that we do not just look like Americans – we drink American, we eat American, we succour American blockbust-ers. And there is no denying that Americans are brilliant at creating addictions and feed-ing them. Ironically many of our young brains are actually encased in baseball caps, a game they probably know little about. No two ways about it, the marketing game is all about identity. Or is it the soul?

So what do we do? Do we try to emulate the Americans to achieve success at the box office? Like Wimpy burgers (the irony of that name haunts me) competing with McDon-alds. And is it worth the effort? In my experience, the price of this Faustian contract is high. It is not the film's soul that is at stake, but your own. So do our film-makers, as Mr Scott suggests, really have a tradition of merging style and soul, however steely that soul may be? And if they do, how in hell's name does the tradition survive in a climate of such cultural and spiritual aridity? I suspect the process has to be totally *subversive*. But I could be wrong – I often am. Let us just be grateful for some of the film-makers included within the pages of this collection – that we had Lyndsay Anderson, Tony Richardson and Derek Jarman, and still have Karel Reisz, Ken Loach, Mike Leigh, Sally Potter, Peter Greenaway, Neil Jordan, Ken Russell, John Boorman, Nicolas Roeg, Terence Davies, Peter Mullan, Lynne Ramsay and others who manage, against the odds, to make films with a *soul* – and an *identity*.

A

Carine ADLER

The work of Brazilian-born Carine Adler is an example of the excellence that has emerged *Under the Skin* (1997) from the British Film Institute/Channel 4 New Director Scheme. Trained at the Central School of Speech and Drama and the National Film & Television School in London, Adler wrote and directed a number of short films, including *Jamie, Touch & Go* and *Fever*, as well as the Channel 4 documentary *Edward's Flying Boat*, before making her feature debut, the stunning *Under the Skin* (1997).

Based on Estela Weldon's 'Mother, Madonna, Whore' (with whom Adler collaborated to attain the film's emotional authenticity), *Under the Skin* is a mesmerising drama which follows the downward spiral into sexual promiscuity of 19-year-old Iris (played compellingly by Samantha Morton in her cinema debut) after her mother's sudden death. Juggling themes of sexuality, loss of identity and sister rivalry, Adler never once passes judgement on her characters.

Evidently influenced by Ken Loach and Wong Kar-Wai, Adler's style is both fresh and uncompromising. Retaining the visual creativity of her short film *Fever*, she employs obscure angles and hand-held cameras. Never simplistic, this style serves to intensify Iris' emotional void. Medium and close-up shots create claustrophobia without being voyeuristic, and the juxtaposition of images serves to underline the confusion of her state of mind. This is most notable in the scene when Iris encounters a stranger in the cinema, which is overlapped by images of the cremation of her mother's casket.

Under the Skin won the Toronto Film Festival Critic's Award, the 1997 Edinburgh Festival Michael Powell Award for Best Feature and the Critic's Award. Adler is one of the few British female directors working today making films about female sexuality from the female perspective. **SK**

John AKOMFRAH

One of the founders of the influential production/workshop group, the Black Audio Film *Handsworth Songs* (1986) Collective, John Akomfrah, born in Ghana in 1957, began his directorial career as part of *Testament* (1988) the wave of young, black film-making talent to emerge in Britain during the mid-1980s. Like his contemporary, Isaac Julien, his film practice demonstrates a thorough grasp of academic debates in both film studies and black cultural studies. As an immigrant, Akomfrah has taken a particular interest in chronicling African diasporic identity, uncovering the personal memories and experiences of people largely excluded from historical inquiry. Juxtaposing actuality and dramatisation, sound and image, at their best his films are formally complex, coherent and communicative.

Akomfrah's first film, *Handsworth Songs* (1986), won him international critical acclaim and to this day remains a landmark documentary film. In his aim to 'document' the 1985 race riots in Handsworth, he turns against a simple recording of events and instead ambitiously attempts to ground these 'spontaneous' events within a much wider frame of post-colonial British history. In doing so, he also strives to capture the subjective (but nonetheless 'real') dimension of the hopes and fears that have characterised the experiences of British immigrants and their subsequent generations. Sinister synthesised music appends grainy reportage, and interviews and anonymous voice-overs give testament to current feelings of ghettoisation and repression. Within this framework the film also weaves elegiac snatches of old Carribean poetry and engaging interviews with the first West Indian immigrants. A brilliant political polemic, it admiringly but unsentimentally glances back at immigrant roots, in the process invoking a profound and heartfelt sense of loss and betrayal.

Whilst retaining something of the admixture of reportage and poesy that characterised *Handsworth Songs*, Akomfrah's two subsequent films, *Testament* (1988) and *Who Needs a Heart* (1991), turn primarily to drama.

It is tempting to view *Testament* as Akomfrah's most personal film given that its story concerns his mother country, Ghana, and the memories it still evokes for a British immigrant. The details of the story, however, make any attempt to trace personal references more difficult. The film concerns a female journalist who returns to Ghana to trace a friend and fellow student activist during the political turmoil of the 1960s. Deliberately problematic – making unclear which elements of the story may be fact or fiction – the film also juxtaposes the rationalising, empirical documentary the journalist is making with the lyrical images and voice that characterise her thoughts and feelings off-camera. Through this poetic contrast, it seeks to evoke the haunting sense of the journalist's irreparable separation from her missing friend and, by implication, her homeland. Although for the most part the film is an engaging and emotive meditation on the feelings of diasporic alienation, it does tend to slip into moments of overbearing piety – particularly when the drama becomes lost in languorous spirituality.

Unfortunately, *Who Needs a Heart* is a real disappointment compared to Akomfrah's other work. Intended as a critique of the career of black British activist Michael X, the film dramatises the personal stories that lay behind his political image. It uses re-enactments to document how the idealism and radicalism of X and his followers also nurtured narcissism and corruption. Sadly, the juxtaposition of political 'image' and political 'reality' is overtly facile and the film fails to offer a wider insight into the racial politics of 1960s Britain or to suggest what relevance a study of these events may be for a contemporary audience. Furthermore, given the tendency of the drama to edge into Warholian ennui, it remains difficult for the piece to sustain any audience interest.

Since the 1990s, with a shift in political climate and difficulties with funding, Akomfrah has turned more towards making 'conventional' documentaries, often financed with the help of international television networks. Despite being more 'linear' and less 'experimental', he has continued to produce exciting material. His film about Malcolm X, *Seven Songs for Malcolm X* (1993), takes the standard chronicle format of interviews and original recordings and mixes it with eerie, dramatic tableaux to subtly allude to something mysterious and mythic behind X's iconic status. Akomfrah has also begun to take his intellectual concern with diasporic experience into new subject areas. His lauded documentary, *The Last Angel of History* (1995) investigates the relation between allegories of alienation, displacement and abduction from black science-fiction and the experiences of African migrants.

Akomfrah's most recent film has seen him return once more to drama. *Speaks Like a Child* (1998) enacts a bisexual, inter-racial love triangle between three friends from childhood. Again with an interest in memory, Akomfrah splits the story across two time frames – adolescent sexual awakenings and a fraught 'reunion' in mature adulthood. Although it suffers from the staginess of made-for-television drama, the film is his most accomplished dramatic piece. The hermetic world of the three children, and the sexual bond that erupts between the two boys, are particularly well handled. However, the film rather disappointingly succumbs to excessive melodrama towards its climax – though this is hardly surprising given the deliberately provocative composition of the triangular relationship. Still, there is much to suggest that Akomfrah will continue his diverse, thought-provoking career, even if it has not quite fulfilled the promise with which it began. **CH**

Kevin ALLEN

Kevin Allen first established himself on the small screen as an actor with 'The Comedy Strip Presents…' alongside his brother Keith Allen, and as a television documentary film-maker. Critical success as a director came with unusually refreshing and energetic documentaries, such as *World Cup Hell* and *On the Road with Bobby's Army*. His feature film career, however, has been less impressive. His role as Andreas in *Trainspotting* (1996) has been the apex of the last decade, which included an appearance in *Spice World* (1997), and the direction of *Twin Town* (1997) and *The Big Tease* (1999), one as nasty and heartless as the other is insipid and self-satisfied.

Twin Town (1997)
The Big Tease (1999)

Twin Town, popularly dubbed 'the Welsh *Trainspotting*', was executive produced by two of the team responsible for the 'original' *Trainspotting*, Danny Boyle and Andrew Mackenzie. Astonishingly, it was intitially conceived as a worthy docu-drama based on real events that emerged during the making of BBC documentary 'Rotten to the Core'. It centres on drug-loving Swansea brothers (played by the Itans brothers, whose acting is a high point) who take revenge on their father's con-man boss.

During the production process, the film mutated into a black comedy; though dark, it encapsulates none of the slick, creative elements which raised *Trainspotting* above its violence and sadism. *Twin Town* is merely violent and sadistic; the lack of redeeming features in its central characters is wholly celebrated. At the time of its release, one critic concluded that it was 'enough to drive the most diehard defender of free speech screaming into the censorship lobby'. Allen himself has likened the film's style to 'the Coen Brothers on Ecstasy', a comment which implies delusions of grandeur, not to mention a bad supplier.

The Big Tease appears to have been an attempt to redress the balance; however, in replacing the violence, Allen goes for a satire with no bite. Gay, Scottish hairdresser Crawford MacKenzie (Craig Ferguson) is invited to the 'hair off', hairdressing's ultimate competition held in Los Angeles, but arrives to compete only to find that he has been asked as an audience member. In order to qualify, he must face some LA style obstacles: bitchy hairdressers, hard-hearted publicists and tough politicos. Displaying little charm or humour, he finally manages to enter with a couple of merely reasonable haircuts – no *Edward Scissorhand* surprises here. A mockumentary along the lines of *This Is Spinal Tap* (1984), *The Big Tease* lacks many of the more effective conventions of the genre. It also manages to add some ineffective ones: the camera gets stuck in the lift doors, and the 'director', who is often in the frame, has no discernible input. Unlike the cult classic *Spinal Tap*, it is only occasionally amusing. Too half-hearted for irony, too tame for kitsch, it has a reasonable baddie, but its 'hero' is neither outrageous enough, nor excels well enough in the competition, ever to engage the audience. **FG**

J.K. AMALOU

A graduate of the London Film School, J.K. Amalou's solitary feature to date is a derivative but energetic crime film that pre-dates the recent glut of British gangster films by a good two years. *Hard Men* (1997) alludes to an array of influences – *Mean Streets* (1973) and *Reservoir Dogs* (1992) among them – adding a few novel twists while never quite establishing a distinctive style of its own. The film's thin narrative draws on the familiar tale of a gangland hardman trying to escape his violent lifestyle. Tone

Hard Men (1997)

(Vincent Regan) is a debt collector for Pops Den (real life career criminal 'Mad' Frankie Fraser) who has just discovered that he is a father. Along with his associates Bear (Ross Boatman) and Speed (Lee Ross), Tone embarks on a final day of crime, gradually coming to the realisation that his associates plan to sell him out. However, what might have been a contemporary tale of betrayal and revenge is stymied by the film's wildly uneven tone. Veering between pitch black comedy and bland pathos, Amalou seems uncertain in which direction he should take his film.

The seedy, multi-ethnic London milieu of cafes, brothels and stark derelict warehouses is contrasted by almost absurdist episodes in which the protagonists kill, maim and steal, seemingly without arousing the interests of the law. The gang's appearance references the familiar, suited gangster look of the Krays era. However, generational criminal conflicts only serve to set up the final round of bloody shoot-outs, ignoring the rich potential the scenario holds for an exploration of the discrepancies between old and new forms of criminality. Caught somewhere between Scorsese's and Tarantino's take on the genre, Amalou's attempts to fuse the former's street level tales of redemption with the latter's pop culture savvy is only partially successful; Tone's split loyalties between his family and criminal associates is handled in far too perfunctory a manner to have any real resonance. Moreover, trivial, throwaway conversations about the pros and cons of Abba lyrics and 'fanny farts', while pointing directly to Tarantino's influence, serve little purpose beyond a self-conscious layering of post-modern detail. Indeed, this reaches its apotheosis when, complete with musical accompaniment, Tone sings a lullaby down the telephone to his baby daughter. Somewhere in the film, there is a worthwhile addition to the London gangster film trying to escape. Regan has an effective, scarfaced, hard man demeanour which might have been better served had the film not been preoccupied with aesthetics of gangster 'cool'. As it stands, Amalou's debut feature demonstrates the difficulties that face film-makers trying to establish a distinctly British, modern gangster film.

Amalou's second feature, *The Salami Man*, remains unreleased.   **NJ**

Jon AMIEL

At first sight Jon Amiel's oeuvre seems an unlikely and distinctly disparate collection. Moving from the gentle satire of *Tune in Tomorrow/Aunt Julia and the Scriptwriter* (1990), his debut Hollywood feature, to the spectacle and big action thrills of *Entrapment* (1999), in the first decade of his film-making career he has shifted between romance, comedy, action and period drama with unusual ease, demonstrating a versatility that can be better understood in the light of his diverse pedigree.

Born in London in 1948 and educated at Cambridge, Amiel started out in theatre, eventually becoming a director at the Royal Shakespeare Company, before moving to the BBC as a story editor. Whilst there he directed 'The Silent Twins', the 1985 docudrama based on the lives of June and Jennifer Gibson, and Dennis Potter's 'The Singing Detective' in 1986, a phenomenal success which won an array of international awards. This background in television and theatre has no doubt contributed to Amiel's reputation as a collaborative director who enjoys close working relationships with both actors and writers. A spell in advertising in the late 1980s, including two mini-dramas for the British government's controversial AIDS-awareness campaign, and his directorial film debut *Queen of Hearts* (1989) followed before Hollywood beckoned.

Although shifting between genres, Amiel's early work maintained a recurrent interest in the unusual and provocative, lending these films an element of risk or inclination towards the unexpected, which distinguishes them from many Hollywood productions. *Tune in Tomorrow*, based on a Mario Vargas Llosa novel, explores the social constraints of 1950s America, specifically centring on the relationship of a younger man and older woman, weaving a surreal and satirical relationship between the lives of these characters and the fictional ones of the radio soap opera that develops within it. The period drama *Sommersby* (1993), with its broody post-Civil War setting and denouement, had many of the trappings of a conventional romance, yet Amiel defied generic and institutional expectations in the film's ending, where the hero sacrifices himself, for capitalism as much as love. Widely seen as a remake of *The Return of Martin Guerre* (1982), the film has an air of myth about it that reflects Amiel's interest in the line between truth and fiction, as both characters and audience ponder who and what to believe.

Next he moved from love story to dark thriller to make *Copycat* (1995), a disturbing but original take on the serial killer movie. Holly Hunter and Sigourney Weaver were cast as the two investigative leads, complicating criticisms that the film took misogynist pleasure in the pursuit of its postmodern murderer, a killer who is replicating the crimes of the twentieth century's 'greatest' serial killers. This premise allows Amiel to open up a reflective look at the genre, making the process of watching familiar territory a critical and uncomfortable exercise. The sequence in which Hunter and Weaver examine scene-of-crime photos of the murdered girls is something of a generic convention, but Amiel's use of ponderous panning and classical choral music here leave the audience feeling distinctly troubled by it.

A return to comedy followed with *The Man Who Knew Too Little* (1997), where a case of mistaken identity propels Bill Murray into an assassination plot. However, Amiel's highest-profile work to date came next with his big-budget extravaganza about a pair of ingenious thieves, *Entrapment*. Amiel proves here that he can also turn his hand to frivolous but spectacular action: Catherine Zeta Jones bending and weaving her way through a web of laser lights to reach her prize is one of the most dazzling moments the genre has produced for some years. Predictions about where Amiel will go from here would be speculative but his career seems likely to continue to surprise and, with a recent production credit on *Simply Irresistible* (1999), to develop along new paths.   **DJ**

Dominic ANCIANO

Final Cut (1999)
Love, Honour and Obey (2000)

Before embarking on a directorial career, Dominic Anciano and Ray Burdis served as producers on a creditable pair of British genre films, *The Reflecting Skin* (1990) and *The Krays* (1990). More recently, they wrote, produced and directed the inventive BBC comedy series, 'Operation Good Guys', set in a London police station. Unfortunately, their directorial collaborations display ambitions that are drowned in a wave of pretension and indulgence; a real pity considering some of the thespian talent involved. *Final Cut* (1998) plays like a student film project dashed together by over-privileged novices who have just discovered the reflexive possibilities of the moving image for the first time. Stretched out over ninety minutes, the end result is often excruciating. Drawing heavily upon a series of improvised scenarios, the film relates the tale of a group of friends gathered at the home of Sadie (Sadie Frost) for a death wake. There, they watch a confessional documentary prepared by their deceased friend, Jude (Jude Law), which will ultimately tear apart the fragile intimacy of the group.

Exploring themes based around the opposition of reality and illusion (for example, all of the principles share the name of the actor portraying them), the film strives to say something about the way in which film or video imagery can record or distort concepts of truth. However, the loose structure simply collapses under the strain of repetition and banality. The film's imagery seems deliberately coarse and ugly to the point where it merely irritates. Furthermore, a talented actor like Ray Winstone looks distinctly uncomfortable having to anchor much of the improvisation. While the film might suggest that its characters' indulgent lives have been irreversibly transformed by the power of the image, it is difficult to see who could possibly care.

Love, Honour and Obey (2000) is something of an improvement, if only for the decision to play the film for broad laughs. On the other hand, as many gags misfire as those that actually work and it seems that the film would have been better suited to the half-hour slot occupied by Burdis and Anciano's more successful television comedy. Focusing this time on a London gangland feud, the sparse narrative is recounted by Jonny (Jonny Lee Miller), a young courier who yearns for the glamorous criminal lifestyle enjoyed by his lifelong friend, Jude (Jude Law). Again the film uses the conceit of having characters share the names of those playing them (Winstone and Frost both return from *Final Cut*), this time for no apparent thematic purpose. The title alludes not only to the criminal code of conduct but to the series of marital jokes (involving impotence, infidelity and S&M kinkiness) which litter the flabby plot. Essentially, the film is a procession of comic sketches, designed to appeal to the lad magazine mindset. The postmodern veneer (which merely intensified the smugness of *Final Cut*) manifests here as knowing parody of current British crime film staples. This is most evident in an absurd shoot out in which Anciano and Burdis themselves (as a pair of pub bouncers) jump out of a van in combat fatigues, wielding an array of military hardware. The film's frequent bouts of throwaway violence are too ineptly handled to have any real blackly comic effect, coming over instead as contrived and mannered. **NJ**

Lindsay ANDERSON

One of the more controversial talents of post-war British cinema, Lindsay Anderson's career was dominated by his strong political beliefs. Ranging from his critical writings and early work in documentary and social realism, to his more polemical and autobio-graphical work, Anderson was never afraid to take chances, which resulted in a colourful, if chequered, working life.

The son of a Scottish Major General, Anderson was born in Raj-era India in 1923, and returned to Britain to study at Oxford University where he experienced firsthand the inequality of established institutions – these would become the focus of his venom in later years. Shortly after graduating, he founded the influential film journal *Sequence* with fellow future film-makers Tony Richardson and Karel Reisz. Through his articles for the journal, as well as his pieces for *Sight and Sound* and *The London Times*, Anderson advocated a more socially conscious cinema. Stepping behind the camera for the first time, he became a major figure in the Free Cinema movement. Harking back to the Italian Neo-Realist movement and with a nod to the pioneering work of Humphrey Jennings, the collective aspired to react to the British film-making practices of that time, which all too often misrepresented public life. The result was a series of pioneering films, often non-narrative, which stripped away the pretence of a happy post-war society, highlighting the troubles faced by working and lower-middle classes. The crowning glory of this period was *Thursday's Children* (1953), a heartfelt documentary about deaf children, which won Anderson an Academy Award.

His first feature, *This Sporting Life* (1963), expanded on the aims of the Free Cinema Movement, and is one of the seminal 'kitchen-sink' dramas that revolutionised British cinema. Set amidst the tough world of mining and professional rugby league, it made a star of Richard Harris and secured Anderson's reputation as one of the major talents of a new, urgent cinema. Harris plays Frank Machin, a miner whose skill as a rugby player keeps him from working in a mine. His lack of popularity is made worse when he embarks on an affair with his landlady, whose husband was killed in the mine. Unable to reconcile his desire for his landlady with his bitterness over the life she has endured, Machin's arrogance and anger, both for the suffering of those around him and for his own feelings of inadequacy, lead him towards self-destruction.

Adapted from his novel by David Storey, *This Sporting Life* presented audiences with an all-too-credible anti-hero. A grittier version of the social climber played by Laurence Harvey in *Room at the Top* (1959), Machin's emotional and physical violence remains a powerful sight; in his stark evocation of a northern mining town, Anderson found a scarred landscape that matched the rocky terrain of Machin's damaged psyche.

Anderson followed the success of his debut with *The White Bus* (1966), a short feature originally intended to be part of a trilogy reuniting Anderson with Reisz and Richardson. When Reisz was delayed by another project, Peter Brook joined the triumvirate, although their films were never shown together. A precursor to the satirical work that brought him international acclaim, and written by playwright Shelagh Delaney, the film follows a girl as she leaves her depressing life in London and travels back to her Northern roots. Blending documentary-style with fantasy, the film is best described by critic David Thompson, who commented that it fitted 'no conventional genre, the offbeat humour often hits the mark as a non-specific satire on British moribundity'.

Following the collaboration with Polish film-maker Piotr Szulkin on the obscure fea-turette *The Singing Lesson* (1967), Anderson made what has become a classic of British cinema. *If...* (1968), based loosely on Jean Vigo's short *Zero de Conduite* (1933), charts the violent rebellion by a group of school pupils against their sadistic teachers at a public school. Malcolm McDowell plays Mick Travis, an unruly and rebellious character, who becomes the bane of the school establishment, incurring the wrath of the head teacher and the respect of his peers. A timely work – it was filmed as student riots were breaking out across the whole of Europe – *If...* is Anderson's finest and most controlled work. Never shying away from an outright attack on the oppressive and hierarchical nature of the British education system that Anderson himself was victim of, the film's success lies in its biting satire, blending the director's social-realist past with Buñue-lesque surrealism. It also broke a number of taboos at the time, including the first display of full-frontal female nudity to be passed by the British Board of Film Censorship. In Malcolm McDowell, Anderson found the perfect image of rebellion, one that appealed to Stanley Kubrick, who chose the actor for the role of Alex in his *A Clockwork Orange* (1971).

Having collaborated with Sherwin on the television play *Home* (1972), Anderson, Sherwin and McDowell reunited for the second instalment of the Mick Travis story, *O Lucky Man!* (1973). A rambling travelogue that takes pot shots at all aspects of British life, with varying degrees of success, Anderson's satire lacks the directorial control he displayed with *If....* The result is a didactic, though frequently entertaining, film.

Entering the workplace as a travelling salesman, Travers is sent to the North of England to sell his wares. Encountering small-mindedness and racism amongst unions and counsellors, and corruption within corporations and the justice system, he becomes the scapegoat for all of society's wrongs. Inspired by Voltaire's 'Candide', *O Lucky Man!* is an admittedly brave attempt to inject new life into the British cinema of the 1970s which, reminiscent of more recent times, was populated by second-rate comedies and gangster dramas. It employs Brechtian theatrical techniques such as the narrative's interruption by footage of the film's soundtrack being recorded and the moment in which Travers is cast as himself in the film of his own life at the finale. An admirable failure, it marked the beginning of an artistically fallow period in Anderson's film career.

Following a further television collaboration with Sherwin on *In Celebration* (1975), a praised adaptation of Alan Bennett's *The Old Crowd* (1979), and *Look Back in Anger* (1980) with McDowell, as well as a series of theatre productions, Anderson, Sherwin and McDowell reunited for the final instalment in the Mick Travers trilogy. *Britannia Hospital* (1982) is the nadir of Anderson's career. Replacing satire with broad comedy, the film fails on every level in its attempt to critique the state of the national heath system in Britain. Here Travers is little more than a cipher in the film, which is made up of a cast that would be more at home in one of the *Carry On* or *Confessions* series. Anderson shows little interest in anything more than presenting clichéd stereotypes and whatever points the film is attempting to make about inequality in contemporary society are superficial and anachronistic.

After a spate of television and theatre productions, Anderson returned to the cinema for *The Whales of August* in 1987. He left behind his political ranting for this quiet, stately and absorbing drama about the autumnal years of two sisters living on an island in Maine. Lillian Gish and Bette Davis offer fine performances, whilst Vincent Price adds light relief as an émigré who lives off the kindness of others.

Anderson's final film, made before his death in 1994, was a return to the style of his early work. *Is That All There Is?* (1993), a mock documentary about his own daily life, is very much the portrait of an artist as an old man. Covering his political views and the struggles he has faced in attempting to get financing for his films, it is a fitting end to an uneven career that nonetheless contributed much to the landscape of political film-making in Britain. **IHS**

Paul ANDERSON

Newcastle-born Paul Anderson graduated from Warwick University with a degree in film studies and an MBA. Early work as writer and director includes *The Spiral Cage*, a documentary about cartoonist Al Davidson, and the short drama *Speed*; he was also principal writer on the crime series 'El CID'.

His feature-length directorial debut, which he also wrote, is *Shopping* (1994), an attractive-looking (if very dark) tale of thrill-seeking car thieves, joy riders, and ram-raiders set in what is presumably intended to be a near-future London, although some

Shopping (1994)
Mortal Kombat (1995)
Event Horizon (1997)
Soldier (1998)

of the cultural references suggest that it is an alternative version of the present. This would-be *Clockwork Orange* (1971) for the 1990s is ultimately little more than a moody melodrama of sullen teenage rebellion and marginal criminal existence in a rubble-strewn post-industrial wasteland, interspersed with some well-staged car chases and scenes of violent destruction. The US version – some 18 minutes shorter – removed much of its pretentiousness along with some of the complexity of the characters and relationships.

Of the several movies adapted from computer games, *Mortal Kombat* (1995) best captures the kineticism and loopy disregard for conventional plot characteristic of the medium. It is a supernatural fantasy featuring a set-up appropriated from *Enter the Dragon* (1973), endless fight sequences, charmless protagonists, humour too broad to be funny, tacked-on platitudes about teamwork and proper motives, and acting so listless and rudimentary that Cary-Hiroyuki Tagawa's performance – more an embodiment of Oriental Evil than a character – seems well-rounded. The fights are unimaginatively choreographed but increasingly well-served by the camera, and the attractive production design and cinematography help Anderson's stylish fragments to cohere.

Event Horizon (1997) is a magnificently silly blend of science fiction and horror in which it is easy to spot elements appropriated from twenty or thirty other movies by directors as varied as Clive Barker, John Carpenter, Stanley Kubrick, Nicolas Roeg, Joel Schumacher, Andrei Tarkovsky, Fred M. Wilcox and Robert Wise. This restless bricolage is anchored by solid performances and, once again, impressive production design and cinematography.

Anderson's next movie, *Soldier* (1998), is something of a backward step. Rumoured before its release to be set within the *Blade Runner* (1982) universe (but not a direct sequel), the two movies are connected by a single passing reference to Tannhauser Gate, but screenwriter David Webb Peoples reworks the central character and situation of his *Blade Runner* and *Unforgiven* (1992) scripts one more time. Kurt Russell, uttering various grunts and growls and less than eighty words, plays a soldier trained from birth who is made redundant by a new, genetically engineered breed of warrior. Left for dead on a garbage planet, he awkwardly integrates into an improbable community of shipwrecked colonists, kills the new warriors, and saves his old comrades. Dubious CGI effects, inept montage sequences, and an excessive use of slow-motion to convey the significance of things, all detract from some attractive visuals. Russell's eloquent silence includes a couple of minor twitches that communicate an appropriate degree of despair.

Anderson is currently in production with *Resident Evil*, starring Milla Jovovich. **MB**

Eileen ANIPARE

A director-writer-producer team, Eileen Anipare (born 1967) and Jason Wood (born 1969) met whilst studying Film at the University of North London and discovered a shared passion for the power of cinema and an interest in documenting the work of contemporary auteurs in an entertaining and informative manner. In 1995 they formed the film-making collective ION Productions as a vehicle to help them finance and produce films that broaden the general audience's knowledge of the work of key contemporary directors.

They immediately started work on their first film, *A Short Film About Decalogue: An Interview with Krzysztof Kieslowski* (1996), a forty-minute profile of the Polish director. In a climate where documentary finance, especially for films focused on cinema, is very scarce, the team used their own funds to fly to Poland and interview Kieslowski shortly after he announced his retirement from directing. Although hampered by its necessary micro-budget, the profile provides a riveting insight into the mind of one of cinema's all-time great artists. It is also the last interview that the director gave to a non-Polish entity before his death in 1996. The film gained wide festival and arthouse exposure in the UK and Ireland.

With a little more money, but still their own, and off the back of their first success, Anipare and Wood were able to make their second film, *Trouble and Desire: An Interview with Hal Hartley* (1997). Shot in New York, it is built around their interview with the American director (*Amateur* (1994), *Henry Fool* (1997)) carried out in May 1997 in the New York offices of his production company. The film provides a fascinating insight into

Hartley's methods, influences and mind, and uses excerpts from his films to amplify and explain. Like their first film, *Trouble and Desire* received significant festival and arthouse exposure and enjoyed sell-out screenings in London and Edinburgh.

In 1998 the Canadian auteur Atom Egoyan was in London directing the Gavin Bryars opera 'Doctor Ox's Experiment' at the London Colliseum. Able to secure an interview with him, Anipare and Wood used it to construct their third film, *Formulas for Seduction: The Cinema of Atom Egoyan* (1999). The pair caught Egoyan in a relaxed and philosophical mood and the piece is even more polished than their second. In the wide-ranging interview, illustrated with extensive clips from his films – including his latest at the time, *Felicia's Journey* (1999) – he talks about the films and film-makers that influence and inspire him, the state of contemporary film-making, the price of both critical and commercial success, his love of opera and his Armenian heritage. With a full endorsement by the director, the film was bought by Alliance Atlantis the Canadian powerhouse distribution and production company, and backer of many of Egoyan's films.

In 2001, heartened by their increasing success and with all of their three films available on DVD, Anipare and Wood have started to plan further films on contemporary film-makers with whom they want to collaborate. Although production finance is still difficult to find, particularly in a 'cinematically challenged' culture like the UK, the team resolve to profile 'contemporary film directors whose output and influence has proven them to be worthy of the attention which major media organisations designate to more mainstream film-makers'. **RT**

Ken ANNAKIN

Ken Annakin was born in 1914 in Beverley, East Yorkshire, UK. After coming of age during the Depression and spending several years exploring Australia, New Zealand and the US, he served with the Royal Air Force in the first year of World War Two. Injured in the great Liverpool bombing, he found a new calling from his days as a mechanic when the British government recognised the importance of film and seized whatever talent was available for film production. Annakin's fate was sealed.

Beginning as an assistant cameraman, he worked on a series of documentaries. His first, *Pacific Thrust*, focused on America's struggle against the Japanese. Annakin was soon working under director Carol Reed, who exerted an important influence upon his early work. *We Serve* followed, which shed light upon the contribution of women to the overall war effort. Sydney Box, another notable mentor of Annakin's, prominent in both production and writing at the 'new' Gainsborough Studios, whose films had also conveyed the pains and drama of war, had urged Annakin at this time to use actors. By 1947, Annakin had all court scenes played out by professionals in his final documentary centring on the British criminal justice system.

Annakin's first films were a dramatic departure from the serious undertones of his earlier work; entertaining escapist comedies, their popularity reflected the desire of the public in post-war Britain to avoid anything too 'heavy'. *Miranda* (1948), a quirky romance about a mermaid's entrapment, was followed by *Holiday Camp* (1948), written by Box. The comedy, set in one of the 'newly established' holiday camps, launched a series of films specifically aimed at Britain's home market: *Here Come The Huggets* (1948), *Vote For Hugget* (1948) and *The Huggets Abroad* (1949). Of little artistic merit, many critics at the time sneered at the films for their overt simplicity; they nevertheless propelled Annakin to new heights. He went on to collaborate with one of the great fiction writers of the century, Somerset Maugham, and moving onto higher-budgeted efforts directed segments in *Quartet* (1949). Cecil Parker wonders who is the subject of his wife's poems; Dirk Bogarde takes drastic action when told his piano playing is below par; tables are turned on Monte Carlo shady lady Mai Zetterling; and kite-flying punctuates a romance, break-up and reconciliation. Like Maugham's psychologically probing *Trio* (1950), the cast included the cream of the theatre in 1940s London.

Annakin's drama, *Broken Journey* (1948), co-directed with Michael C. Chorlton, in which themes of existentialist thought are brought to light, tells the story of a small passenger plane which is forced to crash land in the Alps. Certainly no classic, the film has since been commented upon as a fascinating prototype for all subsequent disaster

Miranda (1948)
Holiday Camp (1948)
Broken Journey (1948)
Quartet (segment, 1949)
Vote for Huggett (1949)
Huggets Abroad (1949)
Landfall (1949)
Trio (1950)
Double Confession (1950)
Mr Know All (1950)
Hotel Sahara (1951)
The Planter's Wife (1952)
Outpost in Malaya (1952)
The Story of Robin Hood and His Merrie Men (1952)
The Sword and The Rose (1953)
The Seekers (1954)
You Know What Sailors Are (1954)
Land of Fury (1954)
Value for Money (1955)
Loser Takes All (1956)
Across the Bridge (1957)
Elephant Gun (1958)
Banner in the Sky (1959)
Third Man on the Mountain (1959)
Swiss Family Robinson (1960)
The Hellions (1961)
A Very Important Person (1961)
The Fast Lady (1962)

films. It is very much a period piece and most of the protagonists are affected by the recently-ended war.

Mr Know All (1950), the third film written by Maugham, centres upon a rather pompous passenger who lays claim to expertise on every subject, in particular fine jewellery. Concluding on a worthy note, the man falsely concedes making a mistake in identifying a piece of jewellery in order to shield a woman's infidelity. After successfully joining forces, Annakin's and Maugham's integrity as a director-writer team was recognised; critics who had previously dismissed Annakin's work as uninspired, shallow and trivial, suddenly found great merit. It was at this point that he began to receive the praise that he deserved yet would find hard to keep constant.

Next, he made the less notable Hotel Sahara (1951), in which Peter Ustinov gives one his best performances as the owner of a hotel set in neutral territory, whose fiancée plays both sides one against the other. Critics commented on the film's wartime stereotypes and its farcical manner. The Planter's Wife (1952), another wartime story, focuses on a socialite who marries a wealthy plantation owner. Displays of boredom soon lead to dreams of extra-marital affairs, until communist guerillas attack and the once social butterfly fights by her husband's side. Issues of loyalty and bonding in the face of the psychological burden of war are well-handled; setting a trend for later work, Annakin's previous attempts paled in comparison. Landfall (1949), also set in the early days of World War Two, reveals the trials and tribulations of an RAF pilot; another psychologically perceptive piece, it penetrates beneath the veneer of an ordinary soldier, an approach lacking in other directors' films at the time. Providing a break in the chain, the crime melodrama Double Confession (1950) proved more of a success. Peter Lorre added some US box-office appeal and Annakin's acute perceptiveness as to the workings of the human mind is once again exhibited.

It was in his first collaboration with Walt Disney that Annakin was given complete creative freedom. The result was two enjoyable and highly profitable historical adventures. The Story Of Robin Hood and His Merrie Men (1952), only the second feature to be produced by Disney studios, and The Sword and The Rose (1953), which appeared on screen soon after, won over audiences. Generating excitement with families worldwide, both are notable for their superb locations and cinematography – a distinctive hallmark of the remainder of Annakin's career.

You Know What Sailors Are (1954), a Cold War naval farce which falls short of Annakin's potential, was followed by Land Of Fury (1955), an average yet distinctive action-adventure set in 1820, superbly shot on location in New Zealand. Dramatising the taming of primitive surroundings by British pioneers, it succeeds in capturing a raw spirit. In a rather ludicrous comedic vein, The Seekers (1954), also filmed in New Zealand, focuses upon a naval officer who, upon stepping ashore is captured by thieves; he is then begged to stay to teach the natives the 'way of the white man'. The humour, though dated, works rather well. Three Men In a Boat (1956), an innocent if somewhat misogynistic comedy, tells of three men who become enamoured with a trio of young women whilst desperately trying to shake off their girlfriends.

More psychological themes are explored, in particular that of the mind's ability to become subconsciously destructive, in Value for Money (1955), which centres upon a young businessman who plunges into the nightclub circuit after receiving a large inheritance. Loser Takes All (1956), the first of two collaborations with writer Graham Greene, explores similar issues. A romantic comedy set in Monte Carlo, it involves a newlywed who is drawn by the lure of the renowned casino and throws his marriage into jeopardy. Annakin's next adaptation of a Greene novel became one of his personal favourites. The drama Across the Bridge (1957) is set around an embezzler's plan to evade the authorities, which backfires when he unwittingly assumes the identity of another fugitive. Annakin followed with Elephant Gun (1958), another treatment of the workings, hopes and delusions of the mind, about a young English woman who arrives in Africa to meet the safari guide she thought she loved.

The next phase of Annakin's career brought him back to the Disney fold to direct two memorable and successful location-shot features. The first, Third Man on the Mountain (1959), breathtakingly shot by Harry Waxman, combines the stunning scenery of the Swiss Alps with the moving story of a young man seeking to surmount the mountain, known as Citadel, which claimed his father's life. Both joined forces soon after in the scenic spectacle *Swiss Family Robinson* (1960), which became one of the highest grossing movies of the era. Adapted from the Johann Wyss novel 'Robinson Crusoe', the story, which some critics considered a little moralistic, centres on a family from Switzerland who are shipwrecked on their way to create an island paradise. It is notable for its distinguished cast, which includes John Mills and Dorothy McGuire.

Annakin developed a special appreciation of Walt Disney during their association and learnt that Disney had one guiding principle – how to move an audience. His mantra, 'I'd rather entertain and hope that people learn, than teach and hope that people are entertained', certainly had a bearing upon Annakin's film-making. The two adventurers never ceased to create new ideas; a visionary duo, they won much public and critical appraisal.

Annakin's one lack-lustre western followed, clearly exhibiting his unsuitability to this genre. *The Hellions* (1961), set in the 1880s, tells of a father and son who ride into a small South African town with vengeance on their minds. The locations and cinematography are of merit but not much interest. Next came the well-received war comedy *A Very Important Person* (1961), the tale of an irascible British scientist who organises his own escape from a German POW camp despite the aid of fellow prisoners. Again the themes of existential thought are touched upon, echoing Vicktor Frankl's classic novel 'A Search For Meaning', which was particular popular at the time.

The Fast Lady (1962), a purely escapist comedy starring Julie Christie, provides light-hearted humour. The story of a dogmatic civil servant and cycling enthusiast who becomes involved with a tycoon and his car-mad daughter, it is by no means Christie's greatest role. Still, her screen presence alone secured the turnout at the box office.

The 1960s were a boom period for Annakin during which he entered into the all-star, epic phase of his career. His versatile films, born during World War Two, gave him a headstart and it was only natural that in the spectacle-orientated 1960s, two decades after the war, film-makers were keen on capturing its history on film. It was around this time that Cornelius Ryan's non-fiction best-seller about the invasion of Normandy linked Annakin with a new mentor, Darryl Zanuck. Zanuck was to prove instrumental in the director's career, exerting much influence upon his mature phase. Many parallels can be drawn between Annakin and his mentors, and just as Zanuck had forged a new style at Warner Brothers Studios, so too had Annakin in his earlier days at Gainsborough. Zanuck's work clearly reflected Annakin's developing philosophies about film-making; his apparent belief that nothing was duller on screen than accuracy proved inspirational for Annakin's subsequent directing.

The dramatic *The Longest Day* (1962) was Zanuck's first independent production. Filmed by three directors – Annakin, filming the British army sequences, Andrew Marton and Bernhard Wicki – it was a mammoth, all-star recreation of the D-Day invasion that won a great public and critical reception. Many commented that it was the most authentic re-creation of what had happened. Filmed on real locations, it stars actual military leaders with English, French and German spoken and subtitled. Due to the violence restrictions that were in place at the time, the war sequences have been criticised for their lack of realism. The film nevertheless won Academy Awards for Cinematography and Special Effects as well as nominations for Best Picture, Art Direction and Editing. Many critics commented that the film was complex and noisy and like D-Day itself went on rather longer than absolutely endurable.

Crooks Anonymous (1963) followed, providing light entertainment with the tale of a thief who is trying to kick the habit but is tempted when he becomes a department store Santa Claus. Annakin's flair for comedic timing is much in evidence in this ironic, satirical British film. The next production, *The Informers* (1965), a drama in which a Scotland Yard investigator makes it his business to trap a gang of bank robbers, is a fine example of how Annakin liked to involve and excite his audiences with the mystery of his tightly woven suspense films.

Annakin's next World War Two action epic, *The Battle of the Bulge* (1965), highlights one of the great conflicts of the war. Many conferences were held between writer Phil Yordan and Annakin until they eventually hit their theme, anti-war. Some critics commented that it was an 'uninspired historical film', others that the battle footage was the best yet captured on film. Reaching the zenith of his career, Annakin soon joined forces with Zanuck again to create two machine spectacles, which exhibited the director's fascination for inventions. *Those Magnificent Men in Their Flying Machines* (1965), the comedy-action epic that tells the story of an air race from London to Paris, proved to be another top grosser of that year.

Annakin's idea, co-scripted with Jack Davies, was nominated for a Best Original Screenplay Academy Award and won a British Academy Award for Best Costume Design. Critics commented that the wonderful contraptions were worth the admission alone. Based on another original idea by Annakin, *Those Daring Young Men in their Jaunty Jalopies* (1969), a slapstick film set in the early 1920s Monte Carlo auto rally was, for the most part, viewed as a fun adventure. Dudley Moore and Peter Cook added laughter, although many critics felt that the film had little humour that really worked.

The Long Duel (1967), another in the action strand, if not one of his most noteworthy, centres upon an archaeologist who becomes embroiled in the troubles of a tribe of Indian nomads. *The Biggest Bundle of Them All* (1968) followed the next year, a weak comedy in which a crew of amateur criminals are conned into helping their captive pull off a daring robbery; Raquel Welch and Robert Wagner star.

Swinging back to action-adventure, *Call of The Wild* (1972), starring Charlton Heston at his best, is another in the long line of Annakin's panoramic films featuring a myriad of beautiful locations. Viewed at the time as a rather poor adaption of the 1903 literary classic by Jack London, it was filmed in Finland and tells of the struggle for survival in the rugged Yukon territory. *Paper Tiger* (1976), with David Niven, tells of a Japanese ambassador's son who must live up to his exaggerated tale of heroism when the boy is kidnapped.

The film explores themes of the strength of the human spirit and the ability to endure and excel. Not long after 1976, splashy, over-produced films were viewed as passé. At this point Annakin turned to American television, directing such made-for fare as *Murder at the Mardi Gras* (1977) and an adaptation of a Harold Robbins' novel, *The Pirate* (1978). Neither of these rather stagnant films show Annakin's potential. He returned with the adventure-themed feature *The Fifth Musketeer* (1977), a remake of the Dumas thriller, the classic about D'Artagnan's involvement in the mystery of Louis XIV's supposed twin brother, *The Man In The Iron Mask* (1939). Although played out by a stellar cast, critics and audiences alike found it rather disappointing.

Institute for Revenge (1979), a made-for-television science fiction pilot, did not spawn a series. Annakin soon forged forward with his feature career, however, with the drama *Cheaper to Keep Her* (1980), in which a divorced man moves into a retirement complex and lands himself a job as an investigator for a feminist lawyer. He soon discovers that most of the men he is assigned to investigate are recently divorced and in the process of being sued, a predicament he himself is facing. As with many of Annakin's later films, this production fell into the unremarkable category.

The Pirate Movie (1982), a family-orientated comedy, loosely based on the classic 'The Pirates Of Penzance' by Gilbert and Sullivan, tells of how the fantasy world of a shy and awkward young girl becomes a reality. Most critics snubbed the film and cited it as a perfect example of how a good operetta can be turned into an inane comedy. Similarily, the *New Adventures of Pippi Longstocking* (1988) was also criticised for its lacklustre musical production numbers. The magically gifted little girl, made famous by Astrid Lindren's book, finds herself shipwrecked in a small coastal town and begins a new life without adult supervision. Some critics argued that on the printed page Pippi was seen as a whimsical free spirit, but on the big screen became annoying and self-centred.

Annakin's final film, *Genghis Khan* (1991), which was to have starred Charlton Heston, never made it to the screen because the ill-fated Vision International production ran out of money during the making of the epic story. Although Annakin's career came to an end on a rather sour note, the adventures of his youth, nevertheless, led to an exciting and challenging career. His films have generated huge international success. His work, encompassing over fifty films, has left a vivid array of pictures in the archive, from upbeat comedies to gripping dramas to the productions for which he will be best remembered, the panoramic action-packed ensemble of far-flung adventures. **ESu**

Michael APTED

Perhaps the most successful and prolific British film-maker to establish himself in the 1970s, Michael Apted's career has continued to be strong and varied. Born in Aylesbury, UK, in 1941, he began at Granada Television working in documentary on the vintage strand 'World in Action'. Thirty years on and his commitment to the documentary form remains, side by side with his feature film ventures, one discipline arguably informing the other. His frequent forays into the thriller genre, has culminated most recently in the James Bond film *The World Is Not Enough* (1999) and the World War Two picture *Enigma* (2001). He has also made a range of biopics and assured dramas.

For British audiences, Apted's most important legacy has been his ongoing real-time documentary series for British television that began in 1963 as '7 Up'. Focusing on a group of seven-year-olds from all walks of life, every seven years since he has returned to chronicle the progression of their lives. Through a series of simple and elegant portraits inter-cutting between talking head interviews and observational footage, the series offers a compelling profile of the British psyche. It is both a personal and social documentary. Apted's investment in the documentary form has led him to direct a piece about native-American activist Leonard Peltier, *Incident at Oglala* (1992), and *Moving the Mountain* (1994) about the student demonstrations in Peking.

In the 1970s Apted segued from documentary into television drama, directing pieces such as 'Another Sunday' and 'Sweet FA', and collaborating with screenwriter Jack Rosenthal in 1982 on 'P'Tang Yang Kipperbang'. Apted's feature film debut, *Stardust* (1974), followed the hits and misses of Jim McClaine and his band The Stray Cats in the mid-1960s and was invested with a documentary spirit. In 1979 he teamed up with Dustin Hoffman and Vanessa Redgrave for *Agatha*, based on the 1926 incident in which the author Agatha Christie disappeared from her home without warning, setting in motion a real-life mystery. This playful film is as tightly wound as one of her own novels and particularly appealing for its lush cinematography, courtesy of premiere Director of Photography Vittorio Storaro.

Apted returned to the subject of music with *Coal Miner's Daughter* (1980), skilfully directing Sissy Spacek in a star turn as country singer Loretta Lynn. She won an Academy Award as Best Actress for the role. The film charts Lynn's life from the early years in Kentucky through to country music success and the tensions and strains that followed. For many, the film's most affecting segment deals with Lynn's country upbringing; had Apted been working in Hollywood in the 1930s and 40s, he may well have excelled in the 'women's picture' genre. Throughout his career he has demonstrated an affinity for natural environments and always seems comfortable in rural American settings, his foreign eye lending the material an added realism in its recreation of time and place. *Coal Miner's Daughter* also features excellent performances from Tommy Lee Jones and Levon Helm, formerly of the group The Band.

In 1981 Apted directed *Continental Divide* for executive producer Steven Spielberg. Starring John Belushi and Blair Brown, it was based on a script with a sense of Hawksian pastiche, written by Lawrence Kasdan. The narrative centres on a Chicago journalist who thrives on his urban life only to find himself transplanted to the Rockies for an interview with an offbeat ornithologist (winningly portrayed by Brown). For all the actors' energy and Apted's obvious fondness for a North American wilderness setting (which he revisited in *Nell* (1994)), the film is a less than surefooted exercise, although, as in all his work, he strongly locates the story, with each environment acting as a character in itself.

With the Moscow-set thriller *Gorky Park* (1983), Apted elicited an appropriately austere performance from William Hurt as the investigator of a series of murders that left victims faceless. Apted worked from a script by Dennis Potter based on Martin Cruz Smith's intricately plotted novel. Proving the value of David Lean's theory that it is healthy for a film-maker to keep coming out of different foxholes, Apted followed *Gorky Park* with *Firstborn* (1984), a well-crafted and potent domestic drama. The film features excellent performances, particularly from lead actress Teri Garr. As with all of Apted's work, a sense of realism pervades the sombre proceedings.

After a couple of misfires, notably the alleged comedy *Critical Condition* (1987), Apted embarked on his most consistent period with *Gorillas in the Mist* (1998). Starring the almost iconic Sigourney Weaver as naturalist Diane Fossey, the film compellingly presents her lifetime commitment to gorilla conservation. Set against a backdrop of expansive African locales, Apted never loses sight of the personal drama that embodies the more political aspects of the story; the romantic aspect of the narrative, however, does halt the film on occasion.

In the mid-1990s Apted directed a cluster of drama-thrillers. In the 1991 film *Class Action*, a father (Gene Hackman) and daughter (Mary Elizabeth Mastrantonio) – both lawyers – go up against one another in court. Mastrantonio's character is another of Apted's strong female protagonists and the action is most engaging in the scenes of her exchanges with Hackman. Apted teamed up with Hackman again in *Extreme Measures* (1996), which centred on the dubious medical practice of a doctor. The movie was produced by Elizabeth Hurley through Simian Films and Apted effectively used Hugh Grant's highly successful screen persona to emphasise the young hero's uneasy quest for truth. The film's grey pallor suitably enhances its menace.

Val Kilmer stars in one of Apted's finest films, the commanding police drama-thriller *Thunderheart* (1992). Set in and around a native-American reservation in the 1970s, it is based in part on an actual event. The drama turns and tightens around a culture clash that benefits from Apted's documentary experience. Kilmer puts in one of his best performances as FBI investigator Ray Levoi, who must find a way to balance both his professional duties with his emerging sense of personal lineage and roots – he is part Sioux. His partner 'Cooch' (Sam Shepard) is far less amenable to adapting to their circumstances.

The film is an edgy and impassioned piece of drama and a rare example of Hollywood engaging, in a contemporary setting, with the racial tensions between white and native Americans. Apted's documentary *Incident at Oglala* makes a suitable companion to this feature.

Having worked in the desert, Apted then moved to the shade and swamp of the American South with *Nell*, the story of a young backwoods woman who has had no contact with the outside world. Apted secures another strong female performance, this time from Jodie Foster as Nell, and Liam Neeson and Natasha Richardson feature as the couple who introduce her to contemporary life. Ravishingly shot, it continues Apted's theme of culture clash. This rural drama was followed by the urban Hitchcockian thriller *Blink* (1994), starring Madeleine Stowe in yet another powerful female role. Playing a woman who has her sight restored only to witness what she believes is a murderer making his escape from the scene of the crime, Stowe must convince the police of what she has seen. Aidan Quinn's cop believes her story and they soon fall in love. The film's real strength though is its application of morphing – Hollywood's 1990s discovery – which Apted uses in an attempt to suggest the way the world looks with new sight. Nothing is what it seems as people regularly slide in and out of focus and perception is constantly in question; the film testifies to cinema's undiminished affinity for stories about looking and seeing.

Apted has recently directed the nineteenth James Bond movie, *The World is Not Enough*, his splashiest example of an action-thriller yet. The film places Bond in the role of bodyguard to the daughter of a murdered oil tycoon and between her and the fiendish villain Renard, played with panache by Robert Carlyle. Bursting with the typical Bond set-piece moments, the film is made far stronger and significant within the series for its confident drama and Pierce Brosnan's new, edgier sensibility. Many consider the film's opening titles to be some of the best ever designed for a Bond movie. Apted has also received positive press for a pair of documentaries, *Inspirations* (1997) and *Me & Issac Newton* (1999) – the first on artists, the latter on scientists – about issues of creativity and problem solving, and the attempt to bridge the left brain/right brain divide.

Apted's most recent film, *Enigma* (2001), a likeable enough adaptation of Robert Harris' novel about the decoding device and its role in British World War Two intelligence, stars Dougray Scott as the crack code-breaker and Kate Winslet as his resourceful accomplice. He is also in production with *Enough*, which is written by Nicholas Kazan. He looks set to continue his capable and assorted career, underlined by a consistently strong and unassuming sense of storytelling and a particular commitment to presenting female characters who are wilful, independent and central to the drama.   **JC**

Christopher ASHLEY

An acclaimed theatre director, Christoper Ashley has carved a niche on the American *Jeffrey* (1995) stage as the purveyor of socially responsible 'message plays', receiving the Lucille Lortel Award for Outstanding Direction for 'Fires in the Mirror'. His only cinematic release to date, *Jeffrey* (1995), is based on the play that originally won him an Obie Theatre Award for Best Direction in 1992.

'I love sex. It's just one of the truly great ideas,' intones Jeffrey (Steven Weber) at the outset. The spectre of AIDS brutally impinges on his hedonistic lifestyle, however, and so celibacy seems to be the only sensible option until he falls for the local gym instructor, Steve, who is HIV-positive. Adapted from his own Off-Broadway play, Paul Rudnick's screenplay opts for a scatter-gun approach in its treatment of the contemporary gay experience. Ashley and Rudnick fill the film with self-conscious theatrical devices (speeches direct to camera, comic set-pieces, and even a cameo from Mother Teresa), but also deal with weightier issues such as the painful loss of friends and lovers. Where Ashley's direction succeeds is in the small vignettes: Sigourney Weaver as the self-help guru; Nathan Lane as the gay priest who believes that Hollywood musicals prove the existence of God; and Patrick Stewart who combines stoicism with a bitchy, barbed tongue. Moreover, *Jeffrey* provides a welcome flip-side to the worthy-yet-wooden *Philadelphia* (1993); here, AIDS and homophobia is explored through humour and self-analysis, and the film seems to revel in the balance it strikes between sincerity and silliness.

Ashley is currently touring America with his theatrical production of 'The Rocky Horror Picture Show'. **BM**

Richard ATTENBOROUGH

One of the great British actors of the century, creator of some of cinema's most enduring *Oh! What a Lovely War!* characters, a perceptive producer, and a director of ambition and epic scope, Sir Richard (1969) Attenborough – now in his seventies – is still a powerful presence in the film-making *Young Winston* (1972) world. Having weathered the various storms of several decades of cinema, with its *A Bridge Too Far* (1977) regular changes of perspective, morals, and personnel, he has forged a distinctive and *Magic* (1978) defiantly individual style. As an actor, Attenborough is best known for his portrayals *Gandhi* (1982) of low-lifes, criminals and cowards, exploring the murky underbelly of a British society *A Chorus Line* (1985) fraught with class barriers and social differences. Mostly modest British pictures, filmed *Cry Freedom* (1987) with small-scale, homespun detail, they charted the struggles of the ordinary man in *Chaplin* (1992) extraordinary circumstances – crime and murder, conflict and comradeship, love and *Shadowlands* (1993) war. His directorial interests are much more expansive, however, still driven by his fasci- *In Love and War* (1996) nation with human experience; often biopics filmed on a David Lean scale, they chart the *Grey Owl* (1999) lives of celebrated historical figures, rejoicing in cinema's dual capacity to deliver both as intimate drama and lavish spectacle. The understated performances Attenborough elicits from his actors contrast with the grandiosity of their treatment within his films, paralleling his fascination with the human faces behind public figures. At best, his style is capable of producing both the eloquent epic *Gandhi* (1982) and the intimate drama *Shadowlands* (1993), at worst, bloated style-over-substance vacuums such as *In Love and War* (1996). Although his ambition in terms of technical skill and narrative scope has more recently waned in favour of disappointing sentimentality, he remains a highly individual director, fascinated with a curiously old-fashioned mode of grand storytelling rarely seen in modern cinema.

Born in Cambridge, UK, in 1923, and fascinated from an early age with the theatre, Attenborough was working as a professional actor by his early twenties. Though baby-faced and small in stature, he was a gifted character actor and, during and following his war service in the RAF, he began to appear regularly in British films. His small but memorable performance in Noel Coward's *In Which We Serve* (1942), as a young coward drafted into the Royal Navy, demonstrated his early capacity for morally dubious characters. His most memorable performances remain that of the violent delinquent gang leader Pinkie Brown in *Brighton Rock* (1947), John Boutling's adaptation of Graham Greene's book, and the serial killer John Christie in *10 Rillington Place* (1971). Close partnerships with actors, writers, producers and directors, both in Britain and abroad, and his parallel career as an insightful producer on films including *Whistle Down the*

Wind (1961) and *The L-Shaped Room* (1962), coupled with his fascination with the power of cinema as a narrative and emotional medium, inevitably drew him towards his own directorial career, which began at the age of 46.

Oh! What a Lovely War (1969), Attenborough's first film, is a curious mix of styles. Based on Joan Littlewood's highly symbolic stage play of the same name, using popular songs of the day to recount the story of World War One, it makes for interesting comparison with his later work. Theatrical and heavily stylised (World War One is represented by Brighton Pier, to which General Haig is selling tickets), it contrasts broad set-pieces, large casts and effects-laden visuals with smaller moments of character and drama. A broad mix of lampoon, musical and morality play, the film teeters between surreal farce (Haig playing leapfrog, theatre audiences roused into song, death totals on cricket scoreboards) and grimy realism (the horrors of trench warfare, field hospitals). Too theatrical to work as cinema, it nevertheless displays some key themes – the fascination with conflict, the struggle for dignity, the schisms of class and rank, and the desire to tell stories on an epic scale with a wilfully emotional punch. It also demonstrates the visual ambition that Attenborough would continue to stretch throughout his career, exemplified by the concluding image, a dizzying crane and track back over a huge field of white crosses.

Young Winston (1972) marks Attenborough's first foray into historical biography, covering Churchill's childhood at Blenheim and early adulthood as a cub reporter in the Boer War. Juxtaposing various aspects of Churchill's life – politics and family, personality and persona – the film is part character study and part historical drama. This is a stylistic mix that all his films struggle to reconcile; the desire to tell a life story in a medium that lasts only a number of hours. The use of key 'dramatic' moments to structure the story, a biographical shorthand he frequently employs, can be both illuminating and deceptive, often saying more about the director's attitude to his subject than the subject itself. There is little doubt here where Attenborough's sympathies lie.

A Bridge Too Far (1977) similarly suffers from its sheer scope in its attempt to retell the sprawling story of 'Operation Market Garden', the failed Allied attempt to seize six Dutch bridgeheads behind enemy lines and bring World War Two to a swift conclusion. It involves an enormous range of stories, including those of British and American Airborne paratroop divisions, infantry battalions, a British tank platoon, the Generals commanding the action, the Dutch resistance, and even various German positions. This makes for a muddled narrative, although the quality of setting, action set-pieces and photography is difficult to resist. Small moments again illuminate the larger story. There are some excellent cameos from star faces, whose rapid appearances and disappearances highlight the chaos of battle (a technique echoed twenty years later in Terrence Malick's *The Thin Red Line* (1998)), and they provide a good contrast between British grit and American gung-ho. They make for satisfying parts, however, in an overblown whole.

Magic (1978), Attenborough's second collaboration with screenwriter William Goldman, is an odd sequel to this trilogy. Starring Anthony Hopkins, his most frequent leading man, it is the well-worn tale of a ventriloquist who is taken over by his dummy. Essentially a psychological horror, gloomily filmed to mirror Hopkins' mental breakdown and the dummy's schizophrenic connotations, the film is unsuited to Attenborough's grand style, although it continues to explore his interest in psychological struggles and internal conflict. His developing style reached its zenith with *Gandhi* (1982), undoubtedly his masterpiece, the fulfilment of a lifelong ambition, and a lyrical portrait of one of the twentieth century's great souls. Its most fascinating aspect is the determination to depict Gandhi as an ordinary man caught up in history, a man whose gift is simply the ability to feel and express the compassion that the British Raj refuses to countenance. Perhaps one of the few stories whose natural drama can carry the full weight of Attenborough's emotional vision, the film is about freedom, oppression and tyranny, the struggle of one man against an overwhelming power, and the demand for equality and dignity. Weighty, moral issues are conveyed with an understated, delicate touch, thanks in no small part to Ben Kingsley's masterful central performance. Charting Gandhi's struggle for equal rights in South Africa as a newly qualified lawyer, his return to India, and the eventual liberation of his homeland, the quality of acting is more than matched by Attenborough's direction. His skill is exemplified by the bookending framework of Gandhi's assassination and the deft command of dramatic pacing in which grand moments are contrasted with the simplicity of the ashram life. Some of the visual sequences – the blood-drenched Amritsar massacre, Gandhi's funeral pyre and procession, and the beautiful closing sequence as his ashes are scattered on the Ganges – are quite stunning. The directorial touches, such as the framing of an ageing Gandhi within huge spaces as a metaphor for his struggle, together with practically every narrative tool in the cinematic handbook, exemplify Attenborough's full-blown approach to storytelling. Long, grandiose and emotive, certainly, but an epic story that deserves its epic treatment, the film is a powerful manifesto of his style and standpoint, political, visual and thematic. It deservedly swept the board at the Oscars®, prompting a torrent of tears from its notoriously lachrymose director.

Another exploration of racial tension, inequality and human viciousness, told with customary epic sweep, *Cry Freedom* (1987) revisits this territory. The story focuses on a white journalist, won over to the cause of black activism in South Africa, who attempts to bring to justice the killers of a black friend murdered in police custody; he is persecuted and forced to flee by his fellow whites. Bold and compassionate, at times sanctimonious, with typically impressive set-pieces and use of landscape photography, the film champions the cause of the oppressed with emotional force and verve. Not quite another *Gandhi*, but a distant second. Attenborough's follow-up to *Gandhi*, a misguided translation of a Broadway hit, *A Chorus Line* (1985), charts the progress of an auditioning group of young dancers who are subjected to the humiliating invasions of privacy by a sadistic, voyeuristic producer. A range of cardboard characters (deprived kid from the ghetto, wannabe starlet, pompous prima donna) give voice to their fears and dreams, while dancing, through ridiculously scripted songs and flashbacks. Replete with embarrassing performances and directorial flourishes, the result is high-camp.

Attenborough's most recent films have all been historical biopics exploring long-held fascinations: the construction of personae; the collision of European and American cultures; the search for romantic and spiritual happiness; and the connections between childhood and maturity. *Chaplin* (1992) also explores Attenborough's love of theatre and film-making. A bold attempt to dramatise a life often obscured by self-made mythology, it follows Chaplin from his early days as a vaudeville performer, through the incarceration of his mother in an asylum, his arrival in America, his various marriages, his extradition from America during the McCarthy trials, and his eventual return for a Lifetime Achievement Award. Again employing a flashback structure, the film inevitably has to employ Attenborough's shorthand; it condenses whole periods into short scenes, rather glossing over the more troubling aspects of a performer plagued by self-doubt and insecurity. His interest in exploring Chaplin legends – the man and the icon, his British roots and American dreams – make for another interesting character study and Robert Downey Jr. delivers a fine central performance.

In Love and War (1996), an account of Hemingway's post-operative love affair with an American nurse in Italy, and *Grey Owl* (1999), the true story of an Englishman who passes himself off as an Indian guide, are stylishly filmed. Both are let down by their central performances, however: Chris O'Donnell cuts a feeble Hemingway and Pierce Brosnan is an unconvincing Native American. Sentimentality comes dangerously close to mawkishness, overshadowing Attenborough's objectivity. *Shadowlands* (1993), made earlier, is infinitely more successful. The low-key, gentle counterpart to Attenborough's epic style, it is the equal of *Gandhi* in many ways. The story of C.S. Lewis' love affair and marriage to American poet Joy Gresham, it features brilliantly realised portrayals of English repression and American sass by Anthony Hopkins and Debra Winger. Attenborough revels in contrasting the cloistered halls and faculty banter with Lewis' increasing emotional liberation as he experiences romantic love with Gresham, and the childhood innocence of her son. A parable of the importance of emotional experience, the film is a study in detailed drama, the honesty and quality of the performances avoid the sanctimony of his more recent efforts. Dealing in grand stories, brimming with content, Attenborough returns again and again to themes of love, class, race, war, politics, and above all, human matters of compassion, dignity, pride, and personality. Old-fashioned, perhaps, and not to all tastes, his style sometimes seems out of step with the modern film-making world. Forthright and candid, sentimental and sensible, he still has an edge.   **OB**

David ATTWOOD

David Attwood has worked mainly in television, directing the police series 'Rockliffe's Babies' and 'The Bill' from the mid-1980s into the mid-1990s, the soap opera 'Brookside', the Screen Two film *Saigon Baby* (1995) and the recent success 'Moll Flanders', for which he and its star Alex Kingston received notice in Amercia.

Prior to 'Moll Flanders', Attwood had made one feature, the comedy drama *Wild West* (1992), which focused on a Pakistani country and western group. Following the disasters and triumphs of Zaf (Naveen Andrews) – a character who wears cowboy-boots and a stetson – and his band as they play the pubs of Southall, the film is essentially comic and likeable. Success only seems imminent when they team up with Rifat (Sarita Choudhury), a woman who seeks escape from her violent non-Indian husband. The band use money from Zaf's mother to make the journey to Nashville (rather than their parents' homeland) to seek their fame but, inevitably, Rifat is picked out for stardom.

Although predictable in its plotting, with disasters positioned schematically throughout the love story narrative, and a falsely cheerful tone, the film hints at deeper themes, particularly the cultural hybridity evident in the mix of Pakistani, Southall and Nashville identities. However, issues of class and race are only briefly addressed because writer Harwant Bains had no desire 'to write a sociological tract about Southall that would impinge on the story'.

Visually, and occasionally narratively, the film parodies the western genre and its frontier values. Too reliant on evoking the optimism and dreams of its central characters though, it fails to fully explore this potential parallel. Avoiding a preachy tone, it opts instead for a light and amusing air, offering a chaotic and often endearing take on the gap between aspiration and reality.

His second feature, *Shot Through the Heart* (1998), was funded jointly by the BBC and the American broadcaster HBO, but not released theatrically. This is the story of two friends (played by Linus Roach and Vincent Perez) – one a Serb, the other a Croatian – who find themselves on opposite sides of the Bosnian war. It was well-received on television. **JD**

Michael AUSTIN

Michael Austin's directorial debut, *Killing Dad* (1989), makes an ineffectual attempt to be darkly satirical. Adapted from Ann Quin's novel 'Berg', it is a hapless ramble into the tribulations of lower-class family life. With a promising premise, set in an out-of-season seaside town with a cast of top British comedy actors (including Anna Massey and Julie Walters), the film could have been an effective black comedy. However, Austin aspires to, but does not achieve, the wit or accuracy of Mike Leigh. The first film funded by Scottish television, it is a desperate story of Ali, a hair tonic salesman (Richard E. Grant) whose dad (Denholm Elliott) is attempting to return to the family nest after deserting Ali as a baby. Still nurturing a deep grudge, Ali feels threatened and decides to kill his dad. Although Austin's first film could have been more tasteful, amusing and compassionate, it is unfortunately patronising and bland.

Five years later Austin returned to direct *Princess Caraboo* (1994), from a script which he co wrote. A palatable fable, successful as a family-friendly light comedy, the film is based on the true story of an esoteric girl (played by Phoebe Cates) who appears mysteriously in the West Country. Her identity is in question: is she a real Princess, or is she an over-imaginative servant girl who has invented this identity to parody the class that exploits her own? A newspaper reporter, Gutch (Stephen Rea), suitably falls in love with the alleged Princess whilst investigating her; however, few sparks fly in this unbelievable romance. Set in the nineteenth century, an era when begging was punished by flogging, the film's superlative moments arise from its satire of class-consciousness. With a darker perception and a more authentic portrayal of the era, Austin's second film could have been more provoking and memorable.

Austin continues to write screenplays. **NI**

B

Stuart BAIRD

Stuart Baird graduated from University College London with degrees in economics and *Executive Decision* (1996)
international relations. After working as Lindsay Anderson's assistant on *If...* (1968), *US Marshals* (1998)
he began a decade-long association with Ken Russell, working as assistant editor on
The Devils (1968), sound editor on *Savage Messiah* (1972); as editor on *Lisztomania*
(1975), *Tommy* (1975) and *Valentino* (1977); and as associate producer on *Altered
States* (1980). During the 1970s and 1980s he edited *The Omen* (1976), *Superman
II* (1980), *Outland* (1981), *Five Days One Summer* (1982), *Beyond the Limit* (aka *The
Honorary Consul*) (1983), *Revolution* (1985), *Ladyhawke* (1985), on which he was also
second unit director,
 Lethal Weapon (1987), and *Lethal Weapon 2* (1989). He received Oscar® nomina-
tions for the editing of *Superman* (1978) and *Gorillas in the Mist* (1988). Working as
Warner Bros.' full-time staff editor during the early 1990s, he supervised the editing of
Tango and Cash (1989), *Die Hard 2* (1990), *New Jack City* (1991), and *Robin Hood:
Prince of Thieves* (1991), among others. More recently, he edited *The Last Boy Scout*
(1991), *Radio Flyer* (1992), *Demolition Man* (1993), and *Maverick* (1994).
 If editing Russell's extravaganzas did not prepare Baird for directing contemporary
Hollywood spectacle, then editing Richard Donner's humorous, hyperbolic and typically
efficient action movies would have. His directorial debut (which he also co-edited) was
the cannily-cast *Executive Decision* (1996), starring Kurt Russell and Steven Seagal.
Despite an ending too many, it is one of the best airborne *Die Hard* (1988) imitators,
playing out its genre twists and tropes with admirable gusto. It is, however, marred by
the anti-Muslim sentiments that have become increasingly common in contemporary US
action cinema.
 Baird's next project was to revive Sam Gerard for a sequel to *The Fugitive* (1993)
called *US Marshals* (1998). John Pogue's screenplay opts to set an innocent, but
eminently proficient, man on the run, and then has Gerard's team – expanded to
include an African-American woman – the main focus of a hackneyed conspiracy narrative. Although the movie is centred on Gerard, his dogged and intelligent character is

rewritten as one who is merely determined and indestructible. Consequently, the end result is as tense as Tommy Lee Jones' lazy drawl. There are some exciting sequences, but the action is mostly laboured, reducing the pretensions of *The Fugitive* to mere plodding. It is perhaps significant that Baird did not edit the movie.

More recently he has undertaken an uncredited co-edit of *Tomb Raider* (2001). **MB**

Roy Ward BAKER

Born in 1916 in London, Roy Ward Baker's career stretches across four decades and a variety of different styles and genres. Having spent a dozen years making as many films, he diversified into popular television and continued to work in both mediums until the late 1980s. He began his film career at Gainsborough Studios in the 1930s, and this firm connection with mainstream British film was never broken. During World War Two Baker was with the Army Kinematograph Unit and worked with stars such as Boris Karloff and Claude Rains, and director Alfred Hitchcock. Directly after the war he commenced his long and fruitful directorial career with one of his strongest films, *The October Man* (1947), which features a landmark performance from John Mills. The first of several collaborations with Mills, *The October Man* deals with the story of a lonely, depressed man in a small hotel. Injured and amnesiac, he is suspected of a local murder, more through suspicion and doubt than any hard evidence. A brilliant mix of tension and character study, Baker shapes an atmosphere of fear and oppression that gradually builds with the film's narrative flow.

Flushed with its success Baker forged ahead producing 19 films over 13 years before helming popular television series such as 'The Avengers', 'The Saint' and 'The Baron' in the mid-1960s, and 'The Champions', 'Randall and Hopkirk Deceased', 'Jason King' and 'The Persuaders' in the late 1960s and early 1970s. From 1970 to 1980, he produced only eight films – not many for the prolific Baker but a lifetime's work for others.

The Weaker Sex (1948), an adaptation of the stage play, provides mild comedy in its observations of the day-to-day life of a well-to-do war widow, but loses something in the translation to screen. *Paper Orchid* (1949) is a passable thriller written by Val Guest about a young female reporter suspected of an actor's murder. The first of his two films of 1950, *Highly Dangerous*, saw Margaret Lockwood suspected of spying in the Balkans, but not to any great effect. For his second feature of the year, *Morning Departure* (1950), Baker teamed with John Mills again. The story of a British submarine hit by a mine and sinking to the ocean bottom, it was uncannily followed by a similar real-life incident. The film's portrayal of a trapped crew slowly realising that they may not all live is thus extremely poignant. Baker creates a terrifying impression, and a sterling cast of British stalwarts, including Richard Attenborough, Bernard Lee and Kenneth More, bring a dignity and depth to the characterisations.

The House in the Square (1951) was better known in America as *I'll Never Forget You*. A remake of *Berkeley Square* (1933), the time-lapse story of a man becoming his own ancestor and falling in love is small-scale but affecting. *Night Without Sleep* (1952) reconstructs a man's memory of a drunken night which may or may not have led to murder, echoing *The October Man*. During a short stint in America, Baker produced films such as *Don't Bother to Knock* (1952), an early vehicle for Marilyn Monroe about a deranged babysitter, and a 3-D revenge picture, *Inferno* (1953), with Rhonda Fleming and Robert Ryan.

Back in England he directed *Passage Home* (1955), a sea-faring melodrama of tension and lust about an attractive young girl aboard a merchant ship. *Tiger in the Smoke* (1956) transferred the melodrama to land as ex-army criminals searched London for hidden booty; it boasts an upright British cast including Donald Sinden and Bernard Miles. Next, Baker produced two of his finest films back to back. *The One That Got Away* (1957) deals with a serial escapee from British POW camps, Luftwaffe pilot Franz Von Werra. Only 12 years after the war, Baker (and his star Hardy Kruger) deconstructed the German stereotypes that had plagued English film and culture, bringing the same dignity to a story of England's enemy as he had to *Morning Departure*. Probably his most remembered work, *A Night to Remember* (1958) is the story of the Titanic's fateful maiden voyage. Now deluged with comparisons to James Cameron's unwieldy and sentimental 1997 epic, it stands the test of time – in much the same way that Baker's other work does. A consummate film, it benefits from a solid narrative, an authentic sense of time and place, and genuine depth of character. At the height of his career and ability, Kenneth More dominates proceedings as the ship's officer trying to stave off the inevitable.

A rush in the early 1960s was followed by a brief respite between 1964 and 1966. *Flame in the Streets* (1961) included another fine John Mills performance. A liberal trade unionist fighting for equal rights for West Indian workers has his progressive front shattered when his daughter decides to marry a black man. Baker recently commented that *Flame in the Streets* is 'a first-class sociological study of what the West Indian community was suffering during that period. A lot of it has changed for the better, but racism is still there, it hasn't gone completely, even forty years on'. Powerful and intelligent, the film struck a chord on its release.

John Mills worked with Baker on another two films. The first of them, *The Singer Not the Song* (1960), is the tale of a priest defying an outlaw in a lonely Mexican town. Lengthy and heavily character-based, the film includes aspects of homo-erotic tension. The war-time thriller *The Valiant* (1962) is about a mined battleship struggling to avert disaster. Not dissimilar to *Morning Departure* and *A Night to Remember*, it has few of their strengths. *Two Left Feet* (1963) stars a young Michael Crawford in an uneventful sex comedy about girl trouble. Baker spent the next three years working in television until a career move which redefined his career – and not always for the best.

Going to work for Hammer Films in the late 1960s, he made a decisive move towards the horror genre. *Quatermass and the Pit* (1967), a watertight adaptation of the television series, shifted away from the stolid direction of the first two films. Andrew Keir plays the first believable Quatermass, and an air of brooding creepiness builds throughout the film to a convincingly frightening final scene marred only by some below-par special effects. Overall, it is another outstanding accomplishment of tight direction and masterfully controlled atmosphere.

In 1968 Baker replaced Alvin Rakoff as director on *The Anniversary*. A black comedy which relies a little too much on its star's performance and less on style and script, the Bette Davis vehicle concerns an embittered one-eyed widow who gathers her sons to her side once a year to mourn her husband's death. 1969 brought the release of the not entirely successful *Moon Zero Two*, a space western which seemed immediately dated in a post-*2001: A Space Odyssey* world. Ingrid Pitt and Peter Cushing liven up *The Vampire Lovers* (1970), a 'lady' vampire tale that includes lesbian love scenes. However, the slow but steady decline of Hammer Films was gradually taking Baker down with it. *Scars of Dracula* (1970) treads the same familiar ground and is notable only for the fact that Christopher Lee and Dennis Waterman share the screen. Hammer's rivals, Amicus Films, poached Baker for several projects in the 1970s; more horror fare in the Hammer vein, most were no great improvement, except, that is, for *Asylum* (1972), a Robert Bloch-scripted collection of chilling tales based around a home for the criminally insane. Another Amicus project, *Vault of Horror* (1973), trapped five characters in the basement of a skyscraper to tell of their recurring dreams, an excuse for an all-star omnibus featuring the likes of Daniel Massey, Terry-Thomas, Tom Baker and Curt Jurgens. ...*And Now the Screaming Starts* (1973), a story adapted from David Case's novel 'Fengriffen', sees a young bride haunted by nightmares of the past. Peter Cushing does his best to bring some gravitas to an overworked but still enjoyable ghost story.

One late Hammer highlight was *The Legend of the Seven Golden Vampires* (1974), an outlandish mix of Kung Fu and bloodsucking, with Peter Cushing's Van Helsing tracking his old enemy Dracula to Chungking, where he is heading a vampire cult. Fun, with plenty of upbeat action, it still carries a cult audience, a reminder that this genre goes back longer than many people remember. The mid-1970s then saw Baker taking a break from film-making to return to television with stints on 'Minder' and 'Danger UXB'. His favourite project, 'The Flame Trees of Thika', made in 1981, starred Hayley Mills. He joined with two old-timers, John Mills and Peter Cushing, for a Sherlock Holmes television film, *The Masks of Death*, in 1984. His last theatrical film, *The Monster Club* (1980), is typical of his later work. An inventive and entertaining collection of stories with a simple framing device, it is well directed and cleverly scripted. A competent British horror, well remembered and well loved, it lacks both the tightness of his 1950s and 1960s work, however, and its dignity.

At the beginning of his career Baker tackled weighty issues, often striking a social chord with uncanny accuracy; his decision to move into television seemed to herald a subtle change of direction into specific genre work and pure entertainment. His skills as a director have remained consistent though, and he has elicited classic performances from many of England's leading actors, making an indelible stamp on British film history. In recent years Baker's influence and importance have been acknowledged: in 2000 the Bradford Film Festival staged a retrospective of his work. Now retired from film-making, he is still vocal about his own experience and knowledge, and his enduring love of cinema.   **IM**

Robert BANGURA

The Girl with Brains in Her Feet (1997) After serving his apprenticeship as a team director of the British hospital drama 'Casualty', and cutting his teeth in the film world with his delightfully whimsical 1995 short, *Sidney's Chair*, Bangura's feature debut, *The Girl with Brains in Her Feet* (1997), immediately catapulted him into the social-realist vein of Ken Loach and Mike Leigh. The tale of a young, mixed-race Leicester girl in the early 1970s learning to cope with adolescence, racism and a fractured home life, it conforms to many of the narrative templates of 1990s British cinema, and Bangura often treads a fine line between didacticism and sympathy for his protagonist. Making his heroine 'Jack' (a fine performance from Joanna Ward) a budding track-star, Bangura also manages to make some interesting points about gender stereotyping and conformity that transcends the occasional one-dimensionality of Jo Hodge's screenplay.

Bangura also captures a strong sense of place and time: Slade and T-Rex reverberate throughout the early proceedings and the claustrophobia of adolescence is neatly reflected in the Leicester environment. Some critics took offence at the change of tone in the film's second half when Jack experiments with sex and drugs, and one might criticise the way in which all adolescents seem to be portrayed as sexually prurient. Yet the film as a whole succeeds because the problems of growing-up are never trivialised. The running metaphor is a particularly clever one: Jack never stops throughout the film, rushing headlong into the perils of adulthood.

More recently, Bangura has returned to his television roots, making the children's drama 'Down to Earth' and the police drama 'In Deep'.   **BM**

Clive BARKER

Hellraiser (1987) Clive Barker is a celebrated name in the literary world, specifically in the areas of horror
Nightbreed (1990) and the *grande fantastique*. Yet his impact on the cinematic scene has been less impres-
Lord of Illusions (1995) sive – and prolific – since his commercial debut as a director in 1987. However, this may have more to do with the constraints imposed on him by both the film studios and the medium rather than any lack of enthusiasm or ability on his own part.

Born in Liverpool, UK, in 1952, Barker entered the world of film indirectly via theatre and fiction. Film was perhaps a natural progression for him, as yet another way of communicating his far-reaching ideas. His little-seen avant-garde shorts, *Salomé* (1973) and *The Forbidden* (1978), reveal many of Barker's preoccupations – sexuality, violence and religion – as well as reflecting his love of puzzles (which would resurface in his maiden feature). The black and white images occasionally recall the expressionist films of Fritz Lang and Robert Wiene – by way of Jean Cocteau's experimental work – but are nevertheless pure Barker, unencumbered by the restrictions of classical storytelling.

Later, the scripts he wrote for *Underworld* (1985) and *Rawhead Rex* (1986), a short story from his challenging 'The Books of Blood', were ravaged by director George Pavlou, and this motivated Barker to make the next adaptation himself. *Hellraiser* (1987) is the result, based on his own novella, 'The Hellbound Heart'.

Remarkably, Barker's first film is also his most accomplished. It is one of the finest horror films of all time, belying its apparent sado-masochistic and video-nasty trappings. Its story is a variation on the Faustian pact, but the movie also contains direct and indirect references to such diverse sources as ancient Greek legends (specifically Pandora's Box), Frankenstein, Hamlet and Snow White. A dissection of the nuclear family from the

1980s with incestuous overtones, *Hellraiser* is extremely visceral in its content – 'Chek-hov with gore' was how one reviewer described it. However, all the skinless bodies and blood never detract from the truly dark atmosphere, which is supplemented whenever the sadistic Cenobite demons are present. It is to Barker's credit that these are his most memorable characters despite the fact that they are only allowed minimal screen time – their leader 'Pinhead' is now a pop horror icon alongside Jason and Freddy. *Hellrais-er*'s ascendancy ensured that sequels would follow, which gradually Americanised the mythos. Barker was involved in these in a purely advisory capacity.

Nightbreed (1990), again from one of his books – 'Cabal' – is a creditable endeav-our, examining the condition of celluloid monsters from an original perspective. Like *Alien Nation* (1988) before it, this film confronts racism and bigotry by substituting the exotic – in this instance the undead – for the true victims of prejudice (it is surely no coincidence that the Nightbreed are located in redneck territory). There is no question as to who the real monsters are, but the heavy-handed battle near the end overstresses this doctrine. In addition, the fragmented narrative and weak performances (particularly from erstwhile director David Cronenberg and lead actor Craig Sheffer), combined with studio interfer-ence, affect Barker's good intentions. Following this catastrophe he emigrated to Califor-nia seeking greater control over his work.

Barker executively produced, rather than directed, his other most successful film, *Candyman* (1992), based on his short story about a hook-handed killer who appears when you look in a mirror and say his name five times. The film raises salient questions about the nature of urban folklore: if enough people believe in something, does that make it real? But by shifting the setting from Liverpool to Chicago, director Bernard Rose also embraces issues of culture and class, the latter most notably through the institutions of academia. Tony Todd gives a strong performance as Barker's tragic villain and Virginia Madsen is perfect as his reincarnated love. Some mention should also be made of Philip Glass' superlative score.

With *Lord of Illusions* (1995), Barker returned to the director's chair. A gratifying, if somewhat laboured, chiller, this piece attempts to marry the noir and horror genres with little success. 'Quantum Leap' star Scott Bakula is Barker's archetypal detective hero Harry D'Amour, and Bond-vixen Famke Janssen is his love interest, exploring the origins of real magic against a backdrop of depthless stage shows. Yet not even the pre-release alterations, made after test screenings, could weed out the blemishes.

Barker has not directed since, preferring instead to concentrate on the written word in books such as 'Everville', 'Sacrament' and 'Galilee'. Tellingly, perhaps, Barker's most recent novel, 'Coldheart Canyon', is set in Hollywood.   **PB**

Mike BARKER

With a background in television, Mike Barker's output includes 'When the Fat Lady *The James Gang* (1997) Sings', 'Go Back Out', 'The Tenant of Wildfell Hall' and 'Silent Witness'. The tone and *Best Laid Plans* (1999) composition of the latter (a BBC forensic science drama) has seeped into Barker's film output, and both *The James Gang* (1997) and *Best Laid Plans* (1999) evoke this strong sense of the grotesque and the unseen rooted in realistic settings.

His debut feature, *The James Gang*, immediately flags itself as a British neo-noir thriller. Its credentials are impeccable: kinetic cinematography, sub-*Lock, Stock* sound-track, and the kind of flashy directorial flourishes that have become de rigueur in these type of films. The story, however, lets the whole venture down. In a 'the-family-that-steals-together-stays-together' narrative, Helen McCrory plays the matriarch who plots to hold her family together by launching one last crime spree. Her husband (John Hannah) remains unconvinced, as all the while a PC (Toni Collette) slowly tightens the noose. It is an intriguing prospect, but one which never gels into a cohesive whole. As in so many crime films, characterisation is lost amongst the flashy visuals and knowing irony. It is thus hard to see why the James children should ever become involved in the whole scheme in the first place.

Best Laid Plans is a taut thriller lasting little over ninety minutes and highly suc-cessful in condensing its intricate plot and carefully sketched characters into a recognis-able time and place. Set in small town Tropico, USA, Nick and Bryce (Alessandro Nivola and Josh Brolin) are drinking in a bar when Lissa (Reese Witherspoon) walks in. After much extended plot convolution, Bryce is accused of her kidnapping and assault. Such a synopsis does not do justice to the myriad of twists and turns that batter the audience senseless. Rarely has a film revelled in its own complexities to tease its audience into first accepting and then rejecting the reality that seems to underpin the narrative. The film thus lives or dies by these twists, and Barker will either irritate or enlighten. Pitched somewhere between *Red Rock West* (1992) and *The Usual Suspects* (1995), the production design is exemplary: a scummy nowheresville that recalls Edward Hopper and the very best of film-noir iconography. The performances too are quietly effective whilst Barker's static camera is skilled at capturing the gritty claustrophobia and grubby paranoia that complements the 'all is not what it seems' mood.

Barker is currently working on a film about Cromwell.   **BM**

Steve BARRON

Electric Dreams (1984)
Teenage Mutant Ninja Turtles (1990)
Coneheads (1993)
Adventures of Pinocchio (1996)
Rat (2000)

A pioneer during the early days of music television, Steve Barron has utilised his unique vision to carve a successful career in television mini-series and feature films. Using special effects, animatronics and puppetry, along with good old-fashioned storytelling, he has continually amazed and awed audiences with his direction and style.

After spending parts of the 1970s working on various film crews, Barron burst onto the music video scene, directing some of the most innovative and highly stylised videos the industry had ever seen. Working with such diverse artists as Adam Ant, Joe Jackson, David Bowie, Eddie Grant and Madonna he quickly became the visionary of the moment. Like his later films, his videos were a unique mix of fantasy and reality. His video for A-Ha's 'Take On Me' is widely heralded as one of the greatest in the business.

In 1984 Barron made his cinema debut with the comedy *Electric Dreams.* The film centres on the relationship between a man and his computer as they both fall in love with the same girl. Using his flare for shaping alternative realities, he successfully created a comedy where the central character, Edgar (voiced by Bud Cort), was a talking computer, delicately and seamlessly blending the human elements with fantasy. Not since HAL 9000 had a computer so devilishly taken over a movie screen. Barron was also prophetic in his depiction of the control that computers would eventually have over life. The film has survived on video and in art-house theatres, becoming a cult favourite.

While continuing to work in music video, Barron collaborated with legendary puppeteer Jim Henson on the short-lived television project 'Jim Henson's The Storyteller'. His segment, entitled 'Hans My Hedgehog', won both him and the series critical acclaim. He took home an Emmy for his effort. The series was a departure for Barron as he moved further away from reality and more into the fantastical. Although he would never abandon humanity entirely, the programme did mark a shift for him.

Turtlemania came next with his direction of *Teenage Mutant Ninja Turtles* (1990). The film evoked the darker feel of the comic book, showcasing Barron's ability to create believable characters out of puppets. Not content with merely translating the animated cartoon show to the screen, Barron gave the film an edge that made it accessible to adults as well as children. It was wildly successful with audiences – spawning two sequels – and received a mixed response from the critics.

After the success of *Teenage Mutant Ninja Turtles*, Barron stepped back into the music video arena, directing several high-profile and innovative videos. His video for the Natalie Cole/Nat King Cole duet 'Unforgettable' won him a Best Director award from Billboard, and his work with Def Leppard earned him several nominations from MTV. He also produced several films including *The Specialist* (1994), with Sylvester Stallone and Sharon Stone, and *While You Were Sleeping* (1995), with Sandra Bullock.

His next feature, *Coneheads* (1993), starred Dan Ackroyd and Jane Curtin. Based on the popular 'Saturday Night Live' skit, the film unfortunately suffered from two major problems. The Coneheads skit was over ten years old and the targeted audience simply did not gravitate to the nostalgia factor of the classic comedy piece. Worse, the story suited fifteen minutes but could not be sustained for ninety. Barron can be praised, nevertheless, for his use of special effects. Next, he directed the strangely mystical *The Adventures of Pinocchio* (1996), starring veteran actor Martin Landau and up-and-coming teen star Jonathan Taylor Thomas. The film, a live-action version of the popular children's story, featured some incredible puppetry work, again by Barron's old associates at Jim Henson's creature shop. Their visual combination provided the perfect surreal atmosphere to service the story. Hardly a box-office success, the film still garnered high praise for Barron's combination of puppetry and live action.

After these average outings, he returned to television in 1998 to direct the mini-series 'Merlin' starring Sam Neill. This epic was a pure visual feast that retold the Arthurian legend through the eyes of one of its most mysterious participants, Merlin the Magician. No longer the foolish, bumbling wizard of the Disney days, Barron created a complex, tortured soul who only seeks to use his power for good but may not always succeed. He received both Directors Guild of America and Emmy nominations for his direction; the mini-series itself also won several Emmy awards for makeup, art direction and special effects.

Quickly capitalising on the success of 'Merlin', Barron directed the made-for-television mini-series 'Arabian Nights', which was aired in 2000. Another slick, epic family piece, it combined great special effects with larger-than-life characters, bringing a touch of the real to the surreal. It was nominated for several Emmy awards and won for Outstanding Makeup.

Adding to an already busy year, Barron then released the film *Rat* (2000). Bringing his career full circle, he utilised his love of music (Bob Geldof worked on the soundtrack) and worked again with the Jim Henson Company, treading a fine line between humdrum everyday life and the bizarre. Eschewing the typical Irish family drama, the piece is a lighthearted morality tale with a biting sense of humour.

Barron is currently working on the mini-series 'Thief of Baghdad'. **JM**

Simon BEAUFOY

Born in 1967, Simon Beaufoy is one of contemporary British cinema's leading lights, due as much to his fondness for all things northern as to the phenomenal success of his screenplay for Peter Cattaneo's *The Full Monty* (1997). Though not an outright successor to Ken Loach's humanistic cinema, Beaufoy's ability to capture small-town life and skilfully invest it with a strong sense of poetry and pain, is highlighted by his apprenticeship in documentaries and short films. A graduate of Bournemouth Film School (where he contributed to the short film *Release Me*, the recipient of five international awards), his first script for *Cello*, about the kidnapping of a cello by a lovelorn football fan, won the Best Script Award at the 1991 Fuji Film Competition. Beaufoy's introduction to the to the public, however, came with the release of *The Full Monty*. In a country still suffering from a collective mourning following the death of Diana, the film tapped into the nation's zeitgeist with clinical precision, mixing warmth and humour with pathos. It plays cleverly on gender stereotypes for it is the male body, in all its shapes and sizes, that is the subject of the gaze, while the women are the breadwinners. Beaufoy also examines the issue of masculinity within a framework of industrial decline and a post-Thatcherite working-class milieu. By mingling young and old, black and white, and blue- and white-collar, he universalises his grand themes of emasculation and disenfranchisement whilst embedding them within a tight-knit community. His screenplay received an Oscar® nomination.

The Darkest Light (1999) *The Darkest Light* (1999), co-directed with Bille Eltringham, is a tender coming-of-age drama set in Beaufoy's beloved North Yorkshire. Seen through the eyes of Catherine (Keri Arnold), whose brother is dying of leukaemia and whose father's cattle are infected with BSE, the film is a tender exploration of the nature of salvation and the endurance of faith. The camera work is simple and steady, with lingering images carrying the weight of the narrative. A strong sense of place suffuses the film and hints at an important new change of location in a British cinema so overloaded with chattering classes in Docklands or gangsters in Soho.

Beaufoy has also written screenplays for *Among Giants* (1998), perhaps the first film to capture the lives of electricity-pylon painters, and *Blow Dry* (2001), in which ex-hairdresser Alan Rickman gets a chance at redemption when the National Hair Championships take place at his home town, Keighley. **BM**

Anna BENSON GYLES

Anna Benson Gyles began her career as an editor for the BBC before producing and directing a variety of biographical films on literary-cultural figures as varied as Virginia Woolf, Harry Houdini, John Malkovich and Vincent Van Gogh. This interest in artistic figures reveals itself in *Swann* (1996), her sole feature film to date. Concerned with the wider meanings generated by artists from the past, the film, based on a novel by Carol Shields, shows how the poetry of Mary Swann (axed to death by her farmer husband) affects the lives of Rose (Brenda Fricker), the guardian of Mary's work, and Sarah (Miranda Richardson), a feminist writer intent on writing a book about the poet. The pain of Mary's life, revealed in snatches of her verse, is contrasted to the various motivations of those who have posthumously championed her work. Furthermore, the precious scraps of paper on which the poetry is preserved (although this in itself takes on great significance) reveal a life of domestic oppression, a detail ironically contrasted to the revelation of the profits to be made from the recycling of forgotten literature. The truth about the surviving scraps of work measures the value of art as antiquated museum display or genuine emotional experience. Strikingly photographed in Ontario, the film unfolds at a measured pace, balancing the layers of experience and realisation inspired by a gifted but downtrodden woman. **NJ**

Steven BERKOFF

Born in London in 1937, Steven Berkoff trained as an actor; prompted by the desire to find good material for performance, he developed a parallel career as a playwright. Over the course of the last twenty-five years, he has become one of Britain's foremost dramatists, an angry man of the theatre, fusing political vehemence with the quest for technical experimentation and innovation. His career as an actor still proceeds, be it as a stock European villain in Hollywood blockbusters or the gangland heavy in the new school of British gangster flicks, to his continued international success on stage, or his own work as a performer-director in the theatre.

As a film director, however, Berkoff has only ventured behind the camera on a single occasion, for a 1994 film version of his play 'Decadence'. The play itself is a typically ferocious Berkoff satire on the British class system. The social argument is polarised through the exploits of two couples (played by the same actors): the adulterous Helen and Steve (representatives of the ruling class), and the working-class Sybil (Steve's wife) and Les (a private detective hired by Sybil to investigate her husband's philandering). Relentless and unforgiving in its attacks on social structures, it neutrally targets the behaviour and attitudes of both the ruling and working classes, suggesting that the existence of the social order can only be maintained by everyone's willing adherence.

As a film, Berkoff's enterprise is not entirely successful: the major problem lies in his decision to play up the inherent theatricality of the project, from the artificial mise-en-scène and predominance of a 'frontal' approach to filming, to the expressionistic and physical nature of the performances. In a theatrical setting, such factors enhance the experience and heighten the social critique; committed to celluloid, it all appears too mannered. Berkoff's performance here is also rooted in his overtly theatrical style, which is not well suited to the medium. That said, his choice of female co-star is interesting; Joan Collins may not always convince but she unexpectedly adapts to the expressionistic style of performance. Along with her role in Kenneth Branagh's *In the Bleak Midwinter* a year later, it does reveal her to be an actress of unexpectedly varied skill.

Garnering no particular success either financially or critically, *Decadence* remains Berkoff's only film to date as a director. With enthusiasm for the theatre, it is quite possible that he will continue to direct solely in that medium. **JP**

Chris BERNARD

Chris Bernard rose from obscurity following the release of his first feature, *Letter to Brezhnev* (1985). Hoping that it would be screened at a few festivals and thus attract funding for a second feature, the film confounded these modest ambitions and went on to become one of the box-office hits of the year. Perversely, it is Bernard's only theatrical release in the UK to date. He was born in Liverpool, UK, in 1955 and started making short films when he was a teenager. In 1976 he became involved in a number of fringe theatre groups in Liverpool, working as both a director and a company stage manager. When the Liverpool-based soap 'Brookside' went into production in 1982, Bernard was employed as script-writer along with fellow Liverpudlian Frank Clarke. After leaving, he wanted to direct a feature film. He raised the £420,000 production costs through payment deferrals and private contributions, and shot *Letter to Brezhnev* in three weeks in 1984.

The story of a Liverpudlian woman who falls in love with a visiting Russian sailor was a daring narrative choice in the 1980s. The Cold War was showing no signs of thawing and Eastern-block countries still inspired fear and loathing in the West. Bernard's film dared to suggest that Western paranoia regarding the Soviet Union was largely the result of ignorance. It was not a viewpoint that the British Government sympathised with and subsequent to the film's release Bernard had his phone tapped by MI6.

Letter to Brezhnev captures Liverpool's visual splendour and its squalor with loving detail: the relentless rain, the ubiquitous fog, the harbour and port with its ferries and tankers. Panoramic views of the city's buildings and rooftops are used as prologues for many scenes. From these elevated perspectives, Liverpool appears almost mythical, like a scale model of a Lilliputian cityscape. This impression is not unsuited to the film's romantic fairy-tale narrative. When the camera comes down to earth these make-believe aspects are contrasted with kitsch lounge-room decor, beige-plain chip shops, dirty lanes and the vernacular of working-class scousers – rich and direct, and unashamedly coarse. The soundtrack is an amalgam of New Romantic rhythms, and the clothes and hairstyles are an indictment of 1980s fashion.

A similar contrast between myth and reality can be found between the film's style and its story. Stylistically, *Letter to Brezhnev* is harsh and unsentimental dirty realism, while the story is a modern reworking of the 'Romeo and Juliet' romance. The imbalance is corrected by Bernard's confident direction, which brings credibility to a fantastic love story.

Following *Brezhnev*'s incredible success, all the big studios in Hollywood wanted to work with Bernard. He was offered dozens of projects, such as *Robocop* (1987) and *Dogfight* (1991), and the producers of *Crocodile Dundee* (1986) wanted to make a film with him. Bernard turned them all down and word got around that he was something of a maverick film-maker who refused to 'play the game'.

Rather than going to America, Bernard waited two years before making the BBC-funded *Shadow of the Earth* (1987). The film was one of David Kane's (*This Year's Love* (1999), *Born Romantic* (2000)) first scripts. It obtained a theatrical release in a number of foreign markets, winning Best Film awards at BANFF and the Tokyo Film Festival, but restricted to a television screening in the UK. Set in 1961, the year when Sputnik went into space and JFK was inaugurated as the American president, the film tells the story of three little boys, two brothers and friend, growing up in a small village in Scotland. The boys become convinced that an albino who lives across the road is actually an alien. He then directed *Shooting Stars* (1991), a Film Four production written by Barry Hines, about a couple of working-class kids who seem to be going nowhere. When one of the boy's girlfriends wins a competition to go on a date with a famous footballer he grows jealous and kidnaps him. Though never released in the UK, the film prompted superlatives from one reviewer in *The Listener*: 'Chris Bernard directed with characteristic grit and panache, one might almost say Bernard has become the deftest and funniest observer of the British social non-consensus we currently have'.

Bernard followed up with *A Little Bit of Lippy* (1992), a black comedy about gender bending in working-class northern England in which a teenage wife discovers that her young husband enjoys dressing up in her clothes. The film was in the Top Ten Films of International Quality at the Cologne Film Festival, received a special commendation at the Prix Futura in Berlin, and featured at the San Francisco Gay and Lesbian Film Festival.

Since 1993 Bernard has worked almost exclusively for television, writing and/or directing productions for Mersey TV, Mellenia Films and the BBC. He currently has three feature films in development with his project company. Given that he is only 45 years old and has already proved himself an exemplary director, the current taste for Northern-flavoured films could mean that his best work is yet to come. **EMa**

Robert BIERMAN

Vampire's Kiss (1989)
Keep the Aspidistra Flying (1997)

Although periodically drawn to the horror genre, Robert Bierman is a director that has few stylistic or thematic threads running throughout his film and television work. Having made his name in 1982 with the BAFTA award-winning short, *The Rocking Horse Winner*, Bierman made his debut feature, *Vampire's Kiss* (1989). His most impressive work to date, it is an underrated hybrid of horror film, comedy and 1980s 'yuppie night-mare' flick. Nicolas Cage gives a truly bizarre performance as the Manhattan advertising executive who believes he has been turned into a vampire by sexy Jennifer Beals and stalks the city in a pair of plastic fangs. Despite the sleek, glossy cinematography and the remarkable central performance, the film is probably best remembered for a scene in which Cage eats a live cockroach. Concerned with gender and office politics, the amus-ing moments where a manic Cage terrorises his secretary make the similar instances in Mary Harron's *American Psycho* (2000) look positively anaemic.

With a script by Joseph Minion (who also wrote the similarly-themed *After Hours* (1985) for Martin Scorsese), it is tempting to see Cage as the main creative force behind the film, particularly in light of his recent executive producer role on E. Elias Merhige's *The Shadow of the Vampire* (2000). Merhige's film is an ironic spin on the making of F.W. Murnau's German horror classic *Nosferatu* (1922), which suggests that the enig-matic lead performer Max Schreck was a real vampire, and Cage has frequently credited the German actor as the inspiration for his 'expressionistic' performance in *Vampire's Kiss*.

Bierman followed with various projects for British television, including 'Frankenstein's Baby' in 1990 and 'The Moonstone' in 1996, a starry adaptation of Wilkie Collins' novel. His only other feature film to date has been the disappointing George Orwell adaptation *Keep the Aspidistra Flying* (1997). Helena Bonham Carter is given little to do, and although Richard E. Grant is fine as Comstock, the clerk who dreams of being a writer, and he certainly looks the 1930s part, his performance is unnecessarily restrained. This is ironic given the barnstorming, almost wilfully undirected, Cage in Bierman's debut. The novel's attack on British bourgeois values of the period (represented by the titular flower) is diluted in Alan Plater's script and it is hard to avoid the feeling that the anger and sarcasm of Orwell's original has been fashioned into yet another British heritage film. When it comes to film funding it would appear that literary adaptations are the preferred choice over a more challenging genre or art cinema, and this somewhat restricting notion of quality seems to have played a part in Bierman's bloodless movie. It is particularly disappointing that a director whose first feature was as wild and odd as *Vampire's Kiss* should have produced a film as tame as *Keep the Aspidistra Flying*. **IC**

Antonia BIRD

Priest (1994)
Mad Love (1995)
Face (1997)
Ravenous (1999)

Born in the UK, Antonia Bird has worked in theatre and extensively in television. Her BBC funded features, *Priest* (1994) and *Face* (1997), address topical social and politi-cal concerns in a relatively conventional realist style enlivened by energetic direction of emotionally intense moments and action sequences. Part of her agenda, similar to Kathryn Bigelow's in films such as *Point Break* (1991), has been to demonstrate that women can direct 'masculine' genres as effectively as men. *Face*'s eventful gangster nar-rative, and the semi-comic, semi-macabre cannibal western *Ravenous* (1999), are proof of her argument. *Face*, however, scripted by Ronan Bennett, is more character-based and introspective than most gangster films. Bird's direction of her favourite star, Robert Carlyle, in *Priest*, *Face* and *Ravenous*, cleverly utilises his persona's beguiling combina-tion of vulnerability and toughness.

Written by Jimmy McGovern, *Priest* is a serious religious drama structured as a clas-sically melodramatic conflict between love and duty with a tearful ending. Father Greg (Linus Roache) is firmly committed to his vocation but torn between his gay sexuality and the Catholic Church's insistence upon celibacy. His compassion for a girl who has

28 Wallflower Critical Guide

confided to him that her father is abusing her cannot lead to action because of the seal of the confessional. Theological, moral and social disputes are conducted through convincingly scripted and acted character interactions and in a climactic, unresolved showdown with parishioners after Greg has been outed by the press. *Priest* resonated with public debate about the Church's attitude towards gender and sexuality in mid-1990s Britain. Stylistic elements allow momentary escape from social constraints: Greg's first sexual encounter with his lover is seductively lit with an open fire in the background; when they kiss on a beach the camera rapidly circles around them. The film's strength derives from its balance of melodrama and realism, and the constant tension it maintains throughout the narrative between love and duty, escape and constraint.

The teenage runaways in *Mad Love* (1995) are a glamourised Hollywood version of the two homeless kids in Bird's earlier British television film, *Safe* (1993). Although *Mad Love* emphasises psychological rather than sociological explanations for the runaways' behaviour, the direction only intermittently attains the emotional intensity which is characteristic of her work. Casting Drew Barrymore and Chris O'Donnell pitched *Mad Love* at the alluring yet often elusive youth audience, but its stars and soundtrack failed to draw them in.

Face, a modest production by Hollywood standards, represents a sizeable BBC investment in a feature film. Robert Carlyle leads an ensemble of talented British actors. Songs by Billy Bragg, Lewis Taylor and Paul Weller provide narrative commentary but are more attuned to an older audience than the one most immediately associated with contemporary gangster narratives. Close-ups of Carlyle's silent, troubled face set the tone for a film which questions the abandonment of political resistance and the relevance of traditional codes of honour among thieves and men in the post-Thatcher era. This is paradoxically mediated through action sequences knowingly indebted to contemporary Hollywood cinema. These include a stand-off reminiscent of *Reservoir Dogs* (1992) and an assault on a police station which pays audacious, low-budget homage to Arnold Schwarzenegger in *The Terminator* (1984).

Bird took over the slight but enjoyable *Ravenous* (1999) after shooting began and directed with gusto. Script deficiencies and incoherencies caused by the interrupted production schedule are compensated for by panicky camera movements, cannibalised corpses, close shots of cooked intestines, and Carlyle's vicious charm. An idiosyncratic Michael Nyman and Damon Albarn score refuses to signpost how the listener should relate to what could be interpreted as a satire on nineteenth-century pioneering. American westward expansion becomes more than a dog-eat-dog scramble; survival and prosperity is only achieved by human eating human.

Thus far, Bird's career has alternated between socially committed realist dramas and genre pieces, with individual films sometimes combining elements of both. *Care* (2000), a powerful British television film, stars Steven Mackintosh and deals with abuse in children's homes.   **MSt**

Andrew BIRKIN

Born in London in 1945, Andrew Birkin is known more for his screenplays than his directing. Launching his career in cinema as an assistant to Stanley Kubrick on *2001: A Space Odyssey* (1968), he began writing screenplays in the 1970s, most of which were turned into television movies, such as *The Pied Piper* (1972) and *The Thief of Baghdad* (1978). He gradually became attached to bigger-budget films, writing the scripts for both *King David* (1985) and *The Name of the Rose* (1986). The former tried to revive the DeMille biblical epic, but director Bruce Beresford's decision to cast Richard Gere as David did irreparable damage to the film. At least Birkin's screenplay for *The Name of the Rose* dispensed with the bulk of Umberto Eco's tortuous murder-mystery prose and fashioned a Grand Guignol spin on Sherlock Holmes. Birkin has also written 'J.M. Barrie and the Lost Boys', a biography of the creator of Peter Pan.

As a director, Birkin rose to prominence when his live-action short film *Sredni Vashtar* (1982) gained him an Academy Award nomination and a BAFTA. *Burning Secret* (1988), his first feature, which boasted an all-star cast, including Faye Dunaway and Klaus Maria Brandauer, made a rather clunky statement about adult cruelty and the loss

Burning Secret (1988)
Salt on Our Skin (1992)
The Cement Garden (1993)

of innocence. When asthmatic Edmund is taken to a remote Swiss spa by his aunt, he becomes entranced with the war exploit stories of the Baron (Brandauer). What he believes to be a budding friendship is really a pretext for the Baron to move closer to Edmund's aunt. Although the snow-bound Marienbad is used to haunting effect, and the stately pace of the narrative allows the action to unfold inch by inch, the overall mood becomes too weighed down with surface beauty, leading to a sense of style over substance.

Salt on Our Skin (1992) was badly received both critically and commercially, once again highlighting Birkin's unease at directing old-fashioned melodramas. Directing his own script (which he co-wrote with Bee Gilbert), the narrative concerns a half-French woman (Greta Scacchi) who reminisces about an old love affair in Scotland that was resumed a decade later. Birkin fails in his attempt to fashion a Merchant-Ivory intimate epic, not least because the credibility and motivations of the characterisations are consistently undermined by poor dialogue and low production values.

The Cement Garden (1993) has proved to be Birkin's most successful directorial effort, due in part, perhaps, to his reliance on the excellent source material, the novel by Ian McEwan. Taking place inside a barren, concrete-walled house on the outskirts of an unnamed British town, the story focuses on an incestuous affair that begins between a brother and sister (Andrew Robertson and Charlotte Gainsbourg) when their parents die. Effecting a gloomy claustrophobia inside the house, Birkin's exemplary timing and characterisation create an unsettling yet seductive mood and recalls 'Lord of the Flies' in its exploration of nascent adolescence in an adult-free world. Less to do with sex and incest, the film seems to conclude that the power of young girls will always be used to manipulate the weaknesses of boys; in short, a 'Lolita' for the 1990s. Birkin seems to have found a perfect collaborator in McEwan, a novelist who always likes to explore the hidden and amoral.

Birkin was awarded the Best Director Award at the 1993 Berlin Film Festival for *The Cement Garden* but has, more recently, returned to writing screenplays, including Luc Besson's *The Messenger: The Story of Joan of Arc* (1999). **BM**

Cathal BLACK

Although Cathal Black launched his career with an experimental documentary, most of his work has been resolutely narrative, though always heavy with the political and social history of Ireland.

His first widely-seen film is the short *Our Boys* (1981), an examination of the abuse perpetrated by the Christian Brothers in their schools. Co-written by experimental novelist Dermot Healy (who has a small role in the film), it shifts between interviews with now-adult abuse victims, fictional sequences about a Christian Brothers' school that is in the process of being closed, and archival footage of the 1932 Eucharistic Congress. Made shortly after the 1979 visit of Pope John Paul II to Ireland, the film's brutal criticism of the Catholic Church's control over Irish life was timely, although it terrified the national television station, Radio Telefís Éireann. Having supported the film financially, when it was delivered to them, they declined to air it or provide any promotional support. *Our Boys* was finally broadcast in 1994

Pigs (1984), Black's first narrative film, centres on Jimmy (Jimmy Brennan), a gay divorcee who takes up residence with a group of squatters in a large, decaying Georgian house in Dublin. His friends include a black pimp, a drug dealer and his prostitute girlfriend, and a schizophrenic. The film's menagerie anticipates the equally provocative family in Joe Comerford's *Reefer and the Model* (1987). The grim, defeated outlook of both films invokes a pessimism about Irish culture's relationship to modernity and its own puritan history, which defined much of the 1980s.

This anxiety about unresolved arguments is also part of *Korea* (1995). Based on a short story by Joe McGahern and set in the 1950s, the film focuses on an embittered old man, John Doyle (Donal Donnelly), who fought on the side of Sinn Féin during the Civil War and now ekes out a living fishing the lakes of County Cavan. His contentedly middle-class neighbour, Ben Moran (Vass Anderson), fought on the side of the Free State and favours rural electrification and a shift to tourism. When Moran's son is killed fighting for the American army in Korea, he gets compensation from the State, making Doyle even angrier. The situation worsens when his son falls in love with Moran's daughter. Heavily loaded metaphorically – emigration, nationalism, modernity, transcendent love and unspoken violence are all present in the complex narrative – it never feels wooden or self-conscious. Indeed, in addition to a compelling story (powered by solid performances) *Korea* has radiant images; Black revels in the lush greens of County Cavan, creating an atmosphere of a world apart.

His latest film, *Love and Rage* (1998), adapted from a novel by James Carney, takes place on Achall Island at the beginning of the twentieth century. Greta Scacchi plays Agnes MacDonnell, a wealthy, liberal Scottish woman who owns a small house on the island and is friendly with the locals and her servants. She begins an affair with James Lynchehaun (Daniel Craig), a highly unstable, vaguely mysterious man who ends up becoming quite violent. He flees the island when their affair goes awry and recreates himself as an exiled Irish patriot in the United States. Like all of Black's work, it is a tightly constructed, visually adventurous meditation on the unresolved historical and political arguments that have long shaped Irish culture.   **JW**

Donald Taylor BLACK

Born in 1951 in Ireland, and educated at Trinity College, Dublin, Donald Taylor Black has been an active participant in the Irish film industry on a committee, council and consultant level for many years.

His first documentary, *At the Cinema Palace: Liam O'Leary* (1983), is a profile of the titular Irish film historian and pioneer archivist. It was awarded a Certificate of Merit at the Chicago Film Festival. He then directed a series of sport and literary profiles, including films on the lives of actor Jimmy O'Dea (1985), playwright Sam Thompson (1986), poet Oliver St. John Gogarty (1987), and on hurling (1989) and other Gaelic games. Though Black's most recent films have been at the centre of debates on social and political developments in contemporary Ireland, he tends to mask his critiques of Irish culture and society with a prosaic visual style.

He directed a film on the history of Dublin City, *In Flags of Flitters – Pictures of Dublin* (1991), which subtly satirises the (then current) vogue for celebrating Irish history. Using footage shot during the 1988 city millennium celebrations, he quietly subverts the ethos of postmodernist nostalgia by exploring some of the historical roots of the events depicted. Black then began to experiment with cinéma vérité styles in a series of three films: *Down for the Match* (1992) focuses on the revels of fans visiting Dublin for the all-Ireland football final; *From Ballybeg to Broadway* (1993) chronicles the production of Brian Friel's 'Wonderful Tennessee'; and *Hearts and Souls* (1995) explores the divorce referendum of 1995.

Black's use of irony and subversion is most pronounced in the latter film. Shot with the co-operation of the so-called 'no' campaign, the documentary allowed its subjects to undermine themselves by using long takes which sometimes captured them behaving foolishly. It raises questions about Irish conservatism without making them explicit, revealing how messages can be conveyed through style rather than overt statement.

His four-part television series on Mountjoy prison, 'The Joy' (1997), follows similar lines. Nominally a profile of the prison, its occupants and its administration, the programme subtly brings several issues to the fore, including the social validity of the prison system on the whole.

His masking technique is at its most pronounced in *Dear Boy: The Story of Michael MacLiammóir* (1999), a profile of the Irish theatre great. The story of an English-born actor who assumed an Irish identity, the film is essentially a study of homosexuality within Irish culture. Just as MacLiammóir had 'played' an Irishman, he had also affected a 'theatrical' persona that made his homosexuality more tolerable to a conservative culture at a time when the subject was not spoken of openly.

Black has worked in theatre, and directed a television opera for Channel Four, 'The Triumph of Beauty and Deceit' (1993), with music by Gerald Barry and libretto by Meredith Oakes. He also directed the BFI Century of Cinema series film on Irish cinema, *Irish Cinema: Ourselves Alone?* (1995), which is written by film historian Kevin Rockett. **HO**

At the Cinema Palace: Liam O'Leary (1983)
Irish Cinema: Ourselves Alone? (1995)
Dear Boy: The Story of Michael MacLiammóir (1999)

Les BLAIR

Number One (1984)
Bad Behaviour (1993)
Jump the Gun (1996)

Born in Salford, UK, Les Blair studied economics at Liverpool University between visits to London cinemas, where he availed himself of the range of art films available: Satyajit Ray's 'Apu' trilogy (1955, 1956, 1959) and Ingmar Bergman's *The Seventh Seal* (1957) became favourites.

His interest in film led him to the London Film School, where he studied in the late 1960s, making several short films reflecting his own experience as a young Northern man away from home for the first time. He found professional work with remarkable speed, producing and editing Salford-born Mike Leigh's *Bleak Moments* (1971). This collaboration was to have a lasting effect on Blair's work as he went on to utilise Leigh's now infamous improvisatory methods in his future television and film directing.

He followed *Bleak Moments* with contributions to the BBC's 'Play For Today' and the ITV network's 'Playhouse' seasons throughout the 1970s. He made a particular impact with G.F. Newman's groundbreaking 'Law and Order' series on BBC2 in 1978, directing all four parts of a show that set new standards for the representation of the police. Detailing events from the perspective of a detective, a villain, a brief and a prisoner, the series utilised real locations, live sound and documentary-style camera work to effect a more realistic portrayal of the justice system than had been previously seen. He continued with the television play directing until making his first feature film in 1984.

Number One, about a snooker player (Bob Geldof) getting an offer he cannot refuse from a snooker promoter who wants him to turn professional, reunited Blair with G.F. Newman. The latter's script references *The Hustler* (1961) and *The Cincinnati Kid* (1965) but lacks the sharpness of these films, rendering instead something of a clichéd melodrama: a potentially unsympathetic ending is undermined by Newman's structure and script. Lively camerawork and the steady, amiable performances of Geldof and Alison Steadman make the film watchable, but away from the constraints of BBC television film-making, Blair seems slightly cut adrift and unsure: the final product retains an unexpected sense of convention. He moved back into television directing with a series on the state of Britain in the 1980s ('The Nation's Health') and a BBC Screen 2 drama about the advertising industry, 'Honest, Decent and True'. At this stage in television work, he demonstrated his political and social concerns via a realistic, documentary approach to camera work.

He directed the television movie of Jack Rosenthal's critically acclaimed 'London's Burning', following with the first series of this fire-fighting drama, before turning back to a subject which, like his advertising industry drama, gave him an opportunity to critique a modern bête-noir: the tabloid press. The 1990 'News Hounds', an improvised drama for the BBC, starred Mike Leigh stalwart Alison Steadman, and demonstrated the lengths the tabloid press will go to for a story to ruin someone's life.

A return to feature film-making saw Blair direct Sinead Cusack and Stephen Rea in a class-conscious comedy, *Bad Behaviour* (1993). Built up from improvisation, the film has a realistic awkwardness about its relationships and scenarios. Reminiscent of Mike Leigh's work in its portrait of both the downwardly mobile and the working class aiming for upward mobility, the film is comically observant when capturing the clash of lifestyles and values. It provides an authentic sense of domestic and work chaos but the documentary style that lends authenticity also renders the film uncinematic.

His most recent feature, *Jump the Gun* (1996), is set in South Africa but largely sidesteps the political implications of the country post-Apartheid. Indeed, Blair claims that 'the characters are not ciphers for political ideas', rather that they demonstrate the everyday lives and problems of a group of people living in Johannesburg. In avoiding the overtly political, Blair manages to convey insight into contemporary South Africa via his mixed-race characters and their problematic lives. The improvised approach works to flesh out characters that could become stereotypes, but does so at the expense of a coherent structure. A loose visual style, free from the kind of severe framing and abrupt cutting which could distract the actors, aids the truthfulness of the performances but ultimately highlights the structural problems inherent in improvised feature films, if not carefully and ruthlessly constructed to avoid self-indulgence.

Unlike Mike Leigh, who has sustained a film-making career, Blair's talent is not as well-formed, and his style appears to be resolutely televisual. He has done some admirable work in this medium, regenerating tired genres whilst conveying his political and social concerns, but is yet to find his true cinematic voice. He has recently completed *H* (formerly known as *66 Days*) which is set in the Maze Prison and details the events leading up to Bobby Sands' death. **JD**

John BOORMAN

Born in London, UK, in 1933, John Boorman has made films in a number of countries and with varying budgets. His output ranges across diverse subjects, genres and aesthetic approaches; nonetheless, certain themes and concerns emerge. There is a strong preoccupation with spectacular landscapes, often ones that are untouched by human civilisation. These are used to underpin an interest in ecological politics and mysticism. The films are visually striking, compositionally strong, and are concerned with the cost incurred by modern life on basic values and communion with the land and magic. Acting as combined director, producer and writer on many of his films means that they often have a personal dimension. The subject matter is usually given an archetypal or mythic framework, in line with Boorman's interest in myth as an articulation of a 'collective unconscious'. There is also a common focus on relationships between men and his films frequently stress psychological tensions, competition and raw emotional states. These themes are played out against locations that have some significance in their own right as well as to the narrative.

After a stint at the BBC making documentaries, Boorman's first feature was in the mode of Richard Lester's *A Hard Day's Night* (1964). *Catch Us If You Can* (1965) is a swinging-London movie starring The Dave Clark Five. The free-and-easy surface of the film is, however, troubled by ominous undercurrents, imbuing it with more interest than other contemporary rock 'n' roll movies and foreshadowing the darker elements of 1960s landmark counter-culture films, such as Dennis Hopper's *Easy Rider* (1969) and *Performance* (Donald Cammell/Nic Roeg, 1970). On the strength of the film Boorman was called to Hollywood where he made *Point Blank* (1967), one of his most visually interesting works. The film has become something of a celebrated cult thriller, consolidated by its re-release by MGM in 1998. Walker (Lee Marvin) is played with a steely coldness which is complemented by the silvery palette used in the film. His mission to regain the money stolen in a bungled heist, during which he is shot and betrayed by his best friend, escalates into a series of raids perpetrated on the 'organisation'. The film represents Hollywood at its most daring. It refuses sentimentality, tells its story in an intensely cinematic way, and constructs a splintered time line that deploys elliptical editing to link Walker's past and present. The unconventional framing and boldly choreographed images are enhanced by tactical use of wide screen. In line with other 'auteur' directors working in Hollywood during this period, Boorman's distinctively taut approach to the 'lone gun'-style thriller leans on the new vocabulary of cinema forged in France by the Nouvelle Vague. The film also resembles Sergio Leone's staccato, pared-down style, with Walker as the cool and calculating 'man with no name' placed in the concrete heart of a west-coast city.

In *Hell in the Pacific* (1968), Marvin features as an American World War Two airman washed up on a pacific island where he encounters a similarly stranded Japanese pilot (Toshiro Mifune). Open hostility subsides into an uneasy peace, in which their cultural difference is used to produce flashes of humour. The intense brightness of the sea, sun and sky impassively overlooks the war played out in miniature on the island lending the film an expressive irony that helps to underpin its anti-war message. The ending is bleak, however: once they muster a heroic escape from the island to another they discover that America has dropped the 'bomb' on Japan, thus resulting in the resumption of open hostility. The producers changed the ending of the film without consulting Boorman; for this reason he has tended to act as producer in an effort to keep control of his product. He returned to Britain for his next film, *Leo the Last* (1970). Set in London's Notting Hill, the piece is an abstract satire on class: the central character (Marcello Mastroianni) is a European noble living in a mansion next to a poor black neighbourhood. During the course of the narrative he shifts from local wildlife watcher to an activist working on behalf of the local black population. The film focuses on Boorman's concern to disrupt middle-class social insularity but, despite winning Best Director at Cannes, some critics have regarded the film as pretentious and unengaging.

Deliverance (1972) is the most well-known of Boorman's films. Set in America, it focuses on four city men and their journey along a river. The river valley is shortly to be swallowed up by the creation of a man-made dam, creating an ecological frame to the story. The documentary quality is potently meshed with the brutality and disturbing otherness of a 'realist' horror film. As with many of Boorman's films the spectacular forest and ravine landscape are the dominant features, locating the action and cutting the men off from 'civilisation'. There are no supernatural horrors here: it is back-woods isolation, fearful paranoia and inbred hillbillies that supply the threat. The four main characters are economically sketched. Lewis (Burt Reynolds) is the 'back to nature' boy, complete with hi-tech bow and arrow, yet it is the mild-mannered Ed (Jon Voight) who finds an inner strength to survive, killing the man he believes held him hostage and anally raped his canoe partner. Powerful and deceptively simple, the film hinges on ambiguities: Ed's actions are based on fear and assumption and the audience never knows if his victim was a perpetrator of the earlier crime. Like other river-journey films, such as Werner Herzog's *Aguirre: Wrath of God* (1972) and Francis Ford Coppola's *Apocalypse Now* (1979), *Deliverance* has a mythic resonance; a rite of passage that works as allegory. Initially the film's distributors Warner Bros. were dubious; they soon realised, however, that the film slotted easily into the climate of challenge and innovation that held sway in auteur-based New Hollywood.

Zardoz (1974), Boorman's next, is a quirky, science-fiction epic that explores a gamut of philosophical ideas which are presented in non-linear mode. In conjunction with Sean Connery's ponytail and droopy moustache, it now looks quintessentially 1970s. Both sublime and ridiculous, it treats Connery's rough challenge to a decadent, elite order of immortals with characteristic brio. Like many of Boorman's films it solicited paeans of praise and damnation from critics and audiences. Turning to the supernatural horror genre, *Exorcist II: The Heretic* (1977), Boorman's sequel to William Friedkin's original (1973) is far from an unimaginative remake of the first film. Boorman's interest in the concept of the 'collective unconscious' is given free reign; Richard Burton's intense priest seeks to renew his faith through an investigation of what happened to Father Merrin, killed in the first film by the demon. Journeying to Africa he discovers that the demon takes the form of a locust, offering a richly resonant means of evoking biblical pestilence and providing a suitably generic Manichean struggle between good and evil. Juxtaposing the narcissistic, shiny surfaces of contemporary New York with the hot, earthy reds of Ethiopia, the film makes ample use of superimpositions, fractured reflections and hallucinogenic visual conceits which, alongside Ennio Morricone's soundtrack, lend the film a Euro-horror feel. The exaggerated, 1970s visual style and non-linearity of both *Exorcist II* and *Zardoz* polarised the reactions of critics and audiences. The films' engagement with ideas and eccentricity, however, still make for a distinctive and multi-faceted cinema experience.

Excalibur (1981) is probably one of the most ambitious film versions of the Arthurian myth. As with most of Boorman's films it absorbs the visual styles of the day, blending romanticism, pre-Raphaelite imagery and late-hippie chic, accompanied by the apt and suitably rousing music of Wagner and Carl Orff's 'Carmina Burana'. Central to the film is the stunning combination of real and artificial landscapes: seasonal changes are integral to the story and filters make the green wood impossibly lush. Dramatising the transition between the old pagan world and Christianity, the film is pervaded by a keen sense of loss as it mourns the passing of magic and invokes a connection between people and landscape. It is through Merlin that the myth is imbued with a 'new age' nostalgia for an imagined world of magic. Nicol Williamson's wizard is a tour de force: witty, laconic and slightly mad, as a magus should be. Nigel Terry's Arthur moves smoothly from ingénue to depleted king. The film is keenly aware of the mythic function of the story and there are frequent references to its importance for the future, bringing a dimension absent from the many Hollywood versions of the myth but taken up later in Steven Barron's *Merlin* (1995).

The Emerald Forest (1985) contains an environmental message in a story about a white boy who has grown up in the Amazon rainforest. The film takes a mythic approach to the subject matter, using it to comment on the modern disregard for the land and for those people who live in harmony with it. Continuing Boorman's romance with the primitive, the film has been criticised for having a nostalgic and stereotypical depiction of the indigenous Amazonian people. Others, however, have welcomed the integration of ecological issues and narrative. Mysticism prevails and the deus ex machina ending of the film can be regarded as problematic: the threat to the 'invisible' tribe is resolved through a storm solicited by magic. While implausible, this ending does sit well with the film's sympathy for an non-rational world-view. There is a typical concentration on male relations, this time between a father and his lost son, which is underlined by the fact that the son is played by Boorman's own son Charley. By contrast, *Hope and Glory* (1987) is set in urban London during World War Two and has a semi-autobiographical focus on the way in which a lower-middle-class family maintains normality in the face of the blitz. The film does not bear the anti-war message of *Hell in the Pacific*; instead, it is shot from a boy's point of view. Only half comprehending, he observes the strange effects on his family, excited by aspects of the war such as local bombsites which are scavenged for war souvenirs. The film is certainly nostalgic yet laced with a humour derived from a profound incongruity of the extraordinary nature of war and the ordinariness of the domestic. The boy's and the director's point of view are neatly merged in the opening of the film as the boy plays with toy knights in the jungle of the garden grass. Those hoping for the usual magic and mysticism were disappointed; nevertheless, the film gained wide appeal and received many more award nominations than Boorman's previous films.

Boorman wrote *Where the Heart Is* (1990) with his daughter Telsche and with the intention of setting the film in London. He failed to raise sufficient funds in the UK, however, and the American studio Touchstone Pictures stipulated a shift of location to New York. Partly based on 'King Lear', this is a moral tale of family life and middle-class investment in material comforts with the main characters based on Boorman's own family. Billed as a comedy, the film's humour is subtle and depends on the audience's tacit recognition of white, middle-class family life. Concerned with art, consumerism, and the sin of lip service paid to political causes, the film depends on a classical rise and fall structure which is given a contemporary flavour through its engagement with bourgeois malaise. Reference to Boorman's romance with archetypes is articulated through the collusion of bodies and paintings used in the film. The film was not well received by critics, partly because of its tendency to treat homelessness rather lightly. Boorman followed the film with another very personal project *I Dreamt I Woke Up* (1991), a short about his own work that was originally commissioned by the BBC. The film interweaves reality, imagination and myth, and features John Hurt as Boorman's alter ego.

Changing tack, Boorman made *Beyond Rangoon* (1995) on a big Hollywood budget and filmed on location in Malaysia. It is an ambitious film that marries the fight for democracy in Burma with an action-adventure narrative. An American tourist, played by Patricia Arquette, seeks escape from the brutal murders of her husband and son having been stranded after losing her passport. Her self-pity dissipates as she becomes aware of the extent of political oppression. The film is certainly intended to inform as well as to entertain thereby incurring the risk of falling between two stools. As with Boorman's other films, the landscape is beautifully photographed; here this helps to underpin the theme of a human-wrought hell located in paradise. *Two Nudes Bathing* (1995), his next project, has not been released on video in the UK and was released in the USA as a short film. The film weaves a narrative around an unsigned French painting, linking it to the sexual education of the two subjects. Boorman also contributed a 52-second entry to *Lumière et Compagnie* (1995), a film made up of shorts by notable film-makers using a very early camera.

The General (1998) received wide distribution and critical coverage. Adopting the rise and fall structure of the gangster format, as forged by Warner Bros. in the 1930s, the film charts the life of Martin Cahill, a professional Irish criminal who was shot by the IRA in 1994. Based in urban Ireland, the film makes much use of Irish dialects and humour. The film takes Cahill's point of view and shows how his identity is rooted in hoodlum-hero mould. As such, the film solicited the same concerns levelled at the 1930s gangster films: the problem of making heroes of criminals. That said, *The General* lacks the seductive glamour of most gangster films. The heists are not framed in terms of Hollywood's slick production values but rather resemble British television drama. It is possible that the choice of subject matter was influenced by the fact that Cahill stole the gold disk award for *Deliverance*'s 'Duelling Banjos' from Boorman's house in Ireland.

Boorman's latest self-produced film, *The Tailor of Panama* (2001), is a version of a John Le Carré novel but strongly echoes the bleak and seedy, yet moral, atmosphere of a Graham Greene novel. It combines the spy thriller with comedy, a mix that has perplexed some critics and viewers who expected, due to the presence of Pierce Brosnan, that the film would be a high-octane espionage-based action piece. Brosnan is cast as a sleazy and immoral British Secret Service operative, which plays nicely against his suave Bond role, characterising the film's satirical approach. Geoffrey Rush plays the tailor who makes good English suits for the Panamanian elite and becomes embroiled in political intrigue. Most of the comedy is based on his and Brosnan's interaction. The film plays into sensitive political territory, with a planned American invasion called off at the last moment. This has led some reviewers to speculate that the lack of a high-profile marketing strategy on the part of Columbia Tristar is due to the film's indictment of US interventionism and British complicity. As with his other films, the fantasy lives of the central protagonists feature strongly in the narrative, and, like most of his work, it has drawn both praise and damnation from critics.

'A dream to some, a nightmare to others', Boorman's films are very personal and repeatedly seek to balance entertainment with a political message. Grounded in liberal values, for some his apparent advocation of a mystical panacea detracts from his political endeavour. Nonetheless, many of the films have an appeal beyond the art-cinema circuit because they render contemporary, moral issues in imaginative and entertaining ways. **TK**

Don BOYD

Born in Nairn, Scotland, in 1948, Don Boyd has created more interesting work as a producer than as a director. In the former capacity, he has contributed to a number of important British films including Alan Clarke's *Scum* (1979), Derek Jarman's *War Requiem* (1989) and the intriguing but disappointing omnibus film *Aria* (1987), for which he also directed the framing story.

As a director, he has often made films with interesting premises but limited success. His debut, *Intimate Reflections* (1974), is an inept psychodrama that reads as a parody of European art-house cinema. Mourning the death of their child, a couple (Anton Rogers and Lillias Walker) are shown in happier times, talking and having sex, while an older couple (who may be the protagonists in the future) deliver monologues straight to camera. The film ends with the four characters together. Though eye-catching, Boyd uses a variety of techniques – slides, direct address and slow motion – to little real effect.

East of Elephant Rock (1977), whilst very different, is no real improvement – a period piece that wastes a great cast (Anton Rogers again, John Hurt and Judi Bowker) in a melodrama that feels twenty years out of date. Set in Malaya in 1948, the film wants to be taken seriously on the one hand and perceived as an ironic curio on the other, as the opening title that asks viewers to 'laugh and smile' indicates. Peter Skellern provides a series of mannered and irritating songs.

Boyd continued to work on the smaller screen, the medium for which he directed the dull television movie *Goldeneye: The Secret Life of Ian Fleming* in 1989, before moving on to *Twenty-One* (1991), his most commercial offering so far. Written by the director and Zöe Heller, this is the tale of the relationships between a New York-based 'modern woman' (Patsy Kensit) and the various loves in her life, including father Jack Shepherd, junkie Rufus Sewell and a married man, Patrick Ryecart. Self-conscious in its attempt to be hip, the film positions Kensit in sub-*Ferris Bueller* mode, addressing monologues to camera, one as she urinates. Boyd and Heller seem to think they are making a profound statement about the 'woman of today' but the tone is too teasing: the central character talks salaciously while carrying on passionless (and with the impotent Sewell character, sexless) affairs. With *Twenty-One* Boyd revisits the territory of 1960s British movies, such as Lewis Gilbert's *Alfie* (1966) and John Schlesinger's *Darling* (1965), but the enterprise as a whole is rather smug, capturing none of the charm or insight that made the earlier films so distinctive.

Kleptomania (1995) reunited Boyd with Kensit in a *Thelma and Louise* rip-off – a psychological drama with Amy Irving playing a wealthy, unfulfilled, bulimic socialite teaming up with Kensit's runaway to commit crimes. A contributor to the wave of 'female buddy' psycho-thrillers made in the last decade, such as Michael Winterbottom's *Butterfly Kiss* (1994) and Bill Eagles' *Beautiful Creatures* (2000), Boyd displays little feel for the genre. Aside from an impressive performance by Victor Garber as Irving's distant husband, there is little on offer here. Amy Irving is a talented actor who rarely gets roles that do her justice and this is no exception. The scene where she masturbates with a stolen necklace is supposed to be disturbing and erotic but it is merely laughable.

After some time spent working once again in television, directing the BBC series 'Ruby Wax Meets...' and episodes of the interesting Channel Four documentary series 'Witness', Boyd returned to features with *Lucia* (1998), casting his daughter Amanda in the lead role. An ambitious piece written by Boyd, the story was inspired by Donizetti's opera 'Lucia Di Lammermoor' and Walter Scott's novel, 'The Bride of Lammermoor'. Kate and Hamish Ashton (Amanda Boyd and Mark Holland) are opera singers who desperately need money to repair their ancestral home. As Hamish arranges a marriage of convenience between his sister and a wealthy American, despite the fact that she is in love with someone else, it becomes clear that events are imitating the Donizetti opera, with Kate as Lucia, a mad murderess. Despite the problems inherent in adapting a nineteenth-century opera for the late twentieth century, Boyd crafts quite an involving tale, creating audacious and stylish material that stands out against the usual crop of British comedies and gangster films. The characters sing live, rather than mime to a pre-recorded track, and his daughter's performance is strong enough to dispel any accusations of nepotism.

Continuing to work with classical material, Boyd is currently directing *My Kingdom*, an adaptation of Shakespeare's 'King Lear' set in contemporary Liverpool. Although not a new idea – Akira Kurosawa made a samurai Lear in *Ran* (1985) and Jocelyn Moorhouse updated the tale in *A Thousand Acres* (1997) – the project is eagerly awaited because Richard Harris stars in the lead role. **IC**

William BOYD

Born in 1952, novelist William Boyd began writing screenplays in the late 1980s (most notably, *Chaplin* (1992)), occasionally adapting his own novels for film. He also wrote the screenplay for *The Trench* (1999), his first, and to date only, project as director.

Entitled *The Somme* in pre-production, the film is set on the eve of that battle and paints a sombre portrait of the average British battalion. With the exception of the final scene, the entire film is confined to a small stretch of trenches (jovially named after some of London's finest streets), thereby successfully evoking a sense of claustrophobia for the audience. Although Boyd rarely strays far from the predictable 'shot/reverse shot', he is adept at creating short bursts of tension. Throughout the scene in which Billy Macfarlane (Paul Nicholls) is shot, for instance, the audience is merely given fleeting images as the camera moves rapidly from the injured man to his distraught brother, thus heightening the sense of chaos and confusion. The most lacking aspect of *The Trench* is its inability to elicit any in-depth knowledge of, or empathy for, the characters. Although the audience may appreciate the futility of their situation and the inevitability of their deaths, the potential shock of their final annihilation is undermined by this weak character development. Solid yet unremarkable, Boyd's direction does nothing to distinguish his film from any other World War One picture. When he does turn his hand to something original, such as the freeze frames of soldiers receiving mortal wounds in the final sequence, this mostly fails to achieve the desired effect.

He is currently writing a television mini-series, 'Sword of Honour', based on the Evelyn Waugh novel. **BPr**

Danny BOYLE

Born in Manchester, UK, in 1956, Danny Boyle directed television programmes before teaming up with producer Andrew Macdonald and scriptwriter John Hodge to break into

The Trench (1999)

Shallow Grave (1994)
Trainspotting (1996)

features with *Shallow Grave* (1994), followed by *Trainspotting* (1996), which consolidated their success. Their films have distinctive visual styles and soundtracks, combining a range of contemporary British music as well as astute selections from pop history.
Both *Shallow Grave* and *Trainspotting* introduced a fresh attitude into British cinema;
their influence is evident in subsequent films, including Justin Kerrigan's *Human Traffic*
(1999) and Guy Ritchie's *Lock, Stock and Two Smoking Barrels* (1998). Having made
such an impact at the start of his film-making career, Boyle's next projects, *A Life Less
Ordinary* (1997) and *The Beach* (2000), were closely scrutinised. With expectations so
high, it was almost inevitable that they would not receive as much acclaim as his previous two.

Shallow Grave opens with accelerated camera movement, one of the team's stylistic
trademarks. Primary-coloured production design and unusual camera angles lend visual
appeal to, both expanding and flattening, the space within an Edinburgh flat shared by
self-absorbed young professionals Alex, David and Juliet. The three rapidly turn on each
other over a suitcase full of money; all they must do to keep it is dismember and bury the
dead man who left it in their flat. Cross-cutting parallels them with two violent criminals
who are searching for the money. Alex is the most consistently selfish character, and the
glint in Ewan McGregor's eyes makes him the most likeable. *Shallow Grave* suggests
that style, and being smarter and quicker with one's greed than everyone else, defines
successful, admirable young characters in mid-1990s British culture. It never presumes
to offer overt judgement as to whether or not this is a good thing.

Trainspotting was the most fêted film of 1990s British cinema. This adaptation
of Irvine Welsh's novel about Edinburgh heroin users is ostensibly quite different from
Shallow Grave's original screenplay. What they share is a fascination with an amoral,
individualistic outlook characteristic of post-Thatcherite Britain. Although set in a less
affluent environment, it is survival and self-interest, rather than social protest, that also
drives *Trainspotting*'s characters. Boundaries between acceptability and criminality blur
for instance when the cynically intelligent, charming Renton (Ewan McGregor) switches
careers from petty thief to London estate agent. Similarly, group solidarity fragments
when serious money is obtained through a fortuitous drug deal. Prior to this, the intense
momentary pleasures as well as dangers of drug taking, provide the film's main focus. In
representing these pleasures *Trainspotting* takes stylistic elements from *Shallow Grave*
to their zenith. Editing and voice-over narration help to sustain a rapid pace over ninety
minutes. The film opens with tracking shots of Renton being chased along Edinburgh's
Princes Street, accompanied by his famous 'choose life' voice-over and Iggy Pop's 'Lust
for Life' on the soundtrack. His speech – 'Choose washing-machines, cars, compact disc
players and electrical tin openers...' – may reject conventional identities based upon
ordinary forms of consumption, but the inescapable lure of consumerism is ambiguously
affirmed at the end. A tease trailer, posters, and excellent soundtrack marketed *Trainspotting* very effectively and helped make it into a profitable multimedia event, one which
extended far beyond the film into fans' lives.

A Life Less Ordinary alludes to Powell and Pressburger's *A Matter of Life and Death*
(1946). Two angels from a bleached-white heaven come to earth to make inept kidnap-
per Ewan McGregor and feisty hostage Cameron Diaz fall in love. In Boyle's previous films
romance is a peripheral concern, and perhaps because it breaks new ground, pacing and
performances in *A Life Less Ordinary* are awkward. Major differences outweigh the film's
superficial resemblance to *A Matter of Life and Death*, in which the Anglo-American
romance carries conviction and, although fantastic, has cultural resonance. *A Life Less
Ordinary* handles its material in a tongue-in-cheek manner, culminating in a bullet of love
shot through the heart and the stars' direct to camera declaration about the wonder of
love. This blank pastiche of romantic conventions leaves a void at the film's centre.

The Beach, the *Trainspotting* team's second adaptation of a popular youth orientated
novel, returns to more familiar territory. Alex Garland's story about a secret Thai island
paradise for Western travellers is reworked into a big-budget Leonardo Di Caprio vehicle.
Darius Khondji's location cinematography and Masahiro Hirakubo's fluent editing compensate for *A Life Less Ordinary*'s stylistic longeurs. Like *Shallow Grave* and *Trainspotting*, *The Beach* charts the dissolution of a small, enclosed community and tests a selfish protagonist's survival skills. The narrative's puncturing of Western tourists' fantasies

sits uneasily with the film's visual allure. The *Trainspotting* team have yet to successfully translate the style and attitude exemplified in their earlier work into bigger budget film-making.

2001 will see Boyle directing two television movies: *Strumpet* and *Vacuuming Completely Nude in Paradise*. An omnibus sci-fi comedy, 'Alien Love Triangle', is also in production for the small screen.   **MSt**

Stephen BRADLEY

Stephen Bradley worked as an assistant to the line producer on Jim Sheridan's *My Left Foot* (1989) and co-produced Paddy Breathnach's art-house feature *Ailsa* (1994). In 1994 he wrote and directed an imaginative 13-minute short entitled *Reaper*, a meta-fictional, black comedy about an apprentice grim reaper (Felim Drew) who comes to claim the old Hollywood actor O.Z. 'Zebby' Whitehead (played by himself). When Zebby shows him that he has already been immortalised in John Ford's classic *The Grapes of Wrath* (1940), the reaper is persuaded that the actor cannot die and the tables are turned against him. Footage of Whitehead as Al Joad appears in the film.

Sweety Barrett (1998)

Bradley wrote and directed his first feature, an Irish-Icelandic co-production, *Sweety Barrett*, in 1998. The story focuses on the dim-witted but kind Sweety Barrett (Brendan Gleeson) who loses his job at a travelling circus and comes to the Irish port of Dockery looking for work. Sweety's nature makes him easy prey in this tough town of poteen smugglers, controlled by a corrupt cop, Mannix Bone (Liam Cunningham). During the day Sweety strikes up a friendship with a young boy; at night, he unwittingly carries out the dirty work for Bone and his gang. When the boy's father is released from prison, Sweety is dragged into a dangerous feud. Although it seems that Bone will get away with murder, Sweety exacts a spectacular revenge, transforming himself into a redeeming hero. *Sweety Barrett* is effectively photographed by Thomas Mauch and has a lush score by Stephen McKeon. Despite a solid supporting cast (including some fine comic turns by Mikel Murfi and Raymond Keane), the script lacks narrative cohesion and relies too much on the physical presence of Brendan to carry it. An uneven and off-beat feature, it nonetheless makes for a promising debut.

Bradley's company, Temple Films, have produced Kirsten Sheridan's *Disco Pigs* (2000).   **KHo**

Kenneth BRANAGH

Born in Belfast, Northern Ireland, in 1960, Kenneth Branagh has already built an expansive career as both actor and director, demonstrating an ambition to work, for the most part, on a large canvas, notably in his highly successful adaptations of Shakespeare.

Henry V (1989)
Dead Again (1991)
Peter's Friends (1992)
Much Ado About Nothing (1993)

Establishing himself as a hotshot actor and director with the Royal Shakespeare Company in the mid-1980s, and securing several high-profile roles in television drama and British films, Branagh made the leap into feature-film directing, carrying his debut movie off with all the bravura and confidence of his screen idol, James Cagney. In 1989 his *Henry V* was released to acclaim and strong box office. In contrast to Olivier's screen version, Branagh's is essentially grittier, infused with an immediacy in its action sequences (partly the result of smaller camera technology) and a more intimate scale than its predecessor. Branagh's film feels like a war movie in its Battle of Agincourt scenes and the film is brazenly emotional throughout, ably amplified by the debut film score of top composer Patrick Doyle. It is a film marked by several set-pieces: the 'Once more unto the breech' speech; and the singing of 'Non Nobis Domine' as the camera tracks with Branagh along a line of dead soldiers in the mud.

Frankenstein (1994)
In the Bleak Midwinter (1995)
Hamlet (1996)
Love's Labour's Lost (2000)

He made confident use of the film's high profile and followed it up with a contemporary thriller, *Dead Again* (1991), produced by Paramount Pictures. Branagh starred with Emma Thompson and Derek Jacobi in the florid thriller that owes a debt to Hitchcock. Robin Williams appears in an unbilled cameo, which he plays seedy and low. The film centres on a contemporary LA gumshoe named Mike Church (Branagh) who becomes involved with an amnesiac who confuses fantasy and reality, soon enough embroiling Church in her confusion and turmoil as he falls in love with her. The film boldly dashes back and forth between black and white and colour, the action amplified by Patrick Doyle's Hermann-esque score.

In contrast to *Dead Again*, Branagh directed the warm and upbeat ensemble piece *Peter's Friends* (1992), a British version of Lawrence Kasdan's landmark *The Big Chill* (1983), written by American Rita Rudner. The story is set over one weekend where a group of thirty-something friends from university gather at a country house. Inevitably tensions, regrets and aspirations fuel the drama and the performances are strong throughout. He then directed a short, *Swan Song* (1992), a two hander starring Richard Briers and John Gielgud in which the drama centres on an affectionate remembrance of the theatre and a consideration of its future.

He followed *Swan Song* with a return to Shakespeare in the sunny adaptation, *Much Ado About Nothing* (1993), a film bursting with good vibrations, marked by the presence of several Hollywood stars – Michael Keaton, Denzel Washington and Keanu Reeves. It features a virtuoso handheld camera shot that begins high above ground before reaching the floor and continuing through a party scene. Branagh's admirable affinity for making Shakespeare multiplex-friendly resulted in one of his best directorial efforts. As with his other films, his commitment to a strong musical presence was evidenced by Patrick Doyle's hit score – notable in the opening of the movie when the men ride in, à la *The Magnificent Seven* (1960). As with his adaptation of *Henry V*, the film appropriately delivers Shakespearean language for a contemporary audience.

With each project gradually becoming more high-profile, Branagh teamed up with producer Francis Ford Coppola and actor Robert De Niro for *Mary Shelley's Frankenstein* (1994). Perhaps a little too frenzied for its own good, and certainly part of a mid-1990s Hollywood interest in the gothic, the film entertainingly combines a certain theatricality (such as the sweeping staircase) and cinematic scale. Branagh himself portrayed the good doctor and his skilful direction is evidenced in De Niro's performance as the monster. For all the attendant hype, however, the film did not do as well as expected, despite its fidelity to the complete story, beginning, as the novel does, in the snowy wastes of the Arctic. That said, it is a film of exuberance, particularly in the moment when Frankenstein creates the monster: the doctor dashes around his laboratory, the camera swirling and swooping, accompanied by Patrick Doyle's musical score which pulsates with appropriate bombast. Branagh's next film, *In the Bleak Midwinter* (1995), was markedly opposite. A small-scale ensemble piece, very much in the spirit of an Ealing comedy, it is about an unemployed actor who tries to find a way to help his sister's church survive by staging an amateur performance of Hamlet. The experience of creating the play brings out other tensions and emotions amongst the villagers. An intimate film, it is brimming with good humour and energy. Shot in black and white, it was re-titled for America as *A Midwinter's Tale*.

Branagh confidently returned to the broad canvas with his unexpurgated *Hamlet* (1996), which he also wrote. Where Franco Zeffirelli's version, made in 1990, was much abbreviated and set in the age it was written, Branagh's is set against the nineteenth-century Franco-Prussian war. The film is arguably his best Shakespeare adaptation yet, himself captivating with bleached blonde hair in the title role and Kate Winslet as Ophelia. Whilst some may find it distracting, Branagh essays supporting character roles to Hollywood big hitters Billy Crystal, Gérard Depardieu, Charlton Heston and Robin Williams. He also draws on his own repertory of actors – including Derek Jacobi (as Claudius) and Richard Briers (as Polonius). The film was relatively well received upon release and looks fantastic, courtesy of Alex Thomson's cinematography. As always, Branagh's core creative team were in place – producer David Barron and composer Patrick Doyle.

His most recent feature, *Love's Labour's Lost* (2000), is an adaptation of the Shakespeare play rendered in the style of a 1930s musical. Like *Much Ado About Nothing*, *Love's Labour's Lost*, another romantic comedy, possesses the same kind of energy and upbeat sensibility. Again, Shakespeare's text is rendered audience-friendly and the action is partly driven by song-and-dance numbers. The film makes a satisfying companion piece to *Much Ado*, and although Branagh occasionally needs to reign in his enthusiasm, it confirms his panache as a director. Committed to making Shakespeare accessible to mainstream audiences, in years to come he may be assessed as one of the cinema's strongest interpreters of the playwright's work.   **JC**

Paddy BREATHNACH

Paddy Breathnach is part of a younger generation of Irish film-makers, which includes Ailsa (1994) Gerard Stembridge and Vinny Murphy, who are heavily influenced by European and I Went Down (1997) American cinema and much less self-conscious than many of their embattled predeces- Blow Dry (2001) sors about politics or their Irish identity. If Stembridge seems to be longing for the days of European psychodrama and Murphy is itching to make genre films, then Breathnach is cutting a middle path between them.

His first feature, *Ailsa* (1994), is a brooding, sumptuously photographed film about a Dubliner who begins to lose interest in his live-in girlfriend, becoming obsessed with the young American, Campbell (Juliette Gruber), living downstairs. Dublin is always dark, rainy or overcast; Breathnach elicits restrained performances from his actors, most nota- bly Brendan Coyle, who plays Miles, the obsessive in question. Eschewing any overt violence, instead he sharpens the mood and tone to convey a sense of restless hopeless- ness. This is an intensely dreary movie, a valuable portrait of the 1990s as a period that was oppressive rather than expansive.

After making the creepy short narrative *The Long Way Home* (1995), Breathnach changed his tone dramatically with *I Went Down* (1997). A revisionist genre film, it tells the story of Git (Peter McDonald), a nice young man caught up with the mob, who needs to pull 'one last job' before he can get out. He is paired with an older, tougher man, improbably named Bunny (Brendan Gleeson), with whom he eventually bonds. The film is filled with the narrative conventions of the gangster film, but they are rendered with such verve and energy that it is difficult to find fault with its essentially derivative nature. There are some distinctively Irish flourishes: a car chase that unfolds on rural Ireland's insanely narrow roads is brilliantly realised; at one point Git walks across a field and for no real narrative reason falls right into a bog. This is genre cinema as it was meant to be – familiar, local and ironic.

Breathnach's new film, *Blow Dry* (2001), stars Alan Rickman as a Yorkshire barber whose flamboyance is awakened by a national hairdressing championship; Natasha Richardson plays his wife. It has been compared with *Strictly Ballroom* (1992) for the way in which it revels in the plastic excess of competitive kitsch-mongers. With only three features, Breatnach has already established himself as one of Ireland's new genera- tion of film-makers, proving to be restless, moving freely across genres and locations. The effect they will have on Irish cinema as a whole should be extremely interesting.   **JW**

Alan BRIDGES

Born in 1927, Alan Bridges, like many of the most talented British directors to make Act of Murder (1965) their first mark in the 1960s, emerged from the training school that was provided by Invasion (1966) television. Also, like many of his contemporaries, he has frequently found a home back The Hireling (1973) on the small screen when cinema work has proved elusive. He has successfully managed Out of Season (1975) to make the transition from low-budget genre entries to sophisticated and well-dressed Age of Innocence (1977) literary adaptations and period pieces. The Return of the Soldier

Nothing could be further from the world of bourgeois manners and class distinctions (1982) evidenced in his later films than the no-nonsense, sparse environment of the budget The Shooting Party (1984) crime dramas that first drew attention. The unjustly neglected 'Edgar Wallace Mysteries' Fire Princess (1990) were produced by Jack Greenwood at his tiny Merton Park production base as strictly 'B' movie programme fillers, but they provided a wonderful training ground for a young direc- tor. Whilst the majority of the series' episodes rapidly ended up on television, Bridges' *Act of Murder* (1965), which clocked in at barely over an hour, was good enough to attract some very positive critical reactions. It remains a model of brisk, tightly constructed genre film-making, with a suitably labyrinthine plot handled with a sophistication which belies its rather lowly origins. It also showed the acute sense of social location that was to become a recurring feature of Bridges' later work.

He proved himself to be equally adept at science fiction with *Invasion* (1966), also shot at Merton Park. The classic sci-fi story of a sleepy English village beset one night by invaders from outer space is told with an attention to detail and conviction which links it to American films such as Don Siegel's *Invasion of the Body Snatchers* (1956). Despite meagre resources and a cast lacking any real star names, Bridges succeeded in imbuing the atmosphere with the same sense of reality that had grounded his earlier crime film. What links these early films to Bridges' subsequent work is his fascination with varying forms of social unease. Although his Merton Park work helped to develop something of a cult reputation for Bridges, he continued to produce television work for the BBC that frequently moved between those dominant paradigms of British cinema, realism and the 'quality' tradition. Pieces such as *On the Eve of Publication* and *Traitor* appeared under the BBC's innovative, socially aware 'Wednesday Play' and 'Play for Today' slots, which had showcased Ken Loach's early work, whilst *The Wild Duck* remained firmly in the category of tasteful literary adaptation.

The move towards his more recognisable later style was confirmed by Bridges' most notable critical success to date, *The Hireling* (1973), which won the Palme d'Or at that year's Cannes Film Festival. Like Joseph Losey's rather similar *The Go-Between* (1971), it was adapted from a novel by L.P. Hartley and deals with the same kinds of sexual and class tensions. In this case these are created by the affair between an upper-class woman, played by Sarah Miles, and her proletarian chauffeur. *The Hireling* is an elegant piece of film-making, with its carefully accumulated period detail, sumptuous cinematography and handsome production design. The acute, not uncritical, examination of social manners and attitudes amongst the 1920s English elite is framed within a nostalgic mise-en-scène. Although this occasionally weakens the social critique, it does allow for the nuances of class difference and prejudice to emerge.

Bridges takes a similar approach in *Out of Season* (1975), where an old romance is rekindled between Cliff Robertson and Vanessa Redgrave in a beautifully observed wintry English seaside resort. Here the passions and tensions that threaten to disrupt the civilised social world are barely contained beneath the immaculate surfaces. *Age of Innocence* (1977), which Bridges made in Canada, works the same kind of vein, centring on the frictions caused by the developing pacifist leanings of an English teacher, played by David Warner, in a narrow post-war community. His disruptive presence breaks the façade of controlled contentment and leads inevitably to violence. Bridges' restrained, but essentially romantic sensibility, and his concern for the conflict between desire and social conventions, pervades all these films; it was quite fitting that he should have become the director of the television version of David Lean's *Brief Encounter* (1974).

The Return of the Soldier (1982), scripted by Hugh Whitemore from Rebecca West's first novel, examines the psychological after-effects of war through the story of an amnesiac soldier, played by Alan Bates. His rekindled affections for an old love (Glenda Jackson), who is working-class, bring to the surface the tensions in his own relationship to his cold, middle-class wife (Julie Christie). The film is a further demonstration of Bridges' continuing fascination with the repressive nature of class and the anxieties caused by a submerged sexuality. *The Shooting Party* (1984), a summation of his achievements as a director, is set amongst the landed aristocracy on the eve of World War One. It is a subtle evocation of a social class on the edge of extinction, unable to cope with the changes that are about to engulf them. Understated as always, Bridges handles his outstanding cast (James Mason, Edward Fox, Dorothy Tutin, John Gielgud) with skill, creating a gleaming image of post-Edwardian Britain that seems poised between affection for a vanished way of life and condemnation of the complacency of the class he is depicting.

Other than the relatively uninteresting commercial assignment of *Fire Princess* (1990), a romantic thriller with Eric Roberts and Jennifer Jason Leigh, Bridges' continued absence from British film production is to be regretted. Although his work has frequently exhibited the kinds of internal contradictions typical of much 'heritage' cinema, with its uneasy combination of social critique and romantic visual techniques, Bridges' best films have succeeded in gently peeling away the veneer of class affectations, uncovering the emotional torrents flowing beneath.   **RS**

Nick BROOMFIELD

Lily Tomlin (1986) Born in London in 1948, Nick Broomfield studied law at Cardiff University and political
Driving Me Crazy (1988) science at Essex University, before attending the National Film School and becoming a
Diamond Skulls (1989) celebrated and controversial documentarist. In a career spanning almost thirty years he
Monster in a Box (1991) has been responsible for some interesting developments in the documentary field which

has led to the receipt of numerous awards, including the prestigious Robert Flaherty *Fetishes* (1996)
Award, the Prix Italia and a British Academy Award. *Kurt and Courtney* (1998)

His noted early works, including *Juvenile Liaison* (1975) and *Tattooed Tears* (1982), were made in collaboration with Joan Churchill. All cinéma-vérité documentaries, they are objective representations of uncompromising subject matter – be it a stark correctional institution, or the work of the Bradford police with young offenders. The principal feature of Broomfield's work – his desire to get extraordinarily close to his subjects – is already a prominent theme here, as is the fact that he seems unwilling to tread softly around the characters that populate his films. This has often led to antagonism. Early controversy was stirred by *Juvenile Liaison*, in which the Bradford police considered their representation to be problematic; they successfully lobbied the British Film Institute for the film's withdrawal.

Two non-documentary films sit oddly in the middle of his career: *Diamond Skulls* (1989) and *Monster in a Box* (1991). The latter is a performance film of Spalding Gray's monologue, a follow up to Jonathan Demme's *Swimming to Cambodia* (1987). Whilst not as groundbreaking as Demme's film, *Monster in a Box* seems to focus more attention on the matter of Gray's performance and the presentation of a subject which is difficult to make visually interesting is successful. By contrast, Broomfield's only genuine fictional film, *Diamond Skulls*, is a lamentable thriller. Critically derided, the most apposite comment is Broomfield's own: 'Yep, well, what can I say. A great cast, a great producer, writer and cinematographer ... But I think I kind of screwed it up.'

It is with later work as a documentarian, however, that Broomfield made his name, and specifically his 1983 film, *Chicken Ranch*, in which he started to develop his 'trademark' style, seeking to investigate a contentious subject by putting himself on-screen right in the midst of the subject to be investigated. There are two modes of investigation. First is the opposition to officialdom. This is shown in such pieces as *The Leader, His Driver and the Driver's Wife* (1991), a portrait of South African, white supremacist Eugene Terreblanche, *Tracking Down Maggie* (1994), Broomfield's portrait of Margaret Thatcher after the end of her career as Prime Minister, and *Kurt and Courtney* (1998), his examination of the death of Kurt Cobain. Second, there is the representation of counter-cultural entities, be it the brothel in *Chicken Ranch* or the sado-masochism club of *Fetishes* (1996). In all cases, the structure is pre-determined; Broomfield and his cameraman attempt to get close to the people they are filming, antagonistically try to pose very difficult questions, and frequently put themselves in positions of peril.

Irrespective of the subject matter, however, there is really only one topic in all these films, and that is Broomfield himself. As the *faux-naif* investigator, Broomfield is willing to imperil himself – as he does with Eugene Terreblanche and Margaret Thatcher's security guards – for the sake of an entertaining documentary where the amusement comes from the mode of investigation, yet is frequently at odds with the way officialdom is presented, almost in hegemonic terms, as a menacing entity. He is the 'agent provocauteur', and in the face of his singular project, the characters in his films become secondary, almost like caricatures. Ultimately, the viewer seems to learn very little about the subjects at hand, and quite a lot about Nick Broomfield himself. That said, he does at least raise interesting questions, leaving the viewer to make their own decision.   **JP**

Kevin BROWNLOW

For many, Kevin Brownlow's legacy will be his dazzling restoration of Abel Gance's epic *It Happened Here* (1966)
historical drama *Napoléon* (1927) – at the age of eleven he possessed his favourite two *Winstanley* (1975)
reels of the film. For some, it might be his film documentaries and books, and for others it *D.W. Griffith: Father of Film*
might be his two impassioned, unusual and engaging feature films. Born in West Sussex, (1993)
UK, in 1938, Brownlow is a landmark film historian and archivist who has contributed much to film culture and an awareness of some of the great film traditions over the past thirty-five years. He is to chronicling Hollywood what film documentarist Ken Burns is to chronicling the American Civil War. Brownlow's commitment to documenting major personalities and movements in Hollywood film history complements and contrasts vividly with his engagement with social British history (actual and speculative) as a rich source for his own feature film work. In 1966, in collaboration with fellow film-maker and friend

Andrew Mollo, he wrote and directed *It Happened Here*, shot on location in London and Radnorshire in mid-Wales. It is an eerie film speculating what might have happened had the Nazis invaded Britain. The drama begins in 1944 and is sparked by Germany having to rely on England's own SS to fuel its armies. English citizens find themselves having to choose between resistance or collaboration. Images of German soldiers marching past famous London landmarks generate a particularly uneasy feeling. The film stars Sebastian Shaw who many years later went on to play Anakin Skywalker in *Return of the Jedi* (1983). Brownlow and Mollo began work on *It Happened Here* in 1956 when Brownlow was just 18 and it stands as a piece of early guerrilla film-making. The film's 'fantasy' is rooted in a realist aesthetic that does what cinema should do – make the unbelievable believable. In its final stages of completion, Brownlow received support from directors Tony Richardson and Stanley Kubrick.

As his career began to take shape, Brownlow worked as an editor and received credit as supervising editor on Tony Richardson's *The Charge of the Light Brigade* (1968). He also directed numerous documentary shorts and worked with Lindsay Anderson on his earliest efforts.

Alongside his fictional film-making, Brownlow has served film appreciation, study and archival work by producing a range of captivating documentaries, including the epic thirteen-part series 'Hollywood', which he co-directed in 1980 with David Gill. James Mason provided a suitably impassioned narration. Indeed, all of Brownlow's documentaries have been strengthened by the narrator's voice – Kenneth Branagh for the Universal horror piece and Lindsay Anderson for the Buster Keaton entry. Most recently, Brownlow directed a documentary about the life and times of Lon Chaney.

As a writer, Brownlow has contributed to analyses of film production and aesthetics, most notably in 'The Parade's Gone By', 'The War', 'The West and The Wilderness' and 'The Pioneers'. These three volumes comprised the foundation of the television series 'Hollywood'.

Following *It Happened Here*, Brownlow once again revisited British history, going far further back to the seventeenth century. The film, made in 1975, was *Winstanley* (based on the novel 'Brother Jacob') – a story set in 1649 when, under the leadership of Gerrard Winstanley (arguably enacting communist principles in his interpretation of what common land was), a community of poor men and women established a settlement in Surrey based on a life of equality. This is a marvellous film that makes one wish Brownlow had found other subjects to dramatise in a feature film format. The film's drama and roots in history are enriched by its realist aesthetic and there is a stillness to the entire piece which recalls the work of Roberto Rossellini, particularly his television film *The Rise to Power of Louis XIV* (1966). *Winstanley* is shot in black and white and lacks any obvious kind of drama. For many this has made the film exemplary of a modernist (perhaps even postmodernist) aesthetic. It is also invested with a political fervour that matched the politicised culture of the late 1960s and early 1970s, harking back to Brownlow's early contact with Lindsay Anderson and Tony Richardson, both responsible for the Free Cinema movement in Britain.

Brownlow's recently published 'David Lean', a biography of the director, is as meticulous as all his efforts and his place in the British film-making firmament is surely secure. **JC**

Nichola BRUCE

I Could Read the Sky (1999) Born in 1953, Nichola Bruce has primarily been associated with documentary film-making. Her documentaries include *The Human Face*, featuring Laurie Anderson for the BBC in 1991, *The Dramatic Art of Steven Berkoff* for Channel 4 in 1995, and *The Monument* with artist Rachael Whiteread for the BBC in 1996.

Her first fiction feature, *I Could Read the Sky* (1999), is an impressionistic reconstruction of Irish immigrant experience in England. Featuring the writer Dermot Healy in the role of the central character, *I Could Read the Sky* is a loose adaptation of the book by Timothy O'Grady and Steve Pyke. In the film, Healy, as the unnamed old man, reminisces about his life, his departure from his small family farm in western Ireland for England, and his subsequent existence as a labourer living in poor bedsits and on the road. As he speaks, digital imagery summons up and dissolves memories from his past, frequently layering one image on the other. The soundtrack is composed of the old man's accordion and extra-diegetic performances by artists such as Sinéad O'Connor and Rí Rá.

Aesthetically and thematically, *I Could Read the Sky* recalls Thaddeus O'Sullivan's earlier avant-garde feature, *On a Paving Stone Mounted* (1978); the themes of Bruce's film are departure and return, past and present. Whilst much of the imagery draws on recurrent Irish cinematic motifs of the bleakness of rural Irish life, in particular the centrality of family and the trauma of loss, its visual aesthetic consistently lifts it out of cliché. Bruce has herself recognised that the film's weakness is its neglect of female immigrant experience, a consequence of her fidelity to the source material.

She is in development with FilmFour on a futuristic journey film.   **RB**

Ray BURDIS
See **Dominic ANCIANO**

Jez BUTTERWORTH
Born in London, UK, in 1969, Jez Butterworth began writing screenplays in 1992, and *Mojo* (1997) in 1995 premiered his play 'Mojo' at the Royal Court Theatre in London. A huge success, *Birthday Girl* (2000) it was adapted into his first film, *Mojo* (1997), at which time Butterworth had already begun developing the screenplay for his next film, *Birthday Girl* (2000).

Mojo was backed by the BBC and British Screen. Set in the London Soho of 1958, in the fictional rock 'n' roll world of the Atlantic Club, the film dramatises the fight between the club's owner and a group of gangsters over the 'ownership' of up and coming star Silver Johnny. The tension leads to sexual rivalry, unrest and, eventually, to murder. The film was criticised for only partially succeeding to shake off its theatrical origins. It deserves praise, however, for stylish camerawork – particularly in the musical sequences – period design, and strong performances from Ricky Tomlinson, Ewen Bremner, Ian Hart and playwright-screenwriter Harold Pinter.

Birthday Girl, backed by Miramax, FilmFour and HAL Films, tells the story of a mild-mannered bank manager from suburban London (Ben Chaplin) who orders a Russian bride (Nicole Kidman) over the internet. She arrives on her birthday, and he soon finds his life turned upside-down, particularly when her two Russian cousins arrive. The film premiered at the 2000 Venice Film Festival and features a score by Angelo Badalmenti.

Butterworth is rumoured to be collaborating on a rock-opera with Blur's Alex James.   **PR**

Ed BYE
Ed Bye has been a noted and respected comedy director of British television throughout *Kevin and Perry Go Large* the 1990s and beyond. He is probably best known for directing 'Red Dwarf', the hugely (2000) successful sci-fi comedy series; also, 'The Detectives', which paired stand-up comic Japser Carrott with Robert Powell as a pair of inept police officers, and 'Bottom' which featured Rik Mayall and Ade Edmonson.

It is the humour of this last series that bears the closest resemblance to his only feature to date, *Kevin and Perry Go Large* (2000). The film is the big-screen outing for Kevin (comedian Harry Enfield) and Perry (Cannes award-winning actress Kathy Burke), characters from the sketch show 'Harry Enfield and Chums', based on how rude, useless and amusing teenagers are.

Kevin and Perry Go Large focuses on their visit to the European party capital Ibiza in an attempt to lose their virginities and become world-famous DJs. In this respect, the film is akin to other teenage sex comedies that emerged in the late 1990s, particularly *American Pie* (1999). It is an endless succession of jokes revolving around bodily functions that go from the slight, smirk-inducing, trouser-busting erections to the disgusting prospect of eating faeces.

A big advert for the Virgin Group and super-club Cream, Bye makes little effort to imbue the film with any cinematic qualities. Only an aerial shot of a suburban nightmare of cars being cleaned and lawns being cut at identical times with identical mowers give an indication that Bye could come up with something more inventive and thought-provoking. Sadly, *Kevin and Perry Go Large* appeals only to the lowest common denominator.

Bye is in production with a feature version of 'Red Dwarf'. **JR**

John BYRNE

The Slab Boys (1997) John Byrne, born in Paisley in 1940, first established himself as an artist and set designer before becoming a playwright and film director. His first play, 'Writer's Cramp', opened at the Edinburgh Festival in 1977 and 'The Slab Boys' premiered a year later. Inspired by his own experiences in the paint-mixing department of a carpet factory in Paisley, the latter won the Evening Standard Most Promising Playwright Award. BBC television subsequently commissioned a six-part series that remains one of the best pieces of television drama of the 1980s, the lyrical 'Tutti Frutti', concerning an ageing rock 'n' roll band. Another series followed, based around the Scottish country and western scene, 'Your Cheatin' Heart'.

Byrne's film version of his own play, *The Slab Boys* (1997), has been criticised for his use of local newcomers; however, his penchant has launched much young Scottish talent. The play's Broadway run established such stars as Val Kilmer, Sean Penn and Kevin Bacon. Further criticism has slated the film as a nostalgic 'vulgar cartoon', too close to its theatrical roots. But vulgar cartoons have of late been the new rock 'n' roll, and 'too theatrical' is often a criticism levelled at directors who reject a classic Hollywood realism. *The Slab Boys* does not romanticise the past or a supposed working-class solidarity; it has a bleak view of the limitations of dreams, aspirations and the attainability of self-fulfillment. Linguistically inventive with a caustic wit, and intertextually referencing British and American popular culture, it retains a wealth of local references. Byrne achieved his aim of a hyper-real fantasy world, a deliciously shoddy glamour, inspired by the technicolour style of Jack Cardiff who gave *Black Narcissus* (1945) such a hysterical visual style. The film is considered by some to fit nicely into the 'dirty magic realism' that has characterised much of recent Scottish cinema. Sophisticated and complexly ironic, *The Slab Boys* could have become a modern classic yet it was critically damned, proved unprofitable, and was denied a release outside Scotland.

Byrne has been chosen as an artist for one of Royal Mail's 'Millennium Stamps' and has recently had a retrospective of his paintings at Paisley Town Hall. He is currently writing another film on the life of R.D. Laing. **FG**

C

David CAFFREY

David Caffrey has had a relatively short yet varied and prosperous career, crewing on *Divorcing Jack* (1998) an assortment of films and television productions. He affirmed his talent for writing and directing with *Bolt* (1997), a short concerning a slap-dash revenge. *Bolt* was a precursor to his successful feature debut the following year, *Divorcing Jack* (1998).

Set in Northern Ireland on the eve of the country's first election as an independent state and based on the inspired premise of mistaken hearing ('Dvorak' not 'divorce Jack'), *Divorcing Jack* is a fast-paced, hard-hitting, black-comedy thriller. Caffrey's obvious skill as a director is stamped on every scene; he has an eye for precision, crafting shots that are aesthetically pleasing in their spacial dimensions. Capable of eliciting the best from his actors, the film is brimming with excellent performances, most notably from its lead David Thewlis, which contribute to the flawless exactitude it exudes. Caffrey put this skill to good use again in the BBC mini-series 'Aristocrats', a well-constructed piece of drama that he directed in 1999. His greatest talent, however, is his aptitude for blending the sinister and the jocular: the audience both laughs at an inept reporter fleeing for his life from the IRA, the UEF, the RUC and the British Army, and also worries about the severity of his situation.

Caffrey has also made *On the Nose*, which has yet to be released.   **BPr**

Simon CALLOW

Born in London, UK, in 1949, Simon Callow made his name as a stage actor, working *The Ballad of the Sad Café* successfully in repertory and then at the National Theatre as Mozart in Peter Schaffer's (1991) critically acclaimed 'Amadeus' in 1979. The inevitable television parts followed and Callow became a household name as the eccentric Simon Chance in the television farce 'Chance in a Million'. He branched into film acting with notable successes including the Merchant-Ivory production of *A Room With a View* (1985) and a slew of Hollywood movies such as Mike Nichols' *Postcards from the Edge* (1990), James Ivory's *Mr and Mrs Bridge* (1990) and Steve Oedekerk's *Ace Ventua: When Nature Calls* (1995).

His early relationship with the Merchant-Ivory team was to prove fortuitous when Ismail Merchant was looking for a director for his film production *The Ballad of the Sad Café* (1991), an adaptation of Carson McCuller's novella. Callow had already exercised his directorial bent with opera and theatre, including Willy Russell's 'Shirley Valentine' on Broadway. Merchant found Callow to be 'a visionary', declaring, 'You just have to take the plunge if you believe in somebody'.

For many, the trust was misplaced, as Callow seemed to find it difficult to direct with imagination and skill for the cinema. The film was criticised for its staginess and lack of style, favouring tableaux above fluidity, and relying on hackneyed cinematic tricks in a lacklustre attempt to avoid theatrics. Perhaps the lack of a distinctive cinematic vision derives from Callow's own limited experience and his view of the work of the director as one who must 'accommodate and weave [the talent] into one texture as discreetly and invisibly as possible'. In doing so, he fails to capture any real sense of the precise evocation of community so integral to the novella's atmosphere.

Although he professes to the desire to make another film, Callow has been kept busy directing a new stage version of 'Les Enfants du Paradis' and the premiere of 'Carmen Jones', and writing acclaimed biographies of Charles Laughton and Orson Welles.   **JD**

Donald CAMMELL

Performance (1970)
Demon Seed (1977)
White of the Eye (1987)
The Argument (1999)
Wild Side (2000)

One of modern cinema's great individualists, Donald Cammell was born in Edinburgh, Scotland, in 1934, son of Charles Richard Cammell, heir to the Cammell Laird shipbuilding fortune, who was also an early, sympathetic biographer of their good family friend, misunderstood occultist Aleister Crowley. As a boy Donald showed a precocious talent for painting and drawing. Embarking on a career as an artist, his picture of the Marquis of Dufferin and Ava was judged society portrait of the year in 1953. Extended trips to New York and Paris and the lure of money failed to sustain his interest in art as a job. Having been caught up in the sex, drugs and rock 'n' roll demi-monde where gutter-class and upper-class mixed freely (and with a walk-on in Eric Rohmer's *La Collectionneuse* (1966) under his belt), Cammell entered the film world by scripting *The Touchables* (1968). A superficial piece directed by Robert Freeman, it was about a pop star captured by girl fans who also falls foul of some gangsters; Ian La Frenais rewrote before it hit the screen. This was quickly followed by the more interesting, hippy, heist screenplay for Robert Parrish's *Duffy* (1968), starring James Fox and James Coburn. Although allegedly based on fact, the film is a frivolous piece very much of its era and Cammell always dismissed it as unworthy of discussion.

Cammell's first directorial project is the one he is forever cursed (or blessed) to be remembered for. *Performance* (1968, not shown until 1970) – co-helmed with Nicolas Roeg – began life as a script called 'The Performers', inspired by the mingling of villains like the Krays with showbiz folk. It was intended to be a project for Mick Jagger and Marlon Brando, but the latter passed and a much-revised screenplay finally mutated into the picture that was released. The film was hated by the studio, who demanded cuts for the US, as well as re-dubbing and re-editing, and the critics, who called it 'worthless … disgusting' (Richard Schickel) and 'sleazy, self-indulgent and meretricious' (John Simon). *Performance* tells of a London thug who kills one of his gangland circle and hides out with a reclusive rock star and his two girls (the menage-à-trois was a Cammell preoccupation) in a bohemian Notting Hill household. He thinks he is tough, but soon finds his sexual identity and his code of testosterone-soaked, bloody masculinity being challenged and chemically re-ordered by wily, game-playing pop star Turner. Gangster Chas (James Fox) finally shoots Turner (Mick Jagger), before he himself is led away to his own end by the mob heavies who have tracked him down. At the last we see that Chas has become Turner; it is Jagger's face that stares at us from the window of the departing Roller. Some critics have interpreted this as a hopeful ending – death affirming life, linking the image of the bullet boring into brain with Cammell's own suicide. Yet *Performance* is so overloaded with meaning that however many names it provokes the critic to drop – Borges, Artuad, Bataille – there is never likely to be one definitive interpretative schema (optimistic, magical, pessimistic, political, pan-sexual) that will triumph. Benefiting from two strong leads, what made this slice of avant-gangsterism a cult film when it was finally issued was Cammell's innovative scatter-gun editing style, not to mention a great soundtrack and the way that this apparently standard, if violent, crime picture turns down a strange alley halfway through. Cammell and Jagger described it as a 'perverted love affair between Homo Sapiens and Lady Violence', and critic David Del Valle later dubbed it 'psychedelic expressionism'. The film certainly yields more with each viewing, and there are many legends about its making and the effects on the makers – Fox for one was said to have been mentally troubled for some years after. For a long time the critical orthodoxy was that the film was primarily the work of co-director Roeg, a canard only recently reversed with the writing of two monographs on *Performance* which explore Cammell's contribution in detail. It would appear that Roeg mainly handled the cinematography.

Living off scripts in development that were never made, Cammell based himself in Hollywood with partner China Kong and only completed three further features. The visually dazzling *Demon Seed* (1977) was supposed to be a comedy about the mating of a computer with a scientist's wife (Julie Christie), but MGM did not get the joke; only the sumptuous images remain as evidence of Cammell's input in what is now a rather lethargic sci-fi thriller. The theme of a computer considering itself superior to humanity was handled far better in Stanley Kubrick's *2001: A Space Odyssey* (1968), but what Cammell's cut of *Demon Seed* might have been like is impossible to determine at this juncture. *White of the Eye* (1987), however, is a marvellous, painterly little film about a gifted hi-fi engineer (David Keith) in the Arizona desert who turns out to be a kind of Jackson Pollock of serial killers, the results of his depravity resembling gory action paintings. A 'painter who happens to make films', as he has described himself, Cammell transforms Margaret Tracy's novel 'Mrs White' into a surreal meditation on the limits of love when confronted by the madness of what Cammell labels a 'psychotic with an aesthetic imagination'. The NPAA (the US ratings board) wanted cuts and an X-rating (commercial death for all but porn flicks), but a timely letter from Cammell's friend Marlon Brando managed to prevent that and save much of his vision.

Donald Cammell's final directorial work was *Wild Side* (1995), a weird, funny and erotic thriller with Christopher Walken and Anne Heche which was widely anticipated but so messed about by the studio that he took his name off the credits. It was finally released straight-to-video with the director credit 'Frank Brauner'. In April of 1996, after writing a note absolving China Kong of any blame, Cammell committed suicide by a gunshot to the head while she was in the next room. He lived for a short time and was lucid throughout – Kong is adamant he did not kill himself due to depression over his career and the *Wild Side* debacle. Ironically, in death Donald Cammell appears to be having more success than he did in life. In addition to the two books on *Performance*, the BBC showed a major documentary on his life and work, *Donald Cammell: The Ultimate Performance* (1998), while Rebecca and Sam Umland are to publish a full biography. Best of all, editor Frank Mazzola – using an old videoprint workprint as guide – restored *Wild Side* to the director's cut; with Cammell's name back on the credits, it had a European release in 2000. It now emerges as one of his best works, an insane, over-the-top and eroticised deconstruction of American film noir territory. Described aptly by one critic as 'beyond incorrect', it shuffles Cammell's trademark concerns of pan-sexuality, ultra-violence and the limits of time, space and gender in a final valediction of his unique genius. Also, during the early 1970s, when he appeared in Kenneth Anger's Crowleyean masterpiece *Lucifer Rising* (1970–80), Cammell shot an experimental widescreen short with Mazzola called *The Argument* (1971). Made to test effects ideas for a projected mega-movie called *Ishtar* (no relation to the Hoffman/Beatty disaster), the exploration of sexuality was, like its big brother, never completed. After the director's death, Mazzola came across the footage and undertook the completion of the film.

A poet of the cinema, one could argue for hours in search of Cammell's themes. Critic Colin McCabe avows that *Performance* is a film which 'demands a very wide range of cultural reference for its interpretation'. His quote from Bataille – 'eroticism ... is the affirmation of life even unto death itself' – which he profers as an apt epigraph for that film, could serve as a credo for Donald Cammell's entire oeuvre. While he admits there is disagreement among the director's friends on the point, McCabe says 'Cammell was not interested in politics but he was interested in magic'. **SR**

Danny CANNON

Born in London in 1968, Danny Cannon began making films when he was sixteen. By eighteen, he had written, produced and directed over a dozen shorts and videos, including a forty-minute piece, *Sometimes*, for television which won the BBC's Film-maker of the Year award in 1987.

He went on to study at the National Film and Television School, where he made two short films to some acclaim. The second, *Strangers* (1991), was bought for television transmission by Britain's Channel Four.

His first feature, which he also wrote, is slightly reminiscent of *Strangers*, again dealing with a gangster lifestyle. *Young Americans* (1993), a British movie with an Anglo-American cast including Harvey Keitel, was clearly designed to call loudly to Hollywood. The film's production style is slickly American, as is its story about a street-wise American policeman sent to London to investigate a drug-ring. A gangster-style thriller set in Soho clubland, the movie utilises MTV-style editing and the steel blues and greys favoured by the makers of glossy Hollywood fare. Its fast pace and youthful energy certainly appealed – Cannon was summoned to direct the $80 million *Judge Dredd* (1995), starring Sylvester Stallone. The studio and star's action-movie sensibilities clashed with Cannon's attempts to produce a film of heightened reality with a symbolic mise-en-scène. It is visually incoherent, a combination of influences from superior films such as *Metropolis* (1927), *Ben Hur* (1959), *El Cid* (1961), and *Blade Runner* (1982), with none of the visual style and clarity of those films.

Like Rachel Talalay's *Tank Girl* (1995) and the Hollywood *Batman* franchise, the film's budget works against it and its director. A cult comic transferred to film cannot count on a mainstream cinema audience, and cult audiences cannot begin to recoup such vast investments, a factor not unnoticed by Hollywood.

With *Dredd* a critical and commercial failure, Cannon was forced to back off from Hollywood for a while, and he returned to Britain where he executive-produced Paul Hills' *Boston Kickout* (1996), an affectionate look at working-class youth. He then directed *Phoenix* (1998) – a drama about the problems of four detectives operating in Phoenix, Arizona – for Sky Television.

Cannon returned to Hollywood to direct a sequel to one of the latest, interminable, horror franchises (of which Wes Craven's *Scream* franchise is the most successful), *I Still Know What You Did Last Summer* (1988). Capitalising on the youth-market dollar and using new stars like Freddie Prinze Jr., Jennifer Love Hewitt and Brandy, the film must serve as something of an embarrassment to Cannon: he was offered and rejected the original, and here he seems duly chastised. The film is a series of slow-turning door-knobs, shadows and 'behind you' mentality; the narrative relies on the 'it's only a dream' excuse too often for its audience to accept the film's events as frightening. Cannon has said that in creating the look and atmosphere of this film he wanted to evoke the terror and intrigue of *The Shining*'s (1980) Overlook Hotel, showing himself to be almost as deluded as the inhabitant of that terrifying place.

At this stage in his career he would do well to discover his own voice rather than attempt to call out to Hollywood with unsatisfactory combinations of other works.   **JD**

John CARNEY

Co-directors John Carney and Tom Hall have been responsible for some of the more interesting of the new wave of low-budget Irish films that emerged in the 1990s. Neither has had formal training in film – Hall briefly studied production whilst Carney has a background in music. This accounts for the striking compositions that have been a feature of the duo's films; *November Afternoon* (1996), in particular, has a moody jazz score that intensifies the decadent feeling evinced by the work.

Shot on video and later, after successful early screenings, blown up to 16mm, *November Afternoon*, filmed in black and white, concerns two couples whose relationships are put to the test during the course of a weekend together. Returned emigrant John's (Mark Doherty) plans for a macho weekend of Dublin drinking are scuppered as an obsessive incestuous liaison between his wife Karen (Jayne Snow) and her brother, Robert (Michael McElhatton) is revealed. Relationships form the basis of Carney and

Hall's second film, *Just In Time* (1998). In this moody piece, a middle-aged academic, Frank (Gerard McSorley), spends a weekend in the country with his painter wife (Frances Barber), leaving his lover behind in London. Their mood of recollection is broken when, to their disapproval, an old friend turns up with his younger mistress. Playing more like French than Irish cinema, *Just in Time* was greeted, as was *November Afternoon*, as a welcome break from the more laboured works of other aspiring film-makers. Since then, Carney and Hall have shot *Park* (1999), a harrowing narrative of abuse that went straight to television.

Working alone, Carney has made the as yet unreleased *Zonad* (aka *The Smiling Suicide Club/On the Edge*) about a group of teenagers who are committed to mental hospital as a result of their shared interest in suicide.   **RB**

William CARTLIDGE

Born in 1945, William Cartlidge (sometimes credited as Bill) has enjoyed a prolific career *An Ideal Husband* (1998) in many different guises. In the 1960s and 1970s he worked principally as an assistant director on some eleven major films including *Alfie* (1966), *Born Free* (1966) and *You Only Live Twice* (1967). Towards the end of the 1970s, he turned his hand to producing, acting as associate, executive or co-producer on films such as *The Spy Who Loved Me* (1977), *Moonraker* (1979) and *Educating Rita* (1983).

His directorial debut came in 1998 with *An Ideal Husband*, a production that was ill-fated from its first conception, destined to be eclipsed by Oliver Parker's blockbuster version of the Oscar Wilde play released in the same year. Like Parker's adaptation, Cartlidge's film boasts an acclaimed cast, including Robert Hardy and Prunella Scales; it failed to receive popular attention however, due, perhaps, to its 1990s updating. Cartlidge's direction is so reverent of Wilde's words that it becomes almost unpalatable to the tastes of a modern cinematic audience, more successfully resembling a clichéd television drama. The first half-hour does nothing to easily instigate the film's journey but the direction and editing improves sufficiently to grant the audience true instances of comedy. The moments, when they arrive, are highly amusing, hinting at Cartlidge's skill. Still, he never quite succeeds in fashioning a well-rounded or evenly paced film.   **BPr**

Michael CATON-JONES

Before the likes of Sam Mendes and Anthony Minghella conquered Hollywood, Michael *Scandal* (1989) Caton-Jones, born in Broxburn, Scotland, in 1958, was arguably one of the first British *Memphis Belle* (1990) directors to move to America and create a string of profitable (if not critic-proof) films. *Doc Hollywood* (1991) With a strong sense of place (whether 1960s London or 1950s Americana) and an abil- *This Boy's Life* (1993) ity to entice the industry's glitterati (Robert de Niro, Liam Neeson, Bruce Willis), Caton- *Rob Roy* (1995) Jones has forged a career in making the kind of summer sleeper hits that constantly *The Jackal* (1997) throw up surprises.

His first feature, *Scandal* (1989), recounts the story of the Profumo affair that rocked the Conservative government in the 1960s. Featuring strong performances (Ian McKellan, Joanne Whalley-Kilmer and particularly John Hurt), Caton-Jones' direction is strong on recreating the milieu – The Beatles soundtrack, miniskirts and tenement houses – but less accomplished when trying to make a wider political statement about the impropriety of government. Indeed, compared to the peccadilloes of the Tories under John Major's leadership, the story now seems a little tame.

Memphis Belle (1990), a factual account of a US Air Force mission in 1943 over Germany, is Caton-Jones' most accomplished film so far, due mainly to the panache and gusto he brings to the initially clichéd narrative. As a throwback to old war films, the direction is tinged with surreal flourishes – such as Matthew Modine's superlative monologue to his plane – and the kind of buddy-bonding that distinguishes the best films of this genre. Never flag-waving or infantile in its exploration of courage and leadership, the film is tightly plotted and uniformly well acted.

Caton-Jones' move to Hollywood in the early 1990s saw a spate of eclectic films that again evoked a specific time and place, and mixed whimsy with brutality. If *Memphis Belle* is Hawksian, then *Doc Hollywood* (1991) is pure Capra-corn. When Michael J. Fox crashes his car in America's Bible Belt, he is obliged to do community service in a small town that is permanently stuck in the 1950s. As an affectionate parody of provincialism and apple-pie homeliness, the film also cleverly juxtaposes the Beverly Hills high-life of Fox to the infinitely more worthy hicksville. Films like this rarely work when the director and cast treat the subject with condescension; here Caton-Jones seems totally committed to the whimsy and (albeit slight) predictability.

Set in 1950s Washington state, *This Boy's Life* (1993), adapted from Tobias Wolff's coming-of-age novel, stars Leonardo DiCaprio and Ellen Barkin as son and mother who move to small-town Concrete. She falls in with amorous suitor Dwight (Robert de Niro); after they are married comes brutality and De Niro moves from shrinking violet to raging bull with each passing scene. Caton-Jones opts to let the action unfold rhythmically, a ploy that pays off when sudden bursts of physical violence jolt the spectator out of their complacency; his static camera and unobtrusive editing add to the sense of futility.

Although *Rob Roy* (1995) had the misfortune of being released at the same time as *Braveheart* (1995), Caton-Jones's film proves a more interesting slice of Scottish myth making than Mel Gibson's historically inaccurate behemoth. Set in the early 1700s, the film concerns the revenge fantasy of Rob Roy (Liam Neeson) after his friend is murdered and his wife raped by Archibald Cunningham (Tim Roth), a foppish aristocrat in thrall to the local landowners and barons. The narrative is dealt with efficiently but it is the mise-en-scène that lends the film its mythic quality. The heather is used to beautiful effect while the rugged landscape and masterly framing recalls Michael Mann's *The Last of the Mohicans* (1992). Roth excels in a role that avoids the high campery of an Alan Rickman or a Gary Oldman and, once again, the collaborative efforts of the cast serve the director well.

The Jackal (1997) is the only film to strike a false note in Caton-Jones' career, due in some way to the excessive homage that it tries to pay the original *The Day of the Jackal* (1973). Where Fred Zinnemann's film is tense and taut, this re-stylisation is both a star vehicle for Bruce Willis and Richard Gere and an excuse for some sub-Bond hijinx and gadgetry. A master of period recreations, it could be the contemporary setting that hampers Caton-Jones; the audience is also asked to sympathise with an assortment of nefarious criminals rather than an identifiable, sympathetic figure. Actors like Sidney Poitier and Diane Venora attempt to lend gravitas, but seem lost amongst the excessively masculine posturing and hyper-charged narrative.

Caton-Jones is currently in production with *City by the Sea*, in which Robert De Niro stars as a police officer who discovers that his son is a murderer. **BM**

Peter CATTANEO

Born in 1964, Peter Cattaneo followed an increasingly common kind of apprenticeship as a film-maker. While still a student at the Royal College of Art, he directed commercials, won a Sony Promo Award for a music video, and saw his short, *Dear Rosie* (1990), nominated for an Academy Award for the Best Live Action Short Film. After graduating Cattaneo turned to television, working on the Channel 4 drama 'Say Hello to the Real Doctor Snide' and directing episodes of 'The Full Wax', 'The Bill' and 'Diary of a Teenage Health Freak', as well as a number of commercials for Paul Weiland's Film Company. His first feature-length project was the BBC film *Loved Up* (1995). Shot on 16mm, it tells the story of a teenage girl's entry into the world of ecstasy and rave culture. Despite – or perhaps because of – its clichéd and platitudinous narrative, it was well received. On the strength of its screening at the 1996 Sundance Film Festival, he was sought out by Fox Searchlight who agreed to finance his follow-up project, *The Full Monty* (1997).

A lightweight comedy-drama, it follows a group of unemployed men from Sheffield as they are driven by circumstances and, although it might seem contradictory, their self-respect to become strippers. The opening sequence contrasts the optimism of the late 1960s and early 1970s with the decimation of the British steel industry, and the concomitant destruction of communities with the steelworks band who still play even though there is no longer a steelworks. Alienated by anxieties about their masculinity, the protagonists are as much concerned with the emotional valorisation of their own degradation as with learning dance steps. Cattaneo's success resides in transforming the emasculation and infantilisation of the group into a childish sense of fun and transgression capable of dissolving class distinctions: although they do not triumph over adversity, they do find a moment of triumph in adversity. The rest – how a movie with a budget of just $3.5 million received four Academy Award nominations and took $200 million at the box office – is history.

Cattaneo's next movie, *Lucky Break* (2001), follows a group of genial convicts as they plan to break out from prison under the cover of staging 'Nelson: The Musical', an amateur production penned by the ineffectual governor (Christopher Plummer). Complications, but nothing resembling narrative or psychological complexity, ensue as Jimmy (James Nesbitt), who has fallen in love with support worker Annabel (Olivia Williams), is forced to choose between escaping or serving his time. An unremarkable blend of mild slapstick and even milder social realism, *Lucky Break* could only offend those who had hoped for more from Cattaneo's second feature.   **MB**

Simon CELLAN JONES

Simon Cellan Jones has a background in quality television, from working as assistant *Some Voices* (2000) floor manager on 'Edge of Darkness' for the BBC to directing episodes of 'Cracker', Jimmy McGovern's excellent crime series for Granada. In 1996 he directed Peter Flannery's epic 'Our Friends in the North' for the BBC. This is an ambitious and impressive story of four friends from Newcastle, which spans three decades, taking in housing scandals, pornography, photo-journalism, terrorism and homelessness. The excellent cast included Mark Strong, Gina McKee, Daniel Craig and Christopher Eccleston, and Cellan Jones brought some cinematic flourishes to Flannery's social realism. Other impressive television work included Oliver Parker's date rape drama 'In Your Dreams', and 'Storm Damage', written by the actor Lennie James.

Cellan Jones' sole cinematic outing to date is *Some Voices* (2000). This tale of a schizophrenic (Daniel Craig) who moves in with his brother (David Morrissey), a café owner, is an adaptation by Joe Penhall of his Royal Court play (and contains a number of themes he would revisit in his subsequent National Theatre production 'Blue/Orange'). Highlighting the failed mental health policy of 'Care in the Community', Penhall's screenplay has Craig abandoning his medication as he falls in love with the free spirited Kelly McDonald while Morrissey struggles to keep business and family together. The performances are excellent: in keeping with Cellan Jones' background in quality television, the two leads had previously impressed in BBC drama, Craig in 'Our Friends in the North' and Morrissey in Tony Marchant's powerful 'Holding On'. Craig (the most charismatic British lead since David Thewlis) has the showier part (in one sequence he wanders naked around West London) and he imbues the character of Ray with both pathos and humour. The shifts in tone are handled well by the director although there is a certain theatricality to some of the scenes and the overall feel of the film is a bit too much like television, albeit good television. London's Shepherd's Bush looks great, a place of uncertainty and urban chaos, and the resolution of the story is pleasingly untidy.

Cellan Jones is clearly an able director but, given the high quality of his television work and the current state of British cinema, he may find that he is better off working on the small screen for the time being.   **IC**

Gurinder CHADHA

Born in Kenya, Gurinder Chadha came to England as a small child and grew up in South- *Bhaji on the Beach* (1993) all, West London. She became a news reporter with BBC Radio before joining Channel *What's Cooking?* (2000) 4 as a researcher. Her first film, *I'm British but...* (1989) was a short funded by the BFI New Directors scheme. Set in the late 1980s, the film uses bhangra music as a backdrop to explore questions of identity and belonging amongst a group of British-born Asians. Chadha uses four Asians from Scotland, Northern Ireland, Wales and England, each with a regional accent, to subvert the stereotypical Asian image.

In 1991 Chadha worked on two television projects and also directed her second short, *A Nice Arrangement*. Partially produced by her own production company, Umbi Films (formed in 1990), this is a drama set in an Indian family's London home on the morning of their daughter's wedding. The film was shown at a number of film festivals, including Cannes, where it was selected for Critics' Week. Chadha went on to direct a number of television documentaries including 'Acting Our Age', featuring Asian Londoners over sixty, shooting and editing their experiences of ageing in Britain.

Chadha became the first British-Asian woman to direct a full-length feature film with *Bhaji on the Beach* (1993). The film was co-scripted with Meera Syal and tells the story of a group of Asian women on a day trip to Blackpool. A variety of Asian female characters are featured, each with their own story: Hashida is caught between her loyalty to an African-Caribbean boyfriend and her parent's expectations; Ginder tries to resolve the tension between being a 'good wife' and trying to escape a violent marriage. The film deals with being Asian and British from a comic perspective whilst focusing on a number of important issues. Elements of *Carry On*-style comedy are juxtaposed with a number of Bollywood-style Indian film fantasies; the music is also a mix of Western and Asian music and includes a Punjabi version of 'Summer Holiday'. Between *Bhaji on the Beach* and her second feature, *What's Cooking?* (2000), Chadha directed 'Rich Deceiver' (1995), a two-part drama for the BBC, and continued to work on documentaries.

What's Cooking? is set and filmed in Los Angeles, yet offers very different representations from those we are accustomed to seeing. The film intercuts between four LA households as they prepare for a Thanksgiving dinner and family get-together. There is a successful yet fractured African-American family, a Jewish family with a lesbian daughter and her lover, a Latino family with a wayward husband and newly-liberated wife, and a Vietnamese family struggling with old traditions and inter-generational conflict. Each of the four families have their own problems to deal with and Chadha uses a different camera technique to convey each. The Vietnamese family, for instance, is filmed with mainly hand-held camera to show the chaos of their lives, whereas the African-American household is shot with a static camera to suggest aspects of control. Chadha was keen to take marginal characters in American society and place them centre-stage; inter-racial couples, and the differences in race and ethnicity more generally, are presented as a given. This is an accessible comedy with well-written and realistic dialogue, dealing with universal issues that could relate to any family. It opened at the Sundance Film Festival in 2000 and recevied enthusiastic praise upon its US release.

Chadha's work is an uncompromising yet approachable documentation of diasporic identity. Influenced by many Western media products, as well as Indian films, she is keen to make films that reflect the world as she sees it, managing to focus on character types that usually find no voice in mainstream cinema. Tackling commercial film-making, whilst still pursuing her own personal projects, she is directing a story about English backpackers trekking across India, *Are You Experienced?*, and *Bend it Like Beckham*, a film about a young Asian girl who is addicted to football. **PR**

Peter CHELSOM

Hear My Song (1991)
Funny Bones (1995)
The Mighty (1998)
Town and Country (2001)

Born in Blackpool in 1956, as a former stage and television actor turned writer-director, Peter Chelsom's film career can perhaps best be epitomised as a kind of rag-bag of competing genres that never fully fuse into a satisfying narrative whole. Although admirers of his genre-bending and lack of convention highlight his ability to coax quirky performances from established stars (Warren Beatty, Goldie Hawn) and attract cult actors to his projects (Oliver Reed, Ned Beatty, Harry Dean Stanton), much of his work is characterised by a no-substance gloss that frequently sinks under the weight of its own expectations.

Hear My Song (1991) – which Chelsom directed and co-scripted with actor Adrian Dunbar – is perhaps the most successful of his films, due in part to its modest aspirations and its narrative orthodoxy. Dunbar runs a nightclub catering for Liverpool's Irish community and aims to fight off his creditors by bringing renowned Irish tenor Josef Locke out of retirement for one last gig. Based on a real incident in which Locke did indeed flee Britain due to tax difficulties, it allows Chelsom – who remembers Locke from his own Blackpool childhood – to fuse a story of redemption and small-town values that is greatly aided by Ned Beatty's performance as Locke. Expertly photographed by Sue Gibson, the images are imbued with a nostalgia and sensitivity that underpins the rest of the story.

With his new kudos, Chelsom remained in the north of England for his next film, *Funny Bones* (1995). Described by *Variety* as a 'postmodern tragicomedy that couldn't find an audience', it typifies Chelsom's film-making: a scatter-gun approach that attempts to fuse a variety of genres into some kind of statement on the nature of comedy. Is it a drama about smuggling, an acerbic riff on the desperation of performance, or a father-son melodrama? Chelsom packs the film with an Altman-esque array of oddballs and losers (Leslie Caron, Oliver Reed, Jerry Lewis, Oliver Platt) and makes interesting visual comparisons between Las Vegas and Blackpool. At just over a couple of hours, *Funny Bones* benefits from the energy of Lee Evans – his part in the vertiginous climax is exhilarating.

Chelsom's next film, *The Mighty* (1998), charts the tentative friendship between two Cincinnati children; one has a father in prison and the other suffers from a bone disease. At times too sentimental, with metaphors sign-posted, Chelsom coaxes powerful performances from his two young leads, Kieran Culkin and particularly Elden Henson. Sharon Stone and Gena Rowlands are also exemplary as the recurring mother figures. Kevin's (Culkin's) love of Arthurian legend is given a neat twist with the sight of knights crossing a bridge (straying just the right side of Python-esque parody) and Chelsom's capturing of small-town Americana befits that of an English director fascinated by the iconography of the unfamiliar. All this is perfectly complemented by Harry Dean Stanton's trademark hang-dog expression.

Chelsom's most recent film, *Town and Country* (2001), highlights his thematic contradictions rather than any cohesiveness. The shoot has already been canonised as one of the most troubled in Hollywood history: re-writes, re-shoots, a two-year delay in release, and fights between producer and director. The comedy about marital infidelity is criminally unfunny; writer Buck Henry's forced one-liners and slapstick shtick are laboriously performed, while the glittering array of acting talent (Warren Beatty, Diane Keaton, Goldie Hawn, Jenna Elfman, Josh Hartnett) is profligate at best. Chelsom tries to inject some quirkiness and physical humour into the mix, but the emotional trials and tribulations fail to find any resonance. The reported clashes between Beatty and Chelsom may go some way to explaining the unevenness of tone. One is left with the sense that Chelsom was merely a director-for-hire, reined in and unable to bring any level of shape or personal slant to what is ultimately a tired and uninvolving attempt at satire.

He is currently in post-production with *Serendipity*, starring Kate Beckinsale and John Cusack as a couple reunited after a ten-year separation. **BM**

Roger CHRISTIAN

Rather like his films, Roger Christian's career has shown pockets of brilliance in a frustratingly incomplete whole. Born in London in 1944, he initially displayed prodigious talent in art direction, graduating to direction in the early 1980s, yet the potential promised by his visual ability has never been fulfilled. Mostly action thrillers, his films employ strong psychological threads to explore the nature of heroism and its conflict with oppression, tyranny and terrorism. However, high-concept ideas, moments of cinematic vision and his panache for sophisticated action direction have too often been betrayed by dreadful scripts and lack of narrative depth, hinting at a director whose enthusiasm for the medium has regularly outstripped his sense of what is cinematically viable. Christian's first break came as art director on Peter Hall's experimental *Akenfield* (1974), a semi-documentary of Suffolk village life contrasted with a fantasy reconstruction of its Edwardian heritage. His command of powerful image was further proved as set decorator on *Star Wars* (1977), transforming earthly locations into otherworldly evocations of Lucas' concept of 'used space' where 'the future is already old'. This experience of mixing futuristic machinery and organic mutation proved vital for his Oscar®-winning, and hugely influential, art direction of *Alien* (1979), which contrasted gloomy futuristic interiors with the Freudian drama of the H.R. Giger-designed alien. His eye for cinematic setting and landscape as image gave Monty Python's *Life of Brian* (1979) a similarly lavish, period-specific look. Christian's greatest strength is his ability to supplement narrative themes with evocative art direction; as director, however, he was to learn that films cannot survive on looks alone.

The Sender (1982)
Lorca and the Outlaws (1985)
Nostradamus (1994)
The Final Cut (1995)
Underworld (1997)
Masterminds (1997)
Battlefield Earth (2000)

Following *The Dollar Bottom* (1980), an intelligent short about a schoolboy protection racket, Christian made his first feature, *The Sender* (1982), a psychological horror involving a madman who telepathically transmits his deranged visions. The film prefaces Christian's later directorial career – an intriguing concept, an impressive look, striking hallucinatory images, let down by below-par acting and periods of derivative, schlocky direction. Christian's interest in psychodrama and the battle with supernatural forces is a recurrent theme in his work, as is his impressive use of visual effects. *Lorca and the Outlaws* (1985) repeats the pattern. A space adventure pitting tyrannous androids against oppressed humans, Christian commands the action and setting with aplomb but the film is too superficial to make any impact. Both films fared badly and Christian's directorial career already appeared to be in terminal decline.

After a gap of several years, during which he gravitated inexorably towards Hollywood, came *Nostradamus* (1994), part biopic, part reconstruction of the famous prophet's life. The psychological trauma of Nostradamus' gift, particularly its estranging effect on his personal relationships, is explored with a bravura range of cinematic tricks – hallucinations, flashbacks, cross-cuts, flash-forwards, slow-motion – and is powerfully evoked by a contrast of styles ranging from documentary to violent fantasy. As an unwilling 'hero' locked in internal conflict, Nostradamus is also a textbook subject for Christian.

The idea recurs in Christian's next three films. In *The Final Cut* (1995) a retired bomb defusal expert is forced to battle a mad terrorist. In *Underworld* (1997) an ex-con plays cat-and-mouse mind games in order to discover his father's killer and in *Masterminds* (1997) a young hacker must outwit a computer wizard holding his friends hostage. Christian identifies the opposed sides as symbiotic doppelgängers, with contrary goals but a necessarily shared mindset in the best serial killer/detective tradition. The psychological battle is as much with internal demons as with real adversaries. As is so often the case, however, the intelligent premises are not fulfilled cinematically; Christian's command of correlating theme and visual image, prevalent in his early work, never surfaces, perhaps due to the new pressures of a Hollywood budget. Instead, competent action sequences, visual thrills and exhaustive editing replace technical innovation and cinematic imagination, turning potentially involving psychological thrillers into pedestrian, forgettable no-brainers. Christian is highly capable of delivering stunning, visceral film-making, however, as displayed in the action sequences he produced as second unit director on *Star Wars: The Phantom Menace* (1999).

His most recent film, *Battlefield Earth* (2000), displays the same talent for broad set-pieces, epic sweep and bone-jarring editing. The flair for apocalyptic future landscapes, the variety of camerawork ranging from noir to war film and the well-worn theme of the triumph of the human spirit, all demonstrate Christian's enthusiasm for the genre and for the art. Sadly, his eagerness to overcompensate for another dire script simply results in another confused, unintelligible film. Christian's films work like production sketches: though full of ideas, there is the inescapable sense that many of them should never have got past the drawing board. **OB**

Alan CLARKE

In a recent FilmFour documentary on Alan Clarke, the playwright David Hare suggested that 'the sort of people that hang around the British Film Institute don't like to admit that almost everything that is good about the British cinema came from the British theatre'. Hare's comment is sadly typical of the British media, reinforcing the ignorant assumption that cinema is in some way more lowbrow than the stage, and goes a long way towards explaining why cinema has never really been accepted seriously as an art form in the UK.

Whilst it may be true that Clarke served a brief stint in the theatre – the Questors in Ealing – the dominant influence, particularly in the work of his final decade, is undoubtedly the films of Michelangelo Antonioni, Alain Resnais and François Truffaut. As with many of his contemporaries who rose up through 'The Wednesday Play' and single drama era, theatre was a way in. Their chief visual and thematic inspirations were from the golden age of the European arthouse, the peak of auteur cinema – Italian Neo-Realism, Czech social comedies and the French New Wave.

Like Rainer Werner Fassbinder's *Berlin Alexanderplatz* (1980), Krysztof Kieslowski's *Dekalog* (1988) or Edgar Reitz's *Heimat* (1984), little matter that the medium was television, Clarke made no concessions to the format he worked on. Ironically his two theatrically released features of the 1980s, the abominable snooker musical *Billy the Kid and the Green Baize Vampire* (1986) and the hilarious yet lightweight *Rita Sue and Bob Too* (1987), are widely considered to be compromised failures. It is all the more tragic then that despite the widespread acknowledgement that television was, and in principle still can be, the great democratic medium, many of Clarke's earlier pieces have either been wiped or sit collecting dust in the archives of the BBC.

Born in Liverpool in 1935, Clarke emigrated to Canada at 21 and soon after enrolled on the Radio and Television course at the Ryerson Institute in Toronto. Upon his return to England in the early 1960s he found a job as floor manager at Rediffusion and, under the auspices of Stella Richman, quickly graduated to directing half-hour dramas. By the end of the decade he had arrived at the BBC where, as he proudly exclaimed, he swiftly earned a lifetime ban from the staff bar.

Clarke's most notable work of this period includes *To Encourage the Others* (1972), the earliest piece to examine the Derek Bentley injustice of the early 1950s, *Penda's Fen* (1974), a surreal tale of a boy beset by angels and devils, and *Diane* (1975), which deals with incest. The turning point in his career came with the decision to ban his borstal drama *Scum* (1977). Written by regular collaborator, Roy Minton, the film is a harsh account of a young offenders centre that makes little attempt to reform its inhabitants. The brutality of authority and the jaded bitterness of the warders negate any possibility of rehabilitation; filled with violence and hatred, the youths are worse leaving the prison than they were coming in. Having toed the line and been pummelled for doing so, Carlin (Ray Winstone) finds himself unable to conform to the institutionalised infrastructure of his environment. He overthrows the system, gains power and becomes corrupted by it. *Scum* introduces the classic Clarke protagonist, the anti-authoritarian alter ego, the man with his back against the wall, the victim of circumstance – 'Survival rules OK', as the poster says.

Although the shelving of the film undoubtedly fuelled Clarke's suspicion and frustration, it ultimately worked in his favour, and he was approached two years later with the offer to adapt it for the big screen. Using most of the same cast, it was remade, virtually unchanged, for cinema release. Naturally, many feel this version to be inferior, preferring the rawness and innocence of the television original. Whilst it does suffer from a fraction more excess and the regrettable exclusion of the scene involving Carlin selecting a 'pretty boy' inmate to be his 'missus', its theatrical run and subsequent video release garnered cult status, giving the film an exposure that much of his other pivotal television work has not been able to enjoy.

The experience of *Scum* hardened and deepened Clarke's work. Where Carlin was more of an everyman forced to rebel in order to survive, *Made in Britain* (1983) presents Trevor (Tim Roth) as an anarchist of choice – more intelligent, more articulate and more violent. Unwilling to let the system beat him down, he submits to it, but stands defiant. Mocking the cycle of options presented to him at the assessment centre, he urinates over his files and gives himself up to his probation officer. He knows the system does not work and, almost to prove it, he seems willing for it to chew him up. When he finally opens up and shows some hint of vulnerability at the stock car derby, he crashes. Feeling compromised, he quickly reverts back to racial hatred and self-destruction. At the dénouement Trevor appears unthreatened by the prospect of beginning prison life, his obnoxious grin revelling in the policeman's words. The freezeframe recalls *Les Quatre Cent Coups* (1959). This misunderstood youth, unlike Antoine Doinel, knows what is in store for him and sees no possibility or desire for escape.

Contact (1985), based on the memoirs of AFN Clarke, deals with the gradual breakdown of a British officer on border duty in Northern Ireland. Despite Clarke's proudly announced disrespect for authority he nonetheless puts aside his judgement and posits the platoon leader in a typical Clarke situation – a man gradually defeated by the tedious pattern of his environment, defeated by the job. With pared down dialogue, more documentary than fiction, Clarke presents a series of encounters and incidents, and builds the drama from this. No one smiles, there is no chirpy banter between the soldiers and no regional accent stereotyping. Sean Chapman's captain, cooped up in the portacabin barrack camaraderie of his soldiers, is, in his head, totally isolated, his blank face registering the insecurity and creeping fear of being shot or blown up. At the end of each day Chapman habitually retires to his room, closes the door behind him and sits upright on his bed, numb with routine. When one of his men is killed, his sergeant informs him, 'Don't get involved boss, its bad for the brain'. Clarke is critical neither of the neither the military nor the terrorists. He takes no sides, yet his unembellished presentation of the process – the vehicle checks, the infra-red night patrols, the futility and even the silliness of the gunfights, where shots are fired in every direction but no-one really knows why – make *Contact* one of the great anti-war films.

Perhaps Clarke's bleakest film of this period is *Christine* (1987). As with *Contact*, there is little or no trace of plot, merely the terminal monotony and boredom of drug-taking. Christine (Vicky Murdock), all blue and white stripes and alice bands – a twisted yet all too real updating of Lewis Carroll's heroine – wanders around a Hounslow suburb with a carrier bag dealing heroin to her friends. Parents and other such authority figures are never seen. In their absence there are risible attempts to organise a party, with sly references to a missing needle from the turntable. Christine belongs in the mould of classic Bressonian heroines from films such as *Mouchette* (1966) or *Une Femme Douce* (1969). She looks on, passively, as the friends she deals to inject themselves. One of them leaves the room and vomits. 'Are you alright?' she asks them all. When nobody comes to the party, she sits down once again in front of Paddington Bear on the television. A harsh indictment of the 'just say no' media campaign of the period, what makes *Christine* all the more grim is that these are not poverty-stricken youths driven to drugs through necessity but lower-middle-class children who choose to live like this.

Despite its Easington Colliery ghost town setting, Clarke's following film, *Road* (1987), adapted from Jim Cartwright's Royal Court hit, offers a more optimistic ending than many of his other key works of the decade. A cross-section of a small northern community, torn apart by the disintegration of industry, wander around the deserted streets talking to themselves about the past. 'Every single thing's a disappointment', one of them cries out. Yet out of desperation comes hope, and music offers them salvation. In the film's final act, two guys in zoot suits pick up two local girls and take them to a deserted house, drink wine and talk only about good things. 'I want magic and miracles, I want a Jesus to come and change things again, and show the invisible, and not let us keep forgetting … I want the surface up and off'; Otis Redding's 'Try a Little Tenderness' liberates them all, giving them voices and moments of clarity previously absent from, or suppressed by, their surroundings. 'I never spoke such a speech in me life,' exclaims Jane Horrocks' ditsy blonde, 'If I keep shouting, somehow, somehow, I might escape'.

His next piece, *Elephant* (1989), takes *Christine*'s lack of dramatic thrust even further, and includes barely two sentences of inaudible dialogue. It follows a series of random murders in Belfast, with Clarke's trademark steadicam sometimes following the victim, sometimes the assassin. Clearly about the 'Troubles', there is no plot, no character identification and no narrative arc – just 35 minutes of pointless killing. It was the culmination of Clarke's style, pure cinema, the bleakest, most uncompromising of all his work, and the cementing of Clarke the auteur. It would turn out to be his penultimate film. With *The Firm* (1989) Clarke comes full circle – the anarchist, the uncontrollable force unto himself, has gone bad. The film deals with football hooliganism yet he is careful never to show a ball in the lens, however, reinforcing the point that the violence has nothing to do with sport and everything to do with the human condition, specifically man's innate hatred of man. Once again, Clarke shows no contempt or condescension for his anti-hero. Gary Oldman's Bex, a thirty-year-old family man, is painted as an attractive character of considerable depth and charm. The lineage of Winstone's borstal boy and Roth's skinhead is clear. Ten years on, this anti-authoritarian is now a respectable member of society with A-levels and a job as an estate agent. Oldman's quest for yob leadership is juvenile and pathetic, yet he believes in it and achieves it. At the film's end, with Oldman's character assassinated, a group of actors assemble, in a gloriously improvised scene, to eulogise him in front of a documentary crew, saying what a visionary he was. One of them aggressively waves a union jacked cloth cap at the camera – the ultimate mirror of British society. 'See that? That's what it's all about.'

In retrospect, *The Firm* seems like the last gasp of honest, political drama, in David Hare's words, rightly so in this instance, 'one of the few authentic television master-pieces'. Shortly after filming ended Alan Clarke was diagnosed with cancer. He died in July 1990. His films were less about the championing of the underdog than they were about the relentlessness of the individual, loners defeated by their environment and soci-ety, a role Clarke clearly identified with – his vocation as uncompromising film-maker paralleling the concerns of his characters. **RCh**

Frank CLARKE

Credited with only one film as director, Frank Clarke established his name and reputa- *Blonde Fist* (1991) tion as a screenwriter with the 1985 hit *Letter to Brezhnev*. Based on his play of the same name, both were directed by his friend Chris Bernard. Made with a budget that was small even by British standards and released at the same time as more expensive and higher profile British films, *Letter to Brezhnev* was a considerable commercial and critical success. The story – a romance between an unemployed girl from Liverpool and a Russian sailor visiting the city as part of a PR exercise – encompasses many of the key themes in Clarke's later work: an overt political perspective on class, and notions of community and urban decline are filtered through a romantic and idealised notion of love.

Clarke began his writing career on the Channel 4 soap opera 'Brookside', which was produced in his hometown of Liverpool by Phil Redmond in the early 1980s. Although he had actually gone to Channel Four seeking funding for *Letter to Brezhnev*, Clarke penned some twenty episodes. He left the programme after two years citing its continu-ing move away from what he felt was a realistic and representative version of Liverpool as the reason for his departure. The success of *Letter to Brezhnev* allowed Clarke to get his second film script made in 1988. *The Fruit Machine* was a story even closer to Clarke's heart and concerns two young gay men who run away together, fetching up in a nightclub called 'The Fruit Machine' whereupon they witness the murder of the owner. The film's director, Philip Saville, who had made the BBC's 'Boys from the Blackstuff', seemed the ideal choice. However, Clarke confessed to not seeing eye to eye with the older director, not least because he felt that Saville was too straight and too middle class.

According to Clarke the decision to make his directorial debut with the self-penned *Blonde Fist* (1991) was far from a daunting experience. He had been intimately involved in the making of *Letter to Brezhnev* and his scripts contained copious direction notes. The titular fist in question belongs to Clarke's sister Margi, who had also starred in *Letter to Brezhnev*; the story concerns a woman who, having spent a spell in prison for assault-ing her no-good ex-boyfriend's girlfriend, goes to New York to find her bare-knuckle-boxing father. She soon discovers that he is now a down and out; in order to raise the fare for her journey back to Liverpool she enters a prize-boxing match for women. Like much of Clarke's work the family becomes the repository of core values with the resources to both survive and fight back. This situation is echoed in Clarke's use of his own family in his work; five of his sisters are in the film.

Blonde Fist is a rather uneasy mix of comedy and social comment, with the latter becoming both sentimentalised and unconvincing. Moreover, the film is episodic, suc-cumbs to too many clichés and, fatally, is too slowly paced – Margi Clarke does not get into her first bout for over an hour. The dialogue still has some jewels however – nobody writes insults like Clarke. **SH**

James Kenelm CLARKE

With his first film, *Got It Made* (1974), James Kenelm Clarke set a precedent that his *Got it Made* (1974) entire career would follow. He wrote, directed, scored and produced, offering glimpses of *Exposé* (1975) the debauched, sexually charged shenanigans for which he would later become known. *Let's Get Laid* (1977) It stars Lalla Ward as a young British socialite whose impending marriage is causing *Hardcore* (1977) her much consternation and whose morals are challenged when she meets a swinging *Funny Money* (1982) couple that change the way she views her mundane life. *Got it Made* is a tale of sexual politics and class war. Not entirely successful, it makes a valiant effort in preaching its serious message.

His second film, *Exposé* (1975), was placed on the infamous video nasty list in the early 1980s. The excessive images of blood on naked female flesh did not please the censor and for a brief period the film gained a notoriety that it did not deserve. It stars European exploitation star Udo Kier, sex starlet Linda Hayden and 'Men Only' magazine regular Fiona Richmond. Kier plays Paul Martin, a struggling author who is suffering graphic hallucinations that depict the savage death of his girlfriend, Suzanne, played by Richmond. Martin hires a new typist, the sultry Hayden, whose ferocious sexual appetite leads to a bizarre mix of murder, rape, mutilation and revenge as she tries to destroy the author's life. The extreme finale finds Kier surrounded by bloody, dead bodies with an unfinished book in his hands. While slow, the film still manages to combine a level of eroticism and drama that is lacking in his two subsequent features.

Continuing his professional relationship with Richmond, *Let's Get Laid* (1977) also stars perennial 1970s soft-core star Robin Askwith as a World War Two soldier returning to a life full of mistaken identity and murder. The highly improbable plot, featuring a cigarette lighter that affects all electrical power, is merely an excuse for Askwith to have his wicked way with a succession of nubile young ladies. *Hardcore* (1977) marked the end of Clarke's association with Richmond. She appears as a 17-year-old schoolgirl who is seduced by her schoolmaster. The attempt to mix moods fails and the film is not aided by the young star's wooden performance.

Over the next few years, Clarke moved away from soft-core features. He wrote *The Music Machine* (1979) and composed the score for *The Wildcats of St Trinian's* (1980). In 1982 he wrote and directed *Funny Money* (1982), a social satire which retained his 1970s sleaziness whilst condemning the 'Me Generation' of the 1980s as credit card buying goes haywire. His final film, *Yellow Pages* (1988), which went straight to video, is a spoof of detective films and stars Chris Lemmon as Henry Brilliant, a private investigator who is hired by wealthy Maxine de la Hunt (played by Jean Simmons) to protect her step-daughter Marigold on a trip to Denmark.

Clarke has produced a distinctive body of work that plays perfectly as a snap-shot of the era in which the films were made. His output of the 1970s, for which he is best known, captures the grimy decadence of the decade and still retains a kitsch charm. His more recent comedies appear facile and hollow in comparison, much in keeping with the decade that spawned them. **DB**

Jack CLAYTON

Although Jack Clayton's career as a director of feature-length films comprises a scant seven titles, his reputation has proved surprisingly long-lived. Born in Sussex, UK, in 1921, and apprenticed to the British film industry from the age of 14, Clayton quietly moved up in the ranks of London Films as a third assistant director, assistant director and editor (1935–40), and saw action in World War One as a commanding officer in the Royal Air Force (1940–46). After the war, he served as a production manager for both Alexander Korda (on *An Ideal Husband* (1947) and *The Thief of Bagdad* (1940)), and lifelong friend John Huston (on *Moulin Rouge* (1952) and *Beat the Devil* (1953)) before testing the directorial waters with short subjects, most notably the sixty-minute *The Bespoke Overcoat* (1955), which won an Academy Award for Wolf Mankowitz's screenplay (based on his own theatrical adaptation of the Gogol short story).

Clayton's 1959 feature-length debut, *Room at the Top* (the first quality film to receive the adults-only 'X' certificate), was an adaptation of the John Braine novel and starred Laurence Harvey as a Northern-born opportunist seeking success within the confines of a small-minded factory town. Harvey's chancer gains confidence through a love affair with an older, more experienced woman (an Oscar®-winning turn by Simone Signoret), only to reject her for a career-making marriage to the boss' daughter (Heather Sears). Screenwriter Neil Paterson also won an Academy Award for Best Adapted Screenplay, and the film inspired two sequels and a television series (with which Clayton had no involvement). Paying great attention to detail and texture, Freddie Francis (later a director in his own right for Hammer Studios and their rival, Amicus) shot *Room at the Top* in black and white. Critical opinion over the film remains sharply divided, with one camp finding it an oversimplification of the novel, and the other (Dilys Powell being an early champion) praising it as both an improvement on its source and a persuasive eulogy marking the decline of the British working class. Although the success of *Room at the Top* helped to instigate the 'kitchen sink' subgenre of British dramas, Clayton opted out of directing the like-minded *Saturday Night and Sunday Morning* (Karel Reisz, 1960) and *The L-Shaped Room* (Bryan Forbes, 1962).

His next project was the first leg in what is loosely considered the director's family trilogy: *The Innocents* (1961), an adaptation of Henry James' 'The Turn of the Screw' by William Archibald (who had turned the 1898 novella into a successful Broadway play) and American novelist Truman Capote. Again employing the services of veteran cinematographer Freddie Francis to shoot in black and white, Clayton imbues the Victorian-era ghost story of a sexually repressed governess (Deborah Kerr) charged with the custodianship of two precocious children (Pamela Franklin and Martin Stephens) with the rank inevitability of a killing jar. Although Francis, who won an Academy Award nomination for his efforts, was reportedly the last to know that the film would be shot in CinemaScope, to this day *The Innocents* remains a breathtaking example of non-epic anamorphic widescreen cinematography. The film is justifiably regarded as a latter-day classic that works both as a post-Gothic chiller and a post-Freudian study of human psychology in extremis. Although James' story has been remade (mostly for television) many times since, *The Innocents* remains the definitive version and is considered Clayton's finest film.

Playwright Harold Pinter provided the screenplay for Clayton's third film, *The Pumpkin Eater* (1964). Based on the 1962 novel by Penelope Mortimer, the film explores the emotional annihilation of a mother (Anne Bancroft) of seven children whose third husband (Peter Finch) proves habitually unfaithful. Clayton again filmed in black and white, this time employing veteran cinematographer Oswald 'Ossie' Morris (with whom he had worked on Huston's *Moulin Rouge*) who works wonders with subtle camera trickery and unusual framing to evoke distance between even the closest of friends and lovers. *The Pumpkin Eater* is a characteristically mature, unrelentingly grim but meticulously drawn study of adult dissatisfaction. Bancroft won the 1964 Golden Globe for Best Leading Actress in a drama, but lost the Best Actress Oscar® to Julie Andrews' *Mary Poppins*. Clayton's theme of a damaged family would carry over again to his next feature.

Clayton's first film in colour, *Our Mother's House* (1967), is based on Julian Gloag's novel about the plight of the seven Hook children when their bedridden matriarch dies within the confines of their Victorian home. Fearing the intrusion of outside agencies and the destruction of their familial unity, the children bury their mother in secret and carry on as if she were still alive. When the children's opportunistic father (Dirk Bogarde, whose performance earned him a BAFTA nomination) arrives on the scene to take advantage of the situation, the children are impelled toward an act of violence that will ultimately propel them toward their adult destinies. To play the agoraphobic Hook children, Clayton cast Pamela Franklin from *The Innocents* and Phoebe Nicholls from *The Pumpkin Eater*, as well as future *Oliver!* (1968) star Mark Lester.

Seven years would pass before Clayton's fifth feature, an expensive remake of *The Great Gatsby* (1974), starring Robert Redford as F. Scott Fitzgerald's doomed hero. Many critics and viewers found the film (at 144 minutes) overlong and Redford wrong for the part, but Clayton's supporting cast is rich in American talent (Mia Farrow, Bruce Dern, Sam Waterston and Scott Wilson). The film is sumptuously photographed by former Ealing Director of Photography Douglas Slocombe; faded textures evoke a sense of distant memories.

Almost a decade would pass before Clayton's next project, the 1983 coming-of-age carnival spooker, *Something Wicked This Way Comes*. Again, the adaptation, in this case of Ray Bradbury's novel, was criticised (even though Bradbury was responsible for the screenplay), but the film is nevertheless handsomely mounted and persuasively acted by a cast that includes Jason Robards, Jonathan Pryce, and a pre-comeback Pam Grier. Shot by Stephen H. Burum, Francis Ford Coppola's and Brian DePalma's preferred cinematographer, the muted, dusty palette of *Something Wicked* befits its Depression-era setting, effectively contrasting with the glittery, primary hues of the insidious travelling sideshow.

Jack Clayton's last feature film was the gentle but dreary and overwrought character-driven drama, *The Lonely Passion of Judith Hearne* (1987). This adaptation of the 1955 novel by Brian Moore stars Maggie Smith as a spinster piano teacher whose binge drinking lands her in Marie Kean's Dublin boarding house, where she is courted by an Irishman (Bob Hoskins) with predictably cheerless results. While the performances drew nearly unanimous raves, the film's abjectly sombre tone (compounded by Georges Delerue's syrupy score) was poorly received, leading to one critical aside that it should have been called *Room at the Bottom*. Jack Clayton wrote and directed one more film for television before his death of heart and liver problems in 1995, less than a week before his 74th birthday.

The thrice-married Clayton was predeceased by friend John Huston, who had once written a letter entrusting Clayton with finishing *Under the Volcano* (1983) in the event of his sudden death. Although Huston (who never sent the letter) regained sufficient strength to complete the feature and two more, his confidence in Clayton stands as testimony to the ultimate act of faith between colleagues.   **RHS**

Sue CLAYTON

The Disappearance of Finbar (1996) Born in Newcastle, UK, Sue Clayton won a scholarship to Cambridge University when she was 17, and from there went to the Royal College of Art to study for a Master's degree in Film. Like several of her contemporaries, she began her directing career in television, making the documentary about the state's attitude to single mothers, 'Women and the Welfare State' in 1977, and several history series. In 1990 she also made a short, *The Last Crop*, which was adapted from an Elizabeth Jolley short story.

Clayton made her first feature, *The Disappearance of Finbar* (1996), after Channel 4 (for whom she had made a number of documentaries) suggested she direct a film. Although they wanted something 'personal', she preferred to avoid what she called 'the small, domestic, interior woman's story', stating, 'I don't think women should feel they can only tell their personal story'. She found Carl Lombard's novel 'The Disappearance of Rory Brophy' after being attracted to the solitude of the flyover on the front cover, and adapted it with the Irish writer Dermot Bolger. She changed the central character's name to allow herself to incorporate a rather weak 'Finn Bar' pub joke into the movie.

The film deals with the disaffected Finbar (Jonathan Rhys Meyers) who disappears off the end of a flyover one day in front of his shocked friends. The residents of the sprawling housing estate on which he lives (Dublin's infamous Tallaght estate, the largest of its kind in Europe) start an action committee to find him. Their quest soon becomes part of the town's life. His best friend Danny (Luke Griffin) chases him to Sweden, having received a drunken phone call from Finbar, and ends up involved with a woman he later discovers to be Finbar's girlfriend. Betrayed by Danny, Finbar disappears again, and Danny chooses to stay where he is. Set in Dublin, Stockholm and Lapland, the resulting film is an ill-conceived attempt to emulate the cross-cultural frameworks that form the subjects of films by directors such as Jim Jarmusch and Aki Kaurismaki. Clayton populates the film with sub-versions of these directors' characters: a Chinese emigrant who compares Dublin to her native city; an Asian couple in a Swedish flat that sing a song about Mongolia; and an old man with tales of world travel.

Attempting a meditation on discontent and the universality of cultural experience, Clayton uses the landscape to effect symbolism of these themes: the estate is a sprawling mass of grey concrete, and Stockholm and Lapland exist as depressive bars and bare settings. Eduardo Serra, whose cinematography invested Iain Softley's *The Wings of the Dove* (1997) with its death sheen, does a brilliant job. Overall, though, the film suffers from its weak script and desultory narrative, and is ultimately rendered an impression of styles borrowed from European and US independent directors.

In 1999 Clayton's career path was documented on Channel 4's 'Upstarts'.   **JD**

Martin CLUNES

Staggered (1994) Martin Clunes will be ingrained in most memories as Gary Strang, the unchanging half of 'Men Behaving Badly'. An enormous hit during the boom of 1990s lad culture, the sitcom parodied the emerging childish yob behaviour of the stereotypical 'Loaded' reader. While the glamorous likes of Michael Caine and Jude Law represented the ideal lifestyle of the magazine's crop of testosterone-fuelled demographics, Clunes and co-star Neil Morrissey were a far more realistic representation of the average subscriber. With his dead-end job, crumpled suit, long-suffering girlfriend and puffy lips, Clunes earned audience sympathy and pity often enough to completely abuse it in the name of comedy.

His directorial output has been a showcase for variations on his Gary persona. His only theatrical release, *Staggered* (1994), is a cross-country farce in which a groom-to-be (Clunes) finds himself stranded on a Scottish island with nothing but a ticking watch. Here Clunes presents himself as an everyman who becomes more shocked and increasingly desperate after every person he relies on for help turns out to be even more perverted, sick or sociopathic. Never really achieving the belly laughs he aspires to, Clunes nevertheless delivers a pacey narrative, proving himself to be a competent journeyman. Attempts to add menace to a flash-forward opening seem out of place, but it is the inherent clumsiness to over-direct that is the bane of many a freshman effort.

Hunting Venus (1999), which was made for television, is a far more a cinematic piece. Unfortunately preceded by his contemporary Brian Gibson's *Still Crazy* (1998), *Hunting Venus* focuses on a faded pop star years after the album got dusty in the bargain bin. Displaying his affection for the subject, the project productively reunited him with Morrissey. Clunes' direction is much more confident; he restrains from using camera tricks that look cheap and nasty on the small screen aspect and budget. A director that knows how to shoot jokes, all he needs now is a decent script.   **BC**

Henry COLE

Henry Cole began his career in film as an actor in Riki Shelach Nissimoff's little-seen *Mercenary Fighters* (1987). By 1995 he had moved behind the camera to direct *Mad Dogs and Englishmen*, a regretful contribution to recent British cinema. *Mad Dogs and Englishmen* (1995)

The film features Elizabeth Hurley, in an early bid for big screen credibility, playing a pampered aristocrat whose heroin habit is beginning to spin wildly out of control. Salvation arrives in the form of C. Thomas Howell's leathery American motorcycle courier and soon Hurley is cleaning up her act. Inspector Sam Stringer (Joss Ackland), however, is adamant that evil drug baron Tony Vernon-Smith (Jeremy Brett, who is criminally wasted) is going down and suddenly Hurley and Howell are dragged kicking and screaming back into the criminal underworld.

Mad Dogs and Englishmen has many of the qualities of a would-be titillating British exploitation flick of the 1970s and as a treatise on redemption and the evils of addiction is damned by its paper-thin characterisation and two dimensional performances. In her defence, Hurley is not the only offender, though her attempts to embrace the low-life are interesting for all the wrong reasons.   **JWo**

Nigel COLE

Like so many of his contemporaries, Nigel Cole began his career directing a range of documentaries and dramas for television. Having made his name with the popular 'Peak Practice' and the award-winning 'Cold Feet', he went on to film the comedy-drama feature *Saving Grace* (2000). The first of BSkyB's movies to obtain a decent theatrical release, *Saving Grace* succeeded in part due to the achievements of Peter Cattaneo's *The Full Monty* (1997), another small and very British tale that did surprisingly well in both the UK and the US. *Saving Grace* (2000)

The film follows the fortunes of Grace (Brenda Blethyn) whose husband dies in a freak accident leaving her with debts and disloyalty – she later discovers his long term mistress. During her attempts to earn an income and thereby keep her manor house, her gardener (Craig Ferguson) asks her for help in tending a special plant. She works her green-fingered magic on what is, of course, a marijuana plant and goes into the dope-dealing business with Ferguson to fund her lifestyle.

This premise attempts to mine its comedy out of the unlikely situation, that of a respectable, middle-aged lady trawling the neighbourhoods of Notting Hill looking for customers. As a result, much of the humour loses its originality as the film's direction and script (by Ferguson and producer Mark Crowdy) struggle to develop the scenarios. The obligatory police interference and stoned Women's Institute members fail to advance a fairly tired idea, as does a prolonged mistaken-identity scene. Blethyn finds her way around a convoluted plot and sentimental, fairytale finale with superb comic timing and realistic humour. Ferguson offers sprightly support.

Cole attempts to fashion a modern Ealing comedy by using upright British characters and situations – the drugs underworld which Grace becomes involved with, for instance, is rendered ordinary and effectively decent – but fails to evoke the darkness evident in some of the best, such as Alexander Mackendrick's *The Ladykillers* (1955) and *Whisky Galore* (1948). It appears that Cole prefers the amiable, unfocused humour of some ill-advised farce. Failing to problematise the response of Grace's community to her crimes, the film ends up lacking in tension; the further it moves from any reality, the more it loses its appeal.

Cole has said 'like all directors I hoped I would do a film one day ... once you have crossed that line you can't go back'. Most recently, he has worked on a wildlife documentary with Julia Roberts. **JD**

Joe COMERFORD

Along with Cathal Black and Thaddeus O'Sullivan, Joe Comerford is part of a group of film-makers who worked on films made by veteran Irish-independent Bob Quinn and then went on to make aesthetically tough, politically-minded films of their own.

Comerford started in the 1970s by making a pair of short experimental films, *Waterbag* (1974) and *Withdrawal* (1984); both are dark, moody portraits of alienation that deal with taboo subjects (abortion, drug addiction). Although he later settled down formally, these early experimental films give a good sense of his interest in the fringes of Irish society.

His first narrative film, the fifty-minute *Down the Corner* (1977), was made with assistance from the British Film Institute and Dublin's Ballyfermont Community Workshop. An extremely grim film, it follows two Dublin kids, showing how economically underdeveloped and hopeless much of the Republic of Ireland was in the 1970s. It alternates between a semi-documentary strategy – somewhere between Italian Neo-Realism and Cuban Third Cinema – and a stark, almost film-noir look.

Comerford's first feature film, *Traveller* (1981), was written by Neil Jordan who was famously unhappy with the results. The film unfolds in an elliptical manner. The narrative – a traveller couple sets off for Northern Ireland to smuggle some televisions into the Republic – takes a back seat to Comerford's interest in revising the conventions of the road movie, offering instead a portrait of Ireland's most misunderstood communities. Several critics have drawn attention to the way in which the film also deals with the delicate subject of Northern Ireland and the bizarre economic differences between the North and the Republic in the 1970s.

His next film, *Reefer and the Model* (1988), also deals with the North, though somewhat more cryptically. Here Comerford centres on a group of smugglers living on a trawler in Conamara: Reefer, the owner of the boat, has an ambiguous criminal and IRA past; Spider is an IRA man on the run; Badger is gay. Reefer meets up with a pregnant, former drug addict and prostitute whom he nicknames The Model and brings into his dysfunctional family. They decide to pull the proverbial 'last big heist', which goes awry. As in *Traveller*, Comerford makes the most of the Irish landscape; here it feels distinctly anti-romantic.

Comerford's most controversial film is also his most recent. *High Boot Benny* (1993) was made just as the peace process was getting underway; this is not clear, however, from the grim, squalid portrait that Comerford paints of the border regions of Donegal. The film centres on a teenager named Benny who, after fleeing from Northern Ireland into a boy's school in the Republic, is terrorised by the British Army, the RUC, Loyalist paramilitaries and the IRA. The family that makes up the school community is, as in *Reefer and the Model*, metaphorically loaded, made up of a priest who has sex with the school's matron, herself a Protestant from the Republic, and a mute girl who smuggles blood to wounded IRA men hiding in the hills. The film caused a storm of controversy in the Republic and the North, and there were some very tense exchanges in the pages of 'Film Ireland' when it was released. Comerford was reportedly hurt by allegations that the film is sectarian. Given the dualistic, often reductive and emotionally manipulative way that the conflict is presented, the assertions are not entirely without justification.   **JW**

Fintan CONNOLLY

In a talk given at the 2001 Galway Film Fleadh, American critic Godfrey Cheshire *Flick* (2000) encouraged Irish film-makers to move away from the straightjacket of 'politics, topicality and prosaic realism', which he felt had been overvalued, and to adopt a more open-minded attitude towards genre films. Cheshire points to an interesting dilemma of recent Irish cinema, one that the younger generation of film-makers are coming up against more and more. Fintan Connolly's *Flick* (2000) is situated at the centre of this debate.

The story focuses on Jack and Des, two friends who are small-time drug dealers in Dublin. Having come upon a huge shipment of Moroccan hashish, they try to use it to hit the proverbial big time. Predictably, their plan goes horribly awry, complete with failed romances, tough talk with mean drug kingpins, and hand-held sequences in crowded, noisy discos. None of this material is particularly original. Although the film has the occasional Irish reference, its setting is non-specific. The film ends with Jack's German girlfriend taking him out of Dublin towards her home on the coast; as they seem to be on the road, he stumbles from the car, vomits, pulls himself together, and mumbles 'west'. This is the last shot of the film and it works remarkably well; the dull dawn light and the awkward framing imbue it with a touching melancholy that is mostly absent.

Whether bald generic imitation and lack of a sense of place is a bad thing is debatable; after all, why should Ireland not have a brand of kinetic-for-its-own-sake, placeless and highly derivative movies? That said, the problems that the natural evolution of Irish cinema inevitably present have been handled with a good deal more grace and style by other members of Connolly's generation of film-makers. Paddy Breathnach's film *I Went Down* (1997), for instance, has a lot in common with *Flick* in terms of adherence to the generic demands of the gangster movie, but is more sophisticated in its cinematic form, use of irony and evocation of place.

However, like Trish McAdam's *Snakes and Ladders* (1996), *Flick* is a solidly made film, has a good sense of visual style and features solid performances, even if it lacks in ambition. Films such as this are likely to continue to provoke much healthy debate about the future of Irish cinema.   **JW**

Alex COX

Although a director in his own right, Alex Cox is probably best known to British readers *Repo Man* (1984) as the host of BBC2's long-running film series 'Moviedrome' (1987–1994). The series *Sid and Nancy* (1986) focused on films that were cultish, obscure, marginal or simply bizarre, and the same *Straight to Hell* (1987) adjectives are equally applicable to Cox's own career. Not unlike Orson Welles, Cox has *Walker* (1987) never been afraid to antagonise the Hollywood studios and has similarly 'started at the *El Patrullero/Highway* top and worked his way down'. *Patrolman* (1992)

Born in Liverpool, UK, in 1954, Cox studied law at Oxford followed by film at Bristol *Death and the Compass* University, and subsequently won a Fulbright Scholarship to study film at UCLA, where (1996) he made a well-received short film, *Sleep is for Sissies* (1980). His debut feature, *Three Businessmen* (1998) the cult classic *Repo Man* (1984), is still perhaps his most famous and admired film. *Kurosawa: The Last Emperor* Inspired by countless Hollywood B-movies (notably Robert Aldrich's 1955 noir, *Kiss Me* (1999) *Deadly*), the film follows a group of car repossessors, sinister government agents, street punks, religious nuts and ufologists, as they chase after a Chevy Malibu with dead aliens in the trunk being driven around Los Angeles by a lobotomised nuclear scientist who may have created the neutron bomb. Besides launching the career of Emilio Estevez (for which Cox later apologised), *Repo Man* has a cast filled with many great character actors (Harry Dean Stanton, Tracey Walter, Sy Richardson) and a soundtrack featuring some of the top west coast punk bands of the period (Black Flag, The Plugz, The Circle Jerks). *Repo Man* is also an important example of Cox's political leanings and his penchant for zany conspiracy theories. The film is fiercely anti-nuclear and anti-Reaganite – its seedy, maniacal characters only care for money – and works as a fine satire of LA's car culture.

Cox's attachment to the punk scene is even more clear in his next project, *Sid and Nancy* (1986), an account of the last days of Sid Vicious and Nancy Spungen, played with total conviction by Gary Oldman and Chloe Webb. More a pure love story than a simple biopic (Cox's original title was *Love Kills*), the film deftly laces documentary-style realism with more abstract, dreamlike imagery. *Sid and Nancy*, however, would mark the beginning of the end of Cox's studio career, which is marked by stubbornness, foolishness and integrity. The film also proved how difficult it is to make explicitly political films in Hollywood.

Straight to Hell (1987) was his most spectacular and interesting failure. Following a fund-raising concert for the Sandinista National Liberation Front, Cox was involved in persuading a number of musicians – including Joe Strummer, The Pogues and Elvis Costello – to tour Nicaragua in August 1986. However, they were unable to raise money for the tour so instead enlisted the musicians to appear in a movie, the result of which is the modern-day spaghetti western *Straight to Hell*. The final film, however, is a shambles.

His next feature was the unjustly maligned *Walker* (1987), starring Ed Harris. In 1855 William Walker, an American, invaded Nicaragua and ruled the country as a dictator for two years. Cox retells these events as an indictment of Reagan's intervention in Central America, even using historical anachronisms (such as helicopters, limousines, Zippo lighters and Walker appearing in contemporary journals) to imply that not much has changed since 1855. *Walker* remains an interesting study of how history is represented and features a haunting score by Joe Strummer. Although it ended Cox's relationship with Hollywood, one must also admire his intentions: *Walker* was conceived as a means of spending as many US dollars in Nicaragua as possible in order to help boost the economy. Today it remains the second highest-grossing movie ever in Nicaragua, after *The Sound of Music* (1965). Since *Walker*, Cox's output has been patchy at best, with little or no distribution. After a five-year hiatus, he returned to directing with *El Patrullero/ Highway Patrolman* (1992), a Spanish-language film made in Mexico. Dramatising the tenet that no good deed goes unpunished, the film follows the struggles of a young policeman to resist corruption, and was shot by Cox using an impressive grasp of the possibilities of the long take. *El Patrullero* garnered his best reviews since *Sid and Nancy*, but was the last of Cox's films to acquire a significant release.

Cox continued his love affair with Latin America in 1996, with an adaptation of Jorge Luis Borges's 'The Death and the Compass', in which Cox himself played Borges. Stylish and provocative, it was expanded from a fifty-minute short film that he had made for the BBC four years earlier. Also in 1996, he made the Las Vegas drama *The Winner*, but subsequently disowned the piece after the producers recut it and replaced the score with what could best be described as porno music. Not long after, Cox was removed from his adaptation of 'Fear and Loathing in Las Vegas' and replaced by Terry Gilliam – although he fought for (and won) a screenwriting credit with his collaborator Tod Davies. In 1997 he formed Exterminating Angel Productions with Davies, and his career would appear to be on the turnaround. The first film from this production company was the Cox-directed *Three Businessmen* (1998), a typically bizarre and existential comedy in which he also stars as one of two businessmen (the third is otherwise engaged) who meet at Liverpool's Adelphi Hotel and spend the evening talking and being mysteriously transported to different cities around the world, including Amsterdam, Tokyo and Hong Kong. Cox has since completed the documentary, *Kurosawa: The Last Emperor*, which premiered at the 1999 Edinburgh Film Festival.

Cox is currently in production with *Revengers Tragedy*, a futuristic version of Thomas Middleton's Jacobean play.   **AS**

Charles CRICHTON

For Those in Peril (1944)
Dead of Night (segment, 1945)
Painted Boats (1945)
Born in Cheshire, UK, in 1910, Charles Crichton began his career in the British film industry as an editor in the cutting rooms of Alexander Korda and worked on films such as *Sanders of the River* (1935), *Things to Come* (1936) and *Elephant Boy* (1937). He first directed on the short *The Young Veterans* (1941).

Crichton started working for Ealing Studios in the early 1940s, establishing his reputation with successful and enduring films such as *Hue and Cry* (1947), *The Lavender Hill Mob* (1951) and *The Titfield Thunderbolt* (1953). Like Crichton, many of Ealing's directors – including Charles Frend, Henry Cornelius and Robert Hamer – served their time in the cutting rooms. Ealing operated on almost a repertory basis, with a number of members of the cast and crew working on many of the films; much of Crichton's work was scripted by Tibby Clarke and a number of his films featured actors such as Stanley Holloway and Jack Warner. Although Ealing is best remembered for its comedies, they made up only a small part of the studio's ouptut. Almost every genre was tackled, with the exception of the musical and the western, and this range of work is evident in Crichton's films.

Between 1944 and 1956 he directed 14 films, 13 of them for Ealing Studios. His first feature, *For Those in Peril* (1944), scripted by Tibby Clarke, is the story of a World War Two flyer who fails to join the RAF and instead joins the Air-Sea Rescue. He co-directed the anthology *Dead of Night* (1945) with Robert Hamer, Basil Dearden and Alberto Cavalcanti. A foray into horror, the film is comprised of five separate ghost stories embedded in a framework of a country-house party; each of the stories is related in turn by the guests and events gradually move into nightmare territory. Crichton's section is the comic chiller, 'The Golfing Story'. The film, an isolated experiment for Ealing, is suitably eerie and was well received. *Painted Boats* (1945), a docu-drama, was the only product of a proposed Ealing studio series to consolidate fiction and documentary. It is a portrait of English canal life that charts the lives of two boat families, examining the demands of traditions and change in the post-war world.

In 1947 Crichton ventured into comedy with *Hue and Cry*. Again scripted by Tibby Clarke, it tells the story of a gang of East End kids who realise that their favourite comic, 'The Trump', is being used as a means of communication by crooks. Harry Fowler is Joe, the leading youth and go-getter, who becomes convinced that a serial he is reading in 'The Trump' is really happening; the police dismiss his findings so he and the boys decide to catch the crooks themselves. Alastair Sim plays the sinister eccentric author of the serial in question, with Jack Warner cast against type as a Covent Garden wholesaler and master crook, Mr Nightingale. There is wonderfully natural acting from the kids, many of who had no acting experience, as the boys who use a variety of childhood pranks in their attempt to solve the case. *Hue and Cry* took Ealing Studios into a new direction of comedy and also made excellent use of vivid London locations; the ending of the film involves the coming together of hundreds of boys to fight it out on a riverside bombsite; their playgrounds are buildings damaged by bombs. The film was a success at the box office and with critics; it has been described as 'English to the backbone'.

Next, Crichton directed a thriller for Ealing, *Against the Wind* (1948), the story of British and Belgian agents helping the resistance movement in occupied Europe during World War Two. With men and women trained as saboteurs, the film includes some semi-documentary training scenes before the group set off on their mission with a traitor (Jack Warner, again cast against type) among them. *Another Shore* (1948) is a comedy set in Dublin. It tells the story of an Irish customs clerk who dreams of moving to a South Sea paradise; an encounter with a wealthy alcoholic offers him the chance but he gives it up for love. Rather unconvincing, it was not one of the more successful Ealing comedies.

Crichton's next film, *Train of Events* (1949), was an attempt by Ealing to recreate the formula of *Dead of Night*, co-directed with Sidney Cole and Basil Dearden. Told in flashback, it is the story of a train crash that brings together three groups of people. Unsuccessful, it was criticised for its use of clichés and flat direction. *Dance Hall* (1950), his next film, signalled another change of genre. A low-key melodrama, it focused on a local dance hall and an upcoming contest, starring Diana Dors and Petula Clark. A slice of-life, it privileged working-class women, a welcome rarity in films of the time.

In 1951 Crichton directed *The Lavender Hill Mob*, one of the studio's most successful films, now regarded as classic Ealing comedy, which won an Oscar® for Best Screenplay. The film stars Alec Guinness as Holland, a humble bank clerk, who befriends Pendlebury (Stanley Holloway), a souvenir-maker. Together the two come up with an unlikely plot to steal a fortune in gold and smuggle it abroad disguised as models of the

Eiffel Tower, along the way gaining the services of two professional criminals, Lackery (Sid James) and Shorty (Alfie Bass). Inevitably, the robbery goes wrong and Pendlebury manages to get himself arrested for stealing a painting off a market stall. However, the main downfall of the four is caused by a box of gold Eiffel Towers getting mixed up with genuine souvenirs on a stall outside the landmark itself and being bought by a group of English schoolgirls. Holland and Pendlebury then have to follow the girls back to England to recover them; the situation becomes more comic when one of the gold Eiffel Towers ends up in a police exhibition and the criminals steal a police car to make their escape.

Crichton made his next film, *Hunted* (1952), outside the confines of Ealing Studios. Starring Dirk Bogarde in a melodrama that deals with the problem of being male in the 1950s, it tells the story of a runaway boy who joins forces with a runaway murderer; the murderer sacrifices himself for the boy's safety.

Back at Ealing Crichton directed *The Titfield Thunderbolt* in 1953 about an eccentric group of villagers who battle to save their local branch line from closure. The villagers take over the railway as a private concern, defying the bureaucrats who want to close down their line. Stanley Holloway is Mr Valentine, the line's alcoholic benefactor, and Sid James is the roguish Hawkins who drives the engine. This film followed the pattern established by previous Ealing films such as *Whisky Galore!* (1949) and *Passport to Pimlico* (1948), dealing with mildly anarchic libertarian energies and demonstrating British parochial values and plucky community spirit. The first Ealing comedy to be filmed in Technicolor, it is given a cosy, romantic glow; the cinematography by Douglas Slocombe shows an idealistic and idyllic version of an England that is no more. Receiving a mixed response at the time of its release, it is now seen as one of the best Ealing comedies.

Crichton's last three films for Ealing spanned a range of genres. *The Divided Heart* (1954) was a complete change of direction; a true life, tug-of-love drama about a Bavarian couple who raise a war orphan as their own child then have to face the consequences when the boy's real mother is traced. *The Love Lottery* (1954) stars David Niven as a Hollywood star worn down by the pressures of stardom. He flees America for Italy only to allow the head of a gambling syndicate to put him up as the prize in a so-called 'Love Lottery'. *The Man in the Sky* (1956) is a suspense drama that tells the story of a test pilot who refuses to bale out when an engine catches fire.

With the closure of Ealing in 1959, Crichton made fewer features, moving instead into British television. He became a prolific director on series such as 'Danger Man', 'The Avengers' and 'Man in a Suitcase'. The British films he did work on were not particularly well-received. *Law and Disorder* (1958) is an amusing comedy starring Michael Redgrave and Robert Morley, the story of crooks rallying around a confederate who is about to be arrested to prevent his son from learning of his father's real career. *Floods of Fear* (1959), which Crichton also scripted, is a melodrama with impressively gloomy production values and performances, featuring two escaped convicts, a warder, and a pretty girl who are trapped by floods in a lonely house. *The Battle of the Sexes* (1960) stars Peter Sellers and Robert Morley in a film about a Scottish accountant (Sellers) who plots the murder of the female efficiency expert who has disrupted the comfortable regime of a traditionally-run Edinburgh tweed cloth factory. A black comedy, it misfires, portraying a negative view of women in business.

The Boy Who Stole a Million (1960), again scripted by Crichton, was, oddly, set in Spain, the story of a young page in a Spanish bank who 'borrows' some money to help his father and then finds that he, the police and a gang of criminals are all after him. *The Third Secret* (1964) focuses on a prominent London psychiatrist who apparently commits suicide; his teenage daughter is convinced it was murder and enlists the help of a former patient to try and find out the truth. *He Who Rides a Tiger* (1966) is a clichéd crime picture featuring a feckless burglar who leaves prison and returns to the old life.

Having ventured to work in Hollywood, Crichton's career suffered a setback when he was forced to leave the set of *Birdman of Alcatraz* (1961) after a row with the star, Burt Lancaster. In the mid-late 1970s Crichton did more work in television, directing programmes such as 'Space 1999', 'The Professionals' and 'Return of the Saint'.

He returned to film when he was asked by John Cleese to direct *A Fish Called Wanda* (1988). A comedy in the Ealing style, this was to be his last film and an international success both critically and at the box office, earning Crichton an Oscar® nomination for his direction. Scripted by Cleese and Crichton, the film starred Cleese and Michael Palin along with American stars Jamie Lee Curtis and Kevin Kline. The film is an old-fashioned farce with Cleese as London barrister Archie Leach, who has been hired to defend a gem thief and becomes the object of attraction for the gangster's moll, Wanda (Curtis). It is a well-scripted and extremely funny film, featuring wonderful performances, particularly from Palin as the stuttering animal-loving dog murderer and Kline as a cruel paranoid who veers between being Wanda's lover and her gay brother.

Crichton's contribution to Ealing's golden age, from the 1940s to the early 1950s, gained him recognition as one of Britain's most important post-war directors. The comedies in particular were part of a series of films concentrating on the determination and resilience of ordinary people, often celebrating their triumph over bureaucracy. With unreal events taking place in a very believable setting, the films have been described as 'realistic fantasy'. Said to have a 'maddening, meticulous perfectionist approach' to his work, Crichton was well known for his professionalism and pursuit of quality, and his ability to elicit fine performances from his actors. He died in September 1999.   **PR**

D

Stephen DALDRY

Like his luminous theatre contemporaries Sam Mendes and Nicholas Hytner, Stephen *Billy Elliot* (2000)
Daldry has reaped extensive critical acclaim for his film debut. Making the notoriously
tricky crossover from theatre, Daldry's *Billy Elliot* was a runaway hit at the 2000 Cannes
and Edinburgh Film Festivals and ensured Best Director nominations at both BAFTA and
Academy Award ceremonies.

Born in 1960, as Artistic Director of the Royal Court Theatre from 1992 to 1997,
Daldry made his name as a producer and director of socially incisive and commercially
viable plays. His 'An Inspector Calls' made the lucrative transfer from the National
Theatre to the West End and the international circuit, whilst his collaboration with David
Hare on 'Via Dolorosa' in 1999 garnered sev
eral awards during its US Broadway run. Handed a three-film deal by Working Title
Films in 1997, Daldry's first attempt was *Eight*, a BAFTA-nominated short about the
story of a young boy coming to terms with the death of his father. Featuring a strong
central performance from Jack Langan-Evans and a tenderly written and expertly directed
relationship with his mother (Gina McKee), *Eight* foreshadows the similarly strong relationship in *Billy Elliot* and highlights Daldry's sensitive balancing of the 'angry young
boy' theme with the implications of an absent parent.

Set against the backdrop of the 1984 miners' strike in a North East colliery town
in England, *Billy Elliot* charts the rites-of-passage of a young boy whose mother has
died and whose father and brother cannot give him the necessary emotional stability and
guidance that he craves. Scripted by gifted playwright Lee Hall, the film is dominated
by Jamie Bell as the sandy-haired Billy, whose combination of poise, spontaneity and
emotional maturity clearly marks him out as a major young actor. A mark of his theatrical
background, Daldry coaxes exceptional performances throughout: Julie Walters gives her
best work in years as the dance teacher who latches onto Billy's potential; the father
and older son pairing of Gary Lewis and Jamie Draven is a mix of menace and emotional
exhaustion. So much more than just a film about ballet-dancing, Bell and Draven
ensure that the narrative is as much about men's feelings of loss as the importance of

self-expression, both cathartically and artistically. The dance sequences are uniformly exhilarating, and the T-Rex soundtrack lends extra texture to the narrative.

Singled out by some critics as manipulative and mawkish, where the film fails to connect is in its socio-political proclamations. The 1984 strike is barely investigated, and Billy's sexual uncertainty is also passed over. In addition, the film's conclusion feels a little truncated – the last five minutes cover a period of around eight years, but the audience is given little clue as to the problems Billy might have had fitting into the (resolutely middle-class) Royal Ballet School hierarchy. As a gender-bending bildüngsroman, the film shares the same faults as Karyn Kusama's *Girlfight* (2000): in both cases, after the triumphant 'two fingers' to the establishment, there is nowhere else for the protagonists to go.

Daldry is currently in production with *The Hours*, a story revolving around three women in different eras who are all profoundly affected by the works of Virginia Woolf. Featuring Nicole Kidman, Meryl Streep, Julianne Moore and Ed Harris, it promises to further cement the reputation of one of British cinema's newest yet most accomplished directors. **BM**

Howard DAVIES

The Secret Rapture (1993) Howard Davies is a renowned and respected stage director with a résumé of award-winning productions at the Royal Shakespeare Company, the Royal National Theatre and on Broadway. Born in Durham in 1945, he broke into stage directing at the Bristol Old Vic in the early 1970s and soon joined the RSC in 1974. As an RSC associate director, he established and managed the Warehouse Theatre, producing and directing such classics as 'Les Liaisons Dangereuses', 'The Iceman Cometh' and 'Macbeth'. Moving to the National in 1987, he continued to direct a variety of classic and contemporary stage productions, including the works of compelling British dramatists such as Nick Stafford, Trevor Griffiths and David Hare.

Davies' first job behind the camera came in 1992 when he directed the BBC television film *Tales from Hollywood*, starring Jeremy Irons. The following year, he made his feature debut with *The Secret Rapture* (1993), an adaptation of Hare's play, which Davies had directed at the National in 1988. A sharp psychological melodrama, Hare's updated screenplay strips most of the rancorous, anti-Thatcherite political allegory from his stage script and focuses on the emotional chaos of diametrically opposed personalities within a family dynamic. Although at times ham-fisted and stagy in its delivery, Davies provides a suitably solemn ambience and successfully guides the film through dense characterisations and complex, unpredictable clashes of goodness, morality, self-righteousness, impulsiveness and love. The film features an explosive performance by Joanne Whalley-Kilmer, a memorable bookend to her earlier acclaimed portrayal of Christine Keeler (of Profumo scandal-fame) in Michael Caton-Jones' *Scandal* (1989).

After receiving a mixed reception to his film debut, Davies returned to the familiar environment of the stage and became an associate director of the Almeida Theatre. Soon to take up his position behind the camera once again, he is scheduled to direct a television film adaptation of William Boyd's novel 'Armadillo' for the BBC and A&E Network, and is attached to a feature film adaptation of Iain Pears' *Rashomon*-flavored mystery novel, 'An Instance of the Fingerpost'. **THa**

Terence DAVIES

The Terence Davies Trilogy Combining social realist, poetic and European arthouse aesthetics, Terence Davies' films
(1984) are of a deeply personal, autobiographical and confessional nature. Akin to T.S. Eliot
Distant Voices, Still Lives (1988) in his sentiment, he is engrossed with the passing and significance of time; the way
The Long Day Closes (1992) in which the past informs the present and future, moulding and haunting people's
The Neon Bible (1995) perceptions, actions and emotions. As such, his films do not always make for easy
The House of Mirth (2000) viewing. Davies' father, who died of stomach cancer when he was eight, was abusive and emotionally unyielding. His own homosexuality, encumbered by Catholic guilt and social convention, caused anxiety and subterfuge. These preoccupations have manifestly informed his early work and, more subtly, his most recent film, *The House of Mirth*

(2000). Though populated by characters that love and support one another, managing to find occasional moments of optimism in their lives, his films do not shy away from representing the miserable aspects of existence: oppressive institutions, pervasive religious authority, physical and emotional violation, and the existentialist reality of being fundamentally alone. He is one of Britain's most genuine, uncompromising and intriguing directors working today.

Born in Liverpool, UK, in 1945, the youngest of ten children (three of whom did not survive into adulthood), he left school at fifteen and worked as an accountant before taking up acting and attending drama school in Coventry from 1971 to 1973. He directed his first short, *Children*, in 1976, on £8,500 from the British Film Institute, and won a bronze Hugo at the Chicago Film Festival of that year. He studied at the National Film and Television School at Beaconsfield and made his second short, *Madonna and Child* (1980). He received funding for his third, *Death and Transfiguration* (1983), from Greater London Arts Association and the BFI. The three together, all shot in stark black and white, form *The Terence Davies Trilogy*, released as a feature in 1984.

The central protagonist and keystone of the trilogy is a young boy, Robert Tucker, an essential character that recurs in different guises in *Distant Voices, Still Lives* (1988), *The Long Day Closes* (1992) and *The Neon Bible* (1995). Exploring the institution of family, Davies tends to focus on its ritualistic aspects, pinning the narrative on key moments of birth, marriage and death, and highlighting rites of passage such as beginning a new school, sexual awakening and leaving home. From *Children*, which focuses on his early schooling and his father's death, through *Madonna and Child*, which highlights his sexual activity and his mother's death, to *Death and Transfiguration*, which ends in his own death, memories and events prompt time shifts – flashes back and forth – in the trajectory of his own life. The dominance of his father and religion, and the burden of his homosexual urges, run thematically throughout the film, shadowing every feeling and impulse.

Davies effectively captures the complexity of Robert's feeling for his father: he smiles when he finally sees him leave the house in a coffin but later stands at the window, viewed from outside, crying. The specificity of his emotion is not made explicit – it could be self-pity, genuine grief, or both – but its intensity is fully felt. The deep bond he shares with his mother, and the enormity of her passing, is conveyed by their mutual affection for one another and his despair as he weeps into her clothes once she has gone. Unable to tell her of his sexual desires, he has always crept from the house late at night to seek out men. Religious iconography looms large, filling the screen, a constant punishing reminder of acts he sees as transgressive and sinful. Acting on his personal desire, and against the tenets of Catholicism, he phones a tattooist to make an appointment to have his testicles illustrated. The call is heard in voice-over as we see shots of a church interior. The camera lingers on paintings and images of suffering and worship; as if to mock Robert further, even the tattooist professes disgust and turns him away. One of cinema's most incisive ruminations on the nature and moment of death occurs at the end of *Death and Transfiguration* when Robert painfully rasps his final breaths, reaching out towards the camera and the light. In ironic juxtaposition an accompanying voice intones: 'When the light goes out, God is dead'.

Stylistically, Davies favours longueurs, holding the camera on empty spaces, faces and set detail. In one long take, Robert is shown as a boy looking out of a bus window as his mother cries next to him. This type of shot recurs again and again in Davies' films – the train sequence at the beginning of *The Neon Bible* is one such particularly memorable moment. Characters are shown looking though windows, out of windows, seen from the street inside a house, framed by doorways, or sitting on stairs and flanked by banisters. It signals their uneasy relationship with the world, the extent to which they are trapped by its conventions or hover at its fringes, negotiating their place within it.

Questioned about the non-linearity of his work, Davies has said 'I'm not interested in what-happened-next, I'm interested in what-happened-emotionally-next'. This preoccupation, and his intention to evoke the essence of complex emotions, is evident in both *Distant Voices, Still Lives* and *The Long Day Closes*. They map similar autobiographical territory as the triology, focusing on family dynamics, and Davies frequently makes use of tableaux vivant to create images of a family portrait. The milieu of the films, pervaded by an intangible threatening male presence, is populated by the very physical presence of females. Women are keen to stay in public houses or at house parties, sharing each other's company, singing together in moments of togetherness, solidarity and spontaneity. The men are more conventional, inflexible and uncompromising, often dampening female pleasures.

Distant Voices, set in post-war Liverpool, won the International Critics' Prize in Cannes and raised Davies' profile. The father figure, more layered here, is still an oppressor. As impressionistic, *The Long Day Closes* revolves around the family experiences of 11-year-old Bud and more explicitly focuses on sexual desire. Music is vital to both films. *Distant Voices* is replete with popular songs, which feature almost as other characters. *The Long Day Closes* is akin to a musical or opera film. It constantly references and uses snippets from other films – particularly those about family, such as *The Magnificent Ambersons* (1942) and *Meet Me in St. Louis* (1944) – radio pieces and songs. On the one hand it is romantic and evocative, yet it also has ironic distance; knowingly, through the use of popular music, Davies critiques a nostalgic impulse. To this extent, his work occupies an interesting position in relation to the popular British heritage films of the 1980s and 1990s. His films are often beautiful but when he lingers on images of curtains or carpets it is not to fetishise or detail the period. Sometimes disorientating, they play with point of view, perception and temporal shifts; keeping the camera steady, trained on one location, Davies signals a change in scene by the turn of the weather or the movement of people in and out of a house.

Relocating to the Bible Belt of America's Deep South with *The Neon Bible*, an adaptation of a John Kennedy Toole novel, Davies evokes familiar thematics and concerns. The story concerns an adolescent, David, and again the father figure is abusive, the mother put upon and worn down. Religion is now of the evangelical kind, but it still pervades. One difference is the character of his Aunt May (played with appropriately distant charm by Gena Rowlands) who comes into his life as the exotic 'other'. A singer down on her luck, her artistic sensibility – signalled by her vivacious personality and colourful clothes – and her striving to realise her dreams, is a direct contrast to the small-town mentality that exists around him. David revealingly comments about the place, 'You had to think what your father thought all his life'. More conventional, both narratively and stylistically, than his previous work, the film is still dreamlike in its tone. Visually and aurally seductive, the jazzy score, the rich tapestry of muted colours, the full moons and night sky full of stars, combine to intrigue and compel the viewer.

His most recent film, *The House of Mirth*, which has been well received by critics, marks a point of departure. Adapted from Edith Wharton's novel, the piece is not discernibly autobiographical. That said, it still deals with social order and outsiders. Lily Bart, the central protagonist, is played by well-known 'X-Files' actress Gillian Anderson (who Davies had reportedly never seen in the television series). She is a character who hovers on the outskirts of high society, never fully accepted because she has neither money nor a name. Desperate to make a good marriage she refuses to settle for Lawrence Selden (a controlled Eric Stoltz), the one man that seems to understand and truly admire her. Juxtaposing deep velvet reds and golden hues with sombre tones, the set and lighting perfectly capture the mood of the story. As Davies has said: 'It had to look like John Singer Sargent portraits, but also the belle époque, which was crammed with stuff, dark, like a mausoleum. It'd stifle the life out of anybody'. The entire cast deliver first-rate performances. Laura Linney and Dan Aykroyd are particularly adept in fashioning subtly insidious and Machiavellian characters.

Despite the originality of his work, Davies has always found it difficult to find funding for his brand of personal, often challenging, film-making. Shockingly overlooked at Oscar® time, whether or not the critical success and international appeal of *The House of Mirth* will affect his status in the long-term remains to be seen.   **HP**

Desmond DAVIS

The 1960s were a watershed in many ways, not least in the world of British film. The environment of artistic and musical experimentation was reflected by an emerging movement of directors – the 'New British Wave' – keen to cast off the dramatic and narrative

chains of the post-war film industry. The 'angry young voices', who had new things to say Smashing Time (1967)
and new ways to say them, suddenly found a financial and creative platform from which A Nice Girl Like Me (1969)
to express themselves. As a result, British films of the time are self-reflective, deeply Clash of the Titans (1981)
rooted in the period and creative environment in which they were produced. Desmond Ordeal by Innocence (1984)
Davis' work, most of which was produced during that decade, suffers under the present
postmodern, ironic gaze. Strongly rooted in the mores and matters of 1960s Britain,
his experimental, earnest style, like that of so many of his contemporaries, now seems
self-important and over-indulgent. Defiantly wearing its heart on its sleeve, it lacks the
objectivity to survive beyond the brief world in which it was forged. However, as docu-
ments of an age, a creative epoch, and a cultural set of attitudes – particularly regarding
the role and psychology of women – his films still bear investigation, particularly if one
is able to look beyond the sepia tones.

Born in London in 1928, Davis began as a clapper boy in the British studio system,
later working for the Army Film Unit during World War Two. He then worked as camera
operator for Tony Richardson, another vanguard of 1960s film-making, on *A Taste of
Honey* (1961), *The Loneliness of the Long Distance Runner* (1962) and *Tom Jones*
(1963). Richardson's style – worthy, heavily mannered and emotionally candid – was to
have a great influence on Davis' burgeoning directorial career.

Having directed a number of shorts in the late 1950s and early 1960s, Davis' debut,
Girl with Green Eyes (1964), is indicative of his preoccupations: a clash of worlds, the
search for self and the liberation of women. The characters – a naïve, young, rural Irish
girl who moves in with a worldly city lass, and the depressed middle-aged writer who
falls for her – are classic fare for an aspiring, 'angry young director'. So too are the
attendant themes: the discovery of intellectual freedom, the rediscovery of youth by the
middle-aged and the maturation of the young. City savvy meets country innocence and
wide-eyed youth meets cynical age. Davis' style, the requisite mix of emotion and issue,
reeks of 1960s chic and now looks oddly cynical. The clash of ages, of childhood innocence and the demands of adult responsibility, recur in *The Uncle* (1965), in which a
seven-year-old boy struggles to come to terms with being the uncle of a seven-year-old
nephew. Davis explores the psychological impact of the boy's inability to reconcile his
two identities, eventually becoming estranged from both, with another overtly stylised
take on the coming-of-age story and pubescent psychology.

I Was Happy Here (1966) is slightly more digestible thanks to its engaging lead,
Sarah Miles. Another search-for-self story, in which a bored housewife who is trapped
in a loveless marriage returns to her home in Ireland and long-lost love, it explores
nostalgia and lost aspirations. Again, the vogueish directorial tricks – non-linear time
sequences, characters from the past stepping in and out of the present, the delivery of
internal thoughts as monologues to camera – now appear self-conscious, overly stylish
and potentially pretentious.

Smashing Time (1967), in which two Northern girls migrate to swinging London
with a variety of comic consequences, is undoubtedly Davis' worst film; he exchanges
earnest self-importance for broad slapstick and scatological farce. The content, including
pie-throwing, paint-squirting, and the full gamut of Mod-and-Mary-Quant pop references,
is indicative of the tone sustained throughout. The inspiration for a mode of cultural
plunder, it is directly responsible for *Austin Powers: International Man of Mystery* (1997)
and *Spice World: The Movie* (1997).

A Nice Girl Like Me (1969) returns to issue-driven drama. The tale of a sheltered,
young woman who decides to see life by embarking on a series of ludicrous relationships, each of which makes her pregnant, the film is an obvious and charmless piece of
romantic socio-drama. It is too admiring of its own unsubtle satire of free love and the
consequences of female sexual liberation. *A Nice Girl* also completes Davis' trilogy of
nostalgic portraits of the loss of innocence and the changing position of women in British
society, a series of films whose desperate desire for progressiveness has ironically made
them museum pieces for an outdated age.

His later efforts, though uncharacteristic, are more successful. Having directed for
television during the 1970s – ironically including episodes of 'The New Avengers', a
show which largely hinged on rehashing pop cultural references from the 1960s – Davis
returned to features with *Clash of the Titans* (1981). An engaging fantasy adventure,

which rearranged Grecian myth with an epic sweep and stop-motion special effects (for the post-*Star Wars* audience), it included a clockwork owl, the Medusa, the Kraken and a flying Pegasus. Davis' last film, based on Agatha Christie's novel (reputedly her favourite), *Ordeal by Innocence* (1984) is a competent whodunnit, evocative of its 1950s setting and an air of repression and social restriction, and laced with an admirably black tone. Davis has since continued to direct for television.   **OB**

Mick DAVIS

The Match (1999) Having received a writing credit (as Michael Davis) on the straight-to-video soft-porn sequel, *Another 9 1/2 Weeks* (1997), Mick Davis took a different path for his directorial debut. *The Match* (1999), which he also wrote, attempts to combine the appeal of Bill Forsyth's early successes (*Gregory's Girl* (1981), *Local Hero* (1983)) with that of the recent spate of British feelgood comedy dramas such as *The Full Monty* (1997). Set in Inverdoune, a picturesque Scottish village where men love their cattle and kilted skin-heads can smell Englishmen through pub walls, Davis fashions a slight tale of tradition vs. modernity. The football match of the title is the hundredth game in an annual event between the teams of Benny's Bar and Le Bistro, the importance of this particular game residing in the fact that the losers must forfeit their watering hole. Having lost for 99consecutive years, the signs for Benny's Bar do not bode well.

While the film attempts to colour its predictable scenario with half-hearted character conflict, it cannot transcend the clichés inherent in this particular sub-genre. The bond between milkman and football-trivia expert, Wullie (Max Beesley) and Rosemary (Laura Fraser), is forged in flashback through their witnessing his brother's death. This hint at darker personal motivations seems incongruous with the overall tone. Indeed, brief references to fulfilment through work and the detail of Wullie's leg calliper seem trite. A gallery of stereotypes pad out the cast, notably Richard E. Grant's wicked Gus (manager of Le Bistro's team, who plans to turn Benny's into a car park) and Neil Morrissey's bitter ex-pro footballer, called 'Piss Off' because of his preferred term of abuse. Alluding to the universality of football, the film still succumbs to the shortcomings of cinematic sport, with stilted choreography and training montages set to musical hits from the past. The film's attempts at whimsy are undercut by an air of cynicism, not only through its adher-ence to feelgood formula but also through the casting of Tom Sizemore, which seems designed purely to make the film saleable in American markets. Conversely, a cameo by Alan Shearer will mean nothing across the Atlantic.   **NJ**

James DEARDEN

Pascali's Island (1988) Born in 1949, the son of director Basil Dearden (*The Blue Lamp* (1950), *Victim* (1961)),
A Kiss Before Dying (1991) James Dearden is chiefly remembered for his Academy Award-nominated screenplay for
Rogue Trader (1999) the landmark film *Fatal Attraction* (1987). While his directorial efforts have also tried to tap into the zeitgeist, Dearden's output thus far suggests that his talents may be better served in the screenwriting arena.

Pascali's Island (1988), his adaptation of Barry Unsworth's novel, works well as a costume drama and is full of the twists and turns that mark his later work. Set on an Aegean island during the last days of the Ottoman Empire, Ben Kingsley plays a Turkish spy who begins to doubt his superiors. In a narrative full of double-crossing, his angst is compounded by the arrival of an archaeologist (Charles Dance). As a debut feature, Dearden's film is undoubtedly ambitious; he exhibits a strong sense of milieu in his period recreation and elicits a range of excellent performances.

A Kiss Before Dying (1991) boasts a strong cast (Matt Dillon, Sean Young and Max von Sydow) but fails on many levels. Dearden's adaptation of Ira Levin's best-selling novel (which had already been filmed in 1956, starring Robert Wagner), focuses on the gold-digging, power-hungry Dillon who marries into von Sydow's wealthy family. When his wife (Young) becomes pregnant, he kills her. Events become complicated, however, when her sister (also played by Young) sets out to solve the crime. The complexities of the narrative, complete with its doppelgängers and exercises in psychopathology, hardly seem suited to the big screen; a definite case of style over substance, it may have benefited from a more modest budget. Though one critic's comment that watching *A Kiss Before Dying* was about as 'exciting as watching someone go bald' seems a little severe, the film's tone is definitely unsure.

After a long hiatus, Dearden directed *Rogue Trader* (1999), a dramatisation of the Barings Bank debacle, which attempted to simultaneously comment on the perils of capitalism run wild and clinically explore the British class system. Ewan McGregor plays Nick Leeson, the man who literally broke the bank in the mid-1990s and absconded to the Far East whilst Britain's best-loved financial institution was left to implode. Once again adapting source material – this time Leeson's published account of events – Dearden's film is technically competent and features a strong central performance. That said, it lacks any deeper exploration of the upper-class system into which Watford-born, working-class Leeson was so desperate to be accepted. Narrative tension is hard to generate with prolonged shots of men in braces shouting numbers and Dearden's treatment of Leeson's wife (Anna Friel) reeks of misogyny. Ultimately, the film has little to say about personal responsibility or the lasting effects of the 'greed is good' maxim.   **BM**

Barry DEVLIN

For the teenagers of the 1980s, Barry Devlin is best known as the lead singer and bassist of the Irish rock group 'The Horslips'. Since then, he has reinvented himself as a director of pop videos (mainly for U2), documentaries and feature films, as well as a television writer. Born in Newry, County Down, in 1946, Devlin settled in the Republic of Ireland in 1972.

All Things Bright and Beautiful (1994)

In the late 1980s he started writing for television. His credits include 'The Darling Buds of May' and 'Ballykissangel', as well as a number of original scripts for mini-series. His first feature film as writer/director was *Lapsed Catholics* (1988), made for Radio Telefís Éireann, a spoof documentary about the return of a progressive rock band for a one-off charity gig. Devlin followed this with *All Things Bright and Beautiful* (1994), a gentle, comic, rites-of-passage story about a young boy, Barry (Ciaran Fitzgerald), who has visions of the Virgin Mary. He attempts to capitalise upon his spiritual insights in order to help the local parish priest realise his ambition and erect a grotto in the village. Allegedly autobiographical, it is set in Northern Ireland in 1954 (the Marian Year) and, with its light, nostalgic touch, bears much resemblance to Devlin's earlier television work. The outbreak of religious excesses that Barry's visions cause is the central source of humour, yet the film never quite dismisses the miraculous in favour of the rational. Even the IRA man (a cameo role for Gabriel Byrne) is treated with some levity, his appearance causing Barry to confuse him with the Good Thief, Barrabas. Although some critics have been dismissive of this rose-tinted view of Ireland's past, Devlin's work has always found an audience.

He currently has many projects in development; most notable, is *The Limo Man*, based on the 'true' experiences of Julia Roberts in Ireland during her post-Sutherland break. He also scripted Suri Krishnamma's *A Man of No Importance* (1994) and Valerio Jalongo's *Spaghetti Slow* (1996).   **RB**

Jasmin DIZDAR

Jasmin Dizdar's first feature, *Beautiful People* (1999), is a flawed but ambitious attempt to make a comedy drama about the conflict in the former Yugoslavia.

Beautiful People (1999)

A Bosnian Muslim, born in 1961, Dizdar came to London in the late 1980s after studying film in Czechoslovakia, and has written a book about the country's most celebrated film director, Milos Forman. He wrote radio plays and worked in BBC television drama before the British Film Institute took an interest in the script for *Beautiful People*.

The film combines magical realism with a Robert Altman-influenced style. Multiple storylines, a large featured cast with no central protagonist and a mix of humour and tragedy – traits that Gilbert Adair has referred to as 'Altmanisation' – have become particularly fashionable in the last decade with *The Player* (1992) and the masterful *Short Cuts* (1993). Dizdar's film sits alongside other Altman homages such as Richard

Linklater's *Slacker* (1991) and Paul Thomas Anderson's *Magnolia* (2000). Set mostly in London, it is concerned with a group of characters that are all, in one way or another, connected to the Bosnian conflict. This is the starting point for an exploration of wider issues such as drug abuse, racism and war. A fight on a London bus between a Croat and a Serb lands them both in hospital where they continue the conflict. A BBC reporter suffering 'Bosnia Syndrome' severs his own leg in sympathy with gangrene victims. In the most interesting (and outrageous) story, a racist skinhead junkie falls asleep in Rotterdam airport after an England vs. Holland football game and is parachuted into Bosnia where he becomes a war hero and learns the error of his racism.

Shot in a frenzied style, some of the performances are irritatingly broad. Collapsing in parts under the weight of too many characters and too many issues, Dizdar cannot be accused of a lack of ambition; although the surrealistic sequences sit uneasily with the trite tying up of loose ends, there is certainly enough here to interest the viewer. The film won 'Un Certain Régard Prix' at the Cannes Film Festival.

Dizdar is currently working on a satirical comedy about juggling the conflicting imperatives of family life and technocratic office space.   **IC**

Simon DONALD

The Life of Stuff (1998)   Born in Lanark, Scotland, in 1959, Simon Donald progressed from regular acting roles in television dramas, such as 'Taggart' and 'Soldier, Soldier', to writing scripts, including the revived 'Dr Finlay's Casebook' and Philip Saville's BBC Screen One drama *Deacon Brodie* (1997). He has also written for features, such as Hugh Hudson's *My Life So Far* (1999) and Bill Eagles' recent *Beautiful Creatures* (2000), and for the stage, basing his directorial debut, *The Life of Stuff* (1998), on one of his own plays.

Badly received, the film was criticised for applying the (very different) styles of Peter Greenaway and Danny Boyle, riding the reputation for movie realism by way of scatological subjects advanced by Boyle's *Trainspotting* (1996) and Paul McGuigan's *The Acid House* (1998), which was also based on an Irvine Welsh book.

Starring Ewen Bremner and Gina McKee, *The Life of Stuff* deals with a group of gangsters in Glasgow's clubbing scene. The claustrophobic setting, combined with the shallowness of the characters, renders it alienating, particularly in light of its convoluted plot of unravelling rivalry among Glasgow's low-life dealers and clubbers. Although the cast makes every effort to invest the characters with some humanity, they fail, in large part because the film is too misanthropic. The humour is grotesque and superficial, lacking either Greenaway's intellect or Boyle's overall coherence of vision. Due to the schlock-horror theatricality of the direction, it struggles to escape its stage-bound roots, and the mix of vile visuals and gallows humour make it an acquired taste.   **JD**

Clive DONNER

The Secret Place (1957)   Clive Donner was born in 1926 in London to a violinist father and a mother who ran a
Heart of a Child (1958)   boutique. He joined Denham studios as an assistant in 1942 and worked as an assistant
Some People (1962)   editor on a number of classic British films, including David Lean's *Oliver Twist* (1948)
The Caretaker (1964)   and Brian Desmond Hurst's *Scrooge* (1951). For most of the 1950s Donner worked as
Nothing But the Best (1964)   an editor on films such as Ronald Neame's *The Card* (1952) and *The Million Pound Note*
What's New Pussycat (1965)   (1953). He always maintained that working as an editor was like being a second director,
Luv (1967)   and believed it to be a far more instructive apprenticeship than being an assistant to the
Here We Go Round the   director. As an editor he was able to see the various stages of a film's production: the
Mulberry Bush (1968)   rushes, the rough cut, the fine cut, the music recording, dubbing and grading of the final
Alfred the Great (1969)   print. While assistant directors are usually tied down with more administrative concerns,
Vampira (1974)   Donner feels an editor's input can dramatically change the ultimate mood and effect of
The Thief of Baghdad (1978)   a film.
The Nude Bomb (1980)   In 1957 he directed his first feature, *The Secret Place*, about a diamond robbery.
Charlie Chan and the Curse   The tension is well maintained throughout the film and the editing is snappy, with a
of the Dragon Queen (1981)   particularly intense climax filmed on the scaffolding of a building site. The film's distinc-
Stealing Heaven (1988)   tion lay in Donner's use of real locations to shoot scenes that, at the time, would have
ordinarily been shot in a studio.

Donner's second film was the sentimental *Heart of a Child* (1958), starring Donald Pleasence, the story of a boy and a St. Bernard dog. While both displayed a keen technical proficiency neither of Donner's first two films were particularly memorable or successful, and he subsequently settled into the role of television director, working on episodes of popular television series such as 'Danger Man' and 'Sir Francis Drake'.

Donner's first taste of critical success came when he directed *Some People* (1962), a film funded by the Duke of Edinburgh's Award Scheme. Attempting to be both entertaining and instructive, its intention was to harness the wayward energy of British youth and direct it toward socially productive rather than destructive behaviour. Such a didactic burden would ordinarily have dragged a film down the scale of dramatic enterprise, but Donner succeeded in making its message subtle and the story engaging. The sense of a youth isolated by its own culture and desperate to find new forms of expression prefigured the whole swinging era of the 1960s. Again Donner chose to shoot much of the film on location in Bristol, and his use of unusual and striking locations provides an engaging realism.

The Caretaker (1964), his next project, was both an exceptional piece of cinema and a seminal venture in funding. The film is an adaptation of Harold Pinter's critically acclaimed play of the same title, in which three men do nothing but sit in a room and talk for a couple of hours. While film is primarily a visual narrative, theatre relies more on the spoken word, and the idea of defying this standard dichotomy with a distinctly theatrical modern play was not something that appealed to financiers. Undeterred, Donner and his producer, Michael Birkett, along with the stellar British cast of Donald Pleasence, Alan Bates and Robert Shaw, set about raising the production budget themselves. Within a week they had collected £30,000 'with no strings attached' from a group of sympathetic investors including Richard Burton, Leslie Caron, Noël Coward, Peter Sellers and Elizabeth Taylor.

Donner was astute enough to realise that the real drama of Pinter's play lay in what was left unsaid between the characters. Such an abstract form of action can only be intimated through the physical presence of the actors, yet Donner did not rely too heavily on basic two-shot over the shoulder close-ups and single close-ups. Nor did he try to compensate for the limited space by filming an array of 'arty' compositions detailing the layers of junk strewn around the small room. To do so would have meant that inanimate objects, as well as the actors' facial expressions, were providing most of the secondary 'action' beside the dialogue. Instead, the comportment and movements of the characters were brought into play, giving the film a dynamic quality it could easily have lacked.

The intense artistic effort required for *The Caretaker*, coupled with its lack of success, may have left Donner a little jaded. Certainly his choice of projects in the following years suggest that with each film he was becoming more and more resigned to the commercial nature of the film industry. *Nothing But the Best* (1964) was a well-scripted social satire in which a working-class yob (Alan Bates), in 'Talented Mr Ripley' style, kills off his wealthy benefactor and assumes his social position under the tutelage of a cynical old Etonian played by Denholm Elliot. The film's black humour is offset by the visual splendour of Donner's direction and the fast-paced editing.

What's New Pussycat (1965) was made from Woody Allen's first screenplay and he has since claimed to have no time for it. Donner had two big stars to work with (Peter O'Toole and Peter Sellers) and he allowed them far too much space for ad-libbing. As one would expect from any film scripted by Allen there are some truly hilarious moments, but Donner's decision to allow for so much improvisation left him with a grossly self-indulgent piece, lacking in any controlled direction.

In his next film, *Luv* (1967), Donner chose to take the British sex romp across the Atlantic. The film was a puerile and painfully unfunny attempt to ride the popular tide of sexual liberalism that qualified the late 1960s. Jack Lemmon and Peter Falk switched roles just days before shooting commenced, and Donner directs with an urgency that borders on desperation in an attempt to prevent the jokes falling flat.

Upon his return to England he directed the more substantial *Here We Go Round the Mulberry Bush* (1968). The film could easily be sluiced into the same lightweight category as its immediate antecedents, but under its surface a deeper human tragedy unravels. The representation of Jamie McGregor (Barry Evans), a frustrated teenager, went beyond the range of permissive fashion and was imbued with an endearing psycho-logical realism. The story is narrated in the first person with Evans speaking directly into the camera, indicating that this is a supremely subjective account of a teenager's life – a life overwhelmed by highly erotic fantasies. The wish-dream colour effects were extremely popular at the time but they also related specifically to the character's state of mind. The film is set in Stevenage and shot largely on location, depicting an England few people thought existed at the time – new housing estates bereft of the character that historical buildings and monuments proffer.

In an attempt to avoid being type-cast as a maker of off-beat sex comedies, Donner made the unfortunate decision to direct a big historical epic, *Alfred the Great* (1969). The story juxtaposed the Saxons' fight to repeal hoards of Viking invaders with a gentle psychological study of Alfred, their troubled leader. It seemed a peculiar choice for Donner, to say the least. Nothing in his prior body of work suggested that he would cope with either the subject or the scale of the film, and he did not. *Alfred the Great* was a mega-budget failure that all but ended Donner's career as a director of feature films. In an increasingly nervous film industry only a handful of directors could have survived such a monumental flop, and Donner was not one of them. The film contains some magnificently staged battle sequences, with helicopters used to provide aerial footage, but the dialogue is simply risible in places. This is, essentially, a problem with the script. A more astute director would have perceived these problems and turned down the offer to direct. Following the staggering commercial failure of *Alfred the Great*, Donner was shut out of the feature film market for five years, directing for American and British televi-sion and even trying his hand at commercials. When he finally did return to directing feature films with *Vampira* (1974), it did little to restore his standing in the industry. The film has no style, no sense of humour and a lamentable script made even worse by Donner's laissez faire direction.

The Thief of Baghdad (1978) is less problematic, but only marginally so. The film boasts an impressive cast including Peter Ustinov, Terence Stamp and a young Ian Holm. It also has lots of eye candy special effects and a bombastic theatricality that Donner employed to compensate for a lack of directorial vision. Donner returned to box-office favour when he directed *The Nude Bomb* (1980), a film based on the popular 'Get Smart' television series. The film's relative commercial success can be credited to the success of the television series rather than the quality of the direction, which fails to make the film look like anything more than an extended episode of the television series.

Throughout the 1980s Donner worked with such acting luminaries as George C. Scott in the made-for-television versions of Dickens' classics 'Oliver Twist' and 'A Christmas Carol'. He directed Ian McKellen, Malcolm McDowell and Candice Bergen in *Arthur the King* (1985) and Drew Barrymore in *Babes of Toyland* (1986). Despite the quality of his television productions, the spectre of *Alfred the Great* still looms large over Donner's oeuvre; his features since then, such as the more recent *Charlie Chan and the Curse of the Dragon Queen* (1981) and *Stealing Heaven* (1988), are notable largely for their substandard scripts and uninspired direction.   **EMa**

Bill DOUGLAS

My Childhood (1972) Bill Douglas is one of the few true auteurs of British Cinema. Feted by critic Derek
My Ain Folk (1973) Malcolm, who hailed his trilogy 'a true masterpiece of poetic cinema', and the winner
My Way Home (1978) of many international awards, he was largely passed over for funding. Although his
Comrades (1987) legacy is apparent in the work of many contemporary film directors, he has also failed to receive much serious acclaim. Born in 1934 in the midst of the depression in the mining community of Newcraighall, outside Edinburgh, Scotland, his early years of poverty and suffering were alleviated by his escapes to the local 'flea-pit'. His entrance was guaran-teed only if he could collect enough jam jars for the return deposit. Failing this, he had to sneak in. 'Up there was the best of all possible worlds,' he wrote in his essay, 'Palace of Dreams: The Making of a Film-maker'. At 17, a friend gave him all the 8mm equipment necessary to fulfil his film-making aspirations and soon he was writing, making costumes and building sets for ambitious projects such as an adaptation of a Chekhov short story. After a stint of National Service in the Air Force stationed in Egypt, where he met life-long

friend Peter Jewell, he moved to London and became involved with Joan Littlewood's Theatre Workshop. A promising actor and writer, he nonetheless believed his vocation was in directing and successfully applied to the London International Film School, graduating in 1970 with first class honours, having made a number of outstanding shorts.

His trilogy – *My Childhood* (1972), *My Ain Folk* (1973), *My Way Home* (1978) – made under the aegis of the BFI, was only enabled after Mamoun Hassan, head of production, saw his work on *My Childhood* and realised Douglas' importance. He subsequently deceived the board into believing a trilogy had been agreed to as a project in order to extract further funds. Douglas' name was later used as an exemplar of talent on a budget to secure government finance for the BFI, but unfortunately he failed to benefit from these funds. Having declared that he detested his upbringing, the trilogy centred largely on Douglas' boyhood landscape. Also professing to hate reality, he was nonetheless drawn to a form of realism, albeit one without precedent. Refusing an easy catharsis, he fashioned an aesthetically distanced and compassionate view which, whilst bleak, is not unrelievedly so. He claimed to be inspired by Chekhov's words: 'I can write only from memory, I never write directly from life. The subject must pass through the sieve of my memory, so that alone which is important or typical remains there as on a filter.' Deceptively simple, his formally composed blocks of images – often entire scenes in one shot – force the audience to make connections between the spare glimpses of emotion and character rather than action and plot. Utilising the distanciation techniques of Russian formalism and Soviet montage style from the individualistic perspective and emotional intensity of European art cinema, he beautifully evinced the locality of his own experience and history.

His final film, *Comrades* (1987), took eight years to be realised. Produced by Merchant-Ivory, it is unlike most British historical epics; no mere exercise in ostentatious production values and romanticised nostalgia, it is political and non-literary. A three-hour tribute to the Tolpuddle Martyrs, *Comrades* benefited from Douglas' knowledge of working-class poverty and played on his passion for pre-cinematic optical entertainments. He introduced a travelling 'lanternist' into the Tolpuddle milieu, injecting a sense of magic realism. The film thus becomes a self-reflexive examination of ways of seeing, a comment on notions of historical fact and the truth of cinema itself as entertainment.

Neither humanist realist in the tradition of British films nor part of the European anti-realist avant-garde, his truly original work excluded him from the rise in academic study and he remained largely neglected. Notorious for his tantrums, and considered obsessive, he failed to fit into a comfortable place within the industry. Mamoun Hassan has described his unique shots and lack of scene coverage from different angles, and his detailed planning which allowed little or no room for collaboration. In later years, teaching at the National Film School, Douglas stated: 'To ignore a bad suggestion is easy: to ignore a good suggestion which is irrelevant is what makes a good director'. His intense, puritanical nature was, however, leavened by an artful sense of humour, which made him an inspired and much-loved teacher. Douglas was diagnosed with cancer too late for treatment and died in 1991. Writing in *Sight and Sound*, Scottish film historian John Caughie finds 'a whiff of institutional guilt' in his reappraisal since his death. His work has still failed to attain wide recognition outside the emergence of Scottish cultural and media studies. A record of his life and work, 'Bill Douglas: A Laternist's Account', was published in 1993. His collection of optical entertainments can be seen at The Bill Douglas Centre for the History of Cinema and Popular Culture, which was founded in 1994. The Centre also contains a tremendous collection of film history. He left at least three unproduced scripts written from 1988–1990: *The Ring of Truth*, *Flying Horse*, about the cinema pioneer, Eadweard Muybridge, and *Confessions of a Justified Sinner*. The latter is considered by many to be his most brilliant script yet it has been passed over by all the British funding institutions.   **FG**

Peter DUFFELL

Peter Duffell began his career in television in the 1960s, directing episodes of the cult series 'The Avengers' and the enjoyable Hammer fantasy show 'Journey into the Unknown'. He has returned to television periodically throughout his career.

The House that Dripped Blood (1970)

England Made Me (1973)

Duffell's debut feature, *The House that Dripped Blood* (1970), was a portmanteau film produced by Amicus, a company second only to Hammer in the British horror film market. Unlike the superior anthology movies – Freddie Francis' *Tales from the Crypt* (1972) and Roy Ward Baker's *Vault of Horror* (1973) – which were inspired by the EC horror comics of the 1950s, Duffell's film incorporates stories by Robert Bloch, the author of 'Psycho'. Despite a good cast – typical for Amicus – of Denholm Elliott, Geoffrey Bayldon, Christopher Lee and Ingrid Pitt, this is pretty disappointing stuff, lacking both the nasty humour and the gore that typically made these movies pleasurable. The mood is dispiritingly light-hearted, particularly in the somewhat campy last story, 'The Cloak', which features Jon Pertwee as a hammy horror star transformed into a real vampire by the titular garment. The only really creepy note is struck by the third story, 'Sweets to the Sweet', with the demonic child (Chloe Franks) using black magic to terrorise Christopher Lee. Effectively spooky material, it seems all the better in comparison to its weaker companions. Originally awarded an 'A' certificate, the film was given an 'X' rating at the behest of Amicus founder, Milton Subotsky, who feared for the marketability of a horror film with no age restrictions.

England Made Me (1973), Duffell's best film to date, was poorly received upon its initial release. In the adaptation of Graham Greene's novel of murky dealings in the world of high finance, Duffell and co-writer Desmond Cory shifted the setting from Sweden to 1930s Germany. The unsuccessful Tony Farrant (Michael York) has an intimate relationship with his powerful twin sister (Hildegard Neil) against a backdrop of the Nazi rise to power, while a seedy journalist (Michael Hordern) attempts to dig up dirt on financier Krogh (Peter Finch). Duffell, who described the film as 'the only thing that has really meant anything to me', stylishly directs the action, particularly in the boating trip scene set on a picturesque lake, accompanied by a Hitler radio broadcast. The main problem with the film is the familiarity of its historical-political backdrop, an echoing of Luchino Visconti's *The Damned* (1969) and Bob Fosse's excellent *Cabaret* (1972), which also starred York. The critical mauling that the film received may be due in part to the international nature of the venture – a British director filming an adaptation of a Sweden-set novel transposed to Germany, financed by an American studio and shot in Yugoslavia.

Duffell followed this with an equally international project, *Inside Out* (1975), an uninteresting heist movie starring Telly Savalas who hatches a plan to spring an aged Nazi from prison as part of a scam to seize looted gold. There is little evidence of the stylish direction apparent in Duffell's earlier work and the chief point of interest is the comically surreal scene where the freed Nazi is drugged and meets 'Hitler' (a member of Savalas' gang in disguise).

Its (deservedly) lukewarm critical reception may have been the reason why Duffell decided to work in television for the next decade. Amongst other eclectic projects, he directed episodes of 'Tales of the Unexpected' and 'The Far Pavilions' for British television. A high point in his work from this period is the television movie *Experience Preferred... But Not Essential* (1982), the amusing story of a waitress set in a Welsh hotel in the 1960s. The piece displayed an appealing feel for comedy, rarely witnessed in Duffell's other cinema projects.

Letters to an Unknown Lover/Les Louves (1985) is a love story set in Occupied France. Filmed in both French and English, this benefits considerably from likeable performances: Ralph Bates as the escaped POW, and Cherie Lunghi and Mathilda May as the sisters he becomes involved with. Deft in his handling of period pieces, Duffell creates an unusual (if not entirely successful) portrait of a grim time.

Duffell's most recent theatrical feature is the family film, *King of the Wind* (1989), a pleasant enough story about an Arabian colt and the stable boy who cares for him as they journey from seventeenth-century North Africa to France. Although the slow pace may be off-putting for many viewers, it is of interest to fans of 'horse movies' (owing something to Anna Sewell's oft-filmed 'Black Beauty') and for the starry cast (Richard Harris, Nigel Hawthorne, Peter Vaughan and Glenda Jackson).

Peter Duffell is a director whose career may have followed a different track had it not been for the (unfairly) hostile reception to his most personal project, *England Made Me*. His recent work has been in television, directing episodes of 'Space Precinct'.	**IC**

Martin DUFFY

Born in Dublin in 1952, Martin Duffy worked as a television editor at Radio Telefís Éireann before embarking on a freelance career. He was responsible for editing a number of key independent Irish films including Margo Harkin's *Hush-A-Bye Baby* (1990) and Bob Quinn's *The Bishop's Story* (1993). He wrote, edited and directed a short film, *Splice of Life*, in 1988, and co-directed *The Cure* (1990) with a group of teenage cancer patients.

The Boy from Mercury (1996)
The Bumblebee Flies Anyway (1998)
The Testimony of Taliesin Jones (2000)

Duffy moved into feature-film direction with *The Boy from Mercury* (1996), which he also wrote. A critical success, the film had a disappointing box-office release. The story concerns a young Dublin boy, Harry Cronin (James Hickey), who believes that he has been sent from Mercury to investigate Earth. His father is dead and in his absence his mother, Mary (Rita Tushingham), calls upon his eccentric Uncle Tony (Tom Courtenay) for help when James insists on addressing her as 'Earth Mother'. When James is bullied at school, his otherwise detached older brother, Paul (Hugh O'Connor), has to step in and restore order. Duffy's period Dublin is shot with gleeful indulgence. The garish artefacts of the 1950s clutter the screen and the highlight of the week is the latest instalment of *Flash Gordon* (1940) at the local cinema.

In 1998 Duffy directed *The Bumblebee Flies Anyway* with Elijah Wood and Janeane Garofalo. A return to the themes of childhood and loss, the story centres on the character of an American teenage boy (Wood) who agrees to a medical experiment to restore the memory loss he has suffered after an accident. The film is shot in Duffy's very distinctive manner with a sense of echoing, empty spaces and an unworldly (in the case of the former film, otherworldly) central character. Certain scenes, such as the finale on the roof of the sanatorium, unambiguously recall the look and mood of *The Boy from Mercury*. *The Bumblebee Flies Anyway* received festival screenings and a cable release In the US.

Duffy's latest film, *The Testimony of Taliesin Jones* (2000), also focuses on a young boy, the Welsh Taliesin (John Paul-Macleod), and a missing parent – in this case his mother (Geraldine James), who has left the family home. He is drawn to a faith healer (Ian Bannen) and to the derision of his schoolmates and discomfort of his family becomes imbued with a sense of religion. Once again, Duffy shows himself unafraid to mix realism with the supernatural, also adding here, a sense of the miraculous. A recurrent motif, the child looking through a window at the night sky in search of meaning, links all three feature films, both visually and thematically. Duffy has also written two novels for young people, 'Once Upon A Universe' and 'Mothership'. **RB**

Martin DUNKERTON

Martin Dunkerton's sole directorial effort thus far, *Brothers* (2000), co-written with Nick Valentine (who also mugs away desperately in front of the camera) and co-produced by brother Julian Dunkerton is, to put it mildly, a work of little merit.

Brothers (2000)

The story focuses on a disparate band of young male Brits who jet off for a week of sun, sand, sea and sex, not to mention copious amounts of alcohol, and in the process attempt to discover the tentative threads that bind their friendship. Much merriment supposedly ensues but what actually follows is a tiresome, overtly misogynistic, would-be meditation on lad culture and mindless hedonism. The attempts at characterisation extend to who can fart the loudest in a long-running competition and who can bed the most women, and the observations on male camaraderie are boorish in the extreme. Subtle it is not – Dunkerton is seemingly from the point-and-shoot school of directing – and one hopes that a proposed attempt to cover similar ground from the female perspective, *More than a Woman*, is little more than a rumour. **JWo**

E

Bill EAGLES

With a background in mainstream television ('Touching Evil III' and several episodes of *Beautiful Creatures* (2000) 'Peak Practice'), Bill Eagles chose to direct a feature debut that would push some very specific demographic buttons. Aimed squarely at *FHM*-boys, fans of Dean Martin, and those who wished *Thelma and Louise* (1992) was more vicious, *Beautiful Creatures* (2000) works with the traditional generic templates of the crime thriller – a muddled narrative, an eccentric supporting cast and photogenic leads. By the end credits one is left with the impression that the film could have been a lot more inventive and innovative. Dorothy (Susan Lynch) and Petula (Rachel Weisz) go on the run when Petula accidentally kills her gangster boyfriend and are forced to adopt unusual methods to survive the resulting fallout. What ensues is a quirky comedy that is unsure which direction to take; it is unclear whether Eagles hoped to make a female buddy movie, a *Lock, Stock*-clone or a comment on police corruption. This ambiguous tone seeps into all levels of the production – Weisz (so enthralling in *The Mummy* (1999)) is made ridiculous in her peroxide wig, while Lynch, last seen as James Joyce's muse in *Nora* (1999), seems ill-at-ease with the butch feminism and retro-gangster chic. There are plus points, such as a visually arresting pre-credit sequence and a relentless soundtrack, but any film that relies on a pink dog to carry the weight of the narrative must be viewed with a certain amount of scepticism.

More recently, Eagles has been directing the television series 'Night & Day'.   **BM**

Adrian EDMONDSON

Many acknowledge Adrian Edmondson as one of the godfathers of late-1970s alternative comedy. Both he and actor-writer Rik Mayall became denizens of the scatological with their immensely successful cult television show 'Bottom'. He is a familiar face (and voice) on 1980s and 1990s British television, with appearances on 'The Young Ones', 'The Comic Strip Presents…', 'Saturday Live' and numerous 'Bottom' spin-off specials. As the husband of Jennifer Saunders, he has also directed her in 'French and Saunders

Guest House Paradiso (1999)

Live' and *Mirrorball* (2000), a television film released to great acclaim late last year.

His film debut, *Guest House Paradiso* (1999), is in essence a feature-length episode of 'Bottom'. With a healthier budget and slicker production values, Edmondson has opened out the initial half-hour concept into what is simply a prolonged series of slapstick routines with toilet humour. He and Mayall play Richie and Eddie, proprietors of the Guest House Paradiso, a hotel where business is notoriously slow. What follows are the extended antics of both owners and guests, and the endless bodily fluid gags that makes *There's Something About Mary* (1998) a paradigm of restraint.

Unless one is a fan of 'Bottom', the film may grate as the self-indulgence of the puerile stars exists simply for itself. There is no weighty pretension or meaning, and the latent homoeroticism between the two men merely carries on a strand of typically quirky humour that began with 'Monty Python' and 'The Morecambe and Wise Show'. As a hybrid of 'Fawlty Towers' and 'The Itchy and Scratchy Show', the film is sado-masochistically successful; Edmondson also seems to be wink-winking at the audience by portraying the English as faux middle-class buffoons and the French as suave and sexy. **BM**

Christine EDZARD

Born in Paris in 1945, Christine Edzard began her career in production design for opera, theatre and then film, decorating the set for Franco Zeffirelli's film *Romeo and Juliet* (1968). She began to write screenplays in the early 1970s, creating a version of *The Tales of Beatrix Potter* (1971), for which she also designed the costumes and sets. In 1977 she directed her first film, a short entitled *The Little Match Girl*, showing an interest in fairytale narratives which had been evident in much of her design and writing. In 1979, the film production company Sands, which she set up with her producer husband Richard Goodwin, released three of her short films under the title *Stories from a Flying Trunk*. This portmanteau-style film included her first short together with work based on 'Little Ida' and 'The Kitchen'. Her next, *The Nightingale*, made in 1981, was based on a Hans Christian Anderson story and mixed live action and animation.

Her first feature, *Biddy* (1983), focuses on a Victorian nursemaid whose life turns to disorder and confusion when her young charges have grown and left the nest. According to one critic, the film is as delicate and incisive as a Victorian miniature, and Edzard demonstrates a keen eye for period detail in the set and costume design. The use of Biddy's voice-over also gives her character some depth, preventing her from being swamped by Edzard's precise, authentic visual portrait of Victorian life.

An interest in period visuals and narratives led her to adapt Charles Dickens' 'Little Dorrit' for her next feature. A mammoth work told in two parts, *Little Dorrit Part One: Nobody's Fault* and *Little Dorrit Part Two: Little Dorrit's Story* (1987), it featured a host of British theatre (and, to a lesser extent, television and film) actors, including Derek Jacobi, Alec Guinness and Miriam Margolyes. Here, Edzard's attention to detail emphasise the film's theatricality and make effective comments about the gulf between rich and poor, demonstrating her concern for social outsiders and class distinctions. Edzard has commented that 'if Dickens was writing today he'd be doing films and television, but he would never have wanted to seduce people as we do now by diluting his message for the benefit of a wider public'. To this end, Edzard's film takes its time, privileging character over plot, resonating with her original intention to make several short films about each of the major characters. The Dickensian themes of poverty and social injustice made for topical subjects during the time of Thatcher's Britain.

Once again drawing on existing material for inspiration, Edzard chose to base her film *The Fool* (1990) on the writings of novelist and social explorer Henry Mayhew. Having conducted research on a cross-section of British society between 1848 and 1861, Mayhew's newspaper articles discussed themes of the privileged versus the poor. Featuring Derek Jacobi as the insignificant clerk who discovers that people's opinions of him change when he passes himself off as the rich reclusive Sir John, the film achieves authenticity in its representations of both squalor and luxury, suggesting that if the dress is right, respect follows instantly.

Edzard's next film, *As You Like It* (1992), put a contemporary spin on Shakespeare's pastoral play. Set in the urban wastelands of Rotherhithe, Rosalind and her cousin Celia are transplanted to an Arden made of cardboard – the Cardboard City of the homeless. Focusing the camera on actors' faces, as though they were portraits in a gallery, the theatricality of the production is again heightened. Although the joy and airiness of Shakespeare's play is diminished, the sense of melancholy is effectively invoked.

Edzard went on to direct a short film version of a children's television opera 'Amahl and the Night Visitors' in 1996 and wrote, designed and directed a short version of *The Nutcracker* (1997) in the IMAX format.

Her most recent project, entitled *The Children's Midsummer Night's Dream*, a collaboration with eight to twelve-year-olds from various Southwark schools in a film production of 'A Midsummer Night's Dream', is due for release in 2001.   **JD**

Bille ELTRINGHAM

Having spent the middle part of the 1990s making short films for television, including the BBC's '10x10' series, Bille Eltringham co-directed his feature debut, *The Darkest Light* (1999), with Simon Beaufoy, writer of the successful *The Full Monty* (1997) and Sam Miller's *Among Giants* (1998). The film draws on Eltringham's creative interest in children as the subjects for his work: his short film, *Yellow* (1996), focused on a seven-year-old who goes missing on a family outing, and Channel 4's 'The Kid in the Corner' (1999) was a well-received and unsentimental series about a hyperactive child. *The Darkest Light* (1999)

Starring Stephen Dillane and Kerry Fox, *The Darkest Light* (also written by Beaufoy) concerns the friendship between two young girls who believe they see a vision whilst playing truant on the Yorkshire Moors. Catherine (Keri Arnold), neglected by her family in favour of her leukaemia-suffering brother, convinces her mother (Fox) of the vision's veracity as they take it as a healing sign. By foregrounding the sickness of the boy, diseased livestock, and the after-effects of Chernobyl, the film attempts to convey a world destroyed by man and in need of considerable spiritual comfort. It achieves a sombre and restrained tone, thanks to its lack of sentimentality and the bleak cinematography of the rain soaked moors. Thoughtful, strong and dramatic, the film makes useful, though undeveloped, references to its time. Tom (Dillane), the father, for example, watches as his cattle are incinerated on the orders of the Ministry of Agriculture, Food and Fisheries. Such rural concerns make a rare change in a world of contemporary British cinema obsessed by cod gangsters and glossy city life. Although the film sinks a little under the weight of its concerns and parallel narratives, it succeeds in rendering a beautiful and well-drawn friendship between Catherine and Uma (Kavita Sungha), using the bond to articulate the need for fulfillment in a crisis-ridden rural community.

Eltringham has formed a company, Footprint Films, with Simon Beaufoy and producer Mark Blaney. *The Darkest Light* is its first, promising, feature.   **JD**

David EVANS

A film-maker and documentarist now living in New York, David Evans is best remembered for his film *Fever Pitch* (1996), perhaps one of only a handful of football films that has ever managed to capture the miasma of emotions that the 'beautiful game' entails. *Fever Pitch* (1997) *Our Boy* (1997) *Dirt* (1999)

His short film *Casino* won him a Fuji Film Scholarship early in his career and he also learned his trade at the Columbia Film School in New York shooting in-situ documentaries and shorts.

Fever Pitch (1996) is based on Nick Hornby's wry account of life, love and Arsenal football club, and Evans manages to capture much of the writer's magic realism and comedy. Colin Firth plays English teacher Paul who attempts to woo Ruth Gemmell whilst hoping his beloved Arsenal can finally win the league. Part screwball comedy, part sports film, Evans cleverly focuses on the human relationships, using football as a metaphor for the whirligig of life. By concentrating on the camaraderie and push-pull fortunes of the football season, Evans makes the film as accessible as possible so that even the most jaded football fan or tormented housewife will find the final-reel revelations a pure rush of adrenaline.

Our Boy (1997) is a complete change of tone for Evans and underlines the human interest that he brings to his films and documentaries. An intense drama, Pauline Quirke and Ray Winstone star as the mother and father of a boy who is killed in a hit-and-run car accident. Examining a family coming to terms with an event of seismic proportions while all the while rooted in a London that never stops moving, Evans pulls no punches with his depiction of their grief. Avoiding maudlin sentimentality, it highlights the strength of human weaknesses, making Sean Penn's similarly-themed *The Crossing Guard* (1995) a cynical exercise in audience manipulation.

More recently, Evans has returned to his documentary roots. *Dirt* (1999) was nominated for awards at various international film festivals (San Francisco, Dinard) and deals with the several community gardens scattered around New York. **BM**

Marc EVANS

Ymadawiad Arthur/Arthur's Departure (1994)
House of America (1997)
Resurrection Man (1998)
Beautiful Mistake (2000)

Born in Cardiff, Wales, in 1959, Marc Evans is unusual amongst many British contemporary film-makers. At a time when the indigenous cinema is increasingly in thrall to American cinematic styles, Evans is concerned with British, or more often Welsh, themes.

This commitment is evident in his short films – for example, *Johnny Be Good*, which has dialogue in English and Welsh – and his debut feature, the Welsh language *Ymadawiad Arthur/Arthur's Departure* (1994). This is a strange science fiction comedy about a group of patriotic Welshmen who travel back in time with the intention of bringing back the ancient national hero, King Arthur, but instead return with a 1960s rugby player whose nickname is 'King Arthur'.

Evans' next film was the 'Welsh Gothic' *House of America* (1997). Edward Thomas adapts his own play, telling the story of siblings Sid and Gwenny (the underrated Steven Mackintosh and Lisa Palfrey) who find some escape from the twin miseries of unemployment and life with their disturbed mother (Sian Phillips) in drink, drugs and fantasies of the US. Inspired by the Beat writers, they adopt the characters of Jack Kerouac and his girlfriend, Joyce Johnson, under the watchful and half-admiring gaze of Boyo (Matthew Rhys). The film shifts from a slice of Welsh social realism to an altogether darker and more lurid affair, culminating in incest and murder. Although not entirely successful, with a slightly unconvincing finale, *House of America* is an interesting melding of grim melodrama and twenty-something angst, depicting a Wales that is far from the national stereotype, with chemical excess and fantasy providing the only release from the industrial wastes and misery. Like Danny Boyle's Scottish-set *Trainspotting* (1996), Evans' film, together with Kevin Allen's black comedy *Twin Town* (1997), attempts to examine the stereotypes of a nation culturally dominated by England and often portrayed as simply picturesque.

Although an intriguing concept, Evans' next film, *Resurrection Man* (1998), was a disappointment. A heavily fictionalised account of the life of a Loyalist psychopath in 1970s Northern Ireland, this is really just a bloody gangster movie, in the mould of Martin Scorsese's *Goodfellas* (1990), with a thin political veneer. Like nearly every film about the Troubles, the film-makers are so loathe to get involved in the messy issues and scared of taking sides, that they end up simply using the backdrop of Belfast, focusing on guns and killings. Even worse, Evans and writer Eoin MacNamee seem to want to make a US-style genre film: the sequence in which the protagonist watches Jimmy Cagney's Warner Bros gangster movies suggests that Hollywood is a contributing factor to the violence in Ireland. Stuart Townsend is undeniably gorgeous and very stylish in the lead, sporting a 1970s haircut and long leather coat, but his extremely explicit murders as one of the real-life 'Shankhill Butchers' are neither shocking or illustrative of anything important, save the quality of the special effects.

Evans is certainly capable of stylish direction – the sequence where a hapless victim is kicked to death to the sound of the glam stomp 'Tiger Feet' by Mud is particularly effective – but the use of freeze-frames, rock music and slow motion count for little in such a relatively misguided movie. There are also some weird comparisons to be drawn in addition to the obvious nods to Scorsese: the Nazi paraphernalia, coke snorting and homo-eroticism of one scene recalls Kenneth Anger's *Scorpio Rising* (1964). John Boorman manages a more successful melding of gangster movie with a contemporary Irish setting in *The General* (1998), but he makes his central character a non-partisan thief, hunted by Loyalists, Republicans and police alike. There are good movies to be made about Ireland, and also some great British gangster movies that are already in existence but, unlike John Mackenzie's *The Long Good Friday* (1980), *Resurrection Man* does not pull these twin strands together.

Evans' *Beautiful Mistake* (2000) is a documentary-concert movie featuring the Welsh rock legend John Cale (who scored *House of America*) and a number of contemporary Welsh acts, such as Super Furry Animals. He has appeared in the documentary *Against the Dying of the Light* (Jack Jewers, 2001), and is currently in production with a new feature, *My Little Eye*, written by David Hilton.

Evans has proved himself to be an interesting director drawn to an eclectic mix of projects, who is capable, on the strength of *House of America*, of crafting movies which are both personal and stylish.   **IC**

Richard EYRE

Born in Devon, England, in 1943, Richard Eyre has made a significant contribution to British theatre, both in his position as former Artistic Director of the Royal National Theatre and as a director working at theatres such as the Liverpool Everyman. His forays into film and television have been surprisingly limited. He produced and directed some of the BBC 'Play for Today' series in the late 1970s, including a television version of his own Liverpool Everyman success 'Comedians', and Ian McEwan's war drama 'The Imitation Game' in 1980. He moved into feature films in 1983, directing *The Ploughman's Lunch* from a screenplay by McEwan.

The Ploughman's Lunch (1983)

Loose Connections (1983)

Laughterhouse (1984)

Set in the world of media, the film follows radio-journalist James Penfield (Jonathan Pryce) as he attempts to improve his professional and social standing by writing popular books on recent British history. Unafraid of big political themes, the film uses Penfield's career and ambitions as a backdrop for discussing contemporary attitudes to history. Penfield himself becomes a metaphor for both private and national deceit: he is duplicitous in his personal relationships, and his most recent book has justified British action during the Suez Crisis. Coming so soon after the end of the Falklands conflict, the film's political resonance presents itself as weary cynicism. The love affair is tacked on and, despite usefully articulating personal deceit, it ultimately detracts from the political themes the film wrestles with. Eyre handles the narrative threads with care, showing a degree of skill in his use of actual footage shot at the Conservative Party Conference. His crowd scenes at the end of the movie provide visual interest but the film's style is predominantly televisual.

For his next film, *Loose Connections* (1983), taken from a script by Maggie Brooks, Eyre attempts to overturn the expectations of two genres – the road movie and the romantic comedy – and applies a fresh approach to both. He said at the time, 'this is my first brush with popular cinema ... I thought this was the kind of thing people would like to see at the Odeon,' explaining that he hoped to alternate between populist and more specialist material (a trend he has continued to follow in his theatre work). Adopting a simple structure, the film shows middle-class Sally (Lindsay Duncan) advertising for a companion to join her on a drive to a feminist conference in Munich in her home-built, customised jeep. Stephen Rea's incompetent Liverpudlian needs a lift and persuades her to take him once he has convinced her (falsely) that he is a gay vegetarian. This setup is amusing, if a little dated, and Eyre tends to favour shots of Rea, thus undermining Duncan's role. Her stony-faced harridan does little to dispel stereotypes that have since begun to diminish. The couple argue and fight their way along the journey; what they learn is echoed by the stripping away of the jeep until it is revealed to be a kit car. The film does not go too far in its attempts to rework generic conventions and the fact that they will end up in a romantic relationship is evident from the start. Small and cosy, Eyre's vision seems more suited to television; lightly amusing, the film is concerned with politics, class distinctions, sexual manipulation and betrayal, as was *The Ploughman's Lunch*. It lacks the political resonance of Eyre's debut, however, preferring instead to address the Odeon audience he mentions.

Eyre's 1984 television working of Ian McEwan's 'Oratorio for Disarmament' was shown the same year as his version of John Gay's 'The Beggar's Opera', starring Roger

Daltrey. He followed with a BBC television film *Past Caring* (1985), the story of an old man falling in love with his younger housekeeper, and *The Insurance Man* (1986), a BBC Screen Two adaptation of Alan Bennett's Kafka-esque story. The latter pair received much acclaim.

During that time, Eyre directed his last feature to date, *Laughterhouse* (1984), in which Ian Holm plays a humane farmer who is unable to transport his geese from his Norfolk farm to London's Smithfield market due to a union mix-up. Taking his daughter's advice, he follows an old tradition of walking the geese to market. Far removed from the self-centred media world of *The Ploughman's Lunch*, the film still conveys a political theme and aspects of contemporary British life, paying attention to detail. The village pubs graduate into boarded-up farmhouses which, in turn, are overtaken by arterial roads and concrete as Holm reaches London. En route, a news camera crew let geese escape in their desperation to find a story, misrepresenting the walk as an attack on the unions. Eyre employs a more sweeping camera to convey rural landscapes. Once his story reaches its conclusion, however, his style reverts to the small images favoured in *Loose Connections*.

Eyre has also co-written Richard Loncraine's 1995 film *Richard III*, and directed the television play of David Hare's National Theatre production of 'The Absence of War'. The latter demonstrates his championing of writers with whom he is keen to work – he has had a long career directing many of Hare's plays. More recently, Eyre has written a book about the contemporaneous history of theatre, 'Changing Stages: A View of British Theatre in the Twentieth Century', and presented the accompanying television series to an enthusiastic reception. He has also directed *Rockaby* (2000) as part of the 'Beckett on Film' series. His reputation as a film director may not be remarkable but his contribution to, and support of, theatre has justifiably made him a central figure in the arts. **JD**

Mark EZRA

Savage Hearts (1995) Mark Ezra began his film career as a screenwriter, co-scripting *Slaughter High* (1986), a low-budget, teen-slasher movie, and *Blind Justice* in 1988. His directorial debut *Savage Hearts*, which he also wrote, was released in 1995. The screwball tale of an East End hustler and an American con-artist who become embroiled in a £2 million theft from the mob, the film was hailed by some reviewers as the 'British *Pulp Fiction*', praised for its black humour and fast-paced action.

Following the casting formula of the previous year's hit *Four Weddings and a Funeral* (1994), *Savage Hearts* pairs an amiable, floppy-haired, young British male (a cockney Jamie Harris) with a sexy American (Myriam Cyr). Here, however, their partnership is a treacherous one that sparks sex, violence and car chases. The American ingredient attracts a non-domestic audience and the setting provides a filmic tour of England's cultural landscape, from the markets of the East End to the stately home of evil Lord Foxley, via a quick detour of the winding roads of the lush, green countryside. Appropriating an American film-making style, *Savage Hearts* attempts to render it distinctively British – the accents are heavy and the cast is peppered with familiar faces from British television, including Angus Deayton as a dry-humoured hit man. Richard Harris also stars as an aristocratic crime boss alongside former Bond-girl Maryam d'Abo

Despite some promise, the direction misses the mark. A chain of betrayals with a predictable conclusion, the film lacks any tangible tension or humour; next to *Pulp Fiction* (1994), it is a cheap approximation of that dark masterpiece. Ezra has continued to write for television – 'Dark Knight' in 1999 – and has a number of screenplays in development. **MS**

F

Martha FIENNES

Born in the UK in 1964, it is somewhat surprising that Martha Fiennes began her career *Onegin* (1999)
making commercials, and even stranger than she directed pop videos for such luminaries
as Boy George, XTC and OMD. Given this MTV-style apprenticeship, her feature film
debut, *Onegin* (1999), belies her background. Full of artfully composed long shots, and
filmed with the expertise of Istvan Szabo or Michael Winterbottom, it strikes a careful
balance between intimate melodrama and epic period piece.

Adapted by Michael Ignatieff and Peter Ettedgui from Pushkin's lengthy prose poem,
brother Ralph Fiennes plays Onegin, a bored aristocrat who falls in love with and then
rejects Tatyana (Liv Tyler). The narrative is often tortuously handled and the film is full of
visual flourishes and painterly tableaux that are often in danger of undermining the entire
piece. The opening shot of a horse-drawn carriage crossing a vast expanse of snow sets
the mood and tone for the rest of the film; rarely has nature been so lovingly captured
by camera. Fiennes uses the stark St. Petersburg locations to expert effect, juxtaposing
them with the lush beauty of the surrounding countryside. The acting is uniformly excellent and, through masterful recreation of the early 1800s, the sense of time and place
are also keenly observed.

Given the excessive reliance on echoing rooms and wintry scenes as a metaphor
for the protagonists' emotional frigidity, one could level charges of self-indulgence at the
director. That said, the film remains a loyal adaptation of a literary source that has so far
presented innumerable textual and cinematic problems to several generations of Russian
film-makers.   **BM**

Mike FIGGIS

Born in Carlisle, UK, in 1948, Mike Figgis was raised in Nairobi, and relocated with his *Stormy Monday* (1988)
family to Newcastle when he was eight. He is an adept writer, composer and musician, *Internal Affairs* (1990)
as well as one of the most innovative and independently minded directors working today. *Liebestraum* (1991)
He is critical of Hollywood and sees it as an environment where creativity and vision *Mr Jones* (1993)

are stifled in order to maximise profits and maintain its hierarchical structure. During his teenage years Figgis' first love was music; he was in a band, Gas Board, with future Roxy Music frontman Bryan Ferry. After moving to London to study music he joined avant-garde theatre troupe The People Show as a musician and performer and toured around the world. After leaving The People Show in 1980, he formed his own theatre company, The Mike Figgis Group. It was at this point that he began his work in film, producing multi-media productions. Some of his early experimental works caught the attention of Channel 4 and they funded his first film, a television feature, The House (1984).

He wrote, scored and directed his breakthrough feature, Stormy Monday (1987). Set in Newcastle's jazz scene, the loving attention to detail and the construction of its edgy, smoky milieu illustrates Figgis' familiarity with, and sympathy for, the environment. It also works as a homage to Hollywood film noir, featuring an impressive cast including Sting, Tommy Lee Jones and Melanie Griffith, as well as some beautiful and highly styl-ised cinematography. The plot, however, moves along at an uneven pace that stifles the momentum. A moderate success, it brought Figgis to the attention of Hollywood.

His first American feature, Internal Affairs (1990), was a hard-hitting tale of police corruption, and here Figgis further perfected the sharp and stylish. The film boasts superb performances from Richard Gere as the creepy crooked cop, and Andy Garcia, his nemesis, resurrecting the former's career and made a star out of the latter. A box-office success, it also cemented Figgis' reputation as a bankable director.

His next feature, Liebestraum (1991), did not fare so well. Critics complained that its plot was convoluted, bordering on the nonsensical. The saving grace of this story of dark family secrets and corruption is the modish, economical way Figgis draws out the psychological agonies of his complicated characters. His next feature, Mr Jones (1993), did not mark a return to form. Trying his hand at romance, he produced an uneven work centring on the romance between Richard Gere, as a charming manic-depressive, who falls in love with his psychiatrist, played by Lena Olin. The film was a commercial flop and critics failed to warm to Gere's unstable charms.

Another commercial failure followed with The Browning Version (1994), a remake of the 1951 classic starring Michael Redgrave, which was adapted from Terrence Rattigan's 1948 play. In Figgis' film, Redgrave's character, Andrew Crocker Harris, is played by Albert Finney. This is no Goodbye Mr Chips (1939); the schoolmaster has no faith in the future, himself, his wife, or his profession. His despair is encapsulated in his poignant rhetorical question, 'How can we mould civilised beings if we no longer believe in civilisa-tion?' Despite sterling performances from Finney, Greta Scacchi, and Michael Gambon, Figgis' Browning Version does not match up to the original. After a period of successive failures, the director finally found the project that would bring him international success. Leaving Las Vegas (1995) earned four Oscar® nominations, and won Nicolas Cage the Best Actor Award. The film centres on Ben Sanderson, an alcoholic screenwriter hell-bent on drinking himself to death in Las Vegas. He forms an unlikely and uncomfortable bond with prostitute Sera, played by Elisabeth Shue. Unable to comprehend why he is so dedicated to his own destruction, he refuses to make her understand. They accept each other as flawed individuals, however; Sera does not save him and we do not know if she can even save herself. The relationship goes beyond the usual romantic love and beyond the Hollywood happy endings. This is a deeply human story of redemption – who receives it, who shuns it, and who deserves it. For Ben, if there were redemption avail-able he would refuse it. Sera's redemption is Ben, or at least the care she shows him, and the dignity with which she does it. Leaving Las Vegas achieved enormous critical and box-office success, particularly for an independent film shot on Super 16mm.

Leaving Las Vegas was a difficult film to follow and Figgis' next project, One Night Stand (1997), did not live up to expectation. It is a weak drama starring Nastassja Kinski, Robert Downey Jr and Wesley Snipes, and was a box-office and critical failure. The film follows Max (Snipes), a successful LA-based professional who arrives in town to spend some time with his friend Charlie (Downey) who has been diagnosed with HIV. Whilst in New York he has an encounter with Karen (Kinski), a married woman – the 'one night stand' of the title. This is a disappointingly weak tale that seems to lead nowhere.

The Loss of Sexual Innocence (1999) marks his first foray into experimental cinema since his days with The Mike Figgis Group in the 1980s. It is an autobiographical, intensely personal portrayal of sexual awakening, longing and experiment, told through the re-working of the Adam and Eve story. Figgis' film caused controversy for casting a black Adam and a white Eve. He had attempted to make the film some years before, but the financial backers were unhappy with the script. He lays the blame at the door of the distributors, saying: 'The distributors basically said, "I don't like the idea of a black man fucking a white woman"'; when they asked him to reverse the roles Figgis, quite rightly, refused.

His stylish direction and experimental concerns are highly evident in *Miss Julie* (1999), his adaptation of August Strindberg's play. The film is thematically concerned with the chasms dividing class and gender, played out against the backdrop of a Swedish Count's estate. Miss Julie, the Count's daughter, seeks love and affirmation after being jilted by her fiancé. Jean is her 'below stairs' lover, an avowed social climber. Each of the characters crave what they perceive the other has to offer; theirs is a pragmatic, selfish kind of love. Figgis used some highly innovative techniques to construct the dense and claustrophobic mise-en-scène. He had a 360-degree one-room stage constructed for the entire film. The action was shot using two hand-held Super 16mm cameras, one in the hands of the cinematographer and one operated by Figgis himself. The action was filmed in sequence, in long, 15-minute takes. A tight space is created around characters, forcing the audience to focus on their expressions, their mannerisms and movements, while the lighting works in expressionistic contrasts of light and shade. *Miss Julie* was not made to achieve commercial success, but rather to continue the director's passion for cinema in all its forms. Some critics disapproved of the film, arguing it was more like theatre than film. Figgis agrees, arguing, 'Theatre is gorgeous and film is theatre – unfortunately most films are bad theatre'.

His most audacious and experimental film to date, *Time Code* (2000), splits the screen into four sections to show four separate but intertwining stories played out in one continuous take using digital cameras, in real time. In the top left-hand corner is Salma Hayek's grasping wannabe starlet. Next to her in the top right-hand corner runs the tale of a down-trodden and lonely wife, played by Saffron Burrows. She is married to a film producer, played by Stellan Skarsgård, who is featured in the bottom left-hand screen at a movie production meeting, and bottom right, escaping the meeting to cheat on his wife with Hayek's character. *Time Code* received mixed reviews: some critics were stimulated by his experimentalism and others saw the split screen as nothing but a gimmick.

Figgis' last two projects have seen him return to his experimental roots after too long in Hollywood. He has recently finished production on *Hotel*, a project set in Venice that is similar to *Time Code*, which involves over thirty actors, including Salma Hayek and David Schwimmer, working without a script. In a period of change generated by digital technology Figgis is excited by new possibilities and also interested in exploring ways of using digital projection to turn any space with seating into a digital cinema.   **SL**

Alexander FINBOW

Alexander Finbow is among many young British directors attempting to make popular films for an international market. His aesthetic choices, however, illustrate the common shortcomings of UK film-makers working in genres which were invented by Americans and have historically been adapted most successfully by Europeans. Finbow set up One World Films with producer Fergal McGrath, in order to 'produce movies the Hollywood and European film-makers alike would be proud of'.

The first film the pair co-produced was the murder thriller *Killing Time*, shot at Pinewood and on location around London in 1997. This was followed by the self-funded feature *24 Hours in London* (2000), a garish melange of gangster movie and science fiction, centring on a convoluted witness protection storyline. Noted for its plagiarism by critics ('without one original idea in its 86 minutes' was *Variety*'s verdict), the film openly steals plot points and sequences from recent popular genre entries – most obviously The *Long Good Friday* (1979) and *The Terminator* (1984) – without establishing a style of its own. Finbow, who directed this and also wrote the screenplay, does create one unusual peripheral character in Samuel (Sean Francis), an organ racketeer forced to assume the identity of his last victim who turns out to be an undercover detective. On the whole,

24 Hours in London (2000)

however, he focuses on the familiar protagonists in this genre: corrupt policemen, hitmen and a sword-wielding gangster (in this case played against type by the late Gary Olsen). The film is set in 2009, the date providing a quasi-futuristic sheen to the production design without significantly contributing to the narrative. As is currently common in films aimed at a young male audience, machismo is ridiculed but appealed to in equal measure, and gun fetishism is ubiquitous. The spirit of Quentin Tarantino looms large, and many of the plentiful deaths are played for laughs. **KP**

Mandie FLETCHER

Deadly Advice (1994) Mandie Fletcher began her career in television comedy, directing programmes such as 'Butterflies', 'The Faint-Hearted Feminist' and 'Brush Strokes' (which she also produced), establishing sharp timing, visual humour and, often, a focus on women. Her most significant television success, the second and third series of Richard Curtis and Ben Elton's 'Blackadder' saga, won her awards and established her as a major talent.

She moved into lengthier comedy with 'Shalom Joan Collins' (1985), a television play made for Channel 4, which focused on a bored homebody in her mid-thirties. The film evokes a fantasy atmosphere when the woman informs her mother (with whom she lives) of Collins' imminent arrival for tea. The ensuing comedy arises out of the dichotomy between the mother's excited response (inviting her neighbours to participate) and the daughter's misgivings. 'Born Kicking', a television drama about a female football player, followed in 1992.

Fletcher's feature debut, *Deadly Advice* (1994), draws on the mother and daughter relationships which are evident in much of her television work, dealing with two sisters who are traumatised by their overbearing mother. Taking advice from Britain's most notorious murderers, conjured from the dead by way of her fertile imagination, one daughter considers the ways in which she might free herself from her mother's grasp.

With its stereotypical, British mix of sexual repression and village eccentricity, it does not provide its cast of British stalwarts – Jane Horrocks and Imelda Staunton as the sisters, and John Mills and Hywel Bennett as two of the murderers – with much to go on. Lacking in humour, pacing and style, the film fails even further in comparison to the British classics it so clearly attempts to emulate, such as Robert Hamer's *Kind Hearts and Coronets* (1949). Realising, perhaps, that her strengths lie in a different type of comedy, Fletcher has since returned to television to direct the progressive and quirky police series about a dope-smoking cop, 'Hamish Macbeth'. **JD**

Bryan FORBES

Whistle Down the Wind (1961) Bryan Forbes (born John Theobald Clarke in London in 1926) was educated at RADA, London, before beginning work as an actor. His career in film has spanned five decades
The L-Shaped Room (1962) and has encompassed acting, writing, producing and directing. He has also enjoyed success as a novelist. Forbes is married to actress Nanette Newman who has appeared in
Of Human Bondage (1964) the majority of his films.
Seance on a Wet Afternoon (1964)
He spent the early part of his career honing his skills as a screenwriter and performer. He wrote *The Cockleshell Heroes* (1956), *I Was Monty's Double* (1958) and *The*
King Rat (1965) *League of Gentlemen* (1960), and performed in *The Colditz Story* (1957), *The League*
The Whisperers (1966) *of Gentlemen* and *The Guns of Navarone* (1961). He also found the time to join forces
The Wrong Box (1966) with Basil Dearden, Michael Relph, Richard Attenborough and Jack Hawkins, setting up
Deadfall (1968) Allied Film Makers in 1959. *The League of Gentlemen* was the group's first film.
The Madwoman of Chaillot (1969)
Forbes made an auspicious debut as director with the highly successful film, *Whistle*
The Raging Moon (1971) *Down the Wind* (1961). It was the first of five low-budget realist films Forbes would
The Stepford Wives (1975) direct throughout the decade, the others being *The L-Shaped Room* (1962), *Seance on*
The Slipper and the Rose (1976) *a Wet Afternoon* (1964), *The Whisperers* (1966) and *The Raging Moon* (1971). The
International Velvet (1978) film was based on a novel by Mary Hayley Bell and seen by the author as a star vehicle
Sunday Lovers (1980) for her daughter, Hayley Mills. Mills plays a poor farmer's daughter who, along with her
Better Late Than Never (1982) friends, mistakes a runaway convict for Jesus Christ. The focus of the film is the fantasy
The Naked Face (1985) world of the children – who were mainly non-actors – but the realist look and setting of the bleak hill farms of the North of England counterbalances any whimsy. The film was

highly successful, making a star of Mills, who had made her debut in *Tiger Bay* (1959), and establishing Forbes' reputation as a sensitive, if stylistically conservative, director.

His next feature, *The L-Shaped Room*, explores the choices open to a young French woman upon her realisation that she is pregnant after an affair with a married man. Jane Fosset (Leslie Caron) arrives in Britain to escape her stifling family in France. She sets up home in an attic bedsit in a house owned by the formidable Doris (Avis Bunnage). Other inhabitants of the house all feel the isolation Jane experiences to varying degrees: Toby (Tom Bell) is a struggling writer with no publisher who is stuck in a day job he loathes, Mavis (Cicely Courtneidge) is a fading music-hall star and army entertainer who is also a lesbian grieving for her lost lover. Upon Jane's discovery of Mavis' secret she is told 'It takes all sorts, dear', a comment that sums up the humanist message of the film. Sonia (Pat Phoenix) is the 'brass in the basement' servicing conference delegates and weary of men, love and sex. She shares a flat with a fellow call-girl who is perhaps the most isolated character of all who is Hungarian and does not speak in the film. Her pain and loss of personal dignity stay silently within her throughout the film, conveyed by the camera in close-ups of her gaunt and haunted expression. *The L-Shaped Room* is social realist in style and setting; street scenes are crammed full with signs and symbols reminiscent of 1960s Britain – red buses, coffee shops and greasy spoon cafés, Capstan cigarette machines, fish and chip shops, young people demonstrating. In dealing with a 'social problem' it neither patronises nor offers any cosy solutions. Jane decides to return to France and face her family; she has not learned to be resourceful but she has realised that comfort and comradeship can be found in the most curious of places. *The L-Shaped Room* is widely regarded as a minor classic of British social realist cinema and attracted good reviews from critics of the day.

Of Human Bondage (1964) is the third and perhaps least successful film version of Somerset Maugham's novel about the inter-class passion between a doctor and waitress. Widely regarded as a dismal failure in comparison to director John Cromwell's sensitive and intelligent original, the film is miscast (Kim Novak, Laurence Harvey and Robert Morley are wasted) and superficial. Forbes' form rallied with his next feature, *Seance on a Wet Afternoon*, a gripping and suspenseful drama centring on psychopathic medium Myra Savage, who is so deluded by her imagined powers she prepares to go public and demonstrate them to the world. Needless to say her plans go awry as by the end of the film she crumbles into total and irredeemable insanity. Despite his earlier successes, it seems *Of Human Bondage* did Forbes no favours. He had difficulties in financing and casting *Seance* (Shelley Winters, Anne Bancroft and Simone Signoret all turned down the role of Myra). Kim Stanley was the final choice and she is strangely lacklustre as Savage. Despite this flaw, *Seance* is genuinely chilling and Forbes demonstrates the benefits of being an actor's director, drawing out superbly overwrought performances from Richard Attenborough and Nanette Newman. Alongside films such as *Peeping Tom* (1959), *The Innocents* (1961) and *The Collector* (1965), *Seance on a Wet Afternoon* was a film that demonstrated British cinema's fascination with madness and obsession in the 1960s.

King Rat (1965) represents a break from Forbes' social realist cycle of films. Based on the novel by James Clavell, George Segal stars in this gripping drama set in a Japanese camp during World War Two. With great sensitivity and power, the film portrays the physical and psychological effects of captivity on soldiers. There is nothing new or groundbreaking about *King Rat* or Forbes' direction. However, once again he demonstrates how effective he is in encouraging often mesmerising performances – most notably here from Segal. Two decades after World War Two, the war film became more critical and less deferential; *King Rat* is a good example of this trend.

For his next feature, *The Whisperers*, Forbes adapted a novel by Robert Nicolson, a sensitive character study of loneliness and old age. The fantasy world of Dame Edith Evan's pensioner works well against the social realist style and setting. Although the film is not considered to be one of Forbes' best, Evans' portrayal of senility and frailty is certainly one of her strongest performances.

A certain light relief came in the form of Forbes' next feature, *The Wrong Box* (1966), a mad-cap black comedy about a family who are divided by an inheritance; one brother (John Mills) co-opts family members into the task of murdering another (Ralph Richardson) for a share of the money. The film features fine performances from Mills and

Richardson, but is also notable for its strong supporting cast including Michael Caine, Peter Cook, Dudley Moore, Tony Hancock and Peter Sellers. Despite at least one critic making a case for *The Wrong Box* to be 'shipped to a desert island and screened continuously to those responsible for it', it is worth a viewing for the supporting cast alone. The direction is somewhat leaden and ham-fisted, however. *The Wrong Box* was Forbes' first big-budget film but only just managed to break even at the box office.

In spite of the relatively poor receipts and reviews of *The Wrong Box,* Forbes did not have any problem getting similarly large budgets for his next two films, *Deadfall* (1968) and *The Madwoman of Chaillot* (1969). The former is a twisted crime caper starring Michael Caine, Eric Portman and Nanette Newman. The film suffers from a weak plot and a certain amount of over-direction, possibly due to Forbes' experiences with the far looser *The Wrong Box* the previous year. *The Madwoman of Chaillot* (1969), with a budget from Warner Bros., also faired badly at the box office. The film is a comedy centring an elderly woman (Katherine Hepburn) who clings to the notion that the world is as rosy as she remembers it from childhood. Hepburn plays a particular type of feisty old eccentric, having made the logical progression from the fast-talking young career women and heiresses she favoured in her early career. In spite of her interesting performance, the film is rather disappointing, and certainly nothing special in terms of direction.

Forbes' next feature, *The Raging Moon*, is an unremarkable, faintly distasteful film focusing on the doomed love affair between two paraplegics (Malcolm MacDowell, Nanette Newman). It was neither a critical nor a box-office success.

After a fallow period, Forbes returned to directing five years later with his masterful and suspenseful chiller, *The Stepford Wives* (1975), adapted from a short story by Ira Levin. Having moved to the suburban town of Stepford, Joanna (Katherine Ross) discovers that some women have no knowledge of the woman's movement. The few women that do gradually become compliant housewives overnight. She realises that the Stepford men of are replacing their imperfect wives with robotic replicas, preferring their women bland rather than bold. Like *Rosemary's Baby* (1968), also based on an Ira Levin story, the film has a bristling, paranoid edge, and can be seen either as a critique of patriarchal capitalism or as a backlash to the burgeoning women's movement.

Forbes' next venture was a major departure from his previous work. *The Slipper and the Rose* (1976) is a delightful musical fantasy based on the Cinderella story. With magical sets and locations, and strong performances from Gemma Craven as Cinders and Richard Chamberlain as Prince Edward (aka Charming), this film is pure eye-candy. It is also notable for its solid supporting cast, which includes Margaret Lockwood as a splendidly vicious wicked stepmother. The film did respectable business at the box office, and the performance of Craven and the musical score drew appreciative recognition from critics.

The director's next feature was the long overdue sequel to *National Velvet* (1944), entitled *International Velvet* (1978). Velvet (Nanette Newman) is now a grown woman living with her partner (Christopher Plummer) and niece, Sarah (Tatum O'Neal). Sarah shows potential for following in the footsteps of her aunt as an Olympic horsewoman. Although *International Velvet* is beautifully shot with excellent performances from Plummer and O'Neill, it was largely ignored by critics. Slightly over-long, it makes an interesting and engaging sequel to *National Velvet.*

Sunday Lovers (1980) saw Forbes directing the British segment of a study of love and sex in four different countries: Britain, France, Italy and the US. Forbes made two more feature films in the 1980s, and neither match the quality of his earlier work. *Better Late Than Never* (1982) is a disappointing comedy about a young heiress and the two old cons who both claim to be her long lost grandfather. Maggie Smith, David Niven and Art Carney do their best with the featherweight script but the film was shunned by audiences and critics. *The Naked Face* (1985) faired little better. The plot centres on psychiatrist, Dr Judd Stevens (Roger Moore), who is suspected of murdering one of his patients by cops Rod Steiger and Elliott Gould. It is every bit as 'straight to video' as this synopsis suggests, and a waste of the (low) budget. Moore is hopelessly miscast as the shrink, and Forbes signposts the clues heavily along the way.

His final feature was made for television and did not receive a theatrical release. It was shown in two parts on Channel 4 and makes for gripping viewing in this format. *The*

Endless Game (1990) stars Albert Finney as a British agent who attempts to uncover the truth about the death of a former lover. The plot twists and turns, and what is interesting is the way Finney's probing not only leads him deeper into international intrigue and high level political corruption, but into his own guilt, sadness and culpability. These feelings of loss and betrayal are superbly realised in semi-hallucinatory scenes in which Finney exudes a clammy intensity. He is supported by a solid cast, including George Segal, Kristen Scott Thomas and Anthony Quayle (in his final screen appearance).

Forbes has long been a stalwart of British cinema and yet his contribution is often overlooked in retrospectives. As a director his style can certainly be viewed as conservative, particularly in comparison to innovators such as Lindsay Anderson or Richard Lester. A study of his career in film is illuminating, however, particularly in the context of understanding the development of post-war British cinema. From the 1950s to the 1990s, his work brought him into close working relationships with key figures such as Basil Dearden, Michael Relph and Richard Attenborough. Indeed, Forbes has produced, acted and written with Attenborough throughout his career. His last screenplay was for the biopic, *Chaplin* (1992). Having survived the 1970s, as the majority of British directors did, criss-crossing between the UK and the US, what his films lack in visual style and flair, Forbes more than makes up for it in his understanding and appreciation of the work of the actor.   **SL**

Timothy FORDER

Timothy Forder's 1993 film *The Mystery of Edwin Drood* is a worthy but ultimately unremarkable attempt to breathe new life into Charles Dickens' novel; first tackled in 1914 by Herbert Blanché and Tom Terris, it was subsequently dealt with more successfully by Stuart Walker in 1935.

The Mystery of Edwin Drood (1993)

The story focuses on Edwin Drood (Jonathan Phillips) and Rosa Bud (Finty Williams) – lovers betrothed to each other by a familial bond brokered by their respective fathers – and Drood's increasing possessiveness which precipitates a deadly jealousy and a mysterious journey into the unknown. As source material, it is fair to say that the novel ranks amongst Dickens' more minor works; the writer died in 1870 before he was able to complete it. Despite a limited budget and resources, Forder – who also adapted the novel – struggles to inject a genuine sense of mystery and drama into the proceedings. Martin McGrath's low-key, atmospheric photography – he is perhaps best known for *Muriel's Wedding* (1994), the visual antithesis of Forder's film – lends the proceedings palpable menace, while Edward Thomas' production design strikes a note of added authenticity. Less successful is the casting: ultimately the film's undoing, it is a bargain-basement pick-and-mix of British character actors, led rather unconvincingly by Robert Powell; Freddie Jones, however, does provide some compensation.

Forder has yet to direct another feature.   **JWo**

Bill FORSYTH

Audiences and critics often associate Scottish film-maker Bill Forsyth with a whimsical and absurdist humour. This is not how he would like his work to be summed up, however, and often feels at odds with the public's view of his contribution to British cinema, which is ironic given that the characters in his films also face a gulf between their own self-image and the images others have of them.

That Sinking Feeling (1979)
Gregory's Girl (1981)
Local Hero (1983)
Comfort and Joy (1984)
Housekeeping (1987)
Breaking In (1989)
Being Human (1993)
Gregory's Two Girls (1999)

Born in 1946, in Glasgow, Scotland, Forsyth began his career in film as an assistant to an eccentric local documentary-maker, Stanley Russell, making sponsored shorts for industry. After Russell's death, Forsyth decided to go freelance, but soon headed to London for a job with the BBC. He was assistant editor on 'Chronicle', 'Z Cars', and 'Play For Today'. After only a year, he headed back to Glasgow, where he made two short experimental films: *Language* (1969) and *Waterloo* (1970). The dire response from audiences and critics to *Waterloo* when it was shown at the Edinburgh Film Festival forced Forsyth to reconsider ways he could more effectively transmit his ideas on weighty issues. In 1971 he set up Tree Films, a company dedicated to making industrial shorts for private companies, with two friends. He was also accepted by the National Film

School. However, due to the work-load at Tree Films, he only stayed at the school for one term. Between 1971 and 1977 Forsyth made short promotional films for clients such as the Forestry Commission and the Highlands and Islands Development Board. By 1977 he felt he had gone as far as he could go with the sponsored film and decided to branch out into features, hoping they could help him expand and explore more creative possibilities.

Between 1977 and 1979 Forsyth wrote scripts for two films he would go on to direct himself: *Gregory's Girl* (1981) and *That Sinking Feeling* (1979). The former was turned down for funding three times by the British Film Institute but, finally, *That Sinking Feeling* was made using £3000 from the Scottish Arts Council. The remaining £3000 needed was obtained through sponsorship from a diverse range of sources, including private individuals, the department store C&A and whisky distilleries. The film centres on a group of jobless youngsters who plan to change their fortunes by robbing a stainless-steel sink factory; a warm and funny film, Forsyth described it as 'a fairy-tale for the unemployed'. *That Sinking Feeling* drew a good deal of critical acclaim, and was the first feature film to be based in Scotland, made by a Scottish director. Yet it failed to grab the attention of national exhibitors and was only released on a wider scale with the success of his next feature, *Gregory's Girl*.

Praised by critics and enjoyed by audiences, *Gregory's Girl* was Forsyth's break-through film. It centres on gawky, awkward teen, Gregory (John Gordon Sinclair), who falls madly in love with Dee (Dee Hepburn), the girl who has replaced him in the school football team. Much of the gentle humour of the film is generated from gender role reversals: girls are sporty, pragmatic and straight-talking, whilst the boys are shown to be clumsy romantic daydreamers. It convincingly recalls awkward teen feelings. The best example of this is in the scene where Gregory is stood up by Dee on a long-awaited date; he stands in front of an enormous clock, each second passing with a heavy clunk as he waits. The film won the BAFTA award for Best Screenplay, beating Colin Welland's script for *Chariots of Fire* (1981).

The success of *Gregory's Girl* was something of a mixed blessing for its writer-director. On the one hand, Forsyth was heralded as a major new talent but, on the other, critics were waiting to see if he was a 'one hit wonder'. The director did not disappoint. Whilst working on a drama for BBC Scotland, *Andrina* (1981), he was also developing his next feature, *Local Hero* (1983).

Local Hero centres on a young American oil executive and his mission to buy a Scottish island at the order of his oil tycoon boss, Happer (Burt Lancaster). Forsyth has said that he loves to turn conventional film structure on its head, to play with audience expectations, and here he does just this: rather than band together as a community to preserve their island from American interests, the islanders are only too happy to sell up at a profit. A critical and box-office success, the film marks a high point in the director's career.

Wanting to move away from the whimsical humour he was now known for, Forsyth took mid-life crisis and conflict as his next subject in *Comfort and Joy* (1984). The film centres on Alan 'Dickie' Bird (Bill Paterson), a local DJ, whose girlfriend leaves him in middle age. He becomes caught up in an ice-cream war between two Scottish/Italian families – the 'Scotia Nostra'. With two stories spliced together, each battles for narrative supremacy and as a consequence neither the Dickie Bird mid-life crisis strand nor the ice-cream war drama are properly developed. Considered deeply flawed by critics, the film did not do well at the box office. Forsyth claims the film was widely misunderstood, that the public expected the humour of his earlier films, and that its deeper concern, a critique of war in general, was entirely missed.

Forsyth's next feature was his first to be set outside Scotland. He moved across the Atlantic for two years to work on *Housekeeping* (1987), based on the novel by Marilynne Robinson. The film focuses on the relationship between two orphaned sisters (Andrea Burchill and Sara Walker) taken in by their strange Aunt Sylvie, played with grace and depth by Christine Lahti. Its location, shot in British Columbia, is beautifully framed; the mise-en-scène successfully conveys a sleepy, backwater Canadian town in the 1950s. Forsyth owned a two-year option on Robinson's novel, and once described the film as 'a promotional video for the book'. Unfortunately, it failed to perform at the box office. This could be due in part to the fact that David Puttnam had commissioned the film during his stint as Head of Studio at Columbia. After his resignation, executives were reluctant to provide sufficient funds to promote films that he had commissioned.

Forsyth's next feature, *Breaking In* (1989), was another American project with a script by John Sayles. The film follows a pair of safe crackers (Burt Reynolds and Casey Siemaszko) as they attempt to collaborate in their shared art. The resulting mishaps are supposed to be humorous, and as a director-for-hire, the studio was keen for the studied character detail and gentle observational absurdism that is associated with Forsyth's work. *Breaking In* turned in a modest profit in the States, but his American experience left him with a bitter aftertaste. He has observed that the greater the budget, the less control directors have. He had been in discussions with American producers to film *Rebecca's Daughters*, from a script written by Dylan Thomas when he was contracted to Gainsborough in the 1940s. He abandoned the project, however, when he realised the studios wanted final approval on casting.

By the early 1990s, Forsyth was ready to quit film-making altogether. The final project in his American odyssey, *Being Human* (1993), was an interesting, if flawed, comic vehicle for Robin Williams. Williams plays the principle character in five stories set in different historical periods, all of which are connected by an exploration of the human condition – its frailties, joys and transience. The direction is both crisp and sensitive, yet *Being Human* suffers from Williams' overpowering presence, which all too often threatens to eclipse every other interesting feature, most notably the fine performances from John Turturro and Lorraine Bracco.

Forsyth's most recent feature, *Gregory's Two Girls* (1999), returns to the gangly, awkward teen of *Gregory's Girl*, now a teacher in his thirties at the same Scottish comprehensive school he attended. Unmarried, unattached and still confused by women, this sequel sees Gregory clinging to fantasy. He lusts after one of his pupils (Carly McKinnon), oblivious to the advances of attractive teaching colleague Bel (Maria Doyle Kennedy). The film's plot is worthy but silly – Gregory and two of his pupils uncover a conspiracy by Gregory's ex-school friend, a local businessman, who is supplying implements of torture to embargoed countries. Audiences were unimpressed at the ham-fisted way the 'local action for global change' message was rammed down their throats at the film's conclusion. In spite of this, *Gregory's Two Girls* is strangely satisfying. John Gordon Sinclair brings his usual edgy, self-deprecating humour to the screen, and offers a convincing portrayal of Gregory's transition into the gangly nerd, Mr Underwood. It received a lukewarm response from critics, however, largely because the script neglects to tie up its loose ends.   **SL**

John FORTE

John Forte's first outing as writer-director was a 14-minute comedy for the BBC called *Mad About Mambo* (2000) *Skin Tight* (1994), about the leading lambeg drummer in Northern Ireland. As the Loyalist marching season approaches, Terry (B.J. Hogg) begins to despair at the poor quality of goatskins available for his drum. Much to the distress of his long-suffering wife, Norma (Marie Jones), Terry decides to buy himself a real-life goat. Forte's script contains some brightly comic moments and is nicely photographed by Seamus McGarvey.

Forte's feature-length debut, *Mad About Mambo* (2000), continues to mine this seam of gentle yet socially-conscious comedy. Danny Mitchell (William Ash), a working-class Catholic schoolboy from West Belfast, dreams of becoming a soccer star. Danny is convinced that if he can improve his sense of rhythm then nothing can stop him from emulating the balletic exploits of his Brazilian idol Pele, or the local Belfast United hero Carlos Riga. With this in mind, he enlists the Mambo dancing talents of a beautiful Protestant girl, Lucy McLaughlin (Keri Russell, star of the popular American television series 'Felicity'). Inevitably, these weekly dancing lessons change the course of Danny's life as young love and sectarian hatred collide in his quest for footballing glory.

Mad About Mambo is a commercial hybrid that deftly combines two popular genres currently in vogue: the sports movie and the dance movie. The casting of Keri Russell, a rising star with an avid young American fanbase, is a telling index of its populist ambitions, but this sop to the American market is tempered by the presence of a strong supporting cast including Brian Cox and Rosaleen Linehan. Equally, as in *Billy Elliot* (2000), which it invariably calls to mind, the comic bathos of the script is counterbalanced by its suitably gritty urban setting. Forte is currently working on a forthcoming feature, *Old New Borrowed Blue*.   **KHo**

Freddie FRANCIS

An award-winning cinematographer who is renowned and sought-after as a director of photography, Freddie Francis' work as a film-maker has often caused him displeasure and embarrassment. He has made a career out of working within the horror genre, and is commonly associated with one studio, Hammer. However, in interview he has commented, 'I enjoyed working at Hammer and the other studios, and I kept making one film after another just because I was having great fun – I didn't realise that they weren't very good films! Oddly, though, while I have some rather good credits as a cinematographer, I get more recognition than you can imagine for those ghastly horror movies.' This attitude towards his own work accounts in part for the inconstancy of his films and a lack of critical respect. His statement betrays a duality about his output. His 'ghastly horror movies', as he calls them, are all renowned for their visual style, accomplished framing and mise-en-scène, and attention to detail. Yet his discomfort with the generic styles and conventions expected of the genres in which he worked often undermined his attempts to create something new.

Born in London in 1917, Francis began his career in cinema at the age of 17 as a clapper boy at British and Dominion Studios. There he worked on a number of low-budget 'quota-quickies' produced by larger American studios in the UK as a means of gaining access to the British market for big-budget, more 'prestigious' Hollywood fare. Drafted into the army during World War Two, he helped to establish the Army Kinematograph Services, making training films with the likes of Carol Reed and Freddie Young. Following the war, Francis began work as a camera operator for Zoltan Korda's British Lion Studios where he worked with Michael Powell on the Archers' *The Small Back Room* (1949) and *The Tales of Hoffman* (1951), a learning experience he insists had lasting influence on his own career and style. After working for American director John Huston on several projects, Francis began his career as a director of photography on *A Hill in Korea* (1956). From there, he quickly became one of the most respected cinematographers in Britain, working on a number of 'angry young man' films from the new generation of British directors working in the early 1960s, such as *Room at the Top* (1959) and *Saturday Night and Sunday Morning* (1960). Working with cinematographer-turned-director Jack Cardiff, Francis won an Academy Award for *Sons and Lovers* (1960) and later went on to work with Jack Clayton on *The Innocents* (1961).

Francis used his prominence as a cinematographer to launch his career as a director; he would go on to make more than twenty films over the next twenty years. *Two and Two Make Six* (1962), his first feature, was a romantic comedy about an American airman stationed in England who goes AWOL after getting into a fight with his sergeant. Taking his girlfriend with him, the two stop at a road-side cafe where they meet another young couple. The serviceman's fortunes begin to change when he accidentally drives away with the wrong girl, who quickly falls for him and persuades him to return to face his punishment. *Two and Two* was poorly received upon its release.

Undaunted, Francis quickly began work on his next project, the horror film *Vengeance* (1962). It marked his first foray into the genre he would become most closely associated with (although he is often credited as having directed large sequences from the 1962 sci-fi movie *The Day of the Triffids*). *Vengeance* was adapted from Curt Siodmak's novel 'Donovan's Brain', and tells the story of a pair of doctors who manage to save the brain of a plane crash victim. The organ begins to take on a life of its own, exerting a strange power over one of the doctors and forcing him to avenge the crash. Francis used the film to begin developing a unique visual style, one that would begin to adapt itself to the conventions of the horror genre. The film was not favorably reviewed; critics called attention to the uneven mixture of horror and science-fiction genres and its outlandish plot.

In 1963 Francis directed *Paranoiac* for Hammer studios, the first in a trilogy of horror-thriller inspired by the success of Hitchcock's *Psycho* (1960). The plot involves the story of a young woman whose visions of her dead brother prompt her to believe she is losing her mind. When the brother actually appears, her madness deepens until it is revealed that he is an impostor attempting to steal the family inheritance. Francis' assured direction managed to find an appropriate tone that matched a showy aesthetic to the bizarre plot twists and red herrings of the story. The film's artistic and commercial success might also be attributed to his work as a director of photography on *The Innocents*. The two films share similarities in both narrative and visual style. *The Innocents* was adapted from Henry James' 'The Turn of the Screw', itself the tale of a woman slowly driven mad by ghostly visions. In both films, Francis was able to capitalise on the strengths of the black and white format, creating a constant play between shadow and light to draw out the tension of the character's slow descent into madness.

Many consider *Nightmare* (1963) to be Francis' finest film as a director. It bore striking similarities to both *The Innocents* and *Paranoiac* in both story and realisation. A young girl in a small town is slowly driven insane through a series of ghostly apparitions staged by her guardians. After a suicide attempt, she is finally taken away. The eerie appearances still continue even after the plotting couple think that they have secured their fortunes; they gradually begin to suspect each other. The film's clever turn of events and startling black-and-white cinematography combine to make *Nightmare* a highlight of Francis' career.

Next, Francis took over for director Terence Fisher on Hammer's Frankenstein series with *The Evil of Frankenstein* (1964). The film provided him with an opportunity to work in colour for the first time and he took advantage of the format, staging elaborate shots of the doctor's laboratory, once again casting the character as a man entrapped by his own passions and paraphernalia. *The Evil of Frankenstein* was poorly received and is generally regarded as one of the poorer contributions to the Frankenstein series. The plot itself deviated from the earlier course set out by the Fisher Frankenstein movies; critics noted that in attempting to diverge from the conventions of both story and genre, Francis' film had in fact done both a disservice.

That same year saw Francis complete his psycho-thriller trilogy with *Hysteria*. The film tells the story of an amnesia victim who hires a detective to put together the missing pieces of his life, only to have it revealed that he is the victim of a ruthless plot to drive him insane. In Wheeler Winston Dixon's 'The Films of Freddie Francis', a fine account of the director's career, he notes that *Hysteria* continued 'thematic preoccupations evident in the earlier work', revealing a suspicion of the wealthier classes and the accoutrements of privilege. Dixon notes that Francis' attention to the details of the main character's apartment and its signs of affluence are at the heart of his thematic concerns. He focuses on these objects and spaces as metaphors for the emptiness of the characters and notes Francis' concern for honesty, accountability, and the rewards of work – all characteristics that the more sinister and suspicious characters in these films lack. After *Hysteria*, Francis directed *Traitor's Gate* (1964), a standard, straightforward heist film involving kidnapping and an attempt to steal the Crown Jewels.

During the next five years Francis completed a series of projects at a prolific rate. The majority of them were made for Hammer, cementing his standing with fans of the horror genre, but prompting continually tepid receptions from critics. *Dr. Terror's House of Horrors* (1965) was the first of Francis' 'omnibus' movies – horror films which comprise a series of stories interwoven around a loose narrative conceit or through an omnipresent narrator. (Francis' other omnibus movies include *Torture Garden* (1967) and *Tales from the Crypt* (1972)). Francis followed this film in close succession with *The Skull* (1965), *The Psychopath* (1966), *The Deadly Bees* (1966), *Torture Garden* and *They Came from Beyond Space* (1967). *The Skull* established Amicus Pictures, a studio rival to Hammer in the 1960s. It was also the first production on which Francis collaborated with horror writer Robert Bloch (who also wrote the story and screenplay for *Psycho*). It tells the story of an eccentric collector who comes into the possession of the Marquis de Sade's skull and sets off a chain of terrifying events associated with the object's evil powers. The film contained fine performances from Hammer staples Peter Cushing and Christopher Lee and stands as one of Amicus' few outright successes. Francis and Bloch collaborated again on *The Psychopath*, the tale of a serial killer who leaves macabre dolls at the sight of the crime. The film's title and plot-line sought to exploit the popularity of Bloch's earlier success with *Psycho*, but few critics found anything noteworthy about Francis' version. Like *The Psychopath*, *The Deadly Bees* bore an uncanny similarity to another Hitchcock film, *The Birds* (1963). In Francis' version, a genetically enhanced swarm of killer bees attacks an unsuspecting pop-singer on holiday in the countryside. *Torture Garden* followed, another Amicus horror film featuring a series of loosely-bound stories based on Bloch's earlier writing. Considered to be the best of Bloch's and Francis' collaborations, the narrative centres on a carnival sideshow and the mysterious figure of Dr. Diabolo who entices visitors with the promise that he will reveal their secret desires, only to have those same desires used against them. With a strong cast that included both British and American B-movie figures such as Cushing, Jack Palance, and Burgess Meredith, *Torture Garden* stands as one of Francis' last commercial and critical successes.

Returning to Hammer, Francis stood in again for Fisher on a studio franchise, directing *Dracula Has Risen from the Grave* (1968). Notable for a few stylistic touches that mark his visual stamp on the series, this version nevertheless failed to appease fans or critics who chastised him for his attempts to do something different with the storyline. In an interview Francis said that he attempted to 'play about with the legend' in an effort to steer his film away from the formulaic and derivative confines of the horror genre and the Dracula series in general. His changes, which included having the infamous Count survive an encounter with a wooden stake and a holy cross, did not sit well with audiences and the series was resumed by a different director in the years to come.

After completing the short comedy *The Intrepid Mr. Twigg* (1968), Francis returned to the horror genre with *Mumsy, Nanny, Sonny, and Girly* (1969). The film stands out again as another attempt by Francis to do something different with the genre, and is notable as much for its black comedy as for the terror it seeks to produce. The story follows an affluent family who play a series of bizarre and deadly games by kidnapping 'friends' and forcing them to follow their rules, until those same rules become their undoing. The film was poorly handled by distributors and received a limited release but it remains one of Francis' personal favorites.

The 1970 film *Trog* tells the story of the discovery of a 'missing link' troglodyte, or caveman, who is brought back to civilisation and runs amok, killing local villagers until it is killed by policemen who track it down and dynamite its cave. The final film of American screen legend Joan Crawford, the camp special effects and clichéd storyline brought little commercial or critical success. It was memorably parodied by American director John Landis in his 1973 film *Schlock!*

Francis followed with *Tales from the Crypt*, a faithful screen adaptation of the E.C. Comics series, *The Creeping Flesh* (1973), the story of a skeleton which grows flesh when exposed to water, and *Tales that Witness Madness* (1973), another anthology film that includes a series of horrific tales injected with doses of black comedy.

He directed a handful of remaining films, *Craze* (1973), *Son of Dracula* (1974), *The Ghoul* (1975), *Legend of the Werewolf* (1975), *The Doctor and the Devils* (1985) and *The Dark Tower* (1989). Of this group, *Son of Dracula* stands out. Francis' final attempt at an update of the popular Prince of Darkness saga, the film came about as the result of a collaboration with Ringo Starr and American pop singer Harry Nilsson (who also wrote the score) and continues to have a large cult following to this day. Francis worked for Tyburn Productions, a film company started by his son, Kevin Francis, on *The Ghoul* and *Legend of the Werewolf*. The company soon went bankrupt, however, and following this failure Francis worked primarily as a cinematographer. *The Doctor and the Devils* and *The Dark Tower* round off his career as a film-maker but, like much of his earlier work, neither movie gained him greater commercial or artistic acclaim.

While Francis' directorial output may never gain him the critical respect of the great visionaries of cinema, he will nevertheless retain a prominent place in film history for his work as a director of photography. From the mid-1970s on, Francis has continued to be highly sought after as a cinematographer. He has worked with David Lynch on *The Elephant Man* (1980) – the last major feature to be filmed in black and white in Britain – *Dune* (1984) and *A Straight Story* (1999), winning another Academy Award for his work on *Glory* (1990). Despite his own lack of success as a director, Francis' work should be remembered for its attempts to challenge generic codes and conventions. **MR**

Stephen FREARS

Stephen Frears is a significant figure in British cinema. Understanding the man and his cinematic vision can be frustrating as he is on record as making so many contradictory statements about his work. Here is a director who sees himself as becoming more English as he gets older, yet within the last decade or so he has directed such landmark American films as *The Grifters* (1990) and *The Hi-Lo Country* (1998). It is perhaps this rich contrast that keeps Frears' work interesting.

His range is remarkable, taking in 1980s social realism, biography, comedy and historical drama within the mediums of film, television and theatre. Frears is often described as a 'writer's director' and has enjoyed long and fruitful working partnerships with a range of quality writers.

Frears was well positioned to helm the series dedicated to British cinema, 'Typically British'. Not many movements and moments have passed this director by – Frears worked with the angry young men in the 1960s, turned to television in the 1970s and 1980s, and in the 1980s worked with the new 'alternative comedians' on the 'Comic Strip Presents...' series for Channel 4.

Born in Leicester, UK, in 1941, after studying Law at Cambridge, Frears became interested in theatre and joined London's Royal Court. His first work in film was as assistant director to Karel Reisz on *Morgan* (1966). A year later he made his first film, a short entitled *The Burning*, which foregrounded some of his later concerns about race and ethnicity.

He continued working as an assistant director for Reisz, Lindsay Anderson and Albert Finney before directing his first feature, *Gumshoe* (1972), starring Albert Finney as a day-dreaming Liverpudlian bingo caller who advertises his services as a private investigator. *Gumshoe* satirises American detective films; having received mixed critical reactions at the time of its release, it has enjoyed something of a renaissance in recent years.

Frears worked mainly in television throughout the 1970s and early 1980s, working with writers like Alan Bennett and Tom Stoppard on plays and films for British television. He has been quoted as saying that 'television gives an accurate account of what it's like to live in Britain – about men and women who lead somewhat desperate lives'. He was to find that he could do this just as accurately and effectively on film.

His next feature, *The Hit* (1984), is a taut, suspenseful, compact crime-thriller which, like *Gumshoe*, has an interesting take on the genre. Terence Stamp plays an informer located by two assassins, John Hurt and Tim Roth, who take him back to Paris to pay for his 'treachery'. It has been argued that for all its style and panache, the film has a disappointingly weak resolution. Whilst this criticism is justified, *The Hit* is about the journey to Paris and, ultimately, the journey to death. The film received some favourable reviews but was not a box-office success. However, as with his earlier *Gumshoe*, *The Hit* is now regarded as a minor British classic.

Through the exploration of relationships which cross boundaries of gender, sexuality, class and ethnicity, Frears' next three features critique Thatcherism. *My Beautiful Laundrette* (1985) was shot in 16mm for £700,000. According to Frears himself, the film was his and screenwriter Hanif Kureishi's swipe at the new entrepreneurial spirit of Thatcherism. Some critics argue that *My Beautiful Laundrette* is the definitive critique of Thatcher's Britain. Others see the film as a direct descendant of the social realist films of the 1950s and 60s, prompting one critic to describe it as 'a story which empties the contents of three kitchen sinks into one washing machine'. The film is set in South London where a thriving Pakistani community lives alongside the hopeless underclass of 'native' England. This tension clearly articulates Frears and Kureishi's concerns in reflecting both sides of Thatcher's economic miracle. The film also critiques the air of sexual repression in Britain in the 1980s via explorations of relationships that call into question family values and the marginalisation of gay men.

Gay relationships and class distinctions are also central to Frears' next feature, *Prick Up Your Ears* (1987), adapted from John Lahr's biography of playwright Joe Orton. Gary Oldman plays Orton, with Alfred Molina as Orton's lover and subsequent murderer, Kenneth Halliwell. Eschewing a faithful biographic approach, Frears focuses on the relationship between Orton and Halliwell rather than mapping the standard chronology. The film begins with Orton's murder, allowing the audience to concentrate on the character dynamics that lead to his death. While not explicitly concerned with class difference and sexual and social inequalities, the Orton-Halliwell relationship articulates the problems of love across class boundaries and against society's norms. The film takes Orton and Halliwell, pitting them first against the system, and finally against each other.

During the 1980s, Frears made several feature films for television (*Bloody Kids* (1983), *Loving Walter* (1986), *Saigon: Year of the Cat* (1983) and two films for the 'Comic Strip Presents...' series, *The Bullshitters* (1984) and the superior *Mr Jolly Lives Next Door* (1988).

His next feature, *Sammy and Rosie Get Laid* (1987), saw him reunited with writer Kureishi. It is a multi-layered look at the social relations of a liberal, mixed-race couple, Sammy (Ayub Khan Din) and Rosie (Frances Barber), and contains similar themes to *My Beautiful Laundrette*. Sexual, ethnic and class politics are dramatised against a carefully crafted backdrop of a decaying, changing England. The action is again based in South London and provides a critique of the repressive morality of Thatcher's Britain. At the time of its release, Frears stated that the film was intended to bring the government down. Of course it did not achieve this, marking the end of his vociferous attacks on the government of the day. The director conceded that he 'did not have anything else to say about England right now'; his films of the 1980s remain among the most caustic cinematic attacks on Thatcherism. In 1988, Frears made his Hollywood debut with *Dangerous Liaisons*, a sumptuous adaptation of a Christopher Hampton play (itself based on Choderlos de Laclos' eighteenth-century novel). Some critics felt it to be too lavish, too highly stylised, and lacking in the cinematic sincerity Frears had become associated with in his British films. However, these criticisms fail to take into account the way the sets, costumes and the stylisation work within the narrative to amplify the superficiality of the characters and their motives.

Frears describes his next Hollywood feature, *The Grifters* (1990), as a cross between Shakespeare and a B-movie. *The Grifters* marries a highly stylised vision of a timeless Southern California with the grittiness that had informed his British films of the 1980s. This curious timeless quality comes in part from the fact that the film is adapted from the novel by Jim Thompson, which is set in the 1950s, while the film is set in the 1980s. The three central characters, Roy Dillon (John Cusack), Lily Dillon (Anjelica Huston), and Myra Langtry (Annette Bening) are compelling. Cusack provides a sympathetic centre for the film, whilst Anjelica Huston's portrayal of Lily, Roy's mother, is perhaps her finest performance to date. *The Grifters* was a success at the box office and was highly acclaimed by critics; it is regarded as a classic of contemporary Hollywood cinema.

His next Hollywood feature is possibly Frears' least successful film to date. *Accidental Hero* (1992) seems to have everything: capable director, major Hollywood-star cast (Dustin Hoffman, Geena Davis, Andy Garcia, Chevy Chase) and an intriguing plot. It should, in theory, work; in practice, it does not. *Accidental Hero* is a comic parable about the nature of heroism, and society's need for the right kind of hero. It focuses on a gruff, shallow petty criminal, Bernie Laplante (Hoffman), who reluctantly saves passengers from the wreckage of a crashed jet plane, only to disappear before taking the credit. Andy Garcia's serene down-and-out, John Bubber, then steps into the frame claiming to be the Angel of Flight 104. A number of factors prevent an interesting script from gaining the momentum it needs: Hoffman's characterisation of Laplante is too much of a caricature rather than a character – somewhere between Ratso Rizzo and Columbo's evil twin. The plane crash sequence is wholly unconvincing, too clean and too bloodless, and the editing is too slow to create the sense of urgency such a scene requires. Frears himself explained that part of the problem with *Accidental Hero* was that he had no conception of how to shoot a plane crash. The film was a commercial failure and failed to ignite the imaginations of the critics, despite fine performances from Davis and Garcia.

Frears' next project, *The Snapper* (1993), was the screen adaptation of Roddy Doyle's book. A minor controversy was caused at the BBC's reluctance to allow the film cinematic exhibition, choosing to air it on television first – all the more galling since the film enjoyed theatrical release in Europe. On the whole, American critics saw *The Snapper* as a warm-hearted Irish comedy and it was generally well received. In Britain, critics tended to compare the film either with the novel or with Alan Parker's *The*

Commitments (1991), the first episode of Doyle's Barrytown Trilogy. From this perspective, the film fared less well critically in Britain. *The Snapper* focuses on Sharon Curley, a young working-class woman who hides the fact she is pregnant until it becomes too obvious to hide. Speculation and rumours fly within her local community as to who the father is, but Sharon refuses to identify him. This is a film about family, love and acceptance, and while the Curleys' are far from the 'ideal family' (they brawl, they gossip, they drink), Sharon's pregnancy serves to bind them closer together. Some critics saw *The Snapper* as a return to Frears' low-budget, social-realist roots, yet the film is too warm, and too uncritical of social and sexual prejudice, the family or community to provide anything other than surface realism. It lacks the biting critique of *Sammy and Rosie Get Laid* or *My Beautiful Laundrette*.

Mary Reilly (1996), starring Julia Roberts, was a box-office failure and was virtually ignored by the critics. The film is based on Valerie Martin's novel, which was itself based on Robert Louis Stevenson's classic 'The Strange Case of Dr Jekyll and Mr Hyde'. The eponymous heroine Mary Reilly, played by Julia Roberts, is the maid who falls in love with Dr Jekyll (John Malkovich). The victim of childhood abuse at the hands of her drunken father, Mary is confused but not surprised by the duality of her employer since she is used to loving and fearing men at the same time. In line with the demands of the story, both Roberts and Malkovich deliver unusually restrained performances. 'Dr Jekyll and Mr Hyde' is, after all, widely interpreted as an allegorical comment on Victorian sexual, emotional and psychological repression, as well as playing out cultural fears about science and progress. The studio wanted a more upbeat ending but Frears held out. Jekyll must be punished and there can be no romantic coupling. *Mary Reilly* was Frears' second collaboration with writer Christopher Hampton, and despite a solid script and Frears' restrained direction, the film received poor reviews.

There are two problems with the film. First, it is difficult to believe that Roberts' character does not recognise her boss to be the evil Mr Hyde. As one critic said: 'That a hairstyle keeps Mary from linking Hyde with Jekyll is as believable as Lois Lane not recognising Superman because he's wearing glasses.' Second, critics clearly struggled to place the film within a generic context: was it Gothic horror, psychological thriller or historical melodrama? With no handy labels available, the critics chose to ignore it altogether, and consequently audiences stayed away. This does the director a disservice as *Mary Reilly* is at least stylish.

His next feature, *The Van* (1996), based on the third instalment of the Barrytown Trilogy, fared little better with critics and audiences. Frears again examines unemployment and its effects on family life. It follows the fortunes of two Dubliners, Bimbo (Donal O'Kelly) and Larry (Colm Meaney), who decide to escape unemployment by investing in a fish and chip van. The van is a big success but this success puts a strain on the pair's friendship. From here the film degenerates into a series of noisy arguments and fights between the two leads and little else. Watching *The Van* it is necessary to remind oneself that it is directed by the same angry voice of the 1980s. Social conscience has been traded in for surface realism and Doyle's sharp, human and insightful humour replaced by cheap gags and pointless screaming matches. *The Van* performed poorly at the box office and critics expressed disappointment.

Frears returned to form with *The Hi-Lo Country* (1998), described by one British critic as 'the finest Sam Peckinpah western the man himself never made'. Set in the 1940s, it centres on the relationship between Big Boy Matson (Woody Harrelson) and Pete Calder (Billy Crudup). It is an atmospheric film that delivers a powerful sense of a decaying old west gradually giving in to a new era, not so much through mise-en-scène, but through characterisation. Despite its 1940s setting, the central plot is classic western material: the hero's hometown is at the mercy of ruthless cattle baron Steve Shaw (Lane Smith). Pete and Big Boy go to work for Shaw's rival, Hoover, played by James Gammon, who represents the town the boys left behind after they received their call-ups. Critics welcomed *The Hi-Lo Country* as a genuine attempt to get 'back to basics', after years of science-fiction cross-overs (*WestWorld* (1973), *Back to the Future III* (1991), *Wild Wild West* (1999)), post-feminist chick-flicks (*Bad Girls* (1994), *The Quick and the Dead* (1995)) and stylistically overblown epics (*Tombstone* (1993), *Young Guns* (1988), *Legends of the Fall* (1994), *Dances with Wolves* (1990)).

High Fidelity (2000) was adapted from Nick Hornby's best seller of the same name. The film drew much criticism from some areas of the British press because of the relocation of the action – Chicago, rather than the North London setting of the novel. Frears himself had reservations about this but later argued that the film 'kept the spirit of the book but universalised the story'. He handles the comedy of Hornby's modern classic with relish. John Cusack plays the list-obsessed Rob Gordon who compiles his top five break-ups. High Fidelity has it all: crackling wit, polished performances and crisp direction.

Frears' next project was an impressive television film, Fail Safe (2000), which caused quite a stir in the States where it was screened by NBC. A Cold War thriller, it asks the audience to imagine a nuclear bomb has been launched by accident on Moscow. It was filmed as if it were 'happening now' in black and white to suggest a 1950s American broadcast.

The director's most recent project, Liam (2000), is a drama set in Liverpool during the Depression. Once again, Frears is concerned with the effects of poverty on family life; here, it is in an historical setting. The story follows the fortunes of Liam (Anthony Borrows) and his family and much of the film's action is filtered through Liam's eyes, as his father loses his job as a docker and they descend further into poverty. Liam's father (Ian Hart) becomes increasingly bitter and turns to a far-right group in order to vent his anger. Scripted by Jimmy McGovern, this film is hard-hitting in places and sincere in its intent to convey a humanist message. Frears' eye for detail is evident in the way he constructs a believable milieu for his characters to inhabit on screen. There are also some genuinely comic moments, mostly concerning young Liam's Catholic education. The film received some modest reviews, but generally critical opinion seems to be that an association between Frears and McGovern should have yielded greater results.

Quintessentially British in the first half of his career, since making Sammy and Rosie Frears has moved back and forth across the Atlantic. His attitude to British, specifically English films, is typical in its apparent contradiction: he believes the central problem with English films is that 'they are only ever about England, and when they're not they're worse'. Well qualified to criticise the industry, he has also been amongst its staunchest supporters. In response to Truffaut's famous swipe at British cinema, Frears said: 'François Truffaut once said that the terms "British" and "cinema" are a contradiction in terms: well, bollocks to Truffaut!'   **SL**

Sidney J. FURIE

Born in Toronto in 1933, and educated at the Carnegie Institute of Theatre, Sidney J. Furie showed early promise writing plays for television performance. His feature-film career began there with a film for which he raised the funds himself: A Dangerous Age (1958), the story of a teenage elopement. Concentrating on character and emotion, with a careful if conventional construction, the film gave an early indication of Furie's later British social-conscience youth movies. This was sustained in his second film, Cool Sound from Hell (1959), which took rebellious youth, jazz and beat poetry, rendering them with harsh and evocative photography and the sensitivity to atmosphere evident in his debut.

Furie moved to England in 1960, where he wrote, produced, and directed several films a year, establishing a penchant for showy camera-work. Doctor Blood's Coffin (1961) and The Snake Woman (1961), both hoary Hammer-style films, were separated by three movies all released in 1961. During One Night deals sincerely with the sexual inexperience of an American soldier in wartime England, suffering the trauma of his friend's suicide; Three on a Spree provides a lively new version of the play (and later film) 'Brewster's Millions'; The Young Ones marked the first of two films with Cliff Richard. The second, Wonderful Life (1964), is also characterised by its stars' toothy zest, jaunty choreography, and implausibly naïve plotting.

Furie's move into more socially conscious work came with The Boys in 1962, a courtroom drama about four East End youths accused of the brutal murder of an elderly garage worker. Flashback details the events of the night and the lives of the boys; the film utilises grainy photography, location shooting and naturalistic lighting, eschewing a manipulative score and traditional happy ending to evoke an austere social commentary.

Following on the heels of Basil Dearden's *Victim* (1961), *The Leather Boys* (1963) provokes careful debate about homosexuality within the boundaries of mainstream cinema. Initially concerned with the story of young newlyweds, the film goes on to introduce issues surrounding male relationships as a young man enters the couple's lives. Shot in close-ups to reinforce the intimacy of the story, the film's ending is necessarily compromised considering the time and the legal status of homosexuality, but overall Furie manages observant, careful direction of a difficult subject.

Furie's reputation was cemented with what remains the highlight of his long career. *The Ipcress File* (1965) (adapted from Len Deighton's spy thriller) launched Michael Caine's Harry Palmer upon a world used to the suave sophistication of James Bond. Shown in thick spectacles, proudly brandishing his East London accent, immersed in cookery and supermarket shopping, Caine's Palmer is an anti-authoritarian counter-culture hero asserting his individuality and investigating the typical establishment spy facade. Furie's visual style became more significant in this film, as he utilises canted camera angles and demonstrates a penchant for shooting through parking meters, rearview mirrors and clashing cymbals to provide a distorted and distinctive view.

Typically, Hollywood sat up and took notice of this surprise success, and Furie moved to the US in 1966. His first studio film (for Universal) was *The Appaloosa* (1966), a western weighed down by Marlon Brando's desire to develop his passion for the plight of the Native American Indians at the expense of the film. Furie's distinctive style edges over into parody with a disruptive variety of oddly angled shots attempting to invest the tiniest of actions with significance.

After directing duties on the J Lee Thompson-credited *The Eye of the Devil* (1967), Furie made *The Naked Runner* (1967), with Frank Sinatra as an ex-spy travelling with his son while Peter Vaughan's dubious boss coaxes him into one last murder. An attempt to mimic the success and style of The Ipcress File, this film revitalises the genre in many ways but suffers from Furie's now intrusive style.

The Lawyer (1970), which he also wrote from an earlier discarded script, went on to form the basis for the television lawyer series 'Petrocelli', starring Barry Newman in the title role. A fictionalised account of the trial of doctor Sam Sheppard (a case which also inspired 'The Fugitive'), the film briefly returns to Furie's more socially concerned period, dealing implicitly with racism and small-town hypocrisy. Here, with a successfully researched legal script, Furie rejects his idiosyncratic style for a keen sense of environment and character detail to some success.

Little Fauss and Big Halsy (1970) marked the beginning of Furie's career re-working popular films at studios' behest. An unoriginal but competently achieved biker movie following two minor league racers on their journey across America, the film borrows from a variety of popular counter-culture sources, including Arthur Penn's *Bonnie and Clyde* (1967) and *Easy Rider* (1969) with no sense of Furie's own concerns stamped over them. A range of disparate elements (the William Burroughs-reading hippy girl; the tortoise and hare fable) are unified self-consciously with a return to Furie's trademark shooting: close-ups of flies on food; races filmed from beneath wheels; shooting the white trash family through their home's screen door.

A biopic of jazz singer Billie Holiday, *Lady Sings the Blues* (1972), an old-fashioned telling of Holiday's eventful life and career, was a box-office hit. Like Furie's *Gable and Lombard* (1976), about the scandal surrounding these Hollywood stars, the movie endorses inaccuracies and composites, using cliché and stereotypes, preferring gloss to grit in a sentimental and unquestioning account of Holiday's life.

Hit! (1973), a film about a Federal agent taking action against the drug gang who killed his daughter, demonstrates Furie's intermittent desire to reinvigorate genre, in this case the thriller, to varying success. *Sheila Levine is Dead and Living in New York* (1975) – an oddity which was buried at the box office was followed by an attempt to replicate Robert Altman's war movie *M*A*S*H* (1970). *The Boys in Company C* (1978) is reminiscent of Furie's early British work in its emphasis on male bonding and social context but avoids any serious debate by placing emphasis on old-fashioned team spirit, and showing how rebellion can be easily re-modelled as patriotism. Even the peace-loving hippy fires up with the rest of them, and 'bad' soldiers were always so, rather than corrupted by a war. Despite its ellipses and overlaps, à la Altman, the film is more confusing than groundbreaking and is ultimately tearfully sentimental.

The Entity (1981), a schlock-horror cashing in on recent cinematic hits, was based on an allegedly true story of a woman terrorised by a supernatural force, and demonstrates how easy it is for a director of erstwhile note to become a hack. There followed Purple Hearts (1984), a simple love story set against a Vietnam hospital, and Furie's involvement with three of the Iron Eagle films (the first, second and fourth, made in 1986, 1988 and 1995 respectively, with the sequels capitalising on the success of Tony Scott's airborne adventure Top Gun (1985)). Endorsing right-wing Rambo-style politics through the unidentified but obviously Middle-Eastern villains, the films are glossy and ridiculous, and a studio-imposed soundtrack (a legacy of Top Gun) reduces the airborne combat to the level of pop video.

In between, he did Superman IV (1987), completing the franchise's box-office decline with a poorly structured, visually disconnected movie. The Taking of Beverly Hills (1992) and Ladybugs (1992) have completed his devolution into jobbing studio hack.

The 1990s saw Furie embark on two film projects which were then partly abandoned: On The Run, which was due to start filming in Ireland in 1995, and In Her Defense, which went into production in 1998 and appears only to have secured Canadian release at present. Top of the World (1997) was about an ex-cop befriending some gangsters on a trip to Vegas was released theatrically, and Tripwire, The Collectors (a traditional crime thriller) and Cord were all completed in 1999, a remarkably industrious year for Furie. He has also busied himself with television films including Married to a Stranger (1997), and The Rage (1999), an FBI-set action thriller. Furie is still hard at work with My 5 Wives, Sonic Boom and A Friday Night Date, finishing and awaiting theatrical release. With Going Back, a story of marines returning to Vietnam as part of a television show, which is currently in production, Furie demonstrates that he has no intention of giving up his career yet.   **JD**

G

Tony GARNETT

Born in 1936, Tony Garnett began his career as an actor and rapidly moved into produc- *Prostitute* (1980)
tion at the BBC. Within a year he progressed from story editing to producing the seminal *Handgun* (1982)
'Wednesday Play', *Cathy Come Home*, in 1966, written by Jeremy Sandford and directed
by Ken Loach. Though better known for his television ouput, Garnett has directed a
number of films: *Prostitute* (1980) and *Handgun* (1982). His body of work, despite
divergence in aesthetic construction, presents a realist and polemical stance maintained
over four decades of production.

As an early example, *Cathy Come Home*'s narrative structure parallels the classic
realist text in its attempt to align the viewer with the protagonist Cathy, yet simultaneously distances itself through specific formal strategies and ideological positioning.
In stylistic and narrative form, *Cathy Come Home* employs many techniques that are
commonly disassociated with the classic Hollywood realist text, in terms of voice-over
commentary, montage, captions quoting statistics, and apparent (though not literal)
direct address to camera. *Cathy Come Home*'s conclusion also unambiguously refuses
to reassure the viewer. Having taken us on the downward spiral into Cathy's enforced
homelessness, the film inverts the usual satisfying placebo of hope on the horizon: her
marriage is unable to survive separation and, in the final harrowing scenes, Cathy's children are publicly snatched from her arms into the 'care' of Social Services.

Such early work demonstrates one of the key characteristics of Garnett's entire
oeuvre: seldom are the main characters mere protagonists, but they are also antagonists.
Cathy Come Home's main characters, in striving to hold their family together, oppose
bureaucratic rules and institutions. Amongst Garnett's Kestrel Productions' work, such
consistency emerges in *Kes* (1969), *The Body* (1970), *Family Life* (1971), *Black Jack*
(1978) and *Prostitute*.

Kes, the most well-known of the Kestrel films, directed by Ken Loach and written
by Barry Hines, tells the tale of a boy's relationship with a kestrel and refuses to offer
the archetypal 'happy ending'. Its final scene shows Billy, the young male lead, burying
the bird which has been killed by his elder brother in a fit of anger. Metaphorically, it is

the end of Billy's emergent free spirit: he soon leaves school to work in the pit. Resisting a satisfying narrative closure, *Kes* underlines the fact that working-class boys like Billy had no way out; schools' custodial function terminated with pupils discharged into the pit and heavy industry. Consequently, such images are ever present in the background. Even the quasi-poetic and comic scene of the football master, fantasising the role of Bobby Charlton on the pitch, is tinged by his spiteful treatment of the boys and the omniscient pit wheels in the distance.

Garnett wrote, produced and directed *Prostitute*, the last of his projects with Kestrel, just before moving to America. The work further demonstrated his belief in the need to unmask and challenge accepted wisdom, this time confronting assumptions about the role of the prostitute. Polemical and aesthetic strategies metamorphosed this unpromising material, offering a radical perspective on prostitution within the community, and considering the nature of our universal 'prostitution' under capitalism. Expectations of representation are thereby challenged: the women's behaviour is not portrayed as deviant, but as uncomfortably conformist. To make the argument compelling, Garnett adopts a primarily conventional aesthetic, interspersed with extensive long-takes and documentary style.

Throughout the 1980s, Garnett elected to work in the USA, completing his second feature as writer-director-producer, *Handgun*. Unlike his previous work, however, the film slips into an overly didactic exploration of the dangers of 'gun culture'. Despite a number of significant scenes, including a protracted rape, the narrative, infused by revenge and the rapist's 'punishment', has a traditionally satisfying ending of the kind that Garnett had so emphatically avoided. It was during this period that he was also involved in an eclectic range of film projects, producing the blatantly commercial 'Sesame Street' movie, *Follow that Bird* (1985), and an exploration of nuclear defence, *ShadowMakers* (1989), among others.

Now firmly back in British television, Garnett is currently chairman at World Productions, successfully producing numerous series and serials from 'Cardiac Arrest', 'Between the Lines' and 'This Life' to 'The Cops'. Under his closely guiding hand, each has unified popularity with a return to the radical stance of his mainstream work: a double sense, perhaps, of 'coming home'. **KS**

Brian GIBSON

Breaking Glass (1980)
Poltergeist 2: The Other Side (1986)
What's Love Got to Do With It (1993)
The Juror (1996)
Still Crazy (1998)

After a brief television career, in which he directed Dennis Potter's 'Blue Remembered Hills' in 1979, as well as 'Murderers Among Us: The Simon Wiesenthal Story' in 1989, Brian Gibson is perhaps best known for his musically-themed films. Having filmed biopics of Josephine Baker and Tina Turner, his most recent, *Still Crazy* (1998), deals with the reforming of a fictional 1970s rock 'n' roll band.

Breaking Glass (1980) was Gibson's first experimental attempt to fuse musical numbers with a linear narrative. Although the well-worn script is clichéd, the story of a pop band and its lead singer who can't stand the pace is sprightly told and makes an explicit connection between punk music and schizophrenia. Late-1970s London is affectionately evoked, whilst the bizarre casting of Phil Daniels and Jonathon Pryce lends an air of improvisation and anarchy to the proceedings.

After such an interesting debut, it was disappointing to see Gibson return to work as a 'director for hire' when he was offered *Poltergeist 2: The Other Side* (1986). Although the sequel is bereft of Steven Spielberg's creative talent and masterly timing – used to such effect in the original film – his spirit hovers everywhere, and Gibson tries to pay homage to him by portraying the nuclear family as the shelter from unspeakable evil. After the death of their grandmother, the Freeling family are again forced to do battle with the spirits of evil. With the help of an elfin clairvoyant and gentle giant Will Sampson, the house becomes the battleground. As so often happens in these pyrotechnic exercises in stupidity, the director is obliged simply to point the camera and allow the special effects to do the work for us (and him). However, in Julian Beck, Gibson has cast perhaps the scariest movie villain in the history of celluloid.

What's Love Got to Do With It (1993) was a return to form for Gibson. In the casting of Angela Bassett and Laurence Fishburne as Tina and Ike Turner, he unearthed two of America's leading black actors at a time when every role was going to Whoopi

Goldberg and Denzel Washington. With Gibson recruiting Tina Turner to be on hand at all times, thereby ensuring fidelity to the source material, the film is more authentic than many other biopics, and the staging of the musical numbers sets it apart from the usual generic offerings. The final transmutation of Bassett to Turner is remarkable and Gibson's handling of the two Oscar®-nominated actors is a joy to watch. Expertly timed and believably characterised, the film works on many levels, not least in its exploration of the development of American music from the 1960s to the present day.

The Juror (1996) was an uncertain film in several ways, due in no small part to the central casting of Demi Moore as the woman in distress. She plays a sculptress who is intimidated by Alec Baldwin into releasing a killer whilst she is serving on a jury. Gibson appears decidedly ill at ease employing the usual generic tricks of the trade, such as point-of-view stalking and dark lighting. Both he and screenwriter Ted Tally (The Silence of the Lambs (1991)) are unable to generate a consistent tone throughout the film, and the laughable climax in Guatemala smacks of desperation. The only high point is Gibson's discovery of Anne Heche, who, in a few brief scenes, all but steals the film from under the noses of her overpaid and bloated co-stars.

With Still Crazy Gibson returned to his musical roots to fashion a whimsical and nostalgic coming-of-age drama. A wry commentary on how the baby boomers of rock 'n' roll are forced to face up to middle age is a lively collaboration between skilled British actors (Timothy Spall, Billy Connolly, Stephen Rea and Jimmy Nail), writers Dick Clement and Ian La Frenais, and Gibson. Putting a clever spin on the notion of taking second chances, the film is a strange hybrid of Rob Reiner's This Is Spinal Tap (1984) and Peter Cattaneo's The Full Monty (1997). **BM**

Coky GIEDROYC

Stella Does Tricks (1996)
Women Talking Dirty (1999)

Coky Giedroyc began making films at Bristol University with the short rave-scene comedy-drama House Party (1988). A move into television led to her directing a series on women in sport for Channel 4 in 1989. She continued in the documentary vein with a piece on Catholics and sex in 1992, and an A–Z series 'Letters From the Homeless' in 1993.

She spent the early to mid-1990s directing television adaptations of Angela Carter's novel 'Wise Children', Joe Orton's 'What the Butler Saw', Jean Genet's 'The Maids', Samuel Beckett's 'Happy Days' and Shakespeare's 'Macbeth', among others. The range of dramatic and comedic subjects, and the focus on female-centred narratives, provided her with the experience and interests to develop her first feature film.

Stella Does Tricks (1996) provided the first post-Trainspotting role for Kelly Macdonald, and as such the film was eagerly awaited. Although marred slightly by a heavy-handed script, it avoided many of the clichés evident in movies about abused teenage girls who become prostitutes, in large part because of Macdonald's performance and the creation of Stella as more than a cipher for 'teen issues'. Inspired by her documentary work on the homeless, Giedroyc and screenwriter A.L. Kennedy flesh events and characters out beyond the limitations of their potential stereotypes; a whimsical flashback and fantasy structure help to strengthen the subject. The film avoids the classic 'loss of innocence' narrative, replacing it with a consideration of how innocence can actually persist even in the most dire of circumstances. As a result, Stella is more than British social realism, employing a winning subjectivity in a bold, assertive and confident first feature.

In Women Talking Dirty (1999) Giedroyc again concerned herself with a female-centred narrative, with the emphasis this time on comedy. Ellen (Gina McKee) is arranging a post-divorce celebration that leads her to review her friendship with a single mother played by Helena Bonham Carter. Still focusing on working-class characters, Giedroyc fails to make more of this self-conscious, confused and unsatisfying film. Notable for its performances, it lacks the flair and style of her debut.

As is often the case with directors who fail to garner much commercial excitement, Giedroyc has returned to television. She has directed the Dawn French vehicle 'Murder Most Horrid', the grim pathologist drama 'Silent Witness' and 'Murder in Mind: Teacher'. All demonstrate her continued interest in strong female characters, with 'Silent Witness' suggesting a link to the dramatic potential of her debut. **JD**

Maria GIESE

Born and brought up in Cape Cod, Maria Giese has come a long way from working as wardrobe assistant on Troma Films' *Chopper Chicks in Zombietown* (1989) but has yet to establish herself as a prominent name in Hollywood. Having wanted to be a socio-political documentary maker, she is best known for the first feature film she made after leaving the UCLA film school, the feelgood soccer flick *When Saturday Comes* (1996), starring Sean Bean, Emily Lloyd and Pete Postlethwaite. She both wrote and directed the likeable tale, a British version of *Rocky* (1976), in which a hero with a dream hits rock bottom only to turn his life around and fulfil his ambitions in front of thousands of screaming fans. The subject matter was suggested by her husband, James Daly, who has a co-writer and producer credit; Daly almost became a professional soccer player himself before moving to the States and the film focuses on Sheffield United, the team that he supports. Christopher Lambert co-produced, having worked with Daly on *Highlander III* (1994).

Displaying a good ear for dialogue, Giese's direction is measured and unobtrusive, although some of the soccer footage seems a little unbelievable. Initially struggling to persuade backers that she could direct a sports film, she has since proclaimed herself happy with the result. Her next two films, however, have yet to secure a theatrical release. *Justice* (1999) and *Hunger* (2000) were co-written and produced by Joseph Culp, son of B-list actor Robert Culp, and both father and son starred in the latter film. *Hunger* is based on the autobiographical novel by 1920 Norwegian Nobel laureate, Knut Hamsun, and a remake of Henning Carlsens's 1966 Swedish film *Sult*. Giese has trans-ferred the plot from 1890 Oslo to modern-day Los Angeles, turning the novelist from the book into a screenwriter writing to survive. Screened only at the 2001 San Francisco Independent Film Festival, it may receive a wider release later in the year.　　**AL**

Brian GILBERT

A graduate of the National Film and Television School, Brian Gilbert made his first feature, *The Frog Prince*, in 1984, developing a love for period detail that was lauded as accurate and illuminating. Set in Paris in 1960, with a screenplay by cartoonist and novelist Posy Simmonds, based on her own experiences, the film offers a lightly amusing and truthful account of the pre-Women's Liberation teenager who had her reputation to worry about. Good performances and spirited direction make this a likeable low-budget oddity.

In 1986 Gilbert directed *Sharma and Beyond* – another off-kilter, winsome piece – which explores the grounding effect that romance has on a flighty sci-fi buff who begins courting the daughter of his idol. A move to America led to *Vice Versa* (1988), a film that deals with a subject already familiar to cinema-goers from John Landis' *Trading Places* (1983) and Sydney Pollack's *Tootsie* (1982): the popular fantasy of being someone else for a period of time. Dick Clement and Ian La Fresnais – best known in Britain as the writers of classic sitcoms 'Porridge' and 'Whatever Happened to the Likely Lads' – offer a tired premise already explored to great comic effect in *Freaky Friday* (1977): a boy (Fred Savage) makes a wish on a golden Eastern skull and he and his dad (Judge Reinhold) end up inhabiting each other's bodies. Trying to deal with the swap, they also have to contend with criminals who are desperate to obtain the skull for their own ends. The comedy lies in the obvious dichotomy of a boy doing manly things – ordering a limo on his credit card and drinking alcohol – and vice versa. Dad playing the fool leads us to the film's moral that even the most workaholic father must find and indulge his inner child if he is to be happy in his relationships.

Curiously, he followed this lightweight, sentimental but amusing film with *Not Without My Daughter* (1991), which has been likened to Hollywood films of the Cold War era in its xenophobia and paranoia. It rests on the premise that anywhere beyond the USA is a dangerous and uncivilised place, particularly if that place is Iran and the American population is already suspicious and primed for racism. Based on a true story, the film follows Betty Mahmoody (Sally Field) as she tries to flee with her daughter from the violent and oppressive regime initiated by her husband (Alfred Molina) on their return to his homeland for a holiday. Directed with a hysterical approach to Iran (which is portrayed as both primitive and excessive), the film borders on US propaganda as the distraught Betty and daughter struggle to find a mountain village which, as luck would have it, is flying the American flag.

Gilbert revisits his period detail in *Tom and Viv* (1994) but overdoes it slightly, packing vintage cars, glowing fields and Oxford architecture into the first few minutes. Adapted by Michael Hastings and Adrian Hodges from the former's stage play, the film spans 1914 to 1947, retelling the story of poet and playwright T.S. Eliot's traumatic and tempestuous relationship with Vivienne Haigh-Wood. Despite the period recreation, the film attempts to portray Haigh-Wood's misdiagnosed menstrual problems and the explicit gynaecological references that accompany them. That said, although Miranda Richardson turns in another of her faultless performances of inspired lunacy and depth, the film still prefers to position Haigh-Wood as a burden to the noble Eliot (Willem Dafoe in an uncanny impersonation). Its strengths lie in the performances and in Gilbert's decent but plodding attempts to highlight the ignorances of the medical establishment.

His most recent film, *Wilde* (1997), is based on Richard Ellmann's acclaimed biography. Gilbert intends the film to articulate how Oscar Wilde's life and experience altered the way society thought. It also attempts to enrich Wilde's image by incorporating aspects of his family life, making much of his relationship with Constance (Jennifer Ehle) and his children; although his wife is a preliminary character her presence, and that of the children, leaves an indelible mark on the narrative. A central focus though is a concentration on Wilde's courage and humanity, as evidenced through his relationships with Robert Ross (a performance of outstanding naturalness from Michael Sheen) and the petulant Bosie (Jude Law). While the film relies on the heritage approach utilised in *Tom and Viv*, which has the effect of rendering Wilde's life and exile in a worthwhile but pedestrian manner, its sexual explicitness does move away from the arena of the traditional costume drama.   **JD**

Lewis GILBERT

One of the hardest working and most consistently commercial British genre directors of the past fifty years, Lewis Gilbert's eclectic output has included several internationally successful British films, including *Reach for the Sky* (1956), *Alfie* (1966), three of the James Bond series, and the adaptations *Educating Rita* (1983) and *Shirley Valentine* (1989). He has also given an impressive range of star names their first major cinematic hits: Laurence Harvey (*The Scarlet Thread* (1951)), Joan Collins (*Cosh Boy* (1953)), Dirk Bogarde (*The Sea Shall Not Have Them* (1954)), Virginia McKenna (*Carve Her Name with Pride* (1958)), Susannah York (*The Greengage Summer* (1961)), Kenneth Moore (*Reach for the Sky*), Michael Caine (*Alfie*) and Julie Walters (*Educating Rita*).

Born in London in 1920 into a theatrical family – his parents and grandparents were vaudeville performers – Gilbert's first foray into the cinema was as a child actor. He moved behind the camera as an assistant at the behest of Alexander Korda, also working with Alfred Hitchcock on *Jamaica Inn* (1939). His own film-making career began during World War Two whilst in the Royal Air Force. Seconded to the US Air Corps Film Unit, where he worked with major Hollywood directors such as Frank Capra and William Wyler. After being invalided out of the services in 1944, Gilbert joined Gaumont-British Instructional Films as a writer-director of short films. He made his first feature, *The Little Ballerina*, in 1947. In his dual role of director and co-producer – in addition to that of scriptwriter – Gilbert established a desire to take greater creative control of his films; a situation that would see him prepared to battle studios in later years, usually over casting.

After a series of very small budget 'quota quickies' Gilbert made *Albert R.N.* in 1953. It was the first of eight features, culminating in the commercial failure of *Operation Daybreak* in 1975, which took the Second World War as their source material. Gilbert would later cite his wartime experiences as a documentary film-maker as the biggest single influence in his life. He also felt that in the decade after the war cinema audiences wanted films that reinforced notions of patriotism and heroism. In satisfying this perceived demand, Gilbert's forays into war established his propensity for depictions of quiet, understated heroism and a focus on character rather than out-and-out action. This was exemplified in films like *The Sea Shall Not Have Them*, set almost entirely in a drifting dinghy in the North Sea, containing four survivors from a downed plane, and *Sink the Bismarck!* (1960), a tense and claustrophobic account of the Royal Navy's hunt for one of Nazi Germany's most important battleships. However, it was two films of individual heroism – *Reach for the Sky* and *Carve Her Name with Pride* – that established Gilbert's storytelling style. *Reach for the Sky* was the most successful British film of 1956 and recreated the life of flying ace Douglas Bader (Kenneth Moore) who lost both of his legs in a flying accident. It now comes across as the archetypal 1950s British war film in its avoidance of some of the battle's more troubling aspects, notably ambivalence about duty and collectivity. That said, its exploration of the role of the individual in the context of the group and the institution established a familiar preoccupation for Gilbert. In *Carve Her Name With Pride* Gilbert perfectly synthesised all of his favourite war themes, eliciting from actress Virginia McKenna the first of a series of excellent female lead performances. As wartime secret agent Violette Szarbo, McKenna is simply brilliant; Gilbert's direction accentuates the tension whilst never losing sight of the moral heart of the film.

His first features were mainly low-budget melodramas set in the seedy milieu of the underworld (*The Scarlet Thread* and *There is Another Sun* (1951)) and his commercial breakthrough came with the film *Emergency Call* (1952). It is the story of three disparate characters, including Sydney Tafler's wanted criminal, who are the only people to have a rare blood type needed to save a young girl's life. Its raw melodrama would provide one of the inspirations for television shows like 'Emergency Ward 10'. After the serviceable but forgettable sub-Ealing comedy *Time Gentlemen Please!* (1953), Gilbert directed and co-scripted the social drama *Cosh Boy*, the first British-made film to receive an 'X' certificate. Though extremely tame by present-day standards, at the time the film was widely condemned for its portrayal of the contemporary myth of the teenage delinquent – the film's explicit moral message of the benefits of corporal punishment clearly sought to compensate for this. The theme of youth and crime was revisited in his next feature, *Johnny on the Run* (1953), an intelligent film for the Children's Film Foundation about the adventures of a Polish orphan on the run from a group of thieves.

Gilbert stayed with the criminal milieu for *The Good Die Young* (1954), an adult melodrama about a mail van robbery with an Anglo-American cast including Richard Basehart, Stanley Baker and a young Laurence Harvey. Though entertaining, the film is largely predictable, unlike Gilbert's next melodrama, the genuinely unsettling *Cast a Dark Shadow* (1955). Here Gilbert casts the matinée idol Dirk Bogarde – still years away from his dramatic breakthrough in *Victim* (1961) – against type as a man who, having killed his first wife for financial reward, attempts to do so again with his second wife. Like many of Gilbert's melodramas, *Cast a Dark Shadow* has moments of suspense but lacks the edge needed to make it truly memorable. However, these films did demonstrate Gilbert's skill in casting relative unknowns and also directing certain stars. Having made *Reach for the Sky*, his career took a further twist as he turned to bigger budget, Technicolor films. He started with *The Admirable Crichton* (1957), again with Kenneth More, co-scripted by Gilbert from J.M. Barrie's fable. The story – Lord Loam and his family are shipwrecked on a desert island whereupon their butler Crichton becomes the master – like so much of Gilbert's output is rather too sentimental. Moreover, the film's production values have a tendency to overwhelm potentially acerbic comment on class relations. In this respect More's rather genial manner as the butler undermines the film to the point where he appears miscast.

Though clearly seduced by the possibilities of both Cinemascope and Technicolor, Gilbert made one last rather idiosyncratic foray into the realm of social realism with *A Cry from the Streets* (1958), a kind of semi-documentary about the life of a welfare officer. His next film, *Ferry to Hong Kong* (1959), was in every way the antithesis of a *Cry from the Streets*. It was his first move away from the traditional subject matter of British films and one of the forerunners of a developing trend that sought (usually unsuccessfully) to appeal to international markets. In this respect it was almost bound to fail: which it did, both commercially and critically. Lovingly shot by Otto Heller and starring Orson Welles and Kurt Jurgens, the film's plot, for what it is worth, concerns an Austrian drifter (Jurgens) who ends up on Welles' ferry in a typhoon. Rumours persist that Welles and

Jurgens despised each other and could barely bring themselves to appear together. Badly acted and badly written, it is a considerable embarrassment for all concerned.

Once again, Gilbert lurched to a completely different subject matter and milieu with *Light Up the Sky* (1960), a comedy-drama set on a searchlight battery during World War Two. Like many of his previous works it succumbs to sentimentality, though the casting of Benny Hill and Tommy Steele as brothers is strangely fascinating. As if to demonstrate his resilience Gilbert returned to the high seas in 1960 for *Sink the Bismarck* and once again in 1962 for the historical costume epic *HMS Defiant*. Starring Dirk Bogarde and Alec Guinness the latter, about a mutiny on an eighteenth-century British naval galleon, was somewhat overshadowed by *Mutiny on the Bounty* which was released the same year. Though impeccable in its art direction and cinematography, and with competent star turns, the film is dull and unmemorable. *Sink the Bismarck* carries a better emotional punch, not least because Gilbert's direction relentlessly focuses on the human dimension amidst the history.

Sandwiched between *Sink the Bismarck!* and *HMS Defiant* was the genuinely interesting, though flawed, *The Greengage Summer*, an adaptation of Rumer Godden's book. One of the film's strengths is in the casting of a young Susannah York as the English schoolgirl falling for a mysterious older man (Kenneth More) whilst staying in a rural French hotel along with her three younger sisters. With the customary high production values, Gilbert's film offers more here: some emotional depth, suggestions of lesbianism and a keen sense of the problems faced by young people during puberty. Yet it grates in its portrayal of a version of Englishness that was becoming increasingly outdated by the early 1960s, especially in the films associated with the 'British New Wave'. Moreover, it is hard to believe that More's character would turn out to be a jewel thief.

Notwithstanding *The Greengage Summer*, *HMS Defiant* is emblematic in many ways of Gilbert's career in the early 1960s: it demonstrates his technical strengths as a film-maker but also his weaknesses with regard to the emotional and narrative potential of cinema. This was also true of his next feature *The 7th Dawn* (1964); like *Ferry to Hong Kong*, it was an attempt to make a big-budget adventure, this time set in Malaya at the time of the uprising. The film is symptomatic of the trend at the time for stories of westerners: here an American plantation owner played by William Holden, encountering romance and troubles in deepest Asia. Its derivative nature extends to the casting of Holden, who had appeared in the vaguely similar *Love is a Many Splendored Thing* (1955), and it recycles all of the clichés associated with the genre.

In 1966 Gilbert showed Paramount Studios a play by Londoner Bill Naughton entitled 'Alfie', based on the radio drama 'Alfie Elkins and His Little Life' about a cockney Lothario. The studio liked it and suggested that Gilbert cast Tony Curtis, though he himself felt that the emerging Terence Stamp was ideal. After a disastrous opening on the New York stage as Alfie, Stamp pulled out leaving the way clear for a young actor called Michael Caine whom Gilbert had seen in a pre-release cut of *The Ipcress File* (1965). The rest is well known; the film became Gilbert's biggest commercial success to date, garnered Oscar® nominations and launched Caine as an international star. Whilst many of Gilbert's films have dated, *Alfie* has stood the test of time, not least because of Caine's performance, particularly in his direct address to camera. Uncomfortably misogynistic at times and with an episodic narrative, the film needs to be seen in its contemporary context, especially in the way it offered the world a very different image of British male sexuality. The closest we get to a stiff upper lip is Alfie's shameless use of his regimental blazer and badge as a tool of seduction. Of course, the moral sting in the tale is Alfie's comeuppance, especially his feelings of mortality and hints at the pain of loneliness. *Alfie* also includes several memorable performances by women including Vivien Merchant as the married woman Alfie seduces and impregnates, Jane Asher as Annie, and Julia Foster as the mother of his baby, whom he ultimately loses in the final scene.

Gilbert's only other film in the 1960s was his first James Bond picture, the Roald Dahl-scripted *You Only Live Twice* (1967), which signalled the definitive move away from the character and storylines devised by 007's creator Ian Fleming. The film's huge sets – the famous volcano alone cost over £1 million – spectacular stunts and exotic locations were proof of Gilbert's technical prowess. The Bond cycle restricts any real individuality on the part of the director, however, and in this Gilbert is no exception.

As if to announce his arrival as an internationally known director, Gilbert then took on that most international of writers, Harold Robbins, with *The Adventurers* (1970), which he also co-scripted, choosing the jet set of South America as a backdrop. Although most of the money is up on the screen, the glamorous sets and international cast cannot overcome what is a ludicrous waste of time, money and effort. The acting is bad, the violence gratuitous, the script clichéd and the direction flat. It is a film with no heart or soul.

With *Friends* (1971), in which two teenagers run away from their dysfunctional homes to a cottage in rural France and have a baby, overblown emotion gives way to unbearable schmaltz. The script is leaden and the story is full of improbabilities. It is depressing to witness Gilbert failing to translate a story that he clearly held so dear to his heart and still he resurrected the characters for a sequel, *Paul and Michelle* (1974), in which we move on three years and follow Paul's search for Michelle and his daughter. Like its predecessor the film seems out of touch with the world of contemporary young people and relies on far too many clichés.

Gilbert's next film, *Operation Daybreak*, focused on the assassination of the Nazi general Heydrich by Czech resistance fighters. Though competently directed, with a realistic edge and with a terrifically affecting ending, it was too dour for 1970s cinema audiences. Following this came *Seven Nights in Japan* (1976), a forgettable story of a romance between an English prince and a Japanese tour guide. As a director-for-hire Gilbert finished the 1970s at the helm of two more James Bond films, *The Spy Who Loved Me* (1977) and *Moonraker* (1979). The former has the distinction of being Roger Moore's best outing as 007 and introducing Richard Kiel as the steel-toothed henchman 'Jaws', whilst the latter managed to spoof both the Bond cycle and a host of space-set films such as *Star Wars* (1977).

If the 1970s proved to be the nadir of his career then the 1980s promised more hope as Gilbert began a series of adaptations of famous plays starting with *Educating Rita*. Here he sensibly relied on Willy Russell's own screenplay and concentrated on the central performances, which are outstanding. As the washed-up lecturer Frank, Michael Caine had one of his best roles in years, yet the star of the film is undoubtedly Julie Walters in her first major film role as Rita. Gilbert's direction is understated and assured but the music score is poor and intrusive.

The promise showed by *Educating Rita* was not fulfilled by *Not Quite Jerusalem* (1984), another adaptation of a play. Essentially a romance between two volunteers on an Israeli kibbutz, the film's episodic structure and wholly unsympathetic characters undermine the narrative. New acting talent in the form of the Polish actress Joanna Pacula stands out. Perhaps it was the commercial and critical failure of *Not Quite Jerusalem* and the success of *Educating Rita* that spurred Gilbert on to work on another adaptation of a Russell play, once again with a strong female role at its heart. *Shirley Valentine* (1989), the story of a Liverpudlian housewife discovering herself in the Greek isles, rests upon Russell's wonderful dialogue as well as Pauline Collins' ebullient central performance. Here, Gilbert fashions a film that is both entertaining and personal.

Stepping Out (1991) is an adaptation of a long-running stage play by Richard Harris about a tap dance teacher who tries to gather a group of amateurs into a coherent troupe for a charity performance. The rather clichéd 'let's put on a show' story somewhat undermines the film. The central performance by Liza Minnelli as the teacher is passable but the film resembles an up-market soap opera, particularly in its handling of the back stage emotional shenanigans.

Gilbert's next film, *Haunted* (1995), draws together several aspects of his work: the desire to try new genres, a focus on old-fashioned storytelling and a demonstration of craft. It also illustrates his tendency to favour the dull, old fashioned and unimaginative. Based on a novel by James Herbert, and with a good cast including Aidan Quinn, the film is a ghost story about a sceptical professor persuaded to visit a house which the owner claims is haunted. It nevertheless seems out of time, with a narrative that is as creaky as the wooden floors in the old house.

He is currently working on *The Memory of Water*, which is due out in 2002. Based on a play by Shelagh Stephenson, it stars Julie Walters, Patricia Hodge and John Hannah. **SH**

Elizabeth GILL

Born in Dublin, Ireland, in 1966, Elizabeth Gill had a cosmopolitan upbringing in coun- *Gold in the Streets* (1996)
tries such as Spain, France and the United States. She studied comparative literature
at Columbia University before moving to New York University to participate on their
undergraduate film production program. She also trained in acting at the Royal Academy
of Dramatic Art, making corporate and music videos while she studied. She wrote the
off-broadway play 'A Woman's Place' and wrote and directed a short film *A Kiss of
Death* (1992). This black comic satire dealt with the misadventures of an acting troupe
attempting a production of 'Hamlet' which goes horribly wrong.

In 1995 Gill worked as first assistant director on Todd Haynes' *Safe* (1995) and
was commissioned by Irish producer Noel Pearson to write a screenplay inspired by the
life and work of Louise Brooks. Pearson also produced and co-wrote the screenplay for
Gill's debut feature *Gold in the Streets* (1996). This is the story of a teenage boy who
emigrates to New York and immerses himself in the hopes, dreams and disappointments
of the Irish immigrant community there. The film was mostly unpopular with Irish critics
even though it toured film festivals in Madrid, New York, Seattle, Arizona and Boston,
and received some positive press. Irish observers saw it as a transparent attempt to
appeal to an Irish American audience. Although performers including Ian Hart and James
Belushi did their best with the material, the film could not overcome the general air of
opportunism with which it seemed to have been assembled. It is also visually unremarkable, blocked off like a stage play (which is the source of the script) and routinely
photographed.

Gill went on to assistant director work in film and television, which she feels has
broadened her ability to work in different genres. She participated in the 1999 Irish
National Writers' Workshop and subsequently completed her first novel. She has also
written for television and is currently developing her second feature, a romantic comedy
called *Goldfish Memory*. **HO**

Terry GILLIAM

Terry Gilliam is best known for films that inventively combine the gothic and romantic. *Monty Python and the*
His trademark soaring flights of fantasy are often set to attack dogged rationality and *Holy Grail* (1975)
grey-minded bureaucracy. *Jabberwocky* (1977)

Gilliam was born in Minneapolis in 1940 and after university his ability to draw *Time Bandits* (1981)
and anarchic brand of humour led him to work for *Help!* magazine (1962–65) in New *Monty Python's The Meaning*
York. Here he rubbed shoulders with cult artists such as Robert Crumb, and met John *of Life* (segment, 1983)
Cleese after seeing him in a pre-Python comedy show, 'Cambridge Circus'. Entranced by *Brazil* (1985)
the presence of real castles and disillusioned with America, Gilliam travelled to Europe, *The Adventures of Baron von*
ending up in London in the late 1960s. His first break came as a resident artist on a *Munchausen* (1988)
television show, followed by some animation commissioned for 'Do Not Adjust Your Set' *The Fisher King* (1991)
(1967–69), a British children's television show featuring several subsequent Pythons. *Twelve Monkeys* (1995)
On joining the 'Monty Python's Flying Circus' team, Gilliam's main task was to create *Fear and Loathing in Las Vegas*
the animated segments that bridged the sketches. Combining cut-outs, often taken from (1998)
medieval and renaissance paintings, with airbrushed caricatures, Gilliam's work lent a
certain surreal richness to the show, as well as adding an extra textural dimension. Working to flout expectations and often using grotesque imagery, Gilliam's animations are one
of the stylistic hallmarks of Python humour.

Python provided Gilliam with the chance to realise his ambition to direct live action.
After dissatisfaction with the treatment of the first Python film, the Pythons sought to
maintain control over their next film by keeping the direction within the team. Sharing
the role, Gilliam and Terry Jones took rather different approaches to the task of directing
Monty Python and the Holy Grail (1975). Gilliam's focus was on creating a film full of
visual interest, whereas Jones and other members of the crew treated the production
process in much the same way as a television show. Despite the problems experienced
by the two neophyte directors, the film was a box-office success and continues to have
cult status. Although largely ignored by critics of British cinema, the satirical technique
of deglamourising the Arthurian legend has been read as bringing politics and history
back into the myth. Since *Holy Grail*'s active rejection of the gleaming and super-clean

Hollywood presentation of the Camelot myth, no Arthurian romance – straight or comic – has ever looked the same again. Gilliam's fascination with the filthy and fetid aspect of the medieval world recurs in his later films. *Holy Grail* fuelled Gilliam's desire to direct, and shortly after he went on to make another medieval comedy based on a nonsense poem by Lewis Carroll.

Co-written by Gilliam, *Jabberwocky* (1977) was carefully storyboarded. The film is an atmospheric, gruesome fairytale set in the middle ages, replete with Pythonesque humour – perhaps because of the pressure to build on the success of *Holy Grail*. For viewers expecting pure Python, the film was a disappointment and it is the only film Gilliam has made that does not enjoy a current video release. It is, however, full of innovative eccentricity as well as a slew of British comedy actors, including Max Wall. Some critics seemed to find the film far-fetched and simply not funny enough. However, for others, its visual invention and unorthodox approach are its strengths. It also seems to have influenced John Boorman, who allegedly studied the film's style before he set out to shoot *Excalibur* (1981). Gilliam did not direct the next Python film, *Life of Brian* (1979), but worked mainly as the film's designer, as well as contributing to the acting, screenwriting and some animation.

Funded by George Harrison's Handmade Films, *Time Bandits* (1981) was written by Gilliam and Michael Palin. The film bends the laws of the physical universe, often using eccentric camera angles, wide-angle lenses and disparate scale, to create a combination of science fiction, fantasy and slapstick that revolves around a small boy named Kevin (Craig Warnock). His adventures begin when a band of dwarves accidentally arrive in his bedroom after having stolen a map of time gateways from God. The film's lesson – that heroes are less than what they seem – lends a wistful sense to the impossibility of any ideal. In many of Gilliam's films fantasy is figured as creative and imaginative escape from reality, but it also carries with it an elegiac undertone. This often evokes a violent and abrupt response, as is the case with the presence of the gigantic squashing foot that appears in the animated Python credits. At the end of *Time Bandits* it is tempting to read the unexpected explosion of Kevin's middle-class gadget-obsessed parents as an expression of anger over the loss of the fantasy world and it potential heroic father figure, King Agamemnon (Sean Connery). This anger, alongside an anarchic pleasure in overturning expectation, prevents Gilliam's films from becoming overly sentimental.

Two of Gilliam's recurring themes, the power of the imagination and the fight against corporate or bureaucratic culture, are taken up in the section Gilliam directed in the last Python film, *The Meaning of Life* (1983). Entitled 'The Crimson Permanent Assurance', it is a tale of swashbuckling on the high accountant sea. After having made the management walk the plank, the anchor is pulled on the City of London building and the rebellious and rather elderly Dickensian crew set sail, with accompanying heroic music, towards the New York corporate accountants to launch a take-over. The mixture of live action and cut-out animation allows the building to become a ship and office furniture to transform into weapons. The sequence provides a pseudo B-movie to the main feature and intrudes on the other film at one point. It is a remarkable piece borrowing from boy's own tales of high romance to stage an attack on and poke anarchic fun at the captains of corporate culture.

Co-written with Charles McKweon and Tom Stoppard, *Brazil* (1985) is perhaps Gilliam's best-known film to date – and it is stylistically stunning. Bringing a 1940s veneer to modern technology, Gilliam produces a technocratic nightmare by revealing the innards of machines, as with the intestinal ducting in all the buildings in the film. Sam Lowry (Jonathan Pryce) escapes the banality, and later horror, of Orwellian bureaucracy and totalitarian control through fantasies of free-soaring flight and heroic deeds. As in many of Gilliam's films, this gambit is double-edged. Lowry's fantasy life acts as a buffer, preventing him from doing anything about the status quo. During the post production of the film Gilliam staged his own battle against the Hollywood studio with a stake in the project. Universal's newly-hired boss would not take delivery of the film for US distribution until it was given a new 'romantic' ending and significantly cut, leaving Gilliam little option as to his course of action. Quality prevailed, however, and after the so-called 'director's cut' won awards and a general campaign, spearheaded by Gilliam, took hold of the American media, the film was eventually released in the US, but with little publicity from the studio. It nevertheless gained two Oscar® nominations. Gilliam's next film, *The Adventures of Baron von Munchausen* (1988), is a wild vision that breaks all the rules of time and scale. Charting the heroic tall-tales of the Baron (John Neville), the film, like *Brazil* and *Time Bandits*, is concerned with the power of fantasy, and the villain is a dogged pragmatist. Set during the eighteenth-century Enlightenment, the film plays with philosophical ideas such as the mind-body split, and juxtaposes earth-bound science with a balloon flight to visit the King of the Moon. There are some outstanding cameo performances in the film, including Robin Williams' hysterical King of the Moon and Oliver Reed's explosive, cuckolded Vulcan. In some ways less bleak than *Brazil*, it still carries a certain sense of nostalgia. Partly funded by Columbia Pictures, the film ran into financial difficulties, halting production and forcing changes to Gilliam's plans, mainly due to poor production management. The grandeur of the sets and the film's rather rambling structure has a capricious charm. Despite its failure to recoup its cost at the box office, it nevertheless stands as testimony to Gilliam's visionary imagination.

The Fisher King (1991) began a cycle of films made in the US that were directed, but not written, by Gilliam. After the ordeal of *Munchausen*, Gilliam launched into an American studio picture based on a screenplay by Richard LaGravenese which focused on characters rather than stunning special effects. Its appeal for Gilliam lay in its status as a modern grail story, the combination of the themes of redemption and love, and its critique of 1980s self-serving values. Robin Williams plays a crazy down and out named Parry, whose personal tragedy and naïve romanticism facilitates the redemption of an ex-yuppie DJ (Jeff Bridges). In this world, events are connected and actions have consequences, making it a type of medieval morality tale shifted onto the streets of New York. The city is transformed into a fairytale landscape, including a castle that houses the grail Jack must retrieve to revive Parry from a coma. Gilliam adds individual touches to the screenplay, such as the Central Station commuters breaking into a waltz. The film benefits from ad-libbed dialogue and largely avoids a mawkish approach, while retaining a sense of human failings and frailties. Bob MacCabe claims that this was the film that 'melded Gilliam's inner vision to the outside world'.

Twelve Monkeys (1995) has Gilliam's trademark textural density and brings his signature gothic technology to the film's vision of the future. Past, present and future are connectively layered into a story that unites love with madness, action chases and desperation. The central character, Cole (Bruce Willis), is a time traveller looking to pinpoint the moment in the past when a deadly germ was released. Confused by the shock of time travel and conflicting messages, Cole begins to believe that he is psychotic, partly as a way of staying with the women he has fallen in love with. Following clues left by the twelve monkeys graffiti, Cole and his girlfriend realise that they have been following a false trail, and that history has mis-read the signs as forewarning the release of the germ. In the closing scenes Cole, as a child, watches himself being shot in pursuit of the germ carrier. It becomes clear that he cannot save five billion people from dying but, unknown to him, his actions mean that the germ can be analysed by future scientists, with the aim of decontaminating the surface of the earth. The film, loosely based on Chris Marker's *La Jetée* (1962), confronts the paradox of time travel and comes out with an innovative and complex approach to pre-determination.

Gilliam's most recent film, *Fear and Loathing in Las Vegas* (1998), is in many ways as close as a Hollywood film can get to stream-of-consciousness form, and this is its strength. Based on Hunter S. Thompson's novella, the film revels in recreating the various drug-induced psychoses experienced by Raoul Duke (Johnny Depp) and Dr Gonzo (Benecio Del Torro). But this is not simply an 'out of it' movie; Gilliam brings a certain ironic distance to the mindless excess that is meant to be the nemesis of the American Dream. Depp's performance is finely tuned, particularly through the inarticulate hand gestures that speak his character's subjective hyper-turmoil. The wide-angle lenses and extreme tilts, which recur in most of Gilliam's films, find a fitting context here, and the hallucinatory sequences are convincingly rendered. While the film might be assigned to the realms of cultdom, it is nevertheless full of surreal intelligence and interest.

From medieval dragons to Las Vegas lounge lizards, Gilliam's films collectively resemble a postmodern bestiary. Offbeat heroes do battle with mind-numbing institutions, grey bureaucracies and psychoses; and no one gets off such encounters lightly.

Setting his mettle against the Hollywood leviathan, Gilliam's skewed visions, coupled with his independent and often uncompromising approach, establish his status as contemporary auteur. *Good Omens*, a comedic fantasy based on Terry Pratchett's novel, is currently in production. **TK**

Alan GILSENAN

The Road to God Knows Where
(1989)
All Soul's Day (1997)

Born in Ireland in 1962, and once considered Ireland's most exciting young documentarist, Alan Gilsenan's more recent work has been less impassioned than his sensational breakthrough, *The Road to God Knows Where* (1989). This is a dark and frighteningly funny look at Ireland in the late 1980s, a time when emigration and unemployment were spiralling and there seemed little hope for young people leaving school. The film is dynamic, self-reflexive and visually haunting, photographed by Thaddeus O'Sullivan. It cuts from stand-up comedy and music performance to images of children playing in refuse-strewn fields in the Dublin suburbs; and it juxtaposes the conceited comments of representatives of promotional authorities with the hands-on experiences of those who had abandoned the country. This all adds up to a powerful polemic quite unlike anything seen on Irish television at that time. Produced for Channel 4 (UK) by Gilsenan's own production company, the film was a major talking point upon its broadcast at home (where it was objected to by the Industrial Development Authority), and catapulted its director to the forefront of non-fiction film-making. The film won a Special Jury Prize at the 1989 European Film Awards.

He followed this work with interesting insights into previously hidden aspects of Irish life including *Stories From the Silence* (1990), about AIDS sufferers, and *Prophet Songs* (1991), about Catholic priests who had rebelled against orthodoxy. In 1996 he directed a high profile series of six films about American authors for ITN entitled 'God Bless America'. Critics observed that his outsider's perspective on American culture gave him a unique and distinctive angle. He also helmed a series of compilations of historical amateur footage under the banner title 'Home Movie Nights' (1996–98).

In 1997 he made an awkward move to fiction with the experimental feature *All Soul's Day* (1997). This piece concentrates on the relationship between the mother of a woman who has been murdered and the murderer himself, now in prison. Deliberately shot with grainy stock, frequently out of focus and shifting from memory to 'reality', the film attempts to make an avant-garde contribution to contemporary Irish film. A weak script blunts any edge it might have had. Although he had directed a number of fiction shorts early in his career and has worked as a theatre designer and director, it was clear that Gilsenan was more at home with documentary. His homage to Irish soldiers who fought during World War One, 'The Green Fields of France' (1998), used some of the same visual techniques employed in *All Soul's Day* to better effect. The poetic, impressionist style blends well with documentary material, giving both an emotional resonance which the fiction film lacks entirely.

Gilsenan was one of three directors of the epic non-fiction history of the Irish diaspora, 'The Irish Empire' (1999), co-produced with Australian television. The series was shot over two years on five continents and featured two episodes directed by Gilsenan himself. Yet even though it touched on subject matter related to *The Road to God Knows Where*, the series was blandly expositional, as were many of the director's subsequent non-fiction works, including *Emerald Shoes* (2000), the story of Irish dancing, *Julie's Journey* (2000), about author Julie Parsons, and *Private Dancer* (2001), a portrait of the lap-dancing scene in modern Dublin. **HO**

Jonathan GLAZER

Sexy Beast (2000)

Acclaimed for his work with Jamiroquai and Radiohead, Jonathan Glazer's feature debut, *Sexy Beast* (2000), breathes new life into the British gangster film. Unwilling to conform to the accepted conventions of the tired genre, through inspired use of casting and location, Glazer elevates his film above the recent spate of British crime movies.

Ray Winstone plays Gal, a retired criminal enjoying life on the Spanish coast, whose tranquil existence is shattered by the arrival of Don Logan, the henchman of his old gangland boss, Teddy Bass. Initially unwilling to leave his idyllic existence, Gal's fear of Logan leaves him no choice but to return to London and his old life.

From the disorientating opening, in which we are introduced to Gal's sun-soaked Eden, *Sexy Beast* plays thick and fast with generic conventions. Betraying his background in advertising and music videos, Glazer successfully blends his dazzling visual style with an intelligent script by Louis Mellis and David Scinto. Referencing films such as *Performance* (1970), *The Hit* (1984) and *Villain* (1971) – the latter in the casting of Ian McShane as Bass – *Sexy Beast* employs all-too-familiar characterisations to undermine audience expectations. Most effective is the casting of Winstone and Ben Kinsley, who plays Logan. Winstone plays against type, swapping his hard-man image for that of a cowardly slob, while Kingsley is convincingly edgy as a psychopath capable of any form of coercion in order to get his own way. Allowing the characters space to develop, Glazer's direction seamlessly shifts between surreal comedy and shocking violence. Much smarter and funnier than Guy Ritchie's *Lock, Stock and Two Smoking Barrels* (1998) and *Snatch* (2000), Glazer's debut is a promising introduction to a new director.   **IHS**

John GLEN

John Glen has been involved in film since the 1950s, having worked his way from dubbing editor to director. Specialising in the action genre, especially in the later stages of his career, he is known primarily for directing the Bond films of the 1980s, having graduated from editing and second unit direction on the series.

Glen's first feature directorial assignment was *For Your Eyes Only* (1981). The eleventh Bond film and Roger Moore's fifth in the lead role, the producers wanted a return to the realism of the series' earlier films and an avoidance of the world domination plots, massive sets and high fantasy which had marked both *The Spy Who Loved Me* (1977) and *Moonraker* (1979). The result is an excellent spy thriller, with a believable plot and hero. Although many would argue that *For Your Eyes Only* is still Bond, but only less of it – in the car chases he drives a Citroen 2 CV – the set-pieces are handled in a taut and thrilling manner. For example, when Bond watches Kriegler (John Wyman) at the shooting range, we feel each bullet hit harder than the previous one; inter-cutting each shot with Bond's reaction heightens the realisation that he is going to be dealing with a professional killer. Similarly, the decision to make Bond's ascent of the mountainous atoll completely silent is an exercise in tension. It is in such moments that Glen's approach as an editor is most effective.

Sadly, the effect is lost on *Octopussy* (1983); for a society that gloried in excess, the world of *For Your Eyes Only* was not enough. Funnier than its predecessor, *Octopussy* was a return to earlier Bond films and is akin to *Diamonds Are Forever* (1971) in placing the comedy first. Glen foregrounds this return in several sequences: Bond's deflection of thrown missiles with a tennis racket whilst being chased on the streets of Udaipur in India; the Union Jack balloon that he uses to gain access to Octopussy's base; and finally, the all too literal Bond-disguised-as-clown at the climax. However, *Octopussy* is still enjoyable and entertaining fare if not necessarily a good action thriller. Glen at least deserves credit for eliciting a passable performance from Steven Berkoff as General Orlov.

A View to a Kill (1985) was Roger Moore's swansong and it shows. Looking too old to play Bond, Moore seems incredulous as 007, particularly when forced to fight the likes of the super-athletic May Day (Grace Jones). As with Glen's previous films, it is the action that really shines. May Day's jump from the Eiffel Tower is spectacular, as is the ensuing chase with Bond driving half a taxi. The film's end takes place on top of the Golden Gate Bridge, San Francisco, with Bond facing-off to Christopher Walken's charismatic Max Zorin, after jumping from an airship. Like *Octopussy*, *A View to a Kill* is not a classic of the series, and virtually everything bar the set pieces is forgotten by the time the credits roll.

A much-needed injection of new blood, Shakespearean stalwart Timothy Dalton replaced Moore. He presented Bond as Ian Fleming intended – reflective, ruthless and almost a complete personality vacuum. Glen must take some of the responsibility for this. Dalton's presence in *The Living Daylights* (1987) is such a difference that either

For Your Eyes Only (1981)
Octopussy (1983)
A View to a Kill (1985)
The Living Daylights (1987)
Licence to Kill (1989)
Iron Eagle III: Aces (1992)
*Christopher Columbus:
The Discovery* (1992)

Glen does not seem to notice or care. When asked if the 'same scene would be set up differently' for the two actors, Glen replied, 'No'. Despite, or because of, Dalton's stoic performance, *The Living Daylights* is closer to the action genre than the comedic Moore movies. Again, sequences such as a cello being used as a sledge and a truck falling out of the back of a Hercules plane are signature moments, usually breathtaking in their execution.

Glen's final Bond film, *Licence to Kill* (1989), was made and promoted during a period of turmoil at MGM, hence its reputation as one of the least seen and rated of the series. Notorious for being the first Bond film to receive a '15' certificate in the UK, it is actually one of the more rewarding. Glen recognises that Dalton's Bond suits his 'rogue' stance, away from her Majesty's Secret Service and driven for revenge. The brutality with which some of the action is displayed is astounding, such as Felix (David Hedison) being thrown to sharks or Bond setting a heavy alight, leaving him to burn to death. It seems as if Glen is determined to push the envelope as far as possible with his final film and surpasses himself with the superlative sequence in which a truck avoids a missile by tilting onto two wheels.

Having left the Bond series, Glen has subsequently made few features. *Iron Eagle III: Aces* (1992) was a needless sequel to an odd series of films. With a plot that involved an international group of pilots, flying World War Two aeroplanes and taking on Peruvian drug barons, it seemed even more outlandish than most Bond movies. Without doubt over-inspired by *Top Gun* (1986), it has nothing relevant to say about the drugs trade. The bandwagon jumping continued with *Christopher Columbus: The Discovery* (1992) and unfortunately proved that Glen was no Ridley Scott. The film, despite having 'The Godfather' writer Mario Puzo on board, is turgid and rather pointless. Glen seems to have concentrated too much on plot rather than addressing the social and cultural issues that Columbus' discovery had on the natives of the New World or even just making such an epic journey exciting.

Glen has recently completed *The Point Men*, but the film's R rating and straight-to-video release suggests that it will not be screened theatrically. Compared to action directors such as Tony Scott or Michael Bay, John Glen's work feels dated; however, some of the cinematic set-pieces he created will be fondly remembered and discussed for years to come. **JR**

John GODBER

Up 'n' Under (1998) Born in 1956, John Godber has worked extensively in television and established himself as one of the most performed playwrights in the UK. As artistic director of the successful Hull Truck theatre company, he also directed the original productions of his plays. His only foray into feature film direction expands one of his popular stage comedies. *Up 'n' Under* (1998) presents a variation on themes familiar from recent British films such as *The Full Monty* (1997) and *Brassed Off* (1996) in which a working class group (in this case, a hopeless rugby league side) faces a seemingly insurmountable challenge. Godber adopts an uneasy balance of stark realism and knockabout slapstick – indeed the film's realist aspirations (all terraced housing, pub interiors and rain-lashed rugby pitches) are in constant tension with its dramatic improbabilities. The re-assertion of the protagonist, Arthur (Gary Olsen), exemplifies the lot of men for whom mini sporting triumphs somehow compensate for unfulfilled professional and personal ambition. Arthur's challenge to a slimy local businessman is borne of his own egotism, but this is a trait the film is reluctant to follow lest it complicates the clear distinctions to be drawn between working-class hero and nouveau riche villain. Indeed, the film tacitly acknowledges that the game upon which Arthur's home and marriage hinge means little in relation to the broader social context, but sweeps this aside in favour of the feelgood climax.

The film also draws from the so-called British 'lad' culture, only gently mocking the sweaty exertions and buffoonery of the overweight, undersexed male group. Indeed, the concession to post-feminism comes in the form of a glamorous gym instructor (Samantha Janus) who is photographed in various states of near or total undress while proving her worth by competing alongside the men on the pitch. Familiar faces from British television comedy – Neil Morrissey, Griff Rhys Jones, Tony Slattery, among others – heighten the sense that the story would have been better suited to the small screen. Godber's direction is largely functional, resorting to slow motion action montages and a rock soundtrack for many of its dramatic and emotional cues. That the characters are shown at one point discussing the British national lottery only slightly contemporises what is essentially an old-fashioned tale.

Recently, Godber's play 'Bouncers' was produced for Swedish television.　　**NJ**

Jim GODDARD

A quick review of Jim Goddard's rather short filmography could be seriously misleading; in a career now spanning five decades, the vast majority of his influential work has actually been for British television. It is here, rather than in his scant cinema feature films, that his real strengths are to be found.

His television output has been astonishingly varied. Among his many titles are Dickens adaptations such as 'A Tale of Two Cities' and 'Nicholas Nickleby', the mini-series 'Kennedy', 'Hitler's SS: A Portrait in Evil', and the award-winning 'The Free Frenchman'. More recently, he has also worked on 'The New Adventures of Robin Hood' and the popular medical drama 'Holby City'. His most striking television work was made in the 1970s when he worked on some of the most memorable crime series of the period. In their different ways, 'Budgie', 'Van der Valk', 'Target', 'Hazell' and 'The Sweeney' helped to contribute to a renaissance in realist British crime drama on television. With their tough-talking, working-class heroes (played by the likes of Adam Faith, Barry Foster, Patrick Mower, Nicholas Ball, John Thaw and Dennis Waterman), their casual attitude to violence and sex, and their real sense of authenticity, they managed to be groundbreaking whilst still attracting a very large popular audience. Goddard's handling of these series had a taut, muscular dynamism which helped to imbue them with a sense of urgency and tension. He also showed a real feeling for location, whether it was the canals and cobbles of Amsterdam in 'Van der Valk' or the housing estates and docklands of 'The Sweeney'. They brought to the small screen some of the qualities to be found in British cinema features like *Get Carter* (1971) and *Villain* (1971), establishing a successful generic formula that could rival American crime shows for their energy and style. Goddard's liking for the genre has continued, albeit in the rather more sedate form of series such as 'Reilly: Ace of Spies', 'Inspector Morse' and 'Hetty Wainthropp Investigates'.

The basis of his reputation as a director of cinema feature films is, for better or worse, centred largely on *Shanghai Surprise* (1986). The film's box-office prospects were certainly not aided by its virulent critical reception. The considerable hostility vented on this essentially lightweight, romantic adventure was probably fuelled by the animosity of those who were waiting eagerly to see if Madonna's acting career would come unstuck. In retrospect, with its story of a missionary and an adventurer in pursuit of a caché of opium in 1930s China, the film is a slightly frantic attempt to recreate the style of early adventure serials, mixing screwball comedy and feisty romance with chases and action scenes. Goddard's perfectly efficient contribution tends to be over-shadowed by the casting of both Madonna and Sean Penn and it has remained difficult for the film to shake off its reputation as one of the major creative and commercial failures of the 1980s.

His only other films remain relatively minor pieces. *Bones* (1984) is a largely inconsequential crime drama with Bryan Brown and Cherie Lunghi, which compares unfavourably with his earlier television work in the genre. The domestic drama of *The House of Angelo* (1997) owes more to the influence of the family of Edward Woodward (it stars Edward, Peter and Sarah Woodward and was scripted by Peter) than to any obvious visual signature from Goddard. This lack of substance in his film work should not obscure the real impact of Goddard's 1970s television work. The time might just be right for the reappearance of Goddard's brand of tough, realist crime dramas, particularly with the success of the BBC's 'Cops' series and *Lock, Stock and Two Smoking Barrels* (1998).　　**RS**

Johnny GOGAN

Johnny Gogan moved from film journalism to film-making with no formal training in either. Born in Sussex, UK, in 1963, he obtained a degree in politics and history at

Bones (1984)
Shanghai Surprise (1986)
The House of Angelo (1997)

The Last Bus Home (1997)

University College Dublin in 1984, after which he wrote for *The Irish Times* on Latin American politics. He was a founding member (with his sister Jane Gogan and Trish McAdam) of The Ha'penny Film Club in 1985. This body later formed part of the roots of *Film Base*, now the leading resource for independent film production in Ireland. In 1987 he was founding editor of *Film Base News* (now *Film Ireland*), which he edited until 1990.

His first short, *Stephen* (1990), is the story of an unemployed Dubliner who believes himself to be famous cyclist Stephen Roche. This tale of the schism between dreams and reality set the tone for his later work. *The Bargain Shop* (1992), a European co-produced television drama, which explores the issues at stake in the redevelopment of Dublin's inner city, examines the destruction of an old man's legacy due to pressure from commercial and political interests causes. The film sounds a note of caution about the changes in Ireland's relationship with capitalism at a time when urban renewal is one of its few visible signs.

By the time Gogan completed the low-budget feature *The Last Bus Home* (1997), the country was fully in the grip of the 'Celtic Tiger' economy. The film is a skeptical reflection on the hollow idealism of the 'new' Ireland, following the formation, brief success, and inevitable self-destruction of a punk band in 1979. A sobering look at both Ireland's past and present, Gogan's concern is with the compromises that come with success and the realisations that come with failure. The film made a virtue of its ultra-low budget by representing the grimy, half-lit world of the punk scene with an authentically rough edge. A striking opening portrays deserted stretches of Dublin suburbia in the bright daylight (when most of the population are attending the Papal visit at the Phoenix Park), which strikes a contrast with the later scenes in dark music venues packed with frustrated teenagers. It won Best Film at the Cherbourg Festival of Irish and British Cinema and obtained international distribution in fifteen territories including Latin America.

His recent work has mainly been in documentary, but he is currently preparing *Mapmaker*, a political thriller set in the border county of Fermanagh. *Paper Tiger* is also in development with the support of the Irish Film Board.   **HO**

Jack GOLD

The Bofors Gun (1968)
The Reckoning (1969)
The National Health (1973)
Who? (1974)
Man Friday (1975)
Aces High (1976)
The Medusa Touch (1978)
The Sailor's Return (1978)
The Chain (1985)

It is probably fair to say that the reputation of Jack Gold still rests heavily on his position as one of the new generation of committed and angry film-makers who emerged from British television into the cinema of the 1960s. Like Ken Loach, Gold was a politically engaged director whose best work showed a real empathy for the outsider and those who buck the system. Frequently charged by dynamic performances, their plain, unadorned style gave them an economy and directness that drew heavily on the lessons learned from years spent working in television drama and current affairs.

Born in 1930, after taking his degree in law and economics at London University, Gold began a six-year stint with the BBC. Working for the news analysis programme 'Tonight', he made more than three hundred short pieces, as well as thirty other documentary and fiction assignments. His documentaries frequently return to the themes of revolt and the politics of the everyday, whether they are centred on a British industrial dispute or on the detention laws of the old South Africa. The common characteristic tends to be a concern with the plight of the oppressed, usually captured in an uncluttered verité style that adds to the sense of outrage.

Many of these same qualities were brought to his feature debut, *The Bofors Gun* (1968). Set in a 1950s British army camp in Germany, the film bristles with a barely suppressed indignation at the idiocies of an imperialist British mindset. Given the task of guarding a now thoroughly redundant piece of weaponry, the tensions between the young soldiers slowly rise to a crisis of futile self-destruction. Gold's direction places the focus of the drama on the performances of Nicol Williamson and David Warner, who play out the contrasts between one person driven to the brink by the values of his society and another who tries to accommodate them.

Williamson is also the star of *The Reckoning* (1969) and brings the same kind of intensity to his role as a successful businessman who moves between the cut-throat financial world of London and the tough working-class streets of Liverpool from which he has risen. Scripted, like *The Bofors Gun*, by John McGrath, it is another bleak view of a social and economic system which seems to have few redeeming features and through which its central character must drive himself with almost nihilistic aggression. In the context of the 1960s, when British cinema frequently tended towards fantasy and stylistic excess, Gold's work was distinguished by its spare, purposeful directness.

From the 1970s onwards, with the increasingly constrained position of the British film industry, Gold returned more and more frequently to television where his most interesting work tends to be found. The most striking of his cinema films from this period is probably *The National Health* (1973), a darkly cynical portrait of a national institution on the brink of collapse. Based on Peter Nichols' stage play, the film heightens the mood of disillusion by contrasting scenes in the rundown hospital with 'Dr Kildare'-style fantasy sequences. The combination of farce and black humour, along with the casting of Jim Dale, led to the film becoming popularly known as 'Carry on Death'.

None of Gold's other 1970s work has quite the same sureness of purpose. *Aces High* (1976) transposes R.C. Sherriff's play 'Journey's End' from the World War One trenches to the war in the air. With a dashing Malcolm McDowell in the lead role and some very fine aerial footage of the dogfights, the film is a slightly uneasy combination of doomed romanticism and realist anti-war message. A further decline is apparent in *Man Friday* (1975), which inverts the Robinson Crusoe story to present Man Friday as the real hero. The casting of Richard Roundtree as Man Friday, and the rather schematic script by Adrian Mitchell, open the film up to accusations of tokenism. The paranormal thriller *The Medusa Touch* (1978), with Richard Burton as a writer who seems to supernaturally cause disasters wherever he goes, looks like a relatively routine commercial chore, and *The Sailor's Return* (1978), a Victorian tale of a sailor returning home with a black wife, received no theatrical release in Britain before turning up on television in 1980. The latter does at least return Gold to familiar thematic territory with its story of prejudice and one individual (Tom Bell) defying the values and attitudes of his own community.

More impressive is the memorable portrait of Quentin Crisp offered in the television film *The Naked Civil Servant* (1975), made for Thames Television. Again centring around a remarkable performance, this time from John Hurt, the film features another of Gold's outsiders, although on this occasion the rebellion takes the form of a camp whimsicality and gentleness in place of the more familiar belligerent aggression.

This move back towards television is even more apparent over the last two decades where, with the exception of the relatively modest *The Chain* (1985), most of Gold's work has been based. *The Chain* presents a series of serio-comic sketches linked by the progress of a removal gang led by Warren Mitchell as they go from house to house. The combination of social observation and broad comedy, and the straightforward visual style, return it to the territory of *The National Health*. Gold's television work has varied from productions for the BBC's television Shakespeare series, to the P. G. Wodehouse adaptation 'Heavy Weather'. Most recently he helped to lay to rest the beloved detective Inspector Morse by filming the last episode of the series and used John Thaw to similarly effecting ends in the sentimental 'Goodnight Mister Tom', which garnered several awards including the BAFTA for most popular television programme of its year.

If this more recent work has seemed to move him further still into the world of mainstream entertainment, this should not obscure the real achievements of his earlier films, distinguished as they were by a tough, uncompromising rawness which made them an essential part of the continuing tradition of British social realism.   **RS**

Sandra GOLDBACHER

The Governess (1990)

The Devil's Chimney (1999)

Writer and director Sandra Goldbacher started her career in television in 1991 with the film *Seventeen*, making her theatrical feature, *The Governess*, four years later. Set in the 1840s, it is the story of Rosina (Minnie Driver), a Jewess who travels as a governess to a Scottish island after the murder of her father where she becomes emotionally involved with a photographer.

The prevailing strength of the film is in the atmosphere that Goldbacher creates through her intriguing screenplay and effective stylistics. The camera's steady treatment of some of the early London scenes makes them appear mellifluous in their antiquity; its more fretful movements suggest a sense of looming unease, which is realised later in the uncovered truth of her father's double life. Like *The Piano* (1993), the film is in danger of alienating (male) viewers with its focus on an exclusively female journey, but saves itself through an engaging exploration of photography and the medium's emotional impact on its central characters. Sultry and seductive, the film itself is akin to Driver's pivotal character, which she plays with a powerful, yet aloof, charm.

Goldbacher followed her debut with the less successful and little acclaimed *The Devil's Chimney* (1999), returning to the familiar themes of female experience and exploration of gender and race struggles. Set in the present day, it focuses on a miserable woman who unravels the intriguing story of a white farmer's wife in South Africa in 1910 who became pregnant through a love affair with her husband's black foreman. Her latest film, *Me Without You*, which she has also written, is currently in production. It stars Anna Friel and Kyle MacLachlan, and traces the lives of two best friends who grow up on the outskirts of London in the 1970s and 1980s. **BPr**

Peter GREENAWAY

Born in Newport, Wales, in 1942, Peter Greenaway is one of Britain's most original and controversial directors. He first trained as a painter and then worked as an editor from 1965, during which time he produced documentaries for the Central Office of Information and began experimenting with film. In addition to his work as a film-maker, he has also produced paintings, written books, had several one-man shows and curated exhibitions worldwide.

An early short, *Windows* (1975), catalogues all the people who died in a small village by falling out of windows, demonstrating Greenaway's interest in lists, which has become a recurring theme in his work. *Dear Phone* (1977) intercuts shots of telephone boxes with shots of scribbled anecdotes from telephone users with the initials H.C. At first these notes are scruffily handwritten but gradually they become more legible; they are read aloud in a documentary-style voice-over (a common device in many of Greenaway's experimental works). The overall effect is both challenging and frustrating for the viewer, as the film's presentation renders the familiar strange. This same strategy is at play in *Water Wrackets* (1978). Here beautiful landscape images are juxtaposed with a harsh, military-style voice-over relaying the story of the 'wracket army' and its strategy to conquer this uncharted area of natural beauty. Image and voice-over are working at cross-purposes, creating a text at odds with both itself and typical constructions of the pastoral.

In *A Walk Through H* (1978) a landscape is constructed out of abstract drawings which, filmed in extreme close-up, have a collage quality; the film's voice-over narrates the stories connected with specific marks. This work also features one of Greenaway's earliest collaborations with the composer Michael Nyman. Music is used beyond its usual cinematic role, here corresponding with the overall structure of the narrative and its tendency towards emphasis and repetition. Works such as *Vertical Features Remake* (1978) and *A Walk Through H* attracted positive interest at various film festivals during the 1970s.

Act of God: Some Lightning Experiences 1961–1980 (1980) consists of interviews with people who have survived lightning strikes. The film is interspersed with ten eclectic 'Apocryphal Stories' told in voice-over and showcases two of Greenaway's burgeoning staples: Nyman's musical score and a series of lists. The lists are presented as running titles at the base of the screen giving, for example, the names of plays that invoke thunder. Greenaway's first feature, *The Falls* (1980), funded by the BFI, is a three-hour mockumentary set in the future. The film relates the lives of 92 victims of the 'Violent Unexplained Event'. As in all his formative films, Greenaway confronts the viewer with both the pleasures and difficulties of counter-cinema, playing with form and content and trifling with the norms of both documentary and classical cinema.

The Draughtsman's Contract (1982) brought Greenaway critical acclaim and, for such an avant-garde film, some limited box-office success. Funded by the BFI and Channel 4 for £350,000, it was important in establishing a place for the British art film. A study of seventeenth-century sexual intrigue set in an English country house, the film tells the story of a draughtsman (Anthony Higgins) who is asked by Herbert (Dave Hill) to paint 12 pictures of the estate as a surprise gift for his wife (Janet Suzman). The draughtsman agrees but on the condition that Herbert's wife gives him daily sexual favours. The intrigue and mystery sets in when Herbert is found dead. The draughtsman is the main suspect and the family believes clues to the murder may lie in his paintings. The film demonstrates Greenaway's concerns with formal parallels and symmetries; each element of the plot is mirrored and repeated a number of times, creating an intricate, baroque structure.

In *A Zed & Two Noughts* (1985) a car accident – caused by a swan outside a zoo – leaves Oliver (Eric Deacon) and Oswald (Brian Deacon) widowers. The two men are identical twin zoologists who then become involved with the female driver of the car, Alba (Andrea Ferreol), who loses one leg in the accident. Grief moves the two brothers into an obsession with death, decay and the creation of life; Oswald is keen to know how long it takes a corpse to rot, where the rotting starts, and how it looks. Greenaway proves more interested in laying out the visual form of the film and its system of signs and allusions than in constructing a narrative. The film is visually stunning, and symmetry is once more a key theme, parlayed through careful framing, meticulous composition and distinctive colour.

With *The Belly of an Architect* (1987) Greenaway continued his interest in the various manifestations of obsession. A middle-aged American architect, Stourley Kracklite (Brian Dennehy), visits Rome to oversee an exhibition in tribute to the eighteenth-century French architect Etienne-Louis Boullée. Dennehy gives an outstanding performance as Kracklite, a man so completely absorbed by the exhibition that he fails to realise his marriage is foundering and that, like his father before him, he is dying of stomach cancer. He becomes consumed by doubt and intrigue about whether his pregnant wife (Chloe Webb) is having an affair with a colleague who is possibly trying to take the credit for the exhibition or is maybe even poisoning him. The film is exquisitely framed and showcases Greenaway's characteristic visual and symbolic rhymes, and elaborate choreography. The themes are typical of his work and include spiritual and corporeal rotting, as well as the fetishisation of the historical, classical and numerical.

Drowning by Numbers (1988) is the story of three generations of women, all named Cissie Colpitts (Joan Plowright, Juliet Stevenson and Joely Richardson), who each murder their husbands by drowning them, helped by the local coroner, Madgett. The film is set during an idyllic English summer in a peaceful village unsettled by disturbing undercurrents of jealousy and revenge. It is full of visual references and evinces Greenaway's perennial fascination with lists: the numbers from the title refer to the strategic placing of the numbers 1 to 100 throughout the film. His love of game playing and punning are foregrounded by both the presence of the numbers and the film's intertwined double entendres of sex and mortality.

Utilising a relatively conventional narrative, *The Cook, the Thief, His Wife & Her Lover* (1989) is one of Greenaway's more accessible films. Albert Spica (Michael Gambon) is a sadistic, foul-mouthed gangster, Georgina (Helen Mirren) his downtrodden wife. Much of the action takes place in a restaurant, La Hollandaise, owned by Spica, where he comes to dine with Georgina and various members of his gang. Spica insults and abuses all of those around him, though his most fraught relationship is with the chef. Georgina catches the eye of another regular diner, Michael (Alan Howard), who sits alone at his table reading; the two begin a passionate affair, meeting for hurried liasons in various locales throughout the restaurant. A study of haute cuisine, adultery and murder, the film is part gangster movie, part revenge tragedy, and ends with an infamous cannibalism scene. Each area of action – the kitchen, the dining room and the lavatory – has a discrete design and colour scheme and the actors' extravagant costumes (designed by Jean-Paul Gaultier) change colour as they move between the areas. The film finds a connection between sex, eating, love, death and decay – and displays Greenaway's interest in each of these.

Prospero's Books (1991) received a mixed reception and has been described as a summation of Greenaway's formal and thematic concerns. Alluding to many of his earlier films, Greenaway reinterprets William Shakespeare's 'The Tempest' as the tale of a mind reviewing its full contents. A commentary on the play is supplied by images of the 24 books Prospero took into exile, and the film is structured around their subject matter – water, cosmology, pornography, ruins, hell, music and so on. The film is centred by an excellent performance from John Gielgud as Prospero, one that fittingly acts as the swansong to his screen career. Michael Clark makes a notable appearance, dancing his way through the film as Caliban. The rapid editing and selection of images are breathtaking, allowing sound and image to constantly blur into each other.

The Baby of Mâcon (1993), his next feature, was one of Greenaway's most controversial; it closed within days of release in the UK and failed to secure a US distributor. The film is a religious satire set in the seventeenth century and follows a church play being performed for the benefit of the young aristocrat Cosimo de Medici (Jonathan Lacey). In the play a withered old woman gives birth to a child. The child's older sister (Julia Ormond) is keen to exploit the situation and claims she is the true mother of the child by virgin birth. When the bishop's son (Ralph Fiennes) investigates the parthenogenesis, the virgin attempts to seduce him. The child causes the bishop's son to be killed and is taken away by the Church who continue the exploitation in a more coldly efficient way. As a virgin cannot be executed the Church exacts a dire revenge, sentencing her to be repeatedly raped. It is mainly because of the rape sequence that the film failed to find a US distributor. Whilst none of the rapes are actually shown on screen they are made even more horrifying and violent through Ormond's tortured and incredibly realistic screaming.

Greenaway deliberately pushed what he describes as the two big themes of contemporary cinema – death and copulation – to extremes. His characteristic visual style is evident; the shapes and tones of early Renaissance high art are combined with the content of late medieval notation-style painting. Lush, painterly cinematography is used, mainly in various shades of red, showcasing the intricately detailed costumes and set design. Depicting organised religion as hypocritical, the film was criticised for blasphemy. Shocking yet compelling, the film was appropriately released to extremely divergent reviews.

His next film, The Pillow Book (1995), courted less controversy. It derives from the classic Japanese text 'The Pillow Book of Sei Shonagon', a diary written by a tenth-century court lady, containing reports of lovers, aesthetic observations and lists of favoured objects and activities. In Greenaway's updated version, a young girl, Nagiko (Vivian Wu), growing up in Japan, participates in an annual birthday ritual: her father, a calligrapher, paints a birthday greeting on her face and her aunt reads to her from 'The Pillow Book of Sei Shonagon'. As an adult, Nagiko has a fetish for calligraphy and demands that her lovers paint hieroglyphics on her body, until she meets a British translator (Ewan McGregor) who offers his body as the surface for her own novel. As most of his work up until this point had been immersed in Western culture and history, the film marked a change for Greenaway.

His most recent, $8^{1/2}$ Women (1999), covers more familiar Greenaway territory and is constructed around a parade of eight-and-a-half archetypes of male sexual fantasy, as represented in Western art practice through the years. It is also intended as a comic homage to the film directors Federico Fellini and Jean-Luc Godard (the first time Greenaway has made explicit reference to his cinematic influences). Philip (John Standing) is a grieving businessman and, as in A Zed & Two Noughts, he deals with his grief through taboos rather than consolation. His son, Storey (Matthew Delamere), returns to the family chateau to comfort his father and in a chillingly rendered twist on Oedipal desire the two sleep together. Twice during the film, father and son watch Fellini's 8 1/2 (1963), a film which focuses on a male director's search for an actress to embody the ideal woman. Having viewed the film, Storey persuades his father to convert the chateau into a private bordello; the destruction of the bordello that occurs later is intended to invoke Godard's deconstruction of cinema. Philip's views on cinema appear very similar to Greenaway's own: 'I hate the cinema' he says, 'everybody feeling the same thing at the same time. It's too intimate.' Greenaway retains control over his films by working independently and generally writing his own scripts. His films are characterised by consummate design, lavish photography (Sacha Vierny often acts as cinematographer) and evocative scores (usually Michael Nyman). His films are dazzlingly original and his background as a painter is evident via numerous references to art history and the studious construction of the frames. He has said that he does not believe film to be a good medium for narrative and has much to offer outside the boundaries of story-telling – he is also frustrated by making two-hour films. His interest in film form is evident in much of his work that, in contrast to Hollywood fare, does not offer solutions, intimacy or condolences. However, despite this, Greenaway maintains that he wants to make mainstream movies for a large audience – but on his own terms.

He is currently working on a multi-media project, *Tulse Luper's Suitcase* – Tulse Luper is an alter-ego he created many years ago – which combines a number of stories variously presented on film, as an interactive CD-Rom and as part of an open website.   **PR**

Paul GREENGRASS

Paul Greengrass has a background in current affairs television, working on shows includ- *Resurrected* (1989)
ing 'World in Action' and 'Cutting Edge'. This experience can be seen as one explanation *The Theory of Flight* (1998)
for his interest in film and television projects about social injustice and political subjects. These concerns are heavily evinced in his debut film, *Resurrected* (1989). A powerful indictment of the military, this film gave the extraordinary actor David Thewlis his first lead role. He plays Deakin, a soldier thought killed in action in the Falklands and given a memorial service with full honours. When he appears, alive and with no memory of what happened, he has to cope with family shame and some grimly staged ritual bully- ing (in the form of a wince-inducing scrubbing brush assault). The acting is strong, not only from Thewlis but from Tom Bell as Deakin's father and Christopher Fulford as an unpleasant squad thug. Greengrass' direction does lean a little toward television-style anonymity but this is in keeping with such an unglamorous subject. The main fault of the film is its ambition: it is about institutional bullying, truth in combat, the Falklands and the close link between bravery and cowardice – the film buckles a little under the weight of this ambition. That said, it was warmly received, winning an award at the Berlin Film Festival.

Greengrass then directed a number of television projects, including 'The Fix' for the BBC, a story about football match-fixing, starring the comedian Steve Coogan in a lead- ing, straight role. *The Theory of Flight* (1998), the director's second theatrical feature, was also financed by the BBC. This is a strange melding of romantic comedy, drama and 'triumph of the spirit' disability movie. Kenneth Branagh is a disillusioned artist obsessed with flight who encounters Helena Bonham Carter's motor neurone sufferer while doing community service. She wants to lose her virginity to a gigolo so he plans to rob a bank to find the cash. Resisting overt mawkishness until the finale, the film is a little on the obvi- ous side. Bonham Carter is surprisingly effective as the feisty wheelchair-bound Jane and it does make a refreshing change to see a disabled woman who wants sex as opposed to the male protagonists of *Born on the Fourth of July* (1989), *Coming Home* (1978) and *The Waterdance* (1992). Despite this, she becomes a saintly figure by the end of the film. Branagh is less impressive, particularly in the cringe-inducing scene in which he rehearses his bank raid. Greengrass directs in a slightly uninspired but effective enough fashion and the film, like *Resurrected*, is at least ambitious with its jarring shifts in tone. In 1999 Greengrass made the BAFTA award-winning 'The Murder of Steven Lawrence' about an infamous racist murder and bungled police investigation in Eltham, London. This is an impassioned drama documentary and ironically, given its television origins, it remains the most overtly cinematic work the director has produced. Shot in a harshly lit, 'mockumentary' style, it is in the tradition of powerful and innovative British television films such as the 1965 'The War Game' and the 1996 'Hillsborough'.

Greengrass is a director who is drawn to interesting projects, but his visual style, too close to a television aesthetic, can be limiting. He is currently in production with a Lot- tery-funded project about the Bloody Sunday massacre, which he is writing and direct- ing; clearly his appetite for campaigning and the controversial remains undimmed.   **IC**

Andrew GRIEVE

From the first time Andrew Grieve read C.S. Forester's seafaring novel 'Hornblower' he *On the Black Hill* (1987)
developed a love of the ocean. After four years in the Merchant Navy he began a career *Letters from the East* (1995)

in cinema; however, before achieving his ambition to bring the nautical epic to the big screen, he had to hone his craft as a director.

After early work as second unit director on *Dead Cert* (1974) and the Steven Spielberg produced *Young Sherlock Holmes* (1985), he was offered his first film as director, *Suspicion* (1987), a television remake of Hitchcock's 1941 original about a young wife who believes her husband is trying to kill her.

On the Black Hill (1987), a touching tale of two identical twins in Wales, was his first theatrical release. His deft handling of the two central characters, and the sumptuous photography of the Welsh countryside fulfilled the promise that his early work had shown. The central performances from Mike and Robert Gwilym are excellent and add to the underlying passion brooding slowly within the small community. It was this sweeping drama that led to Grieve's work on the first of two television series for which he has become highly regarded.

'Poirot' stars David Suchet as the infamous French sleuth. The combination of Suchet's fastidious performance, the attention to period detail and Grieve's subtle unobtrusive direction made the film a huge ratings success and a succession of television films starring the detective followed. He was to revisit the whodunits with 'Murder in the Links', 'Hickory Dickory Dock' and 'The Murder of Roger Ackroyd' in the coming years.

Sean Bean, Clive Owen and Billie Whitelaw starred in his next film, *Lorna Doon* (1990). A seventeenth-century tale of forbidden love between a farmer and an outlaw's daughter, it is beautifully shot but lacks the emotional resonance of R.D. Blackmore's novel. *Letters from the East* (1995) illustrates Grieve's ability to elicit strong performances from his cast – particularly Ewa Fröling as Anna Kaleva – in this moving tale about an Estonian refugee. Once again his handling of the actors and the expansive nature of the script ensured good reviews, but the serious subject matter led to little box-office success.

Grieve was soon to return to television and put his name to another long-running classic. Commander Adam Dalgliesh played, as always, by Roy Marsden once again investigates a sinister murder in one of London's oldest firms in P.D. James' 'Original Sin'. Returing to the novel that inspired him in his youth, he directed the first of many films based on the famous maritime adventurer, 'Hornblower: The Duel', starring Ioan Gruffudd as the eponymous hero sailing the seas looking for action and adventure. The production values are exemplary and the scale of the battles, on land and sea, are inspiring. It was an enormous success and won an Emmy for Best Mini-series.

Greive continues to work on the Hornblower series with 'Mutiny' and 'Retribution', in which the seafaring legend has been promoted to Lieutenant aboard the 74-gun frigate, Renown. Set in the exotic locales of the West Indies and Spain, the juxtaposition of Grieve's lush camerawork with the harsh realities of war is perfectly pitched; it is a fine example of how the director's work has gradually progressed. **DB**

Terence GROSS

Hotel Splendide (2000) Born in London in 1958, Terence Gross has directed commercials, rock videos and promotional works, and written and directed short films, including the award-winning *The Sin Eater* (1996). He is also one of the directors of cult art documentary *London Underground*.

His feature, *Hotel Splendide* (2000), is notable for rich and dramatic visuals which stylistically acknowledge the work of Jean-Pierre Jeunet and Marc Caro (*Delicatessen*, 1991). The imagery centres on the hotel as a lasting and powerful reminder of Mrs Blanche, the now deceased originator of the 'healthy' regime, which consists of boiled fish and enemas. The 'Hitchcockian' theme of the mother as the figure of worship, repression and destruction accounts for the character absurdities of the remaining Blanche family who continue to run the crumbling hotel. After a five-year absence, Kath, the ex-lover of Ronald Blanche, returns to breathe fresh life and colour to the hotel's menu and regime. She is a figure of health and freedom to save Ronald from the matriarchal rule now fanatically continued by his brother Dezmond. Sister Cora is responsible for the mud-baths and treatments; she is restrained from loving relationships or a more expansive life by a deformity of her mother's invention. Exploring the theme of control within the boundaries of sophisticated comedy, the film is a dark comedy rather than heavy drama. The suppression of the body through the encouragement of hypochondria is displayed in an absurd light; still, there is an undertone of sadism in the power relations.

The narrative is structured by the voice-over of Stanley Smith, a guest sent to the hotel because of impure thoughts and trapped through the therapeutic encouragement of a fear of water. Distant from the central tale of star-crossed lovers Kath and Ronald, he emphasises the universal struggle between repression and love, a particularly British theme. Thematically, domineering maternity as an instigator of a self-perpetuating, suppressive lifestyle created by lies, rules and low self-esteem ultimately causes the destruction of the family. Stylistically, the wonderland within the walls of the hotel creates a dank, oppressive and restrictive atmosphere; characters are positioned within frames and watched through keyholes.

Gross' directorial expertise is evident via the captivating cinematography, seamless editing, careful delineation of character and a powerful and well-used musical score. Funny, unique, sad and uplifting, *Hotel Splendide* is an auspicious debut. Gross is currently in production with an HBO film, *The Day the World Ended*. **AHo**

Nick GROSSO

Nick Grosso's entry into feature film production came as a result of his work in theatre, *Peaches* (2000) a milieu to which he may be forced to return following his decidedly uninspiring cinema debut. Born in London to Argentinean parents of Italian and Russian extraction, he was drafted at the age of eight into an Inner London Education Authority programme for gifted children. On leaving school he worked as a photographer before enrolling at the Royal Court Young People's Theatre, where his passion for the discipline of writing flourished.

Having travelled to Berlin in 1994, Grosso wrote the play 'Peaches' in just three weeks. Opening at the Upstairs Theatre at the Royal Court in November of the same year, it was praised by critics for its pithy one-liners and Grosso's ability to capture the cadences of love-struck youngsters, fresh out of university and seemingly adrift on the rocky road of responsibility. His next work, 'Sweetheart', was somewhat darker. Similarly well received, it also centered on a diffident slacker and the tribulations involved in finding direction. With his career established, 'Real Classy Affair' united Grosso with Joseph Fiennes and Nick Moran, in the process igniting his desire to make the transition from theatre to the cinema screen.

The result is the disappointing self-adaptation of his first success, *Peaches* (2000). Produced by the canny Ronan Glennane and Paul Ward, the film's theatrical origins are all too apparent, as is Grosso's evident unease behind the camera. A would-be riposte to *Loaded* culture and archaic male attitudes to the dual Achilles' heels of women and responsibility, the intermittently witty dialogue is suffocated by flat direction and strangely somnambulant performances by a talented young cast, including Matthew Rhys. That said, the production team makes the most of a limited budget and testing schedule, and the Camden locations make for interesting viewing. **JWo**

Val GUEST

Despite the fact that there has been little critical evaluation of his work, Val Guest stands *Miss London Ltd.* (1943) as an important and influential figure in the history of British cinema for a number of rea- *Give Us the Moon* (1943) sons. At the very least, he deserves recognition for his vast cinematic output. In a career *Bees in Paradise* (1944) that spans just over fifty years (from the early 1930s to the mid-1980s) he variously *I'll Be Your Sweetheart* (1945) scripted, directed and produced more than ninety feature-length films. Perhaps more *William at the Circus* (1948) importantly, Guest will be remembered for the role he played in transforming the for- *Just William's Luck* (1948) tunes of England's Hammer Studios. Hammer had been a 'B-rate' movie studio since the *Murder at the Windmill* mid-1930s, churning out standard-issue comedies, dramas and the occasional thriller. (1949) After successfully adapting numerous famous radio and television serials for the screen, *Miss Pilgrim's Progress* (1950) Hammer purchased the rights to Nigel Kneale's enormously popular television serial, *The Body Said No!* (1950) 'The Quatermass Experiment', a science-fiction horror story about alien invasion; Guest was assigned to adapt the series and direct the production, re-titled *The Quatermass*

Mr. Drake's Duck (1951)
Penny Princess (1952)
The Runaway Bus (1954)
Men of Sherwood Forest (1954)
(1954)
Life with the Lyons (1954)
Break in the Circle (1955)
Dance Little Lady (1955)
The Quatermass Xperiment (1955)
(1955)
They Can't Hang Me (1955)
The Lyons in Paris (1955)
It's a Wonderful World (1956)
Quatermass II (1957)
The Abominable Snowman of the Himalayas (1957)
The Weapon (1957)
Carry on, Admiral (1957)
The Camp on Blood Island (1958)
Up the Creek (1958)
Life is a Circus (1958)
Further Up the Creek (1958)
Yesterday's Enemy (1959)
Hell is a City (1960)
Expresso Bongo (1960)
The Full Treatment (1961)
The Day the Earth Caught Fire (1961)
Jigsaw (1962)
80,000 Suspects (1963)
The Beauty Jungle (1964)
Where the Spies Are (1965)
Casino Royale (1967)
Assignment K (1968)
Toomorrow (1970)
When Dinosaurs Ruled the Earth (1970)
Au Pair Girls (1972)
Confessions of a Window Cleaner (1974)
Killer Force (1975)
The Shillingsbury Blowers (1980)
Dangerous Davies – The Last Detective (1980)
The Boys in Blue (1982)
Scent of Fear (1985)

Xperiment (1955). Well-known American character-actor Brian Donlevy was signed to play the lead, a rocket-scientist who discovers an alien infestation of a fungus-like growth that rapidly spreads, threatening London and the world. The enormous success of the film caused Hammer to halt production on its next project, a historical costume drama, launch a *Quatermass* sequel, and begin negotiations to purchase the rights to the Frankenstein character, a shift in production that would bring great success to the studio and forever alter the horror genre.

Born in 1911 in London, Guest began his career as an actor on the British stage and in early silent film. Finding little success there, he worked both as a journalist and columnist, writing for various papers and news agencies and then later as a tipster for American gossip-king Walter Winchell's infamous *The Hollywood Reporter*. He gradually worked his way back into cinema, but this time behind the scenes. A meeting with director Marcel Varnel led to a job as a screenwriter at Gainsborough Studios. From 1934 until the early 1940s, he wrote scripts for a number of British comics including Will Hay and Arthur Askey. Guest debuted as a director with the 1943 Askey musical-comedy *Miss London Ltd*, the story of a young woman who arrives in London from the United States for the purposes of starting an escort service for men. The film was less than a critical and commercial success. Despite the somewhat inauspicious start, Guest quickly began work on his next project, *Give us the Moon* (1943). A 'futuristic comedy' made during World War Two, the film imagines a post-war society in which the hardships and bleakness of life at the time in Great Britain give way to a more hopeful world. The plot concerns a young man who takes up with a group known as 'The Elephants' who devote their lives to avoiding work. When they are called upon to manage a hotel and restaurant, the organisation's dogma erupts with chaotic results.

With *Give Us the Moon*, which he also scripted, Guest established one of his work's primary thematic concerns: the confusion and devastation – either comedic or, as in his Hammer films, horrific – caused by the conflict between opposing groups, lifestyles, careers or philosophies. While these types of conflict are often the drive of narrative itself, Guest deftly foregrounds them through his linear plots and his straightforward visual style, sacrificing individualist 'artistic' tendencies to the service of story-telling. Examples of this formula appear throughout his otherwise varied body of work. There is the man of science whose rationality and reason are tested by the mysticism of the Himalayas and their ancient inhabitants, the Yeti, in *The Abominable Snowman of the Himalayas* (1957). In *The Day the Earth Caught Fire* (1961) the Cold War conflicts and ideology of two nations send the world careering towards the brink of destruction. In *Carry On, Admiral* (1957) the dashing young naval officer meets with an old school chum for a drunken afternoon during which their identities are confused and the officer is forced to see the world from a bureaucrat's point of view. Even David Niven's James Bond in *Casino Royale* (1967) – a film on which Guest was one of four directors – is forced back into the world of espionage by his own government after vowing never to return. Guest explores these conflicted peoples within a variety of genres, showcasing the diversity of his talent even as it resists the easy categorisation inherent to most auteur studies.

He spent the 1940s honing his skill on a number of comedies and mysteries for various studios. Working with a stable of Gainsborough actors, including Askey, Margaret Lockwood, Peter Graves and Max Bacon, Guest directed *Bees in Paradise* (1944) and *I'll Be Your Sweetheart* (1945). The former is a farce about stranded pilots held captive on an island run by women, the latter a romantic musical that revolves around the world of music publishing. He followed with *Just William's Luck* (1948) and *William Comes to Town* (1948), two films based on Richard Crompton's popular children's novels about William, a precocious Welsh schoolboy who continually finds misadventure. In 1950 Guest directed *Miss Pilgrim's Progress*, the story of an American girl who helps save the jobs of British factory workers in a small town. The film was of minor note both critically and commercially, but remains an important milestone in Guest's life and career; it was the first time he worked with actress Yolande Donlan whom he would later marry. They would collaborate on several of the director's subsequent films including *The Body Said No!* (1950), *Mr. Drake's Duck* (1951) and *Penny Princess* (1952).

In 1954 *Life with the Lyons* began what would become a fruitful collaboration with Hammer Studios and one of Guest's most productive and respected periods as a director.

The Quatermass Xperiment followed, earning him praise and launching his next project, *Quatermass II*. The sequel situates Brian Donlevy as the eponymous Professor Bernard Quatermass pursuing alien invaders in the form of tiny organisms with the ability to invade and inhabit human hosts, effectively turning them into zombies whose goal is the eradication of the human species. Like the first film, Guest adapted *Quatermass II* from Kneale's screenplay. The two reportedly had a falling out based on the changes and Kneale was unhappy with the film. Regardless of any production difficulties, whatever tensions arose during the filming fail to blemish the final product; it ranks as a highlight of the genre.

It suspensefully builds to a gradual uncovering of the alien plot as Donlevy's Quatermass pursues a series of clues until he discovers that the alien conspiracy has reached the highest levels of government. Filled with allusions to class tension, a general mistrust of governmental bureaucracy, and a creeping sense of unease, *Quatermass II* is a brilliantly realised portrait of Britain (and the West in general) confronting an unknown future in the midst of Cold War fears and economic unease. Ranked alongside such masterpieces of the genre as Don Siegel's *Invasion of the Body Snatchers* (1956) and Joseph Losey's *The Damned* (1963), it stands as the highlight of Guest's career and, to quote from 'Overlook's Encyclopedia of Science Fiction', it is 'the highpoint of the British Science Fiction film'.

Guest continued to work for Hammer and other studios over the next few years. Projects included *Break in the Circle* (1955), *The Abominable Snowman of the Himalayas*, *The Camp on Blood Island* (1958), *Up the Creek* (1958) and its sequel *Further Up the Creek* (1958), and *Yesterday's Enemy* (1959). Along with the *Quatermass* movies, these films brought Guest a measure of recognition and respect. Among them, *The Abominable Snowman of the Himalayas* stands out as an accomplished piece of atmospheric horror. Guest is able to fashion an eerie sense of foreboding as he did in the *Quatermass* sequel. The casting also helped: Peter Cushing is the scientist who wants to confirm his theories about the ancient snow beasts; American character-actor Forrest Tucker plays the fortune-hunter who wants to capture the monsters and make a profit displaying them back in the United States. The *King Kong*-like plot serves as a device for Guest to explore the theme of rationality and the supernatural colliding with each other through a series of oppositions: the British scientist vs. the American profiteer; Western inquisitiveness vs. Eastern philosophy; and man vs. beast. The film's black and white cinematography and cramped, claustrophobic mise-en-scène, undoubtedly the product of budget constraints and studio sound-stages, still serves to enhance the sense of tension during the hunt for the yeti.

Yesterday's Enemy (1959) and *Hell is a City* (1960), both taut psychological thrillers, were two of Guest's final productions with Hammer. He would make only one more film with the studio, *When Dinosaurs Ruled the Earth* (1970), a quasi-sequel to Hammer's biggest box-office hit, *One Hundred Million Years, B.C.* (1966), starring Racquel Welch. *Yesterday's Enemy* tells the story of a British brigade in Burma that captures valuable information from a Japanese captain. Unable to translate the encoded data, the British commander orders the killing of local civilians in an effort to force the co-operation of the Japanese soldiers. The film stands as a compelling exploration of the boundaries of human cruelty when conditioned by duty and necessity. *Hell is a City* concerns a dedicated police inspector who follows his hunches about an escaped convict to Manchester; the dreary and depressed city serves as an allegory for the state of the protagonists' moral decay and their desire to retrieve their stolen goods at any cost.

In the early 1960s, after leaving Hammer, Guest continued to employ the thriller and science-fiction genres to good effect. *The Day the Earth Caught Fire* (1961) remains a highlight of his career. When the United States and Soviet Union simultaneously detonate nuclear devices during a testing the Earth is thrown off its axis. In an effort to prevent the destruction of the human race, the two nations must set aside their differences and work together. The ambiguous ending leaves viewers with an uneasy sense of foreboding about the conditions of the Cold War and the futility of an arms race between weapons of mass destruction. *80,000 Suspects* (1963), adapted by Guest from an Elleston Trevor novel, served as one of the final highlights of the director's feature-film career. It was a serious and well-received drama about a doctor trying to contain an outbreak of smallpox in the town of Bath while also attempting to hold his failing marriage together.

In 1967 Guest co-directed *Casino Royale*, a spy-movie parody and an attempt to cash in on the James Bond franchise. With five directors, the film suffers from an incoherent script and tampering of too many visions. Even an all-star cast, which includes David Niven, Peter Sellers, Deborah Kerr and Orson Welles, did little to enhance the film's critical or box-office fortunes. During the next few years, his fortunes fell as a feature film-maker and Guest was forced to make a number of soft-core skin flicks, including *Au Pair Girls* (1972) and *Confessions of a Window Cleaner* (1974). He then turned his attention to directing for the small screen, working on a series of projects such as 'The Persuaders', the made-for-television features *Mark of the Devil* (1984) and *In Possession* (1984) until his retirement in the mid-1980s.

In the age of the auteur the term 'craftsman' is often perceived as an insulting reduction of a director's career, yet Guest's stamp as a film-maker is best defined by the qualities that kept him at work over such a long period of time: his professionalism, attention to detail, economy of style and, as Robert Murphy notes in his book 'Sixties British Cinema', his 'middle-brow populism'. These assets infrequently inspire the scholarly interest of critics looking to isolate thematic concerns or a unique and provocative visual aesthetic, but they are characteristics to be championed. Although Guest's name may not appear amongst the canon of cinematic geniuses, his work remains an outstanding example of the rewards of daily toil and consistency. **MR**

H

Piers HAGGARD

The great grand nephew of the author H. Rider Haggard, Piers Haggard is a director whose films tend to be either inspired, displaying a strikingly individual visual style, or simply embarrassing.

Born in Scotland in 1944, he started directing drama for television in the mid-1960s and worked at the National Theatre. In 1966 he was assistant dialogue editor on Antonioni's *Blow Up* and made a brief appearance in the film. His feature directing debut, *I Can't ... I Can't* (1969), is a 'racy' melodrama about a young Irish bride (Tessa Wyatt) whose twin fears of childbirth and contraception leave her unable to have sex with her husband (Dennis Waterman). It touches on some controversial issues; chief among these is the implied criticism of the Catholic Church's stance on birth control. Although the film is afraid to outrightly condemn church doctrine, it was considered shocking enough to arouse anger in the Irish press when it was screened in Cork. Flatly and anonymously directed, *I Can't ... I Can't* is located at the tail-end of the fad for social realism along with Roy Boulting's far superior *The Family Way* (1966) and Peter Collinson's *Up the Junction* (1967).

Little in Haggard's debut could prepare an observer for his next film, *Satan's Skin* (1971), an extraordinary horror movie and the director's greatest achievement to date. A creepy and atmospheric spin on Michael Reeves' earlier *Witchfinder General* (1968), in which the horror is provided by the corrupt and sadistic witch hunters, here it is the eponymous Devil who terrorises. In a seventeenth-century English village, the unearthing of a hairy skull unleashes evil forces. The local children, led by the seductive Angel (17-year-old 'Scream Queen' Linda Hayden), play sex games that end in rape and human sacrifice, people sprout 'Satan's skin' and a disembodied claw roams the village. It ends with a duel between the Devil and Patrick Wymark's witch-hunting magistrate. From this routine British genre plot, Haggard crafts a powerful film which features a number of memorable moments: the eerie credit sequence, set to Marc Wilkinson's excellent score; the surgical removal of the hairy patch of 'Satan's skin' from the thigh of a teenage Michele Dotrice; and the jarring use of a freeze-frame in the climactic duel. He also makes good use of some beautiful scenery. Although there are hints of the strange double standard of Hammer films of this period, where the sex romps of the evil teens are intended to be both titillating and reprehensible, the blood-crazed voracious youngsters also invite comparisons with the Manson family. The clash between wild youth and their 'respectable' elders (here personified by Wymark as the ambiguous, slightly sinister magistrate) reflects the generational split over issues such as the Vietnam War, sex and drugs. Along with *Witchfinder General* and Robin Hardy's *The Wicker Man* (1973), *Satan's Skin* is testament to the inspired strangeness and under-rated achievements of the British horror films of this period. Martin Scorsese spoke of his admiration for the film in the magazine *Film Comment*.

Like too many talented British directors, Haggard went back into television after *Satan's Skin*. Among other projects, he directed the excellent 'Pennies from Heaven' in 1978, Dennis Potter's innovative drama about the power of music and sex. This BBC adaptation, with Bob Hoskins and Gemma Craven, is far superior to Herbert Ross' later Hollywood version with Steve Martin. Haggard also directed the fourth 'Quatermass' outing for television with John Mills playing the titular scientist.

Haggard's next feature outing, the woeful *The Fiendish Plot of Dr Fu Manchu* (1980) was Peter Sellers' swansong. A witless sub-*Pink Panther* comedy, the star plays the dual role of the Oriental super-villain Fu Manchu and his nemesis, Nayland Smith of Scotland Yard. Helen Mirren and Simon Williams (who appeared in *Satan's Skin*) are given little to do and Haggard shows minimal visual flair. Even Sellers delivers a lumbering, laboured performance. He followed with the terrible but entertaining *Venom* (1982), a clumsily-scripted thriller about a bunch of kidnappers trapped in house with a deadly Black Mamba. It looks cheap and Haggard fails to build any real tension. The chief appeal of the film is the starry but oddball cast, including Oliver Reed, Sarah Miles, Klaus Kinski and an overacting Sterling Hayden. Leonard Maltin went someway to summing up the range of performances on display when he said: 'half the big-name cast appears to be drunk; the other half looks as though it wishes it were'. Even this line fails to describe the incredible final scene in which a manic Kinski runs around wrestling a rubber snake. The only hint of Haggard's visual inventiveness are the snake point-of-view shots which still do not counter the myriad close-up reaction shots and ineptly staged action scenes.

After *Venom*, Haggard returned to television and directed, alongside other projects, an Alan Bennett adaptation and the star vehicle 'Liza Minnelli in Sam Found Out: A Triple Play' in 1988. His two theatrical features since *Venom* are more sedate affairs. *A Summer Story* (1988) is a sweet and effective adaptation of a John Galsworthy novel, set in the 1920s, starring James Wilby as the London lawyer who enjoys a rural romance with Imogen Stubbs. The scenery is well photographed and the performances by the two leads are competent. Having to restrain his tendency for flashy visuals, it feels a touch stifled, but is a vast improvement on his other 1980s work.

Haggard's last film to date, *Conquest* (1998), works in a similar vein. Tara Fitzgerald is a touring cosmopolitan type who is stranded in the small Saskatchewan town of Conquest where she overcomes her initial suspicions of country living and is pursued by the love-struck Lothaire Bluteau. Although this fish-out-of-water scenario is familiar from Hollywood comedies such as Jonathan Lynn's *My Cousin Vinny* (1992) and Michael Caton Jones' *Doc Hollywood* (1991), the two leads are attractive and winning; the end result is diverting enough, if a little insubstantial. The film strives to be as 'quirky' as *Summer Story* tried to be 'restrained' but it did deserve better than the hostile reviews it received.

Piers Haggard's career has followed a similar path to many of his genre contemporaries, including Peter Duffell and Alistair Reid, working on wildly diverse projects from promising low-budget work through to polished television programmes.   **IC**

Peter HALL

Sir Peter Hall has been a firm fixture of the British cultural establishment for over forty years, and there is no doubt that his heart and true talent lies not in film, but in the theatre. Born in Suffolk, UK, in 1930, Hall's father was a railwayman – which allowed the budding young theatre fan to get cheap fares on the trains, enabling frequent visits to the theatre in London. He went on to study at Cambridge and, following a stint at the Oxford Playhouse, took over the Arts Theatre in London, where he directed the first performance in English of Samuel Beckett's 'Waiting for Godot'. Hall worked for four years in Stratford with many of the great actors of the day, including Laurence Olivier, and subsequently co-founded the Royal Shakespeare Company in 1960.

Three Into Two Won't Go (1969)

Perfect Friday (1970)

The Homecoming (1973)

She's Been Away (1989)

Never Talk to Strangers (1995)

He spent eight years running the company in Stratford, directing eighteen plays during that time; while there, he also made his first foray into cinema. His films were closely linked to the plays he was working on; however, whereas some theatre directors in the 1960s, such as Tony Richardson, were able to translate their stage work easily into expansive, meaningful films such as *The Loneliness of the Long Distance Runner* (1962), Hall was never able to quite recreate the magic he could weave in an auditorium on the silver screen.

His first film, *Work Is a Four Letter Word* (1967), was a strained attempt to bridge the gap between classical theatre and popular culture. It was based on a satirical play called 'Eh?' and had a potentially strong cast comprising of RSC actors, with the exception of popular singer Cilla Black who was thrown in as the love interest.

Set in the near future, David Warner (controversially cast on stage by Hall as the youngest ever Hamlet two years previously to much acclaim) plays a power station attendant who grows giant mushrooms that produce euphoria when he eats them. He then loses interest in his job and his life, disappearing into a world of his own. Though Hall's sense of the visual does shine through, the film appears extremely static, and the timing of the comedy is hit-and-miss to say the least.

Perhaps learning from his mistakes, the following year Hall embarked on more traditional fare, with a film version of his stage production of *A Midsummer Night's Dream* (1968). Taking advantage of the resources of the RSC at that time, the cast is remarkable. Unfortunately, it is interesting for its performances rather than its direction or cinematography. Diana Rigg, Judi Dench, David Warner, Ian Holm and Helen Mirren all show good promise that they would later fulfil, but the film is little more than a flat reworking of a sparkling stage production, and much of the editing is jerky and unassured.

After he left the RSC, Hall became an independent director, working on both theatre and film as and when he could get the funding. He received backing from Universal Pictures for a gritty but ultimately dull drama about the break-up of a marriage called *Three Into Two Won't Go* (1969), starring Rod Steiger. The film was nominated for the Golden Bear at the Berlin Film Festival, but Universal remained unconvinced and instructed NBC to film extra scenes once Hall had left the project in order to extend the piece to the length of a television movie, which it then became.

Hall returned to unambitious comedy with *Perfect Friday* (1970), a film in which a bank manager (Stanley Baker) plans the heist of his own bank, persuading a rich aristocrat (Ursula Andress) and her oddball husband (David Warner once again) to help his cause. It made little impact, and is now rarely shown.

As he prepared to take over from Sir Laurence Olivier as artistic director of the National Theatre in London, Hall's film career returned to the stage for its inspiration. His most memorable film to date succeeds precisely because of its theatricality and remains fascinating viewing today. Hall had lobbied for some time to get the funding to film a screen version of Harold Pinter's 'The Homecoming', a play that he himself had premiered at Stratford in the late 1960s. Eventually, the money came through and Hall managed to pull together an excellent cast using the core of that original production, including Cyril Cusack and Ian Holm. A friend of the director's, Pinter's terse dialogue and claustrophobic situations transfer well onto the big screen, and Hall succeeded in exacerbating the tension that builds up when a prodigal son returns home to introduce his father and brother to his new wife. The play is riddled with sexual tension and potential violence, brilliantly heightened by Hall with carefully measured framing and precise timing. By interspersing the action with suggestive close-ups and long pauses, *The Homecoming* (1973) is one of the most successful stage-to-screen transfers since Sidney Lumet's *Twelve Angry Men* (1957).

However, this was to be Hall's last film for more than a decade. He did not seem pleased with the reaction to *The Homecoming*, and he moved away from both film and theatre for a while, into the opera house, running the Glyndebourne Opera from 1989–1990.

He returned with *She's Been Away* (1989), which was originally going to be filmed for television on 16mm. At the last minute, Hall and writer Stephen Poliakoff persuaded the BBC producers to switch to 35mm on the strength of the cast, which was, as ever, packed with British theatrical stalwarts. The slow-moving, measured film told the story of an old woman (Dame Peggy Ashcroft, persuaded out of retirement by Hall) who had spent most of her life in mental institutions but, due to funding difficulties, was being sent home to her family. Despite remarkable success at the Venice Film Festival, where Ashcroft and co-star Geraldine James split the best actress award, it was given only a one-week run at a non-West End cinema before being shown, as planned, on the small screen.

Some interesting television work followed, including 'Orpheus Descending' and 'The Camomile Lawn', but apart from an incongrous and poorly-plotted thriller-by-numbers called *Never Talk to Strangers* (1995), apparently taken on as a favour to female lead and producer Rebecca De Mornay, Hall seems to have all but abandoned the big screen to spend his twilight years working on the stage.

Incredibly well connected, with the ability to attract the best in British acting talent, Hall obviously has a keen visual eye and an ear for dramatic dialogue. He has, to date, made some interesting films, which seem likely to remain little more than footnotes to his groundbreaking theatrical career. **AL**

Tom HALL
See **John CARNEY**

Guy HAMILTON

The Ringer (1953)
The Intruder (1954)
An Inspector Calls (1954)
The Colditz Story (1955)
Charley Moon (1956)
Stowaway Girl (1957)
The Devil's Disciple (1959)
A Touch of Larceny (1959)
The Best of Enemies (1961)
Man in the Middle (1964)
Goldfinger (1964)
The Party's Over (1966)
Funeral in Berlin (1966)
Battle of Britain (1969)
Diamonds Are Forever (1971)
Live and Let Die (1973)
The Man with the
Golden Gun (1974)
Force Ten From Navarone (1978)
The Mirror Crack'd (1980)
Evil Under the Sun (1982)
Remo Williams: Unarmed and Dangerous (1985)
Try This One for Size (1989)

Born in 1922 in Paris, Guy Hamilton began his long career as a clapper boy at the Victorine Studio in Nice in 1939. He worked alongside Carol Reed as assistant director on *The Fallen Idol* (1948) and *The Third Man* (1949), with Anthony Bushell on *The Angel with the Trumpet* (1950), with Sidney Gilliat on *State Secret* (1950) and finally with John Huston on *The African Queen* (1951). A capable and professional director, his career peaked in the late 1960s with his involvement in the James Bond series.

His first film, *The Ringer* (1953), was based on the play and novel by Edgar Wallace about a dangerous criminal who hunts the corrupt lawyer responsible for his sister's death. An excellent debut, the mystery thriller proved that Hamilton was able to handle such material; it is widely regarded as the best translation to screen of Wallace's work.

Jack Hawkins starred in *The Intruder* (1954), the story of an ex-army officer who finds that the trespasser in his house is an old comrade fallen on hard times. Rather workmanlike, the film attempts to sum up the troubles of post-war Britain, but falls short. This was followed by *An Inspector Calls* (1954), in which Hamilton skilfully adapted J.B. Priestley's tale of a mysterious inspector visiting justice on a prosperous family, and is a vast improvement. Alastair Sim excels at the head of a refined British cast.

Going on to even greater glory, Hamilton co-wrote and directed *The Colditz Story* (1955), an exemplary recreation of life among British POWs in the Second World War. Perfectly balancing the tragedy and comedy of the situations, Hamilton skilfully crafted a touching tale that would be his biggest success before his first encounter with James Bond. Next came the hit-and-miss musical *Charley Moon* (1956), with Max Bygraves as the music-hall act first shirking and then embracing his roots, and *Stowaway Girl* (1957), a tale of love on the high seas between a steamer captain and a girl of mixed race.

The Devil's Disciple (1959), Hamilton's next, saw him utilising his first star-studded cast; Burt Lancaster, Kirk Douglas and Laurence Olivier starred in the adaptation of a George Bernard Shaw story of eighteenth-century America under British rule. Despite the stellar cast and writing pedigree, the film was not entirely successful, although it contained some excellent moments. *A Touch of Larceny* (1959) fared better, with James Mason and Vera Miles bringing lively performances to the comedic tale of a naval officer faking his own disappearance in the hope that he can sue for libel when he is accused of being a traitor.

David Niven played a British officer in Hamilton's following film, *The Best of Enemies* (1961), befriending his Italian counterpart during the Abyssinian campaign of 1941. A Dino DeLaurentis production, it is mildly satirical and not altogether convincing. *The Man in the Middle* (1964) is a more successful wartime drama of court-martial corruption with Robert Mitchum and Trevor Howard. It is notable for pairing Hamilton with John Barry, the composer he worked with on his next important project.

When Terrence Young, director of *Dr No* (1962) and *From Russia with Love* (1963), left the newly founded franchise over a disagreement regarding percentage profits, Hamilton stepped in to helm James Bond's third outing, *Goldfinger* (1964). His grasp of the quintessential English style and manner, along with his confidence as a director, helped to create the defining statement in the Bond franchise and a milestone in 1960s filmmaking. The film finds secret agent 007 tackling a powerful industrialite who becomes involved with the Chinese government in an attack on Fort Knox. For the first time, everything recognisable about a Bond film came together: the bevy of beauties, the larger-than-life villain, the lethal bodyguard, the secret headquarters, and the spectacular end-battle. These elements have remained fairly constant throughout the Bond films, though rarely executed with such panache and humour.

Before a return to more Bond, Hamilton worked on other projects. *The Party's Over* (1966) is a controversial study of the fate of an American girl who falls in with Beatniks in swinging Sixties London; it became notorious for a scene in which a man makes love to a dead girl and the producers, Rank, disowned the piece. Mock Bond followed with *Funeral in Berlin* (1966), the second outing for Michael Caine as the more down-to-earth spy, Harry Palmer. An intriguing Cold War mystery that built well on the success of *The Ipcress File* (1965), *Funeral in Berlin* captures the paranoia of the era well.

An all-star cast of dozens rescued *Battle of Britain* (1969) from complete failure. A brave attempt to evoke the spirit of the summer of 1940, the film plods along without much success; the many stars including Laurence Olivier, Michael Caine, Christopher Plummer and Kenneth More are quite indistinguishable from one another in the flying scenes.

The next few years were dominated by the sure-fire success of a stream of Bond movies. Sean Connery returned to the role for *Diamonds Are Forever* (1971) whilst Hamilton guided the franchise into the 1970s and a lighter, comedic direction. Pitting Bond against the same villain for the third time in a row should have been a warning sign for the series. *Live and Let Die* (1973) ushered in a new Bond, Roger Moore, but retained some of the gravitas of previous adventures and clever use of American locations. *The Man with the Golden Gun* (1974), however, saw the franchise dip to an all-time low in terms of formulaic comedy and Hamilton left.

Four years down the line came *Force Ten from Navarone* (1978), a tenuous sequel to *The Guns of Navarone* (1961), that bore little relation to the original. With a post-*Star Wars* turn from Harrison Ford, it is the story of a crack commando unit sent to blow up a vital bridge in Yugoslavia during World War Two. Robert Shaw, Edward Fox and Franco Nero do their best, but the film is flimsy and only mildly enjoyable.

Two Agatha Christie adaptations followed. *The Mirror Crack'd* (1980) features Angela Lansbury, Elizabeth Taylor and Tony Curtis amongst the ageing but respectable cast. Murders occur when a Hollywood film comes to an English village, but unfortunately the stars fail to shine in the final product. *Evil Under the Sun* (1982), a more enjoyable adaptation, boasts a more competent cast with Peter Ustinov as Hercule Poirot, and Diana Rigg, James Mason and Maggie Smith in support. *Remo Williams: Unarmed and Dangerous* (1985) is based on a series of novels about a New York cop trained in martial arts and recruited by the CIA. In the film Fred Ward is trained by a distinctly Western Joel Grey to take on an arms dealer. A little plodding and superficial, it is still fun on occasion. Much of Hamilton's early panache and style are submerged beneath overblown action and cod philosophy. *Try This One for Size* (1989), based on the James Hadley Chase novel, is an improvement but, as his last film to date, a disappointment.

Hamilton's career has spanned five decades and he has been involved in several films which are now an indelible part of film history: *The Third Man*, *The African Queen*,

The Colditz Story, *Goldfinger* and *Funeral in Berlin*. He has left a significant mark on the British film industry and his work on the Bond series has influenced generations of film-makers to come. At his best he has been professional, stylish and intelligent.   **IM**

Nick HAMM

Martha Meet Frank, Daniel and A veteran of the West End stage, Nick Hamm won a BAFTA for his 1991 short film *The*
Laurence (1998) Harmfulness of Tobacco. During the next year he moved into television, directing 'Rik
Talk of Angels (1998) Mayall Presents' and feature-length comedy dramas, before tackling feature films.
The Hole (2001)   His first theatrical release was the 1998 romantic comedy *Martha Meet Frank, Daniel and Laurence* starring Joseph Fiennes, Rufus Sewell and Ray Winstone, amongst others. Narrated by Laurence (Fiennes), the tale follows the amorous adventures of the group of three men who find out until late in the day that they are in fact pursuing the same woman. Jumping around through time, the skewed narrative repeats episodes, adding subtle clues each time as to exactly what is going on. Pretty ineffectual, *Martha* is nevertheless a funny and charming film.

Talk of Angels, released the same year, stars Vincent Perez, Frances McDormand and Penelope Cruz in the story of a governess romantically entangled with a man in her employer's family. With a stellar cast at his disposal along with lavish costumes and sets, Hamm made the most of a weak plot, which was based upon the novel by Kate O'Brien. Generally criticised for being full of romantic cliché, the uninspired story hampers what is otherwise a well-executed film.

Hamm's most recent release, *The Hole*, was aided by £1.5 million lottery money. A tale of teenage obsession told in flashback, it centres around the experiences of the soul survivor of a group of four British school teenagers who ventured into a secret underground bunker, with fatal consequences. With Thora Birch taking the lead, straight off the back of her success in *American Beauty* (1999), the film prompted criticism for not drawing on home grown talent and received mixed reviews from critics. Imaginative and thought-provoking, if not entirely convincing, it is nonetheless an affecting thriller.   **LB**

Christopher HAMPTON

Carrington (1995) Born in The Azores in 1946, Christopher Hampton is better known as a playwright and
The Secret Agent (1996) screenwriter than as a director, having forged a career in adaptations of literary classics and period recreations. He adapted Ibsen's 'A Doll's House' for the screen in 1973, updated the Jekyll and Hyde story with *Mary Reilly* (1996), and penned *Total Eclipse* (1995), an unsuccessful attempt to dramatise the famous conjunction of poets Paul Verlaine and Arthur Rimbaud. It was his Oscar®- and BAFTA-winning screenplay for Stephen Frears' *Dangerous Liaisons* (1988) that brought him into the cinematic collective consciousness. Adapting his own play, in turn adapted from Choderlos de Laclos' epistolary novel, Hampton's collaboration with Frears was a triumph of sexual and psychological domination barely hidden beneath a witty yet barbed script.

The spectre of *Dangerous Liaisons* has arguably hovered above Hampton's forays into directing; *Carrington* (1995) was received by one critic as 'less dangerous liaison than safe sex'. While Hampton's adaptation of Lytton Strachey's account of his passionate affair with Dora Carrington is rich in period detail, boasting a strong central performance from Jonathan Pryce, there is a discernible stiltedness and implausibility in their relationship. The love scenes are poorly handled and a mis-cast Emma Thompson functions merely as a cipher; she is only defined by those around her, and thus throws the film off-balance. As a biopic, it is solid if uninspired; and as an account of sexual prurience in the aloof Bloomsbury Group, there are but a few incidental pleasures to be had.

The Secret Agent (1996) is an appropriately grimy and grubby adaptation of Joseph Conrad's novel. Unlike Hitchcock's version (*Sabotage*, 1936), which contemporised the action, Hampton restores the tale to the 1880s. Bob Hoskins stars as Verloc, the double-agent who has orders to blow up Greenwich Observatory. The story is secondary, however, and it is the mood and tone that recommend the film. Atmospherically shot by Denis Lenoir, the murky Victorian streets are apt metaphors for the troubled psyches of the protagonists. Hampton's flashback structure is unwieldy, and the lacklustre treatment of the cameos (Gérard Depardieu, Eddie Izzard, Robin Williams) may disappoint, but as an exercise in faithful literary adaptation and unconventional costume drama, Hampton succeeds in depicting a suitably claustrophobic and paranoid world. He is currently adapting Graham Greene's 'The Quiet American' for the screen.   **BM**

Justin HARDY

Born in London in 1964, writer and director Justin Hardy is the son of *Wicker* *A Feast at Midnight* (1994)
Man-director Robin Hardy. An Oxford graduate and an award-winning short film-maker, Hardy has also directed several television series including 'The Bill', 'Hope and Glory', 'Wing and a Prayer', and the execrable 'London Bridge'.

For his first feature, Hardy teamed up with Yoshi Nishio, who had graduated from the UCLA Producer's Program, to found a film production company and make a quintessentially British film. Although *A Feast at Midnight* (1994) is British, it is also nostalgic and reactionary. Set in the present, it resembles the 1950s; its schoolboys make Harry Potter look like a pupil at Grange Hill. Odd attempts to be contemporary are ineffective and the script never coheres, the tone slipping uneasily between a *Carry On* and a Children's Film Foundation production. It is, however, gently entertaining and often sweet and charming. There are also some smart parodies.

Hardy and Nishio's project is perhaps most interesting for the circumstances of its pre-production. Usual funding processes were avoided and much of the finance was actually raised at City banks from the traders on the day they received their enormous bonuses. The most generous investors had characters named after them in the film. From the runners to the producer and director, the crew were paid a flat rate minimum fee; the boys were mostly non-actors. As Hardy senior persuaded Christopher Lee to work for a pittance on *Wicker Man*, so Justin convinced Lee, and other respected actors such as Robert Hardy and Edward Fox, to join the project.

Although at the finish of *Feast*, Hardy and Nishio were planning to work together again, no such project has yet materialised. Hardy continues with his television projects.   **FG**

Robin HARDY

Despite a slim filmography, Robin Hardy, born in Surrey, UK, in 1929, has a consider- *The Wicker Man* (1973)
able cult following on the strength of his debut, *The Wicker Man* (1973). This extraor- *The Fantasist* (1986)
dinary horror film emerged during the last flowering of an extremely creative period for British genre cinema which also saw the release of Michael Reeves' *Witchfinder General* (1968), Lindsay Anderson's *If...* (1968), *Performance* (Donald Cammell/Nicolas Roeg, 1970) and Mike Hodges' *Get Carter* (1971).

Hardy's film begins as a standard mystery. When police sergeant Neil Howie (Edward Woodward in a career-best performance) goes to the semi-tropical Scottish island of Summerisle to investigate the disappearance of a child, he finds a community of liberated pagans. Amongst the memorable characters he encounters are the lecherous innkeeper (the dancer Lindsay Kemp), his sexy daughter (a dubbed Britt Ekland) and Lord Summerisle (a barn-storming Christopher Lee in a ginger wig). Howie is initially bemused, then outraged, and finally terrified as Summerisle gives up its secrets. The last fifteen minutes are amongst the most frightening in film. Anthony Shaffer's script is both amusing and scary, in a similar vein to the underrated Hitchcock film *Frenzy* (1972), which he also penned. Although Hardy's direction is pedestrian at times, there are many memorable instances and images, from the child swallowing a frog to cure a sore throat to the slow-motion orgy in an abandoned churchyard, and Ekland's sexy nude dance. The superior soundtrack proves folk music's sinister potential and Harry Waxman's photography imbues the film with an eerily clear quality.

Although *The Wicker Man* was mutilated by its distributors (and now exists in a variety of versions), it received a warm critical reception. In Danny Boyle's British thriller *Shallow Grave* (1994) a character watches the fiery climax, and the performers in the disturbing, yet funny, BBC comedy show 'The League of Gentlemen' have frequently acknowledged the debt they owe to Hardy's film. Hardy, since, has worked infrequently, revisiting many of the same themes of belief, sacrifice and strange communities. His only other directorial credit is the strange thriller *The Fantasist* (1986). Newly arrived in a small Irish town, Patricia Teeling (Moira Harris) is plagued by mysterious phone calls. She is both repelled and fascinated by her stalker, who could be Christopher Cazenove's cop or Timothy Bottoms' failed novelist. From an intriguing premise, the film takes a more conventional slasher-movie turn. This ambitious approach to an exploitation piece is reminiscent of *White of the Eye* (1987), Donald Cammell's spiritual slasher movie – *The Fantasist* also had a limited release and remains little seen. There are pleasures to be had from the film, however, such as the collection of grotesque characters and some gruesome murders. Hardy also wrote Zelda Barron's *Forbidden Sun* (1989), a detective psychodrama set in a female gymnastics school in Crete where the rape of a student may be connected to an ancient ritual. The film failed to find an audience but is a further demonstration of the recurrent themes in Hardy's work. Reportedly making a living as a designer of theme parks, he has spoken for some years about his plans for a *Wicker Man* sequel; so far this seems to have come to nothing. In 1994 his son Justin made the old-fashioned family film *A Feast at Midnight* with Christopher Lee.   **IC**

David HARE

Wetherby (1985)
Paris by Night (1988)
Strapless (1989)
The Designated Mourner (1997)

Born in Sussex, England, in 1947, from the 1970s onwards David Hare has developed a critical reputation as one of English theatre's most important playwrights, part of a committed breed of leftwing, politically motivated dramatists such as David Edgar, Howard Brenton and Trevor Griffiths. From 'Plenty' and 'Pravda', through his early 1990s 'state of the nation' trilogy ('Racing Demon', 'Murmuring Judges' and 'The Absence Of War') to his more recent, elegaic works 'Skylight' and 'Amy's View', he is probably best known for his politicised views of English life. His work as a film director, however, has had less exposure.

He made and scripted three films in the 1980s – *Wetherby* (1985), *Paris by Night* (1988) and *Strapless* (1989) – all of which in many ways are fairly unremarkable human dramas. Scripted by Hare, they show a dramatist's concerns with character, dialogue and narrative structure. Each also resonates with the themes that are so important to Hare's stage work. Disenchantment with contemporary politics is embodied in the mysterious young suicide in *Wetherby*, the personification of alienation and disenfranchisement of youth in a Thatcherite-Reaganite culture, or in the ambitious Tory politician Clara of *Paris by Night*, an unsympathetic character who literally believes she can get away with murder. The sterility of human relationships in an age where people are culturally conditioned to 'look after number one' is epitomised by Blair Brown's isolated doctor Lillian in *Strapless* and *Plenty* (1985), Fred Schepisi's film version of Hare's play.

Coming from a theatrical background, Hare uses a limited cinematic palette, but the attention to truthful character development and intelligent dialogue is a genuine strong point. Also, as one would expect from a writer having worked in major theatrical circles, he elicits well rounded performances from his various casts, which have included Vanessa Redgrave, Michael Gambon, Judi Dench, Bruno Ganz and Bridget Fonda. Hare's most recent work as a director, *The Designated Mourner* (1997), is something of an oddity – a film version of Wallace Shawn's avowedly intellectual, coruscating meditation on state brutality and political repression. Hare directed the theatrical production of the play in London and simultaneously committed the work to film. It is a viciously angry work, aesthetically something of an anti-play. Three characters sit round a table and talk in monologues, only intermittently addressing each other; all events discussed in the text have to take place in the viewer's imagination. This time wilfully limiting cinematic style, emphasising the theatrical abstraction of the set and lighting, Hare achieves powerful impact. However, in the extreme close-ups and lengthy takes (that mirror the structure of the monologues), it is the uncompromising nature of Shawn's words that become sharply and uncomfortably focused for the viewer. The film is held together by American film director Mike Nichols' unexpectedly stunning central performance, which is well modelled on Wallace Shawn's own performance technique and delivered mostly as direct address to camera. The closing action of the script when Jack (Mike Nichols) lights a mournful pyre from a paper cake cup – the only moment of a described event actually being visually performed – is thus endowed with a greater significance.   **JP**

Margo HARKIN

Moving easily between documentary and fiction, County Derry's Margo Harkin is, along with Pat Murphy, Ireland's most important feminist film-maker. It is interesting that two of the country's most eloquent ciné-feminists are from the North. Some of the reasons for this are evident in Harkin's first film, *Hush-A-Bye-Baby* (1990), which was made through the Channel 4 supported workshop Derry Film and Video Collective, the body that also produced Anne Crilly's *Mother Ireland* (1998), a documentary meditation on women and Irish nationalism. *Hush-A-Bye-Baby* is set in 1984, a contentious period in the political life of the Republic of Ireland, since it was the year that saw both the 'Granard Babies' case and a referendum on abortion. The action takes place in the nationalist community of Derry, a space nominally part of the UK but whose collective gaze is often fixed on the Republic. The story centres on a 15-year-old girl named Goretti, who starts to date a young man, Ciaran. He is rounded up and indefinitely detained (also a feature of life in the nationalist communities of the North in the 1980s); while he is in prison, she finds out she is pregnant.

Harkin draws on traditional melodramatic forms to show how tough Goretti's situation is; she has no support from her boyfriend who is in prison and, when she finally does tell him, is dismissive. She is terrified to tell any of her girlfriends, her mother, or her sister, whom she thinks will judge her harshly. Like *Mother Ireland*, the film is about traditional nationalism's side-lining of women's problems; understanding life in the North as a simple conflict between the British and the Irish allows for the concerns of women to be ignored, secondary as they are to 'the national question'. It also allows the (often) reactionary elements of politics in the Republic of Ireland to be glossed over in favour of a romanticised vision of unity. Pat Murphy's *Maeve* (1982) dealt with this same question in an avant-garde, slightly didactic way, in the best tradition of European counter-cinema; *Hush-A-Bye-Baby* deals with it in the best tradition of Third World cinema, so often based in politicised melodrama.

Following *Hush-A-Bye-Baby* and the collapse of Derry Film and Video, Harkin returned to documentary film-making under the auspices of her production company Besom Productions. Her film *12 Days in July* (1997) moves between a Loyalist pipe-and-drum band and the anti-Orange Parade organisers in Portadown during the contentious parade season of 1997 – her focus is the Drumcree parade, which happens the week before the 12 July Parades. Her BBC-Northern Ireland documentary 'A Plague on Both Your Houses' (1999) was an intimate, often harrowing look at inter-faith marriages, comprised almost entirely of interviews. She also shot a short documentary in New York, 'NYPD NUDE', funded by Channel 4 in 1995, and portrayed Donegal playwright Frank McGuinness in a short 1998 film, *Clear the Stage*. **JW**

Hush-A-Bye Baby (1990)
12 Days in July (1997)

David HAYMAN

David Hayman is best known as a character actor, playing Malcolm McLaren in *Sid and Nancy* (1986), appearing in Hollywood blockbusters such as *The Jackal* (1997), and more off-beat projects, such as Ken Loach's *My Name is Joe* (1998). He also has an impressive list of television credits, including the acclaimed prison drama, 'A Sense of Freedom' and a lead role in Lynda LaPlante's crime series 'Trial and Retribution'. His imposing, often threatening, persona has led to frequent typecasting as either a heavy or a cop; his directing jobs tend to be similarly dark, brooding affairs.

His debut feature was the startling and original prison drama, *Silent Scream* (1990). Based on the true story of the incarcerated murderer Larry Winters, the film eschews the bleak naturalism of Alan Clarke's *Scum* (1978), offering instead a dazzling, visually impressive combination of crime drama, biopic and drug-induced fantasy. Winters was a traumatised individual, brutalised by religious bigotry in childhood and the twin institutions of the army and prison as an adult. He was one of the first inmates of the Special Unit at Barlinnie prison, where prisoners are encouraged to express themselves through art.

The violent criminal-turned-sculptor Jimmy Boyle is the most famous graduate of Barlinnie and Hayman appeared in the television movie about his experiences. The film dramatises Winters' writings and his drug use (both prescribed and 'recreational'),

Silent Scream (1990)
The Hawk (1993)
The Near Room (1996)

charting a fragmented and expressionistic rendering of his last night before he succumbed to a fatal overdose; screenwriter Bill Beech worked in Barlinnie and planned collaborations with Winters. Part of Hayman's achievement is the way in which the film elicits sympathy for Winters without downplaying the gravity of his crimes, skilfully shifting from the subjective dreams and hallucinations of the protagonist to the objective reality represented by his long-suffering mother. Iain Glen delivers a riveting central performance and was rewarded with a Best Actor award at the Berlin Film Festival.

His next feature, *The Hawk* (1993), is an altogether more conventional affair, inspired by newspaper reporting of the 'Yorkshire Ripper' murders, in which speculation centred on the domestic life of a serial killer and his spouse. Helen Mirren is impressive as a woman whose husband (George Costigan) may or may not be 'the Hawk', a murderer who gouges out the eyes of his female victims. Although the psychological veracity of the film is dubious (Costigan's laddish charmer is far removed from the uncharismatic reality of multiple murderers), it works as a grim Northern variant on slick Hollywood fare such as *Jagged Edge* (1985). Hayman directs efficiently though with none of the stylistic excesses of his debut. The performances are strong but the problem with these 'is s/he or isn't s/he?' stories (including the Joe Eszterhas-penned *Betrayed* (1988), *Music Box* (1990), *Basic Instinct* (1992) and *Jagged Edge*) is that the whole thing is pointless unless the suspect is guilty.

Hayman's most recent film to date is *The Near Room* (1996), a noirish thriller featuring Adrian Dunbar as a character in search of his estranged daughter in the murky world of child porn, blackmail and religious cults. The film is pleasingly atmospheric and expressionistic and it is refreshing to see an attempt to make a Scottish noir. Dunbar (though too lovable to be effective as a hard-bitten hero) tries his best and is given laudable support from Hayman as a sleazy newspaper editor. Ultimately, however, this is disappointing material, flawed by its televisual style and poor dialogue. The film resembles Mike Figgis' *Stormy Monday* (1988) with its melding of US generic conventions and British locations, but compared to Hayman's debut – a successful mix of gritty prison drama and psychedelic art movie – the result is unsatisfying.

Hayman is undoubtedly a talented film-maker and the fact that he has frequently directed episodes of the prime-time television cop drama 'The Bill' says much about the lack of feature opportunities for stylish genre directors in the current climate.   **IC**

Julian HENRIQUES

Babymother (1998) A former arts documentary film-maker, most notably for the BBC's 'Arena', Julian Henriques' first feature, *Babymother* (1998), was produced through Formation Films, a company which Henriques runs with his wife and producer Parminder Vir. The film is a natural progression and expansion of the preoccupations of his 1992 Channel 4 documentary 'We the Ragamuffin'.

Heavily (and slightly misleadingly) marketed as a 'reggae musical', *Babymother*, set in London's Harlesden, was the first feature on Jamaican dancehall culture to receive a commercial release in the UK. Despite being Henriques' first work of cinematic fiction, the film maintains a very strong documentary feel, authentically and convincingly conveying the hard lives and happy times of a certain segment of Harlesden's black community. Vividly rendered and beautifully choreographed, the sequences that focus on the local music industry and the dancehall way of life are by far the film's strongest.

Unfortunately, however, these scenes sit a little uncomfortably with the dramatic and narrative content of the film, which are closer in spirit and execution to the British tradition of kitchen-sink realism. The extravagant, exotic and erotic clothes, hairstyles, music and dancing are sometimes at odds with the realities of complex interpersonal relationships. They counterpoint, not always with success, the difficulties of single parenthood and constant money worries. This is a precarious balancing act carried off with a greater degree of polish by the likes of *Saturday Night Fever* (1977) and *Muriel's Wedding* (1994). Nevertheless, this is a minor quibble in a piece of work that ultimately realises its ambitions admirably.

Henriques is currently working on the screenplay for his second feature which, if all goes according to plan, will be shot on location in the Caribbean.   **AA**

144 Wallflower Critical Guide

Mark HERMAN

Born in East Yorkshire, UK, in 1954, Mark Herman trained as an animator at the *Blame it on the Bellboy* National Film School in London, where he made the short *See You at Wembley, Frankie* (1992) *Walsh*. It won the 1987 Academy Award for Best Student Film. His first feature-length *Brassed Off* (1996) project was *Blame it on the Bellboy* (1992), a lamentable comedy of mistaken identity. *Little Voice* (1998) Work as a writer on the sitcom 'The 10 Percenters' and for the band The Christians *Purely Belter* (2000) followed.

Next, Herman wrote and directed *Brassed Off* (1996), which opened that year's Sundance Film Festival and deservedly won a number of awards: a César for Best Foreign Film, the Peter Sellers Award for Comedy and the Writer's Guild Award for Best Screenplay. It follows the members of a colliery brass band – still struggling to survive a decade after the miners' strike – as they progress through the stages of a national competition while, behind closed doors, the decision is taken to close down the mine. Handsomely shot, and well-performed by a cast of familiar faces, it remains Herman's best film, the apparent ease with which it balances comedy and drama having proven so much more elusive in his subsequent movies. It rarely falls into an excess of senti-mentality and is often genuinely moving. One of its many strengths is its refusal to let the romance between the young leads (Ewan McGregor and Tara Fitzgerald) dominate, enabling a wider focus on several generations of the community being destroyed. The main problem with the film is the uncomfortable position it occupies between a celebra-tion of, and lament for, working-class culture, and the reconstruction of it as just one more component in a commercialised heritage culture. This tension will re-emerge.

In *Little Voice* (1998), adapted by Herman from Jim Cartwright's play 'The Rise and Fall of Little Voice', Jane Horrocks reprises the title role (from Sam Mendes' London production) of a harried young woman whose only escape from her domineering mother lies in the memory of her father and in imitating the singers he most admired. Despite the uncomfortable mood shifts it engenders, this conflict between British social realism and the Hollywood myth of the musical star pays off when LV's magnificent public perform-ance does not constitute the redemptive climax one might have anticipated. However, the recurring notion that the abused are simple and the simple are cute, some mean-spirited characterisations and the image of the North as a repository of the past detract from the film. One is left with the feeling that Herman's reconstruction of elements of 1960s social realism could be part of a tendency in contemporary British cinema to transform our cinematic heritage into heritage culture.

Purely Belter (2000), adapted by Herman from Jim Tulluch's novel 'The Season Ticket', does not resolve these tensions and, like its predecessors, occasionally falls back on Victorian stereotypes of the brutality of working-class life. However, as the transforma-tion of Tim Healy's character by the unsubtle but effective irony of his second appear-ance indicates, there is rather more going on in this story of two teenage boys trying to get together enough money for a couple of Newcastle United season tickets. The film successfully captures the complex interweavings of, and influences on, a depleted community, and although it evokes joy amidst adversity it does not proffer the cliché of delight as a solution to adversity.   **MB**

Peter HEWITT

Born in 1965, Peter Hewitt was educated at the London College of Printing and the *Bill and Ted's Bogus Journey* National Film and Television School. There he made the BAFTA-winning graduation short (1991) called *The Candy Show* (1989), about an undertaker's fantasies. Interestingly, the film *Tom and Huck* (1995) was partly financed by Harrison Ford, Roman Polanski and producer Tim Bevan, later of *The Borrowers* (1997) Working Title, the company who financed *The Borrowers* for Hewitt in 1997. *The Candy* *Whatever Happened to Harold* *Show* provided a calling card to Hollywood. *Smith?* (1999)

As a result, he began his professional career directing the sequel to the successful slacker film *Bill and Ted's Excellent Adventure* (1989), *Bill and Ted's Bogus Journey* (1991), another film in which Death makes an appearance. Well received for its produc-tion design, visual invention and comic detail, all of which were seen as superior to the original, the film was praised for its visual imagination and drew Hewitt even further into Hollywood's attention.

Typical of mainstream Hollywood, Hewitt found himself typecast as a director, being offered *Bill and Ted*-style zany humour projects. For this reason he accepted an offer to direct the first of a six-hour series for American television about a television executive fascinated with the new technology of virtual reality. 'Wild Palms' in 1993, which also had episodes directed by Kathryn Bigelow, Keith Gordon and Phil Joanou, allowed Hewitt to initiate a visual style for the show, described as a surreal soap, part science fiction, part noir, and part 'Dynasty'. Using wide lenses and plenty of moving shots Hewitt was able to set the visual tone for the series.

A desire to shift focus towards more family-orientated drama led him to Disney and *Tom and Huck* (1995). This darkly heart-warming adventure, set in Alabama in 1845, allowed Hewitt to explore one of his interests – looking at worlds removed from the one in which we live now.

The Borrowers would seem a logical move here. Based on Mary Norton's popular children's books about the tiny Clock family, who live under the floorboards and 'borrow' from the resident humans, the story requires a keen inventiveness. Hewitt's technically sophisticated vision, using enlarged sets, digital mattes, computer generated imagery and stop-motion photography, helped create one of the 'other worlds' he is so interested in – resulting in a fantasy-reality hybrid, modern America fused with 1950s Britain. Some bold set-pieces and cartoonish violence (the film's evil lawyer is electrocuted, bug bombed, impaled and scalded) are reminiscent of his previous work.

Hewitt's most recent film, *Whatever Happened to Harold Smith?* (1999), is another work demanding care with the details of setting up and delivering visual jokes and creating the right pop culture look, sometimes at the expense of character and story. It has been reviewed as a quirky and original love story, utilising Hewitt's love of colour in its dream territory production design. The film displays the mix of romance, eccentricity and nostalgia that has been evident in all of his work thus far.   **JD**

Mike HODGES

Get Carter (1971)
Pulp (1972)
The Terminal Man (1974)
Flash Gordon (1980)
Morons from Outer Space (1985)
A Prayer for the Dying (1987)
Black Rainbow (1989)
Croupier (1997)

Born in Bristol, UK, in 1932, Mike Hodges qualified as an accountant, worked in many different labouring and sales jobs, and completed national service in the Royal Navy before his introduction to the world of television in 1957. Enamoured by the industry, he turned his hand to script writing. This led to production and direction on a number of television series, most notably a run on 'World in Action' between 1963 and 1964, which included one of the first reports on Vietnam. A move to the arts series 'Tempo' saw Hodges profiling renowned film directors such as Jacques Tati, Alain Robbe-Grillet, Jean-Luc Godard and Orson Welles; soon after, he produced and directed two television thrillers for Thames, *Suspect* (1969) and *Rumour* (1970).

Hodges' theatrical feature film debut is still his most famous and recognised work. *Get Carter* (1971) is based on Ted Lewis' novel 'Jack's Return Home', and tells the story of a London hitman who returns to his hometown of Newcastle for his brother's funeral and a bloody and brutal investigation into his death. At the time the film was a revelation; an intelligent yet thoroughly violent thriller, stylish and witty, it captures all the grim hopelessness of working-class life in the late 1960s and early 1970s. Hodges' background in documentary film-making had served him well; he brought elements of grit and truth to the film that were unusual for the more traditional thriller. Michael Caine's presence as Jack Carter is one of the key elements of the film; it is hard now to imagine anyone else in the role, although originally Hodges wanted an entirely unknown cast. Caine strides through the film like a casual powerhouse of seething, cool violence, his arrogant demeanour and bitter wit tempered by a genuine emotional connection to his hometown and its people – and to his own grief.

The influence of *Get Carter* cannot be exaggerated. It heralded a sea-change in mainstream British cinema, foreshadowing the harsher, cynical films of the next decade. Hodges could have let this initial success dominate his career but chose instead to continue on his own distinct path, refusing to compromise his ideas. His integrity has led to mixed, though always individual, results.

His second feature, *Pulp* (1972), re-united him with Michael Caine in the antithesis of the Carter role. Caine plays a pulp-fiction writer who is plunged into the shady world of a Mediterranean country. A dark but playful comedy, superficially it bears no resemblance to *Get Carter*; slowly, however, the same themes of betrayal, guilt and exploitation emerge in an altogether different form. Amongst some excellent character cameos, Mickey Rooney excels in a shamelessly self-mocking role as an ageing gangster film star.

Pulp garnered great reviews both in the UK and the US. *Time Magazine* called it 'a minor classic', and *Rolling Stone* 'the best film of 1972'. However, the film was badly distributed in England, and a limited release in the US did not help. Later critics championed it when a New York cinema showed it as the first in a season of 'lost films'. It was the first of Hodges' films to be loved by critics and audiences yet mishandled by movie companies, but it was not the last. Looking back now, it is an odd but sardonically funny film, beautifully balancing comedy with a strange sense of sadness and loss.

In 1974 Hodges made *The Terminal Man* (1974), adapted from Michael Crichton's story of a brilliant computer scientist who, having suffered a serious head injury, undergoes the implanting of a microchip in his brain to control violent seizures. George Segal's character, Harry Benson, suffers from a technophobic paranoia, the fear that machines will dominate humanity.

When he is merged with machines via the electrodes implanted in his head, his paranoia becomes a frightening reality. In a bid to control his 'illness', a consequence of human frailty, he loses his humanity to electronic control. In a chilling scene the electrodes are activated in order to test them. The results range: they induce a certain taste, the urge to urinate, force him into tears with laughter, followed by romantic reverie. The film charts the frightening results of this tampering with nature, mainly through Segal's outstanding performance.

The story is typical Crichton fare and Hodges approaches the material with a clean, clinical style, providing a contrast to Segal's outbursts of violence. Crichton's informed examination of the consequences of technology dovetail well with Hodges' concerns for humanity's condition which is explored, in trademark form, through a single lead character. His first directorial assignment for Hollywood, *The Terminal Man* was not the hit he had anticipated, and though a personal favourite of his, did not receive distribution in the UK until the advent of home video.

Even now the film is not currently available on video and DVD, and the occasional screening on an obscure cable channel does not do it service. It is representative of Hodges' work and his struggles with the movie industry; a strong, uncompromising film left to flounder as the result of the studio's lack of understanding. Hodges has expressed the view that *The Terminal Man* is his best film. The growing stature of the film over the years would certainly attest to this; even Crichton, who originally disliked Hodges' treatment, now believes it to be one of the strongest interpretations of his work.

A second stab at Hollywood fare resulted in further problems. After co-writing the screenplay for the horror sequel *Damien: Omen II* (1978) – the ecological subplot is Hodges' influence – the director's chair was rapidly re-filled after ugly encounters with the studio system and the film's producers. Don Taylor is credited with solely directing the film even though Hodges filmed many scenes; his name is also absent from the screenplay credits, except on the paperback novelisation.

Such pressures may have put off other directors from pursuing Hollywood projects, but Hodges went to the other extreme, accepting an offer from Dino De Laurentiis to helm the multi-million-dollar remake, *Flash Gordon* (1980). Next to *Get Carter*, *Flash Gordon* is the film most closely linked with Hodges, and it is still difficult to believe that the two markedly discrete works came from the same source. Hodges has always asserted that an audience should not be conscious of the director at the end of a film and this goes some way to explaining the diversity of his style.

Flash Gordon is an adaptation of Alex Raymond's 1920s cartoon character, already immortalised in 1930s motion picture serials. For a post-*Star Wars* audience, *Flash Gordon* may have appeared old-fashioned; compared to the innovations of George Lucas' work, its visual effects are undoubtedly dated. The bold strokes of adventure and excitement are enough to appeal to the same core audience, however, and *Flash Gordon* has now taken its rightful place as a cult classic. The film is simple but enjoyable, and Hodges loads enough adult subtext and sexiness into the project to keep all ages interested. The presence of respectable actors (Max von Sydow, Brian Blessed, Timothy Dalton) and larger-than-life performances cannot but help, and a smart, highly quotable script and rock-star soundtrack courtesy of camp favourites Queen all make for a fun-filled romp.

After taking time out to direct television work, and to oversee the English language dubbing of Federico Fellini's *And The Ship Sails On* (1983), Hodges returned to feature-film direction with yet another surprising choice. *Morons from Outer Space* (1985) teamed him with the comic double-act of Mel Smith and Griff Rhys Jones in their transition from small to big screen.

The story deals with the possibility that our first contact with alien life will not bring the hostility of 'War of the Worlds' or the wisdom of *Close Encounters of the Third Kind* (1977), but rather four idiots accidentally crashing a spaceship. Even though Hodges attempts to rein the humour in for the sake of some deeper content, the film is filled with Smith and Jones' brand of broad comedy. As a pleasant comedy with no greater aspirations, the film is successful.

Next came *A Prayer for the Dying* (1987), the finished version of which Hodges disowned when the film was taken out of his hands by the producers and re-edited. A return to more serious subject matter, the film dealt with the story of an IRA gunman (Mickey Rourke) who cannot bring himself to dispose of the witness to his latest killing, a priest (Bob Hoskins). Instead, he confesses his sin, thus ensuring the man's silence. The released version is convoluted, which could be due to studio interference: trying to be a thriller and grasp at something more meaningful, it misses the mark.

Despite glowing reviews, more problems attended the release of *Black Rainbow* (1989): with an impecunious distributor, it received a very limited release in the UK. A film very close to Hodges' heart, it is the story of a medium who channels messages from the dead. Events take a dramatic turn when she receives a message from a man who is still alive, and realises that he will be murdered and by whom. Unfortunately, the killer knows that she knows. Rosanna Arquette, Jason Robards and Tom Hulce form a powerful cast in this engaging and moving thriller, balancing plot and emotion to great effect. Due to lack of distribution, the relatively unseen classic has built its reputation over the years in the home video market.

Difficulties with studios in general, and specific problems with *Black Rainbow* and *A Prayer for the Dying*, led to Hodges taking an almost decade-long break from studio film-making. He filled the early 1990s with television work before encountering similar frustrations with his most recent film, *Croupier* (1997); this time, however, the outcome has been happier.

FilmFour approached Hodges to direct a script by his friend Paul Mayersberg (*The Man who Fell To Earth* (1976) and *Eureka* (1983)). It is the story of a writer who, mid-block, takes a job as a croupier, hoping his life will mend itself. He finds himself becoming obsessed with the job and then dragged into the criminal underworld of gambling, where all his skill on the roulette table cannot protect him from danger. Hodges describes the film as 'a con from a couple of old con-men'. It is intelligent, crafted fare, relying on character and atmosphere. Taking the lead role, Clive Owen has had more praise from Hodges than any other actor apart from Caine.

Despite Hodges' enthusiasm for the project, and its rapid completion, FilmFour initially refused to give it a release. The British Film Institute stepped in to distribute *Croupier* for a very small initial UK release, but a lack of promotion and funding ensured that it disappeared without trace. Hodges sent a tape to a friend in America, who secured a US deal, and the film rapidly became the biggest independent film release of 1999. Word of mouth and tremendous reviews gave *Croupier* momentum; film festival screenings boosted its reputation around the world. A change of management at FilmFour prompted their shift in attitude and the film received a full, deserved release in the UK in May 2001, garnering rave reviews and taking more than respectable amounts of money at the box office.

With *Croupier*'s success, there came a renewed interest in Hodges' work, including complete retrospectives in New York and Los Angeles. Coinciding with its re-release, he directed his own stage play on the London Fringe, 'Shooting Stars and Other Heavenly Pursuits', about the surreal, hopeless world of the film industry. **IM**

Harry HOOK

Born in the UK in 1959, Harry Hook moved to Kenya when he was four years old with his father. He trained at the National Film and Television School in England and emerged as one of the country's great hopes; it seemed clear from early on that his narrative interests lay in negotiating identity in the space between different worlds, and the past and present. His short film, *Unknown Region* (1980), was shot in Africa and concerns the story of a missing British journalist and his obsession with finding links between old and new Africa. Another short, *Sins of the Father* (1982), examines the relationship of an upper-class young man with (what appears to be) a young 'Arab girl', upon the discovery of his expatriate poet father on an Indian Ocean island. Lacking any real comment on colonialism or sexual politics, the film can nevertheless be seen as part of a trajectory that led Hook to his first feature, *The Kitchen Toto* (1987).

The Kitchen Toto (1987)
Lord of the Flies (1990)
The Last of His Tribe (1992)
All for Love (1997)

The film was funded by Cannon and Channel 4 as part of Cannon's innovative, though short-lived, policy of encouraging a select group of new writers and directors every year. *The Kitchen Toto*, which Hook also wrote, deals with a secret society of the Kikuyu tribe, the Mau Mau, and their uprising against British rule in Kenya in the 1950s. Hook chooses to focus on the conflict through the eyes of Mwangi (an excellent Edwin Mahinda), a young Kikuyu kitchen servant, or Toto, who is employed by a British police chief (Bob Peck). As the conflict intensifies the film focuses on the manner in which Mwangi is caught up in the violence, trapped between two worlds. Like many British films about colonialism, it portrays complex socio-political events through the eyes of an innocent, which has the effect of rendering events as less historically comprehensible. Nonetheless, the film has a strong emotional heart and a keen sense of time and place. Compellingly shot by Roger Deakins, and featuring some exceptional acting, particularly from Mahinda and Peck, it presents a less glamorous and romantic image of Africa than the previous year's *Out of Africa* (1985), particularly in its tragic denouement.

The critical success of *The Kitchen Toto*, combined with Hook's ability to elicit naturalistic performances from child actors, brought him to the attention of executive producer Lewis Allen and led to the 1990 remake of Peter Brooks' *Lord of the Flies* (1963). Based on the novel by William Golding, it is an updated version, faithful to the original but with an American cast; Allen hoped this would make the story more accessible to a contemporary American audience. Hook's involvement began with casting 24 amateur actors aged between 8 and 18, who would play the cadets stranded alone on a desert island. *Lord of the Flies* emerges as an interesting take on Golding's book but adds little to Brooks' original, feeling like a somewhat unnecessary exercise. Hook's direction is low-key, suitably benefitting the scenes of disintegration from order into savagery, although the boys' performances are variable. *Lord of the Flies* should have been the film that cemented Hook's status as a young film-maker on the up. Although unsuccessful at the box office, it demonstrated his competence with both a larger budget and the logistics of a Hollywood film. Resisting the temptation to abandon his interest in the dichotomy of the 'savage' and the 'civilised', and thus embrace commerciality, he made *The Last of His Tribe* (1992), for the cable company HBO. The film concerns Ishi (Graham Greene), the last survivor of the Yahi tribe of Native Americans, who is brought to the attention of anthropologist Dr Alfred Kroeber (Jon Voight) in 1911. As in Hook's previous features the production design is handsome and the performances good (particularly *Dances with Wolves*' Graham Greene). As often happens with genre, however, the story is dictated by Voight's character, the white man who learns some humility from the 'other'.

Hook's last film was an Irish/French/German co-production entitled *All for Love* (1997), starring Jean-Marc Barr, Richard E. Grant and Miranda Richardson. Released theatrically in other countries, it was shown on television in the UK, thus precipitating Hook's move away from cinema into television, where he has most notably directed the four-part BBC drama 'Pure Wickedness'. **SH**

Ben HOPKINS

The co-writer of *Janice Beard: 45 Words Per Minute* (1999), Ben Hopkins' two features single him out as one of British cinema's more unconventional talents. His debut, *Simon Magus* (1999), a morality play set in the nineteenth century, tells the story of a Jewish

Simon Magus (1999)
The Nine Lives of Tomas Katz (2000)

outcast who attempts to help a small community build a train station and fight off the scheming gentiles of a nearby town. In order to do so, he enlists the help of the film's eponymous hero, who believes he is in direct contact with Satan. Despite its dour tone, Hopkins builds on the promise of his award-winning short, *National Achievement Day* (1995), assembling an impressive cast and directing with considerable assurance.

His second film, *The Nine Lives of Tomas Katz* (2000), is an anarchic comedy about the end of the world. Referencing everything from silent cinema and club culture to Monty Python and Stanley Kubrick, Hopkins delights in employing all manner of visual effects to create a world on the brink of disaster. Thomas Fisher plays Katz, a prophet of doom who rises out of a sewer to cause mayhem and panic on the streets of London. All that stands between him and the apocalypse is the Metropolitan police, who have transformed from a law enforcement agency into a modern-day equivalent of the Templars. Co-ordinating their battle-plan out of an operations room that resembles some pagan shrine, Ian McNeice's maniacal Chief Constable witnesses with horror the wholesale destruction of his capital city.

More a series of hilarious sketches than a film proper, *The Nine Lives of Tomas Katz* is intermittently successful; what it loses through incoherence, however, it more than makes up for in originality. Moreover, the film shows Hopkins to be a director willing to follow his own vision and prepared to do so on a meagre budget.   **IHS**

Bob HOSKINS

The Raggedy Rawney (1988)
Rainbow (1995)

Once quoted as saying that there were two kinds of films, 'High grade films and Lew Grade films', actor Bob Hoskins' biggest break in movies came in one of the latter. Cast as apoplectic London gangster Harold Shand in *The Long Good Friday* (1980), Hoskins' contributions to the project began during pre-production when he was invited to brainstorm with director John Mackenzie and writer Barrie Keeffe from a hospital bed, having picked up a tapeworm while filming *Zulu Dawn* (1979) on location in Africa. Born in Bury St. Edmunds, UK, in 1942, the only son of a book-keeper and a nursery school cook, Hoskins' stocky 'five foot six inch cubic' frame led him to manual labor as a window cleaner, lorry driver, Covent Garden porter and mango picker on a Syrian kibbutz. His start in theatre happened accidentally when Hoskins was asked to audition for a play while waiting for a scene painter friend to get off work.

Within ten years, Hoskins had established himself as a familiar face in the theatre and on television, and was known to American audiences for his starring role in the original BBC version of Dennis Potter's 'Pennies From Heaven'. Following the success of *The Long Good Friday*, Hoskins appeared in several high-profile productions (*Pink Floyd: The Wall* (1982), *The Cotton Club* (1984) and *Brazil* (1985)) and as Nathan Detroit in the Royal National Theatre's successful revival of 'Guys And Dolls'. Following his Oscar®-nominated turn as a lovestruck ex-con in Neil Jordan's *Mona Lisa* (1986) and his comic portrayal of a bellicose gumshoe in Robert Zemeckis' part-animated *Who Framed Roger Rabbit* (1988), Hoskins had sufficient clout to try his hand at directing.

Co-produced by Virgin and George Harrison's Handmade Films (which rescued *The Long Good Friday* from oblivion), and filmed entirely on location in Czechoslovakia, *The Raggedy Rawney* (1988) is the tale of a World War One army deserter who bluffs his way into the security of a gypsy encampment by allowing himself to be mistaken for a 'magic mad' female shaman – or 'rawney'. The soldier's life is complicated by his affection for the winsome daughter of gypsy chief Darky (Hoskins). *The Raggedy Rawney* was shot by cinematographer Frank Tidy (with whom Hoskins had worked on the comedy *Sweet Liberty* (1986) in America), and boasts a large cast made up of both British personalities – Zoë Wanamaker, Ian McNeice and musician Ian Dury – and native talent. The film's evocative soundtrack is courtesy of Michael Kamen, who had scored several of the films for which Hoskins had provided acting support, with original songs by John Tams of the Albion Band and Sharpe's Rifles.

It would be several years before Hoskins – following a string of increasingly odd projects that found him playing both J. Edgar Hoover to Anthony Hopkins' president in *Nixon* (1995) and a sewer-dwelling, Italian do-gooder in *Super Mario Bros.* (1993) – attempted his second directorial effort with *Rainbow* (1995). Maintaining the same interest in magic and wonder as *The Raggedy Rawney*, *Rainbow* is more overtly childish and self-consciously naïve. When a group of children find the legendary pot of gold at the end of a rainbow in New Jersey, they steal it, causing all of the colour to drain from the world. Attempting to right this wrong before the lack of chlorophyll destroys the world's ecosystem, the kids find themselves carried away to the Midwestern state of Kansas, where they run afoul of a blustery small town sheriff only to be saved through the intervention of an ageing magician (Hoskins). Like David Lynch's *Wild at Heart* (1990) and Jan de Bont's *Twister* (1996), Hoskins borrows imagery from Victor Fleming's *The Wizard of Oz* (1939), in this instance to sell his theme of conservation of both planet and family. Despite the support casting of American comic actor Dan Aykroyd, *Rainbow* (shot by Freddie Francis) remains unreleased in the United States. This is no doubt due to the dubious nature of the film's computer-generated special effects, which prompted Hoskins to lament to an interviewer: 'We had a budget of about three bob. So trying to do special effects with no money was a joke'.

Whether Hoskins will again take to the canvas chair is anyone's guess, and the actor himself seems unconcerned about his prospects: 'I act for a living. That's my day job. I can write a bit and then forget it. But I can't say "This year, I'm gonna spend writing." It's like a hobby. When you see that your ideas work, it's like "Ah, I'm not such a prat then"'.   **RHS**

Peter HOWITT

Born in Manchester, UK, in 1957, Peter Howitt is most familiar to British audiences as a cast member in the popular television sitcom 'Bread'. His directorial feature debut, *Sliding Doors* (1998), which he also wrote, is a fantastical variation on the romantic comedies exemplified by *Four Weddings and Funeral* (1994) and *Notting Hill* (1999), in which American leading ladies are lovingly photographed in a variety of English locations. Utilising a parallel narrative device so that two possible destinies run simultaneously, the film initially presents its protagonist, Helen (Gwyneth Paltrow, complete with an impressive, but indeterminate, English accent), as a PR executive, victim to both personal betrayal and professional sexism. The dual narrative allows the film to contrast Helen's re-assertion and professional flowering with the melancholy of her other existence in which, after being fired from her job, she is reduced to menial work and remains unaware that her partner, Gerry (John Lynch), is unfaithful.

This intriguing split in the presentation of female potential is primarily informed by the dictates of the romantic comedy formula. Paltrow's haircut is deemed crucial not only to the differentiation of each version of her character, but also serves as a prime signifier of her individuality. Both Helens are further contrasted to the brash, predatory Lydia (Jeanne Tripplehorn), the woman with whom Gerry is having an affair. Furthermore, his weakness and deceit are played against the sheer niceness of James (John Hannah) who, for the sake of narrative contrivance, may possess his own spineless streak. The double narrative also allows the film to side step the dilemma of how to resolve the its romantic conundrums: the potential for the fulfilment of one story thread compensates for the tragedy of another. This allows the film to have it both ways, sating the emotional demands of both the 'weepie' and the convention of the 'happy ending'. Presenting a view of English life which partly comprises London wine bars and rowing clubs, the film delivers the requisite clichés (moonlight clinches, reconciliation in the rain) while tacitly acknowledging the gulf between romantic fantasy and reality.

Howitt's follow-up feature, *Antitrust* (2001), is a conspiracy thriller for attentive teenagers, which draws upon recent concerns about the monopolisation of the computer industry and delivers a couple of competent action sequences. Milo (Ryan Phillippe) is hired by Gary Winston, a Bill Gates-like tycoon (an amused and occasionally amusing Tim Robbins), to assist in the development of a new communications system. However, Milo becomes suspicious of his boss' methods when various programmers begin to die every time Winston achieves a breakthrough in his project. The premise is certainly intriguing but the film is severely hamstrung by its perfunctory handling of familiar themes – individual vs corporation, the necessity for freedom of information and the atmosphere of mistrust. Robbins so effortlessly steals the film away from the young leads

Sliding Doors (1998)

Antitrust (2001)

that it is difficult to engage with the hero's final quest to defeat the machinations of big business. Despite its topicality, there is no real connection to the genuine concerns engendered by the global domination of modern communications giants. Ultimately, the film seems stranded in a no-man's land between US teen drama and techno-thriller, too involved for aficionados of the former, considerably lacking for proponents of the latter.

Howitt is currently working on *Johnny English: Rogue Male*, a film starring Rowan Atkinson, written by Ben Elton.   **NJ**

Hugh HUDSON

A director that has never quite fulfilled the promise of his memorable debut, Hugh Hudson has nevertheless matured as a film-maker, specialising in depictions of people who live out their existence in difficult or threatening environments. Born in London in 1936, he served his apprenticeship in television commercials, and was hand-picked by David Puttnam to direct *Chariots of Fire* (1981). The story of Harold M. Abrahams (Ben Cross) and Eric Liddell (Ian Charleson), two athletes preparing for the 1924 Paris Olympics, whilst battling their own personal demons and religious prejudice, it was an Oscar®-winning triumph. Few can forget screenwriter Colin Welland's declaration that 'The British are Coming!' in his acceptance speech. While the film failed to herald a new dawn in British film-making, it still has much to recommend it, not least in the mythopoeic level to which Hudson raises the narrative. He elicits commanding performances and never simplifies the issues by trumpeting patriotism or undermining the division between faith and personal ambition.

Hudson's next piece, *Greystoke: The Legend of Tarzan, Lord of the Apes* (1984), offered a modern spin on the Tarzan legend, with Christopher Lambert as the titular ape-man returning to his Edwardian ancestral home after years in the African jungle. Hudson's direction of the jungle scenes is inspired and the handsome set pieces are lushly photographed. The pace in the film's second half sags badly, however, and it is left to Ralph Richardson (in his final film role) to slide down the stairs on a silver tray, providing moments of genius amongst the general ineptitude.

If ever a moment defined the hokum and narrative bankruptcy of mid-1980s British cinema, it is surely the sight of Al Pacino struggling across a hillside with Dexter Fletcher in tow. Such a mismatch typifies *Revolution* (1985), a work which frequently heads polls for the 'worst film of all time'. The story of a trapper who becomes involved in the American War of Independence is inspired enough, but the whole tone and direction is bereft of originality, focus and narrative coherence. Like Michael Cimino's *Heaven's Gate* (1980), the film proved to be the death knell for a studio – Goldcrest Studios folded, inflicting irreparable damage upon all those concerned. Pacino took a four-year enforced break from acting, whilst Hudson never recovered the kudos that the success of his earlier films had bestowed upon him.

Lost Angels (1989) is the story of a troubled youngster (Adam Horovitz) who is sent to a psychiatric hospital and falls under the spell of his psychiatrist (Donald Sutherland). A necessarily low-key affair after the *Revolution* debacle, Hudson at least succeeds in stamping some kind of authorial marker on the narrative. Replete with bombast and portentous camera tricks, these flourishes nevertheless complement the themes of alienation that the film posits.

Lumière et Compagnie (1995) is a compendium film released to mark the centenary of the Lumière Brothers' film camera. To commemorate the event, forty high-profile film-makers were commissioned to make a film that abided by the 'rules' of film-making a hundred years ago: it could be no longer than 52 seconds, there could be no synchronised sound, and there would be no more than three takes. Hudson's contribution sits a little uneasily alongside such luminaries as Zhang Yimou, David Lynch and Theo Angelopoulos, but the very fact that he is up there in the pantheon of world directors is a testament to his past achievements and the industry's respect.

My Life So Far (1998) was released direct-to-video in America and received only a brief theatrical release in Britain, but the film is accomplished in its depiction of time and place. Based on the memoir 'Son of Adam' by Denis Forman, and adapted by Simon Donald, it is the story of a post-World War One family growing up on a Scottish housing estate whose lives are altered with the arrival of their returning brother and his new French bride. The pleasing collection of international actors – including Rosemary Harris, Colin Firth, Malcolm McDowell, Irène Jacob, Mary Elizabeth Mastrantonio and Tchéky Karyo – is one of a number of incidental pleasures (as is the picture-postcard depiction of the highlands). By concentrating his efforts on capturing the beauty of Scotland, however, Hudson eschews any socio-political or class dissection of the family, failing to probe deeper into the attraction felt by the men towards the 'exotic' Jacob.

I Dreamed of Africa (2000) is as yet unreleased in Britian, due in all probablilty to its box-office failure in America. Billed as Kim Basinger's first outing since her Oscar®-winning turn in *L.A. Confidential* (1997), the film is based on the real-life exploits of Kuki Gallmann who moved from her life of luxurious monotony in Italy to the rugged African countryside. Despite the adventure, her and her family's life is a constant struggle against a hostile environment. Hudson puts Basinger though storms, elephant stampedes and restless natives, but never dilutes the power of his star. Basinger's notorious on-set antics may have hampered Hudson's focus; he captures the harsh beauty of Africa, but never manages to get under the skin of his protagonist. The audience is left with beautifully composed images but little in the way of motivation or meaning.   **BM**

Simon HUNTER

Born in 1969, Simon Hunter graduated in film studies from the West Surrey College *The Lighthouse* (1999) of Art and Design, endowed with a considerable knowledge of film history. In 1999 he made his first feature film, *The Lighthouse*, on a budget of £1.5 million. Set on a small island dominated by a lighthouse, it depicts the atrocities committed by a psychopath killer and is particularly terrifying and sadistic, replete with plenty of blood and gore effects.

An umpteenth variation on the serial killer theme, the film does not come close to any of the best representatives of the genre. Suffering from an unconvincing screenplay, the plot offers few surprises and the characters lack any real depth. However, despite these faults, *The Lighthouse* is much better than most B-movie horrors, in main because of Hunter's direction. The young film-maker has a good command of cinematic language and, in parts of the film, succeeds in creating dynamic tension and a truly frightening atmosphere, efficiently using the claustrophobic atmosphere of the small island and eponymous structure. Containing some key moments, such as the excellent and suspenseful murder scene in the toilet of the lighthouse, the film suggests that he could well have a bright future.

Hunter has reportedly made a two-picture deal with producer Edward R. Pressman (*Wall Street* (1987), *The Crow* (1994)); *Mutant Chronicles* is the first feature on their agenda.   **PLe**

Nick HURRAN

With a career that began with 1980s television staples such as 'Telly Addicts' and 'Boon', *Remember Me?* (1997) Nick Hurran went on to make three cinematic features between 1997 and 1999 before *Girls' Night* (1998) returning to television in 2000 with 'Happy Birthday Shakespeare' and 'Take a Girl Like *Virtual Sexuality* (1999) You'. His first feature film, *Remember Me?* (1997), is a middle-class suburban farce centring around a family whose life is thrown into chaos upon the arrival of the wife's old college sweetheart (Robert Lindsay). Written by Michael Frayn (who also penned *Clockwise* (1996)) the script plays with the American idea of English suburban life and produces some well-developed characters and amusing performances; with Rik Mayall as such a dour husband it is easy to see why Lorna (Imelda Staunton) may find her interests wandering. The film is unassuming yet amusing. The following year Hurran made *Girls' Night,* starring Brenda Blethyn, who had received an Oscar® nomination for Mike Leigh's *Secrets & Lies* (1995). With a plot similar to *Remember Me?*, *Girls' Night* sees the mundane lives of two ordinary factory workers (the second played by Julie Walters) turned around by an unexpected jackpot on the bingo. However, when one of them is diagnosed as having advanced cancer, the girls decide to jet off to Las Vegas to fulfil a lifelong dream. Loosely based upon the real experiences of the writer Kay Mellor, the £4.5million production was originally destined for television until Granada found backing from a US company, the Showtime Network. The result is akin to a television soap-drama in which, critics argued, many scenes resemble those of early 'Coronation Street'. Still, Hurran did receive praise for his structured, if formulaic, direction, and his fusion of the buddy and adventure movie. The strong performances from Blethyn and Walters hold the film together and generate compassion.

Virtual Sexuality (1999), Hurran's most recent feature, is a breezy and undemanding comedy set in and around London. When 17-year-old Justine (Laura Fraser) is unable to find a man to lose her virginity to, she accidentally creates him on a computer programme. Slightly muddled, the plot sees Justine placed into the body of the newly created 'Jake' whilst still existing in her own right and eventually falling for him/herself. The UK's answer to such recent US teen comedies as *Clueless* (1995), *American Pie* (1999) and *She's All That* (1999), *Virtual Sexuality* does not simply transplant the formula, placing themes of transsexuality and acceptance of others at its core. Nevertheless, this is drama-lite, and any lesson that the film tries to offer is second to its saccharine humour and quirkiness. Comic moments come from the scenes where Justine tries to adapt to her new male status – or more specifically her new male anatomy – but there is still the prevailing sense that as a woman Justine was too attractive and fun to have to resort to this. Like the work that has preceded it, *Virtual Sexuality* has Hurran's signature humour that occasionally makes for innocuous viewing. **LB**

Andy HURST

Project: Assassin (1997)
You're Dead (1998)

Andy Hurst has made two features to date, both crime films financed with German money. His debut was the little seen *Project: Assassin* (1997), co-directed with Robin Hill. Promoted with the generic tagline 'the mind is the deadliest weapon of all', this murky thriller did not get a theatrical release in the UK. Producer Marco Weber, who has specialised in low-budget genre pieces, recently produced the higher profile *Igby Goes Down*, which is due for release, with Susan Sarandon and Ryan Phillippe, and *All the Queen's Men* (2001) with Matt LeBlanc and Eddie Izzard. He also produced Hurst's solo directorial outing, the comedy thriller *You're Dead* (1998). This is a would-be Tarantino-esque 'heist gone wrong' story whose plot strongly resembles Roger Avary's inferior *Killing Zoe* (1995). A group of bank robbers (John Hurt, Rhys Ifans, David Schneider) are trapped in a bank vault with a mysterious woman (Claire Skinner) when the robbery becomes a siege. The fragmented narrative, told in (often unreliable) flashbacks, owes something to another popular heist movie, *The Usual Suspects* (1995). Hurst's script is sporadically funny, the pace fast moving and the action occasionally well staged. The acting, however, is wildly variable: Hurt, as always, is excellent; Ifans is satisfactory; and the rest of the cast is merely passable or worse.

With second-rate British gangster films proliferating in the wake of the derivative but successful *Lock, Stock and Two Smoking Barrels* (1998), *You're Dead* suffered critically and commercially. Although Hurst's film is superior to *Love, Honour and Obey* (1999) and *Circus* (2000), it was tarred with the same brush. It certainly falls short of Paul McGuigan's impressive *Gangster No.1* (2000). **IC**

Waris HUSSEIN

A Touch of Love (1969)
Quackser Fortune Has
a Cousin in the Bronx (1970)
Melody (1971)
The Possession of Joel Delaney (1972)
Henry VIII and His Six Wives (1973)
The Sixth Happiness (1997)

For many years Waris Hussein has been referred to as the 'king of the television mini-series', having directed some 49 different productions to date. However, he has also made forays into the feature-film world, although never with the degree of success that he deserves. Born in Lucknow, India, in 1938, Hussein and his family moved to Britain when he was nine, thus beginning the development of the continental split that would mark his work. He attended Cambridge and then began working as a trainee director with the BBC at the age of 21.

His first directorial assignment for the BBC was the opening episode of 'Doctor Who', the world's longest-running science fiction series. A project no one else wanted to touch, as its failure seemed inevitable, Hussein directed a haunting, sinister and mind-blowing story for the family. He progressed to more serious drama, including 'A Passage to India', in 1965. A BBC Play of the Month, it marked Hussein's interest in his homeland and also paved the way for David Lean's version which, according to Hussein, 'borrowed' from his own. In 1969 he directed his first feature. *A Touch of Love* starred Sandy Dennis and Ian McKellen in an adaptation of the book 'The Millstone' by Margaret Drabble. Hussein coaxes good performances from both the method-orientated Dennis and stage actor McKellen to produce a film that is indicative of 1960s middle-class social concerns, focusing on the story of a woman's struggle against an unforgiving society, a theme which would return to Hussein's mini-series work later.

Four subsequent features followed. *Quackser Fortune Has a Cousin in the Bronx* (1970) is a bittersweet romance that centres on the unlikely prospect of Gene Wilder playing a dung collector from a working-class family in Dublin, who is run over by, and falls in love with, American student Margot Kidder. The bizarre romantic comedy streak continued with *Melody* (1971), a film told from a child's point-of-view about two ten-year-olds that fall in love and tell their parents that they wish to marry.

Hussein's next two movies were marked by very different changes of direction. *The Possession of Joel Delaney* (1972) has been compared to *The Exorcist* (1973) as a superior horror film that deals with similar themes. The film (banned in Finland) shows the growing realisation and dread of Shirley MacLaine's character as she realises her brother is possessed by a dead killer. It is worth noting that Hussein again highlights social issues, particularly those dealing with race and drugs, to produce a genre film that has a viewpoint on the contemporary setting in which it is located. By contrast, *Henry VIII and His Six Wives* (1973) is a more traditional historical story. Despite its lavish and accurate costumes and sets, the film fails to become a dynamic piece of cinema, focusing for too long on the deathbed where Henry (Keith Michell) lies for the majority of the time.

Hussein did not direct for the cinema again until 1997, instead concentrating on television mini-series and films. He continued to produce works that dealt with the rich and famous, such as *Edward and Mrs Simpson* (1980) and *Onassis: The Richest Man in the World* (1988), but also worked on true-life extraordinary stories about ordinary people such as *For the Love of My Child: The Anissa Ayala Story* (1993) and *A Child's Wish* (1997). Both tales of triumph-over-adversity in the face of illness, it would be easy to dismiss these films as movie-of-the-week fodder. Hussein is too clever and conscientious a director for this to be the case, however, and often produces compelling and thought-provoking drama that is more suited to the smaller screen.

Hussein returned to the cinema in 1997 with *The Sixth Happiness*. Almost universally praised, the film is the story of Brit, a young Indian born into an anglophile Parsee family who has brittle bone disease and is confined to a wheelchair. Based on the memoirs of Firdaus Kanga, who plays himself as Brit, the story also deals with bisexuality and the middle-class attitudes towards it within the Parsee community. Hussein brings his favourite theme of the minority versus society to the fore and produces a wonderfully touching, funny and poignant film that expands the viewer's horizons and is both entertaining and educational.

Waris Hussein is a director that may not venture into cinema often, yet when he does the results are often surprising and challenging, particularly when these results stem from the drama themselves rather than a disturbance of the form or function of cinematic storytelling. **JR**

Nicholas HYTNER

Born in 1956, Nicholas Hytner studied at Cambridge University and began his theatrical apprenticeship as an assistant producer at the English National Opera. In 1985 he became an associate director of Manchester's Royal Exchange Theatre and, more recently, an associate director at the Royal National Theatre (1990–1997). His critically acclaimed stage productions have ranged from Shakespeare to 'Carousel', which garnered him a 1994 Tony Award. He has also returned to his opera roots, directing 'Don Giovanni' and 'The Marriage of Figaro' across the European circuit. This training has undoubtedly infiltrated his cinematic work; all of Hytner's films fuse a strong visual aesthetic with narrative complexity and powerful ensemble acting.

The Madness of King George (1994)
The Crucible (1996)
The Object of My Affection (1998)
Center Stage (2000)

Hytner's first film, *The Madness of King George* (1994), is an elegant adaptation by Alan Bennett of his own stage success, chronicling the descent of George III into porphyria (a condition that strongly resembled the then-popular concept of madness). The power of Hytner's debut radiates less from history or comedy and more from the performances: Nigel Hawthorne, who obviously sharpened his characterisation of George after playing him for months on the stage, dominates the film; he is ably complemented by a loyal Helen Mirren and Ian Holm's steely doctor. Hytner also captures the inter-necine parliamentary infighting that arose out of the event and imbues his England of 1788 with typically artistic flourishes – sun-dappled meadows and London's grand royal residences. The overall design of the film is sumptuous; aided by Ken Adam's Oscar®-winning set design and George Fenton's clever re-workings of Handel's original music, it achieves a veneer of class and intelligence that typifies the best attempts at theatrical adaptation.

The 1692 Salem Witch Trials are the backdrop for Hytner's next feature, *The Crucible* (1996). Again collaborating with the original playwright, Arthur Miller, Hytner creates a memorably intense version of the classic play, a famous metaphor for the McCarthy witch-hunts of the early 1950s. Where Hytner succeeds is in his careful grasping of the savage ironies inherent in Miller's screenplay and in the generation of passionate performances. Daniel Day-Lewis and Joan Allen as John and Elizabeth Proctor have rarely been better as they slide inexorably to their doom, while Winona Ryder's mature portrayal of revenge hints at a greater emotional range than we have previously seen. Paul Scofield is the real tour de force here, however – a fusion of blind morality and intense ambition that dominates the final-reel exchanges. Again, Hytner's visual concept is stunning; earthy colours, unhurried direction and a cool detachment all help bolster Miller's concept of choosing death over 'life with a bad name'.

After the emotion and raw power of his first two features, Hytner's next film was an abrupt, yet welcome, change of pace. *The Object of My Affection* (1998) is a witty romantic comedy about a heterosexual woman (Jennifer Aniston) who falls in love with a gay man (Paul Rudd). Unlike most mainstream fare, the film tenderly and truthfully dissects the problems and bittersweet anxieties that the subject matter demands. Hytner is true to the spirit and earnestness of Stephen McCauley's source novel and imbues it with a charm that transmits to the acting: Aniston's performance is miles away from that of her lazy 'Friends' persona, and Nigel Hawthorne's acerbic theatre critic doles out the requisite one-liners and truisms that make or break most romantic comedies. With *The Object of My Affection* Hytner proved that he is at ease with crossing genre boundaries, unafraid to try and say something new.

His most recent film, *Center Stage* (2000), is a story about young dancers applying to American ballet school and facing the usual mixture of prejudice, bitchiness, heart-ache and triumph. Despite the rather predictable storyline, the dance sequences are exhilarating; their kineticism outstrips any of the rather tired re-treads of familiar plot strands. Hytner directs a large (mostly unknown) ensemble cast, and captures the daily grind of practice and performance. He also plays with the traditional generic motifs of the dance movie – two young nobodies make it big and someone else sneaks onto an empty stage dreaming of the big time. Hytner's direction is again unhurried, although *Center Stage* sits uneasily alongside Hytner's previous triptych; it is the kind of film that pleases momentarily and then fades after the final credits roll.   **BM**

John IRVIN

Born in 1940, John Irvin served as a documentary cameraman in the Vietnam war, and his directorial career began in television in the 1970s, including such prestigious productions as Granada's 1977 adaptation of Dickens' 'Hard Times' and the BBC adaptation of John Le Carré's 'Tinker, Tailor, Soldier, Spy' in 1980.

Irvin's first four movies were literary adaptations, although from very different sources. *The Dogs of War* (1980), based on Frederick Forsyth's best-seller, fails to successfully transform the structure of the novel, resulting in a number of curtailed movements and episodic stretches. The climactic assault offers welcome release after lengthy procedurals which, although not sufficiently detailed to grip, remain interesting. Despite his trademark tics and mannerisms, Christopher Walken is effective as the mercenary with a heart of gold. Jack Cardiff's cinematography is an advantage; the score is not.

Ghost Story (1981) follows the plot of Peter Straub's novel but, having excised its detail and resonances, fails to replicate its haunting atmosphere. Key scenes are abandoned, losing the organic logic of the original. Laboured 'shock' moments and clichéd flashback sequences further detract from its already modest suspense. The cast, which includes Melvyn Douglas, John Houseman, Douglas Fairbanks Jr., and Fred Astaire, struggles against weak dialogue and unimaginative visuals.

Champions (1983), adapted from jockey Bob Champion's autobiography, recounts the jockey's fight against cancer, driven by the desire not only to survive but also to ride Aldaniti in the Grand National. This potentially intriguing study of a man in adversity is reduced to a rather undignified tear-jerker: on that level it succeeds, courtesy of the conviction of John Hurt's central performance and the strong cast that supports him.

Turtle Diary (1985), adapted by Harold Pinter from Russell Hoban's novel, again takes little more than the plot from its source, but not without good reason. Hoban gives alternating chapters to his protagonists, following the richly patterned and deeply textured free associations of their thoughts and fantasies as they live their quietly desperate lives. Pinter's dialogue – humorous, precise, effective – is in sharp contrast, and his attempts to retain some of the mystery and magic of the tale are undermined by Irvin's unsympathetic and leaden direction. Well-played by another good cast, it is the gentlest of satires on empty middle-class suburban life, and a feeble expression of environmental concerns. Irvin changed tack again with the crude and humourless *Raw Deal* (1986), arguably the weakest and most reactionary of Schwarzenegger's action movies. Very basic in what it offers, it wastes no time delivering the goods, but then bogs them down in half-hearted attempts to intersperse narrative complication between fairly unremarkable set-pieces, culminating in a bloody, disorganised, ludicrous climax. A risible coda follows.

Hamburger Hill (1987), from a screenplay by Vietnam veteran John Carabatsos, follows the 101st Airborne Division as they repeatedly try to take Hill 937 in the Ashau Valley. Intended as a tribute, it makes no mention of the fact that they were ordered to withdraw a few days later, or of the $10,000 bounty US troops put on the head of the colonel who ordered the attacks, and the several attempts made on his life. The movie also suffers from heavy-handed ironies, Philip Glass' intrusive score, and a cast of mostly bland young actors who remain fairly indistinguishable. Bizarrely, despite the film's liberal war-is-hell credentials, it nonetheless perpetuates the myth that it was the Vietnamese, not the Americans, who invaded Vietnam. The revenge-thriller *Next of Kin* (1989) brings Appalachian backwoodsmen into conflict with the Chicago Mafia, lumbering to its predictable climax with unconscionable sloth. Drawn in broad strokes, its attempts to consider the ethics of feuding, revenge, and justice are banal and ultimately meaningless. A good cast and score are poorly served by ponderous direction.

Eminent Domain (1991), a Canadian/Israeli/French co-production shot in Warsaw and Gdansk, is purportedly based on real experiences and events that occurred in Poland before 1979. It tells of Josef Burski (Donald Sutherland), number six in the Politburo hierarchy, who wakes one morning to discover he has been removed from office without any explanation. Opening with an unsubtle depiction of casual corruption and the personal compromises and accommodations made by officials in order to obtain a secure position, it fails to transform into either a Kafkaesque parable or a thriller – it lacks the wit and urgency demanded by the former and the suspense required of the latter. Shot with a palette as murky as the intrigue it depicts, it recalls something of the seediness and boy's-club-gone-wrong atmosphere of 'Tinker, Tailor, Soldier, Spy', but it is not half as gripping.

Widow's Peak (1994) represents another change of direction for Irvin. A period piece set in 1920s Ireland, it veers unevenly from gentle comedy to overblown farce to straight drama. This crisis of confidence, along with the implausible dénouement, leaves the significance of the whole in question. *A Month by the Lake* (1995), based on H.E. Bates' novella, is similarly uncertain as to what it is trying to achieve. Noisy early scenes, in which incident piles on incident, and the frenetic and quirky characterisations, seem at odds with the gentle humour of the tangentially-told period romance. What it lacks in atmosphere and subtlety is compensated for by Pasqualino De Santis' beautiful cinematography. Irvin returned to action cinema with the post-Tarantino thriller *City of Industry* (1997), a minimalist genre movie that could have been stripped down even further. A stylish black and white title sequence gives way to an attractive palette (principally greens and browns), and unfamiliar locations evoke a Los Angeles unique from the typical screen presentation. Once again though, it suffers from an unnecessary coda and an ill-judged score.

Shiner (2001), a rather nasty gangland thriller about an illegal boxing racket, stars Michael Caine and Martin Landau as British and American promoters who are in competition with each other. Highly derivative, it adds nothing new to the genre and features a lazy performance from Caine. *The Fourth Angel* is currently in production.   **MB**

Debbie ISITT

Nasty Neighbours (1999) Debbie Isitt adapted her sole feature to date, *Nasty Neighbours* (1999), from her own successful stage play, which still appears in 'The Guinness Book of Records' for opening in the greatest number of theatres on one single night. The play was praised by critics and enjoyed by audiences, and comparisons with Mike Leigh, inaccurate as they were, quickly followed. The film, however, proved less successful and in most quarters met with harsher criticism. A no-holds-barred examination of the escalating petty squabbles between warring neighbours in middle England, the film – shot on a miniscule budget – attempted to place suburban angst under the microscope. Well served by an experienced cast, not least the estimable Ricky Tomlinson and a typically energetic Phil Daniels, Isitt (who also appears in front of the camera) opts for a televisual documentary approach to create the sense of suffocating claustrophobia. Better suited to the smaller screen, and less sure of itself when the narrative descends into the realms of psychological drama, it is nonetheless a committed and intelligent work that scores a number of telling and authentic observational points about insularity, jealousy and the mundanity of parochial existence. Isitt is currently at work on a film adaptation of her own play, 'The Woman Who Cooked Her Husband'. **JWo**

James IVORY

James Ivory is the undisputed master of contemporary heritage cinema. Despite his all-American origins and his early interest in India and the cultural clash between the East and British culture, Ivory is best known for his literary adaptations of the 1980s and 1990s, which are now regarded as the canonical examples of British costume drama. Sometimes accused of letting the dazzling visuals of setting and costume prevail over the psychological and emotional interplay of characters, Ivory has in fact managed to draw powerful and award-winning performances from his actors (often stage-trained), only enhanced by the immaculate and detailed backdrop of interiors. Although one is led to wonder if Ivory's films would have been the same without long-lasting partners producer Ismail Merchant and screenwriter Ruth Prawer Jhabvala, there is no doubt about the coherence of his oeuvre.

The Householder (1963)
Shakespeare Wallah (1965)
The Guru (1969)
Bombay Talkie (1970)
Savages (1972)
The Wild Party (1975)
Autobiography of a Princess (1975)
Roseland (1977)
The Europeans (1979)
Jane Austen in Manhattan (1980)
Quartet (1981)
Heat and Dust (1982)
The Bostonians (1984)
A Room with a View (1986)
Maurice (1987)
Slaves of New York (1989)
Mr. and Mrs. Bridge (1990)
Howard's End (1992)
The Remains of the Day (1993)
Jefferson in Paris (1995)
Surviving Picasso (1996)
A Soldier's Daughter Never Cries (1998)
The Golden Bowl (2000)

Throughout his productions, from the very beginning of *The Householder* (1963) to the Cannes-promoted *The Golden Bowl* (2000), Ivory has always been a painter of manners and social conventions, portraying individuals forced to choose between clashing cultures, ideologies or classes. His films often have an episodic quality, sometimes overtly following the tableaux structure (as in *A Room with a View* (1986)) and culminating in party or dance sequences. When the interaction between individuals is restrained by the rules of society the conservatism of Ivory's visual style often clashes with the powerful performances of the protagonists, thus exposing the characters' necessity to compromise with social constraints, a sort of rites-of-passage, and the central conflict in almost all his narratives.

Given these haunting themes of self-inflicted exile, sexual repression, and clashing cultures, it is no wonder that American realist Henry James and British novelist E.M. Forster are the main sources Ivory and Jhabvala have used over the past twenty years. The social and cultural discord at play when American and British citizens travel to Continental Europe and discover the unrestrained and passionate way or life of Mediterranean countries, are the core of both writers' work and also of Ivory's films.

Born in Berkeley in 1928 and raised in Kamath Falls, Oregon, Ivory majored in Architecture and Fine Arts at the University of Oregon. He later enrolled at the University of South California, where he graduated in 1957 with an MA in film-making. His master thesis was *Venice: Themes and Variations* (1957), a half-hour documentary shot in Europe, which already displays the extraordinary formalist quality of his later productions. In 1959 he began showing a keen interest in India, with his second documentary, *The Sword and the Flute*. Conceptually similar to *Venice*, this film is entirely focused on Indian miniature paintings in American collections, yet its driving force is the tension between Ivory's role of intellectual observer and his empathetic response to the paintings' exceptional sensuousness and romantic feeling. The success of this film led to a grant by the Asia Society of New York to make *The Delhi Way* (1964) While in India shooting this documentary, Ivory met local producer Ismail Merchant, with whom, in 1961, he founded the Merchant-Ivory Production Company. Their first feature together was *The Householder* (1963), based on an early novel by Ruth Prawer Jhabvala. Jhabvala also agreed to write the screenplay for the film, thus inaugurating a partnership that still lasts today. A satirical comedy entirely shot on location in Delhi, the film is a coming-of-age tale of a young man facing the conflict between tradition and modern life. In 1964

Ivory completed *The Delhi Way*, whose shooting he had interrupted in order to make *The Householder*. Although much less effective than his earlier work, this documentary displays a concern with the passing of time and its effect on cultures, and acts as an effective bridge to *Shakespeare Wallah* (1965), in which time and change are main preoccupations.

Shakespeare Wallah was made with money paid by Columbia for *The Householder*, and is based on the experiences of actress Felicity Kendal's theatrical family, and their efforts to keep the spirit of Shakespeare vivid in post-Independence India, while an Indian cinema is emerging. A humorous film of cultural conflict, it showcases in the company's rootless wandering the great dilemma of Ivory's characters, torn between belonging to a culture and living in another. One of Ivory's best works, *Shakespeare Wallah* was premiered at the Berlin Film Festival and immediately became an international success.

Ivory's third feature, *The Guru* (1969), in a way reverses the theme of the previous film: it portrays a British character travelling to India in search of artistic enlightenment and failing to develop the necessary spiritual qualities. The same structure is present in *Bombay Talkie* (1970), the story of a British artist visiting Bombay hoping for inspiration and discovering the clash between feelings and culture. Shot entirely on location in and around Bombay, the film is at once a psychological drama and a parodic homage to the Indian film scene of the late 1960s and early 1970s. Peculiar in Ivory's career, the feature is really a meta-film – a film about film-making and cinema – in which the viewer is simultaneously involved in what is on-screen and aware of the medium. It also carries forth the classic Ivory themes of cultural misunderstandings that dramatically affect life.

After *Bombay Talkie*, Ivory accepted a commission from BBC Television to shoot a film on Nirad Chaudhuri, a famous Indian polymath. The result was the 1971 television documentary 'Adventures of a Brown Man in Search of Civilisation', where Ivory profiles the 76-year-old scholar while he walks in Oxford and London, professing his love for Western civilisation.

Ivory spent the 1970s going back and forth between America and India. He went to New York to shoot *Savages* (1972), an allegorical tale of people at odds with an unfamiliar environment, inspired by Beechwood, the Colonial Revival mansion, in Scarborough, New York.

He briefly returned to Europe to shoot *Autobiography of a Princess* (1975). Inspired by the research for a documentary on Maharajas, the film tells the story of an Indian princess living in London and the destruction of her nostalgic memories of India, during a tea party to which she has invited her father's former tutor. The film was released after *The Wild Party* (1975), a shrill commercial Hollywood production loosely inspired by a blank-verse narrative poem by Joseph Moncure March about a disastrous Greenwich Village party given by a vaudeville comic. *Roseland* (1977), again based in New York, is chiefly concerned with European exiles dreaming of home in a cavernous and magical New York ballroom. Their three stories, sometimes interconnecting, are centred around the quest to find the perfect dance partner.

In 1977 Ivory was asked by Melvyn Bragg to make a television film for 'The South Bank Show'. The project became almost a detective story, once more about collecting Indian miniatures. *Hullabaloo Over Georgie and Bonnie's Pictures* (1978) was financed by London Weekend Television and proved one of the most difficult collaborations for the Merchant-Ivory-Jhabvala team, with the screenwriter trying to withdraw from the project and shooting beginning before the screenplay was completed. However, upon its release the film received enthusiastic reviews.

The first of Merchant-Ivory's Henry James adaptations, *The Europeans*, was directed by Ivory in 1979. The film depicts the European and American characters reshaping relationships and identities between Puritanism and Continental debauchery, and follows Ivory's own tableaux structure. It displays all the elements that later became hallmarks of Merchant-Ivory costume dramas; the mood-setting use of colours, Ivory's legendary casting instinct (especially as far as actresses are concerned), and the masterful ensemble of interiors and acting.

Ivory's travels between London and America resulted in *Jane Austen in Manhattan* (1980), set in New York and inspired by the sale of a Jane Austen manuscript, the adaptation of which Ivory accepted to direct, only to find out it was just a fragment of a very childish play. However, Jhabvala thought it could be used as the premise for a film in which theatrical groups compete to acquire and produce the Austen play. The film was shot on location with a very tight budget and was closely followed by *Quartet* (1981), an adaptation of the 1928 autobiographical novel by Jean Rhys. The story deals with a love quadrangle between a complicated young West Indian woman, her husband, a manipulative English art patron, and his painter wife. Set in the Golden Age of Paris, with its cafe culture and extravagant night-life, all glitz and intellectualism, the film hints at the sinister core lying underneath the surface, and explores the vast territory between outward refinement and inner darkness. Jhabvala and Ivory's screenplay uses Rhys' novel as a foundation onto which a world is created that is both true to the novel and distinctive in its own right, painting a society that has lost its inhibitions and, inadvertently, its soul.

After completing *Quartet*, Merchant and Ivory returned to India, where they prepared two movies during 1981–82. Ivory directed only the second, *Heat and Dust* (1982), adapted from Jhabvala's Booker Prize-winning novel. The story of two English women living in India more than fifty years apart, *Heat and Dust* cross-cuts between the lives of the women as Anne discovers and repeats the scandal that her independent-minded ancestor caused two generations before.

In 1984 Ivory inaugurated his season of successful literary adaptations with *The Bostonians*, another James novel. The competition of feminist Olive Chancellor (a brilliant Vanessa Redgrave) and a chauvinist lawyer for the affections of a young and passionate speaker is set against the backdrop of Boston's politically active atmosphere – between dinner parties and lectures – and explores the theme already implicit in *The Europeans*. This is the portrait of a nation discovering itself through its arts, ideologies and politics. Two years later, *A Room with a View* (1986) was the first internationally acclaimed Merchant-Ivory production. An outstanding financial success, given its limited budget of $3 million, the film still managed to achieve the lavish and dazzling costumes and sets that won it two of its three Academy Awards (the third went to Jhabvala for her screenplay). The film is a comedy of manners and morals, set in Florence and England, and relies on some career-making performances from Maggie Smith, Daniel Day Lewis and Helena Bonham Carter.

Maurice (1987) was the second instalment of the Merchant-Ivory E.M. Forster trilogy. Following the enormous success of *A Room with a View*, the film manages to capture the struggle of the title character as he asserts his identity in the homophobic atmosphere of Edwardian England. This is yet another variation on the long-lasting Ivory theme of internal conflict shaping the life of individuals. After *Maurice*, Ivory returned to the US for two American films. The first of these was *Slaves of New York* (1989), based on the stories of Tama Janowitz, who also wrote the screenplay for the film. The film was well received in Europe but rather neglected by the American audience, possibly due to the remarkably 'un-American' quality of its cinematography and vision.

The nostalgic *Mr and Mrs Bridge* (1990) followed, which was adapted by Jhabvala from the novels by Evan S. Connell. In a long series of brilliant castings, Ivory called real-life couple Paul Newman and Joanne Woodward to play the title characters, a Midwestern couple struggling with the changing reality around them in 1930s America. An excellent supporting cast manages to create the whirlwind of change around the central pair, while helping to expose the drama hidden behind the inability to communicate one's feelings. The film, shot on location in Kansas City and in Paris, was enthusiastically greeted by both public and critics, and was regarded by some as the best film of the year.

Ivory's next project was *Howards End* (1992), which closes the E. M. Forster cycle with an elegant reworking of his 1910 novel. Again, the film's marvellous looks won the team three Oscars® yet, despite strong and intense performances (especially the award-winning one by Emma Thompson) that make it Merchant-Ivory's greatest financial success, the film lacks much of the conflict and passion present in the book. In comparison, *The Remains of the Day* (1993), reuniting the same central couple of the previous film, is a more quietly intense and dignified period drama. Here the luscious cinematography and the quiet expressiveness of the performances are perfectly balanced in an intelligently and respectfully faithful adaptation of its literary source, Kazuo Ishiguro's

Booker Prize-winning novel. *Jefferson in Paris* was Ivory's next project. Released in 1995, the film narrates the events occurring between 1784 and 1789, when Thomas Jefferson travelled with his elder daughter from Virginia to France as American ambassador. Fundamental years in the history of France on the verge of the Revolution, these also shaped Jefferson's public and personal life. Welcomed by French liberals and intellectuals, which he immediately supported after having experienced the corruption Louis XVI's court, Jefferson became the prototype of the American in Paris, exploring all the artistic and scientific riches that the capital had to offer. The film explores this position and the relationship between American Independence and slavery through Jefferson's relationships with painter Marcia Conway and slave Sally Hemings.

Surviving Picasso (1996) is loosely based on various published accounts, from Picasso's partners, of what life was like at the side of the great artist. The film is the story of Françoise Gilot's literal survival of her relationship (all other women linked to Picasso either went mad or killed themselves); she was the only woman with enough strength of will to leave Picasso. Interestingly, Picasso's estate banned any reproduction of his art in the film.

In 1998 Ivory shot *A Soldier's Daughter Never Cries*, the adapted story of an American family living in Paris in the mid-1960s, and later moving back to North America, told from the point of view of the daughter, Channe. Against the backdrop of their parents' parties, the children experience their own life-making events, narrated in evocative episodes.

Most recently, Ivory returned to Henry James, with the adaptation of *The Golden Bowl* (2000). Replete with Edwardian artefacts, the film's visual splendour never dwarfs the characters; rather, it acts as a constant reminder of what is at stake in the intricate, nuanced love triangle. *The Golden Bowl* manages a depth rarely achieved in the transposition of literary text to screen, capturing Jamesian double meaning. It was acclaimed at Cannes for its richness and performances. **BP**

J

Henry JAGLOM

Born in London in 1941, Henry Jaglom started out as an actor, training with Lee Strasberg at the Actors Studio and performing in off-Broadway theatre. He moved to Hollywood in the late 1960s and was contracted to Columbia Pictures as an actor and featured in a number of films, including Jack Nicholson's *Drive, He Said* (1971) and Dennis Hopper's *The Last Movie* (1971). Jaglom first became involved with film-making working as an editorial consultant on the cult classic *Easy Rider* (1969).

His first film as writer-director, *A Safe Place* (1971), starred Tuesday Weld, Orson Welles and Jack Nicholson. The film is an exploration of the emotions of a young woman (Weld) going through a crisis. Whilst not a commercial success the film was later discovered by Anais Nin who used it in her lecturing as an example of what she called 'the female expression in art'.

Jaglom spent five years getting together $1m to produce his next film, *Tracks* (1976). This film, starring Dennis Hopper and Dean Stockwell, tells the story of an army sergeant returning from Vietnam to accompany a comrade's body home for burial. Whilst crossing America by train he is haunted by hallucinations; the film is about the effect of the Vietnam War on America's psyche and Hopper is outstanding as the tormented sergeant. Jaglom's next film, *Sitting Ducks* (1980), is a comedy road movie which stars Jaglom regulars Michael Emil and Zack Norman as two small-time thieves in a bid to make their childhood dreams come true.

The reasons for Jaglom's involvement with *National Lampoon Goes to the Movies* (1981), co-directed with Bob Giraldi, are unclear. The film goes against the grain of the director's other work. It was badly received by the critics and did not gain theatrical release. However, this was followed by *Can She Bake a Cherry Pie?* (1983), one of Jaglom's more successful films, starring Karen Black and Michael Emil. This is an offbeat romantic comedy with Black as Zee, walking up and down Manhattan streets talking to herself and to the husband who has just left her. At a cafe she bumps into Eli (Emil) and an unlikely, funny and touching relationship develops between the two. Jaglom's next three films all shared the themes of loneliness and the search for love, with Jaglom

A Safe Place (1971)
Tracks (1976)
Sitting Ducks (1980)
National Lampoon Goes to the Movies (1981)
Can She Bake a Cherry Pie? (1983)
Always (1985)
Someone to Love (1987)
New Year's Day (1989)
Eating (1990)
Venice/Venice (1992)
Babyfever (1994)
Last Summer in the Hamptons (1995)
Déjà Vu (1997)

himself playing the main roles. *Always* (1985) is the story of the break-up of a marriage. *Someone To Love* (1987) focuses on people who are alone but looking for someone to love and features Orson Welles in his last performance. *New Year's Day* (1989) is a story about starting over again and moving on in life. *Eating* (1990) starred Mary Crosby in a drama about women and eating. The film has three central female characters who throw a joint birthday party and explores the relationship between women and food as the party progresses and not one of the dozens of women there will take a bite of the birthday cake. In *Venice/Venice* (1992) – half filmed in Venice, California and half filmed in Venice, Italy – Jaglom is Dean, a maverick American film director whose most recent film has been chosen as the official US entry at the Venice Film Festival; the film is about the effect of movies on our romantic dreams.

A drama about balancing a career and children and the ticking of the biological clock, *Babyfever* (1994) was the first Jaglom film to feature Victoria Foyt (now Jaglom's wife). Foyt was critically acclaimed for her role in this film where, attending a baby shower, she meets a diverse group of women in their thirties and forties who share their mixed feelings about having a baby in today's world. *Last Summer in the Hamptons* (1995) stars Foyt and Viveca Lindfors. The story focuses on Oona (Foyt), a successful Hollywood actress who goes to a large country house in the Hamptons, which the owner Helena (Lindfors), a stage actress and ex-movie star, has put up for sale. Helena's extended, talented, theatrical family are all present and have mounted (as is the tradition) a play for a single performance with limited invitations. Oona's unexpected visit wreaks havoc on the group of family and friends. *Déjà Vu* (1997), which Jaglom first wrote as a short story in 1974, is a romantic movie about finding the perfect 'soul mate', starring Victoria Foyt and Stephen Dillane. Foyt and Dillane play two very different people from diverse backgrounds who, against time, location, and previous commitments, find themselves drawn inextricably to one another. This film is more accessible than previous Jaglom works and marking a move away from loose structure to a more straightforward narrative. Jaglom is currently working on *Festival in Cannes* starring Anouk Aimée, Greta Scacchi and Maximilian Schell. Filmed in May 2000, the film will explore the mad world of the international movie business.

Many of Jaglom's films tell women's stories from a female viewpoint. Jaglom feels strongly that women are not represented on screen as movies are still made largely by and for men; hence films about so-called 'women's issues' such as eating and the ticking of the biological clock. Jaglom has been criticised as being self-indulgent and narcissistic yet he is one of the only true mavericks of American cinema, producing his films independently, writing the scripts, often editing the films, and acting in them as well as directing. Jaglom can also be described as an auteur whose films reflect personal concerns and individual issues often overlooked by Hollywood.   **PR**

Derek JARMAN

Sebastiane (1976)
Jubilee (1978)
The Tempest (1979)
The Angelic Conversation (1985)
Caravaggio (1986)
The Last of England (1987)
War Requiem (1989)
The Garden (1990)
Edward II (1991)
Wittgenstein (1993)
Blue (1993)
Glitterbug (1994)

Born in London in 1942, Derek Jarman attended Kings College and the Slade School of Art, where he studied painting. His art studies can be traced through to his later aesthetic, but more immediately affected his career in film when, after a background in theatre design, he became art director on Ken Russell's *The Devils* (1971) and *Savage Messiah* (1972).

As a director Jarman produced films that are personal, political and painterly. Despite the frequent labelling of his work as 'avant garde' or 'art house', and his themes and politics as 'radical', he always considered himself to be a traditionalist. Yet the label of controversialist would be one that followed him until his death in 1994. He was misunderstood, he felt, because he worked within a much older tradition than that espoused and understood by the 'establishment' of his time. His films deal with notions of private, public and cultural identity, and history. More specifically, they often focus on a revisioning of history that establishes a gay lineage across artistic and geographic boundaries. His intensely personal cinema continually demonstrates his belief that 'art is the spark between private lives and the public'.

Jarman's first feature, *Sebastiane* (1976), shot in Sardinia for £30,000, demonstrates many of his outlined concerns. It examines the legend of St Sebastian, but from a much more intimate perspective. Retold, the story focuses on Sebastian's denial of his love for his commanding officer Severus. Gay relationships are the norm on this military outpost and establish Sebastian as that familiar figure in Jarman's films, the outsider and exile. His denial conflicts with the film's overall aesthetic, which is full of homo-erotic imagery. *Sebastiane* was generally well received by critics. Predictably, however, much of the attention focused on the fact that it was the first British feature film to show an erect penis, serving to create Jarman's reputation as the enfant terrible of British cinema.

His next film, *Jubilee* (1978), had the distinction of a parliamentary mention. The categorisation of the film as a 'video nasty' and the general conception of the film as a 'beacon of the punk movement', however, miss the point. The film depicts Elizabeth I and her court astrologer, John Dee, as they travel forward in time to contemporary England. Made in the wake of Queen Elizabeth II's Silver Jubilee, it is a dystopic imagining of (then) contemporary England. This bleak vision shows a country in decline; even Hitler can feel safe living out his retirement in Dorset. Rather than celebrating this decline, the film elaborates on Jarman's concerns about the death of a pre-modern England. The punks in the film are both the victims of this situation and its logical conclusion; it is because they are cut off from art and history that the problems are caused. In his autobiography, 'Dancing Ledge', the director later came to see *Jubilee* as prophetic: 'Dr Dee's vision came true – the streets burned in Brixton and Toxteth, Adam [Ant] was on Top of the Pops and signed up with Margaret Thatcher to sing at the Falklands Ball'.

Often working with Super-8mm and 16mm film, Jarman made a series of shorts throughout the late 1970s that became the film, *In the Shadow of the Sun* (1981). Set to an industrial soundtrack, with an image that is often slowed and manipulated, it demonstrates his early experimentation with techniques which featured more and more in his later work.

The Tempest (1979) is the first of a number of Jarman's films that take high art, and specifically Shakespeare, as their starting point. Both witty and irreverent, it is perhaps best remembered for its chorus of sailors dancing a hornpipe to 'Stormy Weather' as sung by the magnificent Elizabeth Welch. The contemporary allusions are central to this reinterpretation of the play, as is the foregrounding of the relationship between Ariel and Prospero. Themes of banishment, imprisonment and enslavement are also central to the narrative. Shakespeare also forms the basis of Jarman's favourite piece of work, *The Angelic Conversation* (1985). Based around the playwright's sonnets, it illustrates the director's growing unease with conventional filmic narratives. It has a slow-moving, dream-like quality that runs throughout its many layers; the love story, again re-imagined between two men, is perfectly captured by this aesthetic. Sound and image are continually contrasted, held together by the soothing quality of Judi Dench's voice as she reads the poems.

After a decade of planning and trying to raise funds, Jarman finally released *Caravaggio* in 1986. Considering the fact that it is a skillfully realised tale of art, power and sexuality, and the interconnections between them, the reaction to the film was rather low-key. It details the doomed, triangular relationship between the artist and two of his models, Lena and Ranuccio. Beautifully shot and lit, the film again veers away from a more traditional narrative format. The emphasis on the image and Jarman's introduction of modern elements into a historical format – such as a motorbike and typewriter – has a slightly unsettling effect. This interplay of modernity and history is also incorporated into *The Last of England* (1987). Once again, a dystopic future-present is contrasted with a glorious past. Jarman intermingles home movies of his childhood in India with black and white shots of urban decay. Ironic juxtaposition highlights the nightmare vision of things to come. Super-8, a medium that Jarman regarded as documentary, forms a visual link to the home movies and brings a realist style to the portrayal of the present, however unrecognisable or fantastical the events might be. Purposely fractured and disjointed, the film completely eschews any nod to narrative normality and the construction of events is left entirely to the viewer.

The film sparked public debate. Writing for *The Sunday Times*, the historian Professor Norman Stone labelled Jarman's depiction of England as 'sick'. In his response, published by *The Times*, Jarman aligned himself with a high art tradition and cited the cultural influences on his films. He strongly disagreed with Stone's vision of Britain, claiming it was one of 'hollyhocks and beefeaters', asserting that his film accurately reflected the realities of Thatcherite Britain. It was during this time that Jarman announced publicly that he had been diagnosed as HIV positive. The soundtrack of *War Requiem* (1989), Jarman's next feature, is comprised of the reading of Wilfred Owen's anti-war poems, set to Benjamin Britten's 'War Requiem'. It is a moving piece of work that speaks volumes about the personal and public tragedies caused by war, and has also been read as a metaphor for the ravages of AIDS. Jarman followed with *The Garden* (1990), incorporating his battle with illness and his anger with establishment attitudes towards homosexuality and HIV into his work. The narrative is all but non-existent; he focuses instead on striking and highly stylised visual imagery. The beauty of many of his shots of nature and of his own garden at Dungeness hint at a Romantic concern, and help to make the point, even more fiercely, that Britain is a garden neglected.

The intertwining of his work with his opposition to Thatcherism, and specifically to Clause 28, is even more apparent in *Edward II* (1991). The film mixes contemporary politics with history and features an OutRage! demonstration. The refusal of historical specificity makes the point that homophobia is a problem now as it was then. A flawed yet challenging version of Marlowe's play, it was criticised on its release for its misogynistic portrayal of women via the vampiric character of Queen Isabella (Tilda Swinton). Throughout, Edward's relationship with Gaveston is contrasted with his relationship with his queen. While Gaveston and Edward are shot in a golden light, or dancing under the slowly turning reflections of a disco mirrorball, Edward and Isabella's scenes together are noticeable for the coldness of the mise-en-scène. The ending, which sees the prince dancing in high heels and earrings on top of the cage that holds his mother, points to a different future.

Jarman followed with another biopic, *Wittgenstein* (1993). A witty account of the life of the great philosopher, it never loses the depth and weight of the existential angst of its protagonist. The film is a studio-based production that chooses to use props, costumes, lighting and sound effects to evoke different settings. As such, it does at times look rather 'stagy' and theatrical. This is offset though by the script, written by Jarman and Terry Eagleton, which sparkles. Jarman's illness provided the backdrop to his next film, *Blue* (1993), his most striking and experimental film. The visual track features a single, unchanging blue screen. This is overlaid with a soundtrack that is a tide of voices, including Jarman's own; he talks about his illness, his diminishing eyesight, life and death through a consideration of 'blue'. The character 'blue' in the film is many things: the disease, death, a person and a sensation. Jarman's final film, *Glitterbug* (1994), is a posthumous work assembled by his friends – a series of moments from Jarman's home videos. It is a tender and fitting final credit for this champion of 'personal', independent cinema.

Jarman believed that his success as a film-maker was not in the amount of box-office success his films garnered but in the fact he always maintained a free rein over his work. His films demonstrate a keen concern with notions of Englishness, and hark back to a conception of the past that was out of step with the *Chariots of Fire* (1981) nostalgia encouraged in Thatcherite Britain. Cast as the radical, both politically and aesthetically, in actuality Jarman was an arch traditionalist, who arguably had more in common with visionaries such as William Blake than he did with his contemporaries. He has left an enormous legacy as a film-maker, painter, author and campaigner.   **SL & HR**

Vadim JEAN

Co-directed by Vadim Jean (born in 1966) and Gary Sinyor, *Leon the Pig Farmer* (1992) is the kind of delightful fish-out-of-water comedy that referenced the whimsy of the Ealing Comedies and the acerbic wit of Mike Leigh. When a successful Jewish estate agent discovers that his biological father is a Yorkshire pig farmer he goes in search of his roots, encountering all the usual repertoire of skeletons in the closet. Full of wit and pace, the direction focuses on the personal as well as the humorous, and in amongst some rather predictable clash-of-culture and crude racial stereotyping is a film full of warmth. It was rewarded with the International Critic's Prize at the Venice Film Festival and the Best First Feature at the Edinburgh Film Festival. Worthy of note was the directors' pioneering of a deferred-payment scheme to facilitate the film's funding long before the handouts from the erratic Lottery Commission. It came as something of a shock that Jean's follow-up, *Beyond Bedlam* (1993), was part gothic horror and part police procedural. Although this eclecticism is a common strand of Jean's career it has led to charges of uncertain tone and a rehashing of traditional generic codes – both are evident in this film. When a policeman (Craig Fairbrass) enlists a doctor (Elizabeth Hurley) to use her mind-altering drugs on him to unlock secrets in a killer's mind, the film veers into Grand Guignol territory. Like all of his films, *Beyond Bedlam* is skilfully edited and artfully constructed, but features too much style over substance.

Clockwork Mice (1995) is similarly let down by a lack of focus. Ian Hart stars as the idealistic teacher whose attempts to encourage a young boy in cross-country running are met with the requisite suspicion and subsequent tribulation. The structure is episodic and the film falters accordingly. The audience is subjected to an unconvincing mix of fantasy and reality rather than fluid narrative and character development. Although Hart and Rúiadhrí Conroy (as the boy) have powerful screen presence, the wit and tenderness of *Leon the Pig Farmer* is replaced by engineered emotions.

The Real Howard Spitz (1998) returns to the idiosyncrasy of Jean's debut, and also manages to pull off the remarkable coup of eliciting a charming performance from arch-misanthrope Kelsey Grammer. As a failed pulp novelist, his life is changed when he begins penning the 'Crafty Cow' series. The crime-fighting cow becomes a knowing excuse for Jean to indulge in some cunning noir pastiche – swooping cameras and expressionistic shadows – and by focusing on the oddball denizens of Los Angeles, Jean fashions an unconventional, yet wholly believable, paean to quirkiness.

One More Kiss (1999) is a misjudged attempt to humanise the devastating effects of cancer on the individual and the wider community. Jean reels out the usual motifs – walks by the beach, kite flying, embittered bitchiness and blithe spirit – but fails to adequately consider the implications of loss and pain. Sarah (Valerie Edmond) returns home from New York with the intention of spending some time with an old, now married, boyfriend before she dies of inoperable cancer. Obviously her request upsets the marital dynamic. Stilted and too restrained, the film does have moments that transcend the 'terminal disease' genre and manage to plumb the situation's emotional complications.

Jean's next film is a Robert Burns biopic starring Johnny Depp. **BM**

Roland JOFFÉ

Born in London in 1945, Roland Joffé is probably best revealed by the portrait Spalding Gray draws of him in Jonathan Demme's *Swimming to Cambodia* (1987). Gray first met Joffé during casting for *The Killing Fields* (1984) and his vision of Joffé is that of someone possessed: he mesmerises Gray with the story of Cambodia under the Khmer Rouge and of a simple, sustaining friendship between a *New York Times* reporter and his Cambodian translator. Gray plays the perfect foil to the visionary Joffé. In his portrait of a man obsessed with telling the big, important story, Gray reveals both Joffé's strength and his weakness. Joffé is a director with a great vision – his movies are grand and lush; however, his single-minded decision to make a big point impoverishes his characters and the stories that might have emerged from their interactions.

The Killing Fields, Joffé's first feature, displays the director's great skill in building a vast and convincing historical backdrop from meticulous attention to physical detail. *New York Times* reporter Sydney Schanberg (Sam Waterson) discovers that the US has begun a secret bombing campaign in Cambodia, a fact that Joffé links to the subsequent destabilisation of the Cambodian government and the ascendancy of the Khmer Rouge, who were later to carry out one of the most horrible mass killings in human history.

Against these events, Joffé tells the story of Schanberg and his translator Dith Pran (Haing S. Ngor). Schanberg is able to get Pran's family out of the country, but fails to help Pran himself. Considering the rest of the film, its ending is curiously and strangely 'Hollywood'. The message seems to be that love and forgiveness can conquer all; in fact it is more that a good Hollywood ending can efface – or seem to efface – all real complexity. Joffé's next feature, *The Mission* (1986), continues his theme of the evils of imperialism. Spaniards and Portuguese colonists are fighting for possession of a portion of Brazil, waging war against the indigenous tribes, killing and enslaving them in their quest to establish a profitable beach-head in the new world. The tribes' only options are to withdraw further into the jungle, or suffer under profligate conquerors. The sole defenders of the tribe are a group of Jesuit missionaries who enter the jungle with the aim of converting the natives to Christianity. They succeed beyond the realm of cinematic skepticism, establishing a mission that embodies a Socialist visionary's version of Utopia: a completely rational, environmentally sound, loving community devoted to service and the arts. When the mission is destroyed for economic reasons, natives and Jesuits alike are massacred, and the cause of commerce is brutally sustained. Resistance is attempted by a colonist-turned-Jesuit (played by Robert De Niro), who answers with force.

Fat Man and Little Boy (1989) sustains the theme of imperialism, this time focusing not on the application of force but its invention; the characters of the title are not people, but bombs. Specifically, they refer to the nuclear warheads that the US dropped on Hiroshima and Nagasaki in 1945 to end the war in the Pacific. The film is not about Japan, but about the process of making the bombs themselves; it tells the story of the events in Los Alamos that led to the creation of the bomb. The film, as it progresses, has the quality of watching a coal lump transforming into a diamond, with the proviso that the raw materials are pulverised in the process and have little part in the final creation. By portraying the process in slow motion, Joffé illustrates the price to humanity that even the winners must pay to sustain power.

Since Fat Man and Little Boy, Joffé's output has continued to address his signature themes but has been even less subtle – and less well received. The mawkish City of Joy (1992) saw Patrick Swayze as an American doctor who travels in India to find himself, and Joffé's past three outings have been equally disappointing: The Scarlet Letter (1995), starring the perennial exhibitionist Demi Moore as Hester Prynne in a loose adaptation of Nathaniel Hawthorne's novel; Goodbye Lover (1999), a much-maligned detective thriller with Ellen DeGeneres, Patricia Arquette and Don Johnson; and Vatel (2000), starring Gérard Depardieu and Uma Thurman. Vatel tells the story of a chef-entertainer-opportunist in the court of Louis XIV. Made with French money but recorded in English, Vatel was universally booed when it opened Cannes in 2000 and has cast Gaumont, the producing studio, into serious financial trouble.

In the past year, Joffé has been working on a series for MTV and is in the development stage of a science fiction thriller currently titled Animal, about a geneticist and his test subject. As regrettable as his many early excesses were, it is difficult not to hope that Joffé will rediscover his early vision and take up his rightful place in contemporary cinema: the thinking person's Oliver Stone.   **JA**

Niall JOHNSON

With The Big Swap (1998), Niall Johnson attempted to sire that rarest of beasts – a mature, intelligent, British sex drama. While the film is highly commendable for the obvious care and commitment evinced by both cast and crew, it is a pity that what might have been a provocative examination of the alternatives to marriage and monogamy resorts to pat moralising by its conclusion. It hinges on a sexual 'what if' concept wherein five thirty-something couples decide to swap partners during a drunken get-together. Over the ensuing eight weeks, cracks appear in the group dynamic, highlighting a variety of tensions and secrets amongst the friends. The film works effectively in exposing the manner in which unfettered sexuality shatters a middle-class idyll but is limited in its view of sexuality as liberating. Indeed, the sexual swap exposes largely negative characteristics hitherto shielded from friends and partners. The jealousies of Hal, Ellen's eventual affair with a past lover and Julian's embracing of the 'swingers' lifestyle are shown to be wholly destructive. The film does demonstrate a rare optimism in Fi's exploration of her lesbianism, a situation that nevertheless destroys her marriage.

Sequences in which the friends sit around talking about sex (complete with an intrusive, circling camera presumably designed to lend an energy to the claustrophobic interiors in which the film chiefly unfolds) seem contrived and serve to define the characters almost exclusively in terms of their sexual lifestyles. Indeed, the film has barely begun before the narrative gambit is introduced and the characters' back-stories are clumsily pasted on as the film progresses. However, when the group members are actually shown in flagrante, there is a stark, awkward realism to the sex scenes, a refreshing change from the standard, airbrushed conventions in such scenes – nudity is equally dispersed amongst the male and female cast. The exuberance of early sequences is balanced by the concluding passages, in which the group has almost wholly fragmented. Imbued with an air of cloyingly conservative nostalgia, the film holds out for a hopeful future but laments that things will never quite be the same again. Johnson also wrote and produced *The Big Swap*.

In 2000 he directed *The Ghost of Greville Lodge*, a family film based on Nicholas Wilde's novel, 'Down Came a Blackbird'. A ghost story set in the modern day about the adventures of a little boy, its subject matter was entirely different from that of his first film, its tone similar to that of 'The Secret Garden' or 'Tom's Midnight Garden'. Little seen, there is nothing out of the ordinary about the film. **NJ**

Genevieve JOLLIFFE

Raised on the Isle of Wight, Genevieve Jolliffe began working in film-making at an early *Urban Ghost Story* (1998) age. She formed Living Spirit Pictures with Chris Jones and produced their first two features, *The Runner* (1992) and *White Angel* (1993). *The Runner* earned her a place in 'The Guinness Book of Records' as the Youngest British Feature Film Producer at the age of twenty. She made her directorial debut with their third feature, *Urban Ghost Story* (1998).

Urban Ghost Story focuses on 12-year-old Lizzie (Heather Ann Foster) who survives a drug-fuelled car crash (after three minutes of expiration) that leaves her best friend dead. Some months later, her home in a bleak, Glasgow high-rise suddenly becomes the centre of an unexpected wave of paranormal activity.

Shot for a total of £250,000, the film looks rough around the edges, which enhances Jolliffe's attempts to portray a gritty reality, effectively creating a scary atmosphere without using hi-tech graphics. She dispenses with the flying objects and levitating bodies that are typical of poltergeist films and successfully disturbs her audience with some clever editing. By never revealing the cause of the terror Jolliffe slowly increases the anxiety in the film; the camera focuses heavily on a guilt-ridden Lizzie, conveying the emotional turmoil that has engulfed her. Despite much human activity – journalists, mediums and ghost busters – it feels as if the family are completely alone in their nightmare.

Jolliffe plans to work on the third edition of the highly acclaimed 'The Guerilla Film Makers Handbook' and has no immediate directorial projects planned. **SCh**

Chris JONES

Born and raised in the North of England, Chris Jones started his film-making career in *White Angel* (1993) his teens and produced a multitude of Super 8 horror movies. He met fellow film-maker Geneviève Jolliffe at Bournemouth Film School and the two wrote the highly acclaimed 'The Guerilla Film Makers Handbook'. Together they formed Living Spirit Pictures Ltd and Jones directed their first two features.

The Runner (1992), an action thriller set on a remote Canadian Island, premiered at the British Academy of Film and Television Arts theatre. It was successfully marketed and distributed throughout the world by EGM Film International. Jones' next feature, *White Angel* (1993), a tense psychological thriller, was his first to gain a theatrical release. The narrative focuses on Ellen Carter (Harriet Robinson), a successful crime-writer who rents a room to Leslie Steckler (Peter Firth), a mild-mannered dentist. It is soon revealed that Carter murdered her husband three years previously and that Steckler is the local serial killer. On discovering the husband's body bricked-up behind the fireplace, Steckler blackmails Carter into writing his biography, and thus ensues a game of wits.

Offering a very British take on a serial-killer thriller, every aspect of Jones' film is restrained – from the budget to the acting. Reworking old British crime thrillers, there is little gore and scenes develop slowly. The sets are dimly lit, the camera angles tight and the action takes place in a confined space; these three elements work together to create and sustain a claustrophobic tension. Typically, the plot is full of twists, and Jones makes the scenarios even more gritty and chilling by using videotaped footage, a device employed in *Peeping Tom* (1960) and *Henry, Portrait of a Serial Killer* (1986) to similar effect. Steckler confides in the audience, filming himself with his video camera to put across his side of the story by: 'The real problem is the blood. Such a lot of it. Made a terrible mess of my car'. There is nothing extraordinary about Steckler – he could be the man next door. Coupled with Firth's restrained performance, this detail adds a sense of grim reality to the film.

Jones and Geneviève Jolliffe co-wrote *Urban Ghost Story*, which was released in 2001, and directed by Jolliffe. Jones' future project, *Rocketman and Vampire Girl*, is a love story set on a remote Scottish island. There are also plans for a third edition of 'The Guerilla Film Makers Handbook'. **SCh**

Kirk JONES

Waking Ned (1998) Born in the UK in 1964, Kirk Jones established a reputation – and a Silver Lion at Cannes – directing television commercials before embarking on his sole feature to date. Set in the village of Tullymore (population 52), *Waking Ned* (1998) presents a vision of rural Ireland (actually shot on the Isle of Man) heavy on whimsy and laced with picturesque landscapes designed to attract transatlantic viewers with romantic notions of the Emerald Isle. That said, the film is not as saccharine as it might have been and there is a strain of black humour that provides a welcome relief. After discovering the title character expired from shock after a huge lottery win, elderly residents Jackie (Ian Bannen) and Michael (David Kelly) devise a plan to impersonate their dead friend, claim the money and divide it equally between the villagers. Ignoring the potential theme of greed and its effect upon a small community, the film opts to play as a gentle comedy, complete with a couple of diversionary subplots. These narrative distractions – a romance involving Maggie (Susan Lynch) and Pig Finn (James Nesbitt); the relationship between Father Patrick (Dermot Kerrigan) and Maggie's son, Maurice (Robert Hickey) – help to pad out the running time and in one instance provide a neat resolution at the film's climax. Despite the inclusion of humorous interludes involving naked old men on motorbikes, the film never descends into knockabout farce and instead underplays its comic hand. Indeed, it is the nuanced performances (particularly of Bannen and Kelly) that counteract the film's formulaic tendencies. **NJ**

Terry JONES

Monty Python and the Holy A gifted comedian, writer, actor, director and notable academic, Terry Jones also hap-
Grail (1975) pens to be a member of the most successful and widely revered comedy team of all
Monty Python's Life of Brian time – Monty Python – and, like many of his fellow ex-Pythons, has found it difficult to
(1979) escape the overbearing shadow of the famous Flying Circus. Having chosen to continue
Monty Python's The Meaning of his film directing career, often with similarly themed material and starring collaborators
Life (1983) from his Python past, Jones has struggled to emulate the success of the earlier ensemble
Personal Services (1987) films. Less satisfying than his Python work, Jones' later work has continued to display his
Erik the Viking (1989) quintessentially English sense of comedy, in which absurdity is never far from the ordered
The Wind in the Willows surface, a fascination with historical and literary settings and the conflicting realms of
(1996) reality and fantasy, and, most of all, a dedication to the very serious art of being silly.

Born in Colwyn Bay, Wales, in 1942, and having graduated in English from Oxford, Jones found an outlet for his burgeoning comic writing talent working on groundbreaking BBC comedy series of the late 1960s, including 'The Frost Report', 'Do Not Adjust Your Set', and the Marty Feldman showcase, 'Marty'. Monty Python was formed during this period from a coalition of writers and actors all working on similar shows for the BBC, most of whom had appeared in the smash success of the 'Beyond the Fringe' stageshow in London and New York while still at Cambridge a few years before. Instrumental in the new wave of absurdist British comedy shows following in the wake of 'The Goons' and Spike Milligan's 'Q' series, and inspired by an unprecedented culture of opportunity, the Monty Python rise was meteoric. A sketch-show format delivered in stream-of-consciousness style, deliberately making little sense, anarchic, chaotic and ridiculous in tone, 'Monty Python's Flying Circus' (1969) and 'And Now For Something Completely

Different' (1971) created a whole new world of alternative comedy peopled by absurd characters and surreal situations. It was delivered like a shot in the arm to the establishment of a post-war British society still riven by class barriers and social differences. A key performer and writer in conjunction with writing partner Michael Palin, Jones also oversaw the editing which, along with the animations of Terry Gilliam, gave the programme its distinctive narrative style. Both Gilliam and Jones were instrumental in encouraging the group to translate the success of the television show onto larger and more ambitious canvases.

The trilogy of Python films essentially use the same sketch format as the television shows, a broad collaborative mix of visual gags, puns, skits and the requisite silly walks. They are linked by a much stronger sense of shared narrative, however, and a surprisingly serious dedication to accurate depiction of their historical settings. *Monty Python and the Holy Grail* (1975), co-directed by Gilliam and Jones, lampoons both Grail and Arthurian legend with wanton glee, intercutting its stories of a questing and hapless King Arthur and his troupe of horseless knights with a typically absurd, present-day police chase. Spotted with mythological and historical reference points and filmed in a grainy, blood-and-mud, warts-and-all style, with deliberate echoes of Bergman's *The Seventh Seal* (1957), the film's mock-seriousness cuts brilliantly against its ludicrously incongruous comic situations and characters. *Monty Python's Life of Brian* (1979) pulls almost the same trick, but here relocates the action to pre-Christian Jerusalem (thanks to many of the sets left over from Zeffirelli's *Jesus of Nazareth* in Tunisia two years before) and the story of young Brian Cohen's mistakenly Messianic identity. The comic situations all hit the mark, from squabbling anti-Roman coalitions who cannot decide on their name, to unfortunately named Roman generals and crucifixion production lines. The film's startling visual sense of the period, particularly demonstrated in the desert scenes and the crucifixions at Golgotha, provide a much-needed realistic setting. Much lambasted at the time of release, denounced by the Festival of Light as heretical, and still banned in some places, the film makes serious points about religious fanaticism and the vicissitudes of fate and human nature – ironically a modern parable in the Biblical tradition.

Monty Python's The Meaning of Life (1983) is less successful. A sprawling, hit-and-miss patchwork of the cradle to the grave, it is obsessed with sex, death, and bodily functions, from big musical numbers about the sanctity of sperm to live organ theft to the exploding greed of Mr Creosote (played by Terry Jones). Closer to the television sketch format than the other films, and much darker in tone, the film lacks the narrative drive and comic glee of the previous big-screen outings.

The collaborative impetus of Python having waned, Jones' first solo film was a marked change in tone. *Personal Services* (1987), despite the disclaimer at the beginning, is very obviously influenced by the real-life story of Cynthia Payne, the famous madam whose house serviced late 1960s London. The story of a young working-class woman, played by Julie Walters, seduced from a life of mundanity into a secret world of forbidden sexuality, the film contrasts kitchen-sink settings with a rather Pythonesque desire to expose the strange and disturbing forces at work beneath the civilised crust of English society.

Erik the Viking (1989), his next, is a different kind of fantasy fulfilment, adapted by Jones' own Norse saga children's book, a scholarly sideline further explored in his well-regarded academic book on Chaucer's 'The Knight's Tale', and perhaps inspired by the success of *Labyrinth* (1986), which Jones co-scripted. The film marks a return to the medieval world of *Holy Grail*, features several Python regulars, and is shaped by a similar quest narrative in which Erik must search for the Horn Resounding to avert the apocalyptic onset of Ragnarok. It displays the same visual style and childlike delight in the possibilities of fantastic film-making, with plenty of convincing production design and period gags revolving around Erik's viking ineptitude. Caught awkwardly somewhere between child fantasy and adult spoof, however, it lacks the sheer strength of material of the best comic fantasies and the visual extravagance of Terry Gilliam's fantasy films such as *Time Bandits* (1981) and *Brazil* (1985). *Wind in the Willows* (1996) feels similarly uncertain, exchanging the gentle charm of the original story for a spectacular modern update, replete with fascist weasels, unscrupulous developers, and a much darker tone than the source book. Directed in a cartoonish, overblown style, exemplified by Toad's bone-jarring car crashes and the nightmarish phantasmagoria of the dog food factory set up in Toad Hall, the film is too dark to really appeal to its intended audience and too over-the-top to convince adult viewers. It nevertheless provides a wealth of detail for fans of verbal wit and visual grotesque – Python-style – and students of Jones' view of very English eccentricities.

Terry Jones, unlike Terry Gilliam, for whom the comedy has always been secondary to the visual spectacle, has never quite stepped into his own light as a film-maker post-Python. This is partly as a result of the general inability of both public and industry to forget his former identity, and partly because of his own reluctance to transcend it. The prospect of *The Chemical Wedding*, a collaboration with ex-Iron Maiden frontman-turned-novelist, Bruce Dickinson, seems unlikely to break the Monty Python mould, but Jones' place in the annals of British comedy has long since been secure.   **OB**

Neil JORDAN

Angel (1982)
The Company of Wolves (1984)
Mona Lisa (1986)
High Spirits (1988)
We're No Angels (1989)
The Miracle (1991)
The Crying Game (1992)
Interview with the Vampire (1994)
Michael Collins (1996)
The Butcher Boy (1997)
In Dreams (1998)
The End of the Affair (1999)

Neil Jordan's status as a film-maker might best be summarised as enigmatic. He has worked across independent and mainstream markets in both Europe and America, and it is in the former that he has produced his most successful work. While his œuvre does not display any consistent worldview, his films reveal an affinity with literature and literary sources, and he has returned more than once to issues of Irish social and political history. This is not to suggest, however, that Jordan's films lack any pronounced formal aspect. On the contrary, his work has often demonstrated considerable structural and compositional scope.

Born in County Sligo, Ireland, in 1950, but raised in Dublin, Jordan was educated at University College Dublin where he studied Irish History and English. Following a short and critically successful career as a fiction writer, his crossover into movies came as a 'creative associate' on John Boorman's *Excalibur* (1981); he also made a documentary about the film.

Having scripted Joe Comerford's British thriller *Traveller* (1981), he debuted as a feature director the next year with *Angel* (1982), a bleak and violent revenge thriller set in contemporary Northern Ireland. Witnessing a double sectarian killing, a saxophonist played by Stephen Rea – in his first of many collaborations with Jordan – resolutely pursues the killers across Armagh. At the time, Jordan described himself as 'literary sophisticate and a cinematic innocent'. While some critics might have anticipated the resourcefulness of his screenplay, and the film's emphasis on naturalistic mise-en-scène, through its perceived nods towards Buñuelian surrealism, *Angel* was also acclaimed for its formal schemata, winning the director the London *Evening Standard*'s Most Promising Newcomer award.

By most critical accounts, Jordan consolidated his potential with *The Company of Wolves* (1984), the first of many projects with producer Stephen Woolley. Co-scripted with the original story's author, Angela Carter, and shot on a small budget, *The Company of Wolves* is a surreal, expressionistic revision of the Red Riding Hood myth. The film eschews narrative cohesion in favour of a certain dream logic in which classical realism is displaced and ideas of the fantastic – where wolves morph into human form and vice-versa – abound. Given such iconography, and its propensity towards temporal and spatial blurring, the film has often been read as highly symbolic of suppressed, primordial, feminine sexuality and the duality of danger and seduction in the beast/man.

Co-produced by George Harrison's HandMade Films, Jordan's next film, *Mona Lisa* (1986), garnered both critical and commercial success. Ostensibly a noir love story set in a dehumanising contemporary London, *Mona Lisa* casts Bob Hoskins as an artless, ex-petty hood who, following his release from a lengthy prison term, is hired by former boss Michael Caine to chauffeur chic prostitute Cathy Tyson between jobs. Their relationship gives rise to predictable antagonism before the mismatched couple become mutually dependent: Tyson helps Hoskins to re-adjust to the modern world while he agrees to track down her vulnerable teenage friend who continues to work the streets of Kings Cross. Featuring outstanding performances – Hoskins won the Best Actor award at Cannes for his role – and an unsentimental treatment of its subject matter, *Mona Lisa* made excellent use of London locations.

The success of *Mona Lisa* opened doors for Jordan in Hollywood, where he worked on two comedies. The first of these, *High Spirits* (1988), was a $16 million haunted-house sex farce set in an Irish castle, featuring a star cast including Daryl Hannah, Steve Guttenberg, Peter O'Toole and Beverly D'Angelo. A box-office disaster, the film was universally panned by critics. Jordan, who had no post-production input, has since rued the project, stating that he had envisioned 'a kind of *Whisky Galore* [while] the American producers wanted a raucous teenage comedy'. *We're No Angels* (1989), a David Mamet-scripted remake of Michael Curtiz's 1955 movie, was Jordan's first all-American production. A mistaken-identity caper set during the Great Depression, in which Robert De Niro and Sean Penn play escaped convicts who are mistaken for priests and take refuge in a Canadian border-town monastery, the film boasted a revered cast. However, it was not the commercial success Paramount had hoped for. Nonetheless, critics generally warmed to De Niro's performance and praised Jordan for his strong sense of period and location.

Disenchanted by his lack of commercial success and the creative constraints placed upon him by the studios, Jordan returned to home territory and to literary themes for his next film, *The Miracle* (1991). Set in the small Irish seaside town of Bray, the film tells the tale of two male adolescent would-be writers who become infatuated with an American actress (Beverly D'Angelo). A romantic rites-of-passage mystery (and Jordan's personal favourite), the film represented something of a critical resurgence for the director, but another commercial disappointment.

The ordeal of transferring *The Crying Game* (1992) from page to screen lasted some ten years. Initially submitted in partial script form as 'The Soldier's Wife' to Channel 4, the project was passed over on the grounds that the subject matter was too sensitive for the time. *The Crying Game* tells the story of a reluctant black British soldier, Jody (Forest Whitaker), who is abducted whilst drunk at an Armagh fairground and held hostage by members of the Provisional IRA. Jody is befriended by Fergus (Stephen Rea), one of his captors, who agrees to look up Jody's girlfriend Dil (Jaye Davidson) should anything happen to him. Fergus fails to carry out an order to execute his prisoner but Jody is killed by a British armoured vehicle while attempting to escape. Having fled to London, Fergus is court-martialled and sentenced to a suicide mission. He befriends Dil and is pursued by his former paramilitary colleagues as the story follows thriller conventions through to their conclusion. *The Crying Game* fundamentally differs from 'The Soldier's Wife' in the film's striking revelation that Dil is a male transvestite.

Since the script juggled the hot potatoes of race, sexual identity and political violence, the film failed to attract American money. It was eventually co-financed by Channel 4 and a syndicate of European and Japanese distribution companies. Moreover, given the film's generic hybridity, *The Crying Game* proved difficult to market and initially flopped in the UK. In the US, however, the film's distributor, Miramax, marketed the film as a straightforward thriller and traded on the film's gender twist – 'the movie that everyone's talking about, but no one is giving away its secrets'. This strategy, coupled with an enthusiastic critical reception, generated huge audiences. By Jane Giles' account, in the period between its release in November 1992 and the Academy Awards in the following March, Miramax increased the film's release prints from six to more than a thousand. The film was nominated for six Academy Awards, including Best Film and Best Director, won for Best Screenplay, and grossed almost $60 million at the US box office alone.

On the back of the *The Crying Game*'s success, Jordan returned to America where he made the first of three films for Geffen/Warner Bros., *Interview with the Vampire* (1994), an adaptation of Anne Rice's cult gay novel. The episodic events of the film are narrated by a 'reluctant' vampire, Louis de Pointe du Lac (Brad Pitt), who recounts to his interviewer, Malloy (Christian Slater), the details of his two-hundred-year existence. Given its mainstream standing (and a cast including Tom Cruise and Antonio Banderas), the gay sexual overtones of the original novel are predictably reduced to subtext. Considered by some to be narratively laboured, the film is handsomely staged and shot, and did strong business at the US box office.

Jordan chose distinctly Irish themes for his next two films. In the first, *Michael Collins* (1996), he addressed the thorny issue of Irish national history, representing the events surrounding the 1916 Irish rebellion against seven hundred years of British colonial rule. Unsurprisingly, given its politically sensitive subject matter, the film's aesthetic and narrative merits were subsumed by debates over its historical accuracy. Jordan's heroic figuring of Collins (Liam Neeson) – who adopted acts of guerrilla warfare to bring the British to the negotiation table but, in doing so, some have argued, may have created a north/south divide – was particularly criticised. Others took issue with Jordan's unsympathetic representation of the leading figure of the Republican Party, Eamon De Valera (Alan Rickman). Some members of the British press suggested that Michael Collins 'might just as well have been supplied by Sinn Fein's propaganda department' and accused its backers of 'corporate irresponsibility'.

For his next film, *The Butcher Boy* (1997), Jordan turned to an Irish literary source with an adaptation of Patrick McCabe's celebrated novel. Set in a rural Irish community during the early 1960s, the film is an acerbic and breathless coming-of-age picture that depicts events in the life of an orphaned prepubescent, Francie Brady (Eamonn Owens). Rather than dwell upon the often unfettered and romanticised narrative conventions of the genre, the film shows a socially disenfranchised and psychotic boy coming to terms with some terse actualities of adult life – sexual abuse, alcoholism, suicide and class prejudice. For the majority of critics, the film was a successful amalgam of formal expressionism, narrative realism and comedy. For the wider audience, Jordan's obdurate depiction of aberrant childhood proved too much of an affront, and the film failed to make any impact on the mainstream market.

With *In Dreams* (1998), Jordan returned to America and turned his attention toward the supernatural/psychological thriller genre. Annette Bening plays Claire Cooper, an illustrator of children's books, who has psychic powers. A psychotic child killer is at large in rural Massachusetts and Claire has premonitions during which she gains clues to the murderer's (Robert Downey Jr's) identity. Predictably, the authorities roundly dismiss Claire's claims and she is forced to hunt down the killer alone. Narratively, *In Dreams* was critically dismissed as formulaic, but was praised for its unsettling, expressionistic dream sequences, in particular, a much celebrated opening scene in which police divers looking for the bodies of the killer's victims swim gracefully through the perfectly preserved homes of a flooded town.

Jordan returned to Europe – and a revered literary source – for his most recent feature, the period drama *The End of the Affair* (1999). Set in London during the Blitz, the film is a loose adaptation of Graham Greene's semi-autobiographical novel that drew on the author's adulterous love affair with Catherine Watson, the American wife of a wealthy farmer. Ralph Fiennes and Julianne Moore play Maurice and Sarah, the adulterous couple, with Stephen Rea taking the role of Sarah's husband, Henry. Quite apart from the narrative's tragic emotional impact, and its deft use of London locations – producer Woolley referred to the city as the film's fourth character – the film's structure is distinguished by its split narration. Jordan has referred to this process as a 'kaleidoscopic exploration of the same pivotal scenes'. Although *The End of the Affair* enjoyed only a modest commercial success, critically it was viewed as something of a return to form for Jordan. It received ten BAFTA nominations, and a Best Actress Academy Award nomination for Moore. Jordan has continued his association with Moore in a 14-minute film, *Not I* (2000), based on the Samuel Beckett's play.

He is currently in production with *Double Down*, a remake of Jean-Pierre Melville's *Bob le flambeur* (1995), starring Nick Nolte.   **TT**

Isaac JULIEN

Born in London in 1960, Isaac Julien can be seen as the uneasy, black British equivalent of America's Spike Lee. Darling of the British intelligentsia and avant-garde movement, due mainly to his use of subversive political representations of gays and blacks embodied in a tight but fresh aesthetic, he differs from Lee in his experimental approach and his refusal to celebrate black nationalism with its implicit affirmation of heterosexuality. Critics have compared Julien's polemic output with that of Hanif Kureishi, the screenwriter of Stephen Frears' *My Beautiful Laundrette* (1985); Julien himself is more comfortable with this analogy. The most eager critics believe that his cinema follows a Jean-Luc Godard tradition, while others have seen influences of Derek Jarman and Michelangelo Antonioni.

Julien draws on the cultural heritage of the 1960s and 1970s generation of pioneer black British film-makers. Films such as Lionel N'Gakane's *Jemina and Johnny* (1965), Frankie Dymon Jr's *Death May be Your Santa Claus* (1969) and Horace Ové's ground-breaking *Pressure* (1975) lay the foundations of a cinema that placed the black diaspora of Europe in a British limelight. Social realism and the stock race equation of 'prejudice versus class' from an identity crisis point-of-view are the main characteristics of this cinema in its early stage. It gained new colours and complexity with the second genera-tion of film-makers, including John Akomfrah (*Handsworth Songs* (1986)) and Isaac Julien himself.

In 1983, while studying at St. Martin's School of Art in London, Julien founded the production company Sankofa Film and Video Collection with funds from the Greater London Council, which was engaged in institutional responses to the racial disturbances of 1981. He initiated a radical aesthetic based on black plurality and the dismantling of the white racial gaze through cinematic experiments of montage, manipulation of images, and the juxtaposition of documentary, drama and non-linear narratives.

Unlike the first generation of self-made black British film-makers, Julien was intro-duced to film at London's Goldsmith College. He made his documentary debut with *Who Killed Colin Roach?* (1983) while he was still there. Colin Roach lived in the same housing estate as Julien and the piece centred around his controversial death in police custody.

Sankofa's first project, the experimental *Territories* (1985), chose the Notting Hill Carnival to emphasise its complex, multifaceted meanings. Julien intelligently weaves montage, repetitive images, archival footage and traditional documentary conventions to criticise the white passive voyeuristic look at a diaspora culture. Furthermore, Julien denied closure and resolution by destabilising fixed narrative boundaries while intro-ducing the choral refrain 'we are struggling to tell a story'. *Territories* stresses the diver-sity of black experiences by juxtaposing metaphors of public and private spaces, inviting the spectator's active engagement in a semantic connection with the image flow. If Julien is 'struggling' to say something, the spectator is fighting to 'understand' the message.

Co-directed with Maureen Blackwood, the feature documentary-film *The Passion of Remembrance* (1986) was a breakthrough for Sankofa. The film adopts a female point of view and extends *Territories*' concerns through the depiction of the fictional facts surrounding Maggie and her immigrant family, and their interaction with black cultural heritage. The prime motif of *Passion* is the critique of the chauvinism within the black activist movement of the 1970s, expressed through the struggle between the female and the male speaker in a mythical landscape. Weaving non-linear narrative, direct address, varied montage of footage of police oppression and brutality, *Passion* also presents a gay subplot that is more visible and significant than in earlier works. However, unlike *Territories*, *Passion*'s discourse is tied down by its own rhetoric, making engagement problematic. The short *This is Not an AIDS Advertisement* (1987) that came later is notably more fresh in discourse and 'explicit' in its criticism of homophobic safe-sex ads.

Shot in beautiful monochrome, *Looking for Langston* (1988) is arguably Julien's most controversial and interesting work to date. The experimental documentary engages in deciphering homosexual fantasies of the black gay poet Langston Hughes during the 1920s Harlem Renaissance. It was attacked by the Hughes Estate in New York but acclaimed by international art houses. In the film, Julien's gaze idealises gay iconography and black bodies through the use of allegorical tableaux, archival footage, voice-overs of the contemporary black writer Essex Hemphill's poetry and the juxtaposition of Robert Mapplethorpe's photographs to stress the transcendental character of the black nude images. The spectator is invited to participate in this quasi and romantic dream of desire and black unity.

The mainstream feature *Young Soul Rebels* (1991), which won the Critics Prize in Cannes, can be seen as Julien's attempt to preach beyond the converted. Set in London in the Queen's Jubilee year of 1977, the narrative combines an inter-racial gay love story between a black soul boy and a white punk with a homosexual-orientated murder. Like Lee's *Do the Right Thing* (1989), Julien provides a panorama of black subculture in *Young Soul Rebels*, exploring the influence of soul in the white dance-hall. It mixes familiar ingredients such as alternative British style, rap and black body language with an aesthetic that ironically prioritises the three colours – red, white and blue – of the Union Jack. Julien's exploitation of alternative realities during the Jubilee year has the further merit of highlighting a non-official British history. Unlike Spike Lee, however, Julien appears to be unfamiliar with the popular thriller genre, which is evident by his unconvincing portrait of the white murderer as the total embodiment of evil and prejudice. Nonetheless, the film's gay love scene was praised by the critic Stuart Hall for its fluidity and significant acting, and other critics saw it as one of the most powerful homosexual images in cinema.

Young Soul Rebels proved popular, but Julien soon returned to his art-house roots. The short five-minute documentary The Attendant (1993) reaffirmed the black film-maker's preoccupation with form as well as gay desire. Sado-masochist fantasies, death and loss are linked in a net of lavish and flamboyant style that resembles the sensibility of Looking for Langston, in yet another representation and critique of the oppression of the gaze.

Julien's re-engagement with the experimental avant-garde tradition did not exclude the use of conventional cinematic format. The Darker Side of Black (1994) and Frantz Fanon: Black Skin, White Mask (1995) are better placed within a more traditional documentary dictum, exploring juxtaposing images and creative montage. The former focuses on the nihilism and heterosexism of rap by combining facts and interviews with significant representatives of Jamaican, African-American and British black cultures, such as the Jamaican rapper Shabba Ranks. The latter portrays the engagement of the Martinique black intellectual and psychiatrist Frantz Fanon with Algerian politics, drawing on ironic monologues, direct screen address and Fanon's image depicted in various dimensions and juxtaposed with significant players of the story. With influences of Derek Jarman's Wittgenstein (1993), Frantz Fanon is considered by many critics to be Julien's most mature work, exploring thoroughly Fanon's dense ideas and complex personality through the creative combining of documentary realism and experimental lyricism. It is material such as this that makes Julien one of the great British avant-garde directors to date. **CM**

K

David KANE

Scottish film-maker David Kane has written and directed both his features, imbuing each *This Year's Love* (1999) with a similar theme. Prior to this, one of his first screenplays in a long line of shorts, *Born Romantic* (2000) *Shadow on the Earth*, won the Lloyds Bank Screenwriting Competition in 1989. He followed with the little-known *Ruffian Hearts* (1995), a BBC comedy drama about rocky relationships in Glasgow. His first theatrical release, *This Year's Love* (1999), is about a group of single thirty-somethings who mingle around London's Camden Town in search of love and lust. Sometimes light-hearted, it is also cynical and tragic; the film leavens its sadness and disillusionment, however, with reassuring comic spectacle. Established actors such as Jennifer Ehle, Kathy Burke, Ian Hart and Catherine McCormack deliver solid yet quirky characterisations. Aided by the understated dialogue and interactions of Kane's screenplay, Dougray Scott and Douglas Henshall are equally memorable. Choreographing ensemble work is Kane's forte and he develops the episodic plot well, placing equal emphasis on all his colourful characters. Confident but subtle, it is a well-crafted and engaging piece of cinema.

Kane's latest film, *Born Romantic* (2000), is similar but revolves around two pivotal establishments: a Salsa club and a mini-cab firm. Unfortunately, it did not live up to the critical or public acclaim of its predecessor despite the cast of popular actors: McCormack, Henshall, Hart, Jane Horrocks, Jimi Mistry and Adrian Lester. However, using Lester's taxi as a familiar linking device for the abundant storylines, Kane's ensemble direction is again strong. The cinematography creates a hypnotic feel during the night shots of anonymous London, yet even this does not contain the same acuity and realism of Michael Winterbottom's *Wonderland* (1999). Ultimately, attempting to explore three complicated relationships in one hundred minutes, *Born Romantic* has little new to say.

BPr

Marek KANIEVSKA

Marek Kanievska has been described as a director of the 'international style', a term *Another Country* (1984) which hints at his lack of personal or national stylistic touches. Born in England in 1952, *Less Than Zero* (1987)

Where the Money Is
(2000) of Polish parentage, he began his career in the theatre. He attempted to gain entry on director's training schemes for both LWT and Granada, but due to the early curtailment of his education and the lack of a degree, he was considered unacceptable. A directorial break in an Australian television drama led to a Penguin Best Adult Drama Award and on his return to England he embarked upon a successful small-screen career ('Coronation Street' and 'Shoestring') and made an Oscar-winning short, *A Shocking Accident*. His direction of Central Television's 'Muck and Brass' brought him to the attention of producer Alan Marshall, who chose Kanievska to direct *Another Country* (1984), the film adaptation of Julian Mitchell's hit play.

Focusing on the education of spy Guy Burgess – who is called Bennett in the film and played by Rupert Everett – *Another Country* conjectures upon the circumstances which spawned a defector. It posits, somewhat simplistically, that the traitorous seeds lie in the denial of his entry to the school elite due to an indiscreet homosexual love affair, and are carried on the naïve Marxist invective of his best friend, based on Donald MacLean (Colin Firth). The film won Best Artistic Contribution at its Cannes World Premiere for Peter Biziou's cinematography; lush and elegant but also hard-edged and dark, it elevates the film from soft-focused nostalgia. The scenic beauty of Cambridge serves to underline the oppressive, masochistic hypocrisy of the institution. The direction overcame the verbosity and light tone of the play. However, whilst it is claustrophobically tight, forcefully directed and maintains an air of tragedy, the substance of Marxism is trivialised; hypocrisy is revealed but privilege per se is not questioned. This remains the preserve of the scathing satire achieved in *If...* (1968), a superior film on a similar subject.

Kanievska's next project, *Less Than Zero* (1987), a sanitised and even more superficial version of Bret Easton Ellis' novel, was also concerned with privilege. Focusing on an affluent bisexual, Julian (Robert Downey Jr.), and the attempts of his two best friends to prevent his descent into a self-destructive drug-fuelled binge, the film loses the sexual fluidity of the book's character who becomes forced into 'unnatural acts' to avoid his drug debts. The 1980s may have been a shallow decade but the film's brashness disallows any emotional connection. Although the saturated colour is attractive, the gloss convincing, and the constantly moving camera creates a suitably paranoid atmosphere, the drugs are the only chemistry here. *Less Than Zero* is most notable for Downey's performance, particularly in light of his emergent real-life problems. A lack of chemistry is also the problem in *Where The Money Is* (2000), which is only saved from complete obscurity by Paul Newman, who plays a criminal who escapes life imprisonment by faking a stroke. Once hospitalised, his suspicious nurse Linda Fiorentino, desperate to escape her drudgery by a bank raid of her own, sets out to convince him to work on one last job. With little tension, suspense, comedy or action, the film relies on its relationship between Newman and Fiorentino, and her outrageous attempts to goad him out of his 'paralysis' by lap dancing, and finally throwing his wheelchair off a dock. Poorly directed, the film never emerges as anything other than a second-rate Newman vehicle.

Fiorentino is to star in Kanievska's next project *Till the End of Time*, a biopic based upon the love story of Georgia O'Keefe and Alfred Steiglitz, which is currently in production. **FG**

Shekhar KAPUR

Masoom (1983)
Mr. India (1987)
Bandit Queen (1994)
Elizabeth (1998) Born in Lahore, Pakistan, in 1945, Shekhar Kapur began his film career working as a featured actor in a number of Indian films, becoming the country's most popular soap-opera star in 'Handan'. He has directed three films in India, *Masoom* (1983), *Mr. India* (1987) and *Bandit Queen* (1994). A huge box-office success in India, *Masoom* is the captivating story of a New Delhi family who experience difficult times when the presence of an illegitimate child is revealed. *Mr. India*, a well-received musical made for a family audience, contains elements of adventure, comedy and romance. It focuses on Arun, a character who takes in and looks after homeless children on his non-existent income. He is contrasted with Mogambo, the villain who wants to destroy India and take control. Discovering a secret that enables him to become invisible, Arun saves the country and becomes 'Mr. India'. Both films contain fairytale elements and a concern with the nature of dreams and reality. The controversial *Bandit Queen* is very different from Kapur's

earlier work. Based on the true story of Phoolan Devi, the film traces her life from an abusive marriage at the age of 11, to exile in the ravines surrounding her village, before she surrenders to the regional government. Throughout the film, Devi criticises the patriarchal nature of village life, the survival of feudal codes of honour among bandits, and the injustices of the Indian caste system. The events depicted in *Bandit Queen* are not unusual for lower-caste women in Indian society but Devi's resistance is extremely uncommon. Seema Biswas delivers an impressive performance as the resilient heroine and the film shows a very different India to that which is usually portrayed. Banned in India for its excessive swearing and full-frontal nudity, the film won critical acclaim in other parts of the world. At Devi's request, it was also the subject of court action. Although the story was supposed to be based on her own memoirs, dictated whilst she was in jail, she denounced it as a distortion; she later changed her mind. There are some unexplained gaps in the narrative but the film depicts the harrowing and graphic violence – particularly the gang-rape scene – in a harsh style that suits the subject matter. It also features a classical score from Nusrat Fateh Ali Khan.

Despite the success of his Indian films, Kapur felt he was an outsider in an industry dominated by star-driven musicals, revenge dramas and love stories. During this time he also worked on scenes for two films, *Joshilay* (1985) and *Dushmani* (1995), although he asked for his name to be withdrawn from the credits of the latter. For his first English-language film, made outside India, Kapur chose to direct *Elizabeth* (1998). The film is a biographical account of the early years of the reign of Queen Elizabeth I, set in sixteenth-century England, threatened by the Scots, French and Spanish, and divided by the Protestant and Catholic faiths. Starring Cate Blanchett in an impressive central performance, it is a dark period piece; the beautiful, often brutal, images convey the turmoil of her life as 'virgin queen' and the enormous pressure she was under to marry. Powerfully focusing on Elizabeth's personal story, the film also captures a sense of the unrest and violence that prevailed in England at the time. The elaborate style of the film owes much to Kapur's training in Bollywood. Keen to represent the complexity of the plot visually, he used his Eastern sensibilities to stress the melodramatic elements of the story, emphasising colour and shady lighting. In this tale of intrigues, attempted assassinations and executions, the camera is established as the main conspirator. Established from the opening sequence of circular, overhead shots, its roaming becomes one of the main visual motifs of the film – a very different static tableau shots generally used in historical dramas. Kapur was an interesting choice of director for *Elizabeth* and, as a newcomer to the historical drama, imbues it with an original and contemporary feel.

A sensitive, intuitive and subtle film-maker, he often chooses unusual subject matter and works in an unconventional manner. Although *Bandit Queen* and *Elizabeth* deal with controversial subjects, they are not sensationalist. Both films tell the stories of women who struggled within power structures and had to fight to survive. Kapur tends to focus on human stories and, with his background in Indian film, operates on a highly emotional level. He is currently working on a remake of Zoltan Korda's classic British imperialist adventure *The Four Feathers* (1939), starring Wes Bentley and Kate Hudson.   **PR**

Tony KAYE

Born in the UK in 1952, already an acclaimed commercials director, notorious visual *American History X* (1998) perfectionist and self-styled 'lunatic artist', it was only a matter of time before Tony Kaye was approached to translate his distinctive style into feature films. Expansive and visually arresting, his work often flirts with shock and sensation, placing a strong emphasis on the power of the image to suggest, provoke and symbolise. His famous advertising contracts, including Nike, Volvo, Dunlop, Volkswagen and the 1996 Olympic Games, demonstrate a cinematic ambition. The level of detail which he employs, as well as the capacious canvas on which he draws, might also have hinted to eager Hollywood producers – had they chosen to look – that Kaye was unlikely to conform to the constrictive demands of the Hollywood norm. *American History X* (1998), his only feature to date, has become a notorious document of the struggle between a studio and the desire for directorial auteurship. Having had the film wrested from his control by disapproving producers, Kaye publicly disowned it, demanding his name be struck from the film or, failing that, be changed to 'Humpty Dumpty' as 'a metaphor for the fall of man and subsequent events'. He took out full-page advertisements in *Variety* decrying the film, attended meetings accompanied by a rabbi, a priest and a Tibetan monk, and finally unsuccessfully sued New Line. It was eventually edited by its star, Edward Norton.

Kaye is certainly no stranger to self-aggrandisement and, watching the final product, it is difficult to see quite what he was so annoyed about. Confronting issues of American race hatred and the resurgence of White Power and neo-nazism movements in a graphic and provocative way, it is a powerful piece of film-making which, if nothing else, showcases his distinctive visual style. The story of Derek, an angry young man whose rage at the murder of his father leads him into a white vigilante gang, the film is divided between Derek's views before and after a stretch in prison following his murder of two black youths. The present is filmed in naturalistic colour; the flash-backed past is filmed in high-contrast black and white, intentionally symbolic of the film's themes and deliberately fetishised to represent Derek's seductive influence on his younger brother Danny, the film's central voice. Colour and visual symbols – from Derek's swastika tattoos and shaved head to the ostentation of hip-hop styled wannabe homeboys – are employed to powerful effect. The film's strength is its ability to show the dangers and allure of gang mentality at large, be it black or white, as well as the destructive consequences which impact on the individual, and society and the family in general. The device of Derek's Damascene turnaround – the camaraderie and magnanimity of a black fellow inmate – is rather slight, and Kaye betrays his advertising training, overusing slow motion and tending toward technical grandiosity. Overall, however, this is a compelling and engaging document of disenfranchised youth. Whether the book-ending sea image illustrates a bleak future or a turning tide is left suitably open-ended. *American History X* may not be Kaye's complete vision, but the result should be enough to persuade him to direct again.

OB

David KEATING

The Last of the High Kings (1996) As a Celtic nation with a strong historical and mythological past, a legacy often at odds with the realities and pressures of a fast-advancing modern world, Ireland has long provided a rich source of material for authors, artists and film-makers. It is in this milieu that David Keating's sole feature to date, *The Last of the High Kings* (1996), sets its story: in 1977, Dublin, a once great cultural centre that has not yet undergone its renaissance, is worlds away from the flamboyancy and promise of an America to which lead character, Frankie, is constantly turning his eyes. As Thin Lizzy and compatriot late-1970s stadium-rockers blare out their seductive brand of glam, girls and guitars, Frankie is nearing the end of school. He has an uncertain future ahead of him; no identification with his historical inheritance of being descended from the High Kings of Ireland; and, more importantly, no immediate promise of sex and booze. Essentially a coming-of-age drama in which Frankie undergoes sexual awakening, the rediscovery of his cultural identity, and various derangements of the senses, the film displays a refreshing and enthusiastic voice, wistful and comic by turns with moments of melancholia.

Keating has a good understanding for the setting – all bad flares and bad hair – and is intelligently cynical in his attitude toward the packaging and manipulation of Irish culture. Instead, he concentrates on the realities of the situation and the need to break free from enforced identity, incorporating the requisite scrapes, close shaves and fumbles that are the staple of the coming-of-age format. The characters are engaging, the script is fast and funny, and the camerawork is energetic. The directorial style, falling somewhere between the pop sensibility of 'Brat Pack' teen dramas and the seductive nostalgia of television's 'The Wonder Years' is not groundbreaking but it is well made and a better example of its type, sitting comfortably amongst films such as *Rumble Fish* (1983) and *Running on Empty* (1988).

OB

Patrick KEILLER

London (1994)
Robinson in Space (1997) Born in Blackpool, UK, in 1950, Patrick Keiller completed five 16mm shorts in the 1980s – *Stonebridge Park* (1981), *Norwood* (1984), *The End* (1986), *Valtos* (1987)

and *The Clouds* (1989). In his feature-length films, he exposes the political implications of the use of space in England, through an aesthetic informed by modern art. He began work on his first feature, *London* (1994) in 1992. Shot on colour 35mm (Kodak) film, it cost a mere £182,000 to make. *London* is an avant-garde blending of fiction and documentary stylistics, made up of a montage of static camera shots of the city, held together by a post-synchronised monologue narrated by Paul Scofield. The film explores the city through the wanderings of the narrator and his fictional double, ex-gay lover Robinson. As a part-document of London in 1992, Keiller captures the aftermath of IRA bombings, the unveiling of the statue to Bomber Harris, and the re-election of John Major. These present-day images are contrasted with the historical – ranging from Tower Bridge to the houses and haunts of various literary figures – as the film searches for some enduring cultural heritage on which to base the identity of the city.

Devoid of the human agency of traditional narrative films, the city becomes the subject of the film. Place transforms into character through the flaneurial cine-eye of its invisible characters and Keiller's camera. Ultimately, however, the quotidian poetics that the flaneur tradition suggests, is used with an ironic edge. The film concludes that such activity is impossible in present-day London; the traditional English fear of the crowd has left us without public space.

Stylistically similar, his second feature, *Robinson in Space* (1997) leaves the city behind, and searches the 'inbetween' spaces of England. Based upon Daniel Defoe's literary journeys around the country, it is a seven-part episodic tour that debunks the idea that England is merely a service economy which no longer produces anything. A thriving export economy is uncovered, making everything from rubber sheeting for fetish wear to attack helicopters for the US military.

Once again, Keiller juxtaposes historical and contemporary images, this time to reveal the cruelty being practiced upon the land by the (then) Conservative government. A sadism that is inherent within the English country house tradition, the orgiastic extension of this conservative heritage onto the contemporary landscape, is shown in a series of sharp images of fencing, barbed wire, security cameras and radio masts. It is a gothic, S&M vision of the English countryside.

Keiller's third film, *The Dilapidated Dwelling*, is a feature-length, made-for-television film shot on a Beta SX digital camera. It leaves behind Robinson, who no longer functions as a critique of Englishness under New Labour. The problem now is with housing conditions, a space that is transgendered by the voice-over of Tilda Swinton. The film questions why rapid advances in electronic technology, having reduced the price of consumer goods in nearly all areas, have not affected the housing market in the same way; and why are houses still thought of as permanent, despite being so energy inefficient and in need of constant repair?

Stylistically more advanced, accelerated moving shots from cars and trains are used to emphasise the advancement of technology against which the housing market remains static. The film is more documentary than fiction – containing interviews with architects, academics and design engineering manufacturers – and is interspersed with archival footage of previous attempts to revolutionise the housing industry in a pre-fabricated direction. **DMJ**

Justin KERRIGAN

Human Traffic (1999) is Justin Kerrigan's first and only feature to date, a pet project he nurtured and developed for two years upon graduating from film school in Wales. Set in Cardiff, the film focuses on five friends against the backdrop of the local club culture. Eschewing conventional narrative, Kerrigan opts to build the film in a frantic, fragmented style, adopting formal mannerisms familiar from *Goodfellas* (1990), *Trainspotting* (1996) and *Pulp Fiction* (1994). However, the presentation of the highs and lows of a drug-fuelled weekend also gives the film its own voice, mounting a few astute observations on the peculiar rituals of youth culture. The deeper social implications of young people in dead-end jobs, while crudely hammered home (the workers in one burger bar are shown as literal automatons, complete with robotic movement), provide a balance to the chemical highs of the club sequences. One scene, however, wherein the cast sing an alternative national anthem complete with lyrics about youth alienation and isolation, is particularly misjudged, overstating what the film has said more economically elsewhere.

That said, this is a film that is secure in its genuine attachment to the culture it presents – DJ Carl Cox has a cameo as a club owner while Pete Tong is credited as music supervisor. Verbal pot shots at teen pop stars and Sting underline the sense of a generation caught between the carefree hedonism of youth and impending responsibility. With one notable exception, the film refuses narrative resolutions for the various characters. For all of its hyper modernity and sense of irony though, it never really transcends familiar youth movie platitudes – kids are confused, parents don't understand and true love is staring you straight in the face. Despite the film's focus on youth interaction, one cannot help feeling that there is a more substantial film lurking in the barely developed relationships between Jip (John Simm) and his prostitute mother, and Koop (Shaun Parkes) and his father. Attempts by the title sequence to contextualise the film's events amid the social chaos of anarchist riots seem trite and are barely expanded.

NJ

Beeban KIDRON

Born in London, UK, in 1961, Beeban Kidron is an acclaimed film-maker who came to cinema by an unconventional route. The early part of her adult life was traumatic: a runaway at 17, and not long after, a stripper. Whilst still in her teens she became a prize-winning photographer, and earned herself a place at the National Film and Television School. Trained in the British television industry, Kidron has come to specialise in quietly eccentric films that feature interesting character studies. Whilst her fiction features have received mixed reviews, her documentaries are always well observed and provide riveting viewing. She is particularly fascinated by the relationships between women, or pseudo-women, as in the case of the intriguingly titled *To Wong Foo, Thanks For Everything! Julie Newmar* (1995).

Kidron began her career in film-making directing a short fiction piece, *Alex* (1985), and went on to co-direct her first documentary with Amanda Richardson, *Carry Greenham Home* (1984), a political commentary concentrating on a group of women encamped at the notorious Greenham Nuclear Power Plant. The film promotes a clear nuclear disarmament message, but also a sense of the power and solidarity of these strong and committed women. Despite the fact that Kidron was still studying at the National Film and Television School while making the piece, she was so committed to the work that she joined the group at the site for over seven months.

Kidron's first fiction feature, *Vroom* (1988), made for Channel 4, is a likeable road movie set in the grim North of England rather than the wide expanse of America's highways. It was well received by critics, drawing particular attention at the London Film Festival that year. Her next project was a dramatisation for BBC television of the semi-autobiographical novel by Jeanette Winterson, 'Oranges are Not the Only Fruit', about a young lesbian's coming of age in a fanatically religious household. It won the BAFTA for Best Drama, and gained Kidron considerable critical attention. The acclaimed comedy *Antonia and Jane* (1991), which follows the seasoned friendship of two radically different women, was Kidron's first film to be theatrically released in the US.

Her first American-made feature, *Used People* (1992), is a witty ensemble piece starring Shirley MacLaine as a recently widowed woman who is wooed by a handsome Italian stranger (Marcello Mastroianni) who has suffered unrequited love for her for many years at a distance. The strong supporting cast (Marcia Gay Harden, Kathy Bates, Jessica Tandy and Sylvia Sidney), together with Kidron's steadfast and solid direction, make this an enjoyable if somewhat predictable comedy.

Her next feature, *Hookers, Hustlers, Pimps, and their Johns* (1993), saw a return to documentary territory in an uncompromising look at the vice trade in the South Bronx district of New York. It does not take an overtly judgemental stance; Kidron's gentle but straight questioning of the participants and their X-rated activities provides a moving human interest rather than cheap titillation. The film did receive a theatrical release but was first shown as part of Channel 4's Christmas schedule that year where it achieved enormous ratings. In 1994 her film for BBC television, *Great Moments in Aviation*, was screened at the Cannes Film Festival, and was aired on BBC 2 in 1995.

To Wong Foo, Thanks For Everything! Julie Newmar went into production at the same time its generic cousin, *The Adventures of Priscilla Queen of the Desert* (1994) was released. Certainly the subject matter draws a comparison between the two, but in *To Wong Foo*, there are no musical numbers or a tour bus, and none of the three leads are transsexuals. The film is also less risqué, earning a 13 certificate in the States. It follows three drag queens played by Wesley Snipes, Patrick Swayze and the star performer of the film, John Leguizamo, as they set out for the National Drag Queen Beauty Pageant in Los Angeles from New York in an old Chevrolet. Their inspiration is a photograph of Julie Newmar, the actress who played the cat-suited cat woman in the original Batman television series. En route, 'the girls' are stopped by a sleazy cop, bursting with testosterone (Chris Penn), and end up in the sleepy 'nowhere' town of Snydesville where they endeavour to help the locals with their troubles. The message of the film is clear, if obvious and somewhat laboured – people are all different and one should never lose sight of one's dreams. The film was a hit in the US but not in Britain where it received a limited theatrical release. Kidron's next feature, *Amy Foster* (1997), is an adaptation of Joseph Conrad's novel. It is a somewhat overblown affair as Kidron tries, perhaps too hard, to capture the psychological nuances and intensity of the original novel. Rachel Weisz stars as Amy, a nineteenth-century servant who rescues a dashing young Russian (Vincent Perez) from a shipwreck and falls in love. Despite the alluring visual style of the film, it is regarded as something of a disappointment given the strong cast, which includes Kathy Bates, Tom Bell, Joss Ackland and Ian McKellan.

Kidron had intended to direct *Little Voice* (1999) but pulled out. Since 1996 she has been working mainly in television, directing a diverse range of programmes, including a retrospective on the photographer Eve Arnold for the BBC Omnibus series and a production of *Cinderella* for BBC Films.   **SL**

Clare KILNER

A student at the Royal College of Art in the mid-1990s, Clare Kilner began her career in cinema making shorts. *Secret Arthur's Story* (1994), which focused on a man with an eating disorder, was screened on BBC2 as part of their '10x10' short-film strand. It has much in common with *Symbiosis* (1996), a black comedy about food and relationships, which she later wrote and directed for the BBC's 'Screen First' series. Kilner demonstrated her interest in female-centred subject matter with the short *Daphne and Apollo* (1996) which dealt with two women (acquisitions officers at the British Museum) and a sexy plasterer who are brought together by one of the women's memories of an encounter with a beautiful statue.

Janice Beard: 45 wpm (1999)

In 1999 she made her feature debut, *Janice Beard: 45 WPM*, from her own screenplay about a shy misfit who is inhibited by her mother's agoraphobia and moves to London finding employment in an office. An over-complicated plot which takes the film out of the realms of fantasy and romantic comedy and into corporate espionage, is ill-judged: the film's strengths lie in Janice's faked video-letters home which detail her (untrue) travel adventures, luxurious home (actually a show-kitchen), and remarkable (faked) professional achievements. When the plot positions her as an unwitting spy, it loses its way, becoming over-extended and under-developed. The subject and humour bear comparison to John Schlesinger's *Billy Liar* (1963), but *Janice Beard* is slighter in its imagined fantasies, linking them to her low self-esteem rather than a desire to achieve more. Where it does score, aside from the light humour and bold production design, is in its central performance. Eileen Walsh's Janice, with her endearing eccentricity, provides the film with a commendable centre around which a stronger, less complicated plot could have adequately revolved. It was nominated for a Douglas Hickox Award.

Kilner has various projects in development and continues to work with Eclipse, an advertising production company.   **JD**

Peter KOSMINSKY

A product of the BBC's legendary trainee scheme, Peter Kosminsky worked his way through the corporation before moving to Yorkshire Television and starting work as a

Wuthering Heights (1992)
No Child of Mine (1997)

talented and efficient director of drama and feature-length documentaries. Never a film-maker to pull any punches, he soon produced a brave body of work that explored the hardships that life can offer and the strength of human spirit needed to overcome them.

His early work such as 'Afangsti' and 'The Falklands War: the Untold Story' gained rave notices and he was soon directing feature-length drama. 'Shoot to Kill' (1990) was a two-part, four-hour drama starring Jack Shepherd, based on an infamous stalker affair.

He gathered an all-star cast for *Wuthering Heights* (1992) which starred Ralph Fiennes, Sinead O'Connor and Juliette Binoche in the third cinematic excursion for Emily Brönte's classic novel. The film was released theatrically in the UK to critical acclaim and premiered on TNT in the US in 1994. Shot on location, it looked the part and fol-lowed the storyline closely; Kosminsky's documentary style is sometimes as odds with the romanticism of the piece, however, and the lyrical settings were a sharp contrast to the urban settings usually associated with his work. Despite a miscast Juliette Binoche, it featured good performances from its stars, particularly Ralph Fiennes as Heathcliffe.

His feature documentaries, *The Life & Death of Philip Knight* (1993) and *The Dying of the Light* (1994), won awards around the world and led to his BAFTA award-winning *No Child of Mine* (1997). In this harrowing true story, a young child, Kerry (played by Brooke Kinsella), is sexually abused by her parents and their friends and is unable to find help in the children's home she is sent to. A savage indictment of the social services and contemporaneous society, this critique was to become a recurring theme in the director's later works. The childcare phone line set up after the film's first broadcast received 25,000 calls in three hours.

Never a director to shy away from strong subject matters, his next piece, *Walking on the Moon* (1999), is an uncompromising look at bullying in schools and the devastatingly tragic effect it can have on young children. Proving his skill in directing young actors, he elicited truly harrowing yet touching performances.

In 1999 he then returned to the BBC to direct a moving story of young soldiers heading to Bosnia on peacekeeping duties in 1992. 'Warriors' followed the group from Germany to the war-torn country where they were powerless to help as the warring fac-tions destroyed each other. It is a searing drama that pulls no punches with the youth-ful, inexperienced troops naively believing they can help win someone else's war. Once again, Kosminsky demonstrated that the harsh realities which teenagers are faced with in modern society – either at war or at home – could be overcome, but the loss of innocence can never be regained.

As he continues to receive awards and nomination around the world, Kosminsky's work is reaching an ever-widening audience both on television and on the big screen. His next feature, *White Oleander*, is currently in production. **DB**

Andrew KÖTTING

Gallivant (1997) Andrew Kötting's films demonstrate a recurring thematic interest in landscape and its effects on the individual. Often categorised as a psycho-geographer, a term linked with the situationists in the 1950s, his work has been influenced by film-makers as diverse as Humphrey Jennings and Stan Brackhage. Having studied at The Slade School of Fine Art under Chris Welsby, he has also been shaped by his art school training and described his own work as a form of sculptural film-making.

Kötting has directed numerous short films. In work like *Klipperty-Klop* (1984), *Smart Alek* (1993) and *Jaunt* (1995) he uses natural light, juxtaposes sound and image, and edits without a script. These techniques are used to great effect in his 1997 feature, *Gallivant*. The film follows the director, his seven-year-old daughter, Eden, his eighty-year-old grandmother, Gladys, and the crew on a clockwise trip around the coastline of Britain, recording their various encounters on the journey. Kötting's sense and depiction of the landscape is echoed in his interviews with the people that inhabit the coastline; he shows Britain and British people that are rarely represented onscreen. The film becomes a multi-layered exploration of national identity, notions of tradition and history – often an oral history – and a rediscovery of family connections. Running a personal family history alongside a public cultural history, the two strands are unified by the constant presence of the British landscape. As critic Jonathan Romney states, '*Gallivant* is an excursion into wild chance, and unfailingly gravitates towards the unlikely: this is a Britain of sword dancers and harmonica players, tourists with bunions and cafes without table tops. But it's also a very personal record, moving and not a little crazed, the work of a passionately inventive film-maker.' Kötting's second feature, *This Filthy Earth*, which is set in a grim, rural environment, is currently in production. **HR**

Stanley KUBRICK

Stanley Kubrick is one of the rare film-makers whose work and reputation appear to have transcended their medium. Conceptually bold, stylistically precise and technically innovative, his films have simultaneously defined and confounded cinematic epochs while dividing critical opinion. Ambitious and perhaps portentous, some see these characteristics as symptoms of a remote control-freakery which manifests itself as a cold, cynical detachment from his subjects. Either way, Kubrick's work stands as a testament to the possibilities and limitations of the total control of the film director. The recurrence of themes and stylistic choices is so pronounced as to lend ammunition to both those who see him as an astute observer of humankind's essential fallibility or a film-maker whose fatalism is perfectly served by the essential ugliness and pessimism of his vision.

Fear and Desire (1953)
Killer's Kiss (1955)
The Killing (1956)
Paths of Glory (1957)
Spartacus (1960)
Lolita (1962)
Dr Strangelove: or, How I Learned to Stop Worrying and Love the Bomb (1964)
2001: A Space Odyssey (1968)
A Clockwork Orange (1971)
Barry Lyndon (1975)
The Shining (1980)
Full Metal Jacket (1987)
Eyes Wide Shut (1999)

Born in New York in 1928, Kubrick's early work as a photographer and documentary film-maker provided apt training for his stubborn independence, and early feature works clearly display an ambition which seeks to rise above their B-movie status. *Fear and Desire* (1953) remains difficult to see, but its philosophical meditation on men at war prefigured the later *Paths of Glory* (1957) and *Full Metal Jacket* (1987). *Killer's Kiss* (1955) is a stark, minimalist interpretation of film noir staples (the fighter, the femme fatale, the mobster) and while characterisation is limited, it is striking for its merging of visual abstraction with realistic location shooting. *The Killing* (1956) reinterprets the conventions of the heist narrative, fracturing its temporal structure in order to dissect the mechanics of an (almost) perfect racetrack robbery. The film benefits from the presence of an accomplished cast, including Sterling Hayden and Elisha Cook Jr. What these films clearly demonstrate is Kubrick's ability to assert his creative personality in a generic framework, a process that would develop over the body of his career.

Kubrick achieved wider industry recognition with *Paths of Glory*, a World War One drama focusing on the bitter class divide and injustice inherent in military structures. While indicting the French military aristocracy (indeed, the film was banned in that country for many years), its themes are universal. Kubrick makes extensive use of architecture in order to offset and emphasise the conflicts of the film's key characters. The smooth tracking shots, depicting the ravaged trenches of the battlefield, would soon become a familiar stylistic trait. Humanitarian in intent, this impulse is hindered slightly by its emotional aloofness and stark fascination with the order and geometry of the military hierarchy.

Spartacus (1960) marked the only occasion on which Kubrick served as a director for hire, and the sentimentalisation of the Christian revolt against the Romans seems distinctly uncharacteristic. Yet the precise military formations of the battle sequences display Kubrick's talent for spectacle, and the film is one of the more intelligent widescreen epics of the era. Benefiting particularly from its cast (including Kirk Douglas, Laurence Olivier, Tony Curtis, and Peter Ustinov), the film was Kubrick's first major financial success and earned Academy Awards for Ustinov as well as for its costume design, art direction and cinematography.

Kubrick consolidated his new status by adapting Nabokov's scandalous novel of forbidden love, *Lolita* (1962). Overcoming contemporary censorial restrictions by interpreting the story through innuendo, Kubrick transforms Nabokov's prose into a black comedy. This approach was intensified in *Dr Strangelove: or, How I Learned to Stop Worrying and Love the Bomb* (1964). The film again stresses Kubrick's interest in military processes, this time amidst the nightmarish scenario of imminent nuclear destruction. The film's gallery of Cold War grotesques amplifies its satire on the insanity of nuclear annihilation, and Kubrick maintains an icy detachment from his broad caricatures. Nevertheless, the performances of Peter Sellers (in three roles), George C. Scott, and Sterling Hayden transcend the limitations imposed by the striking visual design, sketching the range of paranoid impulses which inevitably collide with devastating results. Less concerned with any political dimension than the inherent human capacity for destructive paranoia, Kubrick presents power structures defined through possession of military technology yet crucially unable to communicate at the most basic human level. Distinguished further by Ken Adam's imposing sets, the film's cynical air is compensated by its often brilliant comedic set-pieces.

2001: A Space Odyssey (1968), while concerned with the metaphysical implications of science and the spiritual, relegates its human figures to mere ciphers. Indeed, the progress from ape to human is presented largely as a technological journey (expressed famously in the jump-cut from a bone to a spacecraft) and the film's most expressive figures are its primitive beasts and supercomputer, HAL. Placing humanity in the midst of its spiritual and intellectual superiors, the journey into infinite space is defined ultimately as one of re-birth and possible re-affirmation. Yet Kubrick focuses attention as much on the mechanics and machinations of objects, most extensively in the extended docking sequence choreographed to the 'Blue Danube' waltz. Famously adopted by the Woodstock generation as a trippy 'head' movie, the film's journey into visual abstraction and obscurantism suggests an unwillingness to fully confront the implications of its initial thesis. Nevertheless, this is cinema as grand, sensory spectacle and the emphasis on imagery to carry narrative bridged a gap between the experimental and the mainstream.

If *2001* ended on a vaguely optimistic note, *A Clockwork Orange* (1971) presents a world in which moral and ethical boundaries have become cynically eroded. Filtered through the eyes of its young, thuggish protagonist, Alex (Malcolm McDowell), the film's dazzling surfaces serve only to further eradicate the sense of a human centre to Kubrick's universe. The core issue of individuality and free will in the face of institutional oppression is somewhat tempered by the essential ugliness of the figures involved, and the satire often emerges as crude and forced. However, the film is brilliantly designed and constructed, particularly in its early section, in which Kubrick forces the audience to confront or accept the sheer amorality of his scenario.

While received initially as a sumptuous but painfully empty 'coffee table movie', *Barry Lyndon* (1975) now appears to be one of Kubrick's most accomplished and rounded works. Eschewing the melodramatic tendencies of the costume drama, Thackeray's picaresque novel of eighteenth-century social climbing is transformed into a sedate meditation on the ritual and process of societal manners. Kubrick effects the light and compositional effects of period art, placing his protagonist (a fittingly blank and passive Ryan O'Neal) as one more slave to chance in a meticulously recreated past. While suppressing heavily intimate interplay between the characters, the film allows its emotional dimension to simmer painfully below its elegant surface. Making extensive use of visual tableaux, natural lighting (utilising a specially designed lens to capture the effects of low-level lighting), and a slow, elegant zoom, the film often seems to physically reduce its characters to a living death, an appearance apt to Kubrick's ongoing fascination with the mechanics of fate.

The Shining (1980) fuses his recurring concerns with staple elements of the horror genre. The film blurs the distinctions between the psychological and the supernatural, each impinging on the other as Jack Torrance (Jack Nicholson) slides steadily into homicidal mania. The film can also be read as an analysis of isolation, and the secluded, ghost-ridden mountain hotel becomes an apt metaphor for Torrance's escalating resentments over his frustrated creativity and dissolving family life. The film's array of subtextual riddles is coupled with an effective implosion of time, and rather than relying on the regular conventions of spooks and dark corners, this is a haunted house whose horrors reveal themselves fleetingly amid well-lit corridors and rooms. Filled with memorable images (a torrent of blood from an elevator door, Nicholson's manic leer through a smashed door frame) and influential, fluid steadicam work, the film also boasts, in Shelley Duvall, one of Kubrick's most impressive, if thankless (an opinion given weight by Vivian Kubrick's fascinating documentary on the film's production) female roles.

Full Metal Jacket presents a cinematic Vietnam unlike any other, shifting the emphasis from jungle to urban warfare. While set against the tumultuous backdrop of the 1968 Tet offensive, the film scales down its action in order to contrast the preparation and enactment of men in combat. An unorthodox structure offsets the extended opening boot camp sequence (in which young men are systematically stripped of their humanity) with the experiences of the recruits in a stark, decimated Vietnam landscape. Narrated by Private Joker (Matthew Modine), the film contrasts the order and precision of the training camp with the chaos of conflict. Intent on producing men fit for war, Drill Sergeant Hartman (Lee Ermey, in an extraordinary role) falls victim to his own creation, a fat, bullied incompetent transformed into a conscienceless killer (Vincent D'Onofrio). Almost in parody of the popular (and revisionist) Reaganite action cycle of the 1980s, the frequent sexualisation of men and military weaponry is strikingly answered in the film's climax in which a platoon is gradually picked off by a lone female sniper.

In light of Kubrick's death during post-production, *Eyes Wide Shut* (1999) seems on reflection an unfinished work. Its take on fidelity, jealousy and dream logic channelled through an array of sub-Freudian motifs appears burdened by its faith to its 1926 source novella, Arthur Schnitzler's 'Dream Story'. The air of sexual melancholy and claustrophobia which permeates the film finds its focal point during an elaborate masked orgy, which may or may not place the film's protagonist (Tom Cruise) in mortal danger. Yet there is an underlying subtlety to the film which takes care to provide all manner of visual and thematic echoes, accommodating the blurring of perceptual distinctions hinted in the film's title. Particularly fascinating is the dismantling of Cruise's established persona, and his often subdued performance is pitched perfectly. Indeed, his central scenes with Nicole Kidman provide an intimacy hitherto absent from Kubrick's work, and their ultimate reconciliation, while somewhat pat in light of the preceding sombre tone, suggests a new, belated optimism in the director's work which alas, we will never see fulfilled.   **NJ**

Hanif KUREISHI

Born in London in 1954, Hanif Kureishi is known primarily as a writer of novels and screenplays such as 'The Buddha of Suburbia', 'My Beautiful Laundrette', 'My Son The Fanatic' and 'Intimacy'. He has dabbled in direction with the 1991 film *London Kills Me*, which he also wrote. His father, a major influence, was a frustrated writer in his spare time and Kureishi himself began writing for the theatre. His first play, 'The King and Me', was staged at the Soho Poly Theatre in 1979. He continued writing and staging plays, eventually becoming writer-in-residence at the Royal Court Theatre, London. In 1985 he worked with Stephen Frears on one of the landmark films of the 1980s, *My Beautiful Laundrette* (1985). Frears appreciated Kureishi's ability to lay bare a community hitherto unknown in British cinema. The two worked together again on Frears' next film, *Sammy and Rosie Get Laid* (1988), and Kureishi's journal of working with the director on the project have since been published. Kureishi clearly enjoyed his experience of film-making enough to try his hand at direction with *London Kills Me*. The film centres on a young man (Justin Chadwick) who is tired of the London drugs scene and wants to live a normal, decent life. In order to get a job, though, he needs one thing: a good pair of shoes, and with no money theft is presented as his only option. The search for the shoes is symbolic of his attempts to better himself, and there is a naïve optimism in this film lurking beneath the grime and deprivation of its surface realism. *London Kills Me* is stylish but, given the subject matter, perhaps a little too stylish. The film was, in Kureishi's words, 'roundly abused' by the critics, most of whom saw it as insincere and inauthentic. One critic went so far as to say it was a promotional video for fast-living and drug abuse. Kureishi has yet to direct another film, although he has continued to work on adaptations of his work for film and television, notably 'The Buddha of Suburbia' for BBC television, and most recently, *Intimacy* (2001), directed by Patrice Chéreau. He seems comfortable in the role of writer and has a unique perspective on the process of film-making and the relationship audiences have with a film text. He has argued that audiences 'require a human truth in order to examine the violence of their own feelings. If they cannot see something of themselves in the story, they are unlikely to see anything else. It should be part of the writer's job to remind the director of this'.   **SL**

London Kills Me (1991)

Richard KWIETNIOWSKI

Richard Kwietniowski began making short films in the mid-1980s, focusing on gay themes and experimental narratives. Amongst these, *Alfalfa* (1987) and *Ballad of*

Love and Death on Long Island (1997)

Reading Gaol (1988) demonstrated elements of the avant-garde approach to narrative, with both offering visual interpretations of existing texts. *Flames of Passion* (1989), a story of two men enjoying a commuting sexual encounter, took its name from the film shown in *Brief Encounter* (1945), making explicit that film's homosexual sub-text.

More short films, television directing (for the Channel 4 'Out' season) and teaching film kept Kwietniowski afloat until he made his feature debut. Slight, funny and charming, *Love and Death on Long Island* (1997) is an adaptation of Gilbert Adair's novel which allows Kwietniowski to explore the gay themes and arguments manifest in his earlier short works. Through its depiction of Giles De'Ath (John Hurt), the intellectual writer who takes shelter from the rain in a cinema, happens upon teen-flick 'Hot Pants College II', and falls for its idol star Ronnie Bostock (Jason Priestly), the film comments on the dichotomy between high and low art. The theme is further developed as De'Ath journeys to Long Island where he ingratiates himself with Bostock's girlfriend and begins a touching friendship with the star, convincing him of his great acting talent.

Kwietniowski and his cast have fun parodying mindless mainstream teenage movies and US daytime soaps, which is reinforced by the casting of 'Beverly Hills 90210' heart-throb Priestly and the suggestion that his character's ability lies beyond his teen stardom. Any darker elements of the story are glossed over as Kwietniowski concentrates on the humour and gentleness of the developing relationship between the widowed intellectual and the gorgeous pin-up. The film's end is touching but refuses to confront any damage done by De'Ath's devious behaviour: Bostock is kind and courteous when he refuses De'Ath's declaration and there is no exploration of the effect of the relationship on his girlfriend.

That said, Kwietniowski demonstrates a finely tuned eye and ear for detail, eliciting poignant performances from his central cast and showing a talent for pathos within a lengthier narrative. The success of the film should provide inspiration for the director to continue in feature film-making, although its more traditional elements may disappoint Kwietniowski's long-standing fans.

He is currently in production with a crime-thriller, *Owning Mahowny*.   **JD**

L

Frank LAUNDER

Born in Hitchin, UK, in 1907, Frank Launder made the move into show business whilst working as a civil servant in Brighton, playing by night as an actor with the Brighton Repertory Company. Realising his performing limitations, he turned to writing. The move was to prove fortuitous for in the late 1930s and throughout the 1940s the British film industry had a healthy production system in need of writers. Launder achieved some considerable success in this role, co-writing screenplays for Alfred Hitchcock's *The Lady Vanishes* (1938) and Carol Reed's *Night Train to Munich* (1940), amongst others. Working in an industry that was able to sustain Hollywood-like studio facilities, he was able to branch out into other areas, teaming with Sidney Gilliat to forge the successful writing-directing-producing double-act of over forty films. Launder explained his success in part due to the organisation of the industry, saying that he felt 'blessed' to have access to so many British stars, some of whom were the biggest of the time. His informal repertory company boasted Joyce Grenfell, Alastair Sim, Patricia Roc and Margaret Rutherford.

Launder and Gilliat directed their first feature in 1943. *Millions Like Us* was designed, as were many British films of the war period such as Alberto Cavalcanti's 1943 film *Went the Day Well?*, to boost morale and reinforce national pride and identity. At the time it was common for short documentary films produced by the Ministry of Information, such as Harold Cooper's *Jane Brown Changes Her Job* (1942) and Ruby Grierson's *They Also Serve* (1942), to deal with women's war effort. *Millions Like Us*, however, proved to be one of the few fiction films dealing with the subject of women in the workplace, in this case, factory workers. Using the character of Celia (Patricia Roc) the film reinforces the importance of love over work in a woman's life as she finds happiness with, and through, a man. It also argues that the work carried out by women, including those in the munitions factory setting, is significant more for the companion-ship and togetherness it brings than for the work itself.

An affinity for female stories seemed to dictate Launder's career progression: his next feature, *Two Thousand Women* (1944), focused on a group of English women

Millions Like Us (1943)
Two Thousand Women (1944)
I See a Dark Stranger (1946)
Captain Boycott (1947)
The Blue Lagoon (1949)
The Happiest Days of Your Life (1950)
Lady Godiva Rides Again (1951)
Folly to be Wise (1953)
The Belles of St. Trinian's (1954)
Geordie (1955)
Blue Murder at St. Trinian's (1957)
The Bridal Path (1959)
The Pure Hell of St. Trinian's (1961)
Joey Boy (1965)
The Great St. Trinian's Train Robbery (1966)
The Wildcats of St. Trinian's (1980)

imprisoned in a makeshift internment camp in a posh hotel during World War Two. Liberated from all signs of men (and therefore male co-stars), the women are able to let loose, until they are accidentally invaded by RAF men whom they have to hide and smuggle out during a concert. A comedy-drama, providing an excellent showcase for British stars such as Flora Robson, Phyllis Calvert and Patricia Roc, the film was not particularly well received by critics. It lacks the attempts at realism of Launder's debut, but has some sharp lines and comic moments, in main because of its cast's talents.

Still centralising women, Launder's next film, *I See a Dark Stranger* (1946), follows the independent Bridie Quilty (Deborah Kerr), who has grown up anti-British in Ireland and takes up work in a pub near a British military prison in order to spy for the Germans. Using her sex appeal, her situation becomes complicated by the British officer who falls in love with her. Vital, secret information, a German agent, the police, and Bridie's internal conflicts make up the slightly rambling narrative which lacks the lightness and concise touch of some of other Launder and Gilliat scripts.

A historical piece, *Captain Boycott* (1947), starring Stewart Granger, focuses on the battle between poor farmers and their abusive landlords in nineteenth-century Ireland. Unsure of where to focus his story, Launder introduced elements of romance and humour that unbalanced the picture. Moving in a new direction, he directed the shipwreck romance *The Blue Lagoon* (1949), the story of two shipwrecked children who grow up to fall in love on the desert island, enduring obstacles which ruin their chances of escape. Necessarily more innocent than Randal Kleiser's 1980 remake, the film is a slow-paced but oddly refreshing romance. Launder's next project anticipated what was to become his most well-known series of films, the *St. Trinian's* movies. *The Happiest Days of Your Life* (1950) is set in a girls' school which, due to wartime restrictions, is mistakenly billeted with a boys' school. It is a lively and energetic farce, thanks mostly to acting calibre of Alastair Sim and Margaret Rutherford, and also the chaotic camera with which Launder captures the split-second timings of his story. Its battle for domination between the sexes, and the 'pulling together' that is necessary for the school's survival provides Launder with the opportunity to explore British society's post-war concerns.

A break from schoolgirls and wartime spirit, *Lady Godiva Rides Again* (1951) focuses again on the subject of women: a local waitress, Marjorie (Pauline Stroud), enters a beauty contest with hopes of breaking into show-business. When she loses a rigged final competition she ends up working nude in a third-rate touring revue until rescued by her family and the man who loves her. An uneven farce, it is a cast of British favourites, including Diana Dors, Dennis Price and Stanley Holloway, who provide the few laughs.

Folly to be Wise (1953) is the story of a newly-arrived camp chaplain (Alastair Sim) who puts on a debate in his role as entertainments officer. Adapted from James Bridie's play, itself written at the height of the 'brains trust', the chaplain stages his own pundit forum, asking 'Is marriage a good idea?' Disorder ensues when the debate gets out of hand, but this brings little excitement to dated and haphazard material.

1954 saw the release of the first of the *St. Trinian's* movies, *The Belles of St. Trinian's*, with its brace of English stereotypes – George Cole's spiv and Sim's blustering headmistress – and chaotic farce. Inspired by Ronald Searle's cartoons, the film sets the standard for the following naughty schoolgirl romps: in an ill-advised get-rich-quick scheme, the irrepressibly mischievous St. Trinian girls use school funds to bet on a horse which, of course, loses. Having been encouraged by the headmistress's brother (both roles are played by Sim), farcical situations ensue as the girls try to save the school. They succeed, sparking a further four films. *Blue Murder at St. Trinian's* (1957), about attempts to run a marriage bureau from the school, combined with a diamond theft plot, relies on slapstick comedy for its appeal. *The Pure Hell of St. Trinian's* (1961) sees the girls saved in an arson trial by a fake professor who is, in fact, an agent seeking wives for the sons of an Emir. Shapeless and tired direction, and the unoriginal humour make this barely watchable. Gilliat joined Launder for the fourth, *The Great St. Trinian's Train Robbery* (1966) which begins with footage of the real robbery, linking the girls' school to this contemporary event. Farcical attempts at humour yield only crude and unsophisticated amusements, and the presence of Sim is sorely missed as one whose comic timing advanced this tired group of films. Launder's final *St. Trinian's* adventure, *The Wildcats of St. Trinian's* (1980), was also his final directorial effort. He brought

Gilliat on board as production consultant and used contemporary comedy favourites such as Sheila Hancock, Michael Hordern, Maureen Lipman and Julia McKenzie. Dealing with a strike, effected as a result of a mistaken identity deception, the concerns of the 1980s cannot be happily equated with the content and form of this distinctly old-fashioned farce. Parodies of rich Arabs border on the racist; portrayals of busty games teachers fall into the trap of sexist stereotyping; and the style seems increasingly ill-advised and exhausted. The film failed to live up to the success of its predecessors.

Between these schoolgirl romps, Launder continued to make workman-like comedies and romances, writing and producing with Gilliat. *Geordie* (1955) is the sentimental tale of a small man whose fortitude pays off when his body-building improves his physique to the extent that he wins a hammer-throwing event in the Highland Games and is asked to represent Great Britain in the Olympics. Reluctant to leave Scotland, Geordie is home-sick and lonely, and manipulated by the media (who sabotage his relationship with his Scottish love). A slight, quirky romantic-comedy, it features appealing performances from Bill Travers (as Geordie) and Alastair Sim, but is ultimately a superficial take on male identity and angst.

The Bridal Path (1959) returns to a Scottish setting wherein the central character, about to marry his cousin, is sent instead to find work and a suitable wife outside his community. Mistaken for a salmon trafficker, farce ensues as he tries to convince of his innocence. An unauthorised advert for the Scottish Tourist Board, the film utilises some beautiful scenery but even this cannot compensate for the slack, if good-natured script, and Launder's uncertain touch.

Joey Boy (1965) returns to the familiar wartime milieu, where Harry H. Corbett's Thompson makes his living through black-market operations and illegal gambling dens. Choosing the army over prison after a police raid, Thompson and his crew successfully transfer their business empire with them. Once returned to civil life they continue as before until another police raid places them under arrest. Laboured, clichéd and juvenile, the film cannot be saved by the mugging of Corbett and his co-stars (Lance Percival, Bill Fraser and Reg Varney); visually ill-conceived, its direction is sluggish.

Proving to be an important figure in British film history, Launder's work is still characterised by an element of laziness as he has allowed the wit and invention of his earlier films to become replaced by tired convention, laboured farce and pedestrian direction. He died in 1997, leaving a legacy of important cinematic artefacts, but little real art. **JD**

David LEAN

Described by biographer Kevin Brownlow as 'The Great British Film Director', David Lean (born in London in 1908, died in 1991), remains one of the country's most admired film-makers. Beginning his career as an editor in 1930, he spent 12 years rising through the ranks of the British film industry, working with the likes of Bernard Vorhaus, Anthony Asquith, Michael Powell and Emeric Pressburger. By the time he came to direct his first film he was regarded as the country's most gifted editor and was frequently requested to assist less experienced directors.

Lean's first directorial credit came with *In Which We Serve* (1941). The inspiration of Noel Coward, who wanted to direct a film based on the experiences of his friend Lord Mountbatten, Lean was brought on as a co-director on the recommendation of Carol Reed. Although offered a script by Pressburger with the backing of Powell, Lean chose to work on Coward's more prestigious production. The decision provoked Powell to accuse him of being 'like a cheap tart walking down Bond Street. You see an expensive, glittering jewel in a window and you just can't resist it'. The jewel Lean chose turned out to be a remarkably successful debut that captured the feelings and concerns of wartime Britain.

In Which We Serve was made as a testament to the strength and endurance of Britain's armed forces and the resilience of the families that awaited their return. One of the finest examples of propagandist film-making from the Second World War, it is rumoured to have been one of Winston Churchill's favourites. Following the sinking of the HMS Torrin, surviving members of the crew, floating on a life raft, think back to the time they spent fighting alongside each other and of their families at home. Drawing on his vast theatre experience, Coward directed most of the dialogue scenes, leaving Lean to

In Which We Serve (1942)
This Happy Breed (1944)
Blithe Spirit (1945)
Brief Encounter (1945)
Great Expectations (1946)
Oliver Twist (1948)
The Passionate Friends (1948)
Madeleine (1949)
The Sound Barrier (1952)
Hobson's Choice (1954)
Summertime (1955)
The Bridge on the River Kwai (1957)
Lawrence of Arabia (1962)
Doctor Zhivago (1965)
Ryan's Daughter (1970)
A Passage to India (1984)

direct the action sequences. Only when Coward was in front of the camera, playing the ship's captain, Louis Mountbatten, was Lean permitted to direct the actors. The resulting film was critically acclaimed by the press and went on to win a special technical award at the Academy Awards.

Lean's second film, *This Happy Breed* (1944), is based on one of Noel Coward's lesser-known works. Focusing on the life of a lower middle class British family over the course of three decades, it was an ambitious project for Lean's solo debut and proves to be only intermittently successful. Above all, however, it highlighted his technical virtuosity: his first colour film, Lean chose to avoid the saturated colours normally associated with Technicolor, opting instead for a more muted palette to reflect the mood of the narrative. Less acclaimed than *In Which We Serve*, Lean's direction was still worthy of critics' praise.

By the time *This Happy Breed* had opened, Coward's play 'Blithe Spirit' was already a phenomenal hit on the West End stage. Once again, Coward invested his trust in Lean. The story of a middle-aged author whose deceased first wife revisits him, re-igniting long-lost feelings of desire and highlighting the dullness of his present marriage, the film's lack of energy highlighted Lean's disdain for comedy and, more specifically, his lack of regard for Coward's comedy of manners. More expansive than the single-set play, *Blithe Spirit* (1945) never quite escapes the staginess of its source. Rex Harrison offers minor compensation, but not enough to sully a disappointed Coward, who complained that Lean 'fucked up the best thing I ever wrote'. Critics were similarly negative in their appraisal of one of Lean's most passionless films.

Success soon followed with *Brief Encounter* (1945). Regarded as one of the finest British films ever made, the film's mood and subject matter were more fitting to Lean's skills than *Blithe Spirit*. The story of an emotionally devastating and unconsummated affair between two people who meet by chance on a railway platform, it was adapted from Coward's playlet 'Still Life'. Escaping the confines of a studio, the film's pivotal scenes were shot at Carnforth train station in Lancashire, which doubled-up for a blacked-out London. In the relaxed, though bitterly cold, environment of northern England, Lean and his crew had more freedom in creating the right mood for the drama.

Brief Encounter also saw the maturing of Lean's talent as a director of actors. He drew out two excellent performances from the leads, Celia Johnson and Trevor Howard, both of whom had little experience in front of the camera. Howard, in particular, needed grooming for the role; the relationship that developed between the actor and director was fruitful enough to see them through a number of future productions, although Howard was never again given a role as rich and demanding as Alec Harvey.

Opening shortly after the end of the war, *Brief Encounter* was a great success amongst middle-class audiences and went on to win the Critics Prize in Cannes. Writing in *The Listener*, critic C.A. Lejeune noted that the film caught 'in words and pictures, so many things that are penetratingly true. The whole colour, the spring, the almost magical feeling of the discovery that someone's in love with you; that someone feels it's exciting to be with you; that is something so tenuous that it's hardly ever been put on the screen.'

Brief Encounter ended Lean's partnership with Noel Coward and Lean chose to visit the work of another great British writer, Charles Dickens. Aside from a remarkably faithful script, which captures the atmosphere of Dickens' novel, what distinguished *Great Expectations* (1946) from previous Dickens' adaptations is a strong, almost expressionistic, visual style. The film draws on influences as diverse as *Casablanca* (1942) – a favourite of Lean's – *Citizen Kane* (1941) and, unsurprisingly, German Expressionist cinema. Set designer John Bryan was attuned to Lean's desire to create striking backdrops for the film. Many of his designs were so extreme they could only be shot from specific angles, drawing audiences further into the claustrophobia of Pip's world. Although Robert Krasker was originally employed as cinematographer, his vision did not compliment Lean's; he was replaced by Guy Green, whose sharp chiaroscuro photography emphasised the film's darker themes, winning him an Academy Award. Along with *Brief Encounter*, *Great Expectations* is the finest achievement of Lean's British career. Cited by many critics as one of the best British films ever made, it proved Lean's ability lay beyond the boundaries of national cinema. *Oliver Twist* (1948) stretched Lean, Bryan and Green's talents further. With the scenes in the workhouse, Fagin's lair and the rooftops of Victorian London, the film's visual style was even darker than its predecessor. Yet it failed to receive the universal praise that had been showered on *Great Expectations*. While critics on both sides of the Atlantic applauded Lean's thrilling account of Pip's life – with the film eventually enjoying a significant run at New York's Radio City – *Oliver Twist* was criticised for its sentimentality. For its planned American run, questions were even raised regarding its depiction of Fagin, the Jewish arch-criminal and leader of the juvenile pickpockets. Coming so soon after the atrocities inflicted upon Jews during the Second World War, the film was deemed to be too insensitive to Jewish sensibilities. In America, its release was delayed until 1951 and only then after 12 minutes had been excised, rendering the film incoherent.

Lean's next film, *The Passionate Friends* (1948), was an adaptation of an H.G. Wells story and very much a companion piece to *Brief Encounter*, with Trevor Howard once again playing the lover, with Lean's wife, Ann Todd, taking over the Celia Johnson role. In one of his best performances, Claude Rains completes the triumvirate as the spurned husband. With its complex flashback structure, the film baffled critics and audiences alike, resulting in poor box-office returns. However, it remains one of the highlights of Lean's British period: a mature, articulate and moving account of a doomed love affair. Commercial failure also awaited his next feature, *Madeleine* (1949). Based on the nineteenth-century trial of Madeleine Smith, who was accused of killing her lover, the film provides a dramatic contrast to *The Passionate Friends*, both in its emotional coldness and in an apathetic central performance by Todd. Savaged by critics, the failure of both films left Lean despondent.

Commercial and critical success returned with Lean's next two features, produced by Britain's answer to David O. Selznick, Alexander Korda. *The Sound Barrier* (1952) was a testament to the bravery of civil engineers and aviators and their attempts to push the envelope of human endurance. Lean's first experience working with a second unit – a factor that would cause him great irritation on his larger films – enabled him to concentrate on the drama, while a more specialised team filmed the many aerial shots. However, he was specific about how he wanted second unit director Anthony Squire to film the sequences. The result was Lean's first true action movie; its elements of drama and myth-making foreshadowed his Hollywood epics.

After his disastrous attempt at comedy with *Blithe Spirit*, *Hobson's Choice* (1954) could have been seen as a foolhardy follow-up to the astounding success of *The Sound Barrier*. A play that had become a national institution, Harold Brighthouse's Northern comedy was acquired by Korda, who offered it to Lean in a remarkable act of faith and confidence. The story of a cobbler whose three wayward children force him to change his outlook on life, it was the romantic story that Lean had been yearning to make. Unlike his previous effort at comedy, it proved his ability in drawing out both the nuances of Northern life and the smart dialogue of Brighthouse's play. Contrasting the sweet-natured romance with the rough terrain of the landscape – an idea recommended to Lean by Coward – gives the film a realistic grounding. Once again, the critics were ecstatic and the film went on to win the Golden Bear at the Berlin Film Festival and the BAFTA for Best British Film.

Lean's last British production, *Summertime* (1955), was also his favourite. Starring Katherine Hepburn, whom Lean had long admired, it is the story of an American woman who meets and falls in love with an Italian whilst on a trip to Venice. Lean saw it as a study of loneliness, which he thought was in everyone: 'It is a more common emotion than love, but we speak less about it. We are ashamed of it.' Shooting on location, Lean found an approach to film-making that appealed to him. As he once said to Korda, in a conversation about the problems of shooting in the studio: 'Those huge doors come down and you are in a pitch black mine. I prefer the sun.' After *Summertime*, Lean went to extraordinary lengths to find the 'sun' for his films. His involvement in *The Bridge on the River Kwai* (1957) began while he was working on *Summertime* when Hollywood maverick producer Sam Spiegel sent him a copy of French author Pierre Boulle's novel. A satire on the effete snobbery of the British military, the film would emphasise the power struggle between Colonels Nicholson and Saito of the British and Japanese armies, rather than attack the British establishment – which Lean had very much become a part of.

It would also show the destruction of the bridge, which remains standing at the end of the novel. Alec Guiness was cast as Nicholson, while veteran Japanese actor Sessue Hayakawa played Saito; the world's biggest film star of the time, William Holden, played the American officer, Shears. Shooting began in late 1956 and wrapped in April 1957. Hardly the happiest of experiences, the heat, illness and bad relations between Lean and his cast and crew left Lean with bitter memories.

The acclaim the film received upon its release, both in Britain and America, was almost entirely unanimous, changing the trajectory of Lean's already successful career. It elevated him from the position of the top British director to one of the world's most sought-after film-makers, winning him the first of his Academy Awards. Visually arresting, with fine performances from the leads, the film now appears anachronistic and all too frequently po-faced. Lindsay Anderson, writing for *The New Statesman*, accurately pinpointed the film's flaw, describing it as 'a huge expensive chocolate box of a war picture. Inside it is perhaps a better and ironic idea; but it takes more than the word "madness" repeated three times at the end of the film to justify comparisons with *All Quiet on the Western Front*.'

Lean sealed his reputation as one of the great epic film-makers with *Lawrence of Arabia* (1962). Less a biopic than an account of T.E. Lawrence's experiences during the First World War, the film won Lean a second Academy Award for Best Director. A remarkable feat, both logistically and creatively, with it he reached the pinnacle of his career. Based loosely on Lawrence's 'The Seven Pillars of Wisdom', the film took almost two years to make and employed thousands in its attempt to re-create incidents from Lawrence's life. Drawing on the skills of his regular crew, who had become used to his rigid, disciplined approach to shooting, Lean travelled throughout the Middle East, North Africa and Southern Spain in search of locations. Aided by cinematographer Freddie Young, he wanted to record images that had never before been screened in the cinema.

Although Albert Finney was seen as perfect casting for Lawrence, Lean chose the relatively unknown Peter O'Toole to play the lead. Startlingly good looking and with an on-screen edginess that resembled descriptions of Lawrence's own persona, O'Toole is adept at playing both the charming and the maniacal sides of Lawrence. So good are his looks that Noel Coward, at the film's Royal premiere, exclaimed that the film could have been called 'Florence of Arabia'.

Now regarded as a classic, receiving rave reviews from critics around the world, the film's only flaw is its occasionally glib analysis of Lawrence's complex personae. Steering clear of his homosexual leanings because of the times, the film paints too simple a portrait of a man at war both with himself and the world around him. However, such quibbles are minor compared with the fact that Lean undertook and succeeded such a feat.

Lean teamed up with writer Robert Bolt again for *Doctor Zhivago* (1965), an adaptation of Boris Pasternak's epic novel. Spanning the history of twentieth-century Russia, the novel was banned in its home country, but was a remarkable success worldwide, winning Pasternak the Nobel Prize for Literature. Lean saw it as the opportunity to make a perfect love story against the backdrop of a tumultuous period of world history. The result is a technically brilliant and visually stunning film that lacks the soul of Lean's earlier work. In his search for a poetic cinema, Lean removed the warmth and emotional power of Pasternak's prose. Both Omar Shariff and Julie Christie are impressive as Zhivago and Lara, as is Alec Guiness, appearing in his fourth film made under Lean's direction. A series of remarkable set-pieces also feature – the signature of a David Lean film. Most memorable is the charge of the dragoons: rather than show the horror of the massacre, Lean cuts away to the expression of horror on Zhivago's face, only returning to the scene of the battle to show the scale of the carnage that has taken place.

Once again, the film was nominated for all the main Oscar® categories, but this time Lean was to lose out. *Doctor Zhivago* went on to become his most commercially successful film, but was savaged by critics. However, nothing was to prepare Lean for the vehemence displayed by critics over his next film, *Ryan's Daughter* (1970). An adaptation of 'Madame Bovary', *Ryan's Daughter* unleashed a backlash against Lean that, even today, appears unduly harsh. Made at a time when the British film industry was suffering from severe cut-backs, Lean's extravagance on the film, which went wildly over budget, produced resentment from all areas of the industry. In addition, his style of film-making was deemed to be out-of-touch with the public taste, a factor which may have explained the film's poor box-office performance. A love triangle between a schoolteacher, his impressionable wife and a young soldier returning from the war, the film ranges from breathtaking storm sequences to unconvincing romantic scenes.

If the critical and commercial failure of the film were not enough, when Lean attended a gala dinner organised by the National Circle of Film Critics, he was subjected to a barrage of professional and personal attacks from some of America's most respected film-makers. Many saw the reaction to *Ryan's Daughter* as the reason for Lean's withdrawal from film-making for nearly 15 years. Although partly responsible, the real reason was far more complex. Over the years, Lean attempted to get a number of projects off the ground. He had cherished the idea of a biopic of Gandhi for over a decade. He also wanted to adapt Joseph Conrad's 'Nostromo' and film a more authentic account of the incidents that led to the mutiny aboard the HMS Bounty. However, all these projects failed to come to fruition. Instead, between his own projects he had often assisted other directors – such as George Stevens on *The Greatest Story Ever Told* (1965) – and directed a documentary in New Zealand.

With his final film, *A Passage to India* (1984), Lean realised his wish to shoot in India and saw his reputation regained both in the eyes of critics and the public. Based on a novel by E.M. Forster, it focuses on the social divide between the British and Indians during the days of the Raj. When a young Indian doctor is accused of sexually assaulting a British woman, justice gives way to bigotry and racial hatred. When it was published in 1924, Forster's novel was seen as a critique of British rule in India. Although not overtly political, Forster's use of the relationship between the doctor and an English schoolmaster enabled him to analyse the injustice meted out to Indians by the British. Less critical than the novel, Lean's film is very much a tasteful period piece. Nevertheless, the film works well in juxtaposing the beauty of the Indian landscape with the brutality of the times.

At 76, Lean was one of the oldest directors to have made a film and certainly the oldest director to make a film on such a scale. Adapting the novel himself, drawing additional material from Santha Rama Rau's stage adaptation, and editing for the first time since *One of Our Aircraft is Missing* (1942), Lean's epic perfectly conveyed the claustrophobia of India under the rule of the British. The only sour note was the casting of Alec Guiness, a white actor, as the Indian Professor Godbole. *A Passage to India* proved to be his swansong. Successful, both critically and commercially, it lost out to *Amadeus* (1984) at the Oscars® but earned Lean widespread praise and introduced him to a new generation of audiences. **IHS**

Mike LEIGH

Along with Ken Loach, Mike Leigh is arguably one of the most important British directors working in Britain today. An idealist steeped in socialist orthodoxy, there is a generosity about his creativity which finds expression in his working methods and the density and amplitude of his observations about English life. His television plays and feature films offer a chronicle of manners and mores which is unsurpassed in popularity by any of his contemporaries.

Bleak Moments (1971)
High Hopes (1988)
Life is Sweet (1990)
Naked (1993)
Secrets & Lies (1996)
Career Girls (1997)
Topsy-Turvy (1999)

The son of Russian-Jewish immigrants, Leigh was born in Salford, UK, in 1943. After dropping out of the Royal Academy of Dramatic Art in the 1960s because of its hidebound methods, he acted, wrote and directed in the theatre before joining the London School of Film and Television. In 1973 he joined the BBC as a writer and director, creating a range of sketches and plays in which he established himself as a shrewd observer of social types and found a degree of critical and popular acclaim.

Central to Leigh's approach is an improvisational method which places the characters and their interaction at the centre of the work. Emerging from an aesthetic revolution engendered by the new cinema of John Cassavetes, the French New Wave, public 'happenings' and the Living Theatre, Leigh 'had an instinct that writing, directing, designing, and film-making could all be combined on the floor rather than at the desk'. Working only partially from a script, director and actor select a real person from the actor's life and begin to evolve a character during improvisations with other actors. All the actors go through the same process and none are permitted to discuss their roles or motivations with anyone other than Leigh. The result is an organic work resonating with the colours and textures of personal history, interpersonal dynamics and socio-historical vibration. During the making of *Secrets & Lies* (1996), for instance, Leigh was careful not to let each actor know more than their character would know, building the film's climactic get-together out of individual histories and perspectives. Since none of the actors knew that the character of Hortense (Marianne Jean-Baptiste) was Cynthia's daughter when the reunion was shot, the actual experience of making the film mirrored the fictional experience. By comparison with the narrative-driven Hollywood scenario with its goal-directed protagonist, Leigh's films are not signposted and appear to be constantly unfolding. In *Naked* (1993) Johnny (David Thewlis) generates an apocalyptic litany out of the recent appearance of product barcodes. Unscripted, the idea came from a cast member who had been harangued outside the studio by a deranged soothsayer.

As accessible and relevant as good soap opera, Leigh's films have succinctly bottled the dynamics which fuel the suburban rituals of the dinner party, the housewarming and the 'barbie'. Although he has become a festival name, found an art-house following in America, and received Academy Award nominations, Leigh's core audience remains the educated middle class that he cultivated for the BBC in the 1970s, and his distributor, Channel 4.

In 1971 actor Albert Finney helped finance *Bleak Moments*. A study of lonely people in which attempts to relate are inept and excruciating for protagonist and spectator alike ('buttock-clenching' is a favourite label for Leigh's fraught exchanges), *Bleak Moments* announced a preoccupation with the search for human solidarity. All his films attend to the crucial aspects of what is said and unsaid: daughters cannot talk to mothers; husbands cannot talk to wives; and girlfriends cannot talk to boyfriends. In *Bleak Moments* Sylvia bemoans the inability to simply touch each other. Twenty years on, the denouements of *Life is Sweet* (1990) and *Secrets & Lies* depend upon characters breaking the silence and owning up to the unsaid that has blighted their relationships.

The stabs at belonging which Leigh's damaged, limited but tough characters under-take are forlorn moments in an 'island culture whose people spend their lives in self-willed social quarantine – not from alien nations but from each other' as noted in *Film Comment*. Constrained by class boundaries and emotionally repressed, dialogue is cramped by the pinched agendas of solitary people, leading to apparently commonplace and vernacular exchanges of unforced poignancy and humour: 'I wouldn't be joking if I wasn't being serious,' a character tells the girl he fancies in 'The Short and Curlies'. When Kitty Gilbert (Lesley Manville) suggests a scenario for her husband's next opera in *Topsy-Turvy* (1999), she is really talking out the dissatisfactions of their marriage. For all his eloquence, nobody responds to Johnny in *Naked*, his tirades being Leigh's most bitter riposte to a cultural establishment which remains infatuated with the possibilities of the language, but shuns a genuine sense of community.

Leigh's project has been to home in on the post-war decline in community values. Some have criticised his characters' tendency towards caricature but, as Gilbert Adair wrote in 1988, 'it has always been Leigh's peculiar genius to demonstrate that there is indeed a reality behind the baffling improbability of other people's lives, to bring even monstrous otherness into intense and startling focus'. His oeuvre seeks to seal the cracks which have fissured post-war England by bringing the English exotic in off the streets. For its portrait of the disaffected Ricky (Mark Benton), *Career Girls* (1997) is one of the more poignant British films of the last thirty years. In *Secrets & Lies* both Cynthia (Brenda Blethyn) and Maurice (Tmonthy Spall) embody the search for community. Lonely and loveless, Cynthia epitomises the beleaguered nurturing woman in Leigh's work, a prin-ciple and focus of cohesion in a society atomised by the allure of social status. The type surfaces again in *Life is Sweet* in the warm and resilient Wendy (Alison Steadman); in *Career Girls* the quiet Annie (Lynda Steadman) and the wary Hannah (Katrin Cartlidge) cling to one another. Leigh often signals a sense of belonging through the similarity of characters' names: Wendy is married to Andy (Jim Broadbent); Maurice and Monica (Phyllis Logan) are the suburbanites of *Secrets & Lies*, their rapprochement being key to its reconciliation of families and classes.

As unobtrusive as a shooting and editing style derived from television, location never becomes spectacle in Leigh's work, as it does in Hollywood films. 'I aspire to the condition of Third World movies,' he has said. 'We're here in a real place: people live, die, work, are unemployed, fuck, shit, drink, and sleep, and so it goes on.' *High Hopes* (1988) is played out against the backdrop of a King's Cross ripe for gentrification; *Life is Sweet* takes place in a relentlessly sunny Enfield suburbia; and *Secrets & Lies* compares the life of working-class terraces with that of the affluent dormitory. Leigh's feeling for life's inhabitants is captured in *Naked's* dedication to Lorraine Phillips, whose death rendered the 'world a duller place'.

It is often commented upon that Leigh's films lack a discernible style, and he does tend to pare the image of anything that might detract from the interaction of his characters. Fond of cathartic scenes, the editing in the revelatory birthday party in *Secrets & Lies* takes on the bravura of a set piece. Only *Naked* and perhaps *Topsy-Turvy* fetishise the image in the style of the arthouse tradition.

Leigh's sensitivity to the past recalls his actors' melding of history and performance. As *Film Review* noted, his films 'should be prescribed viewing for anyone studying the period in which they fall'. Portentously, when *Abigail's Party* aired on BBC in 1977, there were storms across Britain and ITV was on strike. Sixteen million viewers watched. *Life is Sweet* plotted the impact of Thatcherite individualism on grassroots society. *Secrets & Lies* derived its velocity partly from pitching its plea for community in the year before Princess Diana's death saw grieving on the streets. *Career Girls* captured that moment before the Conservative government made university an option for the mature, and not the exclusive domain of the young. *Topsy-Turvy* departed from the preoccupation with post-war Britain to essay a moment in the creative trajectory of Gilbert and Sullivan. Emotional restraint, and the shock of otherness, however, was never far from the surface while the director was at pains to assure critics that it was indeed a Mike Leigh film. **RA**

David LELAND

Born in Cambridge, UK, in 1947, David Leland was educated at Central School of Speech and Drama in London. He started his career in film as an actor and later overcame dyslexia to become a highly acclaimed scriptwriter, moving on to write and direct his own features. Leland's acting career began in the late-1960s and continued throughout the 1970s and 1980s with appearances in films such as *Scars of Dracula* (1970) and *The Time Bandits* (1981). By the mid-1980s, he had begun to channel his creative talents in other directions. He wrote the screenplays for Neil Jordan's highly acclaimed *Mona Lisa* (1986) and former-Python Terry Jones' *Personal Services* (1987) which was based on the life of 'madam' Cynthia Payne. He also scripted two influential 'state of the nation' television features: *R.H.I.N.O.* (1982) and *Made in Britain* (1982) for director Alan Clarke.

Wish You Were Here (1987)
Checking Out (1989)
The Big Man (1990)
Land Girls (1998)

His first feature as director, *Wish You Were Here* (1987), is an impressive debut. Leland wrote the screenplay and some of the music for the film, which is loosely based on the teenage experiences of Cynthia Payne with whom he had previously worked on *Personal Services*. The film effectively plays out the double standards, contradictions and hypocrises that were rife in 1950s Britain. The central protagonist, Linda (Emily Lloyd in her feature debut), meets them all head on; with her quirky rebelliousness and constant challenges to authority figures and their outmoded mores, she is the driving force of the film. Opinion is divided, however, as to the progressive nature of her representation. On one hand, *Wish You Were Here* gives us a gritty, willful heroine who strives to shock everyone around her. By the end of the film, though, she has become a mother (albeit an unmarried one), thus fulfilling the role inscribed for all women at the time, however feisty. The lack of accord between critics points to the film's strength, as it reflects the stark choices available to young women, particularly unconventional curious young women of talent and energy such as Linda.

Leland's next feature, *Checking Out* (1989), a UK-US co-production, stars Jeff Daniels as a man who develops acute hypochondria after his friend dies prematurely from a heart attack. Panned by critics and shunned by audiences, the film's cheap gags are in no way redeemed by its serious subject matter.

Leland followed with *The Big Man* (1990) – retitled *Crossing the Line* in the US. Having recovered from his Anglo-American experience, he shaped a gritty and uncompromising look at the circumstances and situations that lead grown men with families to take up bare-knuckle boxing. The big fight scene is bloody and powerful, and Leland foregrounds his talent for creating sympathetic characters. *The Big Man* also boasts fine performances from Liam Neeson, as the 'Big Man' of the title, Danny Scoular, and Joanne Whalley as his long-suffering wife, Beth. A thought-provoking and well-crafted film, it is deserving of more critical attention. The director's most recent feature, *Land Girls* (1998), stars Anna Friel and Rachel Weisz. Made for FilmFour, the film centres on three young women from different social backgrounds who are sent to work on a small farm in the English countryside during World War Two. Beautifully shot, it is a charming tale of love and labour in harsh conditions. Leland successfully captures the war-time atmosphere and demonstrates his talent for recreating contemporary history. Most recently, he has directed parts of the television mini-series 'Band of Brothers'. Having worked as both an actor and a writer, Leland has an affinity with, and sensitivity for, the complexity of character. He revels in strong personalities and has a director's ability to imagine the landscape that they inhabit and are shaped by. **SL**

Richard LESTER

Richard Lester is without question one of the most important film directors of 1960s British cinema, and his work stands in stark contrast to the realist tradition that dominated British films. Known for his unique sense of visual style, he had sympathy for, and interest in, the vibrant youth culture of the era. Lester did not so much have his finger on the pulse of youth culture – he was the pulse, in film culture at least. His work has been hugely influential and many of the interesting and bold techniques he pioneered in films such as *A Hard Day's Night* (1964) and *Help!* (1965) have become well-worn conventions in pop videos. It is mainly because of this that other aspects of Lester's work have been overlooked. Many of his films can be read as explorations of heroes and the nature of heroism – *Superman II* (1980) and *Superman III* (1983), The *Musketeers* films (1973, 1974, 1989), *Royal Flash* (1975), and *Robin and Marian* (1976).

Born in Philadelphia in 1932, Lester studied clinical psychology at the University of Pennsylvania. After a stint as a television director in the 1950s he took time out to travel around Europe. He settled in England, making friends with two of the more outlandish Goons, Spike Milligan and Peter Sellers. His first film, *The Running, Jumping and Standing Still Film* (1959), was an 11-minute short featuring Sellers which, in a 'home movie' style, does exactly what it says in the title: running, jumping and standing still, to comic effect. Lester's first feature-length film signalled his interest in the vibrant, emerging youth culture as an antidote to post-war stuffiness. *It's Trad, Dad!* (1962) focused on two jazz-crazy youngsters confronting the conventional adult world. It was the director's next feature, *A Hard Day's Night*, however, which brought him acclaim. In hindsight, the teaming up of Lester with The Beatles was one of the defining moments of the 1960s, and helped to shape the future of the music video. Lester captures the exuberance of the Fab Four as they confront an adult world that, to them, is absurd and outdated. He does this through the use of fast cutting, high-angled shots and inventive composition, all fitted glove-like around now classic Beatles songs in 'proto-pop video' sequences. The result is still breathtakingly fresh when viewed today. *A Hard Day's Night* also managed to deliver a strong sense of the growing generational divide. As with his first feature, the older generation are portrayed as joyless old fogies who live by petty rules and regulations which have long ceased to hold any relevance to young people.

Lester followed this with another Fab Four flick, *Help!* (1965), a film full of the same zany exuberance as *A Hard Day's Night*, and every bit as slick. *Help!* is full of the same kinds of gags and visual puns as the previous film, and the action and camera work are just as frenetic. The plot is not the point: it merely provides a context for the wacky Scousers' adventures, and centres on a crazy cult's attempts to steal a sacred ring from Ringo. The film features some great songs and it is here where Lester comes into his own, matching the action to the songs and the stars. *Help!* features 'Ticket to Ride', '(Hey) You've Got to Hide Your Love Away', and, of course, 'Help!'

By the time his next film was released, Lester was considered to be the swinging London film-maker. *The Knack ... and how to get it* (1965) is full of innovative, quirky techniques; so full, in fact, as to be rather distracting, and this was to become a feature and flaw of several of his later films. *The Knack's* content and representation of women is a good deal less palatable now than it would have been in the mid-1960s, and it is curious how the tone and focus of the film change in Lester and Charles Wood's screenplay of Ann Jellicoe's play. The film centres on Colin (Michael Crawford), an introverted, weedy school teacher who imagines he will never be successful at attracting women. He spends much of the first half of the film quizzing the vain, sadistic and pompous Tolen (Ray Brooks) about how to get 'the knack' with the opposite sex. We meet Nancy, played by Rita Tushingham, just arrived in London and confronted by the busy streets and people, and we are struck, through her eyes, of the contrasts between old, ceremonial Britain, and new swinging, shopping Britain. Nancy is naïve but eager to learn about life, love and sex. Colin, Tolen and their surreal Irish flatmate, Tom (Donal Donnelly) fall for Nancy. However, she is intrigued by Tolen's good looks if not by his domineering manner. He takes her to a park and after a disastrous sexual encounter, Nancy begins to scream rape all over town, banging on doors and cheerfully exclaiming 'rape' to the unwitting occupants. The whole issue of the accusation could be interpreted as Nancy's vengeance on Tolen, and this is certainly the way Jellicoe's play interpreted it. Clearly, it is meant as payback for the intimidation Nancy has endured. Yet its comical treatment, coupled with the stylish action and cartoon-like expression, undermine any positive feminist interpretation. Nancy finds her voice, and she wields a certain power, but it is a power based on reaction originating in fear and not an assertion of her sense of self. *The Knack* was highly successful at the box office; critics praised it for its youthful expression and atmosphere of optimism and energy. To contemporary eyes, the camera work and editing are too tricksy, the interior scenes too stage-bound, and its representation of women reprehensible.

A Funny Thing Happened On the Way to the Forum (1966) was Lester's next feature film, based on the stage musical by Stephen Sondheim. Despite a superb cast including Zero Mostel, Phil Silvers, Michael Horden and Buster Keaton, his direction is erratic and the camera too active. Lester's upbeat, innovative techniques go into overdrive as they did in *The Knack*, undermining some of the comic performances. The film was not well received by critics, but did modest business at the box office due to its star-studded cast and Lester's reputation.

Viewed as something of a cinematic trend-setter, he decided to attempt a black comedy. *How I Won the War* (1967) is an anti-war film full of biting satire and razor-sharp observations about class divisions in the British army. The story centres on Ernest Goodbody (Michael Crawford) and his unit's mission to build a cricket pitch for the officers in a remote part of Africa. After the somewhat superficial concerns of his previous films, *How I Won the War* sees Lester toning down his direction so as to avoid saturating the serious underlying message. The film was not a major success for Lester despite the presence of John Lennon as a working-class private, but it did earn him a new respect within the critical establishment.

Lester went to America for his next project, *Petulia* (1968), the story of a marriage breakdown starring Julie Christie, George C. Scott and Richard Chamberlain. Set in San Francisco, the Vietnam War forms the backdrop to this unusually subtle and thoughtful Hollywood film. This may be accounted for by Nic Roeg's stunning cinematography.

Taking a journey back into absurdism, *The Bed Sitting Room* (1969) is a curious and highly original vision of a post-apocalyptic and dystopian society. A black comedy, it has characters who turn into wardrobes and entire rooms. The surreal and absurd content baffled audiences and perplexed critics; the anti-war theme is easily lost in the spectacle on offer. *The Bed Sitting Room* featured an extraordinarily strong cast, including Michael Hordern, Ralph Richardson, Rita Tushingham, Spike Milligan, Peter Cook and Dudley Moore. Still, it did not achieve mass appeal.

Juggernaut (1974), Lester's next feature is a fast-paced and entertaining thriller which manages to maintain an edge-of-the-seat quality largely thanks to the flair of his direction. He takes an essentially formulaic film – in this case, Richard Harris is in a race against time to defuse a bomb on board a packed luxury cruise ship – and injects it with his familiar verve and wit. Hardly a critical or box-office success, it allowed Lester to 'tread water' and keep in with Hollywood during a difficult time for British-based film-makers. After American finance pulled out of the British film industry in the late 1960s, many directors' careers went through a fallow period. Lester spent four years directing television commercials, but returned to film-making with one of his best loved British films, *The Three Musketeers*. The film is an energetic swashbuckling comedy adventure, featuring superb performances from Michael York as D'Artagnan, Richard Chamberlain as Aramis, Frank Finlay as Porthos, and a wonderfully over-the-top Oliver Reed as Athos. A largely accurate, if irreverent, rendering of Alexander Dumas' classic tale, Lester uses humour, fast and furious sword-play set pieces, and sex appeal to bring the story up to date. He followed with the sequel, *The Four Musketeers*. Both films were shot as one project and then divided up, the sequel released a year later.

Capitalising on the success of the Musketeers films, and their irreverent subversion of hero types, Lester directed *Royal Flash*, a film based on the novels of George MacDonald Fraser (who wrote the script) about a cowardly and dishonourable army captain, Harry Flashman (Malcolm McDowell). It was neither a critical nor a box-office success.

The Ritz (1976), a stagy and somewhat overblown version of Terry McNally's play about a man hiding out from his psychotic brother-in-law in a gay spa, faired little better. *Robin and Marian* has been unfairly criticised for its revisionism and accused of taking the magic out of the Robin Hood myth, but it is this latter feature which makes this film so interesting. Robin (Sean Connery) is now in middle age and has returned from exile. He has missed Sherwood Forest, he has missed Marian (Audrey Hepburn) and, upon his return, he finds them all changed; through this, he realises how much he himself has changed. He rekindles his romance with Marian, and there is one last showdown to be had with the dastardly Sheriff of Nottingham (Robert Shaw on villainously fine form). *Robin and Marian* continues Lester's contemplation of heroes and heroism, reflecting at a deeper level a general cultural questioning of myths and legends, good guys and bad guys which seemed to abound in much of the cinema up to the mid-1970s.

The director's next two films were disappointing and failed to make an impact. The prequel, *Butch and Sundance: The Early Days* (1979), is as appalling as it sounds and is a blatant attempt to cash in on the classic original *Butch Cassidy and the Sundance Kid* (1969) a decade earlier. *Cuba* (1979) is a love story set against the backdrop of the fall of the Batista government in 1959, and stars Sean Connery as a mercenary, and Brooke Adams as an ex-girlfriend with whom he falls in love again.

Returning to the updating of heroes, Lester was drafted in to direct the sequel to Richard Donner's hugely successful *Superman* (1978); with *Superman II*, he surpasses the original. Three evil Kryptonian superbaddies (played with 1980s high camp by Terence Stamp, Sarah Douglas and Jack O'Halloran), complete with super powers and nylon jumpsuits, travel to Earth to take over the world and destroy Superman (Christopher Reeve). Working with the evil Lex Luthor (Gene Hackman, revelling in the role), a series of high-octane confrontations between the forces of good and evil take place; the special effects are superb, even now. Lester makes the film appealing to grown-ups and children with its playfulness and irreverent humour. This dual appeal – the star performances and the special effects – guaranteed the film's success with audiences. Critics widely considered that it marked Lester's return to form.

Superman III was not quite so triumphant for a number of reasons: brand fatigue had set in, and the spirited and playful humour of the previous film is lacking, with cheap gags and pratfalls filling the gaps. The bad guys in this sequel are not superhuman but mere greedy mortals; it is science and technology, rather than superpower, which are Superman's enemy here. Gus Gorman (Richard Pryor) is a computer genius who is pres-sured by slimy corporation boss, Ross Webster (Robert Vaughn) into creating an artificial kryptonite to kill Superman. However, Gus deliberately gets the ingredients wrong and creates a kind of kryptonite that turns Superman into an uncaring and destructive thug. It is an interesting premise that wears extremely thin two thirds of the way through the film. Lester followed with the urban morality comedy, *Finders Keepers* (1984), a frenetic and fast-paced farce with some humourous moments imprisoned in an essen-tially uneven, often confounding plot. Tragedy struck Lester's next feature and over-shadowed the film's release. Actor Roy Kinnear, who had starred in the previous two

Musketeer films as Planchet, was killed when he fell from a horse while shooting *The Return of the Musketeers* (1989). The film was completed and dedicated to him, a fitting epitaph for this popular supporting actor of British film and television. Lester's last film, the 'rockumentary' *Get Back* (1991), reunited him with ex-Beatle Paul McCartney for the filming of his 1989–90 world tour. It includes some great performances from McCartney, although a curious nostalgia lingers through the use of vintage Beatles footage. There is a palpable sense that Lester is in some ways seeing his career come full circle – only now, the youth culture is middle-of-the-road culture and the moment has gone. **SL**

Michael LINDSAY-HOGG

The son of actress Geraldine Fitzgerald, Michael Lindsay-Hogg was born in New York in 1940 and has long fought gossip that he is the illegitimate child of close family friend Orson Welles, to whom he bears a remarkable likeness. A distinguished stage and promo director, he has worked with The Rolling Stones, Bryan Ferry, Elton John, Simon and Garfunkel, and directed Paul Simon's 'Graceland'. He received a Tony nomination for Best Director for the production of 'Whose Life is it Anyway?'

Let It Be (1970)
Nasty Habits (1977)
The Sound of Murder (1982)
The Object of Beauty (1991)
Frankie Starlight (1995)
Rolling Stones Rock and Roll Circus (1996)
Guy (1996)
Waiting for Godot (2001)

He first came to Europe to work as a floor manager at Radio Telefís Éireann. A few weeks later, having directed a play for the Dublin Theatre Festival, he was offered a director's contract by Rediffusion. Once they discovered his lack of experience he was relegated to children's programmes, but by spending time with producers he was given an opportunity to direct 'Ready Steady Go!' in the early 1960s. His subsequent visuals for The Rolling Stones' 'Jumpin' Jack Flash' and The Beatles' 'Hey Jude' led to his first two features, *Rolling Stones Rock and Roll Circus*, which was made in 1968 but released in 1996, and *Let it Be* (1970). The former is widely accepted as an epochal concert film. Its homage to Max Ophüls' *Lola Montès* (1955) employed an unsurpassed use of a moving camera capturing the energy and enthusiasm of circus performers alongside the best musicians of the period, such as The Who, Jethro Tull, John Lennon, Eric Clapton and Marianne Faithfull. The fact that it remained unreleased until 1996 earned it the label of 'The Greatest Rock and Roll Film Never Seen'. This was apparently due to The Stones' belief that their performance was overshadowed by The Who due to technical problems. The raw footage was stored, awaiting reshoots – some of it, bizarrely, in a barn. When it finally came to light The Stones agreed to release it.

A month after the former film wrapped, Lindsay-Hogg began work on a television special about The Beatles recording their latest album. Shot on 16mm, *Let It Be* is rough, straightforward cinéma-vérité which, despite its air of sycophancy, is an intriguing document of the disintegration of the mythical status of the band. This film, which won The Beatles an Oscar® for its score, and the landmark, 1980s British mini-series 'Brideshead Revisited' are Lindsay-Hogg's best-known works.

His narrative feature films are offbeat, but not always successfully so. His debut, *Nasty Habits* (1977), was adapted from Muriel Spark's 'The Abbess of Crewe', a satire on Watergate set in a convent. Lindsay-Hogg claimed to be more interested in symbolic power, but many critics found it a one-joke, pointless exercise that added little insight to either Watergate or the clerical life. It is, however, generally regarded as a showcase for most of the acting talent involved, including Glenda Jackson and Sandy Dennis. His next feature, the little-known *The Sound of Murder* (1982), is a witty, deftly directed drama by playwright William Fairchild.

The Object of Beauty (1991), Lindsay-Hogg's follow-up, which he also wrote, is considered by many to be a low point in his career. Although it won Best Picture at the Cairo International Film Festival, it is a failed attempt at screwball comedy. John Malkovich and Andie McDowell play an indolent, wealthy couple who are becoming impoverished and thus remain trapped in a hotel where they cannot pay their bill. Their only asset is a Henry Moore statuette that they discuss selling. When they decide not to, it goes missing. A promising idea, sporting glossy, sleek visuals, it is neither an accomplished comedy of manners nor a witty farce. A listless, self-indulgent drama, critic David Griffen was inspired to write of the film: 'rarely has crass materialism seemed like so little fun'.

Lindsay-Hogg's next feature fared no better. *Frankie Starlight* (1995) was adapted from Chet Raymo's magical folktale 'The Dork of Cork', and follows the life of a French-woman (Anne Parillaud) in World War Two and her difficult escape to Ireland, during which she becomes pregnant. Subsequently she meets Jack Kelly (Gabriel Byrne), a kindly immigration officer who takes her and the child in. Her son (Alan Pentony) prospers despite his dwarfism, becoming a renowned writer and poet, inspired by Kelly's love of astronomy. Impressionistic, it is comprised of multiple time frames and character stories, yet its moments of conventional realism fail to visually capture the poetic mono-logues of the eponymous hero. Glaring plot inadequacies and Parillaud's one-dimensional character are glossed over.

Lindsay-Hogg has said: 'I can't bear to see the prismatic effect of the sun on a lens. I can't bear the use of slow motion. I can't bear the wide-angle lens that distorts. I can't bear any visual grossness like that because I find it detracts from what the actors are doing.' Yet he has felt compelled to explore cinema's visual possibilities: his next feature, *Guy* (1996), attempts an experimental style of mock vérité to delve notions of voyeur-ism and complicity. A woman, whose hand or blurred face we only occasionally glimpse, decides to follow Guy (Vincent D'Onofrio), initially against his wishes, but increasingly with his acceptance. This culminates in his arousal. Fascinating in its early stages, the technical constraints of the film soon begin to pall and the acting becomes a series of poses and somewhat lacking in emotional depth.

Lindsay-Hogg's most recent work has been for television. *Two of Us* (2000), a 'what if' scenario of Paul McCartney and John Lennon meeting up to discuss their errant friend-ship, capitalises on his knowledge of the Fab Two by achieving plausible dialogue, but was severely jeopardised by the background music; no usage rights were granted for the originals. As part of the 2001 Beckett on Film project, he has also directed a well received if slightly over-naturalistic version of 'Waiting for Godot'; shown on television, it will be screened at selected cinemas. **FG**

Ken LOACH

Poor Cow (1968)
Kes (1969)
Family Life (1971)
Black Jack (1979)
Looks and Smiles (1981)
Fatherland (1986)
Hidden Agenda (1990)
Riff-Raff (1991)
Raining Stones (1993)
Ladybird, Ladybird (1994)
Land and Freedom (1995)
Carla's Song (1996)
My Name is Joe (1998)
Bread and Roses (2000)

Ken Loach has sustained a commitment to representing the disenfranchised and exploring controversial social, historical and political issues for nearly forty years. Born in Nuneaton, UK, in 1936, he began in repertory theatre before moving to television, directing for BBC television's 'Wednesday Play' series. Acclaim for *Up the Junction* (1965) and the home-lessness drama *Cathy Come Home* (1966) opened the door to feature films. Loach's career ran into serious difficulties in the Thatcherite 1980s but was revitalised with the production of seven features during the 1990s.

Theatrical and television training impressed upon Loach the importance of good writers, resulting in collaboration with talents as diverse as Jim Allen (*Hidden Agenda* (1990), *Raining Stones* (1993), *Land and Freedom* (1995)), Nell Dunn (*Poor Cow* (1968)), Trevor Griffiths (*Fatherland* (1971)) and Paul Laverty (*Carla's Song* (1996), *My Name is Joe* (1998), *Bread and Roses* (2000)). Famous for location shooting and working with unknown, semi- or non-professional actors, Loach uses various techniques to generate remarkably 'authentic' performances. These include casting people with similar life experiences to their characters, working in a range of dialects and languages, and capturing genuine surprise by revealing only part of the script to actors as shooting progresses. His films seek to represent common experiences and the pleasures and tensions of living as part of an oppressed or underprivileged community. This realist project also involves experiments with different narrative forms in order to dramatise conflicting social and political discourses and examine the typical consequences for groups and individuals of economic determinants.

Poor Cow follows a single mum on the fringes of London's criminal demi-monde. It bristles with stylistic eclecticism and Brechtian playfulness, combining location shooting, intertitles, handheld camera for a bungled robbery, and protagonist Joy's voice-over (revealed at the end as part of a documentary-style interview). Carol White brings resil-ient warmth and directness to the role of a young working-class woman negotiating harsh economic necessities, 1960s permissive attitudes and different versions of masculinity in her husband and lover. Steven Soderbergh's *The Limey* (1999) is a loose sequel starring an older, embittered Terence Stamp. It incorporates footage from *Poor Cow*, confirming its status as a classic 1960s period piece. The central tension of Loach's next film, *Kes* (1969), is between imagination and social constraint. Billy, a Barnsley boy about to leave school and probably work as a miner, finds fleeting liberation through discovering and training a kestrel. Supported by leading independent production company Woodfall, the film is more stylistically consistent than *Poor Cow*. Chris Menges' cinematography employs diffuse lighting for the semi-rural setting rather than highlighting particular characters, thus emphasising how Billy is shaped by and relates to his natural and social environment. Slightly distanced camera placement and simple panning movements allow actors relative freedom of movement. Recurrent shots of Billy running within the confines of his world recall François Truffaut's *Les Quatre Cents Coups* (1959) and the earlier Woodfall production *The Loneliness of the Long Distance Runner* (1962).

Family Life (1971), informed by the theories of counter-cultural psychiatrist R.D. Laing, is the most challenging film of Loach's early period. It extends aspects of *Kes*' observational style into a dissection of power and authority within domestic and institutional interiors. Drama arises from competing discourses: the legacy of 1960s permissiveness, consequent tensions within a respectable, sexually conservative working-class family, and debates between liberals and conservative psychiatrists about the care and regulation of individuals defined as aberrant. The film neither sensationalises nor attempts to draw us into protagonist Janice's schizophrenic subjectivity. Instead, it develops a systematic critical analysis of its formation and possible treatment. *Family Life* concludes with the catatonic Janice subject to the care of a traditional psychiatrist advocating sedation and electro-convulsive therapy. The psychiatrist lectures on his diagnosis to a group of smirking students. The camera places the film's audience uncomfortably in their midst as he asks 'any questions?' in the final shot.

Family Life was the least commercially successful of Loach's early films. This, and the depressed state of 1970s British film production, prevented him from making another feature for nearly a decade. Instead, he returned to television drama, where his major achievement was the four-part 'Days of Hope', made in 1975, exploring the years leading up to the 1926 General Strike. Loach took on an unusual project at the end of the 1970s, a children's film set in the eighteenth century entitled *Black Jack* (1979). The location shooting is typically impressive but the film is awkwardly acted and structured. A concern with the strategies that characters at the bottom of the social hierarchy use to survive fails to gel with the more straightforward moral polarities of a traditional children's tale.

Black Jack marked the last collaboration between Loach and producer Tony Garnett; the two had also worked together on *Cathy Come Home*, *Kes*, and *Family Life*. Garnett's departure was one of several factors that cut Loach adrift in the 1980s. *Looks and Smiles* (1981), scripted by *Kes* writer Barry Hines, revisited familiar territory. One difference is that in Thatcher's Britain the dominant employment issue for the protagonist is not the near certainty of a working life down the pit but whether he will find a job at all. *Looks and Smiles* is a ruminative film, shot in black and white by Menges. Loach felt it neither moved his work forward stylistically nor made the direct intervention into national debates that the violent rightwards lurch in British politics demanded.

Loach attempted to intervene directly into ongoing political struggles through television documentaries on trade unions and the 1984–85 miners' strike. Nervous broadcasters blocked or delayed their transmission. Subsequent films tried to move beyond this impasse by experimenting with different narrative forms. *Fatherland*'s brooding hero and meandering narrative, punctuated by symbolic black and white sequences, place it very much within European art cinema traditions. The initial premise, about a dissident musician leaving East Germany, promises to take off when a West German politician, welcoming him as a fellow German, tries to make political capital out of his defection. The taciturn musician abruptly reminds the press conference that non-white economic immigrants are never invited to enjoy West German freedoms in the same way. Unfortunately, rather than developing a precise critique of existing socialism and capitalism, *Fatherland*'s narrative digresses into a vague, unconvincing search for the musician's father, who is eventually revealed as a tarnished figure who has worked for Stalin, the Nazis and the Americans.

Hidden Agenda (1990), a rare cinematic representation of conflict in Northern Ireland from a socialist perspective, handles its political thriller format more confidently. Given its singularity, the film understandably runs the risk of overloading itself with too wide a range of issues. The murder investigation plot touches upon the British army and RUC's alleged 'shoot to kill' policy, plus the 'dirty tricks' campaign allegedly orchestrated by members of the establishment and renegade security forces to smear British political leaders in the 1970s. Typically for a political thriller, *Hidden Agenda* uses the uncovering of individual conspirators' actions as its central narrative enigma, rather than the broader historical analysis one might expect from a socialist film. Nevertheless, the narrative convincingly plays opposing political discourses off against each other. This includes a cogent argument from some 'dirty tricks' perpetrators as to their reasons for following this course of action. Unlike most 1980s media coverage of Northern Ireland, *Hidden Agenda* did not caricature or silence voices from outside a very limited spectrum. The narrowing of public debate at this time was further evidenced by considerable negative reaction to a film that attempts to widen it. One obtuse Conservative MP shamefully described *Hidden Agenda* as 'the IRA entry at Cannes'.

In the 1990s Loach found sympathetic producers in Sally Hibbin and Rebecca O'Brien and consolidated a regular production team including designer Martin Johnson, cinematographer Barry Ackroyd, and editor Jonathon Morris. *Riff-Raff* (1991), *Raining Stones*, *Ladybird, Ladybird* (1994), and *My Name is Joe* address a constellation of problems arising from Thatcherism: unemployment, poverty, housing crisis and drug epidemics. The appeal of the films partly derives from blending these social and political concerns with comic and romantic plotlines and judicious use of established film and television actors. *Riff-Raff*'s return to the observational style pioneered in *Kes* adds punch to sporadic political discussions and interactions between casualised labourers on an unsafe building site. Ricky Tomlinson, familiar to British audiences from soap-opera 'Brookside', successfully focuses much of the film's humour and political commentary. Robert Carlyle also delivers an impressive early performance. The personal and communal plotlines Carlyle bridges contain many engaging incidents but are relatively divergent within the overall narrative structure.

Partly in comic mode, *Raining Stones* explores the consequences when Bob, an unemployed Mancunian, wants to buy his daughter a Communion dress. This propels him through poorly paid casual work, petty crime, and indebtedness to a brutal loan shark. The observational style locates these experiences as everyday social processes, but humour and narrative surprises arise from individual, spontaneous reactions rather than collective, organised acts of resistance. Bob steals strips of lawn from a Conservative club, accidentally kills the loan shark, and is unexpectedly supported by a priest who condones the killing.

Ladybird, Ladybird, based upon a true story, delves even more deeply into the subjectivity of volatile protagonist Maggie. Her children are repeatedly taken into care by social services. Crissy Rock's compelling performance in close and medium shots brings us nearer to the action than is usual in most Loach films. Extensive flashbacks outline her history of abuse, institutional regulation, and incredible endurance. The film is about her rage and its social contexts. It differs from Gary Oldman's *Nil by Mouth* (1997) by making a female rather than male protagonist central to a narrative involving domestic violence. Partly because of the pervasive focus on Maggie, social services are represented with less attention to internal debates and divisions than was the case with psychiatric services in *Family Life*.

The Spanish Civil War film *Land and Freedom*, a multi-lingual European co-production, reaches beyond personal tragedy and the defeat of the Revolution to propose that debates and possibilities opened up then are still relevant today. It was well received in Europe, particularly Spain, but its comparative lack of success in Britain highlights difficulties inherent in distributing and exhibiting socialist cinema against the grain of a largely apolitical film culture. The narrative hinges around a brilliant discussion scene. Militia fighters and villagers liberated from Franco's fascists debate collectivisation and consolidating the Revolution. David (Ian Hart) and Blanca (Rosana Pastor) are just two voices among many in this discussion. Their romance is not privileged above the changing political circumstances but is constituted by it. Blanca is killed when the anti-Franco forces turn on each other and the narrative ends with David's funeral in 1990s Manchester. *Land and Freedom*'s framing device has David's granddaughter Kim piecing his story together by reading old letters from Spain. David's story begins with his decision to join the international anti-fascist struggle at a 1930s workers' film society screening of a pro-Republican newsreel. Like all Loach's 1990s work, it was mainly screened in Britain in the very different context of 1990s art cinemas. The framing device indirectly reflects this by giving little indication as to who the contemporary collectivity that might act upon this important film might be. Kim's reading of David's letters and the moving final shot where she raises her clenched fist next to two elderly comrades at his funeral are primarily individual, nostalgic acts of remembrance with hopefully proleptic overtones.

In *Carla's Song* Glaswegian bus driver George (Robert Carlyle) decides to follow the enigmatic Carla back to late 1980s Nicaragua to help her search for her lover, Antonio, who has been severely wounded by the Contras. The film attains a touching romanticism when George diverts his bus to drive Carla into the Scottish countryside. Their relationship, although central to the film, is not about George pursuing Carla regardless of everything else but about their undertaking of the Nicaraguan journey together. As they search for Antonio, George interacts with and learns about Nicaraguan peasants and workers who support the Sandinistas. The latter part of the narrative gradually defuses revolutionary romanticism as George realises he has no role there. *Carla's Song* ambitiously strives to integrate *Land and Freedom*'s political debate with *Ladybird, Ladybird*'s exploration of subjectivity. George and Carla's discussions with Nicaraguans and former CIA man Bradley (Scott Glenn) centre on what is at stake in the Revolution. Carla's flashbacks fill out her traumatic personal experience of being directly involved in such a situation.

A return to working class Glasgow in *My Name is Joe* brings together unemployed recovering alcoholic Joe (Peter Mullan) and health visitor Sarah (Louise Goodall). The film's representation of a burgeoning romance between these two ordinary people is sensitively handled. The focus on Sarah's work enables a more nuanced representation of social services than that of *Ladybird, Ladybird*. The grim, virtually predetermined deterioration of their relationship arises from Joe's lack of options within an environment governed by a black economy of drugs and debts. Community values are challenged by destructively individualist economics that allow little prospect of individual or collective change for those at their sharp end. Joe's selfless loyalty to two young drug users undermines his attempts to improve his own life.

Bread and Roses, shot in Los Angeles, extends the internationalist preoccupations characteristic of Loach's 1990s work. Immigrant and ethnic minority janitors struggle to organise themselves against exploitative employers in a cinematically unfamiliar, deglamorised LA of impersonal corporate buildings and red-shirted protestors. Like many of his films, *Bread and Roses* contains one electrifying moment, in this case a confrontation between two sisters, where extreme feelings are communicated through the acting while the observational style creates space for consideration of the wider issues compacted within these emotions. However, across the film as a whole, the personal and the political, the dramatisation of debate and the comedy of defiance, are less effectively integrated than in Loach's best work. **MSt**

Joseph LOSEY

Born in Wisconsin in 1909, Joseph Losey's career divides up into two neat parts: his early career pushed the limits of expression in Hollywood until, in the darkest days of McCarthyism, he was served with a subpoena to testify on his Communist Party association and decided to escape to the relative ideological safety of England. The move across the Atlantic was a reversal of the fate of directors such as Billy Wilder, F.W. Murnau and Ernst Lubitsch; gradually Losey re-established a career in the Old World. Eventually, the cultural cross-breeding in his enforced exile proved to be as fertile as that of his continental forebears, climaxing in *The Servant* (1963), the collaboration with Harold Pinter that spearheaded the challenge to the malaise into which post-war British cinema had fallen. In common with many a prominent American left-winger, Losey emerged from

The Boy with Green Hair (1948)
The Lawless (1950)
The Prowler (1951)
M (1951)
The Big Night (1951)
Stranger on the Prowl (1952)
The Sleeping Tiger (1954)
The Intimate Stranger (1956)
Time Without Pity (1956)

privileged social roots – he was born into a wealthy Wisconsin family and educated at Dartmouth and Harvard – to have his world-view reshaped by the Depression and the New Deal. Roosevelt's funding programmes led to a thriving radical theatre scene in New York in the 1930s, and it was in the heavily political climate of the Theatre Arts Committee, the Living Newspaper and Sinclair Lewis that Losey cut his teeth as a director. The highlight of Losey's stage work was the 1947 production of 'Galileo', involving him in a sometime tumultuous relationship with its author, Bertolt Brecht. Losey never lost touch with his roots in theatre, and went on to stage and film plays throughout his career.

The Boy with Green Hair (1948) was as uncompromising a statement for Losey's Hollywood debut as his background would have led one to expect. This simple, allegorical tale – a persecuted refugee is the boy of the title – of prejudice and individuality has a direct if naïve force, with a preternaturally mature performance by 12-year-old Dean Stockwell at its heart. In later years Losey came to describe its heavy symbolism as 'blatantly sentimental', but the film set out his career stall: to give mainstream cinema a political and sometimes subversive agenda.

Sentimentality was quickly abandoned with a succession of hard-hitting thrillers, such as the mystery-revenge tale The Big Night (1950), which were as well-crafted as their B-movie budgets allowed. The Lawless (1949), a tale of oppressed and underpaid fruit workers, is now of little note, except for its treatment of the racial issues that post-war Hollywood had only barely begun to acknowledge existed. Losey regarded The Prowler (1951) as his finest American feature. It remains a ballsy film noir – policeman Van Heflin is undone by murder and adultery – marked by the classic tragedy of the increasing helplessness of the central character's self-inflicted plight. M (1951) updates the Fritz Lang film's story of a child-killer apprehended by the underworld's combined forces by adding copious amounts of 1950s cod-psychology. It has worn less well with time, perhaps, than the original, but there remains a gruesome horror in David Wayne's killer, and a newly-found sense of urban alienation in the location shooting on the streets of Los Angeles. Throughout this period, Losey continued to work surreptitiously with such black-listed artists as the writers Dalton Trumbo and Ring Lardner Jr. He himself had been under FBI surveillance for many years, particularly since joining the Communist Party in 1946. The clock was ticking and in 1951 the machinations of the House Un-American Activities Committee worked their way down to Losey. His Hollywood career was at an end. Losey came to work in England and discovered the constraints of British cinema's poor production values and even worse scripts at first hand. The forgettable nature of his first European films meant Losey had some reason to be thankful that his earliest credits in exile were pseudonymous (the political scandal associated with his name would have prevented distribution). These included the Dirk Bogarde melodrama The Sleeping Tiger (1954), released under the name of Victor Hanbury, and The Intimate Stranger (1956), under the name of Joseph Walton.

British film began to experience a small renaissance at the turn of the decade and Losey began to show that his early promise had lain dormant and was now ready to be revived. The Criminal (1960), a prison thriller starring Stanley Baker, harked back to his Hollywood grit while displaying the influence of the newly-emerging social realism, in part thanks to the script by Liverpool playwright Alun Owen and John Dankworth's moody jazz score. The result was only undermined by the micro-budget film's lack of continuity and tenuous plot logic. The Damned (1963) is the first of Losey's British films that might be regarded as having the director's auteur touch. This is a bleak vision of a world gone wrong. A group of radioactive children is reared in a top-secret research establishment, their purpose to be the only survivors of an imminent nuclear war. The full horror of their nature is revealed when the outside world breaks in; ordinary people become fatally ill in their presence.

The symbolism and concern with the spoiling of innocence by cruelty and injustice harks back to The Boy with the Green Hair, but now that older naïvety is banished. The Damned takes place in a bleakly violent and hopeless world, both in the person of the army and the teddy-boy gang that attempts to rescue the children. It seemed Losey had learnt how to amalgamate the skills he had honed in his film noir days with the anger of his political vision and despair at the wrongs of the Cold War world. Thanks to the esteem of Cahiers du cinéma culture, Losey had become increasingly vaunted across the Channel, and so the move to international co-production with *Eve* (1962) – a project that was originally to be helmed by Jean-Luc Godard – seemed natural. Unfortunately, the film cannot escape its pulp plot origins: Stanley Baker plays the working-class writer made good who forms an obsessive relationship with Jeanne Moreau's vampish prostitute after they meet in Venice. The fine cast and lavish locations proved inadequate to the task of solidifying this Euro mish-mash.

It was an opportune moment for Losey to leave extravagance behind and focus on something more starkly pared-down. *The Servant* had been an ongoing project of Losey's for several years, since he had first come across Robin Maugham's novelette, but it was when he turned to playwright Harold Pinter, then the brightest young thing of English theatre, that the story came to a critical artistic mass. Together they fashioned a decisive landmark after which nothing could be the same again in British cinema. Philip Larkin wrote that sexual intercourse began in 1963, and *The Servant*, released that year, was to prove both a measure and a maker of such seismic changes.

The young, spoilt grandee Tony (James Fox), and Dirk Bogarde's manservant Barrett, embody oppositions of class, sexual and psychological identities that were at the crux of Britain's transformation. The process by which the servant comes to supplant his master in the hierarchy of power is a perfect encapsulation of a traumatised society, but it would be simplistic to reduce the film to class conflict and nothing else: here the political is made absolutely personal. Every frame of *The Servant* is charged with tension and claustrophobic menace, the image helping the audience to flesh out all that is left so carefully unstated by Pinter's dialogue. The sub-textual homosexual relationship between Barrett and Tony lives more vividly in the memory than many other films' explicitly stated storylines.

Losey elicited uniformly excellent performances, particularly from Bogarde who, for the first time, revealed the previously unsuspected layers of depth and darkness that were to transform his career. Alongside, Fox's naïve emotional brutality was perfectly measured (he went on to star in *Performance* (1970), a study of reversals of identity that bore the marks of *The Servant*'s strong influence). The director had never before been so well served by a scenario that presented the opportunity to reify the characters' interior lives. The orgy scene at the climax may have strayed across the line into hysterical melodrama, but otherwise Losey did not miss a trick. The acclaim was universal and *The Servant* was to be found on just about every critic's top ten for the year. Losey even visited America for the first time in over a decade for the showing at the New York Film Festival. His reputation as a director of international repute had at last arrived.

Dirk Bogarde was kept as Losey's actor of choice in his next few films. *King and Country* (1964), in which a First World War private is court-martialled for desertion, brought together Losey's long-standing pacifism with *The Servant*'s class intrigue. The result was well received, worthy and dull. *Modesty Blaise* (1966) – a would-be cross-gendered James Bond – was a singular departure in the director's career. It showed its big budget in a series of spectacular sets, and veered between fine wit and low camp without ever being quite as fun as its comic book origins suggest it should have been. It was chosen as the official British entry at that year's Cannes Film Festival where it was duly ignored.

With its Harold Pinter screenplay and Bogarde in the lead, *Accident* (1967) reunited the triumvirate of *The Servant*. This was a resplendent unravelling of time and intricately interwoven relationships in the close-knit community of an Oxford college, told mostly in flashback after the starting point of the death of a young male student. It met with an ecstatic reception on its release. Some believe it to be Losey's finest film, but there is a woeful gap between the achievement of *The Servant* and this further collaboration with Pinter, which lacks the former's gritty heart. At this distance, *Accident* appears a worthy companion piece to Antonioni's *Blow-Up*, a contemporaneous release: both are superficially dazzling but artificially complex intellectual structures, and both miss the emotional imperatives required to drive the story and involve the viewer.

The Tennessee Williams adaptation *Boom* (1968) was an outright debacle – chaotic hysteria with a stellar cast – despite which Elizabeth Taylor was happy to immediately work again with Losey. *Secret Ceremony* (1968) was an improvement, a psycho-sexual thriller which leaves a strange and haunting impression on the viewer. By contrast, the sustained existential chase that was *Figures in a Landscape* (1970) is best forgotten. The series of failures sent Losey back to Pinter. Their final collaboration, *The Go-Between* (1971), focuses on a young boy in Edwardian England who finds himself embroiled in the forbidden affair between an aristocratic young woman and a tenant farmer. The L.P. Hartley novel appeared to be rich with the themes of Losey's strongest work: innocence, corruption and the challenge to sexual and social mores. Despite the award of a Palme D'Or in 1971, the film has been criticised for being a blandly superficial simplification of the story. Certainly, Michel Legrand's score is all-pervasive, and there are moments of gilt-edged nostalgia framing the recreation of a long, hot Edwardian summer. Yet the sense of pathos, tension and traumatic shock remain strong, particularly thanks to the fine performance by Dominic Guard as the boy.

Notwithstanding *The Go-Between*'s success, Losey had clearly lost the distinctive edge that had created the unique vision of *The Servant*. With Richard Burton as the exiled leader and Alain Delon as his killer, *The Assassination of Trotsky* (1972) seemed rich with potential for a politically aware director. The final results are far more than disappointing, however, veering between dramatically limp and simply technically inept, as execrable a waste of talent as *Boom*.

Losey made a return to respectability by revisiting the roots of his career in theatre. *A Doll's House* (1973) is one of cinema's most effective Ibsen adaptations. Losey manages to give the play an edgily contemporary resonance; thanks to the tension drawn out by his direction from the performances of Jane Fonda as Nora and David Warner's Torvald, Ibsen's dissection of marriage is revitalised for the modern age.

The 1947 stage production of 'Galileo' had been one of the landmarks of Losey's early work, with Charles Laughton's performance in the title role attracting much acclaim. Some thirty years later, the film version, made in 1974, is undone by the miscasting of Topol, who lacks the conflicted darkness at the core of Brecht's vision of Galileo. Further, unlike its Ibsen predecessor, this adaptation feels stage-bound, but at least stands as a competent document of the play. *The Romantic Englishwoman* (1975) saw Tom Stoppard's witty psycho-games sitting nicely with Losey's splicing of humanity and cynicism. This variation on the old love triangle – Glenda Jackson between Helmut Berger and jealous husband Michael Caine – is given a fresh twist, thanks to Stoppard's literary invention, even if the results are sometimes stiffly portentous. It is slight but watchable.

The story of *Mr. Klein* (1976) – wealthy art dealer Alain Delon is overtaken by a case of mistaken identity in Nazi-occupied Paris – hints at richly familiar Losey territory: the meeting point between politics and the personal. The process by which the Delon character is overtaken by his unseen homonym is fascinating: however, the film never digs deep enough to match the premise, and the Klein character has all the emotional proximity of a slide examined under a microscope. As with so many of his later films, Losey's direction becomes lost within the conceptual abstractions and misses a sense of resonant humanity. The same holds true of *Les Routes du Sud* (1978), a low-key thriller with Yves Montand set at the death of the Francoist regime in Spain.

Some feared that Losey's talent was on the wane, but a final critical success disproved them. Losey's adaptation of Mozart's 'Don Giovanni', released in 1979, is sumptuous to hear and behold, ingenious in its solutions to the problem of staging opera, and every bit the match of Stanley Kubrick's *Barry Lyndon* (1975) in its recreation of period. Telling attention to detail ensures that costumes and design are no bar to a punchy social critique. *La Truite* (1982) is little more than a footnote: a flimsy tale of a young woman (Isabelle Huppert) on a journey of discovery. *Steaming* (1985) is not as worthy a swansong as *Don Giovanni* would have been, but nonetheless Losey's final film is a fine exemplar of the stage-to-screen adaptations of his last years. With a well-used cast including Vanessa Redgrave and Diana Dors, this version of the Nell Dunn drama is an effective demonstration of his facility as an enabler of performances.

Losey died in London in 1984, and it is no disservice to his memory to regard *The Servant* as the pinnacle that towers over the rest of his career, doubling up as both a caught moment in social history and an extraordinarily intense psychological study. The absence of Losey's early austerity in his later films is certainly lamentable; the House Un-American Activities Committee has to answer for a slew of film noir social thrillers that were never made. **BF**

Declan LOWNEY

Time Will Tell (1991)
Wild About Harry (2000)

Declan Lowney began his career as a director with Radio Telefís Éireann, the Irish national television network. He began to specialise in live, multi-camera television events, and recorded concerts by artists as diverse as Luciano Pavarotti, Prince, U2, Van Morrison and the Spice Girls. He also filmed the Velvet Underground during their legendary 1993 reunion tour and made the Bob Marley documentary *Time Will Tell* (1991). Lowney's British television work includes *Orchestra!* (with Dudley Moore), the first series of the romantic thirty-something sit-com 'Cold Feet', and 'The Grimleys'. Lowney's greatest television success was undoubtedly the Irish-based sit-com 'Father Ted', for which he won a BAFTA award in 1996. Written by Arthur Matthews and Graham Linehan, 'Father Ted' ran for two series until the untimely death of its star, Dermot Morgan. With its wonderfully absurdist wit and off-beat ensemble cast (Ardal O'Hanlon, Frank Kelly and Pauline McLynn), 'Father Ted' rapidly gathered a strong cult following. The success of the series was due in no small part to Lowney's supple and intelligent directing, which managed to contain the anarchic excesses of the cast without compromising the comedic integrity of the script. Lowney is also a highly successful commercials director, making popular and witty adverts for Guinness, Tango and Citroen.

Lowney's first foray into film was *Wavelength*, a 17-minute short about the problems faced by a pirate radio station, which he directed, produced and photographed in 1980. However, not until 2000 did he get to direct his first full-length feature, *Wild About Harry*. Written by Colin Bateman (author of 'Divorcing Jack') and produced by Laurie Borg and Robert Cooper (Head of Drama, BBC Northern Ireland), *Wild About Harry* tells the story of Harry McKee (the ever-reliable Brendan Gleeson), a talk-show host fallen on hard times. Once a gentle and loving husband, Harry is now an unfaithful and lecherous drunk. His wife (Amanda Donohoe) has begun divorce proceedings against him, but on the eve of it being finalised Harry falls into a week-long coma. When he awakens he has forgotten the previous 25 years of his life and cannot remember anything since 1974. Although he does not know it yet, Harry has been given a second chance at recovering his wife, his family and his self-respect.

As Harry himself observes in the film, 'The brain is a marvellous instrument'. Indeed it is, but what makes it even more marvellous for film-makers is that audiences seem ever-willing to swallow this amnesiac conceit. Like many contemporary romantic comedies, the script depends on some kind of supernatural intervention which allows the roguish male protagonist a second chance at personal redemption – like Mel Gibson in *What Women Want* (2000) or Nicholas Cage in *The Family Man* (2000). Consequently, the success of such films depends on the audience's ability to suspend its disbelief and to glibly accept the transformation of its leading man from jaded cynic to enlightened innocent. In this context, *Wild About Harry* fares well enough, but one cannot help thinking that such anodyne material falls well short of the comic versatility amply present in Lowney's best television work.   **KHo**

John LYNCH

Night Train (1998)

John Lynch was born in Dublin in 1941 and trained as a stage actor at the Abbey School of Acting in Dublin and the Royal Academy of Dramatic Art in London. He worked in British stage, film and television before returning to Ireland to direct radio drama at RTÉ, Ireland's national broadcaster. In the 1970s, he was director-producer of the children's programme 'Wanderley Wagon', for which Neil Jordan was an occasional writer. Lynch was also director and executive producer of the Irish rural soap 'Glenroe' and directed and later produced the urban soap 'Fair City'.

Lynch moved into feature film direction with *Night Train* (1998), based on a script by Aodhan Madden. *Night Train* stars Brenda Blethyn as Alice, a middle-aged single woman trapped in suburbia whose life is shaken by the arrival of a lodger, Poole, played by a crumpled John Hurt. Poole, it transpires, is on the run from a Dublin criminal gang and spends his days holed up in his room, operating his model trains on a meticulously constructed set. Fantasy and fact merge as Alice and Poole run away together on the Orient Express. *Night Train* was widely acclaimed for its portrayal of love in later life and for its depiction of a suburban Dublin generally absent from Irish cinema. The film's emphasis on character over action and its sense of place reflect Lynch's background in television soap. The same could be said for his empathy with the female characters and his ear for naturalistic dialogue. These televisual qualities do not in any way detract from the film's appeal, however. It is only when it wanders into generic cinema territory – Poole's moment of truth when he faces up to the gangster boss – that *Night Train* ever reflects its director's lack of familiarity with the conventions of feature film-making.

Lynch is currently in production with a new feature set against the backdrop of the Cuban Missile Crisis. **RB**

Adrian LYNE

Born in 1941 and emerging from the group of English directors renowned for their television commercials in the 1970s, Adrian Lyne's most successful films have attempted to tap into the American sexual zeitgeist, often inciting controversy through their crudely provocative narratives.

After the modest teen drama *Foxes* (1980), Lyne achieved a huge popular success with *Flashdance* (1983), a film notable chiefly for its adoption of (then relatively new) pop video stylistics to convey its female underdog narrative. The film carries the distinct imprint of its production team of Don Simpson and Jerry Bruckheimer, with Lyne's advertising background much in evidence in its slick but empty style.

9¹/² Weeks (1985) continued the concentration on surface effects, this time in the service of a tale of obsessive and supposedly sado-masochistic passion. While the leads (Mickey Rourke and Kim Basinger) strike a series of artful poses, their relationship is stymied by the film's refusal to define the nominally dangerous aspect of their affair beyond tease and allusion. The film's stylistic emptiness reduces its characters to the same level of the decorative objects and lighting effects with which Lyne furnishes the film. Perhaps this is precisely the point, but the film seems to want to say something more profound about the relationship between the sex and death drives (as in *Last Tango in Paris* (1972)), a thematic element reportedly severely damaged during pre-release cutting. Conversely, while the film fails as an adequate marker of mid-1980s sexual attitudes, its series of self-conscious compositions at least serve as a useful reference point for cherished items of the so called 'designer decade'.

Fatal Attraction (1987) is a far more accomplished take on the theme of sexual obsession, both through the performances of its leads (Michael Douglas and Glenn Close) and Lyne's more thorough integration of the film's themes with his stylistic choices. However, this is a deeply conservative film which posits the single, hysterical female as a threat to middle-class, patriarchal values. Furthermore, the film has been read widely as a reactionary response to the dangers of promiscuity and infidelity in the AIDS era. Lyne contrasts the warm hues of Douglas's family home with the stark interiors of Close's apartment, and it is left to the latter's skill as an actress to elicit any sympathy for her largely demonised character. The grand guignol climax completes the film's take on the independent woman as monster and such is its manipulative hold that we are implored to cheer her punching, strangulation, drowning and shooting, despite her disturbed, pregnant state. Perhaps there is a half-hearted irony in the final shot of a family portrait, seemingly assuring the reconstruction of the family unit in the wake of devastating attack. Yet the dominant impression is that of an apologia for weak, complacent, white male professionals.

Jacob's Ladder (1990) has proven to be an anomaly so far in Lyne's career. Part paranoid thriller, part hallucinatory nightmare, the film presents another version of New York as Hell on Earth. This is achieved via a scrambled narrative and fractured chronology that attempts to replicate the disturbed psyche of its Vietnam veteran protagonist (played by Tim Robbins), convinced he is being pursued by sinister, masked figures. The film loses its way in the latter stages as the drug paranoia theme is supplanted by a tale of spiritual redemption while never fully uniting these separate strands. The 'twist' dénouement consequently proves something of a damp squib. At least the film provided Lyne with an opportunity to work beyond the confines of slick sex melodramas and Robbins' demonic apparitions are often chillingly realised. Unfortunately, the commercial failure of *Jacob's Ladder* prompted Lyne to return to what he does 'best'. *Indecent*

Proposal (1993) is an incredibly stupid film, presenting its central married couple (Woody Harrelson and Demi Moore) as vulnerable in the face of a vaguely Faustian sexual pact with an amoral, billionaire playboy (Robert Redford). After introducing the themes of female objectification, prostitution and sexual manipulation (familiar territory for Lyne), the film is content to resolve its not inconsiderable moral conundrums through simple recourse to standard romantic reconciliation. There is one effective moment of disorientation as Harrelson, desperate and confused amidst a bank of television screens, imagines multiple racehorses transforming into the image of an orgasmic Moore. Ultimately, however, the film's high-concept gloss cannot compensate for its refusal to tackle its themes on anything other than the most superficial level.

This did not bode well for Lyne's adaptation for one of the most scandalous novels of the twentieth century. However, his 1997 version of Nabokov's 'Lolita' is a commendable effort, despite the inherent difficulties of transforming the book's dazzling prose and moral ambivalence into a workable narrative of forbidden passion. Filmed previously as a cynical black comedy by Stanley Kubrick, Lyne's film adopts a soft-focus veneer that often unfortunately recalls the 1970s sex films of David Hamilton. But the film is anchored by Jeremy Irons' brave central performance as Humbert and is adventurous in its engagement with his seemingly monstrous acts. Lyne walks a delicate line between a gentle eroticism and blatant softcore romance which sometimes oddly compliments attempts to humanise Humbert, an understanding which achieves some level of discomfort. Therefore, given Lyne's catalogue of abused women, his Lo (Dominique Swain) ironically emerges as his most active, rounded female role. The surreal, bloody climax, in which Humbert confronts his nemesis (Frank Langella), sits uncomfortably in the film as it does not adequately develop their antipathy before this moment. Despite this, the film is the best realised of Lyne's career to date.

He is currently in production with *Unfaithful*.   **NJ**

Jonathan LYNN

Jonathan Lynn is probably best known, in the UK certainly, as the award-winning co-writer of the successful television political satires 'Yes, Minister' and 'Yes, Prime Minister' for the BBC in the 1980s. Born in Bath in 1943, he began his career in the late 1960s, acting in television sitcoms like 'Doctor in the House' and 'Doctor in Charge', to which he also contributed scripts to. He continued acting and writing throughout the 1970s, completing a film script for Ken Hughes' *The Internecine Project* (1974). A bad experience curtailed his connection with Hollywood for some years; instead, he continued his television career, performing in the Liverpool set comedy 'The Liver Birds' and writing for British comedian Harry Worth.

Clue (1985)
Nuns on the Run (1990)
My Cousin Vinny (1992)
The Distinguished Gentleman (1992)
Greedy (1994)
Sgt. Bilko (1996)
Trial and Error (1997)
The Whole Nine Yards (2000)

He made two short industrial films in 1983 and 1984. *Mick's People* is about Barclays Bank's scheme to encourage couples to marry and mortgage with the institution, and *The Case of the Short-Sighted Boss* has Sherlock Holmes investigate an international company's loss of profits.

In 1985 he went to Hollywood to write with director John Landis and made *Clue* (1985), based on the popular board game 'Cluedo'. Starring Tim Curry and Lesley-Ann Warren, the film is intermittently amusing but marred by infantile humour and over-ripe performances from its usually dependable stars. In America the film was released with three different endings; on the video version the three endings play one after the other. Although not a great success, Lynn received another job – the chance to make *Nuns on the Run* (1990) for Warner Brothers. When Lynn and the studio failed to agree about the film (originally set in Boston), producers Jon Peters and Peter Guber obtained the project for Lynn, who returned to England to film the newly re-written script with Eric Idle and Robbie Coltrane. Peurile and predictably plotted (borne, perhaps, out of Lynn's sitcom experiences), *Nuns on the Run* relies on the typical visual gags of any film which places two men, disguised as nuns, in the changing room of a convent gymnasium. A modest success, it led Lynn back to America where his relationship with Peters and Guber had at least left him with some development deals. After a brief foray into American television with 'Ferris Bueller', a version of the popular film, Lynn made *My Cousin Vinny* (1992), a film about a hopelessly inept and foul-mouthed lawyer defending his cousin on an inaccurate murder charge. Although the film has a verbally dextrous script (by Dale Launer and polished by Lynn) the direction lacks bite and pace, with some scenes outstaying their welcome for want of judicious cutting. He followed this with *The Distinguished Gentleman* (1992), an Eddie Murphy comeback vehicle about a con-man who takes on a dead Congressman's identity and ends up exposing a political scandal. An unsubtle critique of political hypocrisy and corruption, occasionally sharply scripted and directed, the film aims to make the corrupt politicians who abuse their power, rather than the citizens who vote for them, the centre of the comedy. However, it resorts to slush and sentiment, including the staple 'cute child with incurable disease', and again shows Lynn's inconsistent ability with pace and cutting.

Greedy (1994), inexplicably influenced by Erich von Stroheim's *Greed* (1925), stars Kirk Douglas as the wealthy manipulative patriarch of a family whose members are waiting for him to die so they can inherit his fortune. Spoilt somewhat by mugging and predictably scatological humour, the film saw Lynn consolidate his reputation as a dependable but uninspired director of average comedy.

An unpopular film version of the television show, *Sgt. Bilko* (1996) came next, updating from the 1950s to the present day, and clumsily re-positioning Fort Baxter as a post-Desert Storm base. In its contemporary setting the film uses a few token 'gays in the military' jokes and tries to make comedy out of its gender and racial mix, ultimately to no avail. The film lacks visual wit and, as with Murphy in *The Distinguished Gentleman,* Lynn seems unable to coax an appropriate performance from Steve Martin in a comedy which mixes the sight gag with verbal play, ensemble stupidity and Martin's trademark slapstick to muddled and witless effect.

In the 1997 *Trial and Error*, Lynn returns to the courtroom comedy. This time the hapless lawyer is an actor pretending to replace his drunken lawyer friend. Another predictable script, lacking even the wit of *My Cousin Vinny,* the film is unaided by Lynn's visual style. Soft filter shots are used every time a man's attraction to a woman needs to be suggested, and slow-motion hair waving signifying love helps to slow down the film and smother any humour.

The Whole Nine Yards (2000) takes its influence from Arthur Hiller's *The In-Laws* (1979). A debt-ridden dentist (played by Matthew Perry) befriends his neighbour, a notorious hitman now under the Witness Protection Program (Bruce Willis). Unknown to Perry, his wife is plotting to have him killed and the hitman returned to his former bosses for a tidy financial reward. Another paceless comedy, the film demonstrates that Lynn's career as a director seems to be forever embroiled in the less distinctive end of the mainstream Hollywood market. **JD**

M

Hettie MacDONALD

After studying English at Bristol University, Hettie MacDonald joined the Royal Court *Beautiful Thing* (1996)
Theatre under the Regional Theatre Trainee Director Scheme in 1985. At 24, she became
the youngest woman to direct a play in London's West End with 'The Normal Heart'
at the Albery Theatre and has since racked up an impressive list of theatrical credits,
including her production of Jonathan Harvey's 'Beautiful Thing' at the Bush Theatre.
Channel 4 soon approached her to direct a feature-length film of the play and she
became closely involved in the script development.

Promoted as an 'urban fairytale', *Beautiful Thing* (1996) is a bright, breezy, optimistic meditation on sexual awakening and first love set amongst the close-knit community of a Thamesmead estate in South East London. The two gay 16-year-old boys at the
heart of the film predictably courted comparison with *My Beautiful Laundrette* (1985),
but the similarities between the two films are purely superficial. Where Stephen Frears
focuses on more political aspects, MacDonald is more interested in the personal lives
of her protagonists. The themes of domestic violence and homophobia, and the harsh
concrete and cramped spaces of the council estate, are relegated to the background,
secondary to Harvey's humourous, touching and liberating story. MacDonald deals with
potentially weighty matters with a deft lightness of touch, skilfully interweaving primary
colours, sunlight, rainbows, dancing and the music of The Mamas and the Papas. She
also confidently displays a visual style that opens the story up from its stage-bound roots,
coaxing charming and natural performances from her cast.

Most recently, MacDonald has directed 'In a Land of Plenty' for BBC television and
worked on an adaptation of Patricia Highsmith's only lesbian novel, 'The Price of Salt',
for the big screen.   **AA**

Kevin MacDONALD

The grandson of screenwriter Emeric Pressburger and the brother of mercurial producer *Howard Hawks: American*
Andrew MacDonald (*Trainspotting* (1996), *The Beach* (2000)), Kevin MacDonald was *Artist* (1996)

born in 1967 in Glasgow, Scotland. Initially appearing on numerous television programmes, such as the 1977 'A Matter of Michael & Emeric', to discuss the life and work of his legendary grandfather, an appreciation for the craft of cinema ran deep in the family. MacDonald, however, eschewed fictional film-making and in 1995 embarked upon his first documentary, *The Making of an Englishman*.

Produced for television, the film followed MacDonald on a journey across Europe to find out more about the grandfather he never really knew. Featuring interviews with Michael Powell (the other half of one of the greatest film-making partnerships in British cinema history) and luminaries such as Curt Siodmak and Andre Deutsch, it is an engrossing, affectionate and illuminating work that quickly established MacDonald as a skilled documentary maker and chronicler of film history.

His next documentary, *Howard Hawks: American Artist* (1996), is another magnificent work on a cinema icon. In large part a collaboration between MacDonald and writer-director Todd McCarthy (*Visions of Light: The Art of Cinematography* (1992)), it provides insight into the methodology and life of Hollywood's most chameleon-like of auteurs. MacDonald's next portrait of a film director, *Donald Cammell: The Ultimate Performance* (1998), was sadly completed shortly after Cammell's suicide, its release coinciding with the resurrection of the maverick's final film, the initially mauled *Wild Side* (1999). A revealing and melancholic work, it captured Cammell's struggle to recapture the glories of his debut film, *Performance* (1970), through a mixture of intimate interviews and rarely seen archive footage. *The Ultimate Performance* was to prove a fitting eulogy to a singular talent.

Perhaps MacDonald's most successful and contentious work, *One Day in September* (1999), signaled something of a departure for the director because its subject was not film related. A highly dynamic, controversial and polemical account of the Black December terrorist attack on Israeli athletes during the 1972 Munich Olympics, the film heralded a new approach to documentary storytelling. Justine Wright's visceral, dramatic editing marshals the stock footage of the games themselves whilst the bloody aftermath of the attack and the ineptitude of the German authorities are played out to an emotive contemporary score. Documentary purists complained that it was a manipulative effect, whilst Israeli, Palestinian and German commentators unjustly accused the film of political bias. Aside from the impressive array of interview subjects that MacDonald manages to persuade to speak on camera – his ability to draw information from his subjects remains exemplary – one of the real strengths of the film is the compassion, anger and respect that he extends toward the material. The film deservedly won MacDonald an Academy Award in the Best Documentary category.

One of the most skilful modern exponents of the documentary genre, MacDonald's most recent work is the newly completed *A Brief History of Errol Morris* (2000). A relatively low-key look at the work of a fellow non-fiction alumni, the film features an extended interview with Morris, a master chronicler of American crime and sociological dysfunction whose works include *The Thin Blue Line* (1988) and *Mr. Death: The Rise and Fall of Fred A. Leuchter Jr.* (1999).

MacDonald is also the writer of 'Emeric Pressburger: The Life and Death of a Screenwriter' and the editor of 'Imagining Reality: The Faber Book of Documentary'. The latter book details the work of Humphrey Jennings, the highly distinguished British documentarist who sensitively captured the mood of World War Two Britain. MacDonald, a great admirer of Jennings, has also completed a short film on the director for the BBC. **JWo**

John MacKENZIE

After a lengthy career in television and making small-scale films, John MacKenzie, born in Edinburgh, Scotland, in 1932, first entered the public consciousness with his magisterial gangland thriller *The Long Good Friday* (1979). He had already made four competent, if blandly uninventive films, but it was this gritty gangster piece that made his reputation, giving him a level of success that he has since been unable to replicate.

One Brief Summer (1969) is a downbeat melodrama about a wealthy man who loses interest in his mistress and begins courting his daughter's friend. The film explores the still-taboo subject of incest and underage sexuality with sophistication. MacKenzie's follow-up, *Unman, Wittering and Zigo* (1971), is a bleakly macabre story of a school-teacher who slowly realises that his predecessor was murdered by school boys. *Made* (1972), a social-realist melodrama in the Ken Loach vein, focuses on a girl's attempts to find an escape from her life of drudgery. Full of moments of perception and a strong sense of time and place, the film augured well for the kind of gritty dramas that would typify MacKenzie's style.

The Fourth Protocol (1987)
The Last of the Finest (1990)
Ruby (1992)
When the Sky Falls (1999)

The Long Good Friday has become something of a generic classic, the kind of gang-ster film that today's generation of young British film-makers frequently invoke but never improve upon. Bob Hoskins plays Harold Shand, a classic East End mobster determined to propel himself into polite society by moving from casinos and clubs to property specu-lation. His decision to build an Olympic stadium on the derelict Docklands proved oddly prescient of the future regeneration of one of London's most prized areas of real estate. Standing for a certain type of British working-class anti-hero that thought big but ended up small, he is ultimately outmanoeuvred by both the IRA and the American Mafia. In this respect, the narrative and characterisation recall films such as Howard Hawks' *Scarface* (1932), whilst its evocation of gangster argot and procedures is a mixture of Mike Hodge's *Get Carter* (1971) and *Performance* (Donald Cammell/Nic Roeg, 1970). MacKenzie also slyly dismisses the Thatcherite nouveau riche, thus grounding the piece in a solid socio-political realm. His restless camera and inventive cutting increase the film's edgy paranoia tenfold.

The Innocent (1985) is a mildly interesting diversion in MacKenzie's career trajec-tory, coming as it does in the midst of his spy and police procedural thrillers. Andrew Hawley plays Timothy, a young boy growing up in a Yorkshire cotton-mill town during the depression. As is typical of these coming-of-age dramas, a shifting social landscape proves an apt metaphor for the emotional development of Timothy, while the Yorkshire Dales – where he retreats to escape the travails of home – are beautifully shot. With early performances from Liam Neeson and Miranda Richardson, the film is a curate's egg; full of poignant images and heartfelt acting, it is hampered by 'grim-up-north' clichés and a whimsical plot.

The Honorary Consul (1983) and *The Fourth Protocol* (1987) both starred Michael Caine, and although the sums of their two parts did not necessarily add up to a substantial whole, MacKenzie continued to explore the masculine psyche under pressure from exterior influence. The first, an adaptation of Graham Greene's Argentina-based novel, sees Bob Hoskins drawn into guerrilla warfare when Caine's consul is kidnapped. MacKenzie directs with gusto, and elicits excellent performances from his leads; only Richard Gere's over-the-top machismo strikes a false note in this otherwise efficient thriller. *The Fourth Protocol* is based on Frederick Forsyth's espionage tale of a Russian agent (Pierce Brosnan) who travels to England to blow up a US air base. Like Fred Zinnemann's *The Day of the Jackal* (1973), also an adaptation of a Forsyth novel, the film is concerned less with flashy visuals and narrative invention than with a grainy realism that underpins the procedural aspect of the storyline. Michael Caine is the MI5 operative who has to track the spy down, and this cat-and-mouse scenario is expertly drawn and directed with the requisite pace and 'will-he-won't-he?' tension.

MacKenzie seems totally at ease with this kind of narrative, and his *The Last of the Finest* (1990) is another police procedural thriller that boasts excellent performances. Brian Dennehy stars as the LA police officer who, like Clint Eastwood's Harry Callaghan, is disillusioned with the corruption and compromise on the force. When he is suspended, he fights back. Such a generic plot line could, in lesser hands, have been the usual detec-tive television fodder, but MacKenzie emphasises the relationships between the cops, and his unobtrusive camera allows for more characterisation and less reliance on explo-sions and expletives. His next, *Ruby* (1992) was lost among the brouhaha over *JFK* (1991), but standing alone, the film is an efficient biopic of Jack Ruby that throws in some interesting twists and theories about the assassination of John F. Kennedy. Ruby is the Dallas strip-joint owner, played to great effect by Danny Aiello, whose venality with the Dallas police, the Mafia and the CIA marks him out as a key figure in the events of 1963. Although he has to make do without the tricks of the trade that Stone employed to create his conspiracy film par excellence, MacKenzie firmly roots *Ruby* in realism, seedy mise-en-scène and credible supporting characters.

His 1990s output was mainly made up of television movies: *Voyage* (1993) was a cult collaboration between Rutger Hauer and Eric Roberts; his series 'Looking After Jo Jo' featured a magnificent central performance from Robert Carlyle as an avenging angel, and the same grubby urban decay that has characterised much of MacKenzie's output. *When the Sky Falls* (2000) is based on the life of crime correspondent Veronica Guerin who was murdered after her attempts to expose Irish criminal activity. The film falters under its lack of authenticity. Too often MacKenzie and his screenwriters fuse a number of US crime movies without ever working them into a coherent whole. The clichéd depictions of the underworld are a world away from the originality of *The Long Good Friday*, whose veracity has never really been equalled. This plundering of the Hollywood archives does inject the film with pace and kineticism, however. Its contemporary view of Ireland is unconcerned with rural idylls or charming provincials; the grim claustrophobia of this Dublin is dangerous and teeming with corruption.

MacKenzie's next film, *Quicksand*, which is currently in production, stars Michael Caine and Michael Keaton in the story of a banker who flies to Monaco on business and meets a down-on-his-luck film star. **BM**

Gillies MacKINNON

The Grass Arena (1991)
The Playboys (1992)
A Simple Twist of Fate (1994)
Small Faces (1996)
Trojan Eddie (1996)
Regeneration (1997)
Hideous Kinky (1998)

Born in Glasgow in 1948, Gillies MacKinnon is one of Scotland's premier directors, proving his worth over the last two decades by tackling a wide variety of projects for both television and film. He debuted with the television drama *The Grass Arena* (1991) and claimed industry attention in his handling of a superb Albert Finney performance in *The Playboys* (1992), a romantic-comedy drama set in 1950s rural Ireland. Opening with a succession of water images – a lake, the village water-pipe, holy water, waters breaking as a woman goes into labour – the film establishes unmarried mother Tara (Robin Wright) as the symbol of village fertility. However, the villagers, who superstitiously link local bad luck with Tara's refusal to name her child's father, put constant pressure on her to wed Finney's repressed (and reformed alcoholic) policeman Brendan. The name of the female protagonist is just one of a string of references to Victor Fleming's *Gone With the Wind* (1939), an anarchic staging of which is the backdrop for the dramatic climax of *The Playboys*. Ultimately, Tara must choose between the liberating dream world represented by quixotic travelling-entertainer Tom (Aidan Quinn), or the secure but repressive life offered by Brendan. In this choice, Tara prefigures later MacKinnon protagonists who find themselves caught between emancipatory fantasies and restrictive realities, notably Kate Winslet's Julia in *Hideous Kinky* (1998).

Hollywood immediately took note of MacKinnon but, as with his countryman Michael Caton-Jones, seemed nonplussed by the nature of his talent which lends itself more to the detailed observation of characters and social formations than broad action. His sole Hollywood project, *A Simple Twist of Fate* (1994), is a watchable transposition of George Eliot's 'Silas Marner' to contemporary USA. It features the MacKinnon hallmarks of fine, nuanced performances (from Steve Martin and Gabriel Byrne) and a careful engagement of the viewer's sympathies in the encounter between a recluse, the daughter he adopts, and the politician who contests his own paternity claim on the child years later. However, Martin's script overcooks the emotional struggle between the father figures, a misjudgement that detracts from the film's virtues.

MacKinnon returned to Scotland for *Small Faces* (1996), a small but perfectly-formed urban rites-of-passage tale that, undeservedly, was somewhat lost in the wake of the bolder cinematic claims of Danny Boyle's contemporaneous *Trainspotting* (1996). Families are again on the agenda, MacKinnon's script (co-written with brother Billy) detailing the tribal hazards of growing up in late-1960s Glasgow. The child's-eye view of thirteen-year-old protagonist Lex (an outstanding Iain Robertson) is plausibly captured as he wavers between emulating eldest brother and gang member Bobby or identifying with sensitive, artistic middle brother Alan. In casting Joseph McFadden as Alan, Laura Fraser as his girlfriend Joanne (who is coveted by the local hard lads), and Kevin McKidd, who would become a MacKinnon regular and a talismanic presence in his later films, MacKinnon demonstrated his ability to spot new generations of British acting talent. Excellence of a more mature vintage graced the Irish underworld tale *Trojan Eddie*

(1996) in which MacKinnon coaxed the usual good performances from Stephen Rea and Richard Harris. Playwright Billy Roche's screenplay sets Romany godfather John Powers (Harris) against small-time wheeler-dealer Eddie (Rea), with MacKinnon typically refusing to over-sentimentalise the portrayal of life on the fringes of society. Caught up in the infidelities of Powers' younger girlfriend, Eddie nevertheless comes out on top – the final images show his face beaming out from a cinema advertisement for his successful new business while the defeated Powers looks on.

The director's next two projects, both made under the aegis of BBC Films (reflecting the dependence of modern British cinema on television both as a source of funding and as an exhibition window), were critically acclaimed adaptations of well-regarded novels. *Regeneration* (1997), adapted from Pat Barker's compassionate and intelligent novel (the first in a Great War trilogy that ended with the Booker Prize-winning success of 'The Ghost Road'), deals with the neuroses inflicted on the traumatised victims of trench warfare. Interweaving fact and fictional speculation, the film centres on the attempts of military psychiatrist William Rivers (Jonathan Pryce) to treat patients, among them the pacifist-poet Siegfried Sassoon (James Wilby) and Barker's creation, class-conflicted officer Billy Prior (Jonny Lee Miller). Contrasting Rivers' empathetic, Freudian methods with the inhumane electric shock treatment dealt out by Lewis Yealland (John Neville), a doctor who believes that malingering soldiers can be shocked out of their silence and restored to clockwork 'fighting units', the film explores the psychological effects of war on a generation socially ill-equipped to acknowledge their own emotional frailty. As the 'stiff upper lip' facade peddled by the military top brass is progressively stripped away, the soldiers are revealed as bare husks of their former selves, shellshocked into a silence that Rivers eventually interprets as an eloquent statement against the barbarity and futility of the War. Not only does MacKinnon successfully reproduce the book's compassionate stance towards the victim, it also explores many of Barker's complex thematic motifs, such as the opening up of rigid, socially-enforced gender categories under the stress of war. Rivers points out that the homosexual Sassoon's love for the soldiers in his care could be misinterpreted by his political enemies; for Prior, the caring Rivers begins to embody a double of his mother.

In this fluid nexus of identifications and emotions, sex is associated with death: Prior and his munitions-worker girlfriend, Sarah, share their first intimate moments upon a tomb in a cemetery. War is linked with aesthetic beauty: Sassoon encourages fellow hospital inmate Wilfred Owen to turn his developing poetic skill upon his battlefield experiences. Prior's flashbacks to the trenches are rendered in the same bleached-out, silvery palette that later distinguished the battle scenes in Steven Spielberg's *Saving Private Ryan* (1998), and the opening images of dismembered corpses coalescing into the mud of 'no man's land' are striking. The real strengths of the film, however, lie in its sensitive handling of Barker's thematically rich, multi-layered material, and the coaxing of superb performances from the principals. Miller's defensive, guilt-ridden Prior and Pryce's Rivers, who succumbs to a long-repressed stammer as he increasingly identifies with his patients, are the standouts. *Regeneration* is a morally muscular film, opening up to steely scrutiny a patriarchal system willing to sacrifice its sons with the zeal of Abraham.

The strong sense of place notable in *Small Faces* and *The Playboys* once again played a factor in the accomplishment of MacKinnon's next film, although the Morocco of *Hideous Kinky* is filtered through the awed perspective of two English schoolgirls. Based on the early-1970s adventures recounted in Esther Freud's book, the film charts the inverted relationship of Kate Winslet's Julia and her young daughters Bea and Lucy, who are dragged across North Africa in the wake of their mother's post-divorce mission of self-discovery. Half a world away in geographical and class terms, the girls still share an affinity with *Small Faces*' Lex. In this relationship, the children, retaining a steady grip on their innate school-age scepticism despite the wonders unfurled before them, are forced into the position of guardians to Julia's self-indulgent hippy naïveté. The film never openly condemns Julia as selfish, however, but instead shows her slowly coming to accept her responsibilities as Bea, yearning for structure and propriety, drifts into the care of a Christian missionary. The prevailing mood is one of impermanence and magical illusion, a carnivalesque holiday from regular life that cannot possibly be sustained for all of Julia's self-deception; Christmas is a constant and telling reference point in the script.

MacKinnon achieves this fragile yet seductive atmosphere through stunning compositions and a riotous colour scheme that becomes a valuable signifier of the protagonists' emotional development. As Julia's heady romance with the eastern lifestyle begins to cool, the early reds, oranges and pinks of the Marrakesh street markets are increasingly replaced by more neutral blues, whites and purples. Transvestism, in both a cultural and gendered sense, is an important motif. The girls are regularly seen in masculine dress: Lucy, for instance, wears an increasingly battered Manchester United football shirt to display her attachment to home. Julia adopts the local garments and her sometime partner Bilal (Saïd Taghmaoui) ironically dons that evergreen colonial emblem, the panama hat. Culturally, temporally and personally, the Morocco of *Hideous Kinky* is a true melting pot of values and identities through which MacKinnon deftly critiques 1960s liberalism: transferable parental figures are envisioned in Bea's defection and Julia's nightmares of losing her daughter in the exotic land.

MacKinnon renders narratives where families, both of the biological and less orthodox varieties, and personal relationships figure strongly. This ability has led to his most popular and accessible work to date, the television film *Last of the Blonde Bombshells* (2000), a Golden Globe award-winning success starring Judi Dench as the leader of an all-female swing band whose reformation rekindles memories of World War One.   **MF**

John MADDEN

Ethan Frome (1993)
Golden Gate (1994)
Mrs Brown (1997)
Shakespeare in Love (1998)
Captain Corelli's Mandolin
(2001)

John Madden has come to specialise in a brand of heritage drama favoured by cinemagoers as much as executives; stories of forbidden love, set against the obstructing backdrops of repression, restriction and the rules of society. Using period setting and evocative cinematography to conjure the romantic context, together with passionate performances from his male and female leads, he has woven various versions of his love-triangle tragedies, from the weighty New England melodrama *Ethan Frome* (1993) to the moral minefield of racial love in *Golden Gate* (1994). Madden's affinity for period drama with a literary, literate bent is most notably illustrated by the engaging *Mrs Brown* (1997) and the multiple Oscar®-winning *Shakespeare In Love* (1998). There is the inescapable sense of something pre-packaged about Madden's more recent work, however, particularly exemplified by his decision to direct *Captain Corelli's Mandolin* (2001), the surefire adaptation of Louis de Bernieres' publishing phenomenon. His reluctance to step beyond the cosy confines of period romance or experiment with more edgy styles and material is in danger of making a misty-eyed old romantic seem something of a brighteyed cynic.

Born in Portsmouth, UK, in 1949, initially a director of television and theatre, Madden worked in the early 1990s on British and US television series including 'Inspector Morse', 'The Young Sherlock Homes' and Jim Henson's 'The Storyteller', as well as dramas such as 'Grownups', 'A Wreath of Roses' and the BAFTA-nominated 'The Widowmaker'. Demonstrably a director of considerable dramatic skill, and having additionally directed plays on Broadway, he made his Hollywood debut in 1993 with *Ethan Frome*, an adaptation of an Edith Wharton novel in which New England farmer Frome falls for the cousin of his oppressive, bed-ridden wife. The repressive puritan values of turn-of-the-century New England, mirrored in the film's wintry Vermont landscapes and bleak cinematography, are contrasted with Frome's compulsive love and destructive passion, at once morally illicit and emotionally legitimate.

This is powerful emotional drama of a type much suited to Madden's style, and the various oppositions – love and duty, passion and guilt, emotion and religion – are neatly developed and explored. Less successful is *Golden Gate*, a confused moral drama in which an FBI agent, wracked with guilt over the suicide of a Chinese laundry worker he helped convict, seduces the man's daughter. Set amongst the McCarthy witch-hunts of the 1950s, the film sets out to juxtapose a relationship that contravenes the prevailing mores of both societies, but succeeds only in patronising its audience with simplistic characterisations and over-earnest direction. Madden was yet to hit upon the dynamite formula, though these early experiments illustrate the direction in which he was headed: historical romantic-drama with an evocative setting and a tragic streak of unattainability.

Mrs Brown was Madden's first large-scale success, and is perhaps his most artistically rewarding film. Initially shot for the BBC, the film snow-balled once Miramax, a company whose entrepreneurial stock-in-trade is the sleeper hit, became involved; following its 1997 presentation at Cannes, Madden was effectively launched into the big-league of British directors. Charting Queen Victoria's prolonged period of mourning following the death of her husband Prince Albert – the time which gave rise to her 'Widow of Windsor' pseudonym – and the constitutional crisis her extended absence caused, the film sets out to explore the private face behind her imposing public figure, particularly the prospect of facing life and the throne as a woman alone. Her relationship with gamekeeper and bodyguard-to-be John Brown is the heart of the story; it is an undeclared but palpable relationship of impossible love and the recuperative force which allows her to face up to responsibility. Madden's skill is in conveying the subtle, covert passionate subtext beneath the surface of decorum and duty – he to his Queen, she to her people – with an understated and engaging touch. This is a different Madden love triangle; the third figure here is two-fold, both the spectre of the dead King whom Victoria would never disgrace, and the country to whom the Queen is inextricably wedded. The complex mix of love and friendship, desire and duty, together with superb performances from Judi Dench and Billy Connolly, makes for intelligent, adult cinema.

Shakespeare in Love (1998) is similarly rooted in the contradictory pressures of society and self, but Madden exchanges *Mrs Brown*'s Victorian gravity for an altogether more Elizabethan feel; a bold, sassy, sexy mix of farce, pastiche and romance, a tragi-comedy in the true sense of the word. It is an ironic take on a fictionalised relationship in Shakespeare's life in which he falls in love with a woman betrothed to the Earl of Wessex. Shot through with a whole range of post-modern reference points – Shakespeare going to a psychologist, haggling with recalcitrant actors and struggling with writer's block – and directed in an energetic style, the film manages to capture something of the spirit of Shakespeare's wit, wordplay and invention, thanks largely to Tom Stoppard's effortlessly convincing script. Madden delights in any number of in-jokes, pastiches of the plays, cross-dressings and gender-bendings, and the result is an irreverent dose of Shakespeare-lite. The clever-clever style, slightly smug self-referencing tone and pop casting inevitably leave the sense of a film that thinks it is just too smart to pick holes in. Some purists and factual scholars were critical. Whether the film deserved its shower of Oscars®, and whether it contributes to a wider interest in Shakespeare, is a moot point.

Guaranteed a captive audience, thanks to its origins in a book that reportedly resides in one in twenty British households, *Captain Corelli's Mandolin* shows the same trend as Madden's previous works but none of their charm. It explores the relationship between an Italian captain and a girl on Cephalonia, the Greek island that his army has occupied in World War Two, which flouts not only national allegiances but also her betrothal to simple fisherman Mandras. Comparison with the book is inevitable, particularly given that the film excises large parts of its complex narrative, pares down the subtext love story of Corelli's gay lieutenant for his captain to nothing, and waters down its bleak conclusion to a shamelessly commercial happy ending. Although impressively filmed in Mediterranean hues, and with some exhilarating war sequences, it is badly let down by a simplistic script, some awful accents and the woefully inappropriate casting of Nicolas Cage as the awkward Corelli. Despite having come to the project very late in the day, following original director Roger Michell's heart attack days before the start of shooting, Madden is obviously going through the motions here. **OB**

Sharon MAGUIRE

With her debut feature, *Bridget Jones's Diary* (2001), Sharon Maguire achieves a successful, if undemanding, adaptation of Helen Fielding's book, itself a novelisation of her hugely popular column that appeared regularly in *The Independent* from 1995.

Maguire started out in television, working as a producer and director for the BBC programme 'The Late Show' between 1991 and 1993. She then directed a number of well-received documentaries such as 'The Godfather'. Examining the architect Philip

Bridget Jones's Diary (2001)

Johnson, it was short-listed for Best Documentary at the Montreal Film Festival. Despite the success of her documentary work, Maguire was perhaps a surprising choice to direct. However, given that the character of Bridget's friend Shaz was reputedly based on the director, she was certainly afforded rich insight.

With four million copies sold worldwide, the runaway success of the book and the track record of the film's production company, Working Title Films (*Four Weddings and a Funeral* (1994), *Elizabeth* (1998) and *Notting Hill* (1999)), lessened any risk.

In many ways *Bridget Jones's Diary* is a quintessentially British film. As one critic said: 'no other country in the world would make a film about a woman who hates herself for being womanly in this way'. Maguire does not shy away from showing us a flawed, overweight and self-deprecating heroine. The look of the film is equally specific in its referencing of British culture, from the featured Tesco bags, to crowd scenes with Jeffrey Archer, and the in-joke around the casting of Colin Firth. Maguire's foregrounding of this cultural specificity might go someway to explaining the controversy surrounding the casting of the Texan Renée Zellweger as the eponymous heroine, a choice that was vindicated by the actress' performance.

Maguire demonstrates a light comic touch in her treatment of a zeitgeist book. Together with writers Helen Fielding, Andrew Davies and Richard Curtis, she successfully overcomes the problems of transplanting source material that focuses on the internal feelings of its heroine to the screen. The film has become the most successful British film of all time, to date making more than £34 million in the United Kingdom and $64 million in the United States.

Maguire is now slated to direct a film based on 'Pride and Prejudice', updated by the playwright Wendy Wasserstein.   **HR**

Terry MARCEL

Terry Marcel is a highly successful television director who has failed to make an impact in the film industry on either side of the Atlantic. Born in Oxford, UK, in 1942, he began working as an assistant director on small-scale thrillers, including *10 Rillington Place* (1971) and *Straw Dogs* (1971), as well as (uncredited) assistance on Blake Edwards' *Pink Panther* films.

Marcel's first two films as director, *Why Not Stay For Breakfast?* (1979) and *There Goes The Bride* (1979), are somewhat embarrassing adaptations of Ray Cooney stage farces. Cooney both co-wrote and produced these sub-standard productions, containing elaborate set-pieces that required (and received) steady, albeit unremarkable, direction.

Hawk the Slayer (1980), his next film, is now his most well-known. *Hawk* was one of the first films aimed at the growing audience for post-Arthurian fantasy-science fiction. All the usual suspects are present in the script (co-written by Marcel): dwarves, magic swords and giants make an appearance, as does Jack Palance as the villain Voltan, amidst a supporting cast of UK television actors. Now the film looks dated, the effects are laughable and, although plot flashbacks are well-handled, the direction rarely raises itself above the merely sufficient.

Marcel directed episodes of television series such as 'Bergerac', 'The Bill' and 'Cats Eyes', before returning to features for *Prisoners of the Lost Universe* (1983). Harry Robertson co-wrote and co-produced, as he had done with *Hawk the Slayer*. Like *Hawk*, *Prisoners* was aimed at the fantasy market; again it was let down by dull plotting and uncomplicated but unremarkable direction and casting. More television followed, before Marcel returned to the screen with another co-written venture, a tongue-in-cheek version of Indiana Jones, based on comic-strip heroine 'Jane' published in the *Daily Mirror* in the 1940s and 1950s. The film, *Jane and the Lost City* (1987), features the (somewhat feeble) film-acting debut of UK comedian Jasper Carrott. Although there are some fun set-pieces, and the direction has some of the crisp smoothness of *The Princess Bride* (also 1987), it contains none of the quality of script or acting that made the latter a classic. Marcel gave a nod to his Ray Cooney roots by allowing Jane to lose much of her clothing in an increasingly improbable number of ways. Essentially, however, following its Royal Gala Premiere, the film's uniquely English outlook guaranteed that it would never be a hit.

Embarking on a number of projects in children's television with long-time BBC collaborator Ray Thompson, founder of Cloud Nine Screen Entertainment, Marcel was executive producer on the successful 'The Enid Blyton Adventure Series'. He also directed a television film, *Bejewelled* (1991), for the Disney Channel.

In 1999 he directed the by-numbers sequel to John Dahl's *The Last Seduction* (1994), *The Last Seduction II*, and although he managed to retain some of the biting sarcasm of the original, neither his direction nor the acting succeeded in achieving its pace or dark wit. Marcel's latest project, 'Dark Knight', an attempted serialisation of the classic 'Ivanhoe' by Sir Walter Scott, is unsurprisingly in television.

Marcel is undoubtedly an experienced figure in British television and cinema with a talent for filming complex set-pieces, but it seems unlikely now that his celluloid achievements will ever match his ambition.   **AL**

William MARSH

Born and raised in a relatively old-fashioned suburb of Minneapolis in the 1970s, William *Dead Babies (2000)* Marsh studied psychology, theology and music before relocating to London to take up drama. Highly acclaimed performances as Lenny Bruce and Neal Cassady on the London Fringe led to smaller parts in Hollywood productions such as *Entrapment* (1999) and *Saving Private Ryan* (1998), as well as a career in directing for the theatre and his first short film, *Hotel*.

Marsh's first feature, *Dead Babies* (2000), based on Martin Amis' 1975 novel, had a nine-year gestation period as Marsh struggled to secure funding for the project, no doubt due to its difficult and brutal content. Unfairly and universally reviled upon release, while the film cannot be considered a success it did not deserve the critical butchering it received. *Dead Babies*, the story of a group of English friends and their American guests going mad during a drug-fuelled weekend on a country estate, is drenched in pitch-black humour and a refreshingly raw energy and enthusiasm which is rare in contemporary British film. Unfortunately, the film is rife with caricatures rather than characters; empathy is not encouraged. Given that the source material is very much a product of its time, despite the film's millennial updating, the subject matter leaves it feeling stuck in the 1970s. In the years since the book's publication, audiences have witnessed the release of films such as *The Big Chill* (1983), *Trainspotting* (1996) and *Fight Club* (1999), all of which bear certain stylistic and thematic similarities to *Dead Babies*. It seems that the material has been handicapped by the length of time of time it has taken Marsh to bring his film to the screen. Far too many elements of this nihilistic tale of decadent, disaffected youth flailing aimlessly in a morally bankrupt society have been seen before and executed with far greater impact.   **AA**

Sean MATHIAS

Born in Swansea, Wales, in 1956, Sean Mathias is best known as a theatre writer *Bent (1996)* and director, having won numerous awards for productions on Broadway and London's West End, including 'Indiscretions' (from his own script) and 'Uncle Vanya'. In 1989 he directed a stage version of Martin Sherman's 'Bent' for the gay and lesbian organisation Stonewall. Set in Germany in 1934, 'Bent' centres on Max, a gay Jewish man who is taken from Bohemian Berlin to a concentration camp. Here, his love for a fellow prisoner, Horst, eventually leads him to swap his yellow star for a pink triangle – the Nazi badge of homosexuality. The playwright, Martin Sherman, chose Mathias to direct the film version over such luminaries as Rainer Werner Fassbinder.

Clive Owen appears as Max, and Québécoise actor Lothaire Bluteau plays Horst. Sir Ian McKellen (who played the lead in the 1979 Royal Court premiere) took the role of Max's uncle, Freddie, while Mick Jagger made one of his rare appearances as the mercurial club owner, Greta/George. *Bent* (1997) was shot on location in the UK, with Glasgow streets doubling for Berlin and an abandoned cement factory outside Tring standing in for Dachau. The latter site offered many opportunities to dwarf the actors during their scenes of soul-destroying manual labour. For critics, one moral problem with the film (as with the play) is the implication that Nazis treated gays as lower than Jews, any attempt at relativism in this context being unwise. The script, however, makes it clear that both were treated with contempt. *Bent* won the International Critics award at Cannes in 1997.

Mathias has also worked as a film actor – appearing in *A Bridge Too Far* (1977) and *White Mischief* (1987) amongst others – and published a novel, 'Manhattan Mourning'. He is currently preparing his second feature, *Quadrille*, based on the play by Noel Coward. **KP**

John MAYBURY

Love is the Devil (1998) John Maybury was born in 1958 in London, where he still lives. He studied art at North East London Polytechnic and began designing sets and costumes for Derek Jarman's 1977 film *Jubilee*. It was Jarman who gave him his first super-8 camera, and Maybury went on to make his own avant-garde films from 1982. Experimental and uncompromising, Maybury has worked with avant-garde luminaries such as Leigh Bowery but is better known for his music videos, particularly Sinead O' Connor's 'Nothing Compares 2 U', which won four MTV awards and a Grammy nomination.

His first feature, *Love is the Devil* (1998), is an expressionistic biopic on painter Francis Bacon and his lover George Dyer. The film concentrates more on atmosphere than the detailing of a life, exploring the nature of the creative impulse and its countering destruction. However, the importance of Dyer is significant during a period in which Bacon is considered to have produced his best work. A petty, East End thief, Dyer fell into a far more morally corrupt world than his own, the destructive Soho artist set from 1964–71 centring around Bacon and the Colony Room's Muriel Belcher (Tilda Swinton). In the film he literally falls, crashing through the roof whilst breaking into Bacon's studio, and continuing to fall to his doom. The relationship is brutally eviscerated and decays alongside its representations in paint. Hallucinatory effects – eccentric colour fusions and tortuous perspectives – fittingly convey the skewed relationships; the images are refracted and warped by distorting lenses shot through a nicotine haze. Bacon's actual pictures were denied reproduction by his estate; the painted images in celluloid are reminiscent of his work but never overburden the film. An unsettling score by Ryuichi Sakamoto underpins the visuals.

Maybury's most recent project, a biopic of Elizabethan playwright Christopher Marlowe, has run into financial problems. It has been idly rumoured that he has been approached to direct another artist biopic on the milieu of the Young British Artists, such as Damien Hirst and Tracey Emin, and their rise to fame in the 1990s. Meanwhile, he continues with his fine art career. **FG**

Trish McADAM

Snakes and Ladders (1996) Trish McAdam once told Galway's *Film West*: 'I love films like *All About Eve* and *Whatever Happened to Baby Jane*, films about the tensions between women'. The influences are not suprising given the narrative and the feel of her feature film *Snakes and Ladders* (1996). This is a story about two youngish, arty room-mates in search of love, friendship, success as feminist performance artists and so on. Despite a love triangle scenario, most of the film's energy comes from the complex dynamics between the two women (Pam Boyd and Gin Moxley). This is the most interesting and well-drawn aspect of the film, much more so than the complicated boy-meets-girl plot that sometimes competes for McAdam's attention (the boy in question is played by Sean Hughes).

Overall, *Snakes and Ladders* feels like an episode of 'Friends' as written by Dermot Healy. On one level it a straightforward film, featuring cute young people and hip music; on another, it is a satirical portrait of the odd, painful ways that Irish people try to find some form of individual expression. Bohemia and Ireland tend to be pretty far apart – and not just geographically. Referencing the cultural baggage that makes it hard for men and women to talk to each other, generally *Snakes and Ladders* is a lighthearted, sincere film. Like some of the more recent films of Paddy Breathnach or Gerard Stembridge, it suggests that there is an emergent generation of Irish film-makers that is more confident about being Irish and more interested in making solid, clearly told stories with high entertainment value. This is, in the final analysis, a positive development for Irish cinema. **JW**

Sydney McCARTNEY

Born in County Antrim, Northern Ireland, in 1954, Sydney McCartney attended the National Film School at Beaconsfield for four years. During that time, he trained as a lighting cameraman and worked on sixteen graduation films, two of which won awards at the Edinburgh Film Festival. His initial experiences in the industry were as a director of photography: he worked on short films, music videos and television series including 'The Living Body'. McCartney began directing commercials in the 1980s, winning several awards, wrote and directed a couple of short films, and moved into series direction in 1989 on 'Yellowthread Street' for Yorkshire Television. His first feature film, *The Bridge* (1992), is a period love story set in Victorian times. Based on Maggie Hemingway's novel, it hypothesises a narrative for Philip Wilson Steer's painting of a woman alone on a bridge. A predictable formula is somewhat revived by McCartney's unhurried pace and flair for atmosphere.

The Bridge (1992)
A Love Divided (1999)

His work for television continued steadily, and included 'The Young Indiana Jones Chronicles' for LucasFilm, *The Whipping Boy* for the Disney Channel, the Emmy Award-winning *The Canterville Ghost* for Hallmark/NBC, and 'The Ambassador' for BBC Northern Ireland. His second feature, *A Love Divided* (1999), is set in the 1950s and based around the events of the notorious Fethard boycott in which a couple of mixed religion were ostracised by members of the local Catholic community, leading to widespread sectarian bitterness. McCartney's film explores the effect of the enormous social and religious pressure on the relationship between a Catholic man and his Protestant wife. In some ways the film can also be seen in broader political terms as a study of the fragile nature of the alliances being forged between the north and south of Ireland at the time of its release. Directed and photographed in a workmanlike manner, the film occasionally resembles the work of Frank Capra, particularly in its climactic confrontation scene in which Liam Cunningham addresses a meeting of the townsfolk in defiance of the parish priest. It was nominated for five Irish Film and Television Academy Awards and won Best Film at the Celtic Film Festival. It also won Audience Awards at the Verona, Rotterdam and Emden Film Festivals. **HO**

Joseph McGRATH

Joe McGrath, born in Scotland in 1930, is inevitably associated with two of the most dominant, and often heavily criticised, trends to emerge from the British cinema of the 1960s: the development of anarchic satire and the much derided swinging London films. His work tends to combine a scattergun approach to topical parody, with shots being fired at innumerable and varied targets, and a frenetic, highly stylised visual technique which clearly owes a good deal to the influence of Richard Lester. Much of this may appear dated now, but at the time it seemed to represent the embodiment of all that was new and daring.

Casino Royale (1967)
Thirty is a Dangerous Age, Cynthia (1968)
The Bliss of Mrs Blossom (1968)
The Magic Christian (1970)
Digby, the Biggest Dog in the World (1973)
The Great McGonagall (1974)
Girls Come First (1975)
I'm Not Feeling Myself Tonight (1976)
The Strange Case of the End of Civilisation as We Know It (1977)
Rising Damp (1980)
Night Train to Murder (1983)

Like so many other British directors of his generation, McGrath's training ground was television. He worked as producer and director on 'Not Only, But Also', one of the key comedy sketch programmes to appear in the wake of 'The Goon Show' and 'Beyond the Fringe', and helped pave the way for the innovations of the Monty Python team. It was the beginning of a fruitful association with Dudley Moore and Peter Cook.

His first solo feature film was a direct spin-off of his work with Moore. *Thirty is a Dangerous Age, Cynthia* (1968) is essentially a vehicle for the diminutive comedian built as a series of sketches, written by McGrath and Moore with John Wells, which remain rooted in the format of their television collaboration. McGrath added a barrage of playful cinematic tricks, using wipes, jump cuts and whip pans to enliven, and distract from, what is otherwise a fairly conventional film. This self-conscious foregrounding of filmic techniques, largely brought to prominence by Richard Lester, became the house style of swinging London films, but rarely managed to capture the spirit of spontaneity and irreverence which was to be found in so much British popular culture of the period.

This is painfully apparent in *Casino Royale* (1967), a James Bond spoof on which McGrath is just one of the six directors credited. The film remains the epitome of late-1960s self-indulgence, a rag-bag of overextended ideas and visual puns played out by an all-star cast who seem frequently lost amidst all the Op Art designs and camera tricks.

It nonetheless retains the fascination of a period piece. The same characteristics beset *The Bliss of Mrs Blossom* (1968), a frantic farce with Shirley MacLaine as the wife of a bra manufacturer who hides her lover away in the attic. The paper-thin plot is simply a peg on which to hang a mass of fantasy sequences and pop surrealism. The visual style, like the interior of Mrs Blossom's house, is a swirl of psychedelic colour and movement whose superficiality quickly becomes tiresome. However, the real essence of McGrath's work can still be found in *The Magic Christian* (1970). Scripted by the director with Terry Southern and Peter Sellers, the film assembles an impressive cast including many of those most associated with the satire boom, such as Spike Milligan and several of the Python team. Sellers plays a crazed millionaire who sets out to dispose of his fortune by exposing those who pursue wealth and power. Anarchic, anti-establishment humour is again channelled into a revue-like structure and the film is handled with a crude exuberance that makes full use of deliberately tasteless imagery.

Until this point, McGrath's work succeeded in finding a visual approach to suit the excesses and parodic intent of the material. This mix is not apparent in his subsequent work. In an attempt to modify his usual style and produce a children's comedy, *Digby, the Biggest Dog in the World* (1973) is a much gentler affair. As with *The Great McGonagall* (1974), it afforded McGrath the opportunity to work with Spike Milligan again; retaining some of the inventiveness of Milligan's writing, even this is frequently wilfully shambolic. However, these are certainly preferable to the lame sex farces *I'm Not Feeling Myself Tonight* (1976) and *Girls Come First* (1975); on the latter McGrath is credited as Croisette Meubles.

Little of McGrath's subsequent work has attracted much attention. *Night Train to Murder* (1983) was a modest vehicle for the television comics Morecambe and Wise, and *The Strange Case of the End of Civilisation as We Know It* (1977) features John Cleese as Sherlock Holmes. He showed a rather more deft touch with *Rising Damp* (1980), which at least retained something of the pathos of the original television series. Without the vibrant context of the 1960s to give his work its sense of contemporary relevance, McGrath's later work has become gradually more orthodox.   **RS**

Mary McGUCKIAN

Mary McGuckian's three feature films to date are disparate in both style and content; there are no consistent themes or aesthetic styles running through her body of work. Her first feature, *Words Upon the Window Pane* (1994), showed considerable accomplishment in its cinematography and treatment of narrative, which are reminiscent of European art cinema. Despite some interesting moments, her following two films, *This is the Sea* (1998) and *Best* (2000) have failed to live up to the promise of her debut.

Words Upon the Window Pane, based on a one-act play by W.B. Yeats, focuses on Jonathan Swift's (Jim Sheridan) relationships with his two lovers, Stella (Brid Brennan) and Vanessa (Orla Brady). The stories of these historical figures are told by a medium, Mrs. Henderson (Geraldine James), each séance precipitating a flashback which advances their intertwined narratives. The historical story is juxtaposed with the contemporary story, set in Dublin in 1928, which concerns a heterogeneous group of people who frequent the séances. The narratives of the past and present intertwine dramatically in the final séance in which Mrs. Henderson and her assistant enact a violent conflict between Swift and Stella. By using the device of the séance to access the private and emotional aspects of a well-known historical figure, McGuckian draws attention to the difficulty of accessing these largely hidden aspects of history, and also draws attention to alternative means of imagining and narrating them. The film is also, according to McGuckian, an attempt to address Ireland's Anglo-Irish past.

This Is the Sea is a conventional love-across-the-barricades story set in contemporary Belfast, concerning a romance between Protestant Hazel (Samantha Morton) and Catholic Malachy (Ross McDade). Malachy's friend becomes involved in IRA activities and is killed by a car bomb towards the end of the film. Focusing on the suffering of those caught up unwittingly in political violence, it replicates the opposition between the private world of romance, family and domesticity, and the public world of politics and violence which is set up by the majority of films about the Troubles in Northern Ireland.

This Is the Sea is competently executed and handsomely shot, but offers little variation on the many films which address the effects of the conflict in Northern Ireland.

Best (2000) recounts the life and career of footballer George Best (John Lynch) and includes archive footage of Best playing for Manchester United. The slightly bleached look of the film imitates the quality of 1970s film, and its elliptical editing and use of flashbacks recalls *Words Upon the Window Pane*. A major flaw, however, is the casting of the lugubrious Lynch as Best. Lynch's consistently melancholy air, which is perfect for roles such as the eponymous hero of Pat O'Connor's *Cal* (1984), is inappropriate to the portrayal of Best, a man known for his exuberant charm, wit and sexual charisma. Partly because of Lynch's performance style, the film's interest lies in his gradual descent into alcohol abuse and its effect on his career and his relationships with his fellow players, his girlfriend and Manchester United manager, Matt Busby (Ian Bannen), who emerges as Best's father-figure.

McGuckian is clearly a skilful film-maker with a wide range of interests and one hopes that her next feature will do her talents justice. **FF**

Paul McGUIGAN

Paul McGuigan moved into feature films after a career as a photographer and documen- *The Acid House* (1998)
tarist. Combining an eye for the strikingly pictorial with a social realist aesthetic that *Gangster No. 1* (2000)
underpins a frequent excess of 'style', the skills he acquired are evident in both of his films to date *The Acid House* (1998) is a trio of tales adapted by Irvine Welsh from his own collection of short stories set in modern Scotland. 'The Granton Star Cause' (originally screened as a television short) relates the tale of Boab (Stephen McCole), a young working-class man who, suffering from the proverbial bad day, is given the chance of revenge through a meeting with God. 'A Soft Touch' tells of Johnny (Kevin McKidd), a meek supermarket worker whose prostitute wife betrays him further by taking up with the thuggish neighbour in the flat above. 'The Acid House' is the story of a bizarre personality swap between acid-head Coco (Ewen Bremner) and a new born baby.

Given the film's often absurdist, surreal tone, such synopses do not do full justice to their actual execution. 'A Soft Touch' is the most effective of the trilogy, thanks in no small part to the performances of McKidd and Gary McCormack as Larry, the flamboyant, violent neighbour. Also, McGuigan integrates the dual realist and excessive stylistic modes most effectively in this segment. This allows for greater character insight, ultimately revealing the complicit role Johnny plays in his dire situation. The other segments do not cohere so effectively so there is no real sense of the trilogy forming a greater whole; themes of working-class masculinity, religion and the mundane are scattered across the film without a sense of integration. 'The Granton Star Cause' presents God as a slovenly drunk and 'The Acid House' suggests a link between chemical psychosis and rebirth, yet there is no sense of these events actually imposing themselves and bouncing off each other as thematic strands. While the film invites comparisons with *Trainspotting* (1996), not least for the involvement of Welsh, it wisely treads its own path. However, one cannot help feeling that the stronger aspects of the film evinced in its middle segment might have warranted a greater focus, yielding more rewarding results.

Gangster No. 1 (2000) is a far more assured work that once more draws from a dual realist-expressionistic style, evoking both the twisted psyche of its title figure and the urban ambience of his surroundings. Based on a play by Louis Mellis and David Scinto, it focuses on the seductive allure of evil, power and fear, distinguishing itself greatly from the rash of inferior, 'ironic' British crime films that emerged in the late 1990s. Structured as a long flashback, the film introduces Gangster 55 (Malcolm McDowell, recalling his *Clockwork Orange* voice-over) in the modern era, narrating the tale of his own rise through the ranks of London's 1960s criminal underworld. His young self is portrayed by Paul Bettany, gradually obsessing over the status and position afforded his boss, Freddie (David Thewlis). Such is the young criminal's lust for power, his humanity is stripped away, a characteristic summed by the title's pun on his inner emptiness. Indeed, the gangster is never given a name, identified instead through the twisted ideal he pursues ruthlessly. McGuigan makes striking use of Bettany's staring, pallid features, especially in the moments when he contorts his face into a grotesque death mask. Furthermore, the film's violence has a genuine frisson, achieving a sado-erotic charge in the sequence where the gangster tortures and murders a rival mobster. Here, McGuigan reveals influences such as *Performance* (1970), a source of reference that again sets it apart further from generic contemporaries. Achieving insights amid its melodrama, *Gangster No. 1* suggests directions in which the British crime film might profitably follow.   **NJ**

Conor McPHERSON

Saltwater (2000) Born in Dublin in 1970, Conor McPherson emerged as one of the country's most exciting new dramatists in the 1990s with a series of theatrical monologues and plays, most notably, 'The Weir'. A graduate of University College Dublin, his slippery dialogue and ability to present ambiguous, multi-faceted characters won him almost instant acclaim. As his stage reputation grew internationally (he became writer-in-residence at the Bush Theatre, London, in 1996), McPherson segued into film writing with Paddy Breatnach's *I Went Down* (1997). This was essentially an Irish variant on *Pulp Fiction* (1994), loosely inspired by some of McPherson's own monologues. It features two low-level gangsters who find themselves caught between the conflicting interests and hidden agendas of their superiors. It had a welcome sense of humour and was popular due to McPherson's occasionally witty dialogue and a likable performance by Brendan Gleeson. It screened at the Sundance Film Festival in 1998 and went on to win awards for Best Screenplay from the Irish Film and Television Academy and at the San Sebastian Film Festival.

McPherson's second cinematic outing was his directorial debut *Saltwater* (2000). An adaptation of his play 'This Lime Tree Bower', it concerns the misfortunes of a Dublin family, who are in debt to a local loan shark, and the misadventures of their friends. It is an ethical drama in which the audience is challenged by characters of uncertain morality. However, the play does not convert smoothly to film; the playwright's passages of characteristic dialogue left him little room to create cinematic visuals or to explore and expand upon the original monologues. The result was little more than a series of verbal character vignettes that appeal to his admirers but lacks vision and coherence. Nonetheless, the film won second place in the Best First Feature category at the Galway Film Fleadh and earned McPherson a second Irish Film and Television Academy award for Best Screenplay.

He has since written the play 'Port Authority' and directed an adaptation of Samuel Beckett's 'Endgame' for the 'Beckett on Film' season.   **HO**

Owen McPOLIN

Drinking Crude (1997) Born in 1969 in County Kerry, Ireland, Owen McPolin has worked extensively as a lighting cameraman since his graduation from West Surrey College of Art & Design in 1992, contributing to features such as Nichola Bruce's *I Could Read the Sky* (1999) and Fintan Connolly's *Flick* (2000). He has also worked in fiction and non-fiction Irish and English language television programmes.

His directorial debut, *Drinking Crude* (1997), is a road movie that follows the fortunes of an Irish schoolboy who leaves the provincialism of his native town and country in search of a better life. He moves to London and soon finds himself friendless and victimised. He then meets an affable Scotsman who cleans industrial oil tanks for a living and who offers him a job. Ironically, the work takes them back to his hometown in Ireland, where he must confront friends and family. The film has little to distinguish it visually from scores of other Irish films, but McPolin has enough confidence in the camera to allow several important passages play out via silence and montage.

McPolin is continuing to work on both film and digital video formats.   **HO**

Nick MEAD

Bank Robber (1993) Like many of his contemporaries, Nick Mead has used his love of music and a career
Swing (1999) as a music-video director to launch a successful film-directing career. Creating darkly humorous films, socially aware films, Mead has successfully instituted himself as a competent director within the Hollywood community.

His feature debut, *Bank Robber* (1993), starring Patrick Dempsey, Lisa Bonet and Forest Whitaker, is at first glance a simple film about a bank robber, some cops and a hooker. However, it showcases Mead's ability to slyly comment on social issues within the framework of a straightforward narrative. Utilising modest settings and inspired dialogue, which Mead wrote himself, he allows the characters space to discuss and dissect social mores with ease; the conversations are at the core of an insightful film about crime and fame. Many critics have criticised it for its minimalism, overlooking the way in which the pared-down style allows the dialogue to play a heightened role.

Capitalising on his first film and waiting for his next project, Mead wrote the screenplay for Michael Winner's *Parting Shots* (1998). He continued to work on the script for his next film, the delightful *Swing* (1999), for which he secured a major cast: the popular female singer Lisa Stansfield, legendary saxophone player Clarence Clemons, and Hugo Speer, hot off the success of Pete Cattaneo's *The Full Monty* (1997). This trio ran with Mead's whimsical script about an ex-con who decides to start a swing band despite a great deal of resistance, and Stansfield proved to be a natural actress, sliding easily into her role. Even though *Swing* is much lighter than *Bank Robber*, Mead still provides social commentary, placing emphasis on a character who is trying to rebuild a life after years spent in prison. The film has an optimism that is unusual and refreshing, featuring elaborate dance and musical numbers along with a jazzy score and glossy look, to suggest that the working-class environment is not always so bleak. The film suffered in its similarities to Alan Parker's *The Commitments* (1991), but it portrays the love of music and its barrier-breaking possibilities much more lucidly and hopefully than Parker's film.

Mead is currently working on several projects, including a black comedy, *Falling*, and a musical comedy, *A Fistful of Rubles*.   **JM**

Shane MEADOWS

Born in 1972, Shane Meadows grew up in Nottingham, and his working-class Midlands roots are central to his work, which includes many shorts, an award-winning comedy and two acclaimed feature films.

Smalltime (1996)
Twentyfourseven (1997)
A Room for Romeo Brass (1999)

After educating himself in the technical aspects of film-making, Meadows' came to the attention of producers with his entertaining short *Where's the Money Ronnie?* (1996). Set in a police interview room, where a series of talking heads reconstruct the events that led up to a gang fight, he made the most of the limited resources available to him cleverly employing smart dialogue and quick-fire editing. *Smalltime* (1996), Meadows' first attempt at a lengthier piece of film-making, won the Michael Powell award at the 1996 Edinburgh International Film Festival. A sixty-minute account of life for a group of friends on a Nottingham council estate, Meadows used his personal experience to create a convincing portrait of twenty-somethings living marginally above the breadline. As with his shorts, many of the roles are performed by Meadows' friends, with the director donning a wig to play the idiotic Jumbo. Meadows' two features, *Twentyfourseven* (1997) and *A Room for Romeo Brass* (1999), are very much part of the British tradition of social realist cinema. Once again using non-actors or unknowns, he encourages them to improvise. The cinematography is frequently unobtrusive – long takes and smooth cutting allow scenes to unfold in front of the camera, conforming to conventions of documentary style realism – and the locations arguably become characters in their own right. Frequent shots of action linger long after the characters have left the frame so that the camera dwells on the environment. This explicitly foregrounds the nature of the world that surrounds its inhabitants, and the idea that it is a crucial influence on their lives.

Political as well as stylistic factors also place Meadows' films within this tradition. His films are concerned with the effects of social deprivation on Nottingham's housing estates. While they do not carry the explicit political messages of a Ken Loach film, they do seek to engender a sense of social injustice. Both films also offer social commentaries on the position of men in contemporary culture. In *Twentyfourseven*, the action is centred around a boxing club, an exclusively male space, which is set up to give disaffected young men the opportunity to succeed in a masculine environment.

Romeo Brass presents an even bleaker aspect for the state of masculinity. While the young boxers in *Twentyfourseven* are able to reclaim their lost masculine identity at the club, the men of all generations in *Romeo Brass* have become completely incapable, arguably suffering from varying degrees of mental instability. The women, by contrast, are the only voices of stability in the film, able to hold all their lives together. Cutting between gentle comedy and shocking scenes of brutality with remarkable ease, like all Meadows' films, *Romeo Brass* has its ancestry in the work of another British director, Mike Leigh. **ES & IHS**

Nancy MECKLER

Sister, My Sister (1994)
Alive and Kicking (1996)

Meckler has been the artistic director of the Shared Experience Theatre Company since 1987, and has directed several award-winning adaptations of classic plays, including 'Mother Courage', 'Anna Karenina' and 'The Tempest'. Her film debut, *Sister, My Sister* (1994), is a stifling, claustrophobic film based on the true-life crimes of the Papin sisters in France in 1933. The film stars Jodhi May and Joely Richardson as the two sisters who are maids to a governess (Julie Walters) and her daughter (Sophie Thursfield). Wendy Kesselman adapts from her own stage play but is unsuccessful in breaking out of a conventional upstairs-downstairs narrative. Where the film does score highly, however, is the heated incestuousness between the two sisters in the attic which is juxtaposed with their brutality in the rest of the house. As a ménage-à-quatre, the psychological instability that overtakes the women leads to a pathetic and destructive conclusion, while Meckler's moments of dark humour (like Walter's lip-synching to an opera) tinge the grotesque events with bathos. A hybrid of Robert Aldrich's *Whatever Happened to Baby Jane?* (1962) and Jean Genet's 'The Maids', the film is most successful when it eschews any justification for the crimes; here the banality of evil is simply festering, David Lynch-like, beneath a veneer of bourgeois normality.

Alive and Kicking (1996) is also adapted from a stage play, this time Martin Sherman's tale of a young dancer with AIDS whose relationship with his older lover becomes increasingly strained. Starring Jason Flemyng as Tonio and Antony Sher as his lover Jack, the film is an uncompromising look at gay love and lifestyle that attempts to deal with courtship in the age of AIDS. With its made-for-television production values and gritty realism, it is successful in its shedding of theatrical conventions. Although the spectre of AIDS is never fully relegated, at least the film provides a bitingly witty and realistic portrait rather than resorting to bathos.

Meckler has continued to direct for Shared Experience, most recently, an acclaimed production of 'Mill on the Floss'. **BM**

Peter MEDAK

Negatives (1968)
The Ruling Class (1972)
A Day in the Death of Joe Egg (1972)
Ghost in the Noonday Sun (1973)
The Odd Job (1978)
The Changeling (1980)
Zorro, the Gay Blade (1981)
The Men's Club (1986)
The Krays (1990)
Let Him Have It (1991)
Romeo is Bleeding (1993)
Pontiac Moon (1994)
Species II (1998)

Following his 1956 emigration to England from Budapest, where he was born in 1937, Peter Medak worked as a sound and film editor, second assistant director (Hammer's *Captain Clegg* (1962)), second unit director (*Funeral in Berlin* (1966), *Fathom* (1964)) and associate producer (*Kaleidoscope* (1966)). His directorial debut, *Negatives* (1968), concerns an odd, unmarried couple who pattern themselves on the murderous Dr Crippen (previously the subject of three films) and his wife.

The theme of the mutability of identity is found again in *The Ruling Class* (1972), Medak's adaptation of Peter Barnes' black comedy. Peter O'Toole stars as the fourteenth Earl of Gurney, whose legacy is incumbent on his family convincing him that he is not, as he believes himself to be, Jesus Christ. The family's exhaustive efforts pay off, and O'Toole ends the film not only believing that he is Jack the Ripper, but racking up the body count to support the delusion. *A Day in the Death of Joe Egg* (1972), Medak's adaptation of Peter Nichols' stage play in which Alan Bates and Janet Suzman consider the mercy killing of their handicapped child, was filmed prior to, but released after, *The Ruling Class*.

Medak's light-hearted follow-up, the 1973 pirate comedy *Ghost in the Noonday Sun*, was sabotaged from within by the tantrums of star Peter Sellers, who fired his producers, antagonised co-star Anthony Franciosa and issued the mid-production dictum that his character's name of 'Jack Scratch' be changed for fear of reprisals from the Devil. Despite the desperate hiring of Sellers' ex-'Goon' pal Spike Milligan to enliven the comic possibilities of the disastrous production, the film could not be saved and was barely released by Columbia, which wrote off the debacle as a tax loss.

Medak concentrated on television assignments before teaming up with Monty Python trouper Graham Chapman for *The Odd Job* (1978), in which a suicidal man hires an assassin to do the deed for which he has no courage. When Chapman changes his mind, the hit man is less easily persuaded, with predictably madcap results.

After more television, Medak released his next cinematic offering, the contemporary ghost story *The Changeling* (1980). George C. Scott stars as a composer mourning the loss of his wife and daughter but haunted by the ghost of another child, long dead and possibly murdered, when he retires to a rural mansion. A mature and eerie study in loneliness and accountability, the film is still avidly discussed among genre fans as an example of the Victorian ghost story successfully translated to the big screen.

Medak's next theatrical release was an extreme about-turn from such grim meditations: *Zorro, the Gay Blade* (1981) was an attempt to fashion another lucrative comedy for star George Hamilton in the wake of his unexpected success with the Dracula spoof *Love at First Bite* (1979). Following the cool reception of this problematic lampoon, Medak delved into half a decade of undistinguished television assignments before returning to feature films with the curious *The Men's Club* (1986). Based on the novel by Leonard Michaels (who wrote the screenplay), the film – about a cadre of male friends who form their own encounter group with ruinous complications – was a box-office non-starter despite an exceptional cast that includes Harvey Keitel, Richard Jordan, Roy Scheider, Stockard Channing and Jennifer Jason Leigh.

Having directed episodes of several American series, Medak made a pair of remarkable dramas based on true events in British crime. The first, *The Krays* (1990), is about the infamous twins who ruled the London underworld during the 1960s (played here by Spandau Ballet's Martin and Gary Kemp, with Billie Whitelaw as their frighteningly protective mother). The second is *Let Him Have It* (1991), about the execution of Derek Bentley (Christopher Eccleston) for his involvement in the shooting death of a British bobby (the episode also inspired the Elvis Costello song 'Let Him Dangle'). Tom Courtenay and Eileen Atkins provide solid support as Bentley's troubled parents. Perhaps encouraged by the positive critical response of these two films, Medak continued with two offbeat, unconventional films – the blackly comic neo-noir *Romeo is Bleeding* (1993) and the family drama *Pontiac Moon* (1994). Although capably directed and well-cast, neither production was a critical or popular success, and Medak's only other feature film to date is *Species II* (1998), a crass sequel to a dumb, violent and poorly-received science-fiction film about a murderous mutant running rampant in Los Angeles. **RHS**

Jaap MEES

Born in Rotterdam in 1959, Jaap Mees moved to England in 1989 to study writing *Off the Beaten Track* (2000) and directing at the London International Film School. His first two films there were about Jewish humour (*The Importance of Being Mild*), and beauty (*The Royal Swan*). Matriculating in 1992, Mees' graduation work, *Deeply Estranged from Myself and My Own Song*, was a semi-autobiographical short following the love between a violinist and an alienated man spiritually recovering from cancer.

In 1998 Mees set up Free Spirits production company dedicated to 'quality, passion and integrity'. Under this banner he has directed a series of short documentaries (progressing from VHS to DV, via Hi8 and Betacam), his preferred method being to choose an individual and let them speak for themselves. A favourite with audiences has been *The Singing Conductor* (1998), about Londoner Baysee Rowe, a part-time recording artist who entertains and embarrasses passengers by singing aloud on his daily bus round. *Rainbow Days* recorded the 1997 annual festival of that name (set up in 1994, after two notorious race murders in London), in which music and culture from around the world are brought into local schools to promote racial understanding. Mees then returned to the theme of humour with *Are You Feeling Funny?* (1998).

Most of Mees' films have featured musicians. His longest film to date, *Off the Beaten Track* (2000), is a documentary about Dublin banjo player Tommy Barton, who died in 1972. The project was co-produced by Thomas' son, Billy, whose journey to Dublin from his hometown of Manchester forms the spine of the film. Mees includes background on the Irish 'folk revival' of the 1960s, and provides a clip of Barton's one cinema appearance (in a film called *O'Donoghue's Opera* (1965)), intercutting all this with many talking heads, including local music historian Harry Bradshaw, and Ronnie Drew of folk band The Dubliners. Evincing Mees' love of traditional Irish music, it was selected for festivals in New York and Dublin.

Among other projects, Mees is currently working on a documentary about wood sculptor Ben Wilson, and a feature-length script, provisionally entitled *This Dream Called Life*.   **KP**

Leslie MEGAHEY

The Hour of the Pig (1993) Born in Belfast in 1944, Leslie Megahey began his career producing and directing episodes of the BBC arts show 'Omnibus'. From 1973 onwards, he worked on a variety of projects, including documentaries on Ray Bradbury, Goya and Roger Corman. He demonstrated an affinity for the macabre when he adapted and directed the television film *Schalken the Painter* (1979), a terrifying version of a short story by J. Sheridan LeFanu.

Megahey has directed one feature to date, a BBC production that received a theatrical release; it is such an appealing curio that one regrets he is not more prolific. Based on true events, *The Hour of the Pig* (1993) is a strange hybrid of courtroom drama, historical romp and thriller. In medieval France, an idealistic urban lawyer (Colin Firth) arrives in a rural town to defend a pig charged with the murder of a child. This bizarre (yet fairly common) situation is the springboard for a dense story involving religious hypocrisy, a secret society, a seductive gypsy and an ignorant populace. Megahey handles the film's shift of tone and topic with some skill, crafting a combination of ribald humour (including a sex scene that is simultaneously funny and erotic), Hammer-esque sinister goings-on and some very broad performances from an estimable cast including Nicol Williamson, Michael Gough, Donald Pleasance and Harriet Walter. This ambitious mixture of styles is best demonstrated in the opening scene: a donkey is given a last minute reprieve on the gallows and released 'without a stain on her character', while the animal's owner is hanged. The influence of Peter Greenaway is discernible but Megahey has a striking visual sense and the film's televison origins are well hidden. Produced at a time when British cinema was overly reliant on formula films and tried-and-tested literary adaptations, *The Hour of the Pig* proves all the more impressive.

Since his debut feature, Megahey has directed another television film, *Cariani and the Courtesans* (1987), the absorbing story of a painter who is fixated on a mystery woman, featuring a starry cast – Simon Callow, Charles Gray, Michael Gough and Diana Quick. His most recent credit was as one of the writers for the French-Argentinian-Spanish co-production, *Diario para un Cuento* (1998).

On the strength of his debut, Leslie Megahey is a talent whose background in arts documentaries is reflected in his eclectic choice of projects.   **IC**

Sam MENDES

American Beauty (1999) With his debut feature, *American Beauty*, Sam Mendes became the directing sensation of 1999. Born in Gloucestershire, UK, in 1965, he began his stellar career directing theatre, most notably at The Donmar Warehouse in London, and like many stage directors, was keen to transfer his skills to the cinema. Rather unusually, with just one feature to his name, he has already displayed an acute cinematic sensibility.

Based on a screenplay by Alan Ball (writer on the sitcom 'Cybil'), *American Beauty* received almost unanimous critical praise, winning a handful of Oscars® in March 2000, including Best Screenplay, Director and Picture. Focusing on forty-something Lester Burnham, the film charts his suburban, disaffected meltdown and the subsequent rekindling of his passion for life and desire to live urgently (albeit with some cynicism). A quintessentially American theme, its sentiments have been travailed many times over in other artistic works such as Sinclair Lewis' novel 'Babbitt'. The film's constant motifs of the red rose (an American Beauty) and the colour red provide a vibrant contrast to the softer, inoffensive pastel tones. Mendes demonstrates real confidence in crafting sequences and juxtaposing them – the heart of the film, which revolves around the poetic footage of a plastic bag caught on the breeze, is pitted against the bitter comedy of the dinner scene immediately afterwards. Mendes' theatrical background also results in universally strong performances. Narratively, dramatically, and in its mise-en-scène, the film achieves a sense of completeness. Initially brittle and cynical, it is ultimately warm and generous. The onscreen action is complemented by one of the strongest music scores of recent years composed by Thomas Newman, and the theme music has already begun to find a life beyond the movie.

Mendes' cinema career carries a rare promise for a British director working abroad, similar to that of Ridley Scott and Alan Parker in their early days. His second feature, *The Road to Perdition*, is based on Max Allan Collins' graphic novel. Starring Tom Hanks and set during the Prohibition era in Chicago, it is currently in production.   **JC**

Chris MENGES

Born in Herefordshire, UK, in 1940, Chris Menges belongs to an ever-increasing group *A World Apart* (1988) within the cinematic establishment   the cinematographer-turned-director – ranking *CrissCross* (1992) alongside Barry Sonnenfeld, Jan De Bont and Janusz Kaminski who, under the respec- *Second Best* (1994) tive auspices of the Coen Brothers, Paul Verhoeven and Steven Spielberg, have forged *The Lost Son* (1999) new careers in Hollywood. Before turning to directing, Menges was already a two-time Oscar® winner for Best Cinematography for *The Killing Fields* (1984) and *The Mission* (1986). He joined ITV's 'World In Action' team in the early 1960s and became a jour-nalist and cameraman for several important documentaries about South Africa. He also began a fruitful collaboration with Ken Loach, first of all as camera operator on *Poor Cow* (1967) and then as cinematographer on *Kes* (1969).

His directorial debut, *A World Apart* (1988), is often compared to Richard Attenborough's *Cry Freedom* (1987) for its passionate and honest account of apartheid in 1960s South Africa. Menges' film ranks above its counterpart, however, due to an extraordinary central performance from Jodhi May and its muted tone which eschews the sensationalism and generic platitudes common to many socially worthy films. When Molly (May) is ostracised by her school friends after her mother's imprisonment for collu-sion with the ANC, the mother-daughter relationship becomes fractured and distant, as much because of May's incomprehension of events, as her mother's (Barbara Hershey) total allegiance to the cause. These kinds of martyr films or issue statements are often hamstrung by bloated liberalism, guilt complexes or sheer historical inaccuracy, but *A World Apart* successfully navigates through its incendiary subject-matter with compas-sion and warmth. The film garnered acting prizes for May and Hershey at Cannes, as well as the prestigious Cannes Jury Prize.

CrissCross (1992) undermined much of Menges' kudos. A slow-moving domestic drama about a 12-year-old boy who turns to crime to help his mother who is struggling as a waitress, the only incidental interest here is Goldie Hawn's portrayal of a woman faced with the ugly realities of her existence.

Second Best (1994) marked Menges' return to form. Casting William Hurt as an introverted Welsh postman who adopts a young boy, he crafts a small-scale drama that quietly showcases the underused talents of Hurt, depicting a shy character who is emotionally freed by the arrival of the child. Far from ostentatious, the direction is almost invisible; the camera is frequently static and makes the most of the ensemble acting – Hurt plays alongside Jane Horrocks, John Hurt and Keith Allen.

The Lost Son (1999) is an important film, not least in its tackling of taboo subject matters – paedophilia and child prostitution rings – but also in offering French actor Daniel Auteuil his first attempt at an English-language film. He plays a retired policeman, Xavier, who is residing in Soho and inadvertently discovers a child prostitution ring, an operation he decides to bring down from within. He becomes mixed up in a child prostitution ring and decides to attack the gang from within. The film is surprisingly generic, with several film-noir motifs flagged from the outset – the disillusioned ex-cop, the friendly call-girl, the travelogue locations, and the final twist. Menges plays it straight, however: there is no condescension or soft-peddling of the subject matter, and Auteuil's embittered hero is played with just the right balance of cynicism and compassion to temper the film's cardboard-cut-out characterisation and narrative implausibilities.

In recent years, Menges has continued to work as a cinematographer, lensing *Michael Collins* (1996), *The Boxer* (1997), *The Pledge* (2001) and Penny Marshall's forthcoming *Riding in Cars with Boys*. **BM**

Ismail MERCHANT

In Custody (1993)
The Proprietor (1996)
Cotton Mary (1999)

Born Ismail Noormohamed Abdul Rehman in Bombay in 1936, Ismail Merchant graduated from St Xavier's Jesuit College, Bombay, in 1958, with a BA in the Arts. The same year, he travelled to New York, where he began a Business Administration MA at New York University. It was here that Merchant became enthralled by the cinema of European auteurs. Despite professing a love for popular Indian cinema, he felt the need to make humanist films that drew on the culture of the subcontinent but were aimed at an international market. He graduated in 1961, but during his study had made the Oscar®-nominated fourteen-minute film, *The Creation of Woman*.

On the way to France, Merchant chanced to see *The Sword and the Flute* (1959), a documentary on India by James Ivory. He was so impressed by the Oregon-raised director's sensitivity to the subcontinent that he arranged a meeting later that year. These two names are now synonymous with verbose films that gently criticise the values of a (usually bygone) era whilst luxuriating in its finery. The first Merchant-Ivory film, *The Householder*, appeared in 1963. The company subsequently released 25 films over 25 years (gaining wide recognition with *A Room With a View* (1986) and *Maurice* (1987)), functioning in a truly independent manner – ploughing the proceeds of each picture into the next. Merchant set up the company's first office in New York in 1967; despite working out of England for many years, he did not establish a London office until 1982.

Merchant has received nine Oscars®, none for directing. His first attempts at directing came with two docu-dramas made for television: *Mahatma and the Mad Boy* (1973), concerning a monkey wallah and a shore-side statue of Gandhi, and *Courtesans of Bombay* (1982), depicting the women he knew as a child. His debut feature, *In Custody* (1993), was adapted by Anita Desai and Shahrukh Husain from the former's novel. Set in present day India, it tells the story of a brusque teacher's ill-fated trip to Bhopal to honour an Urdu poet (Shashi Kapoor) and record his voice for posterity. Merchant made the film in order to focus attention on the dying Urdu language, which he feels provides a much-needed link between Hindus and Muslims. It may have displayed Merchant's ability to secure talented actors, but was marred by repetition in the recording sequence and digressions for local colour. Merchant remained in the modern day for *The Proprietor* (1996), in which novelist Adrienne Mark (Jeanne Moreau) is haunted by memories of World War Two, and leaves her New York home to return to a France riven by racial tension. The critical response was worse than that for *In Custody*, and *The Proprietor* was barely released in Britain. His third film, *Cotton Mary* (1999), is set on the Malaber Coast in 1954. Greta Scacchi plays white colonial, Lily Macintosh, whose inability to breastfeed her baby becomes the catalyst for the neurotic breakdown of her nurse, 'Auntie' Mary (Madhur Jaffrey), who is one of the many Indians to identify with the British colonisers. All three of Merchant's features are marked by unimaginative use of camera, clumsy establishing of onscreen geography, and the inability to generate emotional climaxes or satisfying pace. All were released under the Merchant-Ivory banner, although Merchant himself did not take producer credit on any of them. He also eschewed any working partnership with frequent Merchant-Ivory collaborator, Ruth Prawer Jhabvala, who would have provided much needed rigour and structure.

He has recently finished shooting an adaptation of V.S. Naipaul's novel, 'The Mystic Masseur'. Set in Trinidad, the film is a comedy that details the rise to fame and fortune of a struggling schoolteacher. **KP**

Saul METZSTEIN

Late Night Shopping (2001)

Born in 1970 in Glasgow, Scotland, Saul Metzstein studied architecture before working as a production runner on Danny Boyle's *Shallow Grave* (1994) and *Trainspotting*

(1995), and directing several shorts, one of which, *Magic Moments*, stars Dougray Scott. His Channel 4 documentary, *The Name of this Film is Dogme 95*, an exploration of the film-makers' manifesto, is presented by film journalist and author Richard Kelly, and includes interviews with directors such as Kristian Levring, Harmony Korine, Lars von Trier and Søren Kragh-Jacobsen.

A FilmFour project, Metzstein's feature debut, *Late Night Shopping* (2001), was made on a budget of £1.5 million. Set in an unspecified city, the film focuses on four friends who work night jobs and meet up in a café in the early hours of the morning to swap stories and avoid their problems. The protagonists – all anxious about their twenty-something dead-end existences – are realistically flawed and engagingly confused. Sean (Luke de Woolfson) no longer knows if his girlfriend, who has a day job, still lives with him; Vincent (James Lance) cannot resist sex; Lenny (Enzo Cilenti) thinks of porno-graphic images at inopportune moments; and Jody (Kate Ashfield) loses her job and feels sidelined. Refreshingly funny, with the humour emanating from the characters' insecuri-ties rather than their situation, the film never becomes farcical, even in the second half when it opens up spatially: moving away from the confines of the café and work environ-ments, it turns into a road movie as the friends journey together to a seaside town to reunite Sean with his girlfriend. Although laced with whimsy, *Late Night Shopping* still has flashes of social realism, but Metzstein subtly works through issues of employment and commitment rather than heavy-handedly sign-posting them. **HP**

Roger MICHELL

As the BAFTA-award winning director of 'The Buddha of Suburbia' (1993) and *Persuasion* (1995), Roger Michell is skilled at evoking a strong sense of place and time, exploring the repressed emotions and quirky foibles that characterise a stereotypical Britishness. After moving to England from South Africa, where he was born in 1957, and graduating from Cambridge, he was assistant director to both John Osborne and Samuel Beckett at the Royal Court Theatre. Whilst resident director at the Royal Shakespeare Company, he directed 'Hamlet', and most recently the National Theatre's version of Harold Pinter's 'The Homecoming'. His first venture into film was a television version of the stage play 'My Night with Reg', which he had previously directed in the theatre.

Titanic Town (1998)

Notting Hill (1999)

His feature-film debut, *Titanic Town* (1998), was loosely adapted from Mary Costello's semi-autobiographical novel. When the Catholic McPhelimy family move to Belfast in 1972, their housing estate is descending into a battle zone between the British Army and the IRA. Matriarch Bernie (Julie Walters) is galvanised into political action when one of her friends is killed in the crossfire and the film recounts her efforts to halt the violence, appealing to Stormont officials and IRA leaders alike. Michell's debut is a confident one, not least in its handling of the actors and its narrative innovation. Telling the story from the point of view of daughter Nuala O'Neill, he combines the earnestness and honesty of a child with a certain partisanship. Unlike *Some Mother's Son* (1996), the film does not take sides; instead, it is content to allow the action to unfold exponen-tially. Where Michell falls down is in his inability to satisfactorily marry the opposing tones and moods of the film. The hard-edged, gritty realism (underpinned by John Daly's cinematography) sits uneasily with the broad humour that differentiates Walters from her haughty neighbours. This failure to resolve the myriad of narrative strands weights the film; it is more a portmanteau of arresting images and slapstick humour than a worthy political statement.

Michell went on to *Notting Hill* (1999), on the surface the kind of schmaltzy cinema that relies on the charm of its two leads and the knockabout comedy and meaningful drama of its screenplay. Yet on closer examination, Michell's follow-up to Mike Newell's *Four Weddings and a Funeral* (1994) is a minor triumph, replete with directorial flour-ishes that mark it out from the usual moribund romantic-comedies. When Hugh Grant accidentally spills orange juice all over Julia Roberts, an unlikely romance begins; the outcome, however, is never in doubt. Along the way, Michell, and screenwriter Richard Curtis, offer a plethora of ideas and narrative threads – an America-versus-Britain cultural debate, housemates from hell, disability, job dissatisfaction, Portobello Road well-to-dos, and a dissection of 'stardom' – throwing them all into the comedy melting pot. Although the exercise in creating a feelgood film may rankle, it is hard not to be taken in by the gusto of Michell's direction and the performances he elicits. Grant and Roberts are on top form and their chemistry is genuine. Michell's set-pieces – the car chase through London, Grant as a Horse and Hound reviewer, and the scene in which the seasons change in one long tracking shot – lend an accomplished feel to the rest of the film.

Michell's health problems prevented him from directing *Captain Corelli's Mandolin* (2001) and John Madden stepped in at the last minute. His next project, *Changing Lanes*, is the story of a road-rage attack in New York, starring Samuel L. Jackson and Ben Affleck. **BM**

Scott MICHELL

The Innocent Sleep (1996) Scott Michell is an example of someone who rose very quickly, only to disappear almost without trace – by no means an unusual tale. He began as a voluntary PA and Script Reader for the First Film Foundation, which gave him the contacts to work as assistant to the actor Peter Capaldi on *Soft Top, Hard Shoulder* (Stefan Schwartz, 1992).

Michell then wrote, directed and co-produced a 22-minute short called *Seeds* (1993) which was shown at the London Film Festival and subsequently bought by LWT. Having assisted on Bill Britten's short film *One Night Stand* (1993) and Vadim Jean's *Beyond Bedlam* (1993), he was granted funding based on the success of *Seeds* and started planning his first feature, *The Innocent Sleep* (1996).

As an inexperienced director and producer, much faith was placed in Michell. The plot of the film – a moody thriller in which the suicide of an Italian banker turns out to be murder – sounded promising. In the ensuing battle for the truth, a journalist unwittingly uncovers a complex web of international crime. Even better, it was based on a true story: the Roberto Calvi affair of 1982. The story allowed Michell to film tense Hitchcockian scenes in unusual locations across London, using familiar techniques to heighten the suspense. Unfortunately, it did not succeed. Though the pace of the film never flags, and some of the cinematography suggests a good eye for detail, the plot simply is not tight enough; in addition, the casting often seems misplaced. Most memorable is the score by Mark Ayres, who also wrote the music for *Seeds*. The sweeping arias, with solos by Lesley Garratt, are beautiful, but woefully over-extravagant for a thriller. The film's backers struggled to make their money back on *The Innocent Sleep* and Michell's planned film, *Redemption*, for Sunlight Pictures, was never made. **AL**

Christopher MILES

The Virgin and The Gypsy (1970) The brother of noted British actor, Sarah Miles, Christopher Miles has worked on a number of projects, often with a literary bent. He made a notable debut with the Oscar®-nominated short *Six-Sided Triangle* (1963). His first feature, *The Virgin and the Gypsy* (1970), was an adaptation of a D.H. Lawrence novella in which Franco Nero smoulders as the wandering titular vagabond who seduces the daughter of a priest; she, in turn, is punished for her carnal transgressions. Although the film is handsomely shot, capturing the atmosphere of Lawrence's 'philosophical bodice-ripper', it pales next to Ken Russell's Lawrence adaptation, *Women In Love* (1969). Russell was at his stylistic peak in 1969; Miles, though able, simply could not match him. With a script by the noted television playwright Alan Plater, the film was still warmly received.

A Time for Loving (1971)
The Maids (1974)
That Lucky Touch (1975)
Priest of Love (1981)
The Clandestine Marriage (1999)

Elements of the erotic and the sophisticated are also present in his next film, *A Time for Loving* (1971), an overly tasteful French sex comedy which is clearly inspired by Arthur Schnitzler's saucy 'La Ronde'. Aside from the obvious thematic similarities (sophisticated Europeans coupling in lavish surroundings), Miles' film is written by Jean Anouilh, who had adapted the Schnitzler play for Roger Vadim in 1964. Its attractive, voguish cast – Britt Ekland, Phillipe Noiret, Mel Ferrer and Susan Hampshire – helps.

Miles stayed with highbrow French material for his next film, *The Maids* (1974), an adaptation of Jean Genet's study of sex and power. Despite a heavyweight cast (Glenda Jackson and Susannah York as the maids, Vivien Merchant as their employer) the material is pretty poor. The claustrophobia that Genet creates in his play is dissipated by Miles' pedestrian direction. Even the performances are irritatingly mannered and the film as a whole is rendered uncinematic (unlike Nancy Meckler's later version, *Sister My Sister* (1994)).

That Lucky Touch (1975) was a change of pace for Miles. Set in Belgium, an odd plot pitches a stilted Roger Moore as an arms dealer who romances Susannah York's investigative journalist. This is likeable enough, if a bit plodding. It is particularly noteworthy, however, for an excellent Lee J. Cobb performance, his last role before his death the following year. *That Lucky Touch* was marketed with the unbelievably bad tag line, 'When a No-No Girl Meets a Go-Go Man – WHAM!'

After working on the television show 'Roald Dahl's Tales of the Unexpected', Miles made *Priest of Love* (1981). Returning to the subject of D.H. Lawrence, the film is a biopic that dwells on the last years of the author, after he found notoriety with 'Lady Chatterley's Lover'. Ian McKellen plays the author and Janet Suzman his wife. Penelope Keith, John Geilgud and Ava Gardner provide impressive support. The picturesque, if sedate, events take place against an international backdrop (the US, Mexico and Italy). Palatable enough, it lacks ardour, which is ironic given the passionate nature of Lawrence's scandalous writing. McKellen is good, though, if a bit miscast, and the photography by Ted Moore is visually engaging.

The director's interests in classical/period stories manifested itself with two projects made for telelvision, *Lord Elgin and Some Stones of No Value* (1987) with Nigel Havers and a pre-stardom Hugh Grant, and a documentary, *Love in the Ancient World* (1997). He has also worked on the Lenny Henry sit-com 'Chef'.

His most recent feature, *The Clandestine Marriage* (1999), is a period comedy with a starry cast, including Joan Collins, Nigel Hawthorne, Timothy Spall and Tom Hollander. The tale of a couple that attempts to stage a marriage of convenience in order to rescue their ancestral home, it is mildly funny. The humour is an uneasy mix of slapstick and verbal wit, however, and Collins gives a wildly over-the-top performance with her strangulated German-accented delivery.

Miles is not an untalented director. At best, he injects many of his films with a personal touch, but too often notions of 'quality' and 'sophistication' render his output a little dull.   **IC**

Gavin MILLAR

Born in Clydebank, Scotland, in 1938, Gavin Millar has worked in television and feature films as a writer, director and occasional actor since his 1970 debut, *The Eye Hears, The Ear Sees*, a documentary about the artist Norman McLaren. He then worked in television, directing plays such as Dennis Potter's 'Cream In My Coffee' and Alan Bennett's 'Intensive Care'.

The Eye Hears, The Ear Sees (1970)
Secrets (1983)
Dreamchild (1985)
Danny, the Champion of the World (1989)
Complicity (2000)

In 1983 he directed the twee *Secrets*. This was billed as a 'tempting tale of eroticism and desire' but in reality amounts to is a mildly risqué comedy about a schoolgirl who causes consternation when she finds a packet of condoms and thinks they are balloons.

Millar returned to television until *Dreamchild* (1985). This is an adult variant of 'Alice In Wonderland' with Coral Browne as Alice Hargreaves, the inspiration for Lewis Carroll's celebrated children's tale, now aged eighty and visiting New York to celebrate the author's centenary. The film takes place both in 1930s Manhattan, where Mrs Hargreaves attempts to adjust to her fame, and an England of seventy years earlier in which Carroll (Ian Holm) pursues his platonic but disturbing obsession with her. She is tormented by nightmares and fantasies in which the creatures of Carroll's creation are sources of fear as well as wonderment. Although not always successful, *Dreamchild* is notable for the combination of Dennis Potter's screenplay (with his characteristic themes of childhood, fantasy and disturbing sex) and Jim Henson's creatures. The low budget shows and there is a corny and unnecessary romantic subplot involving Mrs Hargreaves' travelling companion (Nicola Cowper) and a newsman (Peter Gallagher). Coral Browne is great in the lead, however, and the whole enterprise is to be commended for its ambitious mix of childhood, literature and nightmare.

After *Tidy Endings*, a 1988 television adaptation of Harvey Fierstein's play, Millar made the British television film *The Most Dangerous Man in the World* (1988) with

Martin Shaw and Tom Radcliffe. *Danny, the Champion of the World* (1989) is a pretty enjoyable adaptation of Roald Dahl's children's novel that teams Jeremy and Sam Irons as a father and son who outwit the sinister Squire (Robbie Coltrane.) Some good performances (particularly Michael Hordern and Lionel Jeffries) make this watchable but it does fall far short of other Dahl adaptations such as Mel Stuart's *Willy Wonka and the Chocolate Factory* (1971) and Nicolas Roeg's creepy *The Witches* (1990). The film was made for British television but was released theatrically in the US.

In the last decade Millar has worked fairly consistently in television, directing episodes of the American show 'The Young Indiana Jones Chronicles' and the BBC projects 'Pat And Margaret' with Victoria Wood and Julie Walters, and the superior Iain Banks adaptation, 'The Crow Road'.

Millar's only other feature to date is another Banks adaptation. *Complicity* (2000) features Jonny Lee Miller as Cameron Colley, a screwed-up newspaper hack on the trail of a serial killer with a social conscience. The film's credibility hinges on the central character: Colley is a gambler, a coke fiend, a chain smoker and a computer games nut who is having an affair with a married woman (Keeley Hawes). Miller is too young to be convincing as a hardboiled addiction freak and he sleepwalks his way through the whole thing; the dysfunctional Colley is reminiscent of the far superior, noirish television show 'Cracker' and Miller pales beside the slobbish Robbie Coltrane creation, Fitz. The stylish direction of 'The Crow Road' is largely absent here; it looks too much like pedestrian television. Without the strong interior voice of the novel, this is really another anaemic serial killer movie, distinguished only by the high quality of the supporting cast (Brian Cox, Bill Paterson). The film was released direct to video in the UK but received a theatrical release in North America.

Although Millar has made some enjoyable features, he has produced most of his best work for television, working with talents such as Alan Bennett, Harvey Fierstein and Dennis Potter. He has also acted in Peter Chelsom's impressive *Funny Bones* (1995) and co-written a book on film editing with fellow director Karel Reisz. **IC**

Sam MILLER

Among Giants (1998)
Elephant Juice (1999) Born in Suffolk, UK, in 1962, Sam Miller began his career as an actor with a role in the BBC adaptation of Olivia Manning's Balkan trilogy 'Fortunes of War' and a regular part in the popular police soap 'The Bill'. He began to direct episodes of the latter in 1994, next turning to hospital drama 'Cardiac Arrest' and the cult legal lifestyle drama 'This Life'. He also achieved success with the television movie *King Girl* (1996), a tale of adolescent sexual identity wherein a neglected, bereaved girl abandons her femininity and is bullied with devastating consequences.

Having appeared in Gary Oldman's searing autobiographical drama *Nil By Mouth* (1997), Miller briefly returned to television with 'King Leek' before making his feature debut, *Among Giants* (1998). The film, written by *The Full Monty* (1997) screenwriter, Simon Beaufoy, mines a similar subject to that success, and utilises the settings of Beaufoy's directorial debut *The Darkest Light* (1999) which he co-directed with Bille Eltringham and also wrote. In subject – a working-class gang of tough men working cash-in-hand painting pylons – the film belongs to Beaufoy rather than Miller, although the latter directs with his television trademark of hand-held cinematography, favouring a mix of intimacy and distance in his use of the camera.

Set against the towering pylons of the Yorkshire Moors, *Among Giants* follows a traditional love story between unlikely lovers Rachel Griffiths and Pete Postlethwaite, with the concerns of unregulated work and its dangers as a sub-plot. At times affecting and alarming, the film ultimately suffers because of a common Beaufoy touch: the affectionate attitude to his characters that overlooks any confrontation of the potentially darker aspects of the script.

Miller's second foray into feature directing arose from his connection to 'This Life' creator Amy Jenkins: he directed her screenplay of thirty-something angst, *Elephant Juice* (1999). The film travels the increasingly well-trodden path of commitment-phobia more successfully achieved on the small screen in shows such as 'Ally McBeal' and 'Sex and the City'. That its title refers to the similarity betweeen the phrase 'elephant juice' and 'I love you' when silently mouthed should give some indication of the level at which the film and its scenarios are pitched. Dinner party cod-sophistication provides the structure for the film, utilised to articulate debates surrounding the uselessness felt by these insecure child-adults, whose relationships (a smart demographic array which includes gay, straight and bisexual) are unnecessarily complicated.

Its attempts to move away from a televisual style – overhead shots to signify distance and dissatisfaction, and episodic inter-titles to effect cinematic narration – failed to impress. Predictable, and lacking in emotional resonance and veracity, the film was lamented as a prolonged, self-indulgent whine wasting the coruscating persona of the brilliant Daniela Nardini.   **JD**

Anthony MINGHELLA

Anthony Minghella is a director whose romantic style and epic vision seem almost *Truly, Madly, Deeply* (1991) anachronistic. Criticised on the one hand for his melodramatic rendering of passionate *Mr Wonderful* (1993) emotions, he has been conversely praised for the considered and intellectual manner *The English Patient* (1996) of his approach to film-making. Paying homage to an earlier cinematic era, although *The Talented Mr Ripley* (1999) by no means old-fashioned, Minghella is at his best when dealing with weighty issues. Allowing his actors time to fully develop their characters, and nuancing details of plot and dialogue, he is capable of under-playing a scene to best effect.

Born in the Isle of Wight, UK, in 1954, Minghella worked as a script-writer and editor for such television stalwarts as 'Eastenders' and 'Boon' before creating a fantastical television series in association with Jim Henson Productions entitled 'The Storyteller'. Mixing real action with special effects, and including trademark Henson puppetry, the series was based on folk tales and myths; as with most folk tales, the episodes had their dark side and sinister undercurrents.

Minghella's first feature film, *Truly, Madly, Deeply* (1991), was greeted with mixed reviews. Juliet Stevenson plays Nina, who sees her world falling apart after the death of her lover Jamie (dryly acted by Alan Rickman). Nina becomes depressed and goes into therapy, rats move into her flat, and she is dogged by an Eastern European with an unlikely accent. One day she is alone in her flat, picking out a mournful tune on the piano, when she hears a cello join in. Looking around she sees her dead lover, returned to watch over her. *Truly, Madly, Deeply* dips into surreal waters as other ghosts join Jamie in the flat, making demands on Nina to rent classic movies on video and keep the central heating turned to maximum. Meanwhile, she falls in with therapist Mark (Michael Maloney) and they make tentative steps towards a relationship. Their courtship includes one of the film's most pilloried moments when the two hop along the South Bank, revealing details about their personal life. *Truly, Madly, Deeply* is moving, but Minghella surrenders to schmaltz a little too often.

Mr Wonderful (1993) is not considered to be one of Minghella's more successful films; however, it did get him a foothold in Hollywood. Directing Matt Dillon as the lead helped, as did choosing the most popular American genre: romantic comedy. Perhaps Minghella needed more edge and substance in his subject matter to prove what he was capable of.

The English Patient (1996) was adapted from Michael Ondaatje's celebrated novel. Minghella took an intricate and poetic work and made a magnificent feature, deservedly winning an Academy Award as Best Director. The eponymous character, played by Ralph Fiennes, is horrifically burnt and lying in an Italian villa, which has been appropriated as a war hospital. He is attended to by a French-Canadian nurse, Hana, played by Juliette Binoche, who also picked up an Academy Award as Best Supporting Actress. The villa is peopled with emotionally scarred and shell-shocked characters, including the thief-turned-spy Caravaggio, who suspects that the patient is really a Nazi collaborator. Replete with poignant moments, *The English Patient* is unrelentingly tragic, but always beautiful. Shot with a rich palette, it sometimes loses itself in its own lushness, but many consider it one of the few great films of the 1990s.

Minghella's most recent work, *The Talented Mr Ripley* (1999), is an adaptation of Patricia Highsmith's acerbic, cynical novel. A period psychological thriller set in the 1950s in Italy, it is another directorial tour de force which has assured Minghella's premiere status. Tom Ripley (Matt Damon) is a young man who lacks the necessary connections and money to progress in society. When he meets socialite Dickie Greenleaf, assuredly played by Jude Law, he learns to crave his lifestyle so much that he murders him – an adult's version of 'The Prince and the Pauper'. Somewhat remarkably for such a popular film made for Hollywood, *The Talented Mr Ripley* suggests strong homo-erotic undertones in the relationship between Ripley and Greenleaf. But it functions not only as an investigation of sexuality, which further involves Greenleaf's girlfriend Marge (Gwyneth Paltrow) in the triangle, but also explores issues of class and wealth in American society. Rather than pick the blockbuster of his choice, Damon chose a tough, ambiguous role; it is Law, however, who really steals the show. Period details are well observed, lending an authenticity and weight to the plot. Where dancehall classics provided the soundtrack for *The English Patient*, here jazz becomes the motif for the characters' carefree, increasingly unhinged, existence. Disappointingly ignored by the Academy, the film marks Minghella as one of the most interesting, commercial and accessible directors working today.

He has recently directed an adaptation of Samuel Beckett's 'Play' for the 'Beckett on Film' season, and returns to war drama with his next feature, *Cold Mountain*, which is currently in production. **HPe**

Paul MORRISON

Solomon and Gaenor (1999) Throughout the 1970s Paul Morrison made his name as the director of community-based documentary films. These works followed under-privileged children from housing estates and local authority care as they engaged in arts and culture programmes designed to educate and entertain them. A film-maker committed to social concerns, he made films on dyslexia, children with special needs and related community projects.

His only feature to date, the Academy Award-nominated *Solomon and Gaenor* (1999), the story of a forbidden love affair between the Welsh daughter of religious mining stock (Nia Roberts) and an Orthodox Jewish man (Ioan Gruffudd), came late in his career. It demonstrates Morrison's interest in the strengths and weaknesses of community, particularly those at the lower end of the class ladder. The separate communities are portrayed with a necessary reliance on their religious practices. Importance is placed on tradition as emphasised in one particular scene: images of a pub full of laughing and drinking Welshmen entertaining a reluctant Solomon (known to the Welsh by the less obviously Jewish name of Sam) are intercut with those of his sombre Jewish family, sitting silently at the dinner table waiting for him.

The film's love story demands that Solomon hides his Jewishness from Gaenor and her family, necessitating the kind of deception which (as in Thomas Hardy's work) effects a tragic end. Both families are shown to be moralistic and judgmental, rejecting the young couple because they have contravened their respective laws. Morrison evokes this sense with calm skill, allowing the pleasingly defiant Gaenor some dignity as she is banished from her chapel.

Morrison films landscapes which recall Charlotte Bronte and Hardy, visualising the doom and tragedy evident in the plot; like another character, the scenery becomes part of the story as we trace Solomon's journey from his culture into Gaenor's by way of rain and snow-soaked country fields. Morrison avoids the film's potential for 'heritage drama' with some beautifully sensual and modern touches: a naked and visibly pregnant Gaenor sits astride Solomon in one of the film's sex scenes; later, she strips naked and gets into his sick-bed to spend their final night together. Sentimentality is thus kept to a minimum.

The performances are affecting, particularly those of the two leads, who depict the growing relationship with an awkward charm and an unusual honesty. Overall, the film is an ambitious, if slightly pedestrian, evocation of doomed romance amongst religious enemies, and the violence and hatred this can promote. **JD**

Elijah MOSHINSKY

Genghis Cohn (1993) Despite his unusual upbringing, Elijah Moshinsky is a common breed: the stage director who occasionally directs films for television, some of which may also receive a theatrical release as and when the producers (in Moshinsky's case, always the BBC) see fit. Born in the French quarter of Shanghai in 1946, he is the son of Russian Jewish émigrés. He was brought up in Melbourne, but lives in London. Such a multi-cultural background has imbued Moshinsky with an openness towards different attitudes and cultures, as well as an understanding of the importance of historical background across the world. He has also learned that nothing can be taken as absolute in life – particularly when approaching a script.

He studied history at Oxford and directed a student production of 'As You Like It'; its success landed him a job as staff producer at the Covent Garden Opera House in London. Moshinsky then began to cement a successful career as an opera director. In 1980 Jonathan Miller (a friend from the Oxford and Cambridge Players troupe) invited him to direct one of a new Shakespeare series on television that he was planning with the BBC, intending to create 'definitive' screen versions of classic texts.

Moshinsky directed five plays onscreen over a period of four years, including one of the jewels in the Shakespearean crown, *A Midsummer Night's Dream* (1981). These television films showed the promise suggested by Moshinsky's stage successes, and certain preoccupations run concurrently throughout all of his work. He believes in the importance of establishing a background of social reality and has the ability to allow major stars the freedom to interpret roles. Interesting and intelligent end product stems from a manner of working where certain interpretative ideas are stated at the start of rehearsal and can then be explored with the cast until a cohesive whole is formed.

Moshinsky is also skilled at maintaining a swift pace in films that have the potential to drag. Although he has had some interesting television failures, such as the farcical thriller *The Green Man* (1990) and the so-called comedy *Brazen Hussies* (1996), one success that marked Moshinsky out as one-to-watch was the highly charged *Genghis Cohn* (1993), his only work to have a theatrical release. In this controversial comedy, the ghost of a Jew (Anthony Sher) murdered in the concentration camps returns to haunt the German who killed him (played by Robert Lindsay, a Moshinsky regular on both stage and screen). The Jew ends up helping his nemesis to solve an important crime, during which the German unintentionally picks up Jewish sensibilities. The blackness of the comedy, the economy of its early sequences, and the controlled power of Lindsay's performance, make *Genghis Cohn* stand out as an unusual and worthwhile piece.

Although Moshinsky has worked with many of the biggest names in the business his onscreen work for the BBC seems likely to remain little more than an interesting footnote to the mixed fortunes of an influential stage career.   **AL**

Malcolm MOWBRAY

Following *A Private Function* (1985), Malcolm Mowbray's promising debut, he was fêted by Hollywood and subsequently travelled stateside for a glittering career which has not yet come to fruition. A dreamy British eccentric, he struggled in Hollywood and seems to have been ruined by it, as have so many other nascent talents.

Self-critically exacting, Mowbray left art school in 1972 because, it is said, he was not up to his own artistic standards. He went on to the National Film School and graduated in 1976. For his first job he adapted a short story by Tolstoy for David Puttnam. In 1980 he wrote 'Days at the Beach' for David Rose at BBC Birmingham, receiving much praise and a letter from renowned playwright Alan Bennett. A correspondence sprung up between them, and a mutual interest in post-war austerity and butchery eventually resulted in the co-written *A Private Function*; Mowbray, however, received little credit for the writing. Produced by Mark Shivas, and shot for under £2 million on location in Yorkshire, this diverting comedy about a particular form of priggish, British snobbery in times of hardship became a minor British classic. The slight story about a plan to slaughter a stolen pig to celebrate the coronation of Elizabeth II is brought to life by some sharp dialogue, superlative acting and Mowbray's deft direction. It has a particularly European sensibility, likened by Shivas to that of Milos Foreman, and sets the scene of 'ordinary' people in extraordinary situations with the comedy arising from the characters' reactions.

The notable lack of special effects and comedic devices in *A Private Function* would have served Mowbray better in his subsequent features, all of which have been weakly

A Private Function (1985)
Out Cold (1989)
Don't Tell Her it's Me (1990)
The Revengers' Comedies (1998)

scripted and ill-cast. The director's quirky nature has not seemed suited to fare such as *Out Cold* (1989) and *Don't Tell Her it's Me* (1990); in their continued attempt at celebrating the ordinary, both go badly awry. The plot of the former suggests a kitsch *Blood Simple* (1984), but an underwritten script belies any interest that the concept may suggest. The latter manages to be both flavourless and cloying, its plot reminiscent of *The Nutty Professor* (1963), and *Grease 2* (1982), with only a couple of running gags to enliven the embarrassment. Mowbray himself admitted: 'Some directors get typecast on their strengths. I'd prefer to concentrate on my weaknesses and improve across the board.' However, even his latest offering, which on paper should have worked to his strengths, was not well received. *The Revengers' Comedies* (1998) was based on two acclaimed Alan Ayckbourn plays and had a suicidal *Strangers on a Train* (1951) plot. Made for the BBC and backed by Miramax, the original five hours of the plays have not benefited from a cut to feature-film length. The impressive cast included respected actors Sam Neill and Kristin Scott Thomas, and such comic genius as Steve Coogan, but the resultant farce is hampered by leaden action. Helena Bonham Carter is miscast and desperate comedy touches such as bad wigs and goofy teeth are laughable. Lacking the acidic dialogue of *A Private Function*, and its pacing and sure touch, one cannot help but wonder whether this early success was due more to Bennett's input than Mowbray's.

In the early 1990s, *Sight and Sound* described Malcolm Mowbray as the 'most depressing British Casualty in Hollywood'. It would be a shame if he were to remain one back on his home turf. He is currently in production with a romantic comedy, *Portofino*, starring John Lithgow and Diane Weist.   **FG**

Peter MULLAN

Orphans (1997) Born in Glasgow in 1959, Peter Mullan is widely respected as an actor having starred in number of films, among them Ken Loach's *Riff Raff* (1990) and the acclaimed *My Name is Joe* (1998), for which he won Best Actor at Cannes. With the support of Scottish Television, he wrote and directed two First Reels – *Close* (1994) and *Good Day for the Bad Guys* (1995) – before making a Tartan Short with the support of BBC Scotland, *Fridge* (1996). Cinematographer Grant Cameron, producer Frances Higson, editor Colin Manie and actor Gary Lewis all worked on *Close* and came back together for Mullan's first feature, *Orphans* (1997), which again he both wrote and directed.

Despite winning four awards at the Venice Film Festival, *Orphans* suffered from distribution difficulties because FilmFour felt that there was little audience for the film. Given its problematic history, it is rather ironic that it is one of the more absorbing, intelligent and entertaining British films of recent years. Set in Glasgow, the narrative focuses on the events that occur in the lives of four grieving siblings the night before their mother's funeral. At odds, each feels the burden of familial responsibility, realising their difference in attitude, and experiencing guilt and loss. Her death an emotional and spiritual catalyst, they embark on a journey through a series of misadventures. The central performances – particularly those of Douglas Henshall and Gary Lewis – are uniformly complex and stirring, and well supported by a cast of oddball Dickensian characters. Mullan has commented in interview: 'When people don't know whether to laugh or cry, those are the moments I like'. Never shying away from showing the miserable aspects of human existence, he always leavens the situations with flashes of black humour and magic realism. Seamlessly combining personal drama with social commentary, he touches on issues of class, religion, emasculation and the disintegration of the family. On a hopeful note, the family finally reunite at the end, coming to terms, and better able to deal, with their love for one another and their need for intimacy.

Mullan is currently in production with *Magdalene*, a film set in Ireland in the 1960s about women who were imprisoned for promiscuity and subjected to terrible treatment.   **HP**

Laura MULVEY

Penthesilea: Queen of the Born in 1941 in Oxford, UK, and currently occupying the scholastic position of
Amazons (1974) Professor of Media Studies at London's Birkbeck College, Laura Mulvey has given much

to cinema, both in terms of her career as an academic and theoretician – particularly *Riddles of the Sphinx* (1977)
her research into psychoanalytic film theory – and her structurally provocative directorial *Amy!* (1979)
output. Often collaborating on screen with Peter Wollen, an equally important figure in *Crystal Gazing* (1982)
the annals of academia, Mulvey's work not only offered an important feminist discourse
but also dragged British cinema into fertile new territory previously occupied only by
continental political provocateurs such as Jean-Luc Godard.

Mulvey's first film, *Penthesilea: Queen of the Amazons* (1974) (co-directed, written and produced with Wollen) was a groundbreaking polemical piece that took as its
starting point the mime performance of a Henrich von Kleist play about the eponymous
Queen of the Amazons. The film weaves elements from Kleist's personal life into a compelling treatise on the craft of acting, female emancipation and the dynamics of relationships. A thought-provoking, multi-structured work, it manages to avoid didacticism,
emerging as illuminating, perceptive and quite unlike anything else in British cinema at
the time.

Another collaboration with Peter Wollen, *Riddles of the Sphinx* (1977) remains
Mulvey's most celebrated work. It represents a crystallisation of her approach to cinema,
politics and gender. Ostensibly the examination of the relationship between a mother
and her rapidly maturing child, who is increasingly suppressed, the tale is imbued with
a keen awareness of Freudian interpretations of the relationship and the female uncon-
sciousness. The mythological tale of Oedipus acts as a backdrop to the increasingly
fraught familial alliance. Mulvey (who also appears in the film) and Wollen advance the
story through a synthesis of literary and visual allusion, producing a compelling work of
rare intelligence, insight and uniqueness of form.

Solely credited to Mulvey (though Wollen was certainly involved), *Amy!* (1979) is
a strange, perplexing but nonetheless engrossing work, often described as an anti-docu-
mentary, that takes as its loose subject the acclaimed American aviator, Amy Johnson.
However, rather than just chronologically regurgitating historical facts in an attempt to
recreate her life and major achievements, the film creates a labyrinthine jigsaw puzzle
in which divergent forms and visual representations, heavily informed by feminist psychoanalytic theory, briefly connect to signify meaning and import. A complex and multi-
layered work, it remains a strange but beguiling entry into the 'documentary' genre.

Mulvey and Wollen's next work, the more conventional and linear *Crystal Gazing*
(1982), looks at the different opportunities open to two men and two women in the
London of Thatcher's Britain. A contemplative and, given the milieu, necessarily sombre
work, it is also an honest and evocative portrayal of suffocated aspiration and ambition in
a climate hostile to collective regeneration and growth. There is a dark humour at play in
some of the writing and the film interestingly incorporates a monologue written by actor-
comedian Keith Allen. *Crystal Gazing* sadly seems to have marked Mulvey's final foray
into feature productions. *Frida and Tina* (1983) and *Disgraced Monuments* (1996), two
shorts, have since emerged but, in an environment hostile to providing funding for films
which refuse to defer to the dictates of commercial imperatives, there seems to be little
room for someone of Mulvey's obvious commitment and intelligence. As an adjunct to
her academic career, Mulvey is also an acclaimed author – her texts include 'Fetishism
and Curiosity' and a BFI modern classic on *Citizen Kane* – whose place in British cinema
history is firmly assured.   **JWo**

Pat MURPHY

Pat Murphy emerged in 1981 with her film *Maeve*. Coming out as the conflict in North- *Maeve* (1981)
ern Ireland was reaching a fever pitch, it focused not on the explosions and masked men *Anne Devlin* (1984)
that were filling British and Irish television screens, but on the effect that both the mili- *Nora* (2000)
tarism of the UK and the hyper-masculinist attitudes of the Irish Republican community
had on the lives of women. Her symbolically-named heroine Maeve – in Irish saga, the
Queen of Connaught who tried, unsuccessfully, to conquer Ulster – tries hard throughout
the film to reconcile nationalism and feminism; it is, to say the least, an unhappy marriage. Drawing upon a highly self-conscious style, it often makes metaphorical use of the
landscape of Belfast. Yet Murphy never fully enters the realm of the avant-garde, as did
many of the French and British political film-makers of this era.

Her next film, *Anne Devlin* (1984), continued both her interest in the role women have had in the struggle for Irish independence and evinced her fondness for an intense, brooding style. Bríd Brennan, who also played Maeve's sister Roisín, plays Anne Devlin, a servant in the home of Robert Emmet who, in the disastrous aftermath of the 1798 United Irishmen rising, refuses to give the name of any of the participants to his 1803 rebellion. Like *Maeve*, *Anne Devlin* makes extensive use of long takes and slowed-down, sometimes elliptical narrative form. The latter film looks more rich and vivid than the drab *Maeve*, which serves to make the repression visited upon the stoic Devlin – repression that comes from all sides of the conflict – seem all the more painful.

Murphy recently returned to cinema with *Nora* (2000), a meditation on the relationship between James Joyce and Nora Barnacle. Joyce is played by Ewan McGregor, signalling a move into the big time that once seemed unthinkable given the political and formal radicalism of her work up to this point. **JW**

Vinny MURPHY

Accelerator (1999) Born in 1961 in Dublin, Vinny Murphy joined City Workshop as an actor and musician in 1982. In 1987 he made his first short film, *Late*, set in London. In 1993 he wrote and directed three shorts, *Football*, *Trouble* and *Hairspray*, which were performed on an improvisational basis by his students from the Jobstown Screen Acting workshop. *H for Hamlet* was a longer venture (77 minutes) which relocated Shakespeare's play in a post-apocalyptic future. He has acted in a number of films including Geraldine Creed's *The Sun, the Moon and the Stars* (1996) and John Boorman's *The General* (1998).

Murphy's first feature, *Accelerator* (1999), is a low-budget production which follows two groups of marginalised teenagers who challenge each other to a road race in stolen cars from Belfast's inner-city to Dublin. With stylistic nods to Francis Ford Coppola's *Rumble Fish* (1983), the film also bears generic comparison with recent European explorations of similar themes such as Konstantinos Giannaris' *From the Edge of the City* (1998). Made with many of the current and previous members of the Jobstown workshop, the film challenges its viewers to empathise with its inner-city protagonists. The central tension is between the two leads, Whacker (Gavin Kelty) and Johnny T (Stuart Sinclair Blyth). Where Johnny T dreams that his winnings will free him from his Belfast surroundings and allow him to travel to Barcelona, Whacker's ambitions are more circumscribed. Their environment is filmed in strong colours, as if to counter the notion that these are abandoned, lifeless spaces, and much of the action takes place at night. Cutting between the couples in the cars, the film emphasises, without stating, the similarities between the inner-city teenagers of Belfast and Dublin. Inevitably, tragedy looms as they come up against the limitations of their experience.

Murphy continues to teach in conjunction with Ireland's 'filmbase', an organisation invested in all facets of film and video making. **RB**

N

Bharat NALLURI

Born in India in 1966, and raised in the UK, Bharat Nalluri is a budding contemporary British film-maker with a stylised aesthetic cultivated from time spent in television and commercial advertising. His interest in directing stirred early when he and schoolmate Paul Anderson discovered a Super-8mm movie camera in a cupboard at school. Anderson, who Nalluri jokes he is 'three years behind', is now a successful director himself, having helmed the Hollywood genre actioners *Mortal Kombat* (1995), *Event Horizon* (1997), and *Soldier* (1998). After studying business and film in college, Nalluri cofounded the production company Pilgrim Films with producer Richard Johns in 1993. Based in Newcastle upon Tyne, Pilgrim, with Nalluri as its principal in-house director, built its business on producing television commercials, corporate videos and television dramas, including the Nalluri-directed shows 'Driven', 'In Bed With Jimmy Monty', and 'Pressganged'. Pilgrim expanded its scope to feature films in 1995 by commissioning the development and production of two scripts, *Downtime* (1997) and *Killing Time* (1998), both to be directed by Nalluri.

Downtime is a moderately successful blending of American-style action-disaster and kitchen-sinker with independent panache. Milking every drop from its bare-bones budget, Nalluri achieves grungy realism via the film's on-location setting (Liverpool passing for working-class Newcastle upon Tyne), and introduces genuine moments of tension and suspense without the benefit of big-budget flash. The film's central weaknesses – aside from the flawed ending, which is a disappointing bookend to its amazing, nail-biting opening – is Nalluri's decision to ignore the socio-economic possibilities of the script's interesting mishmash of genres. *Killing Time* is a derivative 'bullets and babes' riff on Tarantino material, a hybrid of Italian spaghetti westerns, *La Femme Nikita* (1991), *Reservoir Dogs* (1992) and *Pulp Fiction* (1994).

Although stylishly executed and stunningly photographed, the film's tired, nihilistic black comedy, lack of suspense and bland production design diminishes the pleasure of the film. A lacklustre misfire, on the macro level, *Killing Time* does not work as action, comedy or camp.

Downtime (1997)
Killing Time (1998)
The Crow: Salvation (2000)

With his next feature, *The Crow: Salvation* (2000), a $25 million-budgeted third installment to the gothic film series, Nalluri made his American directorial debut. Hampered by an awful script, it is full of cliché, dreadful dialogue and one-dimensional characters. Soon after, Nalluri returned to Newcastle and resumed his duties at Pilgrim Films, directing an episode of the Channel 4 contemporary genre series 'Shockers II', entitled 'Cyclops'. He is also reuniting with old classmate and friend Paul Anderson as the 2nd unit director on Anderson's *Resident Evil*, a film realisation of the popular, Capcom zombie action-horror video game series. **THa**

Ronald NEAME

Take My Life (1947)
The Golden Salamander
(1950)
The Card (1952)
The Million Pound Note (1953)
The Man Who Never Was
(1956)
The Seventh Sin (1957)
Windom's Way (1958)
The Horse's Mouth (1958)
Tunes of Glory (1960)
Escape from Zahrain (1962)
I Could Go on Singing (1963)
The Chalk Garden (1964)
Mister Moses (1965)
Gambit (1966)
A Man Could Get Killed (1966)
Prudence and the Pill (1968)
The Prime of Miss Jean Brodie
(1969)
Scrooge (1970)
The Poseidon Adventure
(1972)
The Odessa File (1974)
Meteor (1979)
Hopscotch (1980)
First Monday in October
(1981)
Foreign Body (1986)
The Magic Balloon (1990)

Ronald Neame has been one of the most prolific and commercially successful directors to come out of Britain in the twentieth century, and also one of the most difficult to categorise. The quality of his films has been inconsistent, to say the least, and those he made in the second half of his directorial career have never quite lived up to the promise of his earlier achievements. After a long apprenticeship as a cameraman, Neame proved himself a capable if not spectacular director in a range of genres, from war films to light comedies to disaster epics. A handful of his films, such as *Tunes of Glory* (1960) and *The Pride of Miss Jean Brodie* (1969), are recognised classics, while others, such as *Meteor* (1979), are forgettable drivel. Throughout his career Neame has eschewed any idiosyncratic or distinctive style behind the camera, retaining a simple, unobtrusive standard of direction that is most attentive, particularly in his earlier films, to the actors' efforts in realising their character.

He was born in 1911 in London. His father, Elwin Neame, was an occasional film director and photographer, and his mother was the actress Ivy Close. When his father was killed in an automobile accident in 1923, Neame was forced to leave school and look for work. After a short stint with an oil company his mother used her connections in the film industry to find him a job at Elstree Studios. He first worked as a focus-puller and later as an assistant cameraman, most notably on Hitchcock's first talking picture, *Blackmail* (1929).

Neame's first mini-break came in 1934 when he was working as a cameraman on Arthur B. Woods' *Drake of England*. He then worked as cameraman on a string of 'quota quickies' throughout the 1930s, also acting as house cameraman on the highly popular George Formby films.

During the war years Neame worked as a cameraman on a number of memorable films, including Gabriel Pascal's *Major Barbara* (1941) and Powell and Pressburger's *One of Our Aircraft is Missing* (1942), for which he received his first Oscar® nomination. David Lean and Neame made a hat-full of movies for the Army, Navy and Air Force during the Second World War, with Lean directing and Neame working as cinematographer. In 1943 the two men formed a production company with Anthony Havelock-Allen, and Neame earned his second Oscar® nomination as cinematographer for the Noel Coward project *Blithe Spirit* (1945).

In 1944, when the entrepreneur J. Arthur Rank decided to invest serious money in the British film industry, it was decided that Neame would travel to Hollywood on a fact-finding mission. The journey was propitious for his future career in film. The knowledge he gleaned from the Hollywood Industry made him reluctant to return to the relatively undemanding role of cinematographer. He wanted a greater challenge and subsequently told Rank that he would like to try his hand at producing. In 1946 he was both co-writer and producer of Lean's *Great Expectations*. It was a runaway success, earning a string of Oscar® nominations, winning in two minor categories and proving that British films were commercially viable on both sides of the Atlantic. Even in the 1990s, by which time Neame was based in Hollywood, the residuals from *Great Expectations* were still paying for his yearly holidays to England.

Following its success, he logically progressed to work as a director. *Take My Life* (1947) was a competent debut without being spectacular. Having already worked in film for twenty years before attempting to direct, Neame had a sound understanding of the practical side of film-making. He never had to rely on cameramen or the editing process to compensate for any technical ignorance. A disadvantage of this experience was that it compromised his ability to consider visual narrative far beyond standard interpretations. The subtle framing and restrained camera movements in his early films enabled viewers to focus unswervingly on the relative circumstances of the main characters. However, if the main characters failed to engage an audience so too would their circumstances, leaving the film's weaknesses exposed. Neame's second film, *The Golden Salamander* (1950), is a case in point. A predictable thriller about gun running in the North African desert, the only thing worth noting is the fact that it was filmed almost entirely on location; Neame believed that, wherever possible, a film should be shot in this way for the sake of realism.

It was with his third feature, *The Card* (1952), that Neame began to prove his worth as a director. The film is a class-based Ealing comedy that details the ambition of a laundress' son, played by Alec Guinness, who wants to attain both wealth and respectability even if it requires morally reprehensible behaviour to get there. Though hardly deserving of superlatives, the film proved a minor hit at the box-office and highlighted Neame's unqualified strength: an ability to extract first-rate performances from his actors and actresses.

The 1950s were, artistically if not remuneratively, Neame's most rewarding decade. Following the success of *The Card,* he made two films in succession with Hollywood stars. First he directed Gregory Peck in *The Million Pound Note* (1953), a classic comedy about a bankrupt American travelling abroad, and next *The Man Who Never Was* (1956), a rather plodding war drama starring Clifton Webb.

The success of these two films precipitated Neame's first directorial foray into the Hollywood studio system. In 1957 he was called to Hollywood to direct a remake of *The Painted Veil* (1934) called *The Seventh Sin* (1957). It was a far from pleasant experience. The studio was unhappy with Neame and eventually replaced him with Vincent Minnelli, who refused a director's credit despite Neame's insistence that he wanted none himself. It was the first substantial failure Neame had experienced. Rather than slip into obscurity, however, he returned to London and, after steadying his resolve with *Windom's Way* (1958), went on to direct what were, arguably, his two best films, *The Horse's Mouth* (1958) and *Tunes of Glory*. The latter is consistently cited as his best film and was his own personal favourite. John Mills won a best actor award at the Venice Film Festival, and Alec Guinness could easily have won one himself.

In 1963 Neame directed Judy Garland in her last film, *I Could Go on Singing*, handling her moody and demanding persona, and inspiring a remarkable final performance. His skill with actors was first acknowledged at the Academy Awards in 1964 when Dame Edith Evans was nominated for a Best Supporting Actress Oscar® for *The Chalk Garden* Some five years later he went one better, directing Maggie Smith to Best Actress Oscar® in *The Prime of Miss Jean Brodie.* Vanessa Redgrave had already played the character of Jean Brodie in the theatre, but Neame wanted Smith for the film role and it proved a prescient choice.

After the critical and commercial success of *The Prime of Miss Jean Brodie*, it was only a matter of time before Neame was lured to Hollywood to helm a big studio film. The attraction of Hollywood's mega-budget zeitgeist was that money no longer stood between a director's vision and a producer's realism. That said, freedom from economic constraints came at a price – the commercial nature of the films that were offered big budgets.

In 1972 Neame was chosen to direct the seminal 'disaster epic' *The Poseidon Adventure*, about ten passengers on an ocean liner who fight to find their way out of the ship when it is overturned by a freak wave. Shelley Winters won an Oscar® for her role as an overweight woman who dies saving her fellow survivors in the final stages of the dramatic escape. The film also picked up a Special Achievement Award for its special effects and a handful of other technical awards. An imaginative, expensive and stylish production, it was a big box-office success. There are few films that create a new genre, but Neame never let the *Poseidon Adventure's* remarkable reception convince him the film was anything other than a commercial success; he never expressed any lasting fondness for it. Only the evident technical assurance was a source of pride. This is a harsh judgement of his own work: great special effects and great actors are rarely enough to make a film enjoyable. What audiences found gripping about *The Poseidon Adventure* was the way in which the different aspects of each character's personalities and histories unravelled, and the subsequent changes in the group dynamics.

The Poseidon Adventure marked a dubious point in Neame's career. Not only did Hollywood's big-budget production values take him away from the films he most wanted to make, but it also took him away from the culture he was most able to make them in. Having cut his teeth as a director during the Golden Age of British cinema in the 1940s, he was primarily interested in character studies.

Over the next two decades, the quality of Neame's films deteriorated markedly as he began to focus more on action. He has held the studios responsible, intimating that these were the only kind of films that he was able to make in the 1970s and 1980s. *The Odessa File* (1974), a thriller based on the Frederick Forsythe novel and starring Jon Voight, is watchable, with slick production values and a reasonable plot. The characters are superficial, however, and the pace and tension uneven.

Neame's next film, *Meteor*, was woeful, confirming that *The Poseidon Adventure* was far more than a special effects film. By his account, Neame felt pressured into directing it because he had refused to make the sequel to *The Poseidon Adventure*. A year later, *Hopscotch* (1980) provided better characters and two fine actors (Walter Matthau and Glenda Jackson) for Neame to work with. Matthau is superb as the grumbling and disgruntled CIA operative who, having being demoted to a desk job, proceeds to leak his memoirs to rival intelligence agencies. Following the enjoyable on-set experience of *Hopscotch*, Matthau was keen to work with the director again; they were reunited a year later in *First Monday in October*.

While *First Monday in October* is a fairly pedestrian effort, it would still have been a reasonable swansong to a brilliant career. Unfortunately, Neame went on to direct *Foreign Body*, the story of an Indian immigrant who poses as a private doctor. Perhaps Neame believed the film marked a welcome return to more character-based work, but no amount of sympathetic directing could have saved the diabolical script. This was Neame's penultimate film, the last being a children's adventure fantasy, *The Magic Balloon* (1990), which was an experiment in Showscan that sunk without a trace because few cinemas were capable of screening the relatively new 70mm film format.

The French writer Gustave Flaubert once wrote that good writing is like polishing a window – the more you polish, the less you see the glass. Neame adopted a similar philosophy to film-making. He believed that a director should never draw attention to the camera, and consciously avoided any stylistic flamboyance. Despite an extensive filmography (or perhaps because of it), Neame's oeuvre gives the impression of a director who never managed to make the film that would give him lasting critical recognition, unlike his contemporary and sometime collaborator David Lean. In the later stages of his working-life, he chose to direct less inspired, more commercial projects, becoming increasingly disillusioned with the industry. After a remarkable career spanning eight decades, BAFTA-Shell rewarded Neame with an Honorary Membership to the British Cinematographers Society in 1990 for his outstanding contribution to the British film industry. **EMa**

Anthony NEILSON

The Debt Collector (1999) Born in 1967, Anthony Neilson studied at the Welsh College of Drama and Music in Cardiff. He subsequently wrote for television (contributing to the series 'Cracker') although his theatrical excursions have had a higher profile: verbally violent, his plays are also marked by a sharp wit. In 1997 he caused a furore with 'The Censor', which focused on the confrontation between a film censor and a female pornographer.

That controversy foreshadowed the response to Neilson's brutally efficient film debut, *The Debt Collector* (1999), which he wrote and directed. Set in Edinburgh, but shot largely in Glasgow (due to a subsidiary deal with the Glasgow Film Fund), *The Debt Collector* was described by Neilson as a 'Scottish urban western'. Billy Connolly plays ex-hardman debt collector Nickie Dryden, based loosely on Glasgow's Jimmy Boyle, who served 15 years for murder and was a beneficiary of Barlinnie prison's art therapy programme. Dryden visited violence on those who would not pay debts; when they were uncooperative, he turned on their relatives. Surprisingly, he emerges as the victim of the piece. It is Ken Stott who provides the brooding menace, playing Gary Keltie, the detective who arrests Dryden, and is determined to make his victims become spectres at his every feast. The situation intensifies through the actions of Flipper (Iain Robertson), a young gangster manqué who idolises Dryden and tragically emulates his methods.

Neilson stated a desire to examine the effects of violence, but his focus on the spiral of cause and effect – coupled with increasingly grotesque acts – makes *The Debt Collector* play like a Jacobean revenge tragedy. The women in the lives of Dryden and Keltie (wife and mother respectively) provide an opportunity to humanise both characters. Ultimately, however, they serve as victims of – and catalysts for – ever more cruelty.

Neilson has continued to write for the theatre.   **KP**

Chris NEWBY

Born in England in 1957, Chris Newby came to prominence with his short, *Relax* (1991). This is the blackly funny story of Steve, a gay man anxiously awaiting the results of his HIV test, scrubbing between his toes with his toothbrush and picturing his own death; needless to say, the film's title is ironic. *Relax* won an award at the Berlin Film Festival and was included on the compilation tape, *Boys' Shorts: The New Queer Cinema* (1993).

His first feature, *The Anchoress* (1993), the story of Christine Carpenter (Natalie Morse), a fourteenth-century peasant who is obsessed with the Virgin Mary, owes much to Andrei Tarkovsky. She is persuaded by a lecherous priest (Christopher Eccleston) to become an anchoress, a holy woman who is walled up in order to receive visions and bless the villagers. When she rebels against his malign influence, he has her mother tried as a witch. This is stark and sombre material, ravishingly photographed in tinted black and white by Michel Baudour, which benefits from a strong cast (Eccleston and Pete Postlethwaite in particular). Newby has a natural eye, and the harsh settings and heavily composed mise-en-scène are reminiscent of Ingmar Bergman's medieval movies (*The Virgin Spring* (1960), *The Seventh Seal* (1957)). Although the painterly quality of the images and deliberate pacing might be off-putting to some, this is a provocative examination of the clash between individual faith and organised religion.

Newby's second feature, *Madagascar Skin* (1995), is about Harry (John Hannah), a young gay man who is hung up about a vivid birthmark on his face (the 'Madagascar skin' of the title). He flees from his hometown to a beach where he rescues a man, Flint (Bernard Hill), buried in the sand. The two move into an empty cottage, become friends, and then lovers; Flint, a liar and thief, may also be a murderer. Despite its thriller plot, the film is presented as a love story between two misfits. Newby resists any urge to tie loose ends together, offering instead an enigmatic, (often maddeningly) cryptic, mood piece. Although the two leads are impressive, the appeal of *Madagascar Skin* is a stylistic one. Like *The Anchoress*, this is slow, but the unashamedly poetic images are seductive. The only major flaw is the suggestion that Harry would be so rejected – 'I'm going to die and no-one's ever touched me' – because of his skin blemish; John Hannah simply is not disfigured enough for his alienation to be plausible.

Like Richard Kwietniowski (*Love and Death on Long Island* (1997)), Newby has made the transition from gay-themed short films to features with success.   **IC**

The Anchoress (1993)
Madagascar Skin (1995)

Mike NEWELL

Like many fellow British directors, Mike Newell's career has been a delicate balancing act. A true survivor of the treacherous waters of British film-making, having consistently worked in television and cinema for the past forty years, Newell has juggled the demands of personal vision and commercial return with varying degrees of success. Employing neither the full-blown, big-budget style of a Ridley or Tony Scott, nor the resolutely, dogmatically home-grown approach of a Mike Leigh or Ken Loach, his best work has a broad crossover appeal. It combines the commerciality of formula with a very British attention to the finer details of character and intimate emotional drama. Moving from modest but well-crafted domestic stories, to the larger canvases allowed by Hollywood budgets, with a concurrent shift of focus from British to American subjects, Newell was a key figure

The Man in the Iron Mask (1976)
The Awakening (1980)
Bad Blood (1981)
Dance with a Stranger (1985)
The Good Father (1987)
Amazing Grace and Chuck (1987)
Soursweet (1988)
Enchanted April (1992)

in the revival of fortunes of the British film industry in the mid-1990s. This was due in the main to the phenomenal success of *Four Weddings and a Funeral* (1993), his most widely-known work which inspires vitriol and veneration from its audience in roughly proportionate numbers.

The film's light, shamelessly romantic style is actually unusual for Newell who, else-where, is more restrained and often downbeat. The accuracy of tone, however, together with the focus on a strong character-driven script and an emphasis on British issues – relationships, class and codes of behaviour – are indicative of his preoccupations. At his best, Newell is capable of truly brilliant film-making of an old-fashioned, dramatic type, as in *Donnie Brasco* (1997). A worthy addition to the mob film canon, its fluent explora-tion of split loyalty and betrayal, and brilliant central performances rank alongside the technical wizardry of *Goodfellas* (1990) or the epic grandiloquence of *The Godfather* (1972).

Born in St. Albans, UK, in 1942, Newell attended Cambridge University, followed by a three-year Granada Television training stint. His initial intention had been to gradu-ate into theatre directing, but he soon found himself directing for television, an occupa-tion which was to largely sustain him for the next twenty years, beginning with *Sharon*, a documentary, in 1964. His basis in television direction, with its focus on domestic issues and settings, and an exclusively British target audience, laid the groundwork for close dramatic work that concentrates on character and situation rather than technical virtuosity. His direction of television plays penned by writers such as David Hare, John Osborne and Jack Rosenthal was particularly formative.

After his version of *The Man in the Iron Mask* (1976) was deemed good enough to warrant a theatrical release, Newell began to make tentative moves towards the world of feature-film production. His first two efforts were undistinguished schlock pictures produced by a British industry desperately trying to compete with the Hollywood action-horror market. *The Awakening* (1980), a mummy picture in which an obsessive archae-ologist believes the spirit of an evil Egyptian queen has possessed his new-born daughter, borrows heavily from seminal horror films *Don't Look Now* (1973), *The Omen* (1976) and *Rosemary's Baby* (1968), but lacks any of their subtlety or verve. *Bad Blood* (1981) is a slightly more convincing thriller, based on the story of Eric Stanley Graham, a farmer who shot several people dead in his isolated community in the 1940s and became the subject of New Zealand's most notorious manhunt. Newell uses the bush setting to heighten the unnerving atmosphere, and handles the climactic chase involving Maori trackers and police well enough, but the film marks his last experiment in the genre.

Also based on a true story, but more compelling, is *Dance with a Stranger* (1985), a film about Ruth Ellis, the last woman to be executed in Britain. Here, Newell finds himself in more familiar dramatic territory. Ellis – a young Miranda Richardson in her debut role – is a social climber, a working-class girl burdened with a ten-year-old son, who becomes embroiled in the seedy world of Soho nightlife in 1950s Britain and an obsessive relationship with high-roller David Blakeley. Austere, grimy London and post-war repression contrast the red-blooded desire of the story, a desire fuelled by lust and the drive to escape the trappings of working-class identity. Filming in a neo-documentary style, Newell is fascinated by Ellis' predicament and by the louche corruption and degen-eracy of the world Blakeley represents, playing with visual and dramatic representations of sleaziness and self-destructive behaviour. To indicate her downmarket character, par-ticular emphasis is placed on Ellis' coarseness and lack of social niceties; the true moral degradation is played out around her. London – and Britain – has never felt dirtier.

The Good Father (1987) is no less critical of British strictures and structures, but is much funnier in its treatment. It is a battle of the sexes in which Newell explores the emasculating developments of 1960s liberalism and 1980s feminism and their impact on family relationships. In opposition are an emotionally inept father, aided by another ex-husband casualty of female empowerment out for revenge on the sisterhood, and the former's liberated lesbian wife. The film charts their child-custody battle with an unerr-ing comic eye, laying emphasis on the unhealthy motives of all involved. It is especially accurate as a study of male anger and repressed emotion of a peculiarly British type. The intelligent comic tone – half-satire, half-farce – signals Newell's later comic efforts, *Four Weddings and a Funeral* and *Pushing Tin* (1999).

Soursweet (1988) examines relationships in Britain from the perspective of an immigrant Chinese family finding their way in a foreign land. It is a clash-of-cultures film in which each generation of the family experience some sort of revelation. British society becomes an agent of change rather than a stagnant and repressive force, and the 'old' way is represented by the Soho Triad gang who pursue an unfulfilled debt, threatening the development of the family's new way of life. Impeccably acted and directed, emotional bite is provided by Ian McEwan's script. *Soursweet* is a strong conclusion to a trilogy of films that demonstrate Newell's fascination with emotional drama, relationships, and the trammels of class, sex and society – sometimes circumstantial, and sometimes self-imposed.

Newell revisits these ideas in *An Awfully Big Adventure* (1995), the story of a love triangle set in a post-war Liverpool theatre, in which a young working-class stage-hand is caught between the intellectual desire for social respectability and the emotional need for love and excitement. Hugh Grant, in an unusual role as the Machiavellian, snobbish theatre owner, represents the former urge, and Alan Rickman's suave, enigmatic lead actor, the latter.

Appropriately enough for a director fascinated by entrapment – an idea explored very differently in *Four Weddings* and *Donnie Brasco* – Newell is also interested in methods of escape. *Amazing Grace and Chuck* (1987), a comic fantasy of wish-fulfilment, examines one form of release, demonstrating cinema's Capraesque potential to transport its audience from the realities of the everyday; and reality doesn't come much more real than mutually assured nuclear destruction. A young American boy strikes from his 'little league' baseball team in protest against a local missile silo, gaining national notoriety and inspiring basketball star Amazing Grace Smith and fellow sports stars to follow in his suit and lobby the president.

Newell revisited the idea of fantasy intruding upon reality in *Into the West* (1992). The contrast in the film becomes intentionally stark, comparing the effect of the grim environs of Irish tower-block life on two children with the fantastic resonance of a white horse brought home by their grandfather. It is Newell's most visually ambitious and striking work, invoking the mythology of both Irish folklore and the Western frontier as metaphors for imaginative liberation and for the rediscovery of family and identity. *Enchanted April* (1992) demonstrates a more realistic form of escape, and revisits Newell's interest in the psychology of repressed and oppressed women. Four 1920s archetypes – a snobbish widow, an aristocrat, a bored housewife, and the unfulfilled wife of a writer – escape from their constraining circumstances to an Italian castle, where their disparate characters, and the contrasting emotional sensibilities of England and Europe, collide. The development of this side of Newell's style – the ability to mix sharp comedy, well-drawn character and drama with sentimentality – was soon to prove financially, as well as artistically, rewarding.

Both of Newell's best films – *Four Weddings and a Funeral* and *Donnie Brasco* – incorporate his talents as a comic entertainer and character director. *Four Weddings and a Funeral* has become something of a pop phenomenon. Instrumental in convincing various movers and shakers of the potential viability and commerciality of home-grown British product, the film is the perfect example of Newell's comic side. It is well-scripted and performed, entertaining and immensely marketable, its characters teetering on the cusp of character and caricature. The central character of a 'serial monogamist' – Hugh Grant in full stumbling schoolboy flow attempting to overcome the binds of English emotional ineptitude in professing his love for a frank American – is a classic Newell protagonist. He is manacled in emotional chains of his own making, as are the sugar-coated issues of repressed love, English reserve, class and character. Newell's skill is in mixing the requisite comic mishaps with emotional punch. The array of neatly packaged British stereotypes – bumbling fop, cheeky Cockney and hell-raising Scot – overtly panders to an American audience and is too much for some to stomach. Where Newell has the charm and wit to carry it off, later imitators do not. While laying much of the groundwork for the international reception of modern British film-making, *Four Weddings* has also been instrumental in creating some of the straightjackets of subject and character by which those films are bound. It has spawned formulaic romantic comedies and Cockney posturing – outdated stereotypes and one-size-fits-all film-making of the worst kind.

Quite the opposite, *Donnie Brasco* is an understated, unsentimental character study that seeks to break down, rather than perpetuate, well-worn stereotypes, in this case those of the American Mafia. Taking an almost scientific interest in the rules, rituals and routines of low-level mob life, the film follows Donnie, an undercover cop, and the development of his relationship with Lefty Ruggiero, a long-serving foot soldier who becomes his mentor. Newell's interest is in the dramatic potential of Donnie's split loyalty. He contrasts his home life and the increasingly complex world in which he becomes embroiled, portraying the conflicting demands of profession and friendship that must inevitably come to a head. There is also an affectionate, comic touch at work in the fascination with Mafioso language and Mob etiquette. Sayings like 'fahgedabuoudit', 'fugazi', 'stand-up guy' are explained; the distinction is made between 'a friend of ours' and 'a friend of mine'; nicknames such as Sonny Black, Sonny Red, Lefty Two Guns abound; and at Christmas, both Donnie and Lefty exchange cards with identical wads of cash inside. In their own way, these rules of conduct are as restrictive and defining as the British codes which Newell has explored elsewhere. With its cinematic nods to *Goodfellas* (Scorsese-style montage sequences cut together with a pop soundtrack) and a domestic, low-key approach that deconstructs *Godfather* mythologising, the film is Newell's most compelling drama and his most fluent exploration of the dramatic possibilities of film. It features outstanding turns by Johnny Depp and Al Pacino.

Pushing Tin is another glimpse into a parallel, male-dominated world: the testosterone-fuelled profession of air traffic control. It is a high-pressure, competitive environment charged with the type of masculine ego exemplified by top-man Nick Falzone, whose supremacy is threatened by the Zen-like, Indian feather-toting calmness of new man Russell Bell. Another study of male codes of behaviour, the film once again showcases Newell's fluent style and comic timing, as well as his fondness for the slushy ending that *Donnie Brasco* thankfully lacked.

A commercial director in both the positive and negative senses of the word, Newell is a consistently reliable and intelligent film-maker who focuses on cinema's capacity to entertain and emotionally engage rather than provoke or enrage. He is currently in production with *How to Lose a Guy in 10 Days*. **OB**

Allan NIBLO

Loop (1997) Judging by the sheer volume of formulaic romantic comedies that continue to spill out from the beleaguered British film industry, indistinguishable from each other in style or direction, trammelled by a tired, outdated and grossly unimaginative format, the school of quirky British romantic comedy has a lot of students. It is a school that is very good at producing very bad films. Unlike Hollywood, who fashion the modern-day Meg Ryan mega-hits, producers in Britain, particularly since the leviathan success of *Four Weddings and a Funeral* (1993), continue to search for the dynamite formula of charm comedy and chemistry. Allan Niblo's debut *Loop* (1997) represents one such concoction: the dysfunctional romantic comedy, fuelled by edgy humour and a faint hint of farce, some ludicrous characters, and a narrative in which events descend into chaos and then come out smelling of roses.

The characters are off-the-shelf: a hard-to-get, sassy heroine with a thing for wild men, her tomboyish sister, a wet suitor who thinks he loves the former but falls for the latter, a troubled kid and her wayward artistic father. Throw in an eccentric disabled mother, her even more eccentric husband, and the heroine's maniacal ex-boyfriend out for revenge, a range of badly realised romantic subplots between the main characters, and the inevitable happy ending.

Obviously filming on a minuscule budget, with sound recorded on set and the camera rigidly fixed in place, Niblo uses very short scenes and quick editing to try to inject pace. He is scuppered by some dreadful performances, however, and a bad script which uniformly falls on the wrong side of the fine line between cringe-worthy cliché and cultural comment. Producer of *Human Traffic* (1997), Niblo is no stranger to this. *Loop* reminds you that good films are increasingly hard to make, and with countless projects languishing in development or distribution hell, it is difficult to see how this ever made it to the production line. **OB**

Adrian NOBLE

A Midsummer Night's Dream (1996)

As a former artistic director of the Royal Shakespeare Company, with an enormous number of fine theatrical productions under his belt, there is little doubt that Adrian Noble has the talent to translate his success under the proscenium arch onto the silver screen. However, as innumerable examples in cinema's history have attested, the two art forms are different, bearing their own individual acting styles, settings and artistic demands. Unfortunately, Adrian Noble's sole film effort is a textbook testament to the pitfalls of cinematic adaptation. Originally a hugely successful stage production, much praised for its bold use of colour and staging, *A Midsummer Night's Dream* (1996) is essentially a straightforward export of the original with a slightly abridged text.

Fairies ride about on umbrellas, sporting coloured, electric-shock hair-dos, dressed in various garish shades; the Players zip about on a motorbike, looking like the unholy offspring of the Mad Hatter and Wallace & Gromit; the forest is a huge, wooden sound stage dressed with light bulbs; and the lovers perform slapstick antics through free-standing doors to highlight the farcical tone of their story. Though imaginative, these are essentially theatrical tricks designed for a visual impact that does not translate well into film, resulting in a form of high camp that even John Waters would eschew.

Noble possesses a strong command of Shakespeare's text and directs the action with flair. He fails, however, to adopt cinematic devices, such as editing, camera movement and focus, to counteract the over-the-top theatricality of his images. A needless attempt to frame the story as the contents of a child's imagination adds little, merely reminding us of the toy-box production design. Misjudged references to *E.T.* (1982), *The Wizard of Oz* (1939) and the Disney version of *Peter Pan* (1953) provide the only hints that Noble is directing a film rather than a stage play. Understandably, he has since played his dramas out on more familiar stages. **OB**

Christopher NOLAN

Following (1998)
Memento (2000)

Establishing himself as an original talent with his debut feature, *Following* (1998), Christopher Nolan swiftly capitalised on his critical success with the acclaimed thriller *Memento* (2000). Favouring small, intense, character-driven stories, his work is heavily influenced by noir narratives and aesthetics. Fashioning protagonists that become the detectives in the mysteries of their own lives, both films incorporate flashback narratives.

Born in London in 1970, Nolan experimented with home videos from the age of seven, studied English Literature at University College London, and made three- and four-minute 16mm shorts. *Following*, a hit at Toronto, Slamdance and Rotterdam film festivals, is shot in documentary-style black and white, and runs at an economical seventy minutes. Like *Memento*, its plot seems convoluted but is actually simple. An aspiring writer, Bill (Jeremy Theobald), tells the story: having become obsessed with following strangers his life takes a dramatic turn when one of his subjects, Cobb (Alex Haw), approaches him and leads him into a life of petty crime. Featuring the customary characters – gangster boss and femme fatale – and the requisite double-crossing, the theatricality of the piece tends towards the melodramatic and at times the acting seems stagey and stilted. However, given that the shoot of twenty days took place over a year, with only one or two takes of each set-up, this is hardly surprising. Variously touching on issues of class, identity, voyeurism and the nature of illusion, the film is well sustained by its intriguing premise.

Nolan's subsequent film, *Memento*, screened in competition at the 2001 Sundance Festival and won the Waldo Salt Screenwriting Award. Based on a short story by Nolan's brother, Jonathan, about a polaroid image which fades rather than reveals itself, in the director's own words it is a 'dis-linear' thriller 'dealt to us in reverse chronology by a protagonist coping with a trauma-induced condition that prevents him from making new memories'. Guy Pearce plays Lenny, the protagonist in question, perfectly creating a sense of the character's complex past and empty, searching present; with an unreliable memory he tattoos his body in order to remind himself of the important details of his life. Extremely stylish, it cuts between black and white and green-tinged colour to delineate time shifts. Like *Following*, it rarely features establishing shots, focusing close in on Lenny's face to heighten the sense of his entrapment and claustrophobia. Joe Pantoliano is suitably ambiguous as Teddy, the contradictory figure who could be friend or enemy, and Carrie-Ann Moss, the spiky, enigmatic love interest, contrasts well with the soft-focus image of Lenny's dead wife.

Since moving to Los Angeles in 1997, Nolan has written a screenplay for an adaptation of Ruth Rendell's 'The Keys to the Street', which he may direct. He is currently in production with *Insomnia*, starring Al Pacino, Hilary Swank and Robin Williams, a remake of the Norwegian film of the same name by Erik Skjoldbjaerg (1997), adapted by Hillary Seitz.   **HP**

Trevor NUNN

Hedda (1975)
Lady Jane (1986)
Twelfth Night (1996) Born in Ipswich, UK, in 1940, Trevor Nunn's theatrical credentials are impeccable. Artistic Director of the Royal Shakespeare Company before Adrian Noble, and Artistic Director of the Royal National Theatre since 1997, he began with Cambridge Footlights and quickly established a reputation as a wry and witty adapter and director of the classics. His productions of the late 1970s Shakespeare-for-television films (*Antony and Cleopatra* (1974), *The Comedy of Errors* (1978) and *Macbeth* (1979)) were groundbreaking in their innovation and visual flair. His three feature films have shown similar command of both word and image.

Nunn adapted *Hedda* (1975) from Henrik Ibsen's play 'Hedda Gabler', and the dropping of the 'Gabler' for the film version is a clue to his approach to the eponymous anti-heroine. Played to the hilt by Glenda Jackson, Hedda is bored by her husband and revolted by the idea of carrying his child. Yet her schemes for revenge rebound on her. Placing too much deference on the original play, much of the time is spent on clinical analysis and lingering close-ups; the rest of the supporting cast are subsequently a little wasted. There is a hypnotic tension in Nunn's direction, however, and his theatrical training is impeccably harnessed to the medium of film, with his camera observing, Sphinx-like, the unfolding predetermination of it all.

Lady Jane (1986) focuses on an intriguing historical figure in Edward VI's second cousin. An overlong biopic, it is ultimately stymied by the miscasting of Helena Bonham Carter as Jane and, more damagingly, the way in which rural England is depicted as some Monty Python-esque Arcadia. The casting of RSC stalwarts such as Joss Ackland, Jane Lapotaire and Patrick Stewart lends much-needed weight, but at a time when witty Merchant-Ivory costume dramas were beginning to assert themselves on the cinematic map, this film is dreary and excessively dependant on high-falutin language and sentiment.

Twelfth Night (1996) updates Shakespeare's classic comedy of sexual confusions to an unspecified Edwardian period, and contains some of cinema's best ensemble acting. This time, Bonham Carter is perfect in the role of Olivia. She is admirably complemented by Toby Stephens, Richard E. Grant, Ben Kingsley and Nunn's wife Imogen Stubbs. The director avoids what could have been a facile attempt at gender-bending antics, although the US publicity campaign was keen to market the film as *Some Like it Hot* (1959) meets *Tootsie* (1982). The pace and humour is fast and frenetic, and compared to a work such as Kenneth Branagh's leaden and overly-beholden *Hamlet* (1996), it succeeds in transposing age-old themes to jaundiced modern audiences.

Nunn's most recent work includes television directions of National Theatre shows, such as 'Porgy and Bess' in 1993 and 'Oklahoma' in 1999.   **BM**

O

Joe O'BYRNE

Joe O'Byrne was artistic director of Dublin's Co-Motion Theatre Company from 1985 to *Pete's Meteor* (1998)
1998 where he wrote and directed several critically-acclaimed productions, including
'Departed', 'The Ghost of Saint Joan', and 'The Sinking of the Titanic and Other Matters'.
He also directed the award-winning 'Frank Pig Says Hello' (adapted by Patrick McCabe
from his novel 'The Butcher Boy') which was performed in New York, Melbourne and The
Royal Court in London. O'Byrne has since directed two other McCabe plays: 'The Dead
School' and 'LocoCounty Lonesome'.

He began his film career as a script editor on Johnny Gogan's low-budget *The
Bargain Shop* (1992), and worked as a member of the video crew on Jim Sheridan's *In
the Name of the Father* (1993). He wrote the screenplay for Cathal Black's 1995 award-
winning feature *Korea* (adapted from the short story by John McGahern), a powerful
rites-of-passage parable about the bitter clash between tradition and modernity in 1950s
Ireland.

In 1998 O'Byrne wrote and directed his first feature, a children's film entitled *Pete's
Meteor*, starring Brenda Fricker, Alfred Molina, Dervla Kirwan and Mike Myers. Set in
inner-city Dublin, *Pete's Meteor* tells the story of the Devine family – three orphaned
children and their grandmother – whose lives are altered when a meteor lands in their
back garden. As O'Byrne had never directed even a short film prior to *Pete's Meteor*,
co-producers Liam O'Neill and John Lyons (producer of Paul Thomas Anderson's *Hard
Eight* (1996) and *Boogie Nights* (1997)) wisely insisted on the need for an experienced
cinematographer. The film is smartly photographed by Canadian-based Paul Sarossy
(Atom Egoyan's *The Sweet Hereafter* (1997) and *Exotica* (1994)) and this visual poise
compensates somewhat for the essentially mawkish storyline. It was first shown at the
1998 Dublin Film Festival, and earned a Special Jury mention (Children's section) at the
1999 Berlin Film Festival.

O'Byrne is a skillful and imaginative translator of literary drama, although it remains
to be seen whether or not he can apply this talent to his film work. He is currently
working on a stage adaptation of Oscar Wilde's 'The Picture of Dorian Gray' and a

translation of Bertolt Brecht's 'Mother Courage'. Forthcoming film projects include directing his screenplay *The Rocky Road* in the summer of 2001. **KHo**

Pat O'CONNOR

Born in Ardmore, Ireland, in 1943, Pat O'Connor left school at 17 and travelled to England before moving to the United States. He enrolled in a liberal arts programme at UCLA then continued his education in Canada. He returned to Ireland in 1970, when he began work with Radio Telefís Éireann. After a six-year stint in documentary, he moved to drama. He directed several television plays and wrote episodes of the serial 'The Riordans'. In 1982 he directed the acclaimed BBC/RTÉ co-production 'The Ballroom of Romance'. This is a dark, atmospheric tale of repressed sexuality in 1950s rural Ireland written by William Trevor. It won several awards including a BAFTA and a silver award at the New York Festival.

After further television projects co-produced by Channel 4 and the BBC, he came to the attention of David Puttnam, who produced his feature debut, *Cal* (1984). Based on the novel by Bernard MacLaverty, this is the story of the romantic relationship between an IRA getaway driver and the widow of the man his unit have killed. Impressively acted by Helen Mirren and John Lynch, it followed some of the metaphysical threads of 'The Ballroom of Romance', employing similar imagery to evoke a sense of enclosure and oppression. Although some observers criticised the film for retreating from the political context, most responded positively to its passion. It was nominated for the Palme D'Or at the Cannes Film Festival.

O'Connor's next project, *A Month in the Country* (1987), based on the novel by J.R. Carr, is about the tentative friendship which grows between two World War Two veterans who are working on different archeological projects in a Yorkshire village in the 1920s. Like *Cal*, its focus is more on emotions and relationships than issues or politics. Its delicate portrayal of Englishness and the English countryside was admired by both audiences and critics. It won a Silver Rosa Camuna at the Bergamo Film Meeting, and helped to establish the screen careers of Colin Firth and Kenneth Branagh.

O'Connor's promising career began to turn sour with his move to the United States. *Stars and Bars* (1988) features Daniel Day-Lewis as an art dealer who encounters eccentric characters while pursuing a Renoir painting. Based on the novel by William Boyd, the film attempts an atmosphere of black comic whimsy that it fails to achieve. It was neither a popular nor a critical success. The situation did not improve with *The January Man* (1989), a mismatch of comedy, thriller and romance with Kevin Kline as a goofy amateur sleuth in search of a serial killer. In both films it appears that O'Connor had no genuine interest in or connection with the material. They share a concern with outsiders and eccentrics but lack any real insight into the characters and their worlds. By comparison with *Cal* and 'The Ballroom of Romance', they are also visually bland. The most notable result of the film was O'Connor's subsequent marriage to its female lead, Mary Elizabeth Mastrantonio.

O'Connor returned to more familiar ground for his next project. *Fools of Fortune* (1990) re-united him with William Trevor in an adaptation of his historical novel about an Anglo-Irish family who attempt to remain outside politics as Ireland fights for independence. Aided by a strong cast and an emphasis on complex relationships between disparate characters, it is a respectful, delicately rendered and handsomely photographed film. It lacks personality, however, falling too easily into the category of 'heritage film'. It was thus eclipsed by the Merchant-Ivory collaborations that were popular at the time of its release.

O'Connor then began a five-year hiatus from feature film-making and worked in television, directing a film on the life of Zelda Fitzgerald for TNT in 1993. He finally returned to the big screen with *Circle of Friends* (1995), a crowd-pleasing adaptation of Maeve Binchy's novel. This US-Irish co-production was supported by a wave of investment in the Irish film industry following changes in the legislation covering tax relief for international financiers. O'Connor's nationality was an asset in getting the project approved and he was also clearly more comfortable with the subject matter. The film introduced Minnie Driver as a small-town girl who attends university in Dublin in the late 1950s. It is a tale of romance, relationships and coming-of-age of a type familiar to international audiences, and features beautiful images of Ireland and the Irish countryside. Its mixture of warm humour and winning performances proved to be box-office gold. *Inventing the Abbots* (1997) was an eagerly anticipated follow-up that once again featured a young and attractive cast and was set in the late 1950s, this time in America. It follows the story of two working-class brothers who attempt to ingratiate themselves with upper-class girls. Based on a short story by Sue Miller, featuring a cast including Liv Tyler, Joaquin Phoenix and Jennifer Connelly, it promises much but delivers little. O'Connor is more concerned with romantic universals and family dynamics than with the particulars of class and society. The result is lushly photographed but empty; the film did not generate significant box-office returns.

Dancing at Lughnasa (1998), an adaptation of Brian Friel's acclaimed play, provided the director with both an Irish setting and a focus on family. It charts the experiences of five unmarried sisters in rural Donegal in the 1930s following the return of their brother from the missions in Africa. Evoking a rich sense of time and place, it features a talented group of actors including Meryl Streep, Kathy Burke and Brid Brennan. Yet despite superficial thematic and visual similarities to 'The Ballroom of Romance', it remains stagebound at the cost of potential cinematic dynamism. It was nonetheless nominated for a Golden Lion at the Venice Film Festival and won a Best Supporting Actress award for Brennan at the inaugural Irish Film and Television Academy Awards.

O'Connor's most recent film, *Sweet November* (2001), is an unremarkable remake of the 1968 version. It is a romantic comic drama starring Keanu Reeves and Charlize Theron, the latter as a woman with commitment issues who is pursued by a persistent suitor. **HO**

Damien O'DONNELL

Having received over thirty awards for his short film, *35 Aside* (1995), the story of a boy's life at a new school, Irish-born Damien O'Donnell found further success with his feature debut, *East Is East* (1999). Based on the sell-out play by Ayub Khan Din, who also wrote the screenplay, the film is set in the north England town of Salford in 1971 and focuses on the experiences of a Pakistani family and their attempts to negotiate a sense of their own identity within British culture. Om Puri plays the father, George Khan, the patriarch who left his first wife in Pakistan and now runs a chip shop with his second wife, a British woman, Ella (Linda Bassett), the mother of his seven children. Hypocritically, he is determined to cling to his belief system and marry his sons off to Pakistani wives. His harsh actions naturally lead to discord within the family. The eldest son runs away at the beginning of the film to live his own life and the next two in line are less than enamoured with the idea of a marriage of convenience.

Touching on themes of immigration, tradition, progress, religion and race, the film refers to, rather than foregrounds, the political landscape of the early 1970s – Enoch Powell is referenced, for example, as is the 'war' in India. Tonally light, darker aspects of the script, such as George's abusive tendencies, are outweighed by a mix of amusing situational and observational humour. Vibrant colours enhance the film's cartoon-like aspects and its energy. As much a rites-of-passage movie as it is a piece about assimilation, on the whole the protagonists are realistically drawn, only occasionally slipping into caricature. Nominated for six BAFTAs, *East Is East* won the Alexander Korda Award for Best British Film and the Evening Standard Award for Best Film. O'Donnell has also directed *What Where?* (2000), which stars Gary Lewis and Sean McGinley, as part of the 'Beckett on Film' season. **HP**

East Is East (1999)
What Where? (2000)

Gerry O'HARA

Since his days directing 'The Avengers', Gerry O'Hara has built up a body of work that will enthral both the cinematic scholar and the avid cult television enthusiast. With a mixture of action, science fiction, exploitation and melodrama, he has proved himself to be adept at every genre he tackles. Few examples exist of his early work on the embryonic 'The Avengers' series; Patrick McGee and Ian Hendry often recorded the show live

That Kind of Girl (1963)
Game for Three Losers (1964)
The Pleasure Girls (1965)
Maroc 7 (1967)

and the BBC's notorious policy of wiping tapes was in full effect. It was, however, a perfect show for O'Hara to launch his career; the recurring spy motif in almost all his early repertoire first emerged here and the show's quirkiness had a definite influence on the look and feel of his subsquent work.

That Kind of Girl (1963) and The Pleasure Girls (1965), a couple of sordid tales of debauchery in the swinging Sixties, predated O'Hara's work in the late 1970s. The first is the story of a promiscuous young Austrian girl who seduces a small community, which soon collapses in a storm of adultery, venereal disease and pregnancy. In direct contrast to the decadent sexuality portrayed in O'Hara's later work, the film condemns the actions of the vivacious, young paramour. The Pleasure Girls follows four flatmates on their desperate search for fame. Mistreated and taken advantage of, the girls naïvely place their hopes on a variety of dubious characters in the turbulent world of fashion and glamour.

In 1967 O'Hara returned to television with Man in a Suitcase (1967), the story of a jet-setting detective, McGill (Richard Bradford), who travels Europe solving crimes but always causing trouble. Maroc 7 (1967) is a convoluted spy thriller about a fashion editor who uses her position as a front to smuggle diamonds. Starring Gene Barry and Leslie Philips, the brisk plot is set against a beautifully shot Moroccan landscape. Rapidly becoming typecast as a director of spy thrillers and detective yarns, O'Hara went on to film the screen adaptation of Nicolas Freeling's novel 'Love in Amsterdam', entitled Amsterdam Affair (1968). A moderate success, it stars Wolfgang Keiling as detective Van Der Valk who is investigating a mysterious case of murder among the picturesque canals of the Dutch City.

Next came a typically British tale, All the Right Noises (1969), in which a happily married electrician, played by Tom Bell, is having an affair with fifteen-year-old Val (Olivia Hussey). Following in the footsteps of such British classics as This Sporting Life (1963), it lacks the anger and passion that made them such masterpieces. It does stand out amongst O'Hara's oeuvre, however, for its subtle characterisation and gritty location.

The cult television series 'The Professionals' marked a breakthrough period in O'Hara's career. The ultra violent, non-PC adventures of Bodie and Doyle were a huge success; sales of Capris were on the increase and shaggy perms were the ultimate fashion accessory. This hard-hitting show pulled no punches and with episodes such as 'Blood Sports' and 'A Hiding to Nothing', he gave the show a gritty style rarely seen on mainstream television.

His following film, The Brute (1977), starring Hammer starlet Sarah Douglas as a glamour model desperately trying to escape the evil clutches of her brutal husband (Julian Glover), is a genuinely disturbing view of matrimonial strife. Leopard in the Snow (1978) stars Susan Penhaligon as a young girl trapped in a severe blizzard in Cumberland and Kier Duilia as the reclusive disfigured racing driver who rescues her; romance soon blossoms. A shameless tearjerker, the film was the first adaptation of the Harlequin Romance series.

Possibly O'Hara's most infamous film as writer and director is the Brent Walker production The Bitch (1979). The sequel to The Stud (1978), it once again stars Joan Collins as Fontaine Khaled who, along with Michael Corby as elegant con man Nico Canatafora, is caught up in diamond smuggling amongst the high-flying jet set of London's West End. The film greatly benefited from the early days of home video, and the heady mix of kinky sex and thrilling intrigue made a star out of Joan Collins. A return to the style of his earliest films and the diamond smuggling plot of Maroc 7, it is the seedy and decadent world that his naïve heroes frequent which always wins in the end.

Following this big success, he returned to television to write for the detective show 'Bergerac'. Four years later he directed a new version of the classic German tale, Fanny Hill (1983). The adaptation may look handsome and the all-star cast – Shelley Winters, Oliver Reed and Wilfred Hyde White – may look the part, but the erotic charge of previous encounters with the innocent young Fanny Hill is sadly lacking. Considering the panache with which O'Hara usually handles the erotic scenes in his films, this is surprising. 'Press Gang', his last foray into the world of television, was a far subtler affair featuring early performance from the likes of Dexter Fletcher and becoming compulsory viewing for young teenagers that year. His final film to date, The Mummy Lives (1993), is a substandard reworking of the mummy legend starring Tony Curtis as the eponymous anti-hero who wreaks revenge on the cursed explorers that have opened his tomb.

With a body of work that delves into so many varied genres, it is strange that O'Hara is not more widely known as a director. From today's vantage point much of his work seems to embody the very meaning of the word cult and deserves to be seen by generations to come. **DB**

Gary OLDMAN

Born in London in 1958, Gary Oldman began his cinematic career acting in British films, *Nil by Mouth* (1997) such as Alex Cox's *Sid and Nancy* (1986) and Alan Clarke's *The Firm* (1988). He quickly moved on to establish a niche for himself playing villains in Hollywood and Luc Besson films. His sole work as a director to date is the visceral *Nil by Mouth* (1997).

A semi-autobiographical narrative of South London working-class life, *Nil by Mouth* is dedicated to the memory of Oldman's father. Mobile camerawork often frames protagonists, particularly abusive father Ray (Ray Winstone), in close shots. Other stylistic devices include staging action behind a pane of glass inside the house where Ray beats his wife, Val (Kathy Burke), into miscarriage. This could imply a child's view; unavoidably close to and furtively glancing at, yet not fully comprehending, horrendous events. Ray's insular arrogance allows him to regret, after beating Val, his own father's denial of affection. Communication between women in the film, often through touch or silent looks, provides an alternative emotional focus. Ending the film with Val confronting her abuser, rejecting victimhood, would have been politically correct. Instead, the final sequence opts for a more ambiguous conclusion. It reiterates Val's new confidence whilst hinting that Ray, hugging his child for the first time in the film, might also be able to change.

Oldman has continued his acting career, but despite the critical praise that *Nil by Mouth* received (including two BAFTA awards), he has no directorial projects currently planned. **MSt**

Ronan O'LEARY

Born in Dublin in 1959, Ronan O'Leary's early credits reflect an interest in theatrical *Fragments of Isabella* (1989) and literary material. He began his career as a drama producer-director for PBS in Los *Driftwood* (1996) Angeles in 1983. His first work in Ireland was *Fragments of Isabella* (1989), in which solo actor Gabrielle Reidy reprises her stage interpretation of Isabella Leitner's book of the same name (published in 1978). The story of a family of Hungarian sisters imprisoned in Auschwitz in World War Two, *Fragments of Isabella* recreates the events of the period through a combination of actuality footage and staged reconstruction. Structurally, it combines passages of extreme lyricism with an almost hysterical rendition of the events. By focusing on the Holocaust's violation of intimacy rather than attempting to depict its wider ramifications, O'Leary's film perfectly fits its low-budget, studio-bound format.

It was unfortunate for O'Leary that *Driftwood* (1996) was to become better known for its production history than its content. Financed under Ireland's Section 35 (now Section 481) tax-break system, *Driftwood* became the centre of a series of allegations of misappropriation of finance. O'Leary lost control of the final edit, which passed into the hands of British-based Goldcrest Films. When the film was released, he disassociated himself from it although he remains credited as director, editor and scriptwriter. The finished product is a thriller shot in an arthouse style which overtly references *Psycho* (1960) and bears many similarities to the Stephen King adaptation *Misery* (1990). Starring Anne Brochet and James Spader, it concerns a young man who is washed up on an Irish beach and becomes the obsessional focus of his rescuer, French sculptor, Sarah (Brochet).

Spader plays the role with his usual passivity while Brochet avoids over-investing her part as the manic woman with the kind of hysteria that characterises this genre. That said, the film still leaves itself open to accusations of misogyny. Perhaps deliberately, *Driftwood* does not foreground the beauties of the Irish scenery and instead presents it as a bleached-out and constricting landscape. It is all the more surprising, then, that the local inhabitants are caricatures of the idiot peasant, with Barry McGovern as the unlikely McTavish, grimacing and cavorting to the inevitable soundtrack of traditional Irish music. Somewhat unfairly dismissed by critics, the film has since enjoyed an extended life on video.

O'Leary also co-scripted Michael Lindsay-Hogg's *Frankie Starlight* (1995), a film marred by both miscasting and unimaginative direction. He has recently returned to his interests in theatre with the completion of a documentary entitled *Hold the Passion* (2000), about Dublin's Focus Theatre, whose founder, Deidre O'Connell, introduced the Stanislavsky Method to a generation of Dublin actors. **RB**

Stuart ORME

The Wolves of Willoughby Chase (1988)
The Puppet Masters (1994)

Born in Derby in 1954, Stuart Orme is primarily a director of television films, dramas and music promos. His pop work was initiated whilst making a Genesis documentary for Granada and he went on to make videos for, among others, Whitney Houston, Dave Stewart, Joy Division and James Taylor. He also directed a well received music series for television in the early 1980s, 'Futurama Rock'. He had a hand in the boom of 'alternative' comedy, directing two programmes at the inception of many comedians' careers: the acclaimed 'Wood and Walters', (Victoria and Julie, respectively) and 'Al Fresco', which introduced the careers of Ben Elton, Stephen Fry, Hugh Laurie, Emma Thompson and Robbie Coltrane.

His most notable drama series include the award-winning 'Inspector Morse', 'The Sculptress', the rousing 'Ivanhoe' and the acclaimed 'The Last Train'. 'The Fear', a five-part serial set in Thatcher's London, was reminiscent of movies such as *Scarface* (1983) and *The Long Good Friday* (1980), and was a fresh depiction of working-class villainy. His style is flashy, but at its best, often gripping. His two feature film releases to date, however, have not revealed the talent he has shown in his television work, perhaps constrained by budgetary limitations, studio half-measures and poor scripts.

Orme decided to direct following graduation from drama school and began his career at Thames Television in 1970, working as a floor manager. He then moved to Westward in 1978. From 1980 to 1985 he freelanced, directing for Granada, Thames and other independent companies. In 1985 he and his wife established a production company, Red Rooster, to enable a more regular production process. Subsequently, he united with US director Marcelo Anciano and producer Martin Wyn Griffiths to form Anciano Wyn Griffiths Orme (AWGO). He hoped this alliance would increase the likelihood of him being offered features with 'small crews and good stories ... for a bigger market'.

Toward the end of the decade Orme finally directed his first feature, *The Wolves of Willoughby Chase* (1988), a children's drama based on Joan Aiken's classic tale of two children left in the care of a fearsome governess in a fantasy nineteenth-century England overrun by wolves. It should have been enjoyably creepy, but was predictable, badly acted and failed to create the filmic world necessary for the suspension of disbelief.

After more macabre and gripping television mysteries and thrillers, including the feature-length television film *A Question of Guilt*, based on the best-selling novel by Frances Fyfield, his next feature was sci-fi horror *The Puppet Masters* (1994). This was Disney's first foray into horror after their studio re-vamp nearly ten years before. Unfortunately, although quite dark for a Disney film, it was not well realised; a weak, thoroughly predictable screenplay delivered a standard action movie with neither innovation nor much in the way of sci-fi iconography.

Casting Donald Sutherland in the lead role was a nod to the remake of paranoia movie *Invasion of the Bodysnatchers* (1978), but this served merely to underline the derivative plot inspired by the superior film. Here, the story of alien parasitic slugs invading the mid-west and taking over human brains starts well, has some nice touches and is occasionally scary, but degenerates into an awkward action romance. In addition, the dated theme and the hackneyed devices, while original and shocking in the McCarthy era, in the 1990s render the film pointless.

Orme is currently at work on his next project, a television mini-series of Sir Arthur Conan Doyle's 'Lost World'. Shot on location in New Zealand, it stars Bob Hoskins, Peter Falk, animatronics and digitally enhanced 'terrible lizards'. **FG**

Thaddeus O'SULLIVAN

Thaddeus O'Sullivan's films are, to say the least, formally diverse; throughout his career, *December Bride* (1990) however, he has been interested in the vicissitudes of the Irish experience, seeking to *Nothing Personal* (1995) move beyond the misconception that Ireland is a mono-culture. *Ordinary Decent Criminal* (2000)

His early shorts were experimental, sometimes semi-documentary explorations of the Irish in Britain, partially funded by the British Film Institute. *A Pint of Plain* (1975) is a wandering narrative in which a number of Irish people living in London cross one another's paths and then go their separate ways. It has an improvised feel, and seems to take a pleasure in the evocations of these displaced souls. *On a Paving Stone Mounted* (1978) is a more formally demanding work, and also has a heavier, sadder feel about the results of emigration. O'Sullivan's first foray into narrative was *The Woman Who Married Clark Gable* (1985), an adaptation of a Séan O'Faoláin short story. This 25-minute film, starring Bob Hoskins and Brenda Fricker, is a gentle, richly detailed portrait of the escape that Hollywood glamour provided from the repressive cultural climate of 1950s Ireland.

These films were part of a moment in Irish cinema, led by veteran independent director Bob Quinn, where politically engaged, formally adventurous independent film-making seemed to be emerging. O'Sullivan's work both as a film-maker and a cinematographer figures centrally in this period: he shot Quinn's series 'Atlantean', and in 1984, shot Cathal Black's *Pigs* and Pat Murphy's *Anne Devlin*. The first two from the Republic, the third from the North, all are adventurous pieces, little seen outside Ireland but crucial for an understanding of the nation's cinema.

After making a number of television films, O'Sullivan returned to feature-length narrative with *December Bride* (1990), a beautifully photographed exploration of Ireland's rural Protestant communities. The story centres on Sarah (Saskia Reeves), a Catholic woman who works as a servant housekeeper for two Presbyterian brothers (Donal McCann and Ciarán Hinds). When she has a baby she refuses to name the father, instead opting for an odd kind of ménage-à-trois with the brothers. Overall, O'Sullivan evokes the extremely complex, and often misunderstood, interaction between landscape and politics in the Irish province of Ulster. Like a lot of film-makers of his generation, he is interested in de-romanticising Ireland, making it clear that the pastoral visions of the eighteenth and nineteenth centuries were hopelessly simplistic. He is unwilling to entirely abandon these images and attempts to uncover the ambiguity, pain and possibility that they always contained.

His most recent features have been crime films of sorts. *Nothing Personal* (1995), set in the mid-1970s, centres on three young Belfast guys, two of whom are working their way up in a Loyalist paramilitary organisation and one of whom is a Catholic who crosses their path when he wanders into the wrong neighbourhood. It is a violent, visceral ride through the no-go areas of Belfast during a particularly rough period in Northern Ireland; in short, a significant departure from the cool, painterly contemplation of *December Bride* (and even further away from the experimentalism of *A Pint of Plain* and *On a Paving Stone Mounted*).

His latest film, *Ordinary Decent Criminal* (2000), a German-Ireland-USA co-production, is a more straightforward crime piece, starring Kevin Spacey and Linda Fiorentino. It is based on the life of gangster Martin Cahill who is also the subject of John Boorman's 1997 film *The General* and David Blair's 1998 work *Vicious Circle*, although this version is more of a comedy. With a script by Gerard Stembridge, who in the last few years has made more commercial cinema, it is a far cry from O'Sullivan's earlier avant-garde, political works. **JW**

P

Tony PALMER

A seminal and prolific director of television films and documentaries on musicians, Tony Palmer has also been an author, critic, journalist, radio presenter and tea boy for Franco Zeffirelli. His impressive diversity of musical subjects ranges from Andre Previn to Frank Zappa and his visual equivalents for the musical scores are often impressively original. However, with only a few cinematic releases he has attracted little critical attention.

Glad All Over (1971)
200 Motels (visuals, 1971)
Bird on a Wire (1972)
The Space Movie (1979)
Testimony (1988)
The Children (1990)
England, My England (1995)

Born in London in 1941, his introduction to film came whilst at Cambridge University working for Patrick Garland as a German-English translator for a film on the Salzburg Festival. This experience led him to apply for a General Traineeship Scheme at the BBC. Warned by Garland to have an unusual interest to ensure his place, Palmer memorised the greyhound-racing page of his paper by heart on the way to the interview and was accepted as 'useful in Sport'. He did, however, vehemently express his desire to assist Ken Russell; ending up in BBC Radio Nottingham displeased him greatly. He resigned immediately but, working out his three month's notice, realised that he actually enjoyed the job. Subsequently Zeffirelli's 'assistant', he was then taken on by Humphrey Burton at the BBC where he bided his time before assisting on Russell's television feature *Isadora Duncan, the Biggest Dancer in the World*. This taught him enough for a producing role on *Alice in Wonderland* (1967) with Johnathan Miller, but creative disagreements led to a demotion. He then assisted Burton on an Omnibus film about Benjamin Britten; when Burton left the BBC, Palmer took directorial responsibility for the project. Luckily for him it became the first BBC film to be networked in America and his career soared at the age of 26.

Aware that Palmer's first musical love was classical, but that he was also a staunch defender of popular music's cultural significance, the BBC asked him to make a film about the emergence of the phenomenon of the 1960s. This became *All My Loving* (1968), subtitled, somewhat disingenuously, as 'a film about pop music', which incensed many due to its use of Vietnam War images juxtaposed with the music and flower-power rationale of 1968. Mary Whitehouse assisted Palmer's notoriety by commencing legal action against the BBC over the film. Controversy continued in his weekly television series 'How It Is' which built on his reputation established by his pop music criticism for *The Observer* and as an underground diarist for *The Spectator*.

His television feature, *Glad All Over* (1971), was shown at The London Film Festival. A film scenario set around a visit of 'The Living Theatre' to a sex fair in Denmark, it did well in the US, but could not get a distributor in Britain because, Palmer believes, 'nobody could understand it'. Another, on which he directed the visuals as an experiment in the potential opticals of video electronics, was Frank Zappa's rock opera, *200 Motels* (1971). Palmer described it as 'a kind of mixture of childhood fantasies, adolescent fantasies, and now grown up fantasies, all somehow strung together to make some sort of enormous nightmare that he may or may not have had at some point in his life'. Although visually arresting, making history as the first feature shot on video tape to be granted a commercial release, it met with disdain. It was even criticised in *The Spectator* by the film critic, Palmer himself.

In 1977 his definitive 16-part documentary, 'All You Need Is Love', detailed a history of popular music. He also directed documentaries and films about Maria Callas, Chopin, Leonard Cohen (*Bird on a Wire* (1972)), Cream, Dvorak, Handel, Yehudi Menuhin, Mozart, Rachmaninov, Stravinsky and Tangerine Dream amongst many others. Few of his projects have not been about music and musicians, although two pieces that have strayed from his usual arena feature Mike Oldfield's score as a vital element: *The Space Movie* (1979) celebrates the tenth anniversary of the Moon landing; *The Children* (1990) is based on an Edith Wharton novel about a man infatuated with the daughter of an old friend. His preferred genre has also tended to marginalise him, although these films pay as much attention to socio-political contexts as the biographies and the music. *Testimony* (1988), for example, detailed the turbulent relationship of Dmitri Shostakovich and Joseph Stalin. *England, My England* (1995), written by John Osborne and Charles Wood, puts the life of Purcell into a modern perspective. A group of actors in the 1960s are performing Shaw's play set in the 1660s, 'In Good King Charles's Golden Day', and decide to investigate the earlier period that in many ways closely resembles the exciting turmoil of the 1960s. It moves between both periods, enabling an individualistic and acute viewpoint.

Palmer's underground sensibilities have often found him at odds with the moral majority; humanising the romanticised images of musical idols has caused much controversy. His film and television work informed by 'the new journalism', his book on the 'Oz' trial and his arts presenting and criticism have all contributed to a unique exploration of history and popular culture. He appeared in *Stanley Kubrick: A Life in Pictures* (2001) giving a homage to one of his heroes. His latest project is *The Lord of the Dance*, a movie version of Michael Flatley's hit stage show, co-written by the star, which is planned to go into production in the autumn of 2001.   **FG**

Nick PARK

Born in Lancashire, UK, in 1958, Nicholas Wulstan Park (CBE) became interested in animation at school; aged 13, he started to experiment with stop animation in his parent's attic. One of his first efforts, *Archie's Concrete Nightmare*, was shown on BBC Television in 1975. In 1980, having completed his degree in Communication Arts at Sheffield Hallam University, he went on to study animation at the National Film and Television School in Beaconsfield. When he invited Peter Lord and David Sproxton, the founders of the inspirational Aardman Animation, to guest lecture at the School, they were so impressed by his enthusiasm and talent that they asked him to join them. He was finally able to complete his graduation project, *A Grand Day Out* (1992), under their auspices. This was the first outing for his signature figures, the eccentric, cheese-loving inventor, Wallace, and his loyal dog, Gromit.

Often accused of nerdish, self-satisfied whimsy, Park's work has a gentle, old-fashioned and quintessentially English tone – it is frequently parochial. However, absurdist slapstick and attention to detailing, and a combination of witty, parodic puns and precisely nuanced characterisations, enables total suspension of disbelief. For the young in spirit, it grants a rare treat. The characters capture the popular imagination more and more at each airing, even managing to vastly increase the sales of Wallace's favourite

Wensleydale cheese. Aardman have made a fortune in merchandising tie-ins, from radios to backpacks, and such is the company's power in the animation market that it has retained control of the merchandising and its profits despite their alliance with Dream-Works SKG.

Park is now a partner in the firm; he and Aardman have received over one hundred awards for their shorts, commercials and music-video sequences, including Peter Gabriel's 'Sledgehammer', made in conjunction with the Brothers Quay. In 1990 Park won an Oscar® for *Creature Comforts*, an engaging animal 'claymation' visual with a human documentary audio track. Two more Academy Awards followed for *The Wrong Trousers* (1993) and *A Close Shave* (1995), the latter a science-fiction romance mystery. In both shorts, Park increasingly experiments with ever more cinematic lighting, sound and score, working toward an eventual full-length feature.

The team pitched the idea for this feature, *Chicken Run* (2000), over a dinner with Jeffrey Katzenburg and Steven Spielberg (who has a chicken farm) of DreamWorks SKG. Referring to a range of classic movies from the patently obvious *Great Escape* (1963), one of Spielberg's favourites, to *Frankenstein* (1931), *Alien* (1979) and *Terminator* (1984), *Chicken Run* is, for the most part, a delight: funny, and never patronising. It is, however, overlong and occasionally laboured, seeming to suffer a little from its division into several set-pieces, possibly because Park did not have enough control over the movie as a whole. Originally a hands-on animator, working every frame himself, Park found that he functioned more as a director the more complex the shots became. On *Chicken Run* this involved overseeing a team of hundreds of animators. That said, a wealth of comic detail holds the interest on the moments where the plot flags and a beautifully designed milieu maintains the sense of surreal, nightmarish tension.

Since Aardman's deal with DreamWorks, the studio is ensured a place in the big league alongside such corporations as Disney, whilst retaining its independent status, its Bristol base and, hopefully, maintaining the cottage industry, handmade feel.

Park is set to make a further four films with the DreamWorks studio. Aardman's next feature will be *The Tortoise and the Hare*, on which Lord and Park will executive produce, whilst Park himself develops a Wallace and Gromit movie. **FG**

Alan PARKER

Born in London in 1944, Alan Parker is a vociferous and uncompromising figure in British cinema. Very much the 'working-class boy made good', he entered the film industry via the world of advertising, once describing himself as an 'accidental film-maker'. Starting out as a post boy for an advertising agency, Parker quickly worked his way up to junior copywriter, later to become something of an innovator in the world of television advertisements. He particularly contributed to the development of humour in British commercials, which he thought they lacked, and was responsible for the memorable Leonard Rossiter/Joan Collins Cinzano promotions. Between 1969 and 1978, he made in excess of five hundred television commercials, winning every major industry award. Indeed, Parker's vivid style owes much to his early advertising experience.

In 1973 he wrote and directed a fifty-minute film, *No Hard Feelings,* which the BBC bought and aired several years later. His first film produced for the BBC, *Evacuees* (1975), attracted attention from the theatrical marketplace and David Puttnam persuaded him to stand in as a director for a few days on a film he was producing, *That'll Be the Day* (Claude Whatham, 1973). However, Parker's big break into features came with *Bugsy Malone* (1976), a story he wrote with his own children in mind; with 'it being several years before Disney got its act together', there was nothing for them to watch. The film is a delightful musical spoof of gangster movies with a cast made up entirely of children.

Parker's second feature, *Midnight Express* (1978), is based on the true story of an American arrested in Turkey for drug smuggling. It is a powerful and harrowing film; the forbidding locations coupled with dramatic lighting work to create the prison environment in detail. It features superb performances from Brad Davis as Billy Hayes, the hapless amateur drug smuggler, and John Hurt as Max, an eccentric Englishman who acts as a constant reminder to Billy of the ways in which the prison can crush him. *Midnight*

Bugsy Malone (1976)
Midnight Express (1978)
Fame (1980)
Pink Floyd: The Wall (1982)
Shoot the Moon (1982)
Birdy (1984)
Angel Heart (1987)
Mississippi Burning (1988)
Come See the Paradise (1990)
The Commitments (1991)
The Road to Wellville (1994)
Evita (1996)
Angela's Ashes (1999)

Express earned Parker international acclaim, picking up six Oscar® nominations and winning Best Screenplay for an adaptation and Best Original Score. He followed this with a stylish, up-tempo, contemporary musical, *Fame* (1980), a film that spawned the long-running and highly successful television series of the same name.

Shoot the Moon (1982), Parker's next feature, is the first film in which he seems to have invested a great deal of himself. It has been described by some critics as autobiographical, and although he has denied this, he does not deny that its uniquely personal feel comes from his own experiences upon the break up of his first marriage. What possibly added fuel to the autobiography fire was the uncanny likeness of the two leads (Albert Finney and Diane Keaton) to Parker and his wife.

Moving away from the intimate towards the public, Parker's next film, *Pink Floyd: The Wall* (1982), is the masterful expansion of Pink Floyd's concept album. Over the years the film has become both a rock classic and an indication of the size of former Floyd front man Roger Waters' ego. However, this does both the film and Waters a major disservice. Parker himself commented on the ego issue when discussing the experience of making *The Wall*, saying, 'Can you imagine, three megalomaniacs all used to getting their own way'. *The Wall* is a stunning, intelligent piece of film-making, with Parker's direction matching up to the imagination of Pink Floyd's mind-expanding music. Gerald Scarfe's exemplary animation sequences – the giant marching hammers, the school teacher squeezing children into a mincer – would surely figure in any list of the most iconic and enduring images of the early 1980s.

The critically acclaimed *Birdy* (1984), which followed *The Wall*, does not make for easy viewing, with the narrative flow constantly being disrupted by long flashbacks and montage sequences. Nevertheless, it is a moving story directed with sincerity and sensitivity. The film centres on two best friends who have returned from the war in Vietnam: Al (Nicolas Cage), the former high school romeo, and Birdy (Matthew Modine), a quiet and withdrawn man with an obsession for birds. Both are wounded by their experience of war. While Al's damage is physical, Birdy's is psychological; he withdraws into himself, in his mind becoming a bird, perching, cooped up and caged. It is a curious film, traumatic, yet hauntingly beautiful. Once again, it is the strong central performances, combined with Parker's use of location and lighting, that renders *Birdy* so powerful and potent.

With his next feature, *Angel Heart* (1987), Parker courted controversy, taking on the MPPA single-handedly for awarding the film an X rating, provoking many Hollywood executives. *Angel Heart* focuses on a private investigator, Harry Angel (Mickey Rourke), who is hired to trace a debtor for Louis Cyphre (Robert De Niro). The superior twist to the film is that Angel realises the person he is seeking is also responsible for a string of grisly murders – a dark, subconscious side of himself. Initially, Parker wanted to shoot *Angel Heart* in black and white, but settled for regular film stock and draining the colour. The stark contrasts between light and dark, and the many shades of grey in between, mirror the film's themes and concerns, signalling Angel's state of mind.

Parker again invited controversy with his next feature, *Mississippi Burning* (1988), a glossy recreation of a famous, civil-rights murder case. The film was praised for its fine performances (most notably, Gene Hackman as a veteran FBI man) but criticised for its flat and inaccurate reworking of history and its perceived anti-Americanism. Parker, however, claimed that *Mississippi Burning* was a polemical film, intended to create debate; to this end, it succeeded. With subject matter that also had the potential to be contentious, *Come See the Paradise* (1990) certainly had an untold story – that of the internment of Japanese immigrants to the United States in camps at the outbreak of World War Two. With a loose script, the film rambled, failing to capture the imaginations of both audiences and critics. It was also heavily criticised for its historical inaccuracies, seen by some as an exercise in historical revisionism.

In his next film, *The Commitments* (1991), the story of the rise and fall of an Irish soul band, based on the first book in Roddy Doyle's Barrytown trilogy, Parker exploited his love for soul music. *The Commitments* is enjoyable but lacks the grit of the novel and other adaptations of Doyle's stories such as Stephen Frears' *Snapper* (1993) and *The Van* (1996). The soundtrack is exceptional – indulging Parker's obsession for Otis Redding – but this is a feelgood film, amusing for its duration, with little aftertaste.

Following this, Parker both wrote and directed *The Road to Wellville* (1994), adapting it from a novel by T. Coraghessan Boyle. The film centres on Eleanor and Will Lightbody (Bridget Fonda and Matthew Broderick), a couple who journey to Battle Creek, Michigan, at the turn of the century to Dr. Kellogg's renowned sanitarium to partake of his cures. A quirky, at times grimly humorous, film, it frustrates more than it satisfies, instituting a number sub-plots then leaving them hanging in mid-air without resolution or explanation.

Parker's next project, *Evita* (1996), was a slick film version of the Andrew Lloyd Webber/Tim Rice musical. Given his lyrical visual style and his adept handling of 'musical films', he was the natural choice to direct. The film did well at the box office but received mixed critical reviews, as projects involving the talents of Madonna invariably do. Whatever the reasons for some critics' dislike of the film, *Evita* is a pleasing and visually alluring piece of cinema. Parker's most recent offering, *Angela's Ashes* (1999), is based on Frank McCourt's bestselling autobiography. It follows the fortunes of Frankie (Robert Carlyle) and his young family, as they struggle to overcome poverty in the slums of 1930s Limerick. The atmosphere of decay reinforces and reflects the spiritual, social and moral decay that Frankie must overcome in his struggles against unemployment, prejudice, and cultural and religious intolerance.

Once known for his frequent lambasting of the British film industry, it seems that the maverick has mellowed. In spite of his documentary, *A Turnip Head's Guide to British Cinema* (1986), which ridiculed the critical mentality of the industry in Britain, Parker has been charged with regenerating the British film industry and recently became Chairman of the newly formed Film Council.   **SL**

Oliver PARKER

Othello (1995)
An Ideal Husband (1999)

Born in 1960, and best known for his extraordinary reinterpretation of *Othello* (1995), Oliver Parker began his career as a television actor, appearing in such classic mid-1980s fare as 'Poirot' and 'Lovejoy', as well as small roles in *Nightbreed* (1990) and *Nuns on the Run* (1990).

Screen adaptations of Shakespeare arguably live or die by their inherent cinematic qualities – mise-en-scène, thematic relevance, performance and running time. Parker's *Othello* obeys all of these rules: he pares the playwright's bleakest musings on the human condition down to an audience-friendly two hours, coaxes out of Kenneth Branagh one of his finest screen performances to date, and utilises picture-postcard Italian locations. Maintaining the location and time period of the original play, the film gives us a far clearer insight into the characters of Othello and Iago than many of the more prestigious versions (Welles' in 1950 and Olivier's in 1965). The film's length has meant a number of textual excisions (numerous subplots are omitted), but this paradoxically creates a more fulfilling narrative experience; the universality of betrayal and jealousy are brought to the foreground with devastating emotional effect.

The central performances are uniformly excellent – Laurence Fishburne as Othello lends his early scenes a timidity and introspection that contrast well with his latter explosions into anger. Irène Jacob's Desdemona looks suitably doomed, her alabaster fragility neatly balanced by the passionate bed scenes (shot in flashbacks). At the film's centre is the banality of Iago's evil. Where both Parker and Branagh succeed is in never revealing the reasons for his jealousy; instead they are teasingly suggested by Branagh's frequent asides to the camera, implicating the audience in his schemes while at the same time revelling in his own malice.

Parker's follow-up was another literary adaptation, *An Ideal Husband* (1999), based on Oscar Wilde's drawing room comedy about politics, marriage and blackmail. The film succeeds in the lively, energetic performances of a first-rate cast, including Cate Blanchett, Minnie Driver, Julianne Moore and Rupert Everett, and the way in which Parker has been able to take elements of the play's original farce – comic misunderstandings, near-misses, beautifully timed punchlines – and replicate them in the film. *An Ideal Husband*'s subject matter also strikes a chord with 1990s political life. Jeremy Northam as the happily married MP who is suddenly confronted with an immoral deed in his past is somewhat reminiscent of the Clinton affair – the film was released in the US in the midst of the Lewinsky scandal. There are shortcomings, however: Parker often seems unsure as to whether the film should be an all-out frenetic farce or a more subtle exposé of Anglo-American relations, while the necessities of Wilde's chaotic to-ing and fro-ing is not always successfully transposed. Nevertheless, Parker is inventive and has a sharp eye for detail (aided by Michael Howells' design).

Parker is currently in production with *The Importance of Being Earnest*, his second adaptation of an Oscar Wilde play for which he has assembled another glittering cast – Colin Firth, Rupert Everett, Tom Wilkinson and Judi Dench as Lady Bracknell. **BM**

Willi PATTERSON

Don't Go Breaking My Heart (1998) Starting out in advertising, Willi Patterson earned a nomination from the Director's Guild of America for Best Commercial Director in 1992. He had moved to Los Angeles, but returned to the UK in 1997 partly to provide a better environment for his children, and partly to get a feature film into production, having been frustrated by the laborious American studio process. He had previously helmed two full-length dramas – *Dreams Lost, Dreams Found* (1987) is a mystery love story, *Out of the Shadows* (1988), a thriller set in Greece – which were made for US and UK television respectively.

His theatrically released feature, *Don't Go Breaking My Heart* (1998), is an amiable but unremarkable romantic comedy, set in a middle-class London suburb, and reliant on many actors familiar from British and American television. It stars Jenny Seagrove as Suzanne, a middle-aged mother who is recently widowed, but not looking for a man to fill the gap. Her dentist and supposed friend, Frank (Charles Dance), has other ideas; during hypnosis sessions in the surgery room he attempts to brainwash her into falling in love with him. The plan backfires, and Suzanne falls for Tony (Anthony Edwards), an ailing sports therapist whose relationship is on the rocks. Luckily, Tony is also in love with Suzanne. The film has little to say – except that if you try very hard you might succeed – but it is rare to see the love life of a forty-year-old woman figure centrally. Patterson, however, proves better at developing the subplot between Tony and Ben, Suzanne's son, who has become dispirited since his father's death.

Patterson is keeping his film and commercial directing concurrent. He set up the advertising company Slim Pix in March 1999 to exploit digital camera technology. One of his next feature projects, *The Godmother*, is an adaptation from the novel by Wesley Burrowes; the other, *Lord of the Dance*, is in production. **KP**

Pawel PAWLIKOWSKI

The Stringer (1997) After the success of *The Last Resort* (2000), the British Film Industry told writer-director
The Last Resort (2000) Pawel Pawlikowski that it would be a wonderful stepping stone to making a 'proper' film. The exposure of the 75-minute drama has certainly perplexed the BBC, who made it on a shoestring £320,000 as part of a low-key experiment, and it speaks volumes about an industry that refuses to accept that a film of such modest scale – with no obvious demographic appeal and no huge built-in marketing strategy – could possibly break through. Yet there is more honesty and cinematic purity in one frame of Pawlikowski's film than in virtually any of the other 'proper' British films released in the last year.

Born in Warsaw in 1957, Pawlikowski came to Britain as a 12-year-old Polish refugee. In the late 1980s he began making documentaries for the BBC. No mere hagiographies, his pieces for 'Bookmark' – *From Moscow to Pietushki* (1990), *Dostoevsky's Travels* (1992) and *Serbian Epics* (1992) – stand out from this period. However, aside from their original transmission date, and with one-off screenings at London repertory cinemas, barely ten years on they remain the sort of films rapidly phased out by the 'Pride and Prejudice' era. His feature debut, *The Stringer* (1997), premiered at Cannes but has been little seen since. The featurette, *Twockers* (1998), followed a year later. Originally planned as a documentary on child burglars, it soon mutated into a drama, clearly setting the tone for his second feature proper.

Filmed in Margate, with landscapes straight out of Tarkovsky, *The Last Resort* paints a Britain of administrative ineptitude and chip shops that serve batter without any cod. Everyone is a refugee, everyone a victim. The oppressor, the antagonist, is society itself.

In the middle is Tanya (Dina Korzun), a Russian twenty-something with a ten-year-old son in tow, abandoned at the airport by her British lover and awaiting deportation in a seaside town surrounded by barbed wire and CCTV cameras. Pawlikowski never falls back on easy stereotypes and cheap laughs – heroes and villians are non-distinguishable. Just as the police are portrayed in a fairly sympathetic light, so too is the pornographer, played by real-life 'Ben Dover' with considerable charm and humour, who genuinely wants to help Tanya escape. Alfie (Paddy Considine), the bingo compere with a sideline in dodgy phonecards, falls for Tanya while introducing her to the staple British delights of Benson and Hedges and Chicken Tikka, but his violent past resurfaces in a fit of rage that speaks more of his frustration at his social status and lot in life than of any chivalry or moral rightness. Even Tanya is flawed, uneasily warranting her fallen angel status when it is revealed that she was a bourgeois children's book publisher in her native land.

Pawlikowski's methods set him apart from most. He lives in a small rented flat with the crew during production, has no patience for industry notions of script editors or development by committee, and chooses close friends as collaborators rather than track-record professionals. He is scathing in his belief that most British film-making is lamentable: 'I see all these guys running around that are all technique. They have nothing to say and the stupid thing is that they are not even curious and they don't care. Everything is either plot, plot, plot or style, style, style, and when they try to do something that reflects life or tells a story it turns into some awful issue-based thing. It is really frustrating when you want to see something original, something different.' **RCh**

Ron PECK

On the strength of his two feature films, it is difficult to make a case study of Ron Peck, an East End film-maker most famous for his controversial debut, *Nighthawks* (1978). The story of Jim (Ken Robertson), a closet homosexual who teaches geography in a comprehensive school while cruising bars and discos by night, the film was championed for its honesty and lack of emotional breast-beating. Groundbreaking as the film was, however, it trailed Spain's first feature about a sympathetic and sexually active gay male – Eloy de la Iglesia's *Hidden Pleasures* – by two years. Conceived by Peck and co-written with Paul Hallam (who assisted with direction), *Nighthawks*' use of mostly non-professional actors suggests (particularly when Robertson interacts with his pre-teen students) the unstructured feel of Michael Apted's '7 Up' documentary series. Robertson's pivotal performance is refreshingly nuanced: Jim is neither a wallflower nor a predator, neither a role model nor grotesque.

Nighthawks (1978)
Empire State (1987)
Strip Jack Naked (1991)

At its heart, the film is more about affiliation than sexual preference, bringing Jim into contact with other young men from the North who have similarly abdicated 'the fundamental role of the male of the species', trying to reinvent themselves in a somewhat more permissive milieu. Time and distance have currency in their lives, with pickup lines consisting of little more than 'How long have you been here?' and pillow talk that consists of 'How long have you been in London?' Despite its use of (fleeting) frontal nudity and (non-graphic) male lovemaking, *Nighthawks* impresses most by disallowing eroticism in its bid to show how simply the other ten per cent lives. When Jim climbs into bed with a pickup, he is unfailingly polite, asking 'What time do you have to get up in the morning?' In its banality and normalcy, the comment is a more revolutionary act than all the attendant press of flesh.

A subtext of *Nighthawks*, Great Britain's booming enterprise culture of the 1980s, came to the fore in Peck's belated follow-up, the crime drama *Empire State* (1987). Like John MacKenzie's *The Long Good Friday* (1980) and Mike Figgis' *Stormy Monday* (1988), *Empire State* concerns the support of Thatcherite gentrification by foreign interests – seen here in the form of Martin Landau's ugly American investor. It is a vampiric performance that anticipates the actor's later Oscar®-winning turn as Bela Lugosi in Tim Burton's *Ed Wood* (1994). Pitting cockney London against real-estate developers out to demolish lower-class neighborhoods (symbolised by the Canary Wharf district) for yuppie apartment blocks, Peck's screenplay identifies the ageing gangster Frank (Irish actor Ray McAnally) as its hero. Owner of the eponymous Docklands nightclub, he refuses to sell out to the Americans. He is betrayed by his own protégé (Ian Sears), who seizes ownership of the club and mockingly threatens to put his former mentor on display so that tourists can marvel at 'all that East End chat, the filthy language and the threats of the old violence'. Frank rather brutally wins out in the end, however, able to maintain traditional values. Coming as it did after the unapologetic *Nighthawks*, *Empire State* was criticised in some quarters as a pretentious, modern film noir and in others for using gay characters as mere adornments. Despite its bigger budget and the presence of known actors, this more commercial product is ironically the rarer of Peck's two features, much less seen or discussed.

Peck has also directed the comic short *What Can I Do With a Male Nude?* (1975), about a photographer's discomfort when his subject is a muscular adolescent, complete with post-Benny Hill and pre-Austin Powers genital camouflaging. His most recent project of note is the 1991 documentary *Strip Jack Naked*. Conceived as a 'making-of' look back at his landmark 'homo promo', the end result – shot in 16mm, in both colour and black and white – is an impressionistic semi-autobiography, with Peck reliving moments from his life that he would later fictionalise for *Nighthawks*.

Spanning three decades in the life of a committed and passionate gay artist, the documentary engenders hope that Peck will step behind the camera once more, if only to show how the story ends. **RHS**

Mark PEPLOE

Afraid of the Dark (1991)
Victory (1995) Mark Peploe has worked as a screenwriter on a number of interesting European films, including a gothic version of *The Pied Piper* (1972), directed by Jacques Demy, and Michelangelo Antonioni's *The Passenger* (1975). Co-written by Peter Wollen (amongst others), the latter stars Jack Nicholson and Maria Schneider in a sparse story about a journalist who switches identity with a mysterious dead businessman. Peploe has also co-scripted two Bernardo Bertolucci films, *The Last Emperor* (1987) and *The Sheltering Sky* (1990). Bertolucci is married to Peploe's sister, Clare, herself a writer and director (*Rough Magic* (1995)).

His debut feature was the engaging, if flawed, psychological thriller, *Afraid of the Dark* (1991). Lucas (Ben Keyworth) is an adolescent who is awaiting an operation to save his sight. He is tormented by anxieties and nightmares, and fears that a stalker who is killing blind women will target his mother. Although the premise suggests an interesting combination of mood piece and slasher movie – as in earlier British films such as Michael Powell's *Peeping Tom* (1960) and Roman Polanski's *Repulsion* (1965) – the story does not really go anywhere. Lucas spends much of the film wandering; when the (fairly predictable) final revelation arrives it is less than absorbing. That said, it is atmospheric and full of familiar faces, including Frederick Treves, Fanny Ardant and David Thewlis. Although Peploe does have a problem with pacing (a legacy, perhaps, from his time spent working for Bertolucci), he has a good eye for striking imagery, managing to make the film at once eerie and monotonous.

His only other feature to date, *Victory* (1995), is a French-financed adaptation of a Joseph Conrad novel with a starry international cast including Sam Neill, Willem Dafoe, Irène Jacob and Simon Callow. Set in the Dutch East Indies in 1913, this is the story of Heyst (Dafoe) who rescues Alma (Jacob) from the hideous San Giacomo (Callow) who has 'bought' her. Although they escape to an idyllic island retreat, they are pursued by sinister fortune hunters (Neill and an exaggerated Rufus Sewell). A fairly faithful adaptation of the source novel, much of Conrad's psychological complexity is nevertheless sacrificed for the screen, particularly the characterisation of Heyst. Although beautifully shot, as a piece of 'heritage cinema', it verges on the sterile. It does not help that Conrad's writing is difficult to transpose to the screen; the most successful adaptations of his work – Alfred Hitchcock's reworking of 'The Secret Agent', *Sabotage* (1936), and Francis Ford Coppola's version of 'Heart of Darkness', *Apocalypse Now* (1979) – have been the loosest. Even performers that are usually reliable, such as Dafoe and Neill, are hamstrung by the stifling nature of Peploe's screenplay. Having taken a while to get a theatrical release in the UK, the film then received lukewarm reviews.

Although his directorial outings are not without interest, Mark Peploe's work as a screenwriter remains his most distinguished. **IC**

Chris PETIT

An unusual and intelligent film-maker, Chris Petit is one of Britain's best and yet least-known experimental writer-directors. Although he is currently making a moderate living from journalism and writing quietly intricate thrillers in novel form, he has always made it clear that film is his first love. It was his desire to get closer to his dream of being a director that made him take a job as *Time Out* film critic in the mid-1970s. He worked there for five years, during which time he was given the opportunity of interviewing acclaimed director Wim Wenders. At the end of the interview, Petit showed him a treatment for a film and asked if he would be interested in backing it; Wenders agreed to put up part of the money. Moving away from funding avant-garde experimental films, the British Film Institute chose Petit's *Radio On* (1979) as the first film to be made under the new regime of accessibility.

Radio On remains Petit's most well-known piece; it often fills schedule gaps at British film festivals. It is a remarkable road movie that follows a young man who travels from London to Bristol to investigate the suicide of his brother. The narrative itself is minimal, but its fascination with the beauty of urban concrete scenery, not to mention its dark, moody soundtrack, featuring Kraftwerk and David Bowie amongst others, have made it a quintessential post-punk cult film. Sting features as a petrol pump attendant. The sensitivity with which the concrete landscape is represented shows the hand of a director who has extraordinary confidence and sensitivity.

His next film, *An Unsuitable Job for a Woman* (1981), is a film noir of sorts, loosely adapted from a P.D. James novel about a female detective who becomes obsessed with the victim of a murder she is investigating. The film is both moody and stylish and, like *Radio On*, deals with memory and death, two themes that can be seen in many of Petit's books and films. It was nominated for a Golden Bear at the Berlin Film Festival, the city where Petit made his next two thrillers back-to-back: *Flight to Berlin* (1983) and *Chinese Boxes* (1984) which, although tightly plotted, marked the beginnings of his disregard for linear narrative. Although his German films were met with some critical acclaim, his move towards deeper experimentation into the nature of filmic narrative may have troubled investors.

A hiatus followed. Film work dried up and he was forced to resort to making documentaries on bank managers and air-hostesses for the BBC, as well as an episode of 'Miss Marple'. Having returned to writing, it seemed that Petit might not work in film again. Visiting a second-hand bookshop, however, he struck up a conversation with the shop assistant, who turned out to be another artist on a downturn – the novelist Iain Sinclair, who has since made a name for himself with dark, unusual tales set in and around London. They first worked together on the television thriller 'The Cardinal and the Corpse' in 1992, and again on *The Falconer* (1998) and *Asylum* (2000).

In the early 1990s, unencumbered by film commissions, Petit had started experimenting more and more with found images. He had taken to carrying around a Polaroid camera, and became fascinated by the peripheral nature of images on CCTVs and camcorders. Despite the careful plotting of his novels, on film Petit began to explore the use of images beyond narrative. He considered the nature of the image in the public domain and, in the instance of *London Labyrinth* (1993) and *Surveillance* (1993), which was partly inspired by Chris Marker's sci-fi short *La Jetée* (1962), used found footage from CCTV cameras to create films in their simplist form. His belief that images had been 'shot to death' is evident in the almost totally inscrutable short film *Dead TV* (1999), a deconstruction of two important television moments of the early 1990s, and also in his meditative short film which revisited his first success, *Radio On (remix)* (1998). The latter scrambles the narrative of the original to fully explore the technological possibilities available in the editing suite, without a single frame of new footage being shot.

Petit soon stopped working on 35mm film, preferring to use digital video because of the freedom, cost benefits and speed it allowed him. He expressed his desire to work at the pace of Godard or Fassbinder, away from the restraint of cumbersome film crews or completed scripts. His films became increasingly experimental, in some instances (such as *The Slaughterhouse Tapes* (1997)) being made for display in art galleries rather than screening rooms. Working more with Sinclair, the two of them shared both writing and directing credits as they played around with narrative and tried out different ideas as they went along. A prime example of their adaptability can be seen in *The Falconer*; low overheads meant they could use development money to make the entire project. Working with Keith Griffiths, a hands-off producer Petit has used throughout his career, both he and Sinclair set out to make a 'fictional documentary' about a real-life former 1960s icon, the film-maker and counter-culture shaman Peter Whitehead. Though Whitehead was thoroughly unimpressed with the result, *The Falconer* is now recognised as a ground-breaking synergy of arts on film, not least in its use of both experimental music and layered graphic designs. Some of this only came about because of their ineptness with the camera microphone and the poor quality of some of the Hi-8 and re-filmed Super 8 footage they shot.

The Falconer is not available on video, but its entirely fictional narrative about a real person deals in black magic, incest, murder, drugs, egg smuggling and foul play; it almost led to Petit and Sinclair being charged for conducting a Satanic ritual on National Trust property.

Petit followed with a short film, *Negative Space* (1999), about a journey to discuss the perfection of image with well-respected film critic Manny Farber (who lives in southern California), and sharing the same discussion with Dave Hickey, a writer on art and architecture who lives in Las Vegas. Petit includes clips from classic films (including some from Godard) that the pair use to illustrate their arguments, but Petit seldom runs the clips straight, framing them in boxes, slowing them, abstracting them until one is forced to examine every element of the image itself as well as its context.

Back in the UK, the uproar over *The Falconer* led Sinclair and Petit to subtitle their next project, *Asylum* (2000), somewhat pessimistically as *The Last Commission*. Made for Channel 4, it provides further rumination on reality and fiction, extending some of the ideas raised by *The Falconer*. With a cast of real-life people – writers, a poet, a mythologist and the film's sound editor – Petit and Sinclair also make an appearance. Petit plays a shadowy film-maker called Kaporal, Sinclair a spymaster hiding in a second-hand book shop. Set in a future where a virus has wiped out the planet's cultural history, the heroine tries to solve a murder by piecing together aural clues to her fate. But the film is about much more than that – the thriller plot-line is soon laid to one side as people who fascinate the film-making pair are brought in, playing both themselves and other characters. Petit himself casts a shadowy melancholic figure in the film, and the piece is shot on both digital and Super-8, with 3D digital sculptures from the same artist who worked on *The Falconer* often mixing in with the images. The soundscape is also unconventional, mixing the noise of aeroplanes, shopping trolleys and dialogue with careful confusion. It seems that *Asylum* itself is set in a parallel universe where genres and linear theories do not exist, and where the differences between reality and fiction are constantly blurred. Happily, despite *Asylum*'s subtitle, both Petit and Sinclair have been given a new commission by Channel 4 to make an as yet unnamed film based on Sinclair's new book about the M25.

It is a great shame that those who fund film art cannot regularly find money to pass on to such an experimental writer-director as Petit. Whatever else the result may be, the film is guaranteed to be thought-provoking, intelligent and absolutely unique. **AL**

Stephen POLIAKOFF

Born in 1952, Stephen Poliakoff's career to date has completed a strange arc. Starting out as a BBC television writer of considerable repute, he quickly made the transition to feature film writing and directing, producing intellectually provocative works of intelligence and guile. The abject critical and commercial failure of his last feature, however, *Food of Love* (1997), heralded a swift return to television work, where he seems once again to have struck a rich vein of form.

Poliakoff's first television script, *Stronger Than the Sun*, in 1977, was part of the highly reputable 'Play for Today' series. Directed by Michael Apted and featuring a stellar cast led by Tom Bell and Francesca Annis, it put Poliakoff's name firmly on the map and quickly led to an offer to write a feature script for *Bloody Kids* (1979), which was directed by another BBC alumni, Stephen Frears. A state-of-the-nation address about the chaos of Thatcherite Britain, the themes of confusion and sociological ennui would prove to be recurring motifs in Poliakoff's work. The following year, he returned to television, penning the 1980 *Caught on a Train*. An observational piece about fractious relationships and cultural divide, Peggy Ashcroft featured in one of her finest small screen roles. 1982's *Soft Targets*, directed by Charles Sturridge, completed a concentrated run of writing success for Poliakoff. A year later both he and Sturridge teamed up again for *Runners*, the tale of a father's fraught, obsessive search for his missing daughter – both are excellently played by James Fox and Katie Hardie. Ostensibly a realistic thriller, lent extra gravitas by Sturridge's impressively low-key direction, the film also examines the role of the media in creating a wave of hysteria over the disappearance. Like much of Poliakoff's later work, it makes striking use of London locations.

In 1988 Poliakoff directed *Hidden City*, a film inspired by an article that appeared in *Time Out* magazine concerning the existence of a building that was used as a base from which prisoners were interrogated during the war. Amongst the writer-director's finest efforts, it is a taut, thrilling, atmospheric affair that depicts the capital city as a receptacle of suppressed history and a subterranean catacomb of fear, secrecy and paranoia. Poliakoff wrote his next film, *She's Been Away* (1989), and Peter Hall directed. The first 35mm film to be wholly financed by the BBC, like much of Poliakoff's writing it seeks to get beneath the veneer of seemingly contented relationships and examine their true dynamics. Peggy Ashcroft portrays an elderly woman institutionalised at an early age for vaguely feminist leanings who senses that the relationship between her nephew (James Fox) and his beautiful young wife (Geraldine James) is not all it should be. Potentially stodgy fare, Poliakoff's intelligent, gently acerbic script lends it wit and insight.

Close My Eyes (1991) remains Poliakoff's most fully realised work as both writer and director. The tale of a brother and sister (Clive Owen and Saskia Reeves) parted in childhood by divorce, who embark upon a torrid, incestuous affair, it was a timely exploration of the end of the 1980s and physical and moral decay. Beautifully photographed by Witold Stok, whose languid photography captures both physical and metaphorical heat, it takes an adult approach to the most taboo of subjects and to sexuality in general. Alan Rickman excels as Reeves' cuckolded husband. Poliakoff's follow-up, *Century* (1993), was an ambitious undertaking that saw him going back in time to the turn of the century to tackle the thorny subjects of eugenics and the rising female demand for emancipation. The film operates within the framework of a romantic drama and ultimately buckles under the weight of its own aspirations to be educational, enlightening and entertaining. Turns from Clive Owen, Charles Dance and Miranda Richardson leaven the heady brew but the film still met with a muted critical response.

Food of Love (1997) was a lighter affair that did little to alter the gentle downward spiral of Poliakoff's cinematic career. The story focuses on a jaded, yuppie bank assistant (Richard E. Grant) who retreats to a rural idyll to stage a production of 'Twelfth Night', which he had originally staged in the same village some ten years before. Accompanying him are members of the original production – similarly disaffected on the perpetual treadmill of London life – and some streetwise urban youths from the acting class Grant teaches. A culture clash ensues in which the idyll is revealed to be little more than a mini-metropolis, complete with hostility, bigotry, and crass commercialisation and consumerism. Though directed with a keen eye for the minutiae of modern life, Poliakoff's script is atypically weak, relying as it does on two-dimensional, stereotypical characterisation. That said, many of the observations are pertinent and pressing enough, and Grant, as always, offers good value. More recently, Poliakoff has returned to writing and directing for television, a decision that seems to have resuscitated his obvious talents. 'The Tribe', 'Perfect Strangers' and particularly the beautifully realised 'Shooting the Past', aired in 1999 – a distillation of the key Poliakoff themes of the complexities of relationships and the influence of the past – are undoubtedly major works and evidence of a fertile, perceptive and daring talent.   **JWo**

Sally POTTER

Sally Potter's career can be divided into two distinct phases: an earlier period committed to feminist theory film-making and a later adoption of more mainstream practices. Her artistic pursuits also extend into areas of music and dance.

Thriller (1979)
The Gold Diggers (1983)
Orlando (1992)

Born in London in 1949, she trained as a dancer; indeed, one of her first shorts, Combines (1972), focuses on dance and screened at The Place contemporary dance theatre. In 1979 she established her profile as a feminist director with *Thriller*. Along with others such as Julie Dash, Laura Mulvey and Yvonne Rainer, her work was aligned with the rise of academic film studies and the growing prominence of intellectual investigations of women's relationship with the cinema and other art forms. *Thriller* has since become a classic independent feminist piece, developing a strategy for an alternative cinema that rejects the pleasures of mainstream fare predicated on the objectification and exploitation of the female image. It defies narrative cinema's spatio-temporal linearity and references other films and texts. For instance, it features Alfred Hitchcock's *Psycho* (1960) soundtrack and quotes directly from academic feminist writing. Shot in black and white, with lighting effects reminiscent of expressionist conventions, *Thriller* explores the construction and treatment of femininity in the opera 'La Bohéme'. In particular, the film questions why the working-class heroine has to be sacrificed to an early death and creates a new scenario: Mimi, the new action heroine who is subject and investigator, becomes reconciled with the old passive heroine.

The Gold Diggers (1983), Potter's first feature-length film, extends *Thriller*'s investigation and explores the connection between the circulation of gold, money and women in patriarchal economies. Foregrounding music, it relieves reliance on the verbal. Both *Thriller* and *The Gold Diggers* employ similar strategies to subvert classic narrative conventions that represent stereotypical feminine images. *The Gold Diggers* turns the table on these stereotypes and presents the male characters as one-dimensional caricatures. Potter's casting decisions in these two films are also interesting. Colette Laffont, who plays Mimi in *Thriller,* also plays one of the two lead female characters in *The Gold Diggers.* That Potter casts Laffont, a black actress, in two leading roles, points to her attempt to subvert the casting of black actors in peripheral parts within mainstream cinema. In casting Julie Christie as Ruby, she explores the economics of beauty and the star. While Ruby circulates amongst men, Celeste (Laffont) aids the circulation of money in a bank. Later, Celeste decides to take on the role of investigator when she is denied knowledge of her function in this economy. Delving deeper into issues relating to sexual politics, *The Gold Diggers* makes a political statement of how the colonisation of women as objects with exchange value parallels the colonisation of the landscape in the search for gold.

Potter's short film *The London Story* (1987) depicts a conspiracy against the government. Unlike its predecessors it marks a shift in Potter's commitment to feminist film theory's didacticism in line with a general diminishing of 1970s activism. Coming close to her idea of a feminist musical, she tells the dystopian story through dance numbers: the scene at the ice rink features a sequence in which a co-conspirator obtains information to comic effects; at the end, two male co-conspirators dance alongside her by the river Thames.

With a decent budget, quality production values and its status as a European co-production, *Orlando* (1992), adapted from Virginia Woolf's novel, marked Potter's entry into mainstream film-making. The film is an entertaining historical romp through four hundred years of British history and tells the story of Orlando who lives from 1600 to the present day, and switches gender when the film enters the Victorian era. When Orlando becomes female, she looks into the camera and deadpans: 'No difference at all. Just a different sex'. It marks yet another phase in Potter's film-making practice: in contrast with the cinema of 'unpleasure' that her earlier films attempted to create, here she negotiates between feminist concerns and the enjoyment of entertainment cinema.

The Tango Lesson (1997) is semi-autobiographical, with Potter herself starring as the director who has to juggle her professional and personal life. An account of her relationship and collaboration with the dancer Pablo Verón, who also plays himself in the film, it features magnificent sequences of tango dancing, choreographed by Verón. As the two negotiate their relationship, their encounters with each other are represented through the dance. When Potter sees Verón for the first time on stage, she trains her eye on him from the audience, subverting the notion of the masculine gaze that objectifies feminine images. This reversal is foregrounded through strategic use of mirrors and the moment when Potter asserts her female 'look' in the conversation with Verón at the barber shop, and her eyes are unequivocally associated with that of the camera. Expressing Potter's feminist politics and interest in formal film aesthetics, *The Tango Lesson* also gives voice to her professional concerns, notably in the scene of her meeting with Hollywood producers. Towards the film's end, somewhat abruptly, it brings up issues of identity: Potter's Jewishness and Verón's position as an outsider, an Argentinian living in France.

The Man Who Cried (2000) is Potter's attempt at an epic Hollywood film. Using historical chaos as a backdrop, she paints the themes of *The Tango Lesson* onto a larger canvas. Christina Ricci plays a young Russian Jew who is searching for her long-lost father. Johnny Depp is the love interest, a romanticised gypsy freely associated with love and music; like Vernón he is an outsider, hovering at the edge of Parisian society. Potter loses the plot halfway into the film, taking her personal obsession a little too far; in a rather unconvincing conclusion, Ricci's character finally finds her father in Hollywood, where he has made a name for himself.

Despite the disappointment and contrivance of her most recent film, Potter is undeniably a thought-provoking film-maker whose works are deeply personal and political.

ST

Udayan PRASAD

Born in India in 1953, Udayan Prasad emigrated to the UK at the age of nine. He is an *Brothers in Trouble* (1996) experienced director of television drama whose work, much of which has been for BBC's *My Son the Fanatic* (1998) Screen 2, has dealt with a wide range of subjects. His first project as a television director, *They Never Slept* (1990), was a comedy from a script by Simon Gray. He went on to direct *102 Boulevard Haussmann* (1991), which examined a period in the life and work of the French writer Marcel Proust. *Running Late* (1992), tells the story of George Grant, an egocentric London television show host, who is going about his daily business when an urgent telephone call from his wife sends him on a journey which leads him to question events in his life. *Femme Fatale* (1993) is an entertaining comedy about a beautiful and charming young Italian woman who bewitches a handful of English villagers.

Next, Prasad went on to direct *Brothers in Trouble* (1996), a portrayal of the lives of the early Pakistani, Indian and Bengali immigrants to Britain. Amir is an illegal Pakistani immigrant smuggled into England in the 1960s. He moves into a boarding house with a number of other men under the supervision of Hussein Shah (Om Puri). The household is shaken by the arrival of a young white girl, Mary (Angeline Ball), who affects the lives and relationships of the men. In the early part of the film, sombre lighting enhances the paranoid atmosphere with many scenes taking place at night. When Mary arrives she literally brings light with her, rigging up electric bulbs, which the illegals have never dared use. This is used as a metaphor: through her warmth and friendliness, Mary brings out something unexpected in the men. From this point the lighting in the film changes and there is a direct contrast in the final section which is filmed in broad daylight in the streets and on the edges of the countryside. It powerfully conveys the sense of hopelessness and fear in which illegal immigrants live.

My Son the Fanatic (1997) is Prasad's most well-known and successful work to date. From a script by Hanif Kureishi, the film is about Parvez (Om Puri), a married, middle-aged Pakistani taxi driver who has many prostitutes as clients. He begins a relationship with one of them and, in many ways, appears to have assimilated himself into Western society; however, his son Farid feels like an unwelcome visitor in Britain. Slowly rejecting his father's liberal attitudes, Farid opts out of marriage to a white girl and retreats into a lifestyle taught and practiced by an extremist's school of Islam. Framing plays an important part in illustrating Parvez's conflicted point of view. Puri gives a terrific performance as a middle-aged married man in crisis; his position within the frame demonstrates his increasing disorientation from everything he knows (much of the film is shot using handheld camera to suggest movement and instability). Both *Brothers in Trouble* and *My Son the Fanatic* appear to be more personal works for Prasad. They are about the British Asian experience, show contradictory representations of Asian identity in Britain, and demonstrate a progression in narrative theme and his style as a director.

More recently, he has directed an episode of Alan Bennett's 'Talking Heads 2' and number of episodes of the Carlton TV drama series 'Big Bad World'. He is currently working on *Gabriel & Me* (2001), a drama about a young boy who believes he can save his dying father if become's an angel.

PR

Q

Stephen and Timothy QUAY

Identical twins Stephen and Timothy Quay were born in 1947 near Philadelphia in an *Institute Benjamenta* (1995)
area with a high proportion of European immigrants. This exposure to a more cosmo-
politan culture interested them greatly, and led to their move to Britain to study at the
Royal College of Art, where they started to develop a style of animation that has become
their trademark. Utilising puppetry, stop-motion photography and a genuine sense of
the surreal, the Brothers Quay, as they are known professionally, have become critically
renowned for their work – even if their self-consciously obscure narratives have placed
them at the extremes of public appeal.

As animators, their surreal style, achieved through a particular form of animation
(puppetry and artefacts), as well as minutely constructed design and photography, is
heavily influenced by the work of the great Czech animator Jan Svankmajer. Their narrative leanings are inspired by the writings of European authors with a bias towards the
expressionistic and dreamlike; notable inspirations include Franz Kafka, Robert Walser,
Bruno Schulz and Lewis Carroll. The renown that the Brothers Quay have achieved is
based on a number of celebrated short-films, including *The Cabinet of Jan Svankmajer*
(1984) and *Street of Crocodiles* (1986), which led to the production of their one feature
film to date, *Institute Benjamenta* (1995) – otherwise known as *This Dream People Call
Human Life*. Primarily a live-action movie, *Institute Benjamenta* is a starkly odd creation. In basic narrative terms, it concerns the life of Jakob Von Gunten (played compellingly by Mark Rylance), who 'wants to be of use to someone in this life'. To achieve
this end, he enrols in the dilapidated Institute Benjamenta, a school for servants where
the curriculum involves only a single lesson, endlessly repeated, intuitively grounding the
students in willing monotony and subservience.

Beyond this simple outline of plot, the film is a remarkable triumph of monochrome
photography, chiaroscuro lighting, fastidiously precise and attentive production design,
and expressionistic modes of performance. In many ways, the texture of the film becomes
more important than the narrative drive. Clearly the ambition is to realise the singular
texture of dreams; the visual image is sometimes combined but frequently at odds with

the audio detail, and music and diegetic sounds do not necessarily match what is seen. This disharmony creates a film which is at once haunting, disquieting and unsettling, and at times illogical, irrational and impenetrable. The primary narrative concern is an absurdist exploration of 'the human condition', an investigation into what existence actually means. Jakob Von Gunten's willingness to devote himself to the monotonous and dehumanising existence of servitude is countered by his defiant need to be an individual, and his growing infatuation with the school's proprietor, Lisa Benjamenta (played by Alice Krige). Ultimately, Lisa is stirred from a meaningless and loveless existence; becoming aware of that emptiness, she chooses to stop living. It is a bleak conclusion to a unique film, a piece that celebrates the artfulness of cinema to an extreme.

Never likely to be troubled by mass appeal, the Brothers Quay seem content to remain within the realms of the avant-garde, as one of their most recent short films *In Absentia* (2000) – a collaboration with Karlheinz Stockhausen, a titan of avant-garde classical music – would seem to suggest. Given the painstaking aesthetic of their work to date, and the fact that their work may never realistically pull in huge commercial audiences, any future feature-film work from the Brothers Quay could be a long time coming.   **JP**

Bob QUINN

Although he may not be Ireland's most famous film-maker, Bob Quinn has been behind the scenes of the country's now vibrant independent cinema for three decades. Starting in Ireland's State-owned television service Radio Telifís Éireann in the 1960s, he helped to instigate structural changes and tried to make the station more friendly to independent film-makers. In 1969 he left the station and Dublin for the remote, Gaelic-speaking region of Connamara, founding an independent production company called Cinegael.

The first widely circulated film made by Cinegael was *Caoineadh Airt Uí Laoire/ Lament for Art O'Leary* (1975), an Irish-language fifty-minute feature that retold the famous Irish poem of the same name. A formally rigorous work, it moves freely between the eighteenth and twentieth centuries, linking the cultural imperialism of England with its domination of territory and property. It forms part of the international flowering of politically militant, aesthetically innovative cinema that is unique to the 1970s and belongs alongside projects such as Godard's Dziga-Vertov work.

Quinn's full-length fiction work, *Poitín* (1979), was the first filmic narrative made entirely in Irish Gaelic. The story centres on an old poitín maker (Cyril Cusack) and the two henchmen (Niall Tóibín and Donal McCann) he employs. These two moonshine-middlemen are extremely poor and halfway through the film launch an ill-conceived plan to cheat their boss. He punishes them and regulates his own illegal trade in a way that the incompetent police never manage to. It gradually becomes clear that Quinn sees Connamara as a tough, insular community that has responded to centuries of underdevelopment in often brutal ways.

Quinn is probably best known in the Republic of Ireland for his Atlantean series, made for RTÉ. The first set of (three) installments was produced in 1983, and centred on Quinn's search for the North African and Middle Eastern roots of the Irish. He also wrote a book called 'Atlantean: Ireland's North African and Maritime Heritage' as a companion to the series. The second series (called 'Atlantean 2: Navigato') was produced in 1997 and focused on the Baltic region. These are odd works, sometimes appearing to be standard science documentaries (featuring maps and interviews with experts), at others feeling quite subjective (including an image of Quinn trying to do an elaborate Egyptian dance).

The line between his 1987 film *Budawanny* and his 1993 film *The Bishop's Story* is a little blurry; the latter is ostensibly a re-make of the former. Both deal with a priest (Donal McCann) on Clare Island who has a dalliance with his housekeeper (Maggie Fegan). *Budawanny* tells this story in a linear way, shot on black and white 16mm, with English dialogue. *The Bishop's Story* tells the story of the fallen cleric as a flashback bookended by images of him in a drying-out home for priests. The images of Clare Island are sepia-toned, the dialogue is in Irish Gaelic and translated by silent-film-style intertitles, and the whole film is on 35mm. Blowing up the footage from the 16mm,

Budawanny gives *The Bishop's Story* a textured, grainy look; even the small amount of new footage shot on 35mm has a certain roughness to it.

Budawanny feels like a very interesting sketch, well observed, but still waiting to be filled out; *The Bishop's Story*, on the other hand, is clearly Quinn's masterpiece. It is an anti-romantic portrait of an isolated culture struggling both to hang on to its distinctive elements and deal with modernity. It also has a highly innovative visual schema, quite unlike anything else to come out of Ireland or Europe in the 1990s.

The backbone of Quinn's career has been the countless small documentaries he has made mainly for television, which are infrequently shown outside of Ireland. Among the most recent of these was *It Must Be Done Right* (1999), a portrait of Donal McCann that was finished just before McCann passed away. **JW**

Paul QUINN

Paul Quinn was born in Chicago, Illinois in 1960, and began his career in theatre as a *This Is My Father* (1998) teacher, actor and director. He moved into cinema with parts in Barry Levinson's *Avalon* (1990), Tim Robbin's *Bob Roberts* (1992) and Mike Figgis' *Leaving Las Vegas* (1995). Quinn's first feature, *This Is My Father* (1998), is something of a family affair. Starring his brother, Aidan, in the lead role, the film was photographed by another brother, Declan. The family's roots, in both Ireland and America, form the thematic centre of *This Is My Father* which tells the story of an ill-fated romance in rural Ireland in 1939. A simple farmhand, Kieran (Aidan Quinn), meets the high-spirited Fiona (Moya Farrelly) and the two fall in love. Circumstances of history and birth conspire to bring the relationship to a tragic conclusion and Fiona leaves for America. When her son, Kieran (James Caan), faces a crisis in his own life, he travels with his nephew to Ireland to find out the truth of his parentage. An ambitious first feature, the film is at its most successful where it explores the cruelty of an older Irish generation towards its own members. Declan Quinn's conjuring of the countryside as dark, gloomy and constricting in the past, and bright and garish in the present reinforces this theme and Aidan Quinn's performance as the first Kieran is one of his best on film.

Quinn might have resisted the temptation to load the narrative with so many plot twists – the curse on Fiona's family, for instance, and the inclusion of John Cusack as an American pilot whom the couple encounter on the beach are details which the film could do without. *This Is My Father* performed well at the Irish box office and took a number of awards on the festival circuit.

Quinn is currently working on his second feature, *Never Get Outta the Boat*. **RB**

R

Michael RADFORD

Born in New Delhi, India, in 1946, raised in the Middle East, educated in Britain, and Another Time, Another Place
later residing in France and Italy, with regular excursions to America to court financial (1983)
moguls, it is no wonder that Michael Radford's films are an eclectic mix. Cosmopolitan in *1984* (1984)
setting and story, they explore the collision of worlds, both geographical and emotional. *White Mischief* (1987)
They are human dramas that are concerned with the desire for freedom, stifled creativity *Il Postino* (1994)
and emotion, the enigmatic search for happiness and fulfilment, and the desire to liberate *B Monkey* (1998)
the boxed-in, pent-up and beaten-down. Less well known than he deserves, Radford is a *Dancing at the Blue Iguana*
detailed and expressive director, more suited to the European mode than the kitchen-sink (2000)
tendencies of his homeland. He often implicitly contrasts a cloistered, unmistakably British, sensibility with a more liberated European emotion; in the latter part of his career,
he has developed an almost expressionist approach toward storytelling and cinematic
narrative.

The best example of his style of film-making is also his greatest success. *Il Postino*
(1994) is a gentle, character-driven work that deals with lofty matters: exile, emotional
frailty, the search for freedom of expression, and the rediscovery of the important aspects
of life. Its main character is also something of a textbook Radford hero – a simple,
uncomplicated man, seized and buffeted by emotions that are beyond his ability to
express, whose discovery of liberation carries with it a tragic price.

Initially educated at Oxford, and having worked as a teacher in Edinburgh, Radford
enrolled as one of the 25 inaugural students at the National Film and Television School
in 1971. He made his first experimental short films during this time and, upon graduating, directed several documentary films for the BBC, including *Madonna and the Volcano*
(1976) *The Last Stronghold of the Pure Gospel* (1977). Radford wrote and directed *The
White Bird Passes* for BBC Scotland. Part documentary and part fiction, the film's poetic
and prosaic strands vie to relate the life of Scottish writer Jessie Kesson. *Another Time,
Another Place* (1983), his first full-length feature, was partly financed by the burgeoning film wing of Channel 4 and originally shot for television but awarded a cinematic
release. In rural Scotland in the last year of World War Two, a trio of Italian POWs, forced

into tasks of fruitless labour, meet with the menial existence of a Scottish woman locked in a loveless marriage. The shared need to escape, bordering on desperation, and the characters' concurrent modes of imprisonment – actual and psychological – play out in a fluent exploration of desire and cultural identity, set against an austere landscape that cuts against the red-blooded passion bubbling below the surface.

The same schematic is used in Radford's *1984* (1984), an impressive translation of George Orwell's novel, filmed presciently during the exact dates specified in the source material. The film features meticulous sets of bombed-out streets, crumbling concrete buildings, and bleak, soulless rooms which are strongly reminiscent of post-war Britain with its peeling paintwork and postered sloganeering. Using the milieu to represent the intellectual and emotional sterility of Winston Smith's 1984 world, Radford once again stresses the necessity to penetrate surface phenomena and get at the hidden truth beneath. Monochrome realism contrasts with Technicolour flights into an imagined world of escape. Radford pays particular attention to the potential falsity of what we see, as in the fictitious propaganda newsreels and television screens, reminding us of the schism between external representation and inner psychology. The implication of film as a tool of manipulation – both film and sound have central roles in the 1984 world – also adds an interesting slant to Radford's own attitude to the dual properties of cinema to conceal as well as explicate. It is really the suppression of freedom of expression – vocal, written and thought – that interests Radford, however. The slate-like impassivity of John Hurt's central performance counterposes his discovery of love as a redemptive, liberating force. Though Winston's freedom inevitably wreaks its own destruction, Radford – unlike Orwell, whose ending is more ambiguous and downbeat – suggests that the experience of love and liberty is crucial, however brief and unsustainable it may be.

Based on the scandalous love triangle of Diana Broughton and fellow aristocratic expats in 1940s Kenya, *White Mischief* (1987) turns this idea inside out. Here the landscape becomes the natural, uncorrupted depiction of beauty and transcendence against which the human story – normally the Radford focus – becomes ever more desperate, empty and destructive. Freedom of expression – the unhealthy lust between Diana and Erroll – results not in liberation but in entrapment, as jealous husband Sir Jock murders her lover Erroll, shoots himself, and leaves Diana to take the fall. The voyeuristic camerawork, complete with shots in murky bedrooms, through keyholes, and in morgues, conjures a sickly ambience. The drugs, drink and decadence of the upper-class ex-pat lifestyle – exploitative, indulgent, and impure – are the focus of criticism. With its irredeemably unpleasant characters, and rather didactic tone – Radford's resolutely socialist standpoint coming obviously to the fore – the film lacks the subtle touch of his better work and flopped badly.

During a subsequent seven-year hiatus, Radford emigrated to Italy, where he struck up a close friendship with Massimo Troisi, collaborator and star of his best, most lyrical film, *Il Postino*. In its story of a simple-minded postman who meets Pablo Neruda, the exiled Chilean 'poet of love', Radford finds his purest expression of the inspirational power of emotional freedom, and the rediscovery of the beauty of life in its simple forms – in poetry, the landscape, friendship and love. Loosely structured and unusually paced, the film skips about in time to lay emphasis on the rhythms of the growing relationship between the 'great' and the 'little' man. It is a meeting of worlds in which mutual lessons are learned: for Neruda, the pleasures of simple friendship away from his self-subsuming fame; and, for Mario, a world beyond the confines of his community which opens his eyes to the beauty of the everyday. Human failings – Neruda's return to fame and his neglect of friendship, and the political strong-arming which silences Mario's new-found poetic voice – bring a downbeat conclusion to Radford's gentle tale. The emphasis, however, is on discovery rather than loss, suggesting the appropriateness of life ending at the very moment it has really begun. Though wilfully manipulative, the sheer charm of Radford's film, and its refusal to romanticise the rural setting, are inescapably persuasive.

His subsequent films, although well made, inevitably pale alongside their predecessor. *B Monkey* (1998) is a romantic thriller in which a bookish teacher falls in love with a female criminal, again exploring the collocation of disparate worlds. The film feels unusually generic for Radford; it mixes action and romance sequences with typically convincing art direction and a variety of styles, but lacks the emotional punch of his best work.

The experimental *Dancing at the Blue Iguana* (2000) follows a week in the lives of several female dancers. A pet project developed from improvisation, it is filmed in an intimate, documentary style that attempts to portray an Altman-esque snapshot of its characters' lives. Convincing and well acted, it suffers from a lack of structuring and precision, but demonstrates his developing experimentation with storytelling form, and his further interest in an expressionistic exploration of character. Radford is that rare breed in British cinema – a director willing to try new routes and challenge the rules, though tellingly, like his characters, he has rarely found that freedom at home.   **OB**

Lynne RAMSAY

Born in Glasgow, Scotland, in 1969, Lynne Ramsay began her cinematic career direct- *Ratcatcher* (1999) ing short films. Located in her hometown during the 1973 bin-men's strike, her first feature, *Ratcatcher* (1999), eschews macro-historical analysis of a moment when the army intervened in a political dispute in mainland Britain, opting instead to vividly register the micro-historical textures of a working-class environment. Soldiers clearing rat-infested rubbish form part of a series of fascinating experiences in a film based around children verging on adolescence.

The film begins with the death of James' friend Ryan in a polluted canal. That this could easily have been him is reiterated in *Ratcatcher*'s dual conclusion where James floats in the canal but is also shown arriving with his family at a new house in the countryside. Although social comment is implicit, *Ratcatcher*'s concern is with how this environment looks and feels to young protagonists oblivious to danger or social determinants. This is established in the sensual opening shot of Ryan inexplicably wrapping himself in a net curtain. These small acts of enjoyment, tenderness and callousness, both in and around children's lives, recall fellow Scot Bill Douglas' autobiographical trilogy – *My Childhood* (1972), *My Ain Folk* (1973) and *My Way Home* (1978). James' father (Tommy Flanagan) is portrayed as a mercifully more complex character than the brutal working-class egotists typically played by Ray Winstone in earlier 1990s British films such as *Ladybird, Ladybird* (1994) and *Nil by Mouth* (1997): he is shown rescuing a boy from the canal and then hitting his wife after being attacked by a street gang.

With such an intriguing first feature, the critical success of *Ratcatcher* suggests that Ramsay could very well go on to become an important director. She is currently in production with her second feature, *Morvern Callar*.   **MSt**

Karel REISZ

It is interesting to consider how the phenomenon of the reviewer-turned-writer sprang out *We Are the Lambeth Boys* (1958) of the post-war European critical intelligentsia. In all probability it is due to a simultaneous sense of frustration and admiration for the domination of American cinema, and a *Saturday Night and Sunday* belief that the medium had to be recaptured for the continent's new generation. Nowhere *Morning* (1960) can that sense of frustration have been greater than for the cine-literate viewer confronted *Night Must Fall* (1964) by the cultural impoverishment of post-war Britain – quota quickies and the aptly-named *Morgan: A Suitable Case for* J. Arthur Rank's numerous mediocrities. While *Cahiers du cinéma* may have yielded *Treatment* (1966) François Truffaut and Jean-Luc Godard, almost a decade before their careers began, and *Isadora* (1968) with a sense of urgency, Karel Reisz founded *Sequence* magazine while studying chem- *The Gambler* (1974) istry at Cambridge. Born in Czechoslovakia in 1926, he had fled mainland Europe aged *Who'll Stop the Rain* (1978) 12. *The French Lieutenant's*

By the mid-1950s, he and Lindsay Anderson (who also worked on the magazine) *Woman* (1981) graduated to film-making. Reisz had a formidable background in film academia, includ- *Sweet Dreams* (1985) ing his authorship of the standard text 'The Technique of Film Editing'. He and Anderson *Everybody Wins* (1990) were the leaders of Free Cinema, the radical rallying cry of British film which combined a belief in the power of social realism with a strong political agenda in a society that, barring the odd Aldermaston march, was still intensely conservative. Reisz's documentary *We Are the Lambeth Boys* (1958) may now seem pallid and innocuous; at the time, it was unprecedented as a depiction of working-class life on-screen, a shocking contrast with the staid fictions of British film. The conceptual substance of Free Cinema has been questioned in retrospect and as a cinematic movement it quickly burned itself out; however, its real influence can be seen in television of the 1960s, both documentaries and popular programmes such as 'Play for Today'.

The movement's next logical step was a feature film. *Saturday Night and Sunday Morning* (1960) launched the careers of Reisz and its star Albert Finney. Critics seized upon the gritty Alan Sillitoe-scribed tale of a Nottingham factory worker as evidence of Britain's very own answer to the nouvelle vague: here was a new kind of cinema that was unflinching in its treatment of provincial life and abortion. Unfortunately, in retrospect, the good intentions of the makers have not prevented the film becoming extremely dated; there is an emotional gulf that makes it impossible for the viewer to empathise with the characters, regarding them rather with an anthropologically observational interest.

By the mid-1960s such hard-edged realism had been overtaken by eye-catching visuals, from the invention of the Czech new wave to the television advertising that made up a large part of Reisz's income. The surreal imagery and dark comedy of *Morgan: A Suitable Case for Treatment* (1966) was borne out of this confluence of fashions. The effect is superficially interesting but never nears boiling point, while the script repeatedly spills over into self-indulgence. Still, one is thankful for any film that gives the arrestingly dotty David Warner a lead role as the madman of the title.

Isadora (1968) was advertised as 'The Lives and Many Loves of the Most Exciting Woman of Our Times'; Reisz's roots in realism were buried out of sight as he undertook this over-inflated biography of Isadora Duncan. Despite – or perhaps because of – the lack of radical chic, this conventional big-budget production was Reisz's most watch-able feature to date, thanks in particular to Vanessa Redgrave's dominating performance. *Isadora* may be overlong, but then extravagance was never a stranger to the free-thinking dancer's life.

The Gambler (1974), Reisz's first American film, is an intense, absorbing and exis-tential account of the alternating pleasure and struggle of addiction. James Caan's epony-mous lead character is an English Literature professor who seems to be as possessed by the urge to be in debt as the will to win; the James Toback script similarly veers between compelling intensity and macho pretension. The film's real strength is in the details: it is a cool and observational look at the gambler's world, aided by a marvellous supporting cast, in particular Paul Sorvino.

Who'll Stop the Rain (1978) was a far bleaker and more desperate look at the American underbelly. It packs the biggest punch of Reisz's career, successfully address-ing the crisis of the country's post-Vietnam psyche. Here the heart of darkness has come home: war reporter Michael Moriarty quickly finds himself in over his head in a heroin deal and is forced to enlist the help of Nietzchean veteran Nick Nolte to protect himself and his wife. The sense of fear and corruption is pervasive; this is a film without moral absolutes. Its conviction springs out of a sense of confusion and ordinary lives over-taken by events. A sparsely populated thriller, it is far more telling than the big-budget Vietnam War epics of the 1970s and 1980s.

It seems that the only consistent note to Reisz's career was the unpredictable vari-ety of his chosen subjects. A costume drama with contemporary interludes, *The French Lieutenant's Woman* (1981) succeeded, at least conceptually, where other directors had failed in repeated attempts at adaptations. Still, the ingenuity of Reisz's achievement, in collaboration with Harold Pinter, does not disguise the fact that the essence of the John Fowles novel does not transfer well to another medium. The film's greatest strengths, the Dorset visuals, are thanks to cameraman Freddie Francis. The Patsy Cline biography *Sweet Dreams* (1985) is essentially a showcase for fine performances by Ed Harris and the great Jessica Lange, for which it cannot be faulted.

With an Arthur Miller script bringing together Reisz, Nick Nolte and Debra Winger, it was inconceivable that *Everybody Wins* (1990) could be a failure. Yet the small-town corruption thriller proved to be an unmitigated critical and box-office disaster, and appears to have put paid to Reisz's career. Its reputation is undeserved. The plot is far less obscure than some have claimed, and Debra Winger's depiction of bewildering mad-ness is the outstanding performance around which the film pivots. A thriller with a politi-cal edge, it is a worthy successor to *Who'll Stop the Rain*.

He has recently directed *Act Without Words*, an adaptation of Samuel Beckett's play, for the Beckett on Film series. **BF**

Peter RICHARDSON

Peter Richardson first found fame writing, acting in and directing for 'The Comic Strip *The Supergrass* (1985) Presents...', showcasing a group of comedians, among them Dawn French, Jennifer *Eat the Rich* (1987) Saunders, Adrian Edmondson and Rik Mayall. Parodying Enid Blyton stories ('Five Go *The Pope Must Die* (1991) Mad on Mescalin') and Hollywood blockbusters (including a vision of what an American version of the 1985 miners' strike would look like in 'Strike'), they found their natural home on the (then new) Channel 4, developing television comedy from its sketch-based formats into more imaginative short films.

Buoyed by the success of the television shows, and undeterred by the dwindling fate of British cinematic comedy, The Comic Strip moved into feature films with Richardson writing, acting in and directing *The Supergrass* in 1985. Despite a cool critical reception, the film achieved good box-office results on the back of the Comic Strip reputation and the cast of usual suspects: Daniel Peacock, Nigel Planer, French and Saunders, and Edmondson.

The story focuses on a hapless man (Edmondson) who is overheard by the police lying to his new girlfriend about his drug dealing business in order to impress her, and having to act as a 'supergrass' in order to escape punishment. The plot is periodically implausible, and the characters often fail to convince despite the good-natured playing of the central cast. Visual and toilet humour predominate, weakening the film's chances of pulling off a clever farce, although there are attempts by Richardson to invest the film with a darker subtext, as Edmondson's dream turns into a nightmare.

Richardson's following film, *Eat the Rich* (1987), demonstrates his interest in the state of Britain in the 1980s, but failed to provide a consistent and funny satire in its unstructured tale of a class war raged by a malcontent who advocates the eating of the middle and upper classes in a restaurant renamed Eat the Rich. Over-cameoed (Paul McCartney, Bill Wyman and Angie Bowie) and under-developed, the film lacks a consistent style and is repetitive in narrative and comic attempts.

The poor box-office of the film led to Richardson's next – *Five Go to Hell* – being scrapped, and his following feature effort, *The Pope Must Die* (1991), was originally written as a three-part series for Channel 4 who backed down soon after the script was completed. That it was re-written for the big screen may go some way to explaining its structure: some elements are padded out and others so undeveloped that they hardly register with the viewer. Erratic and heavy-handed, the film failed to live up to the controversy hoped for by the film-makers. An attempt at religious and gangster satire, it stars Robbie Coltrane as a mistakenly elected Pope who has to clean up the Vatican whilst securing his own dubious past. The lame script and frenetic direction are ill-matched and the result is a chaotic waste of Paul Bartel, who invests this movie with its only real comic effects.

That Richardson and his co-writer Pete Richens so readily admit to a love of childish, vulgar humour is unsurprising when one casts a critical eye over their cinematic output. Lacking maturity and experience, the films seem more suited to a late-night television slot than proper cinematic distribution.

Having contributed to the decreasing popularity of 'The Comic Strip Presents', Richardson has returned, with more success, to television directing with the cult BBC2 series 'Stella Street'. **JD**

Tony RICHARDSON

Tony Richardson, born Cecil Antonio Richardson in Shipley, UK, in 1928, was educated *Look Back In Anger* (1959) at Wadham College, Oxford, where he studied English. He is an important figure in Brit- *The Entertainer* (1960) ish cinema. An original 'angry young man', and co-founder of the Free Cinema Movement *A Taste of Honey* (1961) in the mid-1950s, he is also a key figure in terms of production, forming Woodfall Film *The Loneliness of the Long* Productions in 1958 with playwright John Osborne and Bond producer Harry Saltzman. *Distance Runner* (1962) He is the father of actors Natasha and Joely Richardson, by his first marriage to Vanessa *Tom Jones* (1963) Redgrave. *The Loved One* (1965)

Richardson began his career with the BBC as a director in the early 1950s. He *Mademoiselle* (1966) left to pursue a career in the film industry, co-directing a documentary film, *Momma* *The Sailor from Gibralter* *Don't Allow* (1955), with Karel Reisz. Along with Lindsay Anderson and Karel Reisz, he (1967) developed the Free Cinema movement, partly to allow them to exhibit their challenging, energetic, experimental, low-budget films. The movement took its name from a series of six programmes of screenings held between 1956–1959 at the National Film Theatre. Included under the Free Cinema banner were three examples of 'New Wave' film-making from France, United States and Poland, and three low-budget films made in Britain; the majority of the latter were documentaries. The Free Cinema directors shared an interest in communities, and a particular respect for the traditional working class. They had an interest in the developing youth culture, counter-balanced by a genuine concern for the nature and effects of leisure activities and the erosion of the traditional working class in post-war Britain. The Movement was in many ways both a continuation of, and a reaction against, the Griersonian documentary realist project of the 1930s and 1940s.

During this time, Richardson had helped to set up the English Stage Company at the Royal Court Theatre, where he had directed John Osborne's 'Look Back In Anger'. He believed a film adaptation of this successful and controversial play would at last open up a way for he and his Free Cinema colleagues to get into the mainstream film industry. After hearing that Richard Burton had agreed to play Jimmy Porter on screen, Warner Brothers decided to finance the film. Richardson set up Woodfall Film Productions, with Osborne and Saltzman, to produce the film. *Look Back In Anger* (1959) brought the angry young man to the screen, and Richard Burton's Jimmy Porter is the epitome of 'angry': he paces, snarls and broods his way through the film, targeting his existential angst on everyone and everything around him. Despite Burton's smouldering appeal and forceful performance, and the heavily hyped 'sex angle', *Look Back In Anger* did not catch the imagination of the critics or the cinema-going public.

Richardson's next venture for Woodfall was *The Entertainer* (1960), again based on a highly successful stage play by John Osborne. Laurence Olivier had played the lead, Archie Rice, a fading music hall comedian, in the theatre, but attempts to reconstruct Archie on screen failed dismally. Filmed partly on location in Morecambe, *The Entertainer* follows the fortunes of a theatrical family, charting the downfall of music hall entertainment through the demise of Archie, and vice versa. The film received hostile responses from critics who felt it to be overblown and technically flawed. By this time, Woodfall was in serious financial difficulties, and Richardson abandoned plans to shoot a film based on Shelagh Delaney's best-selling novel 'A Taste of Honey'.

However, with the success of *Saturday Night and Sunday Morning* (1960), directed by Reisz, Woodfall and Richardson could afford to begin work on *A Taste of Honey* (1961), one of the important British films of the 1960s. The film is set in Manchester and centres on a working-class heroine, Jo (Rita Tushingham), who, just a child herself, becomes pregnant and tries to strike out on her own with the help of her gay friend Geoffrey (Murray Melvin). The film was shot entirely on location, a decision that reflected Richardson's views of studios at the time: 'I hate studios, I no longer even want to shoot interiors in studios, I would rather work in the limited conditions which a location imposes upon you'. Richardson, and cameraman Walter Lassally, create a certain poetic realism which at once binds and yet sets the figure against the urban landscape, so that visually at least all struggles, however everyday and ordinary, are grand, human conflicts fought with dignity and nobility. Critics responded positively to this poetic realism, and to the strong central performance of Tushingham, and those of Dora Bryan as Jo's mother, and Melvin as Geoffrey.

Richardson did not fare so well critically or commercially with his next feature, *The Loneliness of the Long Distance Runner* (1962), an adaptation of a short story by Alan Sillitoe. However, with the surge in interest in British film both past and present, it has since received the serious critical attention denied to it at the time of its release. Using a flashback narrative structure, the film focuses on Colin Smith (Tom Courtney), who is sent to borstal for theft. Colin is a troubled adolescent filled with fury against the world, society, his mother and the authorities. As the film moves towards its end we become aware, through flashbacks, of at least some of the reasons for his delinquency: lack of a strong father figure and a mother too interested in consumer goods and television to be of any use to him. Whilst in borstal, Colin's talent for cross-country running emerges and he is promptly given special training privileges so he can compete for the reform school's honour in a race with the local public school. His special training runs give Colin time to be himself, and a space in which he can be a free individual. The camerawork reflects this, and some of the film's more experimental and uplifting moments come as we accompany him on his training runs through the damp woodland. Indeed, it was the camerawork – swirling treetops and jagged panning shots set to a lively jazz score – which most upset the critical establishment. These stylistic, poetic moments were seen as gimmicks or shallow trickery that aped the techniques of the French New Wave.

Richardson's next film, *Tom Jones* (1963), is considered by some to be the director's masterpiece. It is a pivotal film of British cinema in the 1960s, moving away from the depiction of working-class realism and into the swinging Sixties. *Tom Jones* is an adaptation of an eighteenth-century novel by Henry Fielding, adapted for the screen by John Osborne. It tells the story of Tom Jones (Albert Finney), an orphan taken in by a kindly old squire and later disowned. Tom is mischievous, self-serving and lustful, and encounters equally lustful females along his bawdy way. The kind of mad-cap action and energetic optimism permeating *Tom Jones* marks it out as a kind of proto-swinging Sixties film, even if the historical subject matter seems to preclude it from such a categorisation. A rambunctious 'bustiers and breeches saga' it may have been, but bubbling under its historical setting is a sexy spirit. The camerawork of Walter Lassally and imaginative use of locations also set this film apart and excited critics. *Tom Jones* earned almost £25 million and won three Oscars® for Best Film, Best Director and Best Screenplay. It is undoubtedly Richardson's most critically acclaimed film.

After the success of *Tom Jones*, he embarked on a change of location and then a change of cinematic direction. *The Loved One* (1965) was his first American project, a deliciously dark adaptation of Evelyn Waugh's novel about a British colony of expats in Los Angeles. Robert Morse plays Dennis Barlow, a young poet who travels to America for the funeral of his uncle. Intrigued by the strange people he encounters, Dennis decides to stay and finds work as an assistant in a pet cemetery. Widely advertised as the film with 'something to offend everyone', *The Loved One* is a masterpiece of the macabre. It is easy to see why it proved so difficult to adapt the book for the screen and also to see why luminaries like Luis Buñuel tried. That said, the film is decidedly uneven, delivered as a swirl of ideas through strong imagery that would become increasingly characteristic of Richardson's work from this point. *The Loved One* was a hit with critics, but received a lukewarm response from audiences. However, its darkly quirky and irreverent tone makes it a minor masterpiece of Hollywood film-making of the period.

Richardson made a sharp cinematic break with his next two features, *Mademoiselle* (1966) and *The Sailor from Gibralter* (1967), collaborating with Jeanne Moreau on both. They received hostile notices from critics, and their experimental nature guaranteed restricted exhibition.

His next feature, *The Charge of the Light Brigade* (1968), earned some praise for its unromanticised portrayal of Victorian army life and its anti-war sentiments. The film is also notable for a strong performance from Vanessa Redgrave, Richardson's then wife. However, shortly after the release of the film, Redgrave filed for divorce, citing Jeanne Moreau in a highly publicised suit.

Richardson's *Hamlet* (1969) is 'sexed-up Shakespeare for the Sixties' in which Nicol Williamson plays a purposefully unattractive and surly Hamlet, with Marianne Faithful as a tremulous and delicate Ophelia. The film received cool reviews from critics who were unconvinced by Williamson's Hamlet and irritated by the claustrophobic use of close-ups.

Laughter in the Dark (1969) was based on Nabokov's 'Lolita' and centres on a wealthy married man (Nicol Williamson) and his obsession with a young girl (Anna Karina). His fascination leads him into mounting psychological danger, with never a thought for his 'prey'. Critics largely ignored the film, and audiences exercised their good taste by staying away from this unpleasant, sordid piece of exploitation cinema.

Ned Kelly (1970), the director's next feature, tells the story of the infamous Australian outlaw of the title. Mick Jagger turns in a splendid, understated performance as the eponymous hero and the film uses the story to explore the historic tensions between the British and the Irish, with some success. The camerawork, in complete contrast to his previous film, *Hamlet*, creates more space around the characters and allows for an appreciation of the setting and the breath-taking scenery. Despite the presence of Jagger,

Ned Kelly was not a box-office success, although critics did appreciate the film's visual style and Jagger's performance, as well as the Shel Silverstein soundtrack.

Richardson's next project took him to the United States. *A Delicate Balance* (1973) stars Katharine Hepburn, Lee Remick and Paul Scofield in the screen adaptation of the Pulitzer Prize-winning play about a highly strung Connecticut family whose friends come to stay indefinitely, causing tension and animosity. Even Hepburn's superb performance as the cranky matriarch failed to impress critics, and the film was a commercial failure.

After *Dead Cert* (1974), a thriller set in the world of horse-racing, Richardson made *Joseph Andrews* (1977) in an attempt to repeat the winning *Tom Jones* formula. Based on another of Fielding's novels, Joseph Andrews starred stalwarts of British farce Jim Dale, Michael Hordern and Beryl Reid. However, critics saw it for what it was – a some-what half-hearted attempt to cash in on the success Richardson had enjoyed over a decade earlier.

After the failure of *Joseph Andrews* and the critical lambasting Richardson received, he moved to the United States where he stayed until his death in 1991. He made a number of television movies (*A Death in Canaan* (1978), *Penalty Phase* (1986), *Shadow on the Sun* (1988) and *The Phantom of the Opera* (1990), a British-American co-production, shown in two parts). Richardson also found time to make three more features. *The Border* (1982) is notable for Jack Nicholson's portrayal of a guard on the US-Mexican border patrol who decides he has had enough of being a cog in the system; he resolves to right just one wrong by helping a young Mexican girl (Elpidia Carrillo) enter the country illegally. *Hotel New Hampshire* (1984), the tale of an eccentric Connecticut family and their extended network of in-laws, has a sparkling script and a dynamic cast – Rob Lowe, Jody Foster and Beau Bridges. Richardson's daughter Joely makes her screen debut as a waitress in the film.

The director's final film, *Blue Sky* (1994), was completed in 1991, shortly before his death that year, and released posthumously. The release was held up by the collapse of Orion who financed the film. *Blue Sky* is a fitting finale for Richardson and many crit-ics saw it as a return to his previous form. About the relationship between a military man and his family, it has a distracting political thriller sub-plot. Major Hank Marshall (Tommy Lee Jones) is an army careers officer and nuclear scientist who moves to a new base at the film's start. We soon become aware that there are serious tensions within his family caused by his wife, Carly (Jessica Lange), an unconventional, flirty, social but-terfly living in a fantasy world. Beneath her attractive and energetic kookiness lies deep emotional instability, which Hank acknowledges but does not tackle. He is punished for this as Carly begins an affair with the base commander (Powers Boothes). In order for him to pursue Carly he must dispense with Hank and sends him to monitor nuclear tests in the Nevada desert. This is where the conspiracy-theory sub-plot takes off. *Blue Sky* is a touching, sensitive film. A little unevenly directed, full of more ideas than it perhaps needs, this is part of the director's distinctive signature. Jessica Lange won a Best Actress Oscar®.

Tony Richardson's contribution to British cinema cannot be over-stated. He directed some of the landmark films of British cinema in the 1960s, brought the angry young man to the screen, pioneered Free Cinema and the British New Wave, as well as co-founding Woodfall Films, one of the most important production companies of the 1960s. Being so closely linked to the fortunes of the British industry overall, Richardson was affected by the changes that occured in the late 1960s when American finance pulled out. Along with Richard Lester, he is one of the few directors to have enjoyed the continuing support of the American studios long after their love affair with swinging London ended.   **SL**

Alan RICKMAN

The Winter Guest (1997) Alan Rickman's hawk-like face and basso profundo vowels have been employed for the last decade by Hollywood whenever 'suave English villain' has appeared in the casting notes. His rise to prominence was facilitated by his role as Bruce Willis' nemesis in *Die Hard* (1988), but he will probably be forever remembered as the Sheriff of Nottingham in Kevin Reynold's *Robin Hood: Prince of Thieves* (1991). Kevin Costner was so dismayed at what he saw as Rickman's consummate scene-stealing – the performance veers from pantomime hamminess to genuine menace – that Rickman's character was severely cut from the final film.

Born in London in 1946, despite training as a graphic designer as the Royal College of Art, a three-year stint at the Royal Academy of Dramatic Art was followed by a variety of work for the Royal Shakespeare Company. Rickman then gained critical acclaim (and a Tony nomination) on Broadway playing Valmont in 'Les Liaisons Dangereuses'. His only directing credit has been an adaptation, *The Winter Guest* (1997). After Rickman directed the play in London's West End in 1995, he teamed up with playwright Sharman McDonald and co-adapted the script for the film. Retaining Phyllida Law as the meddling Elspeth who tries to rekindle her strained relationship with her daughter Frances (played by real-life daughter Emma Thompson), the film is a confident debut by Rickman. Although *The Winter Guest* ultimately fails to break out of its stagebound origins (its Pinteresque pauses quickly grate), his portrayal of a fractured relationship set against a harsh Scottish landscape is both acutely aware of the brooding tensions and finely attuned to the cinematic possibilities of the environs. Rarely have images of ice and snow been so imbued with metaphorical resonance, while the ending, though smacking a little too much of redemption, reinforces the gentle optimism and gallows humour that stipples this confident debut and augurs well for the future.

Rickman recently returned to the stage, playing Antony in the RSC's 'Antony and Cleopatra', whilst adults and children alike are eagerly anticipating his appearance as Professor Snape in the new Harry Potter film.   **BM**

Philip RIDLEY

Born in 1960 in London, where he grew up and continues to live, Philip Ridley is a dark poet and teller of children's tales. Keenly interested in writing and drawing from an early age, he wrote and created the artwork for ten novels by the age of thirteen. He suffered through much of his childhood afflicted with asthma so severe that he was intermittently bedridden in an oxygen tent. Feeling detached from the outside world and without any close friends (his schoolmates nicknamed him 'Alien'), he found solace in comic books, his favorite being the mutant superhero group 'The X-Men'. Ridley eventually pursued formal training in the arts at the St. Martin's School of Art, where he studied painting.

The Reflecting Skin (1990)
The Passion of Darkly Noon (1995)

In the mid- to late-1980s, his focus shifted to the cinematic arts when he directed two short films, *Visiting Mr. Beak* (1987) and *The Universe of Dermot Finn* (1988), for Channel 4. His prodigious writing output did not ease, and this period marked a dense period of creative productivity for Ridley. Between the years of 1988 and 1992 – not including film-related projects – Ridley published three novels and three children's books and had two stage plays and three BBC Radio plays produced from his scripts. In the midst of this period, Ridley tasted critical acclaim for his screenplay for *The Krays* (1990), a brutal biographical tale of the British 1960s-era twin-brother gangsters, directed by Peter Medak. Ridley's feature debut as director, *The Reflecting Skin* (1990), which he also wrote, is a surreal, gothic phantasmagoria of 1950s rural America as viewed through the terrified eyes of its eight-year-old protagonist. Entirely visceral, Ridley brushes vivid, colour-saturated images of the disturbing and the beautiful. His horrific vision painfully strips the skin from the fable of childhood innocence and reveals a grotesque, fiery nightmare. Too lyrical for the horror crowd and too gut-wrenching for the art-house crowd, *The Reflecting Skin* is at times inaccessible and difficult to digest; still, Ridley's exceptional grasp of the cathartic power of cinema cannot be denied.

A fable about a troubled teen orphaned from a religious cult, again penned and directed by Ridley, *The Passion of Darkly Noon* (1995) treads similar mythic neo-American Gothic territory but cuts to more overt fairytale imagery around a perverted 'Beauty and the Beast' framework. Another surreal, visual masterpiece, Ridley continues his idiosyncratic but mesmerising emphasis on aesthetics over narrative and adds stylised film editing, non sequitur images and overstated sound effects to the mix to further advance his alluring brand of cinematic madness. He makes no apologies for his unconventional excesses, retorting 'the tyranny of being liked doesn't honestly interest me at all'.

Since 1995, Ridley has primarily focused on writing and illustrating novels for children; his ninth children's book, 'Vinegar Street', was published in 2000. He is currently working on scripts for two feature films for the British production company Kennedy-Mellor, including a film adaptation of his children's book 'Krindlekrax'. **THa**

Aileen RITCHIE

The Closer You Get (2000) After graduating from Glasgow University, Aileen Ritchie began writing for the stage and later became Artistic Director of Clyde Unity Theatre in 1990. Following a film writing course at the National Film and Television School, she wrote several shorts including *Icing on the Cake* (for BBC Scotland), *One Sunday Morning* (first screened at the 1996 Edinburgh Film Festival), *Magwana* (a 1998 Cannes Short Film award-winner), and *Drifting* (for Channel 4). In 1996 she wrote and directed the short film *Double Nougat* for BBC Scotland, which won the Herald Guardian Angle Award at the 1996 Edinburgh Film Festival. On the strength of this, Uberto Pasolini (producer of Alan Taylor's *Palookaville* (1995) and Peter Cattaneo's *The Full Monty* (1997)) approached her to direct her first full-length feature, *The Closer You Get* (2000).

The Closer You Get is a romantic comedy set in a small village on the Donegal coast. Due to a perceived shortage of eligible women, the local herd of bachelors, led by thick-headed butcher Kieran McDonagh (Ian Hart), place an advert in the Miami Herald hoping to entice American women over for their annual St Martin's Day celebrations. Unbeknownst to the men, the postmistress steams open the ad before sending it, and informs the local women of the conspiracy. The story ends in fairly predictable fashion, with the lads discovering that true love lies closer to home.

As *Sight and Sound* noted, '*The Closer You Get* is yet another innocuous provincial comedy radiating feelgood sincerity and cleanly packaged for an international audience'. Despite a strong supporting cast – including Sean McGinley, Niamh Cusack and Ruth McCabe – William Ivory's thinly-plotted screenplay is fatally afflicted by a rash of jaded stereotypes and crude 'Oirish' clichés. Robert Alazraki's cinematography is pretty but cloying, and cannot disguise the narrative vacuity. There is no doubting Aileen Ritchie's potential, but her work might be better served by engaging with more original and worthwhile material. **KHo**

Guy RITCHIE

Lock, Stock and Two Smoking Barrels (1998)
Snatch (2000) Born in Hertfordshie, UK, in 1968, Guy Ritchie entered the film industry in 1993 as a runner, and quickly moved into directing music videos and commercials. He completed a short film, *The Hard Case*, before writing and directing *Lock, Stock and Two Smoking Barrels* in 1998. The film was a box-office success, due in part to an aggressive advertising campaign, and also the effective marketing of one of its stars, well-known footballer, Vinnie Jones.

Lock, Stock and Two Smoking Barrels is set in the criminal underworld of London's East End, a world of violence, gangs, big-money card games, strip clubs and drug dealers. This subject matter and the sepia tint of the film stock hint at nostalgia, suggesting a generic referentiality to British gangster films of the 1960s and 1970s. In this respect, *Lock, Stock* sits firmly within an already established tradition of British crime films.

However, the visual style and energy of the film indicate a shift away from the social realism that has often been the dominant aesthetic of British cinema. Clearly influenced by his early career in pop videos and advertising, Ritchie uses techniques such as stop-motion photography, disorienting dissolves, and the mixing of different film stocks. Contradicting realism's tendency to render these processes invisible, like Danny Boyle's *Trainspotting* (1996), *Lock, Stock* draws attention to the image and the processes of representation. Both films also share a specific sense of the cultural moment in which they were made. The representation of gender in *Lock, Stock* is interesting within the context of 'new laddism'. Like the magazines and television programmes frequently associated with the 'movement', the film is preoccupied with the aggressive attempts of young men to reaffirm their heterosexual identity. The 'new' visual style is central to this mode of representation: the images of youthful masculinity are accompanied by spirited contemporary music; off-kilter camera angles take the point of view of the hard-drinking males; and fast cutting emphasises their energetic, forcible natures.

Ritchie's second film, *Snatch* (2000), embodies similar themes and stylistic tendencies. Like *Lock, Stock*, *Snatch* is rooted in London's violent, working-class East End. The key locale is an illegal boxing club, a predominantly masculine milieu; it provides the perfect location within which to examine the expression of working-class masculine identity.

As in the earlier film, *Snatch*'s visual style foregrounds 'newness' and youth; the soundtrack is startlingly modern and loaded with deliberate contemporary references. It is also nostalgic, however, for the atmosphere of old British crime movies, as suggested, once again, through the use of sepia-tinted film stock. Ritchie also makes cultural references that are now anachronistic. In the past, London's East End was characterised by a concentration of Jewish immigrants; by the 1960s many of these inhabitants had moved, giving way to new waves of immigrant communities from the Indian subcontinent. Centralising Jewishness as a motif in the film, *Snatch* manages to be ultra-contemporaneous whilst still nostalgically recreating the past.

The characters and the locations are unashamed stereotypes. In true postmodern style though, they are stereotypes of people and places that only ever existed in film and media of the past. Ritchie's use of such referentiality is explicit and self-aware. The audience is invited to laugh in self-conscious appreciation of the multiple layers of referential representation when an American character describes London as 'fish and chips, cup of tea, bad food, bad weather, Mary Poppins' – a stereotype describing a stereotype.

Although Ritchie's films may be viewed as culturally regressive, he has an energetic approach to film-making that challenges conventions of narrative, style and sound. It is his willingness to experiment with colour, editing and a wealth of cinematographic techniques that marks him out as an innovative director.   **ES**

Bruce ROBINSON

Bruce Robinson is an enigma. One of the most distinctive voices to emerge in the British film industry in the last twenty years, he has been practically silent in cinematic terms for the last ten. A writer equally adept at drama and comedy, he finds inspiration for both forms in the lyrical expression of his rage at the injustices of the world. He is a director for whose 'return' devotees secretly await with the fervour of the Second Coming, despite the fact that he has never managed to repeat his early success – largely thanks to the caprices of a sanitising Hollywood. He is the writer-director of one of the most original and adored British films ever, the enduring *Withnail and I* (1987), which is revered and endlessly quoted by critics and fans alike. He has never quite been able to escape its brilliant, deranged, inescapable shadow. Although *Withnail and I* is undeniably Robinson's best film, it is interesting to wonder how his career might have developed had it not garnered the level of devotion it did. Instead, he was inevitably courted by Hollywood, an industrial machine in which a warped cog like Robinson was more liable to become a spanner in the works; since his sole Hollywood feature, *Jennifer 8* (1992), flopped, and several other of his scripts were mauled beyond recognition, he has become disillusioned with the expense and restrictions of film-making, turning his attentions to the creative freedom and more reliably monomaniacal process of novel writing.

Withnail and I (1987)
How to Get Ahead in Advertising (1989)
Jennifer 8 (1992)

Born in Kent, UK, in 1946, and trained at the Central School of Speech and Drama, Robinson initially worked as an actor, appearing most notably in Zeffirelli's *Romeo and Juliet* (1968), Ken Russell's *The Music Lovers* (1971), and Truffaut's *L'Histoire d'Adele H* (1975). During this time – in the inevitable periods of 'resting' which were to recur in *Withnail and I* – Robinson began seriously writing scripts, one of which, *The Killing Fields* (1984), written for David Puttnam, was directed by Roland Joffé and eventually landed Robinson an Oscar® nomination. A buddy movie at heart, the story of an American journalist and the Cambodian aide he is forced to leave behind amidst the Khmer Rouge massacres, Robinson's script is lyrical, character-driven and moving without being manipulative. It concentrates on the intimate relationship that grows between men in the chaotic mess of war, combining astute criticism of political machination and the futility of conflict with a strong command of situation and character. Rage and outrage are the driving forces of the story, with the script treading a finely observed line between human drama and larger themes.

It is this precision of tone that really makes *Withnail and I*: the ability to combine high comedy with a rich vein of pathos; the tale of two out-of-work actors at the fag-end of the 1960s, desperate, addicted to and repulsed by their predicament, averting their eyes to avoid staring real life in the face. In a sense the film is not funny at all, a tragic story of the destruction of ideals ('they're selling hippy wigs in Woolworths, man'); of the enforced loss of love and friendship; of the search for fulfilment in an unfulfilling, divisive, and probably futile world, Hamlet's 'quintessence of dust'. But *Withnail* is, of course, undeniably, unavoidably, stomach-achingly funny, perfectly illustrating Robinson's oft-quoted mantra that comedy is really a very serious business indeed; a study in mania and desperation, a very British rejoicing in the comedy of melancholia and misanthropy, in which, crucially, Withnail and I are pathologically unable to see the joke. The delicate frisson of knowing that any moment Withnail is liable to explode into a vitriolic, bilial attack on anything and everything furthers Robinson's fascination with a world which does not see Withnail's talent, which throws problems in his way, and which cussedly refuses to answer for itself. The 'I' character – actually called Marwood in the script – is the touchstone from whose point-of-view the film is largely seen, the passive rock against which Withnail breaks his head, and who grounds the grotesquerie of the other characters – predatory homosexual uncles, panda-eyed dope dealers and vindictive farmers. The film is essentially a rites-of-passage story: Withnail and Marwood retreat to the country, forced to grow up from adolescent, self-obsessive agonising into a world of real hurt, as Withnail the consummate actor, striker of theatrical poses and played-at emotions, finds himself confronted by the real thing at the film's conclusion. Robinson's camera also contrasts the squalid degeneracy of their London life with the natural beauty of Yorkshire that exposes their vulnerability and mutual dependency. But it is the magic script, half-hysterical, half-lyrical, and the fine degree of pathos, that make this such a precise and involving fable of love, mania and loss – while the Hamlet overtones, particularly the final, brilliantly apposite soliloquy delivered to the wolves at London Zoo – 'Man delights not me; no, nor woman neither' – add an extra poignancy to the complexity of the central relationship.

How to Get Ahead in Advertising (1989) is just as angry, and often just as funny, but lacks the same charm due to its more overtly political agenda. A critique of the advertising industry and consumer culture, the film follows Bagley, an ad executive whose cut-and-thrust, money-hungry lifestyle drives him to the point of madness. The development of an evil talking boil may or may not be the product of his overactive imagination in the throes of nervous breakdown. The same command of comic scenes is there – Bagley destroying every trace of advertising in his house rivals Withnail drinking lighter fluid for hysterical, manic glee. The script is just as sharp in its targets, revelling in the potential of Bagley's battle with his pustulous alter-ego as a source of comic mishap. Again, rage and disgust are Robinson's motivations; rage at the manipulativeness of the ad-men, disgust that we let ourselves be manipulated by them; the attempt to make a stand against the overwhelming injustice of the world, the madness and frustration at the wrongness of it all are, as in Withnail, the keys to Bagley's story. The capacity for hysteria and psychotic episodes might also be a key to Robinson's. The final polemic speech about the corruption of Thatcherite Britain, as well as the dreadfully made prosthetic boil, are particularly hard to accept. Fascinating, but very strange, the film lacks the glorious subtlety and lyrical edge that distinguished *Withnall and I*.

Driven abroad largely by the lack of financial support for film-making in Britain, *Jennifer 8* (1992), the only Hollywood feature Robinson has directed, marks a return to the serious, character-driven territory of *The Killing Fields*. It is a serial-killer thriller about a hard-boiled cop digging into the murky past of small-town Eureka, California, and his growing relationship with the sole witness, a blind woman, and an inscrutable FBI observer. Strikingly filmed, with particular focus on the metaphorical waste and decay of the town – witness the rain-soaked opening on a rubbish dump – the film again displays Robinson's understanding of character and dialogue. Also in evidence is his fascination with modes of self-denial and self-corruption. The film feels straightjacketed, however, and Robinson's fluency is strangled by the constraints of a generic format and an oppressive Hollywood regime. The film dived and Robinson, disgusted by the whole affair, turned his back on directing.

Other Hollywood screenplays have showed little trace of his distinctive voice; *Fat Man and Little Boy* (1989), a pot-boiler about atomic bombs, *Return to Paradise* (1998), about western travellers imprisoned for drugs possessions in Malaysia, and *In Dreams* (1998), a serial-killer film involving second sight, did moderate business but were, in Robinson's words, 'artistic disasters'. The voice, however, is gloriously manifest in Robinson's 1998 novel, 'The Peculiar Memories of Thomas Penman', a wonderfully written fable of – in his own words – 'a boy and his grandpa, life and death, sex and hate, dog's meat and cancer. It is also … about love'. Hopefully, the lunatic gaze will turn again to cinema; until then, as Withnail – and Hamlet – might say: 'The rest is silence'.

OB

Franc RODDAM

Born in 1946, Franc Roddam's greatest achievement as a director remains the youth culture classic *Quadrophenia* (1979). A dramatisation of the rock opera by The Who, the film betrays the narrative limitations of its origins, but Roddam's direction stands out as the element that keeps its considerable energies in check. These energies are the problem with the film; bequeathed no more than a skeleton storyline by the original concept album, co-writer Roddam has to use all of his imaginative talent to negotiate the problem of translating protagonist Jimmy's primal generational rebellion into something more substantial. Successfully rooted in the period feel of mid-1960s London and Brighton, the mod context nevertheless fails to provide the kind of social background against which Jimmy's rage could be understood and evaluated. This is not the conceptual territory of Stanley Kubrick's *A Clockwork Orange* (1971). Jimmy's drama of self-identity may be played out around the same dramatic fixtures – parents, crime, drugs and tribal mentality – but the sense of a brutal society sowing the seed of discord in its youth is entirely absent. A few cardboard reactionary figures aside, the drama is confined to Jimmy's circle. The film is all the better for this concentration of its resources on the mod subculture, giving an unflinching picture of how the glorious camaraderie is based not in genuine fraternity but in the details of a style: the right haircuts, Levi's, scooter and records. That this style is appropriated in the first place from black America renders the casual racism of Jimmy and his friends all the more ironic.

Arguably, the film runs out of steam when Jimmy veers from the gang path and the focus tightens on his emotional struggles. A promising subtext that links the schizophrenia alluded to in the title with Jimmy's family history comes to nothing – Roddam crafts an astute visual emblem of the film's title in a shot where Jimmy's reflection is splintered into the four mirrors affixed to the front of his scooter. Yet the final images of Jimmy tearing along the edge of the cliffs on his bike are exhilarating, redeeming some of the narrative rawness. The film remains in currency as a marker of British youth culture (as its 1997 re-release as *Quadrophenia: A Way of Life* suggested), and Roddam deserves credit for introducing a generation of working-class British actors to the public. Phil Daniels, Ray Winstone and Phil Davis have all gone on to produce fine work in television and film.

Roddam's subsequent cinema work has been rather overshadowed by his strong debut. With military conspiracy thriller *The Lords of Discipline* (1982), he attempted his first American production; fans of Pat Conroy's novel declared themselves frustrated by his interpretation. The plot involves cadet David Keith stumbling across a secret society controlling physical and racial abuse in a respected military school.

Roddam returned to Britain for a reworking of the Frankenstein legend, *The Bride* (1985). Notable for its bizarre lead casting – Sting as the Baron and Jennifer Beals, fresh from *Flashdance* (1983), stepping into Elsa Lanchester's shoes as the Bride – the film can be commended for seeking inspiration from the James Whale/Universal horror classics rather than contemporaneous slasher/schlock formulas. For horror fans in the 1980s, though, the histrionic love story of *The Bride* seemed too much.

Portmanteau movies are risky propositions for even the biggest film-makers, and the much-hyped and rather pretentious *Aria* (1987) suffers from the usual wild variation in quality. However, Roddam's contribution to this collection of operatic arias visually interpreted by name directors is arguably the finest segment in cinematic terms, and in no way inferior to the muddled contributions of heavy-hitters Robert Altman, Nic Roeg and Jean-Luc Godard. Inspired by Wagner's 'Tristan and Isolde', from which Roddam's musical selection 'Liebestod' is extracted), it stars Bridget Fonda as one of a pair of star-crossed lovers. A short and affecting piece, it uses an evocative Las Vegas backdrop to ironically reflect upon the folly of love.

Roddam's most recent cinematic outing is the mountaineering drama *K2* (1991), starring James Cameron favourite Michael Biehn. Generally praised for its breathtaking vistas of Pakistan and British Columbia, the film is equally condemnable for its indulgence in climbing-as-the-route-to-self-knowledge cliché. Whether Roddam, never truly comfortable on genre territory, has lived up to the raw, early promise of *Quadrophenia* is debatable; he has worked more fruitfully in television, acting as deviser and executive producer of British series 'Making Out', a factory-set comedy-drama that was equal parts Alan Bleasedale and 'Coronation Street'. Recently, he has directed versions of 'Moby Dick' and 'Cleopatra' for US television.   **MF**

Nicolas ROEG

Performance (1970) Born in London in 1928, Nicolas Roeg is one of the most visually inventive directors
Walkabout (1971) of contemporary British cinema. A former cinematographer (he photographed films for
Don't Look Now (1973) directors including François Truffaut (*Fahrenheit 451* (1966)) and Richard Lester (*Petu-*
The Man Who Fell to Earth lia (1968)), he has produced a body of work over three decades that has both compelled
(1976) and confounded film critics. Intrigued by the possibilities of disrupting the way we think
Bad Timing (1980) about temporality, Roeg has described cinema as a 'time machine'. His use of editing to
Eureka (1982) challenge received notions of the relationship between past, present and future is daring
Insignificance (1985) and provocative, although he has been criticised for his refusal to adhere to linear nar-
Aria (segment, 1987) rative structures. While his detractors complain that his work is pretentious and often
Castaway (1987) incoherent, cinephiles admire his undisputed mastery of montage and mise-en-scène.
Track 29 (1988) Experimental and unpredictable, Roeg's body of work explores the themes of sex and
The Witches (1990) death in often uncomfortable ways. Frequently set against a supernatural backdrop, his
Cold Heaven (1992) films push against the boundaries of fantasy and reality, exploiting cinema's potential as
Two Deaths (1995) a dream text made up of clues and images.
Hotel Paradise (1995)   *Performance* (1970) marked Roeg's sensational feature debut. Co-written and co-directed by artist Donald Cammell, this cult favourite features Mick Jagger in his first film role. 'Even the bath water's dirty,' a shocked Warner Bros. was reported to say upon viewing the psychedelic drug scenes, the homoeroticism and the gender bending. Made in 1968, the film was shelved for two years. Set in 1960s London, Chas Devlin (James Fox) is a performer (a hired killer) on the run from gangsters. He hides out in the basement of the house of reclusive rock star Turner (Jagger), whereupon he becomes embroiled in a series of complex and ultimately murderous identity games with Turner and his two girlfriends, Pherber (Anita Pallenberg) and Lucy (Michele Breton).

Australia is the site of Roeg's first solo effort, the acclaimed *Walkabout* (1971). When their father inexplicably kills himself in the middle of the Australian outback, two English children (played by Jenny Agutter and Luc Roeg, the director's son) are stranded. The film tracks one of Roeg's main thematic interests: the conflict between nature and civilisation. To its credit, it attempts to avoid any easy resolution of this age-old dispute, although at times it does succumb to obvious messages about the inherent goodness of Aboriginal life, as represented by the young boy who helps the children, and the corruptness of the modern city. Although the film's extended zooms and freeze frames may appear somewhat dated, its photography of the outback – seething with lizards, scorpions, kangaroos and birds – is stunning. Another point of interest is the subtle but powerful exploration of the sexual tension between the girl and the Aborigine. In one noteworthy scene, which occasioned considerable controversy at the time for its full frontal nude footage of a 17-year-old Jenny Agutter, the English girl swims nude in a lush natural pool.

Don't Look Now (1973), based on a Daphne du Maurier short story, is Roeg's masterpiece. Shot in Venice, and starring a young Donald Sutherland and Julie Christie as bereaved parents, this haunting, complex and enigmatic film deals with death, loss and memory. Arguably the best of his films at expressing the portent of the otherworldly, it is pervaded by a powerful sense of foreboding and doom. It contains one of the most famous love scenes ever filmed. Roeg presents scenes of the couple getting undressed (taking showers, brushing teeth) and intercuts images of their passionate sex with scenes of them getting changed and ready for an evening out. The scandalously explicit nature of the scene led to rumours that Sutherland and Christie had become carried away during filming.

The Man Who Fell to Earth (1976), featuring a perfectly-cast David Bowie, is the second of Roeg's films to feature a major rock star. The beautifully photographed Bowie plays the role of an alien who comes to earth searching for water for his drought-stricken planet in this unusual and confusing film. Despite its striking visuals, it is too self-indulgent, sacrificing a coherent narrative in favour of lyrical images. Continuing to explore his fascination with intercut sex scenes, in contrast to the inventiveness of *Don't Look Now*, the film's images of love-making seem gratuitous and contrived.

Bad Timing (1980) is a penetrating and mesmerising study of obsessive love between two Americans in Vienna. Focusing on a police investigation into the attempted suicide of Milena (Theresa Russell), the story is told largely in flashback as a police detective (Harvey Keitel) interrogates the suspected Dr Linden (Art Garfunkel). Drawing complex parallels between psychoanalysis and the law, the film is a sustained exploration of memory and guilt. A well-edited, intelligent film, *Bad Timing* nonetheless fails to convey any human intimacy or sympathy for its characters. Its portrayal of a sexual relationship is perhaps one of the most pessimistic of contemporary cinema. Shortly after the filming of *Bad Timing*, Roeg married Theresa Russell, who subsequently starred in his less well-received films of the 1980s (the couple have since divorced).

As is the case with many of Roeg's later films, *Eureka* (1982) met with serious distribution problems; shelved by its studio, this rather pretentious film had a limited release in 1985. *Aria* (1987), described as 'the first MTV version of opera', brings together ten short pieces by ten different directors (including Robert Altman and Ken Russell). Roeg's vision of Verdi's 'Un Ballo in Maschera' stars Theresa Russell, made up as a man, in a story based on the attempted assassination of King Rog of Albania in 1931. Recalling the visual brilliance of *Walkabout*, Roeg's 1987 film, *Castaway*, with Oliver Reed and newcomer Amanda Donohoe, contains extraordinary footage of Turin, the setting for this story about a couple who live on a desert island for a year. *Track 29* (1988), while a seriously flawed picture, is nonetheless the most interesting and thought-provoking of this period of Roeg's career. Dennis Potter's script makes a fascinating match with Roeg's direction and the film is preoccupied with the blurring of the uncertain boundaries between the real and the imagined. Like many of Roeg's films, it openly invites psycho-analytic commentary.

The Witches (1990), based on a book by Roald Dahl, is Roeg's first children's film. The last feature film to be produced by the late Jim Henson, *The Witches* is the most straightforward of Roeg's films to date, and also one of the most entertaining. With superb performances from Anjelica Huston as the Grand High Witch, and Mai Zetterling as the grandmother, the film is instantly absorbing. Like all great children's films, it is directed at both adults and youngsters, with a humorous but quite sinister story about a young boy's attempt to save the world's children from the horrible fate of being turned into mice by witches.

Unfortunately, the films that have followed in the 1990s have not been nearly so fresh or inventive. Pursuing Roeg's ongoing fascination with sex and death, *Cold Heaven* (1992), his adaptation of Brian Moore's novel, is a supernatural thriller that attempts to match the Gothic intensity of *Don't Look Now*. Although the first half of the film is gripping, the frankly outrageous conclusion lacks the subtle, more haunting force of Roeg's earlier work.

Two Deaths (1995) is a pretentious, over-plotted story of obsessive lust and violence set against the background of civil unrest in Romania during 1989. The little-seen *Hotel Paradise* (1995) is a short film about a soon-to-be-married woman (Theresa Russell) who wakes up in bed with a chained and naked stranger. She remembers nothing and the stranger begins to tell her what happened last night. An erotic tale, the film is indicative of the disappointing direction Roeg's film-making has taken in recent years, with an increasing turn to the production of straight-to-video soft-core porn releases such as *Full Body Massage* (1995). **TH**

Bernard ROSE

Few as they are, all of Bernard Rose's major films are marked by a memorable stylish-ness. Born in 1960, a graduate of Britain's National Film and Television School, he was the winner of a BBC award for young film-makers as a teenager. After directing a televi-sion movie and his first features, Body Contact (1987) and Paperhouse (1988), he went on to release his first notable international film, Chicago Joe and the Showgirl, in 1990. It stars Kiefer Sutherland as a World War Two soldier stationed in London who falls into committing petty crimes and murder with a British tart, played by Emily Lloyd. Although not marked by the same audacity as Immortal Beloved (1994), or even a consistent spark of energy and creativity, critics did take note of the film's unusually stylised violence.

Based on a Clive Barker story, Rose's next feature, Candyman (1992), had the mis-fortune of being released during a period in which the gory horror film was out of fashion. However, in Rose's hands, Candyman turned out to be a few steps above some of the horror genre's popular predecessors that were spawned in the 1980s. In fact, his care-ful pace and build up to the first appearance of Candyman, as well as the reverence for urban myths to create genuine chills, suggests that Rose has more in common with Val Lewton than Wes Craven. The film's decidedly adult female protagonist, played by Virginia Madsen, provided a refreshing change from the empty-headed bimbos who have been carved into slabs of meat by movie monsters Freddy Krueger, Jason Vorhees, and the like. While the movie certainly delivers the gory goods – a necessity of the genre's conventions – Rose injects a style that is more indicative of a personal touch. With the rich, evocative score by Philip Glass, the washed-out cinematography – depicting the urban projects and the appearances of Candyman with equal dread – and the plot that has its roots as much in urban film noir as it does the horror genre, Candyman is raised well above the level of a B-movie production. It is a testament to Rose's talent that he could turn stock material into something fresh, unique and absolutely terrifying.

Moody, evocative and stylish are the three words that best describe Rose's biopic of Ludwig van Beethoven, Immortal Beloved. Centred around the fictional mystery of an unknown woman who inspired furious passion in Beethoven the man and his music, the film is a psychological study of Beethoven as played by Gary Oldman. Rather than follow a conventional biographical telling of the composer's life in strict linear fashion from one year to the next, Rose brings a mystical sense of wonder and mystery to the story. Aided immeasurably by Oldman's ferocious performance, Rose paints a portrait of Beethoven not simply as a conflicted artist – like Van Gogh in Lust for Life (1956) – but as a tragic man unable to hear his own passion for life that is so evident in his music.

Adapted from Leo Tolstoy' novel, Anna Karenina (1997) is Rose's most recent pic-ture, starring Sophie Marceau, Sean Bean and Alfred Molina. With a visual style influ-enced by high-class British television productions, Rose fuses the visual beauty of the film with energetic and ravishing musical motifs based on Tchaikovsky's 'Pathetique' Symphony. His next feature is another Tolstoy adaptation: an update of 'The Death of Ivan Ilyitch', entitled Ivansxtc (2000), which is made by the rules of the Dogme 95 Manifesto. It has yet to garner a major release. Quoted as saying, 'Film is dead. Long live cinema,' this visually evocative film-maker is set to be an important proponent of the digital media. **SM**

Benjamin ROSS

Born in London in 1964, it was after graduating from New York's Columbia University in 1991 that Benjamin Ross (along with playwright Jeff Rawle) came up with the idea for The Young Poisoner's Handbook (1995). The film is based on the life of Graham Young who was sent to Broadmoor in 1962 (aged 14) after he poisoned his family. Released for 'no longer being a danger', he began his poisoning spree again. The narrative follows this path – Young is played with verve and panache by Hugh O'Conor – and where the film succeeds is in its expert melding of gruesome horror and pitch-black wit. Coming across as a hybrid of Kind Hearts and Coronets (1949) and Roald Dahl's 'George's Marvellous Medicine', the film scores in its telling evocation of 1970s domestic kitsch, while also poking fun at the medical establishment, incarnated here by a befuddled Antony Sher.

It displays the kind of control of tone and sureness one associates with directors such as John Waters or Peter Jackson, and whilst Ross still has some way to go before joining those celebrators of kitsch kitchen-sink horror, there are some impressive visual and narrative flourishes.

Ross' recent television movie, *RKO 281* (1999), is worthy of mention, not least for its attempt to demythologise the making of *Citizen Kane* (1941) and to get under the skin of the enfant terrible Orson Welles. Under the aegis of Ridley Scott and HBO, the film recounts the making of the film – 'RKO 281' was its working title because Welles did not want to draw the attention of William Randolph Hearst. The film is part history lesson, part film-about-film, and the starry cast (Liev Schreiber, John Malkovich, Roy Scheider) lend extra gravitas to Ross' kinetic and caustic tale.

Ross is scheduled to direct *Jack Sheppard and Jonathan Wild*, starring Harvey Keitel and Tobey Maguire as the eponymous eighteenth-century London bandits.   **BM**

Tim ROTH

Born in London, England, in 1961, Tim Roth has been astonishing audiences with his *The War Zone* (1999) gutsy, on-screen performances since the early 1980s. Using his extensive experiences to inform his directorial debut, he created a work of harrowing intensity, *The War Zone* (1999), an incest drama that has garnered international praise and awards.

Adapted by Alexander Stuart from his novel of the same name, *The War Zone* focuses on a seemingly typical family that has recently moved from London to an isolated Devon home. Essentially a four-person piece – Ray Winstone (Dad), Tilda Swinton (Mum), and newcomers Lara Belmont (Jessie) and Freddie Cunliffe (Tom) – it juxtaposes wide, art-house landscapes with microscopic familial relationships, each fraught with an unsettling sexual tension. Tom, a 15-year-old boy trying to come to terms with his own burgeoning sexuality and place within the family, is the audience's guide into the story. He is often set apart, shown alone and idle until the climax, at which point he is compelled to take action against his father. Avoiding movie-of-the-week cliché, often eschewing loudness for silence, Roth's depiction of incest is all the more distressing. The film is murky. Everyone here is exposed – all manner of naked, ambiguous flesh – but impossible to see; Roth keeps it dark, literally and figuratively. Throughout, his camera is still and wide as a window; his mise-en-scène is never about judgement or even explanation, but rather quiet observation. This is most notable during the rape scene set in a bunker: the frame encompasses two gun turrets lit like eyes, impassively watching the horror in front of them. Rather than end the film neatly, Roth finishes with a question from Tom: 'What are we gonna do?' With that, the bunker door is closed, and Roth and his camera are gone.   **DHo**

Simon RUMLEY

Although it failed to secure a full theatrical release, *Strong Language* (1998), the debut *Strong Language* (1998) feature of writer-director-editor Simon Rumley, was auspicious enough to secure an *The Truth Game* (2000) extended run at London's National Film Theatre and announce the arrival of an ambitious and industrious new talent.

Hampered by a low budget, in this case necessity proved to be the mother of invention; Rumley's intelligent editing and unusual aesthetics make the film an evocative, if acquired, taste. A zeitgeist, fragmented look at the assembled lives of various, disparate London misfits, marooned in the cultural wasteland of the late 1990s, *Strong Language* utilises a vérité approach, having the characters address the camera directly on subjects such as sex, politics, money and movies. At times wayward and off-target – the naturalistic performances vary wildly in quality – it is driven by a sense of urgency, and the result is undeniably funny, ambitious and perceptive.

Strong Language was to prove the first of a trilogy of films marked by intensity and a quest for emotional honesty. *The Truth Game* (2000), the second part, treads a similar path, albeit with slightly diminishing effect. Showcased at the NFT after UK distributors failed to pick it up, it similarly focuses on the raw reality of the relationships between six twenty-somethings as hostility begins to gnaw at the fragile fabric of their friendship.

By turns repellent, egotistical and charmless, Rumley's film exposes the ugliness that underpins their lives with a cinematic style that makes up in directness what it lacks in subtlety. The performances are of a markedly higher quality, but the viewing experience in general feels slightly second-hand.

Club Le Monde, featuring Danny Nussbaum (Tim in *TwentyFourSeven* (1997)) and purporting to be an exploration of club culture, is currently in production and will complete the trilogy.   **JWo**

Ken RUSSELL

Madness, sex, death, power, Christianity and classical music – a fair summation of the obsessions of one of Britain's most obsessive directors, Ken Russell; an abrasive, provocative iconoclast with a lunatic streak, the self-styled enfant terrible of British cinema who declared himself 'unbankable' in a recent South Bank Show. There is no mistaking a Ken Russell film. 'The Russell treatment' is a favoured phrase of both disparaging reviewers and eager video-sleeve copywriters, equally capable of expressing admiration or disgust depending on its context. Whatever the standpoint, it acknowledges Russell as a unique stylist, an individual cinematic voice which is, if nothing else, inimitable and unmistakable. Brash, garish, loud, frequently maniacal, sometimes shocking and frequently hilarious, Russell has been forever marked by the films he made in the 1970s. Deliberately provocative and heavily mannered works such as *Women in Love* (1969), *The Music Lovers* (1971) and *The Devils* (1971) are heady concoctions of sex and psychodrama. They showcase his style – a broad, gaudy combination of directorial flourish, overblown performance and lurid, sledgehammer imagery; skulls, crucifixes and scantily clad women are de rigueur Russell.

Slated by critics, disregarded by the public, and despised by penny-counting studios, Russell's inability to rein in or adapt his approach to anything less than high-pitched hysteria has ironically enslaved him to a style which was genuinely groundbreaking and revolutionary in its day, challenging the accepted standards of BBC-dominated film-making. He is a bombastic pioneer whose steady degeneration into unimaginative genre flops in the 1980s and 1990s has conveniently placed him back on the shelf, safely out of harm's way. Certainly histrionic, definitely excessive, pathologically unsubtle and quite possibly unhinged, Ken Russell – whatever one's opinion of his work – is a true original.

In Russell's self-made television autobiography, *A British Picture* (1989), the child Russell is fascinated by the process of film-making from an early age, gleefully projecting classic films to friends and family as the bombs of the Blitz fall all around, making short films with borrowed cameras and appropriated funds. Mixing fantasy, film homage and rosy-tinted biography, it is one of Russell's most successful films of the 1980s. It demonstrates a restrained return to his documentary roots whose low budget (and close-to-home subject) steers him away from visual excess into more imaginative use of camera and editing, a trend often upheld throughout his career.

Born in 1927 in Southampton, UK, following stints in the Merchant Navy, the RAF, as a dancer in the Ny Norsk Ballet, and an actor in the Garrick Players, Russell became a freelance still photographer for various illustrated magazines. He produced several short amateur films during this time, inspired by early heroes Cocteau, Murnau and Eisenstein: *Peepshow* (1956), *Amelia and the Angel* (1957) and *Lourdes* (1958). Experimental fables, they preface Russell's interest in creating mood and psychological state through a combination of image, music and editing.

Russell freelanced for the BBC over the next ten years, mostly for the groundbreaking flagship BBC arts series 'Monitor', directing many documentary films, most notably his profiles of classical composers, which are his only real area of expertise outside cinema. The films show an early desire to break the restrictive boundaries of the format within which he was working. The documentary and biopic, hitherto staid variations of factual, received pronunciation reporting, in Russell's grasp became much more expressive and visually arresting platforms for giving a sense of the creative and personal context from which art springs. *Prokofiev* (1961) and *Elgar* (1962), while still framed by an explanatory voice-over, used impressionist reconstruction and stylised editing to underpin the musical score, to give a sense of historical and emotional origin as well as the straight facts. *The Debussy Film* (1963) similarly uses an unusual narrative framework, a 'film within a film', in which the actors play actors trying to reconstruct Debussy's life, a technique echoed in *Looking for Richard* (1996) over thirty years later. Other subjects included Bartok, Délius, Strauss and Isadora Duncan. The constraints of funds and medium actually forced Russell into creating some of his most original and interesting work.

Russell made his film debut while he was still working largely in television. *French Dressing* (1963), a slapstick farce pitched somewhere between Jacques Tati and the American-style buffoonery of Keaton, Lloyd and The Keystone Kops, aims to satirise the St Tropez-French Riviera scene by relocating it to Gormleigh-on-Sea, with direction more reminiscent of Benny Hill than Buster Keaton. *Billion Dollar Brain* (1969) was another experiment, the third instalment of the successful Harry Palmer series, overseen by Bond producer Harry Salzman and starring Michael Caine, intended as a calling card with which to fund the Tchaikovsky biopic Russell had been planning for some time. A genre spy story pitting a megalomaniac against ex-secret agent Palmer, the subject says little about the director. Its treatment – gaudy and loud, with a dash of smut and violence, and plenty of late-1960s style – was perhaps a hint of things to come, but proved too much for regular Palmer fans, who deserted in their droves. Lacking the big-bucks negotiating power he had hoped for, Russell's next film was initially another hack job, a contract script he accepted to facilitate other things. It was some time before he read the source novel on which the script was based, and realised that he had found the ideal platform from which to proclaim his distinctive vision to the film-making world.

Women in Love (1969), along with his two following films, is the exemplar of Russell's burgeoning style and intention. Frustrated by the bland uniformity of the majority of British film-making, and inspired by the controversy his television experiments had caused, his new vocation was to shock. He wanted to explore the outermost reaches of taste, acceptability and censure, to provoke and enrage. This strain of self-aggrandisement, the sense of an imposed directorial personality that runs through all his films, makes for uneasy viewing. One cannot help but suspect that the more outrageous scenes, the more gratuitous directorial touches and the often ludicrously high nipple count are present for purposes that have little to do with narrative. Nevertheless, these three films show some of Russell's best direction, particularly his skill in marrying music and score with action, and his rich ability to create striking cinematic image. The grandiloquence, the bombast and the ludicrously overblown style are all tempered here by a tangible desire to deliver something new, different and exciting.

Women in Love is based quite faithfully on the D.H. Lawrence novel which in its day was far more controversial than its film version could ever hope to be. A steamy, sensuous exploration of sexuality, juxtaposing two love affairs which inevitably wreak emotional havoc and self-destruction, the film sees Russell in full homo-erotic flow, drawing parallels between various states of passion and obsession and the omnipresent danger of crossing over into violence, destruction and delusion. Lavishly produced, with some fascinating non-verbal narrative scenes using only sound, music and image to progress the psychological content of the story, the film is also a restrained and intelligent re-invention of the period drama whose immediacy and contemporary verve was rightly admired, earning Russell an Academy Award nomination. The film also contained one of the most infamous scenes in cinema history – the fire-side wrestling scene between Alan Bates and Oliver Reed, nude, sweaty and a sensational word-of-mouth selling point around which, as in many other Russell films, a whole bible of myths has sprung up.

The link between sexuality and creativity, and the concurrent potential of passion spilling over into madness, is more fully explored in *The Music Lovers* (1971). Russell's long-held pet project, a biopic of Tchaikovsky, which he was finally able to direct following the commercial success of *Women in Love*, was secured with a pitch famously quoted as 'the nymphomaniac meets the homosexual'. Following Tchaikovsky from his early days as a struggling composer through to his eventual death from drinking cholera-contaminated water, the film is perhaps, along with *The Devils*, the best example of Russell's cinematic style. Three key sequences demonstrate his work at its lunatic best. The virtuoso opening, dominated by long pull-backs and tracking shots, punctuated by quick edits to focus on the story's key characters, is set entirely to Tchaikovsky's music. As the camera swoops, various images hint at the content to come, a kind of overture to the story. It is a Bacchic society, dominated by rampant sexuality, grotesquerie and death – a drunken woman being leered over by soldiers, masked revellers and various other pagan symbols – and a thinly-disguised undercurrent of hysteria, through which Tchaikovsky moves aloof and estranged. Two other key scenes – as Tchaikovsky performs at the Conservatoire and Russell cuts between the various major influences on his life, and the psychotic sequence following Tchaikovsky's abandonment by his patron – similarly demonstrate Russell's attempt to use music and image to evoke emotional states. In context it is a gleefully indulgent perspective and style of storytelling which few directors would have the nerve to produce. Other sections – a sub-Freudian train sequence in which Tchaikovsky is forced to confront his sexuality by the naked figure of his wife rolling around the compartment for example – demonstrate cod psychology of an embarrassing order. It contains the best and worst of the Russell vision.

The relationship of creativity, sexuality and madness are accompanied in *The Devils* (1971) by Russell's other obsession – religion, or more specifically, Christianity. Based on an Aldous Huxley novel, the film is Russell's most infamous work; widely banned, denounced by the Festival of Light and deplored by critics. It is the source of some of the most notorious rumours, including allegations of sexual assault of female extras, devil worship and on-set intercourse during filming. In reality, the film is Russell's only truly disturbing work, a dark, downbeat film in which a convent of nuns in seventeenth-century France, goaded by their sexually repressed hunchback Mother Superior, become obsessed by a charismatic priest, Grandier. They accuse him of black magic, for which he is eventually burned by a team of Catholic exorcists. It is a parable of power, both of the manipulation of doctrine by Church representatives and the ineffectual whims of royal favour, and a moral tale of the impossibility of denying physical desires – Grandier's healthy sexuality, naturally filmed, is contrasted with the austere interiors of the white-tiled convent. The film carries all the Russell trademarks. Phantasmagoria is best demonstrated in the hysterical possession scenes as naked nuns career around the convent, wailing, crying and blowing raspberries, and the 'purging' of the Mother Superior, filmed in a white-tiled cell to look like 'a rape in a public lavatory'. The visuals, particularly the lavish Derek Jarman sets and bludgeoning Gothic imagery, are striking. There are also moments of pure Jacobean farce – protestants dressed as blackbirds used for target practice, an overacting Torquemada, and a rampantly homosexual King Louis. The result is the ultimate Russell sensory overload, an assault on the senses and sensibilities quite unlike anything before or since, a bloody, fiery grotesque whose sheer lunacy the director would never equal.

By now, the Russell image was fixed in the public imagination: a controversial, declamatory director of excess, tramping the outer limits of sex, surrealism and fantasy in search of the next sensational story with which to raise the hackles of conservatism. His fascinations were to continue through his films of the 1970s, but never with the incendiary force of his early works. *The Boy Friend* (1971) was an artistic disaster of some measure. It is a pastiche of British musical theatre in the 1920s, with heavy-handed attempts at show-tune satire, extravagant dream sequences, and a leaden Busby Berkeley treatment, although the contrast of Twiggy as an impressionable young ingénue with the sleazy glitz and glitter all around is intriguing. *Savage Messiah* (1972), another art film both in subject and treatment, follows the heady relationship of young sculptor Gaudier with older author Sophie Brzeska. Intense and dislocated, evocatively filmed by Derek Jarman, it again examines Russell's interest in the correlation between sexuality and the compulsion to create, and the waves the angry young artist causes in polite Edwardian society. *Mahler* (1974) is a return to the low-budget biopics of Russell's BBC days, interpreting the composer's works through a series of set-piece scenes from his life, treated with customary Russell exclamation.

The next two films foregrounded the figure of the creative martyr, with both starring Roger Daltrey as an obvious Messiah figure. *Tommy* (1975), another key Russell film, is the big-screen version of the seminal The Who rock opera: the story of the deaf, dumb and blind kid who becomes a pinball wizard, gains global fame, and rescues the world through music. Grandiose, symbol-ridden and incomprehensible, but blessed with a soundtrack of genius, the subject was ideal fare for Russell. He duly gave it the full 'treatment' – post-war austerity exploding into psychedelia, Daltrey racing through technicolour skies, baths of baked beans, and a plethora of over-the-top performances from its all-star cast. *Lisztomania* (1975) was a blatant attempt to repeat the formula, but employed Rick Wakeman to rearrange Wagner and Liszt into a poor relation of the rock opera which had preceded it. This was a career low, from all points of view.

With the American revolution in 1970s cinema continuing apace, producing contemporary, hard-hitting stories under the technical guidance and narrative innovation of Scorsese, Coppola et al., Russell's visual style was beginning to look dreadfully out of date. What had seemed exciting and different at the start of the decade now seemed woefully overwrought, a grotesque and flabby Huguenot compared with the lean and hungry feel of *Taxi Driver* (1976) or the psychotic grandeur of *Apocalypse Now* (1979). Contemporary British directors like Nic Roeg had produced intelligent, stylish works that lacked Russell's pretentious and patronising tone. Bluster and bombast, tits and titillation, were not enough to satisfy audiences anymore, and Russell was struggling to keep up.

Valentino (1977) tried to win back audiences with the promise of the sexual antics of the eponymous hero; although unusually controlled, a dreadful performance from its recalcitrant star, Rudolf Nureyev, and various regurgitated Russell mannerisms leave the film feeling like a seedy and hollow stab at tabloid exposé. *Altered States* (1980) essentially sealed his fate with the story of a maverick scientist whose experiments with sensory deprivation backfire, cueing a multitude of hallucinogenic glimpses beyond the cosmic pale. A cynical attempt to cash in on the sci-fi trend and blockbuster mentality set in motion by *Star Wars* (1977) and *Close Encounters of the Third Kind* (1977), and afforded a massive budget, the film allowed Russell to indulge every deluded fantasy he could imagine. Multi-eyed goat-men are crucified and massed hordes undergo eternal torment in fiery pits. Ridiculous, hilarious, and lacking even a tentative grounding in plausible story, the film bombed spectacularly, taking the best part of Russell's career with it.

Over the ensuing years, Russell continued to direct, achieving sporadic successes such as *Crimes of Passion* (1984), an engaging sex thriller reminiscent of David Cronenberg's *Crash* (1997) in its use of gloom, doom and perversion in the neon glare of modern life. Mostly he has produced derivative and unimaginative rehashes of earlier successes. Adolescent sub-mythological horrors like *Gothic* (1986) and *The Lair of the White Worm* (1988) employed the woefully clichéd imagery and hysterical acting style which represent his worst. Passable period pieces like *Salomé's Last Dance* (1988) and *The Rainbow* (1988) hark back to *Women in Love* with a faint hint of sauce and sleazy psychology. *Whore* (1991), a deliberately unglamorous exploration of the seamy world of street prostitution, desperately tries to recapture a controversial edge but manages only to be vaguely unpleasant. The sense of unpredictability that drives his early films, of firing off in every direction, of a world that, like its director, might at any minute spin gloriously and dangerously out of control, has been reduced, ironically, to crushingly predictable formula.

Russell apparently plans to reinvent his career by making his new films 'irresistible' to internet users; this could translate as cramming in as much salacious sexual content as the average breathy adolescent can handle. Quite how the early footage of blood-drenched naked nuns and *Rocky Horror*-style overacting translates into *The Fall of the House of Usher* (2001), Ken Russell's adaptation of Poe's masterpiece of the macabre, of course, only he could possibly know.   **OB**

S

John SCHLESINGER

John Schlesinger's films have brought a dazzling array of dreamers, losers and fighters to the screen; a character of contradictions, he describes himself as 'a romantic cynic'. Born in London in 1926, he was subsequently educated at Balliol College, Oxford. When World War Two interrupted his studies, he joined the Combined Services Entertainment Unit. During this time he made an amateur film, *Horrors*, and upon resuming his studies, chose to follow an acting career, joining the Oxford University Dramatic Society and becoming president of the Oxford Experimental Theatre Company. An encounter with Roy Boulting during Schlesinger's acting career re-ignited his interest in film-making. This led to a 15-minute documentary, *Sunday in the Park* (1956), that in turn attracted the attention of the BBC.

Schlesinger went on to make a series of documentaries for the BBC – 26 in total – most notably *Terminus* (1961), an acutely observed documentary about visitors to London's Waterloo Station. *Terminus* went on to enjoy commercial distribution and won a Venice Film Festival Golden Lion Award and a British Academy Award.

His first feature, *A Kind of Loving* (1962), is a social realist text based on the novel by Stan Barstow that uses locations in the industrial north of England. The film is the first indication that Schlesinger's oeuvre was concerned with character observation – the politics of the personal rather than the social. The story centres on Vic Brown (Alan Bates), who embarks on a relationship with Ingrid Rothwell (June Ritchie); when it fails the couple go their separate ways, until Ingrid tells Vic she is pregnant. They marry and move in with Ingrid's mother (Thora Hird). The marriage is an unhappy one and Vic takes up the 'angry young man' mantle. Like all angry young men, Vic grows up and he and Ingrid walk off into the uncertain, smog-filled horizon, hand in hand.

Schlesinger's next feature, *Billy Liar!* (1963) tells the story of Billy Fisher (Tom Courtney), a young man in a dead-end, routine job. Billy is ambitious but lazy. Without sufficient application in the real world, he lapses into moments of fantasy. The film features fine performances from a solid British cast including Courtney, Julie Christie and Wilfred Pickles. *Darling* (1965) also starred Julie Christie, this time as the hip youngster,

Diana Scott. Diana is never satisfied and flits from modelling, through acting and into the arms of an Italian prince via a series of affairs, flings and an orgy. Her voice-over narration should bring us closer to the workings of Diana's mind, but the superficiality of her character prevents the audience from empathising with her. The film is strangely disjointed because of this, but the superb performances that Schlesinger extracts from his cast, the tight editing, and the film's style and settings make this a classic of 1960s British cinema. *Darling* won several Academy Awards – Best Actress (Christie), Story and Screenplay (Frederic Raphael), and Costume Design (Julie Harris).

Schlesinger's next project, *Far From the Madding Crowd* (1967), again starred Julie Christie and Alan Bates in a big-screen adaptation of the novel by Thomas Hardy. The film elicits exceptional performances from its principle cast members, including Christie, Bates, Peter Finch and Terence Stamp. Lovingly recreated and beautifully shot, the film never achieved the critical acclaim it deserved. *Midnight Cowboy* (1969), however, brought Schlesinger international recognition. With his interest in characters re-ignited, the result is two of the most moving characterisations in contemporary cinema. The film follows the fortunes of Joe Buck (Jon Voight), a young country boy who heads for the bright lights of New York to make it at as a gigolo. He is soon down on his luck and reluctantly pairs up with Enrico 'Ratso' Rizzo (Dustin Hoffman), who teaches him how to survive in the city. New York is filmed as a grimy, seedy and shallow place. It was praised for its realism upon release, but has since been criticised for its perceived anti-Americanism. However, the film's setting could, broadly speaking, be any big city in industrialised society, where poverty and deprivation are neighbours with wealth and opulence. Schlesinger employs many interesting camera techniques in the film. Described in recent years by some critics as 'gimmicky', the experimental work was bold and compelling. *Midnight Cowboy* won several Academy Awards – Best Director, Best Screenplay for Waldo Salt, and Best Picture, the first X-rated film to do so. *Midnight Cowboy* is an influential and powerful film, and its impact can be seen in films such as Susan Seidelman's *Smithereens* (1982), Gus Van Sant's *Drugstore Cowboy* (1989) and Jerry Schatzberg's gritty *Panic in Needle Park* (1971).

Schlesinger returned to the UK for *Sunday Bloody Sunday* (1971) to continue his exploration of characters at crossroads in their lives – only in this film, their roads are intertwined. It centres on an unusual love triangle between divorcee Alex Greville (Glenda Jackson), a gay doctor, Daniel Hirsh (Peter Finch), and their mutual lover, a young sculptor, Bob Elkin (Murray Head). The film received a muted critical response but did respectable business at the box office. He also directed the final segment in *Visions of Eight* (1973), a compendium of eight different directors' views of the 1972 Olympic Games in Munich, including Milos Forman, Arthur Penn and Mai Zetterling.

Schlesinger followed with *The Day of the Locust* (1975), an adaptation of a Nathaniel West novel, about the underbelly of Hollywood in the 1930s. The film received mixed reviews upon its release and was not a major box-office success. More well known is *Marathon Man* (1976), an adaptation of the popular novel by William Goldman. Schlesinger is reunited with Dustin Hoffman, who plays young Jewish graduate Babe Levy, foiling a gang of Nazi thieves in New York. The film is as fast-paced and furious as thrillers come and features perhaps the most painfully memorable scene of cinematic dentistry in film history. His next feature, *Yanks* (1979), took American GIs stationed in Britain during the Second World War as its subject. While it creates a certain rosy nostalgia that some critics saw as pandering to American audience sensibilities, *Yanks* is effective but too long and overly sentimental in places.

If *Midnight Cowboy* was Schlesinger's high point then *Honky Tonk Freeway* (1981) has to be his all time low. A comic road movie, it has the dubious honour of nearly bankrupting the studio. Schlesinger never attempted another comedy in his film-making career. Licking his wounds from his *Honky Tonk* experience, he then embarked on two projects for British television, *An Englishman Abroad* (1983), and *Separate Tables* (1983), an adaptation of Terence Rattigan's play.

His next big feature, *The Falcon and the Snowman* (1984), was based on the true story of two young Americans who sold America's secrets to the Soviet Union. Plot is secondary to characterisation and there are echoes of *Midnight Cowboy* in the relationship between clean-cut government office boy Christopher Boyce (Timothy Hutton) and his jumpy, drug-dealing friend and co-spy Daulton Lee (Sean Penn). *The Falcon and the Snowman* was well received, particularly in the US.

The Believers (1987) marks the director's only foray into the horror genre. It has some slick moments, and Schlesinger shows how adept he is at manipulating audience emotions. However, despite the presence of Martin Sheen, it is a disappointing film. His form rallied again in his gentle and intelligent film, *Madame Sousatzka* (1988). Once again, plot takes a back seat as Schlesinger takes his time to explore the relationship between an eccentric piano teacher of Russian decent, Madame Sousatzka (Shirley MacLaine), and her young student Manek (Navin Chowdhry).

Schlesinger's next project, *Pacific Heights* (1990), might be best described as a 'yuppie nightmare film'. The film centres on a young couple (played by Melanie Griffiths and Matthew Modine), who buy a property and rent out a couple of the apartments. Enter Carter Hayes (Michael Keaton), the tenant from hell, who arrives complete with jig-saw, to make their lives a misery. The problem with *Pacific Heights* is the lack of back-story, leaving us to guess as to why Keaton's character is so off-kilter. *The Innocent* (1993) was a German/UK co-production. A Cold War spy thriller, it is unusual in its emotional force; the central protagonist is a young British engineer (Campbell Scott), caught between the seductive influence of a German agent, Maria (Isabella Rossellini), and the duplicitous, fast-talking CIA man, Bob (Anthony Hopkins). Despite its respectable status, *The Innocent* did not achieve release in the States until 1996. He followed with *Cold Comfort Farm* (1995), which was made for the BBC.

Schlesinger's last feature was the brutal would-be post-feminist vigilante shocker, *Eye for an Eye* (1996). The film re-works the *Death Wish* (1974) scenario by making the avenging parent the mother (Sally Field), whose daughter is murdered by the irredeemably evil Robert Doob (Kiefer Sutherland). Often described as 'exploitative', the film certainly milks every negative emotion and the attack scenes are rather grisly, but it is redeemed by some interesting and imaginative camera work and lighting, and strong performances from Sutherland and Field. However, as a film it looks like a better-than-average television movie, lacking the grandeur of some of Schlesinger's earlier work.

His most recent feature, *The Next Best Thing* (2000), did good business at the box office, but drew mixed reactions from critics. The title refers to the unconventional family created when Abbie (Madonna), a straight yoga instructor, and Robert (Rupert Everett), a gay horticulturalist, conceive a child after one drunken night of passion. They agree to stay together to raise the child; all goes well until Abbie falls in love with Ben (Benjamin Bratt) and is given her a chance to form the 'traditional' family. *The Next Best Thing* is a well-meaning, credible attempt to explore contemporary definitions of 'family' raising difficult questions within a mainstream context. It nudges tentatively at boundaries, not merely in terms of its themes, but also through its use of multi-generic narrative. The film has all the hallmarks of romantic comedy, but soon becomes a mixture of tragedy, courtroom drama and melodrama – a kind of 'Will and Grace'/*Kramer versus Kramer* hybrid. It is in the handling of these diffuse elements that Schlesinger ultimately fails. The majority of the film's detractors, however, chose to focus on the performance of Madonna, applying the usual adjectives to her acting style – wooden, lightweight and amateurish.

John Schlesinger's contribution to cinema has been remarkable and enduring: an innovator in documentary early on in his career, a contributor to the British New Wave, and the director of some of the most influential contemporary films. Many of his films have been interpreted from various political standpoints by critics and theorists. Yet, surprisingly, Schlesinger has little interest in politics or social messages: 'I agree with Goldwyn – if you want to send a message send it Western Union.' **SL**

Peter SCHWABACH

Having begun his career as an Art Director on Michael Hoffman's *Privileged* (1982), Peter Schwabach made his directorial debut, *The Secret Laughter of Women*, which was produced by the UK's venerable Handmade Films, over a decade later in 1998.

The writing debut of Missan Sagay and O. O Sagay (a former paediatrician), the film tells the tale of Nimi (Nia Long), who leads a relatively peaceful life amongst a

The Secret Laughter of Women (1998)

female-dominated Nigerian community in a picturesque coastal town in southern France with her eight-year-old, excitable son, Sammy (Fissy Roberts). Nimi's unmarried status and illegitimate son are frowned upon by her traditionalist neighbours and her bustling mother, Nene (Joke Silva), is keen to marry off her wilful daughter to confer her with respectability. When the handsome Reverend Fola (Ariyon Bakare) moves into town and shows interest in Nimi, Nene wills a relationship with the black padre. However, the arrival of a comic book writer, Matthew Field (Colin Firth), to whom both Nimi and Sammy take a shine, precipitates a less welcome relationship.

Louise Stjernsward's Nigerian costumes and Martin Fuhrer's attractive camerawork boast a beautiful array of tones and colours, which ensure that *The Secret Laughter of Women* is always beautiful to watch. However, Schwabach's cross-cultural comic romance still feels stilted, in large part due to some hesitant performances, not least from Firth, and some clumsy dialogue. Moreover, the film's attempt to mine the romantic comedy genre prevents it from fully realising the potentially transgressive nature of the material, leaving it with little to say about the subjects of race or sexuality.　　**JWo**

Stefan SCHWARTZ

Soft Top Hard Shoulder (1992)　A co-founder of The Gruber Brothers comedy duo, Stefan Schwartz has continued to
Shooting Fish (1997)　create entertaining films with his production company. Surrounding himself with talented producers and writers, he has become a leader in the British film community, producing and directing television and feature films. Together, he and his production partner, Richard Holmes, have become one of the strongest forces in the British Film Industry.

Schwartz attended York University where he met Holmes and spent time working on several short films. After being turned down by the National Film School, he successfully moved into television, directing commercials and short films such as *Bonded* and *The Lake*. His first feature film, *Soft Top Hard Shoulder* (1992), is a road movie that suffers from its use of a clichéd story and simplistic plot. Featuring some stunning visual imagery, it makes the most of the Scottish countryside and benefits from tremendous acting performances, particularly that of Peter Capaldi, who also wrote the script. Although not a huge success with audiences, it went on to win a London Film Festival award.

Schwartz returned to television to direct the political satire *Giving Tongue* (1996) for BBC Screen 2. In 1997 he wrote and directed the feature *Shooting Fish* (1997). Centring on two con men, portrayed by Dan Futterman and Stuart Townsend, and a con woman, played by Kate Beckinsale, the film was carefully scripted and executed. Schwartz reportedly wrote over ten drafts before filming. Still, the film is loose, fast and extremely funny; peppering the comedy with jokes, plot twists, humorous incidents and delightful characters, Schwartz fashioned a feelgood film which some have called 'bubblegum'. While most young British directors were making dreary looking, heavily plotted films, he presented a fun, hip, lighthearted movie with a touch of heart. Vividly coloured, it has a great sense of energy. Beckinsale is excellent as Georgie, the woman who cons the con men. Firmly establishing Schwartz as a feature film-maker, it had the biggest opening weekend for a British-financed feature in the UK.

Having continued his involvement in producing, including the 1998 smash *Waking Ned Divine*, Schwartz is in production with his next directing project *The Abduction Club* (2001), a romantic drama about a group of men who abduct a woman to obtain their fortunes.　　**JM**

Jake SCOTT

Plunkett and Macleane (1999)　Prior to his feature debut, Jake Scott, born in 1965, established an extensive list of music video credits, directing promos for REM, Oasis and The Verve, amongst many others. Son of Ridley Scott, his single film to date exhibits much of the baroque, textured visual design of his father's work, but none of the thematic richness and subtlety that distinguished both *Alien* (1979) and *Blade Runner* (1982).

In fact, *Plunkett and Macleane* (1999) is a relentlessly oppressive film, not only through its grimy period detail but through its tendency for stylistic overkill which suffocates some of its more agreeable content. Set in 1748, the tale of two highwaymen ('they steal from the rich ... and that's it!' ran the poster tagline) is infused with a postmodern sensibility. Contemporary slang, a techno-influenced soundtrack, explosive action sequences and 'new laddisms' are presumably designed to entice a jaded youth market to whom a bawdy Georgian romp would normally offer scant appeal. Despite their best efforts, Robert Carlyle and Jonny Lee Miller are given little opportunity to breathe life into the title characters, and their interaction seems laboured as they struggle to provide some much-needed depth. Admittedly, the film seeks to present its eponymous figures as iconic and spares no chance to visualise them in a series of striking poses. However, the supporting cast (Alan Cumming, Ken Stott, Michael Gambon and Liv Tyler) are lumbered with particularly shallow roles, simply fulfilling a variety of stereotypes. Touching superficially on themes of class and sex (the foppish Macleane is alarmed to discover he has contracted a STD from a rich woman), these also come across as stilted and mannered. One sequence in a brothel recalls Robin Askwith and the *Confessions of ... sex* comedies of the 1970s. An impressive set-piece, which recreates the Tyburn gallows, generates a tension absent throughout the rest of the film. Replete with allusions to other films (including Ridley Scott's own debut, *The Duellists* (1977)), Scott's first film is ultimately stymied by its self-conscious excess, from its mud spattered exteriors to its lavishly art-directed interiors. Funded through the Arts Council of England with National Lottery money, the film demonstrates the difficulties inherent in re-imagining British historical adventure with one eye fixed permanently on the American box office. **NJ**

Ridley SCOTT

Born in Durham, UK, in 1937, and trained at the National Film and Television School, Ridley Scott has had a successful career in television and advertising, and is one of Britain's most successful mainstream directors. Often derided by critics for his tendency to emphasise style over substance, particularly in the use of inexplicable, though atmospheric, light sources (a quality he shares with his brother, Tony), Scott has created a vision of the past, present and, most dramatically, the future, that has influenced a whole generation of film-makers.

The Duellists (1977)
Alien (1979)
Blade Runner (1982)
Legend (1985)
Someone to Watch Over Me (1987)
Black Rain (1989)
Blade Runner – The Director's Cut (1991)
Thelma and Louise (1991)
1492: Conquest of Paradise (1992)
White Squall (1996)
G.I. Jane (1997)
Gladiator (2000)
Hannibal (2001)

His feature debut, *The Duellists* (1977), loosely based upon a Joseph Conrad story, is a flamboyant exercise in period style. Harvey Keitel and Keith Carradine play two French officers who embark upon a series of duels with each other, across the war-torn devastation of Napoleonic Europe. Beautifully composed, with the leads coping as well as they can with a perfunctory script, the film is interesting, if only for the attention lavished upon every aspect of period detail. Though visually impressive, it is a dull drama that offers little more with repeat screenings.

Moving away from the ponderous into the fast lane of mainstream Hollywood cinema, Scott directed *Alien* (1979). Skilfully blending the stalker genre with the space movie, the film is a testament to his ability to transform the most rudimentary material into something more complex and suspenseful. Novelist J.G. Ballard noted the difference between the script's clichéd dialogue and the completed film, identifying its strengths as 'one of the most original horror movies ever made, the throwaway dialogue perfectly set off the terrifying vacuum that expanded around the characters'. Emphasising their solitude in the vastness of deep space, Scott creates a static environment where lives are trapped in a suspended state. The most banal functions of living appear to take hours and each day bleeds uneventfully into the next, creating a monotonous existence. Even the Nostromo spaceship limps listlessly through the vast reaches of deep space. Looking less like a craft capable of travelling to the furthest corners of the universe than some decaying behemoth, the combination of leaking pipes, dank chambers and under-lit corridors bear more resemblance to the haunted houses of old B-movies than the result of technological advancement. Camouflaged in such an environment, H.R. Geiger's monstrous creation is the embodiment of the fears and desires of the Nostromo's crew, as it violently and mercilessly hunts them down.

Also helping to elevate the film above the realm of the conventional horror/sci-fi movie is Sigourney Weaver's remarkable central performance as Ripley; succeeding in subverting generic conventions, she presents a complex female character as much a predator as she is a victim. Setting the ground for future female action characters, such as Sarah Connor in the *Terminator* series, Weaver's presence ensured that the *Alien* series would continue beyond Scott's involvement.

Scott remained in the future for his next project, *Blade Runner* (1982), an adaptation of Philip K. Dick's story 'Do Androids Dream of Electric Sheep?' and the film that launched a thousand doctoral theses. His best to date, it remains a triumph of vision and intelligence. Once again, Scott plays with generic conventions, positing the murky world of the noirish detective thriller within the confines of dystopian science fiction. The Los Angeles of 2019 is envisioned as a melting pot of past, present and future, with 1940s fashions colliding with eastern cuisine, and architectural styles ranging from Mayan to Bauhaus. The hectic streets, illuminated by neon lights and littered with wastrels, urchins and black marketeers, are dominated by the over-designed super-structures of a faceless corporate technocracy. Scott successfully created a world immediately recognisable yet simultaneously alien and exotic. The lack of geographical perspective added to the otherworldliness of the environment, unwilling to map out the locations within the sprawl of the future LA. As a result, the audience remain as confused and lost as the film's protagonist, Deckard (Harrison Ford).

Released in 1982, the original *Blade Runner* was different to the version Scott had originally conceived. Responding to test audiences' confusion and dissatisfaction with the narrative and downbeat ending, studios demanded a voice-over to accompany the action, the removal of certain scenes and a happier ending. Although the voice-over accentuated the noirish feel to the film, it emptied it of its subtlety and ambiguity, whilst the closing moments appeared as inauthentic as the androids themselves. With his director's cut in 1991, Scott removed both the voice-over and the end, inserting the famous unicorn sequence, which raises interesting questions about Deckard's identity as a 'replicant'. More satisfying than the original, it reasserted Scott's film as a masterpiece of science fiction cinema.

After *Alien* and *Blade Runner*, *Legend* (1985), his next film, was something of a disappointment. An attempt to rework the fairytale for a modern audience, it tells the story of a boy whose infatuation with a young forest girl offers the Prince of Darkness the opportunity to plunge the world into permanent night. Too violent for infants, yet too infantile for adults, the film is overlong and a waste of Scott's undoubted talent. Both Tom Cruise and Mia Sara are hardly credible as the leads, while dozens of extras are corralled into a spectacular display of hackneyed Irish accents and impish expressions. Only Tim Curry, stunningly made-up as the film's villain, manages to rise above the mediocrity, breathing life into a one-dimensional role. Limping from one expensive and pointlessly picturesque sequence to the next, no amount of style can help a film that borders on the tedious. It is Scott's weakest and most self-indulgent work. His next, *Someone to Watch Over Me* (1987), was the first with a contemporary setting and something of a pleasure after *Legend*. Transforming a dull and dreary 1980s Manhattan into a glittering metropolis, Scott combines the elements of a thriller with a domestic drama: a love triangle between Mimi Rogers' wealthy murder witness, Tom Berenger's cop, and Lorraine Bracco's suspecting wife. It is most effective when contrasting the ordinary lives of Berenger and his wife against the fabulous lifestyles of Rogers and her friends. Both the Guggenheim Museum and Rogers' apartment offer Scott opulent backdrops to the drama, emphasising the emptiness of Rogers' life and her vulnerable position both as a witness and the object of a married man's desires. An intelligent and entertaining thriller, *Someone to Watch Over Me* proved Scott's ability as a director able to work effectively on something other than an effects-driven spectacular.

Scott stayed in the present with *Black Rain* (1989), although he goes to extraordinary lengths to transform Osaka into a futuristic urban landscape; small compensation for the crude representation of Japanese culture. From the scenes in a steelworks to the film's climactic shootout in a rain-drenched countryside, Scott ensures his locations have an otherworldly feel. Unfortunately, there is little quality in the writing, which posits a maverick, super-hero American cop against a host of racial stereotypes. Michael Douglas plays Nick Conklin, a 1990s Dirty Harry who is ordered to work with the Japanese police force after a high-ranking Yakuza member escapes from his custody. A lazy reworking of the fish-out-of-water theme, *Black Rain* is a thinly plotted thriller whose intermittent visual elegance fails to hide the tasteless American imperialism lurking beneath.

Deservedly, Scott achieved enormous international success with his next film, *Thelma and Louise* (1991), one of his best to date. A clever variation on the conventional road movie, it posits Geena Davis and Susan Sarandon's eponymous heroines against the men in their lives, who have cheated, robbed and abused them into become fugitives from a repressive patriarchal society. In many ways Scott's most conventional film, his directorial style appears equally at ease in the vast open plains of Midwest America, as it is in the heart of urban life. The expansive landscape, beautifully shot by Adrian Biddle, becomes a metaphor for the women's recently acquired freedom, where they find themselves as free and as powerful as the men who oppress them. A well-paced film, it offers the leads enough room to create a convincing bond of trust and loyalty, and with excellent support from mostly male cast of boyfriends, husbands, lovers and cheats.

In contrast to *Thelma and Louise*, *1492: Conquest of Paradise* (1992) is a visually stunning, but dramatically leaden epic. Released to coincide with the 500th anniversary of Christopher Columbus' arrival on American shores, it stars Gérard Depardieu as the explorer, sent by Sigourney Weaver's Queen Isabela in search of land and wealth to expand Spain's immensely powerful empire and its already burgeoning coffers. An attempt to balance Columbus the myth with the man who brought destruction upon a civilisation, the film is too enamoured with the former, carving out a heroic figure of the explorer. Although efforts are made to account for the genocide that followed in the wake of the Spaniards' arrival, the perceived heroism of Columbus' actions prevents any scathing portrait of one nation's barbarism. However, Scott succeeds in creating a number of impressive set-pieces, even if he fails to give the film an even pace.

Scott's next film, *White Squall* (1996), begins as a traditional rites-of-passage drama, but soon transforms into a terrifying fight for survival, affording him the opportunity to employ his trademark skill as a visually arresting director. Set in 1960, it tells of the disaster that befell the captain and teenage crew of The Albatross when they encountered a hurricane in the usually calm waters of the Caribbean. After a passable first half, in which each member of the crew is introduced and indulges in bonding and kinship, the film steadily gains pace as the storm moves in on the Albatross. A riveting piece of film-making, disorientating and emotionally devastating, Scott pulls out all the dramatic and technical stops to show the Albatross' last, terrifying moments. Ending with a court scene that attempts to investigate the skipper's liability for the boy's deaths, *White Squall* is a remarkable feat of suspense and drama trapped in an all too ordinary film.

Scott's most controversial work, *G.I. Jane* (1997), bears close resemblance to Tony Scott's work for 'high concept' producers, Jerry Bruckheimer and Don Simpson. Marketed as a female version of *Top Gun* (1986), and equalling the earlier film in terms of its lack of intelligence and reliance upon a collection of overused clichés, it is a loud, brash and ultimately depressing film. It follows Demi Moore's transformation from an officer in the US Naval Ops room to a hardened member of the Marine Corps, charting the political minefield she has to traverse to get there. Unable to hold a shot without cutting every few seconds – a signature of the production team of Bruckheimer and the late Simpson – the film attempts to create a drama out of every scene. Even the sight of Moore shaving her head warrants the use of rousing music and an aggressive, cod-masculine expression from the film's star. Any lucid attempt to analyse the place of women in the modern fighting force is lost through shallow characterisation and a risible script. *G.I. Jane* is a reactionary, unsubtle and an all-to-frequently offensive piece of film-making.

Gladiator (2000), however, is Scott's best film since *Thelma and Louise*. A tour-de-force of special effects and old-fashioned storytelling, it succeeds through the careful blending of the familiar and the new. The awe-inspiring sets that dominated the old epics are made more impressive with the use of CGI effects, as are the monumental battle scenes, including a chariot race that echoes *Ben Hur* (1959). Also present are the scheming siblings, political intrigue and clichéd dialogue. However, these elements are updated, to satiate the appetite of a more knowing, contemporary audience. Scott draws fine performances from a large cast, including Russell Crowe and Joaquin Phoenix, and never allows the battles to dominate the drama.

Following *Gladiator*, hopes were high for Scott's version of Thomas Harris' best seller, 'Hannibal'. Although Jodie Foster refused to reprise her role as Clarice Starling, the FBI agent who forms an intimate, yet dangerous, bond with the renowned serial killer, Hannibal Lecter, Julianne Moore's involvement guaranteed the presence of another strong female character actress. However, *Hannibal* (2001) is a veritable cornucopia of Scott trademarks. From a surprisingly lazy adaptation by David Mamet and Steven Zallian, Scott drowns the film in atmospheric lighting and morning mists, accompanied by a bombastic Hans Zimmer score. As a result, the film never achieves the sense of menace that haunted both *Manhunter* (1986) and *Silence of the Lambs* (1990). Best are the scenes in Florence, where Anthony Hopkins' operatic performance is matched by the surrounding architecture, whose decadent past suits the flamboyant psychopath. Once the action returns to America, the film becomes a routine cat-and-mouse thriller. Hopkins' campiness looks out of place, while Moore flounders in a role that seems to have lost its sense of purpose. Only the scenes with Gary Oldman, who plays Lecter's surviving victim, and the final, grotesque dinner scene, provide the macabre mood that the rest of the film desperately lacks.

Scott is currently in production with *Black Hawk Down*, an account of the disastrous Battle of Mogadishu, when over one hundred marines were killed in attempt to overthrow a Somalian warlord.   **IHS**

Tony SCOTT

Tony Scott is probably the ultimate post-MTV film-maker. Born in the UK in 1944 and educated at the Leeds College of Art and Royal College of Art, he formed part of a wave of British-born Hollywood directors emergent from the field of advertising in the 1970s (including his brother, Ridley). Scott's films have been unashamedly commercial and, working mostly within the action-thriller genres, he directed some of the most financially successful features of the 1980s for the production team of Don Simpson and Jerry Bruckheimer. This creative collaboration helped to re-define commercial American cinema, placing emphasis on slick, high-concept narratives while drawing heavily from the diffused, neon-tinged visual style of music videos and commercials, complete with rapid-fire editing and prominent rock soundtracks. Seemingly crass and impersonal, the films have nevertheless been hugely influential, both in their stylistic bombast and their ultimate reduction of the action genres to pure masculinist fantasy. Ridley Scott has defined his brother's aesthetic as 'rock 'n' roll' while the critic John Harkness called him 'the crown prince of the inexplicable light source'.

Scott's first feature is in many ways one of his most interesting. *The Hunger* (1983) puts a fresh spin on the vampire myth, cushioning its thin narrative of immortal lovers in a series of emptily sumptuous visuals. Its modish surface design outweighs any deeper engagement with the vampire mythos but it is a commendable attempt to update the sub-genre. Unusually for Scott, the film centres on two female characters (played by Catherine Deneuve and Susan Sarandon) but the sexual dimension to their relationship is too entrenched in male fantasy to be completely convincing. The film also provides David Bowie with one of his best screen roles.

Scott subsequently embarked on his Simpson and Bruckheimer period, testosterone-fuelled action fantasies in which the signature of the production team was as prominent as that of the director. *Top Gun* (1986) clumsily appends Reaganite Cold War politics to a male rites-of-passage saga, its homo-erotic undertones in constant tension with its hyper-masculine form. Dubbed memorably by one critic 'Phallus in Wonderland', the film is the neo-conservative military fantasy par excellence, shamelessly manipulative but depressingly schematic in its conflict resolutions. However, its impressive aerial action sequences lend the film genuine excitement and it consolidated Tom Cruise's status as a major star. Unfortunately, both *Beverly Hills Cop II* (1987) and *Days of Thunder* (1990) are abysmally retrograde films, the former diluting the social force and humour of its predecessor, the latter failing spectacularly in its attempt to transfer the narrative project of *Top Gun* onto a car racing scenario. The film also brought the collaborative blockbuster success of Scott, Simpson and Bruckheimer to a temporary halt.

Revenge (1990), a male-centered melodrama starring Kevin Costner, was little seen upon its release. The straightforward action thriller *The Last Boy Scout* (1991) was a much more confident work, however, benefiting from a flip, profane Shane Black script and some amusing interplay between leads Bruce Willis and Damon Wayans. The film gleefully sends up the dynamics of the buddy-action genre while delivering the requisite brutality in regular doses. The film's philosophy is summed up by the sequence in which Willis reduces a potential assassin to hysterics with a stream of wise-cracks before plugging him full of bullets. Scott carried this new sense of irony and parody over into *True Romance* (1993), resulting in his best film to date. Working from Quentin Tarantino's script and taking advantage of an eclectic cast which includes Dennis Hopper, Brad Pitt, Gary Oldman and Christopher Walken, the film achieves the allusive, pop culture sensibility of its writer's directorial work while retaining Scott's familiar visual design. Drawing from a 'lovers on the run' (played in a strangely touching fashion by Christian Slater and Patricia Arquette) scenario, the film veers between extreme violence and comedy, fusing these elements brilliantly in the fatal verbal showdown between Hopper and Walken. Yet there is little in the film of genuine, tangible substance beyond its relationship to the popular culture it regurgitates.

Scott's subsequent work in the 1990s has been patchy and not always confined to the screen. In 1994, he headed a consortium – along with brother Ridley – to buy Shepperton studios, evidence perhaps of a desire to establish a solid production base in his home country. However, he continued to work as a director exclusively in the commercial American industry. *Crimson Tide* (1995) is a suspenseful military thriller that benefits from a pair of strong lead performances by Gene Hackman and Denzel Washington. Although its Cold War themes seem a little anachronistic, it handles the attendant masculine conflicts in a much more delicate fashion than *Top Gun*. *The Fan* (1996) only scrapes the surface of its potentially rich material, the study of sports celebrities and their relationship to fans giving way to standard psycho-thriller conventions. The film relies on Robert De Niro's title performance, an interesting variation on his gallery of unhinged loners, albeit one that does not match similar material in Scorsese's *King Of Comedy* (1983). The Will Smith vehicle *Enemy of the State* (1998) is a high-tech thriller in which any genuine paranoid frisson is negated by standard chase scenes and explosions. Gene Hackman's presence, in a role that recalls his character in Coppola's *The Conversation* (1974), only serves to remind the viewer of a time when conspiracy thrillers actually inspired the audience to think.

Scott's most recent film, *The Spy Game*, is due for release at the end of 2001. It stars Robert Redford as a retired CIA agent who returns for one last mission in order to rescue his protégé, played by Brad Pitt.   **NJ**

Ian SELLAR

Few British directors of the last twenty years have made a more striking feature film debut than the Scottish film-maker, Ian Sellar. *Venus Peter* (1989), which he also co-scripted with the author of the original novel, Christopher Rush, joins a rare list of films including the Bill Douglas trilogy and Terence Davies' *The Long Day Closes* (1992) in achieving a clear-eyed yet evocative recreation of a remembered childhood. If his subsequent career has never fully built on that achievement, this may be traced to his decision to channel his talents into developing the abilities of others; in 1996 he became Head of Directing at the National Film and Television School.

Perhaps his sensitivity in depicting the interior world of the child stems from his early involvement with Bill Douglas; his film career started as a runner on Douglas' *My Childhood* (1972) and he was assistant director on *My Ain Folk* (1973). He brings something of the same acute sense of place and community to his picture of a small fishing village in *Venus Peter* that Douglas does to his portrait of a mining town. He also exhibits a visual style which, while being entirely his own, has the same feeling for the possibilities of expressive film-making found in Douglas' work.

As well as working with Douglas, Sellar was assistant to Kevin Brownlow on *Winstanley* (1975), and wrote and directed two short films, *Leicester Square* and *Southwark* (both 1980), before entering the National Film and Television School to study directing in 1981.

Venus Peter is both an elegiac portrait of the passing of a now largely vanished way of life and a hymn to its virtues. Sellar's achievement lies partly in his sensitive handling of the actors – he coaxes a lovely performance from his young lead George Anton and a predictably fine one from Ray McAnally – and in his ability to enter into the imaginative life of a young boy. Billy's experiences of growing up in a narrow community that is both supportive and restricting are rendered in frequently striking visual images which capture the boy's naïve attempts to make sense of his world. This involves the creation of a level of romantic fantasy through which he compensates for the areas lacking in his own life.

Something of the same visual flair is apparent in *Prague* (1992), which was an official selection for the Cannes film festival, but the film suffers rather from the uncertainties of tone that have often dogged European co-productions. Most of his subsequent film work has been as a scriptwriter and includes co-authoring the BBC-backed adaptation of Patrick Gale's novel, 'Kansas in August'. **RS**

Don SHARP

Born in Tasmania in 1922, Don Sharp has worked across a number of genres but is best known for directing a clutch of British horrors for Hammer Studios and their various rivals during the mid-1960s. A stage actor in his native Australia, Sharp emigrated to the UK after World War One. He found work screenwriting for, and occasionally performing in, films aimed at the matinee audience, few of which were seen outside England.

After dabbling in television, he directed his first directorial assignment of note, *Kiss of the Vampire* (1963), an attempt made by Hammer to produce successful vampire pictures without Christopher Lee. Sharp and producer Anthony Hinds (whose screenplay was credited to the pseudonymous John Elder) cast stage actor Noel Willman as the sanguine Herr Ravna, who seeks to add newlywed bride Marianne Harcourt (played by Jennifer Daniel) to his blood cult. Her modern-minded but ineffectual husband (Edward de Souza) is forced to reclaim her, adopting the counter-magic of the melancholic Professor Zimmer (Welsh actor Clifford Evans). A plot point rejected from Terence Fisher's earlier *The Brides of Dracula* (1960) – which also considered the notion of vampirism as a social disease – is recycled as the heroes call upon the powers of darkness to send a plague of bats on Willman's coven. Unreleased in England for two years, the film is stodgy but handsomely shot in colour by Alan Hume. One standout scene of a masked ball attended exclusively by the living dead inspired a similar set piece in Roman Polanski's 1967 spoof *The Fearless Vampire Killers*.

Following the Tommy Steele save-the-orphanage vehicle, *It's All Happening* (1963), Sharp directed the armada-era swashbuckler *The Devil-Ship Pirates* (1964) for Hammer. The British-Warner-Pathé release (distributed in America by Columbia) starred a bearded Christopher Lee – in the first of many assignments for Sharp – as a Spanish cut-throat who must quash local resistance when his vessel runs aground off the coast of Cornwall. Targeting the school holiday crowds, *The Devil-Ship Pirates'* diet of floggings, hangings and swordplay pushed its 'U' certificate to the limits. Still, the film remains a spirited romp performed by a cast of familiar British faces including Andrew Keir, Ernest Clark and Michael Ripper. Although the forty-ton, motor-operated galleon constructed for the film (anchored a mile from Bray within a man-made lake) capsized one afternoon during a tea break, no one was seriously injured and the film found favour with both critics and moviegoers.

Sharp returned to supernatural themes with *Witchcraft* (1964), which was shot in black and white for Lippert Films and starred an ageing Lon Chaney Jr. as a warlock bedeviling real estate developers with an ancient curse. Though no classic, the feature has achieved a cult status and benefits from one of Chaney's last serious performances before he wasted a decade playing halfwits. Sharp teamed with Christopher Lee and producer (and uncredited screenwriter) Harry Alan Towers for *The Face of Fu Manchu* (1965). The British-German co-production was filmed on location in Ireland and proved sufficiently profitable to inspire an immediate sequel, *The Brides of Fu Manchu* (1966). Lee reprised his turn as the controversial archvillain, with Douglas Wilmer replacing the departed Nigel Green as Scotland Yard's indefatigable Sir Denis Nayland Smith. Not based on the Sax Rohmer book of the same name, the sequel has been fobbed off as 'a publicity stunt' by star Lee, who nonetheless went on to appear in three more sequels without Sharp on board.

Between *Fu Manchu* films, Sharp was lured back by Lippert to direct *Curse of the Fly* (1965), the second black and white sequel to Kurt Newman's successful Technicolor shocker *The Fly* (1958). Even more downbeat than the original, this installment attends the increasingly diminished returns of the benighted Delambre family, whose father (American actor Brian Donlevy) continues to experiment with matter disintegration/reintegration, despite horrific negative results and a locked stable bursting with malformed freaks. Rarely seen since its release and unavailable on video, *Curse of the Fly* is another cult oddity; bootleg prints are much sought after by collectors. *Rasputin the Mad Monk* (1966) marked Sharp's last feature-length work for Hammer Studios, and reunited the director with star Christopher Lee. Of dubious historical accuracy – lawsuits threatened by the descendants of Rasputin's alleged assassin necessitated script changes – the film is further hampered by a tight budget that restricts the action to a series of cramped interiors. The production benefits from a characteristically intense central performance, and capable support from Richard Pasco and Barbara Shelley. Sold by Hammer as a horror film, the feature was double-billed with John Gilling's more overtly horrific *The Reptile* (1966).

The comic *Our Man in Marrakesh* (1966), released in the United States as *Bang! Bang! You're Dead!*, was an unmemorable bid to cash in on the vogue for spy films. Working again with producer Harry Alan Towers (author of the original story), Sharp directed an international cast including Tony Randall, Senta Berger and Klaus Kinski. Location shooting helped to take the sting out of this overly familiar tale. Towers and Sharp attempted comedy yet again with *Rocket to the Moon* (1967), a film inspired by the writings of Jules Verne and encouraged by the burgeoning interest in cinematic science fiction. The story of a bid to reach the moon in the nineteenth century, it was shot in Ireland with another international cast made up of Burl Ives, Gert Fröbe, Dennis Price and Klaus Kinski (as a Russian spy). It was sold under a number of alternate titles – *Blast Off*, *Those Fantastic Flying Fools* and *Journey that Shook the World* – in an attempt to curry favour with an audience it never found.

Sharp returned to television work at the end of the decade, following this stint with a string of low-budget pictures: *The Violent Enemy* (1968), about an IRA plot to destroy a British power plant; *Taste of Excitement* (1969), a suspense piece set on the French Riviera; and the supernatural-laced *Psychomania* (1971). Taking advantage of the trend for American motorcycle pictures instigated by *Easy Rider* (1969), Sharp's black comedy follows a British biker gang (led by Nicky Henson's bitter child of affluence) from dissatisfaction to suicide to rebirth as an undead army spreading mayhem through the home countries. Released in America as *The Death Wheelers*, the film is by turns anarchic, amusing and cringe-inducing. It is best remembered today for its support performance by former leading man George Sanders (cast here as a satanic family retainer), who committed suicide in Spain shortly after completing the project. Co-star Robert Hardy worked for Sharp again in the more serious-minded horror outing, *Dark Places* (1974), as a mental patient making life impossible for a top-billed Christopher Lee. Critical reaction to the film ran the gamut from 'tepid' to 'dreary'.

Following his direction of *Callan* (1974), a theatrical extrapolation of the British television series featuring Edward Woodward as a government agent with a conscience, Sharp made one of his few 'A' pictures, the political thriller *Hennessy* (1975). Rod Steiger stars as an Irish family man whose grief over the accidental deaths of his wife and daughter (mowed down in Belfast amidst crossfire between the IRA and the British military) urges him towards a doomed plan to blow up Parliament. Despite the presence of an excellent support cast (Lee Remick, Richard Johnson and Trevor Howard), the film was denounced by critics as overblown and unbelievable. Sharp's *The Thirty-Nine Steps* (1978) was more faithful to John Buchan's source novel than Alfred Hitchcock's classic 1935 thriller (also remade in 1959 by Ralph Thomas). It was neither sufficiently inventive nor exciting enough, however, to attract audiences away from the flashier George Lucas-Steven Spielberg productions that were fast marking the end of, not only a decade, but the era of low-budget adventure and suspense film-making in which Sharp had made his reputation.

A similarly outdated feeling dogs Sharp's final theatrical endeavours. *Bear Island* (1979) was a star-studded adaptation of the arctic espionage novel by Alistair MacLean, featuring Donald Sutherland, Vanessa Redgrave, Richard Widmark and Christopher Lee (in his last film with Sharp). It was heavily altered, in part by Sharp, who had previously directed the second unit motorboat chase that perked up Geoffrey Reeve's otherwise dreary 1972 MacLean adaptation *Puppet on a Chain*. Shot in British Columbia and Alaska (with interiors filmed in the cosier confines of Pinewood Studios), the feature was given a minimal theatrical release, attracting cool-to-hostile critical reaction and audience indifference. *What Waits Below* (1984), the story of a group of cave divers (led by Robert Powell) who discover a mutant subterranean race, had the same fate.

The remainder of Sharp's output consists of made-for-television work (occasionally for the 'Hammer House of Horror' anthology series of the early 1980s). Never merely a hired hack, but far from being a stylist, Don Sharp's reputation rests on a handful of thrillers which, however compromised by rushed schedules or limited budgets, remain thoroughly entertaining a generation later. **RHS**

Jim SHERIDAN

Jim Sheridan is one of the key figures in the Irish film 'renaissance' of the 1990s. Born in Dublin in 1949, the eldest of seven children, he graduated from University College Dublin and the Abbey School of Acting, and later co-founded Project Theatre under the aegis of the influential Project Arts Centre. After Dublin Corporation denied him an arts grant for hosting a visit by Gay Sweatshop, a flamboyantly 'out' theatre group, Sheridan moved to New York with his family in 1981. He became artistic director of The Irish Arts Centre, where he worked as a director, playwright and actor until 1987, and provided a platform for several Irish writers (including his later collaborator, Terry George).

He began his film career in 1988 when, after only an eight-week film production course at New York University, he directed *My Left Foot* (1989), based on the autobiography of Christy Brown, a physically disabled Irish writer and painter. It was nominated for five Academy Awards – Best Film, Best Director, Best Adapted Screenplay (by Sheridan and Shane Connaughton), Best Actor (Daniel Day-Lewis) and Best Supporting Actress (Brenda Fricker). Both Day-Lewis and Fricker won Oscars® for their deeply moving performances. The largely unsentimental portrait of Brown's impoverished Dublin childhood clearly benefited from Sheridan's own Northside upbringing, as well as his years of work in the theatre. Very much a product of his Irish experience, Sheridan combines firm political commitment with a strong sense of the emotional power of drama.

All of Sheridan's subsequent films deal with emotive Irish issues, allegorically structured in terms of familial – usually Oedipal – conflict. In 1990 he wrote and directed *The Field* (adapted from the play by John B. Keane), a grim allegory of the emotional legacy of the Famine on the subsequent generations of Irish people. Set in Kerry in the 1920s, *The Field* tells the story of 'Bull' McCabe (Richard Harris), a tenant farmer who has spent his life cultivating a small field in a barren and inhospitable landscape at the expense of his long-suffering son (Sean Bean) and wife (Brenda Fricker). When a sauve Irish-American (Tom Berenger) attempts to buy the field, 'Bull' opposes him by fair means and foul, culminating in the American's brutal murder. The film deviates substantially from the original play, not least in its ending (derived from W.B. Yeats' 'On Baile's Strand') in which 'Bull', insane and utterly alone, wades into the sea and fights the waves. Featuring a tour-de-force performance by Harris (who received an Oscar® nomination for Best Actor), the film solidified Sheridan's reputation as an 'actor's director'. However, this is also the film's essential weakness, as Harris' often overwrought, Shakespearean intensity threatens to overpower the rest of the film.

In 1992 Sheridan wrote the screenplay for Mike Newell's *Into the West*, a gentle yet stirring fable about two traveller children who escape their dingy Dublin life on the back of a mystical white horse. His writing deftly blends harsh social realities – poverty, alcoholism, discrimination – with an enchanting magical realism (drawn from Celtic mythology), though on occasion the film does stray into sentimentality.

The same year Sheridan directed, produced and co-wrote (with Terry George) his most controversial – and in many respects his most accomplished – film, *In the Name of the Father* (1993). Based on Gerry Conlon's autobiography, 'Proved Innocent', the film recounts the wrongful arrest and 14-year imprisonment of Conlon (Daniel Day-Lewis) and several others for the IRA bombing of a Guildford pub in 1974. As the title suggests, Sheridan has taken a controversial subject and given it a wider audience by focusing on the Oedipal drama of a father and son who also happen to be political prisoners. The film provoked media condemnation in Britain, where Sheridan, Day-Lewis and co-star Emma Thompson (who played the solicitor, Gareth Peirce) were accused of making an anti-English film, and of distorting the factual record. Indeed, certain liberties were taken with the facts of the case. Conlon and his father Giuseppe (Pete Postlethwaite), for instance, were never imprisoned together. This poetic licence seems more than justified, however, raising important social and political questions about the British justice system.

In 1996 Sheridan and Terry George co-wrote George's directorial debut *Some Mother's Son*, the story of two mothers (Helen Mirren and Fionnuala Flanagan) whose sons took part in the 1981 IRA hunger strike in Northern Ireland's Long Kesh prison. Predictably, the film was attacked by the British establishment for being pro-Republican – much was made of the fact that George himself had served three years in Long Kesh for IRA offences – although the screenwriters were keen to stress the veracity of their narrative and its fidelity to actual events. Sheridan's guiding hand is visibly present in the relentless series of ironic cross-cuts and penetrating juxtapositions between the personal and the political: as the mothers bond on the outside, the prisoners bond on the inside; when the two women dance together out of loneliness, the prisoners dance out of solidarity. Within the context of the newly evolving peace process, the film was a timely reminder of the traumatic complexity of the Northern Irish conflict.

Sheridan's most recent film, *The Boxer* (1997), completed the Northern Irish trilogy (again, it was co-written with Terry George), and reunited him with Daniel Day-Lewis. Lewis stars as Danny Flynn, a former Belfast boxer who is released from prison after serving 14 years for his involvement in an IRA bombing. Danny has renounced his political past and dedicates himself to re-opening a non-sectarian boxing club. His former teenage sweetheart, Maggie (Emily Watson), is now married and raising her son while her husband is in prison. Their relationship is rekindled despite the fact that they must keep their affair a secret both from the community and from Maggie's father (Brian Cox), who is an IRA leader committed to upholding the ceasefire against extremists within the republican movement. This polemical portrayal of the crisis in Republican politics lacks the assured dramatic touch of Sheridan's previous work – the relationship between Lewis and Watson is oddly lacklustre – but its humanist vision of a devastated community struggling to achieve some kind of normality is typical of Sheridan's integrity and commitment. The balance between emotional drama and political debate is always a difficult one to sustain and, throughout his career, Sheridan's use of conventional three-act structures is occasionally laboured. More than any other Irish director, however, he ably demonstrates that commercial cinema can both entertain and educate.

Sheridan has since acted as co-producer for Angelica Huston's *Agnes Brown* (1999), and is currently working on *The Notebook*, an adaptation of the best-selling novel by Nicholas Sparks. **KHo**

Julian SIMPSON

Displaying ingenuity, precision and a thorough knowledge of the machinations of the conspiracy genre, *The Criminal* (2000), self-confessed cinephile Julian Simpson's auspicious debut, is a deeply flawed but undeniably smart affair that augurs well for his future cinematic career.

Jasper Rawlins – a surprisingly good Steven Mackintosh – is a feckless musician whose life takes a sinister turn after meeting a femme fatale, Sarah (Natasha Little), in a London bar. Before anything happens between them Sarah is brutally murdered and Rawlins finds himself drawn into a murky, nightmarish world – courtesy of Nic Morris' brooding photography – in which he is chief suspect in the hunt for Sarah's killer. To make matters worse, Bernard Hill's foul-mouthed Inspector Walker is particularly unhelpful in Rawlins' quest to establish his innocence.

A former film school student, Simpson's main asset is his knowing, sophisticated and witty script, which exerts a powerful grip, particularly in the film's opening 25 minutes.

His penchant for the elliptical is also refreshing and wholly appropriate for the film's central subject matters: paranoia, subterfuge, duplicity and the oppressive power of the State. Despite the odd twist and turn too many, there is a confidence and élan at work here that invokes the work of the director Christopher Nolan, whose success Simpson, with careful nurturing, could well go on to emulate.   **JWo**

Iain SINCLAIR
See **Chris PETIT**

Gary SINYOR

Born in Manchester in 1962, Gary Sinyor's directorial career began in 1992 with *Leon the Pig Farmer* and encompasses five films to date. Writing and producing some of his early features, Sinyor has remained within the realms of comedy.

Praised by critics as an admirable first feature, *Leon the Pig Farmer*, which he co-directed with Vadim Jean, collected the Chaplin Award for Best First Feature at Edinburgh in 1992 and the FIPRESCI Award the same year at Venice. It tells the story of Leon Geller, a Jewish man dissatisfied with all areas of his life, not least when he finds out he is the product of artificial insemination and his father is a Yorkshire farmer. Drawing praise for its sharp performances, wit and innovative visuals, its ideological stance caused some confusion. However, its sheer off-the-wall humour ensured festival circuit popularity and audience approval.

In 1995 Sinyor directed *Solitaire for Two* from his own script, a battle-of-wits tale starring Mark Frankel as a body-language expert trying to woo a mind-reading palaeontologist (Amanda Pays). With glossy cinematography of the advertising quality, and a weak plot, *Solitaire for Two* is a disappointing follow-up to Sinyor's initial success.

Stiff Upper Lips (1998) is an enjoyable parody of Merchant-Ivory films in which Georgina Cates plays an Edwardian lady who is dissatisfied with her suitor and finds alternative love with a well-endowed local peasant, George (Sean Pertwee). Peppered with such lines as 'I want my sexual awakening and I want it now!', *Stiff Upper Lips'* wicked humour plays off of the corseted, snooty aristocratic canon of literary adaptations that British cinema seems to have endlessly flogged. Silly as the humour is, it is precise in pinning down the exact idiosyncrasies of the genre it affectionately spoofs.

The next year Sinyor directed *The Bachelor*, a remake of Buster Keaton's *Seven Chances* (1925), the story of a would-be millionaire who must marry within 24 hours in order to inherit his fortune. Pursued by a mob of suitors, Jimmie (Chris O'Donnell) must decide between money and marriage, and whether to commit to his ex-love Annie (Renée Zellweger). With a plethora of amusing cameos from people such as Mariah Carey and Peter Ustinov, the film is overtly comic. Most of its humour hinges on the absurdities of the dating game by playing on romantic-movie clichés, many with relative success. What lets the film down is the weakness of the two leads. O'Donnell has neither the comic knack nor charisma to carry off the role; he is not aided by Zellweger playing out her vulnerable sweetness once again. The incisive humour of *Stiff Upper Lips* makes *The Bachelor* seem vapid by comparison. Relinquishing the comedic bite, Sinyor creates a truly average film.

Love Hurts (2000), Sinyor's most recent film, has not had a theatrical release. **LB**

Brian SKEET

Born in 1966, Brian Skeet began film-making in the late 1990s with *The Misadventures of Margaret* (1998), a British, American and French co-production based on 'Rameau's Niece' by Cathleen Schine. Parker Posey, queen of late-1990s indie comedies, plays Margaret, a dizzy, popular novelist, opposite Jeremy Northam as her British professor husband. Suspecting him of straying, Margaret flits between fantasies of various affairs including a femme fatale-like professor (played by Brooke Shields) loosely based upon an eighteenth-century philosopher's diary she has been adapting. Intending to evoke the golden age of screwball, effervescent comedies of the 1940s and 1950s, Skeet never quite manages to capture or sustain the audience's interest in either the characters or plot. His script aims to be chic and sophisticated – in keeping with the retro kitsch style of its St Etienne soundtrack – but ends up being self-conscious and inert. Premiered at Sundance in 1998, it attracted little interest and Posey's performance drew some harsh criticism.

Adapted by Skeet from the novel by Peter Cameron, his next film, *The Weekend* (2000), won the New American Cinema Award at the Seattle Film Festival. Financed and executive-produced by Granada Films, *The Weekend* takes place as a group of friends reunite for a dinner to mourn the loss of their charismatic friend Tony to AIDS a year previously. With enjoyable performances from Gena Rowlands, Brooke Shields, James Duval and Deborah Kara Unger, this ensemble piece illuminates the tensions that lie beneath the friends' grief, examining how each attempts to come to terms with it. Swapping settings between two upmarket houses north of New York, the film is stylishly photographed by Ron Fortunato, whose previous credits include *Basquiat* (1996) and *Nil By Mouth* (1997). The pain and loss and eventual emotional showdown between the group is juxtaposed against the salubrious and misleadingly idyllic environs. Critics, who disliked its anachronistic Chekhovian subject matter, deemed the film's depiction of high society as pretentious. Despite its engaging performances, the ponderous pacing does tend to create a soporific atmosphere. **LB**

Jimmy SMALLHORNE

Jimmy Smallhorne grew up in Ballyfermot, a disadvantaged working-class area of Dublin. *2by4* (1998)
After spending time in rehabilitation for a teenage gambling addiction, he moved to New York in 1990 to pursue a career in acting. For several years he worked on various construction sites before co-founding the Irish Bronx Theatre. Despite having no experience whatsoever of film-making, Smallhorne came to prominence in 1998 with *2by4*, a gritty and provocative feature about a group of Irish construction workers living in contemporary New York.

2by4 is a remarkable debut by any standards, not least in the manner of its production. As director, co-writer (with Terence McGoff and Fergus Tighe) and lead actor, Smallhorne comes close to making this a vanity project, but it remains a testament to his restless energy and vision that he avoids any hint of self-indulgence. Initially intending to shoot it on Super 16 and a small budget, Smallhorne managed to secure $500,000 from first-time producer John Hall. Using a strong ensemble cast, he then workshopped the improvised script for six weeks.

2by4 tells the story of Johnny (Smallhorne), whose chaotic life revolves around the building sites and bars of the Irish ghetto in New York. Johnny works as a gangerman for his uncle, Trump (the late Chris O'Neill), whose gruff bonhomie masks a mean and insidious nature. On the surface all seems fine until Johnny's hectic lifestyle and recurring nightmares force him to confront the grim ghosts of his past. Although set in New York, *2by4* is the first explicitly gay Irish film, revealing a sexual sub-culture which directly challenges the more conventional Irish stereotypes. Beginning as a personal voyage of discovery it also ends up revealing the hypocrisy and bigotry of an older generation of Irish-Americans. The film featured prominently in several festivals, including the New York Film Fleadh, the Dublin Gay and Lesbian Film Festival, Raindance, and the Verzaubert International Gay and Lesbian Film Festival (where it was nominated for Best Feature). *2by4* was nominated for the Grand Jury Prize at the Sundance Film Festival in 1999 where it won a prize for Best Cinematography (Declan Quinn). **KHo**

Mel SMITH

Born in London in 1952, Mel Smith formed part of the new wave of comedians to burst on to the television scene in the early 1980s and one half of the trio Smith and Jones with Griff Rhys Jones. He parlayed his obvious comic talents into directing features in the late 1980s, all of them comedies.

He debuted with *The Tall Guy* (1989) in which an American actor, down on his luck with women, lands a staring role in a musical version of 'The Elephant Man' and falls

The Tall Guy (1989)
Radioland Murders (1994)
Bean (1997)
High Heels and Low Lifes (2001)

in love with a nurse. The film is a confident first venture into feature territory, aided by Richard Curtis' script. Although relatively popular, its American-in-London premise did not spark a success on the scale of the previous year's *A Fish Called Wanda*. *The Tall Guy*, like other work by Curtis, is notable for the richly drawn supporting characters.

Following *The Tall Guy*, Smith went to America and directed for television's 'Dream On', a series about the exploits of a thirty-something man with a vivid imagination. In 1994 he collaborated with George Lucas on *Radioland Murders,* which starred the actor Brian Benben who has appeared in 'Dream On'. Based on an idea of Lucas', harking back to the early 1970s, the film is a comedy set in the 1930s in the behind-the-scenes milieu of showbusiness. A frantic slapstick piece, it focuses on the opening night of a Chicago radio station where a murderer is at large. It is packed with verbal and visual jokes and a host of personalities – Bo Hopkins and Cindy Williams from Lucas' *American Graffiti* (1973) are in the radio audience – as various acts strike up over the airwaves. Christopher Lloyd and Ned Beatty also feature. The film's subplot is a romance between two protagonists (portrayed by Benben and Mary Stuart Masterson) who bicker and wisecrack throughout the film. It is written by Willard Huyck and Gloria Katz who worked as writers on *American Graffiti*, *Howard the Duck* (1986) and *Indiana Jones and the Temple of Doom* (1984). *Radioland Murders* is frenetically paced and dialogue-heavy, in the manner of a 1930s screwball comedy. Made very cheaply, partly as an experiment for Lucas, and to push the boundaries of digital film-making, it failed to make any impact at the box office despite its energy and good humour. A small film, it is worth rediscovering, demonstrating as it does Smith's ability to construct visual gags.

Based on a script by Richard Curtis and Robin Driscoll, Smith directed *Bean* (1997) with collaborator Rowan Atkinson, a movie expansion of Atkinson's popular television character Mr Bean, a mute, comically inept man. A very popular release, *Bean* is driven by visual humour and slapstick, making the character ripe for the film format. The concept does feel slightly overstretched, however: in an attempt to rid themselves of their disaster-prone employee, Bean is sent as a visiting scholar by a London art gallery to an equivalent in LA. Comic misadventures abound.

Smith's most recent film, *High Heels and Low Lifes* (2001), stars Minnie Driver and Mary McCormack. A breezy crime caper comedy about two young women who stumble upon plans for a heist and try and outfox the criminals, it is similar in tone to the old Ealing films. Energetic, it is carried by the female leads, with Smith displaying his trademark affinity for comic contortions of plot. **JC**

Iain SOFTLEY

Backbeat (1993)
Hackers (1995)
The Wings of the Dove (1997) Iain Softley was born in 1958 and educated at Queens College, Cambridge, where he gained a reputation as an accomplished theatre director. He burst onto a rather lacklustre British film scene in 1993 with his first feature, *Backbeat*, produced by Stephen Woolley, the true story of the fifth Beatle Stuart Sutcliffe and the band's formative days at the Star Club in Hamburg in the early 1960s. Softley immediately established himself as an actor's director, eliciting stunning performances from Stephen Dorff as Sutcliffe, the artist who turns his back on the band before dying of a brain haemorrhage, and Ian Hart as Lennon. Sheryll Lee gives a career best as Astrid Kirchherr, Sutcliffe's muse and creator of the mop top image for the Beatles. Although the Star Club sequences are cartoonish and the narrative sags in the middle, the film balances a lively sense of fun with emotional intensity. Softley makes excellent use of composition and colour; although his painterly eye would come to the fore in *The Wings of the Dove* (1997), his sumptuous adaptation of Henry James' novel, it was not before he had made *Hackers* (1995), an over-hyped computer conspiracy thriller that simply added to a plethora of bad computer movies. Although lifted once again by Softley's sensitive direction of actors – Jonny Lee Miller and an inexperienced Anjelina Jolie perform well and perfectly capture the hacker zeitgiest – the movie is empty and very much of its time.

Softley's next film, the triple Oscar® nominated *The Wings of the Dove*, pulls together the disparate strengths of his earlier works. While the golden hues and luxuriant Venetian set-pieces sometimes look like expensive adverts, the grand passions of the protagonists are never swamped. Set in 1910 in England and Venice, it tells the story of a poor couple's plot to get their hands on a dying heiress' fortune. Journalist Merton (Linus Roach) woos her so that he and Kate (Helena Bonham Carter) can eventually inherit the money. Softley is a great director of women: Carter's Academy Award nomination is richly deserved and relative newcomer Alison Elliott, who plays the dying heiress, is never allowed to display too much sentiment. This is film-making of great maturity: the protagonists are complex and morally ambiguous, and the audience is never talked down to.

Softley is currently in production with *K-Pax* in which Kevin Spacey plays an inmate of a psychiatric hospital who claims to be an alien from the planet K-Pax and has an extraordinary effect on his fellow patients and doctor, who is played by Jeff Bridges. **SP**

Richard SPENCE

Having spent his childhood in Belfast, Richard Spence directed television at the BBC and worked on two drama-detective series, 'Bergerac' and 'Poirot'. He also directed episodes of 'Making Out', which was awarded best drama series at the BANFF Festival 1989. More recently, Spence's work has ranged from cutting edge made-for-television films to Hollywood features starring A-list players.

You, Me, and Marley (1992)
Blind Justice (1994)
Different for Girls (1996)
New World Disorder (1999)

Many of his earlier films did not secure a theatrical release. His first film, the BBC production *Night Voice* (1990), was based on his own story. Its gritty style owes more to the underground cinéma vérité, reminiscent of the New Wave approach of the late 1950s, with the narrative emphasis on recounting realities of working-class life. The fact that this had been Spence's reality gave the film a distinctive and believable edge. *Thacker* (1991), his second film shot at the BBC, centres upon strange goings-on in the depths of rural England, telling the story of dark powers in the Cotswolds and the search for long lost love. Less grainy, it was still sensitively filmed. *You, Me, and Marley* (1992), another perceptive piece made by the BBC, is set in Spence's IRA-dominated hometown and revolves around a gang of teenage car thieves; it went on to win the Michael Powell Award at the Edinburgh Film Festival that year.

Spence followed with *Skallagrigg* (1994), a dramatisation of the book by William Harwood about the search for the mythical figure Skallagrigg, who is the hero of stories told by disabled people in hospitals and housing. It features a cast of over twenty actors with disabilities and was awarded a BAFTA for Best Single Drama. *Big Cat* (1998) a love story-thriller was the final television film Spence directed; starring David Morrisey, the film won critical acclaim for fine performances and an intriguing dialogue.

Blind Justice (1994) provided Spence with his first taste of big-budget Hollywood. The film, a spaghetti western, is well written by Daniel Knauf. It recounts the story of Canaan (Armand Assante), a gunfighter blinded during combat in the Civil War, who becomes burdened with the protection of a baby and wanders into a small old West town on his way to deliver the child to prospective parents. He then inadvertently becomes mixed up in a scheme to collaborate with the Cavalry to save the town from a gang of Mexican bandits and earn two hundred pounds of US silver. The film received glowing reviews but failed to draw in the numbers at the box office and only did marginally well.

Different for Girls (1994) focuses on two old school friends who meet for the first time in 17 years; one is shocked to discover that the other has undergone a sex change. Spence, and writer Tony Marchant, approach this potentially tricky subject with appropriate care. It was subsequently much praised by critics as one of the more distinctive odd-couple romantic comedies. The film won notorious acclaim for its leads at Sundance; Steven Mackintosh tackles his difficult role with aplomb and Rupert Graves, who is unquestionably a fine actor, is quite remarkable. Some critics did feel that the cast was made up of simplified characters but it remains an enjoyable film for fans of intense, close-up, witty character portraits.

With *New World Disorder* (1999) Spence ventured into Hollywood territory for the story of an old school detective (Rutger Hauer) who finds himself out of his depth when he is assigned to investigate the theft of cutting-edge technology from a computer company. His partner for the investigation, the beautiful tech-savvy detective (Tara Fitzgerald), with whom he shares great screen chemistry, learns that they have to put their differences aside to capture the ruthless hackers. Andrew McCarthy makes a fine villain and the film is fun for Hauer fans. However, many critics commented on the predictability of the storyline. *Déjà Vu* (1999), Spence's most recent film funded by Channel 4 for television, is a thriller staring Kerry Fox. *Cutler* is soon to have a release and *A Nice Easy One* is currently in production. **ESu**

Bob SPIERS

That Darn Cat (1997)
Spice World (1997)
Kevin of the North (2001)

Best known as a prolific director of British television comedy since 1968, Bob Spiers has moved into features relatively recently. Amongst his television credits are highly regarded shows such as 'Dad's Army', 'The Comic Strip Presents...', 'Absolutely Fabulous' and 'Fawlty Towers', and the strange comedy-drama 'Upline', which he made in 1987.

His first theatrical feature, the Disney movie *That Darn Cat* (1997), was a remake of an earlier (and superior) movie of the same name from 1965. Notable chiefly for the appearance of Christina Ricci in the lead, this is an uneventful, slapstick would-be comedy-thriller for the family audience. A kidnapping plot is foiled by the titular feline but some 'cynical' one-liners – such as Ricci's explanation of her penchant for wearing black clothes: 'It matches my soul' – cannot disguise the dated nature of the whole enterprise. Particularly dispiriting is the lack of any feel for comedy, which is ironic given the director's background in (often excellent) sitcoms.

The same year, Spiers directed *Spice World* (1997). A vehicle for the pop group The Spice Girls, the film is clearly indebted to earlier British pop movies, particularly Richard Lester's Beatles movies *A Hard Day's Night* (1964) and *Help* (1965), and Sidney J. Furie's *The Young Ones* (1961). The Spice Girls' doubledecker bus can even be seen as a homage to the latter film. Although the plot is a lightweight concoction about touring and a film-maker (Alan Cumming) who is making a documentary about the band, the whole thing is inoffensive enough, with cameos from Meat Loaf, Bob Geldof and Kevin Allen. The band's manager is played by Richard E. Grant who is not at his best here. The band themselves are passable, playing characters that emphasise their personas – 'Baby' is naïve and sucks lollipops, for instance, and 'Sporty' is into football. Most of the jokes are either given to, or are at the expense of, 'Posh'; 'Scary' is by far the most grating. Though pretty forgettable, there is enough here to hold audience interest, particularly that of young fans of the band; watched four years later as the band disintegrates, it begins to look more like a snapshot of an era. Well-timed to catch the band at their most popular, *Spice World* was an enormous success at the box office.

Spiers' next film, *Kevin of the North* (2001), was little seen. A strange cast (Skeet Ulrich, Natasha Henstridge, Rik Mayall and Leslie Nielsen) feature in this comedy-adventure about a man who enters a race across the snowy wastelands of Canada to inherit a fortune. Spiers' direction, never showy at the best of times, is unremarkable. His most recent film, *Doin' The Splits*, is unreleased at the time of writing. Having produced such inspiring television work as 'Dad's Army' and 'Fawlty Towers', Spiers' features thus far would seem to suggest that he is better suited to the small-screen format. **IC**

Roger SPOTTISWOODE

Terror Train (1980)
The Pursuit of D. B. Cooper (1981)
Under Fire (1983)
The Best of Times (1986)
Shoot to Kill (1988)
Turner and Hooch (1989)
Air America (1990)
Stop! or My Mom Will Shoot (1992)
And the Band Played On (1993)
Mesmer (1994)
Tomorrow Never Dies (1997)

Born in Ottowa, Canada, in 1947, Roger Spottiswoode began his career as a successful television and documentary editor in Britain, before embarking on a career in America. His early work in Hollywood included editing three of Sam Peckinpah's films – *Straw Dogs* (1971), *The Getaway* (1972) and *Pat Garrett and Billy the Kid* (1973) – before making his directorial debut with *Terror Train* (1980). Despite a patchy period in the 1990s, Spottiswoode has proved himself to be a safe and capable pair of hands with a big-budget project – the Bond film, *Tomorrow Never Dies* (1997).

Terror Train is a *Halloween* (1980) clone, and also features 'scream queen' Jamie Lee Curtis as one of a band of teens at the mercy of a psychopath, as they party the night away on a moving train. His next, *The Pursuit of D.B. Cooper* (1981), is a comic chase caper starring Treat Williams as an escaped robber who parachutes from a hijacked plane with thousands of dollars, hotly pursued by law enforcers, including Robert Duvall. Having suffered a series of problems during its making – several directors and major re-writes of script – the film is disjointed.

Spottiswoode finally had the opportunity to demonstrate his considerable abilities Devil's Pale Moonlit Kiss with *Under Fire* (1983). Set in Nicaragua in 1979, during the last days of Somoza's (2000) dictatorship, it is a graceful and spirited tale centring on three American journalists and *The 6th Day* (2000) their reactions to the revolution taking place around them. Fine performances from an exceptionally strong cast (Nick Nolte, Gene Hackman and Joanna Cassidy) make this a gripping and passionate piece of mainstream cinema. Spottiswoode directs with exceptional style and flair. *The Best of Times* (1986) followed, which saw him reunite with Ron Shelton, who had written *Under Fire*. The film is essentially a buddy movie about Jack (Robin Williams) and Reno (Kurt Russell), two former high school football-team mates, and Jack's inability to live down a humiliating sporting defeat in his youth. Jack obsesses about re-staging the game and, as the two draw closer together, enormous strain is put on their respective marriages. Successfully avoiding syrupy-sweetness, *The Best of Times* did little business at the box office.

Spottiswoode ventured once again into the territory of the buddy movie with *Shoot to Kill* (1988), a film that features two male protagonists who are brought together but have nothing in common. It is worth more than a passing glance for several reasons. First, it marked Sidney Poitier's return to acting after ten years behind the camera. Second, the performance of Clancy Brown as the villain of the piece is chillingly superb; it is easy to see how he has carved a career out of such roles (*Highlander* (1986), *Shawshank Redemption* (1994)). Finally, Spottiswoode's background in editing informs every shot and sequence, making it a textbook example of mainstream Hollywood film-making. Despite this, *Shoot to Kill* did only modest box-office business.

His next feature was popular with audiences but much maligned by critics – and rightly so. *Turner and Hooch* (1989) is an appalling cop flick starring Tom Hanks as an anally retentive detective whose only witness to a murder is a slobbery, clumsy dog named Hooch. Despite the ridiculous premise, audiences flocked to the cinema to see one of America's favourite stars acting with a dog. Spottiswoode does a fairly standard job in terms of direction thus ensuring his stability in Hollywood. That said, the cinema-going public were not to be fooled by Spottiswoode's next two offerings – both action comedies, and both huge flops, despite the presence of top stars. *Air America* (1990) features Mel Gibson and Robert Downey Jr. as pilots working for the CIA during the Vietnam War. *Stop! or My Mom Will Shoot* (1992) stars Sylvester Stallone as a cop who has just split up with his lover and boss (JoBeth Williams). His mother, played by Estelle Getty, of television's 'Golden Girls' fame, comes to comfort her son. Spottiswoode's direction is ham-fisted and clichéd; it is further handicapped by a script that is at best light-weight.

His next release, *Mesmer* (1994), is a biography of the eighteenth-century Austrian physician, Franz Anton Mesmer. Despite a solid performance from Alan Rickman as Mesmer, it is plodding and episodic. Spottiswoode did not make another cinematic feature until 1997, though during this time he made two respectable television movies – *And the Band Played On* (1993) and the Canadian/Japanese collaboration, *Hiroshima* (1995) – which also received limited theatrical releases. He redeemed himself in the eyes of studios and their accountants, however, with the James Bond film, *Tomorrow Never Dies* (1997). As with the majority of films in the Bond series, it was highly successful in terms of its world-wide box-office receipts, and generally rated amongst critics. Spottiswoode handles the Bond brand with style and its trademark action sequences feel particularly safe in the hands of a director with the sharp eye of an editor.

His next feature, *Devil's Pale Moonlit Kiss* (2000), is set during the end of the Cold War and centres on an American porn publisher's attempts to help a young East German ice skater to defect. Spottiswoode's deft hand raises the somewhat flimsy plot to an average level of film-making, yet it is somewhat disappointing after the high-octane thrills and spills of *Tomorrow Never Dies* (1997). Spottiswoode's most recent work capitalises on current debates in science surrounding the issue of cloning. *The 6th Day* (2000) is set in a near-future America, where scientists have developed cloning technologies. Despite the fact that the world's leaders and scientists have agreed that every form of life can be cloned, with the exception of humans, mad scientists and their pay-masters are happily and covertly cloning people for their own evil needs. Arnold Schwarzenegger plays Adam Gibson who returns from work to find that he has been replaced by a clone of himself, the result of an accident that occurred during a terrorist attack. Spottiswoode seems content to put all his faith in the impressive special effects. Robert Duvall turns in a characteristically fine performance as the scientist, which unfortunately throws Schwarzenegger's lack of acting ability into sharp relief. Although it enjoyed a moderate success at the box office, the film was panned by critics for its pump-action, and somewhat vacuous, delivery.

Roger Spottiswoode has proved himself to be a capable director in terms of producing films in the New Hollywood. Despite a low period in the early 1990s, his career as a Hollywood film-maker seems to be on an upward curve. His films are stylish and unpretentious, but he has yet to deliver work of the directorial standard of his earlier *Under Fire*, which is Spottiswoode at his best.   **SL**

Paul SPURRIER

Underground (1998) An actor from the 1970s, Paul Spurrier appeared most notably in the 1970s television version of 'Anna Karenina', and in a variety of disparate film and television projects, among them, *Max Headroom* (1985), Peter Duffell's *King of the Wind* (1989) and *The Wild Geese* (1978).

When he turned to feature film-making, after a stint as assistant director to Jack Gold on *The Chain* (1984), he did so after a huge gap, typical of independent film-making; within the usual traditions of first-time, no-budget directors, he also wrote, photographed and edited *Underground* (1998). Starring the late Ian Dury, the film is concerned with the drug culture of a London dance club, the titular Underground.

Set against a story involving teenage drug dealer Rat (Billy Smith) and his south London patch, it develops into a tale of overdoses, revenge and sex, all taking place over one night. Although the club setting and the drug storyline has led to comparisons with Justin Kerrigan's *Human Traffic* (1999), this film is different in tone and intention, erring on the darker side of drug use in the clubbing underworld.

It succeeds in its ability to merge the social realism of British cinema's reputation with the commercially viable plot necessary if the film is to be seen outside its country of origin. Spurrier uses a handheld camera to afford mobility and immediacy to the story, offering a vivid sense of location. From the opening travelogue images to the final shots of Rat battling across the Thames against suited commuters, the film employs images of the city to illuminate the story. Bare, grim council estates, the smoky club and deserted parks all feature as part of Rat's world.

With a heavy score which reinforces the film's dark tone, it demonstrates real promise. Spurrier has since made a short film, *Live on Arrival* (1999), about a man pronounced dead in hospital despite being able to walk and breathe. It suggests an offbeat vision that may flower if given the opportunity to develop.   **JD**

Richard STANLEY

Hardware (1990) A progenitor of cyberpunk cinema, Richard Stanley constructs his highly inimitable proj-
Dust Devil (1992) ects from the fabric of mysticism, magic and myth. Born in South Africa in 1966, to a mother versed in ancient religions and folklore and a father obsessed with British crime author Edgar Wallace, Stanley spent his formative years exposed to the interestingly parallel influences of alternative spirituality and genre cinema. Stanley's introduction to the horror genre came quite early as a toddler during his father's repeated viewings of *King Kong* (1933), a film developed from a Wallace story.

After graduating from a Catholic military cadet school, Stanley eventually pursued a career in film with his enrolment at the Cape Town Film and Video School. He left South Africa for London after graduating to escape mandatory military service. He continued sharpening his cinematic skills by directing short films, two of which, *Rites of Passage* and *Incidents in an Expanding Universe*, were honored with a prestigious Institute of Contemporary Arts Gold Seal Award. Stanley worked professionally as a music video director for Wicked Films, hammering out cinematic pop-promos for punk, pop and goth acts such as Public Image Ltd., Renegade Sound Wave, Pop Will Eat Itself and Fields of the Nephilim.

After completing a documentary on the Soviet-Afghanistan War, entitled *Voices of the Moon* (1990), Stanley wrote and directed his first narrative feature, *Hardware* (1990), for Wicked Films. Based on a student project from Stanley's Cape Town days and shot on a modest £1 million budget, it quickly achieved underground cult status for its heady blend of high-tech post-apocalyptic visuals, cryptic religious references and energetic camerawork. *Hardware* is a cautionary, twenty-first century 'technology vs. humanity' tale. It concerns a government-manufactured android and a deadly fascist population control tool that is unwittingly recovered from a salvage yard by a returning soldier as a Christmas present for his cloistered artist girlfriend. Short on substance, *Hardware* is a pop mythology hodgepodge pinched from contemporary science fiction classics such as *The Terminator* (1984), *Alien* (1979), *Blade Runner* (1982) and *Brazil* (1985). Not even Wim Wenders' *The State of Things* (1982) is safe from Stanley's cinematic pickpocketing. Stanley calls *Hardware* his 'monster child', and has said: 'I felt a little ashamed that, having gone to all that trouble, what I ended up with was just a reasonable *Alien-Terminator* rip-off. I don't know whether to be proud of it or to reject it'.

Dust Devil (1992) is Stanley's personal and poetic follow-up to the more commercially palatable *Hardware*. An existential South African horror film, it was shot on location in Namibia on a budget of £2.8 million. The story is loosely based on the legend of a real African serial murderer called Nhadiep, a killer whose reputation elevated to the supernatural realm over time because of his elusiveness and mysterious demise. Stanley meshes the cinematic embodiment of Nhadiep with the spaghetti western figure 'The Man with No Name' and to the urban folklore mythos of the 'disappearing hitchhiker'. The film's genre structure serves as a framework for deeper explorations of Gnostic spirituality and, to a lesser extent, the South African-condoned policies of racism and sexism, resulting in a uniquely absorbing experience for viewers able to see beyond the film's blood-spattered surface. Stanley's penchant for wearing his cinematic inspirations on his sleeve remains – Andrei Tarkovsky, Sergio Leone, Dario Argento, Alejandro Jodorowsky and Wim Wenders are all along for the ride. Unlike in *Hardware*, however, Stanley makes them the inspirations for his own work rather than cobbling them together to create a hybrid Frankenstein. *Dust Devil* was drastically edited by 19 minutes for its US release, culling most of the spiritual elements and turning the film into a straight-up serial killer tale. Stanley's original cut is sometimes referred to as the 'final cut' or the 'European cut'.

In 1994 Stanley completed a filmic interpretation of the British prog-rock act Marillion's concept album 'Brave', about a suicidal girl on a bridge, on a budget of £100,000. It was broadcast on RTL Television and later released on video. After completing *Dust Devil*, Stanley was hired by American producer Ed Pressman to write and direct a contemporary adaptation of H.G. Wells' 'The Island of Dr. Moreau'. After devoting four years to pre-production work, Stanley was fired four days into filming and replaced by director John Frankenheimer after losing a power struggle with actor Val Kilmer.   **THa**

Frank STAPLETON

Frank Stapleton is an example of that rare kind of director that is aware both of his own *The Fifth Province* (1999) strengths and what it is that he wants to direct. That said, only one of his films, *The Fifth Province* (1999), has been released in the cinema. All his work to date signals his preoccupation with surreal suggestiveness, imaginative freedom and fantasies that have their seeds in small Irish communities. As one critic has aptly noted: 'Stapleton's films are always about Ireland, an ironic, postmodern Ireland, lampooning both ancient pieties and modern fashionable poses, an unreal Ireland that captures the essence of the one we inhabit'. Steadfastly refusing to embrace the trendy attempts to re-brand his country of birth, Stapleton's *The Fifth Province* is wonderfully deadpan. It not only shows off his expansive film knowledge, 'borrowing' many images from all manner of classic movies, but also takes a well-aimed swipe at the self-important intellectualism that surrounds the study of the medium. Its wild, imaginative story, co-written by Stapleton, involves a simple lad whose dreams overlap into reality, his love for the black poetry-reciting Irish President, and a Danish intellectual with an unhealthy obsession for the shower scene in *Psycho* (1960).

The film makes stunning use of shots of rain and pseudo-religious light; its surrealistic aspects – of which there are many – are played straight, never becoming too elaborate. Despite its excellence, the film has been unjustly overlooked by the majority of people living east of the Irish Sea. Stapleton continues to work, however, and hopefully will soon gain the recognition he deserves.   **AL**

Gerry STEMBRIDGE

Guiltrip (1996)
About Adam (2000)

Born in Dublin, Ireland, in 1960, educated at University College Dublin, Gerry Stembridge worked for Radio Telefís Éireann for five years, but shot to fame as one of the writers and performers of the controversial radio series 'Scrap Saturday' in the late 1980s. This fast-paced political lampoon also featured the talents of comedian Dermot Morgan, but was withdrawn from the air in 1991 at the height of its popularity.

Stembridge made his feature-film debut as writer and director of the drama *Guiltrip* (1996), one of the most successful Irish films of its time at the Irish box office. This dark tale of an abusive relationship between a controlling soldier and his wife makes use of a flashback/flash-forward structure and a visual sense of enclosure to explore the frustration and claustrophobia of contemporary small-town Irish life. He expanded upon this theme recently in the television drama 'Black Day at Black Rock', which deals with the events which transpire when it is announced that a group of African emigrants are to be moved into a tightly-knit Irish community.

In 2000 he wrote and directed the romantic comedy *About Adam* which, like *Guiltrip*, demonstrated that an Irish film could be both Irish and universal at the same time. This romantic comedy depicted the seduction of three sisters by a handsome young Dubliner who is engaged to one of them. It illustrates how different people can have varying perspectives on the same events; Stembridge made this point visually resonant by matching the style and tone of each encounter to the personality of the sister in question. Like *Guiltrip*, the film also toyed with narrative structure, making it something akin to a comic Irish *Rashomon* (1950). *About Adam* was widely distributed in Europe and the US where it gained positive notices as an exemplar of the 'new' Irish cinema. Stembridge has worked on shorts and in theatre as a writer and producer. He has also served as screenwriter on Thaddeus O'Sullivan's *Ordinary Decent Criminal* (2000) and Pat Murphy's *Nora* (2000), based on the relationship between Nora Barnacle and James Joyce.   **HO**

David A STEWART

Honest (2000)

Born in Sunderland, UK, in 1952, and most famous for being one half of the successful rock band The Eurythmics, Dave Stewart began composing film music in 1989 for *De Kassière*. He has also worked on Paul Verhoeven's *Showgirls* (1995) and Ted Demme's *Beautiful Girls* (1996). In 2000 he released his first feature as a director, *Honest*, which he co-wrote with Dick Clement, Ian La Frenais and Karen Lee Street.

Set in London in 1968, *Honest* is the story of three sisters from the East End who masquerade as men at night to rob nightclubs and jewellers. Inevitably, events do not run smoothly: after accidentally involving an aspiring American writer in their escapades, the girls make dangerous enemies with both the local gangsters and a crazed, Colombian cocaine dealer. The film received much of its commercial interest for casting three members of the pop band All Saints in their screen debut. Although the posters and marketing relied on their glamorous looks, the film itself is less exploitative – in drag, the girls look uncannily like the Beatles in their early days.

Honest is a fast-paced, urban adventure that switches back and forth between the grey terraces of the East End and the psychedelic West End. Thematically, it attempts to cover too much ground. Both a love story and a crime story, parodying the free-love ethos of the swinging Sixties, it tries to create moments of touching family drama whilst simultaneously commenting on the liberation of women and the gaping social distance between East and West London. Relying too heavily on caricature, it was heavily criticised in the press for the mediocre performances of its central stars. Many cinemas pulled *Honest* from their screen after a very poor opening weekend (£111, 309 from over 200 screens), but Stewart's efforts are not entirely wasted. An impromptu music festival allows him to display a moment of directorial authority, and he handles the ethereal, often disturbing, experience of taking hallucinogenic drugs with confidence and visual innovation. **MS**

Brian STIRNER

Having written and directed only one feature film, many people may not know the name of Brian Stirner, yet he has been acting in film and television for over twenty years. If *A Kind of Hush* (1997) is any indication of his talent, he should certainly start to become more widely recognised outside the UK in the years to come.

A Kind of Hush (1997)

The film, based upon Richard Johnson's book, centres on a group of young boys who have all been sexually abused by someone in their life and form a gang to stalk out sexual predators. Using a largely young, unknown cast, Stirner successfully handles the delicate social mores, displaying great courage where other directors might have balked at depicting the harsh realities of the issue. Unlike Barry Levinson's *Sleepers* (1996), to which it bears loose similarities, the beauty of *A Kind of Hush* is that Stirner does not treat the vigilantes as people who have everything covered. There are no Brad Pitts or Jason Patrics in this film, getting their revenge and then partying with Minnie Driver or Robert De Niro. Instead, they are simply a mess, and certainly not heroes.

Stirner does give one character a chance to explore his gang-like ways and possibly a glimmer of hope. Stu, played by Harley Smith, is a young man struggling with his past and trying to resolve his future. He may be the hero of the piece but he is not a lawyer or a writer; he works in a kitchen. Ultimately, the film deals less with the effect that abuse has on these youngsters and more with their hopes for the future. It is not just a film about revenge then, but also about growing up and learning to accept the frailties of life. Rather than allow the material to become sentimental, Stirner retains a gritty edge, finding a truth that few first-time directors have achieved. All his years of acting seem to have created a director of conscience and craft. **JM**

Charles STURRIDGE

Charles Sturridge entered the film business with a small acting role in Lindsay Anderson's *If...* (1968) and joined ITV's 'World In Action' team in 1974. After a television directing apprenticeship on 'Coronation Street', he scripted the LWT series 'Troubles', based on J.G. Farrell's novel, in 1980. Arguably his most important contribution to the television and film world came in 1982 with the release of 'Brideshead Revisited'. Adapted and directed by Sturridge from Evelyn Waugh's novel, the series won seventeen international awards, including the coveted BAFTA for Best Series, two Golden Globes and eleven Emmy nominations. The eleven-part series is frequently invoked by cultural commentators and critics as a defining moment in British television. Not only did it help forge a number of illustrious careers (most notably Jeremy Irons'), but its combination of period drama, literary gravitas and global commercial appeal became the template for the British 'heritage movie' of the 1980s and early 1990s. It undoubtedly paved the way for the spate of Merchant-Ivory adaptations of the classics, and contributed to the style and tone of a very specific facet of British cinema.

Runners (1983)
Aria (segment, 1987)
A Handful of Dust (1988)
Where Angels Fear to Tread (1991)
FairyTale: A True Story (1997)

Sturridge's feature debut, *Runners* (1983), starred James Fox as an anxious father looking for his runaway teenage daughter on the streets of London. The film is well-suited to Sturridge's television credentials, as the seedy realism and gritty urban feel of the narrative is cleverly teased out by his slow-paced, revealing direction. The film is also adept in its attempt to dig deeper beneath its tabloid-style sensationalist storyline. Although after two years of a fruitless search the media may have called off the search, the relentlessness of Fox's father makes a defiantly unambiguous statement about personal responsibility.

Sturridge's 'La forza del destino' segment in the portmanteau film *Aria* (1987) sits uneasily alongside those of luminaries such as Jean-Luc Godard, Robert Altman and Nicholas Roeg. John Hurt is the man wandering the streets of Italy, his own personal odyssey punctuated by the marrying of operatic arias and glossy visuals. Due to the highly individualistic talents of the directors, it is hard for any consistent narrative tone to emerge, and the spectator is relegated to the level of cipher, reacted against rather than reacting to.

A Handful of Dust (1988) is another Sturridge adaptation of an Evelyn Waugh novel. Kristin Scott Thomas stars as the frustrated aristocratic wife who rejects her husband (James Wilby) and begins a passionate affair with a young man-about-town (Rupert Graves). The film fails to register Waugh's savage irony. The novel, set in the 1930s, inevitably punishes the wife's infidelities by having her young son die, but the direction here is so in awe of the beautiful scenery and ugly aristocratic manners that any hint of a satirical indictment is lost amidst the surface gloss. This is the worst kind of costume drama – impeccably acted, perhaps, but rife with hollow moralising and a blatant misunderstanding of the source material.

Where Angels Fear to Tread (1991) recounts the tale of a brother and sister who travel to Italy to retrieve the young child of their sister-in-law who died during childbirth. Adapted from the E.M. Forster novel, the film emotionally connects much more than *A Handful of Dust*, and again boasts fine ensemble acting. Helen Mirren dominates the film when she is on screen; Judy Davis excels as a neurotic spinster. Again, however, one is left with the impression that this is television masquerading as cinema; that behind all the surface gloss and impeccably mannered performances, there is a fundamental detachment from the proceedings and a staccato pace that seems ill-suited to film.

FairyTale: A True Story (1997) was, along with Nick Willing's *Photographing Fairies*, one of two 1997 films that was inspired by Elsie Wright and Frances Griffiths' photographs of the fairies at the bottom of their Cottingley garden. Whereas *Photographing Fairies* used the sensation to explore imagined realities and the effects of World War One on the public psyche, Sturridge's film takes the point of view of the children, melding fantasy and reality with some excellent special effects and ultimately uplifting messages. As Spielberg will testify, these kind of films work only when the film-makers themselves believe in the fantasy of their subject matter; it is to Sturridge's credit that he firmly empathises with his material, fashioning a heart-warming film.

Sturridge has recently returned to television. 'Gulliver's Travels' won five Emmy awards; 'Longitude', adapted from Dava Sobel's novel, was also released to great critical acclaim; the forthcoming 'Shackelton' will star Kenneth Branagh as the titular Antarctic explorer. It seems that the small-screen format is best suited to his talents – the more stately pace, richer tonality and broader characterisation that television entails is a sina qua non for the kind of tales Sturridge wishes to tell. He is currently in preproduction with *Disgrace*, an adaptation of J.M. Coetzee's Booker Prize-winning tale of a South African university lecturer and his affair with a student.   **BM**

Eric STYLES

Dreaming of Joseph Lees (1999)
Relative Values (2000) After studying at the National Film and Television School, Eric Styles began his career directing documentaries for the BBC. His association with BBC Cardiff was marked by 'Last Days at Fforchwen' and 'The Dream', for which he received a nomination for a BAFTA Cymru Best Director Award in 1995. His television debut *All Mixed Up* (1996) won several international awards, including Best TV Feature at the San Francisco International Film Festival and three BAFTA Cymru Awards; his 1997 short film *Birdbrain* won the Kodak Award for Cinematography at the British Short Film Festival. Styles' single drama films for the BBC have included *Love in the House of the Lord* (1997) and *Washed Up* (1998).

His feature-film debut came in 1999 with the release of *Dreaming of Joseph Lees*. Starring a host of up-and-coming actors (Samantha Morton, Rupert Graves and Lee Ross), the story centres on Eva (Morton) who secretly pines after Joseph (Graves), the boy who left her behind when he left to pursue his career. Harry (Ross), her new suitor, completes the triangular relationship. This intriguing, romantic psychodrama is marked by a strong central performance by Morton, who has quickly become British cinema's most exciting and talented actress. Catherine Linstrum's screenplay, however, is frustratingly unwilling to explore the wider connotations of events: the reasons for Eva's infatuations are never satisfactorily explained; and the conflict between duty and passion is dealt with in a perfunctory manner. With judicious cutting and stronger characterisation, the film may have been more successful in breaking free from its made-for-television trappings.

Relative Values (2000) boasts higher production values and a more impressive source in Noël Coward's play. Like *Dreaming of Joseph Lees*, Styles sets the action in the 1950s, and his affinity with the traditions of this era is evident in both films. *Relative Values* chronicles the fortunes of the Marshwood family and the Countess's reaction to the imminent marriage of her son to a Hollywood star, Miranda. A basic comedy of manners, it is concerned with social and class distinctions and the fraught relationships of a tightly-knit family. Styles coaxes excellent performances from his actors – Julie Andrew as the Countess combines the matriarchy of *Mary Poppins* (1964) and the materfamilias of *The Sound of Music* (1965) to witty effect – whilst the combination of Stephen Fry, Colin Firth and Jeanne Tripplehorn ensure the right balance of humour and mayhem. Clever tricks abound: like the servant, the audience is cast in the role of voyeur in the aristocratic shenanigans; the bright-red kitchen walls hint at the underlying class warfare. **BM**

Sara SUGARMAN

Sara Sugarman first achieved prominence as an actor, appearing on television ('Juliet Bravo', 'A Very Peculiar Practice') and in features (*Sid and Nancy* (1986)). She began directing with the stylish short, *Anthrakitis* (1998), which received a BAFTA nomination. Given this achievement (and her ability as an actor), expectations were high for her debut feature. Sadly, *Mad Cows* (1999), an adaptation of the novel by Kathy Lette, can only be seen as a disappointment. Although Lette's story of an Australian twenty-something living in London who is impregnated then abandoned was a success in print, it does not translate well to the screen. The first big problem is the casting of Anna Friel, who does not stand a chance, hampered with an awful (phoney) accent. She does try hard, as does Joanna Lumley (although she is basically reprising her role from television's 'Absolutely Fabulous') as the friend who helps her avenge herself on her baby's feckless father (an awful Greg Wise). Sugarman uses lots of music video techniques (speeded up action, weird angles, pop soundtrack) but to little avail: although the model would seem to be swinging Sixties movies like those of Richard Lester (such as *The Knack* (1965)), this falls far short of the similarly staged *Spice World* (1997). Another problem is the distracting, would-be 'wacky' cameos from Noel Gallagher, the models Jodie Kidd and Susie Bick, Harrods owner Mohamed Al-Fayed and 'It Girl' Tara Palmer-Tompkinson. There are some talented performers caught up in this (such as Anna Massey and Phyllida Law) but they are given little to do. Much of Lette's writing relies on painful puns, so it is difficult to see why anyone thought this would work on screen.

For her second feature, *Very Annie Mary* (2001), Sugarman returns to the Welsh setting of *Anthrakitis* with the story of a young woman (the excellent Australian actor Rachel Griffiths) who tends to her father (Jonathan Pryce) after his stroke, despite his crushing her dream to be an opera singer. This is pleasingly far from the 'Cool Britannia' setting of a London peopled with models and socialites, and the cast (which also includes Ioan Gruffudd and Matthew Rhys) is talented, in its entirety, the film is unsatisfying. Pryce is a vital performer and when his character has a stroke the film loses a lot of its energy. Griffiths tries hard and is a winning actor but she ends up occasionally mugging. The screenplay is bitty and composed of a series of loosely connected vignettes and Sugarman seems to be aiming for Ealing-esque whimsy, but fails. **IC**

Mad Cows (1998)
Very Annie Mary (2001)

Stewart SUGG

After an undistinguished career directing documentaries about trains, Stewart Sugg wrote, produced and directed his feature debut, *Fast Food*, in 1998. Starring rising British talents Emily Woof and Douglas Henshall, it deals with Benny's return to his home city of London to find that serious changes have occurred. His friends have turned to petty crime, enabling them merely to exist, as the title suggests, on a diet of fast food. The title attempts to work as a metaphor for the disposable cheapness of the gang's lives, as evidenced by their casual attitudes to violence and crime. The inevitable love

Fast Food (1998)

story between Benny (Henshall) and Letitia (Woof) also takes place, resulting – rather incredibly – in the blind Letitia re-gaining her eyesight.

With its crime-based plot, fast talk and energetic approach to violence, the film is essentially derivative, mining other established genres in a bid to gain credibility. Reviewers have pointed to the noirish story, the references to Martin Scorsese's *Goodfellas* (1990) and Stanley Kubrick's *A Clockwork Orange* (1971) in the beating of a tramp, and the verbatim quotes from Brian De Palma's *Carlito's Way* (1993). The hand-held camera work that permeates the film lends a sense of urgency but is still too derivative to evoke originality. The steals fail to illuminate any aspect of the story, instead distracting and concealing, leaving little room for the characters to develop beyond stereotypes. The plot twists and turns but ultimately, by sacrificing plausibility in favour of a most unlikely narrative resolution, wraps the film up far too comfortably.

Sugg is currently working on his second feature, *Kiss Kiss Bang Bang*, about a washed-up hitman forced out of retirement. Chris Penn, Paul Bettany (capitalising on his remarkable performance in Paul McGuigan's *Gangster No. 1* (2000)) and Sienna Guillory are due to star. **JD**

Poitr SZKOPIAK

Small Time Obsession (2000) At first glance, Poitr Szkopiak's debut, *Small Time Obsession* (2000), appears to be another in the long line of recent films by young British director's dealing with petty theft and other underworld dealings. Closer inspection, however, reveals Szkopiak's interest in exploring the interaction of people with Polish roots living in their small London community rather than their world of crime. Though nefarious, their actions do not define them as people. A social drama-comedy, it should not have been compared to *Lock, Stock and Two Smoking Barrels* (1998).

Szkopiak's writing and film-making is delightful, employing inventive camera angles, loose dialogue and beautiful locations to delve into the characters' relationships. It is not a slick film by any means but one that shows a great deal of vision in its small scale. This enhances the audience's visual perception of the film and an understanding of the protagonist's day-to-day realities. Few freshman directors would have the nerve to include a wealth of information in such long takes; despite several scenes of substantial length, Szkopiak should be applauded for privileging complex detail and motivation over fast cutting.

Szkopiak has also co-produced and edited Ian Diaz's *The Killing Zone* (2000), which has been released on video and DVD. **JM**

T

Julien TEMPLE

Julien Temple can be seen as representative of the over-hyped and short-lived renaissance of the British cinema in the 1980s. Having worked in video for the pop music industry in the early 1980s, he followed in the wake of figures such as Alan Parker who moved from advertising and television into film-making. He later departed for Hollywood for a short, troubled career before returning to British film and television co-production in the late 1990s.

Temple's feature films span a variety of genres, often displaying verve and wit as well as a flair for imaginative visuals. Very much a poor man's enfant terrible, he has frequently parodied cultural icons and subverted genre conventions in line with what he calls his 'joyous cynicism'. However, this has often been at the expense of narrative, plot, sound and characterisation, resulting in frequent box-office failures. Critics have generally been hard on his feature film work. Mark Le Faun's comment that Temple is 'a slick skilled producer of images ... rather than a film-maker' epitomises critical opinion.

Born in London, UK, in 1953, Temple studied at King's College, Cambridge, and The National Film School during the mid-1970s. Among his first works were a number of promising shorts such as *Punk Can Take It* (1979), a defense of punk and a parody of Humphrey Jenning's World War Two propaganda classic *London Can Take It* (1940), and some television documentary work, most notably *It's all True* (1982), an irreverent exploration of the video phenomenon for the BBC.

Temple gained critical attention with his stylish pop-promo video work for the likes of the Rolling Stones; the controversial *Undercover* (1983) artfully combines performance footage and a tight comic-strip style narrative alluding to political oppression in Central America. He directed his first feature, *The Great Rock 'n' Roll Swindle*, in 1979. This wry film charts the rise and fall of punk rock group The Sex Pistols in quasi-documentary style, using a frantic mix of live action, newsreel and animation in different formats to convey the punk spirit and bricolage aesthetic. The group (all except John Lydon aka Johnny Rotten) play themselves, accompanied by such diverse figures as the notorious train robber Ronald Biggs and 1970s porn star Mary Millington. Despite its innovative

The Great Rock 'n' Roll Swindle (1979)
The Secret Policeman's Ball (1979)
The Secret Policeman's Other Ball (1982)
Absolute Beginners (1986)
Aria (segment, 1987)
Earth Girls are Easy (1989)
At the Max (1991)
Bullet (1995)
Vigo – A Passion for Life (1999)
The Filth and the Fury (2000)
Pandaemonium (2000)

style, however, it is not free from the clichés of the pop musical sub-genre, such as a loose narrative structured around a succession of songs and the svengali manager, appropriately played by the film's narrator Malcolm McLaren, the Pistol's real-life handler.

Eschewing his usual excesses, *The Secret Policeman's Ball* films (1979 and 1982) are solid, workman-like recordings of live Amnesty International concerts featuring comedian John Cleese among others.

Temple's next full feature, *Absolute Beginners* (1986), was produced by the ill-fated Goldcrest company and stars David Bowie. Although beset by financial and production problems, this is an energetic, colourful musical based on Colin MacInnes' 1959 novel of the same name which explored the emerging youth culture in London during the 1950s; class and race tensions are evoked by a crude sub-plot in the film. Temple and numerous scriptwriters turned the novel into a boy-wins-girl story – Eddie O'Connell as Colin and Patsy Kensit as Crepe Suzette – using a mix of dramatic and musical sequences, often shameless pastiches of classic Hollywood musicals such as *West Side Story* (1961). It was a costly box-office flop, its attractions marred by a poor script and a disjointed structure.

For the ten-piece compendia *Aria* (1987), Temple joined such luminaries as Jean-Luc Godard and Robert Altman in a filmic interpretation of operatic arias. His segment (also released separately as the short *Aria: Segment IV*) transposes extracts of Verdi's 'Rigoletto' into a story of infidelity set in a kitsch American motel; a typically camp affair, it employs sweeping steadicam shots.

His rather inauspicious Hollywood debut, *Earth Girls are Easy* (1989), is a satirical sci-fi musical-comedy on West Coast suburban values and lifestyles. Jeff Goldblum and Jim Carrey star as hapless extra-terrestrials involved with a lovelorn Californian bimbo played by Geena Davis. Gleefully garish with a slender narrative and characters, one critic described it as 'vacuous entertainment'.

Temple returned to the pop music industry in 1991 as location director come creative consultant on *At the Max* (also known as *Rolling Stones: Live at the Max*), a well-received, rapidly-edited film of a Rolling Stones concert. Shot in a modified IMAX format, it benefits from a sharp, high-volume digital soundtrack and images of remarkable clarity. His next feature, *Bullet* (1995), quickly went to video. An urban crime thriller, it starred the late rap-star Tupac Shakur and an over-the-top Mickey Rourke as a recidivist ex-con involved in drugs and gang warfare in New York. Although based on a true-life story of a disintegrating Brooklyn family, excess violence and a dubious subtext of racial conflict between Jews and blacks do little to redeem it.

Temple's next film *Vigo – A Passion for Life* (1999), is an apparently sincere biopic of the French avant-garde auteur Jean Vigo. Partly funded by Channel 4, it featured James Frain as a tubercular Vigo. A mediocre script and episodic plot repeating romantic clichés (the artist as a poor misunderstood tragic genius) combined with lack-lustre performances and a concern with Vigo's personal life rather than a critical exploration of his film-making, ensuring a panning from the critics.

Temple returned to surer ground and finer form with *The Filth and the Fury* (2000), a deliberately tendentious documentary on the Sex Pistols aimed at countering the McLarenite version of events. Consummate editing juxtaposed revealing interviews – most memorably with John Lydon compounding punk mythology and nostalgia – and blistering concert footage. Intercutting this with television archive material, he produced a poignant montage-style portrait of the band and disaffected working-class youth in a moribund Britain of the 1970s.

Temple's interest in the rebellious continued with *Pandaemonium* (2000), a rather unconventional historical drama and biopic based on the professional and sexual rivalry between the English Romantic poets Samuel Taylor Coleridge and William Wordsworth. Linus Roache and John Hannah play the characters with considerable sensitivity. Shot on location in the West Country and Lake District, the lyrical film features fine cinematography which admirably visualises the poetic imagination and troubled mental state of an opium-addicted Coleridge through the use of slow-motion sequences and time ellipses. Typically flouting the conventions of period drama, Brechtian-like, Temple also included anachronistic elements to convey what he sees as the modernity of a poet's vision and its 'great resonance for today'. **PJ**

Edward THOMAS

To anybody remotely concerned with both the heritage and future potential of the British crime film, Edward Thomas' sole feature to date, *Rancid Aluminium* (2000), is a profoundly discouraging experience. Its presentation of a London wide-boy publisher (Rhys Ifans) in conflict with the Russian mafia certainly contains all manner of cross-cultural potential. Instead, the film indulges a variety of lad-mag gangster fantasies, comprising big guns, horny secretaries and sultry, sub-Bondian Russian nymphomaniacs. Furthermore, the film is incredibly stodgy in its plotting (a central narrative bluff is a particular misfire), a fault compounded by its chaotic pacing and sudden shifts in tone. The current trend in post-Tarantino, British crime films to paste layers of 'irony' on to their scenarios, here merely serves to further enhance the vacuum at its centre.

The grafting onto the soundtrack of recent pop hits (from the likes of Robbie Williams and Elastica) simply adds to the air of desperation and contrivance that permeates the whole production. From the self-conscious, 'hard boiled' voice-over to the procession of ethnic and gender caricatures, the film fails to engage either as a thriller or a comedy. In supporting roles, Joseph Fiennes (with a particularly shaky Irish accent), Sadie Frost, Steven Berkoff and Tara Fitzgerald all appear indifferent to the shambles around them. As co-producer and screenwriter (based on his own novel), James Hawes must share a portion of the blame for this depressing mess of a film.

Thomas has also worked as a production designer (on *Resurrection Man* (1998), for instance) and as a writer (on *House of America* (1997)). **NJ**

Rancid Aluminium (2000)

Jeremy THOMAS

One of the most distinguished British film producers of the last thirty years, Jeremy Thomas, born in London in 1949, has an impressive body of international work behind him. As a producer he seems to have a particular affinity with controversial directors, working with David Cronenberg (*Crash* (1996), Bernardo Bertolucci (*The Last Emperor* (1987) and Bob Rafelson (*Blood and Wine* (1997). He has also worked with figures as diverse as Julien Temple, Takeshi Kitano and Johnny Depp (on his impressive but little-seen directorial debut, *The Brave* (1997)), and produced off-beat gems like *The Shout* (Jerzy Skolimowski, 1978), *Eureka* (Nicolas Roeg, 1983) and *The Hit* (Stephen Frears, 1984).

Fittingly for someone so drawn to the obscure and offbeat, his sole directorial credit to date is the weird drama *All the Little Animals* (1998). This is an ambitious psycho-drama about a damaged young man (Christian Bale) who flees from his demonic pet-killing stepfather, whom he calls 'The Fat' (a scary Daniel Benzali) and takes refuge with an animal-loving man of the woods (John Hurt). Bale is taught to respect all life, joining Hurt on his expeditions burying roadkill until 'The Fat' reappears and sparks a violent climax. The performances are strong, as one would expect of a talented cast, and the film is pleasingly odd and difficult to categorise. Part 'tree-hugging' animal rights tract, part character study, it ends bloodily like a Hollywood thriller. Perhaps due to Thomas' inexperience as a director, the film does not hold up to much analysis, although Hurt's character in particular is intriguingly ambiguous, both sage and psycho.

Having made his name as a producer of unusual fare, Thomas should be credited for his attempt to direct similar material; it is promising enough to make one look forward to any future projects he undertakes. **IC**

All the Little Animals (1998)

J. Lee THOMPSON

Born in Bristol, UK, in 1914, John Lee Thompson began his life in the arts as a stage actor with the Nottingham Repertory Company while still a teenager, eventually turning his hand to writing. Enjoying some success on London's West End, he was encouraged to adapt several of his plays for the screen and eventually to write original screenplays. In 1950, after wartime service with the RAF and having turned out a handful of original scripts, Thompson was invited by Associated British to direct his first feature film, *Murder Without Crime* (based on his own play, which had enjoyed runs in both London and New York), featuring Dennis Price.

Murder Without Crime (1950)
The Yellow Balloon (1953)
The Weak and the Wicked (1953)
For Better, For Worse (1954)
As Long as They're Happy (1955)
Alligator Named Daisy (1955)

Throughout the 1950s, Thompson helmed 13 films ranging in content and style from efficient 'small' pictures to more ambitious projects. In *The Yellow Balloon* (1953) William Sylvester stars as a hoodlum who manipulates a young boy wracked with guilt over his involvement with the death of a mate. Diana Dors appeared several times for Thompson: in the women-in-prison film *The Weak and the Wicked* (1953), the quasi-musical *As Long as They're Happy* (1955), about a Wimbledon mansion turned upside down by the visit of an American song-and-dance man, the madcap beast-on-the-loose comedy *An Alligator Named Daisy* (1955), and in the downbeat *Yield to the Night* (1956), which took the true-life murder case of Ruth Ellis as its inspiration. Thompson explored the uncertainties of young newlyweds in *For Better, For Worse* (1954), starring Dirk Bogarde, and contemplated the other side of the coin with *Woman in a Dressing Gown* (1957), a thoughtful study of mid-life marital dissatisfaction starring Yvonne Mitchell and Anthony Quayle (who would appear several times in the director's films). *The Good Companions* (1957) was an adaptation of a J.B. Priestley novel about the travails of a travelling troupe of variety performers. Sylvia Syms received a BAFTA nomination for her lead role in *No Trees in the Street* (1958), a slice of lower-class British life, while Haley Mills enjoyed her first starring role in the tension-filled *Tiger Bay* (1959). Curt Jürgens took the lead in *I Aim at the Stars* (1959), Thompson's fictionalised account of the life and American emigration of former Nazi scientist Werner von Braun.

When director Alexander Mackendrick quit the production of *The Guns of Navarone* (1961) after disagreements with executive producer-scenarist Carl Foreman, the producers decided to replace him with Thompson. They were understandably impressed by his nervy direction of the Africa-set World War Two drama *Ice Cold in Alex* (1958), his handling of the locomotive chase set-piece of *North West Frontier* (1958) and his comfort with filming in such trademarked widescreen processes as VistaVision and CinemaScope. With only ten days of preparation, and filming mostly on the sound-stages and backlots of Shepperton Studios (location shooting being done in Greece), Thompson made a quantum leap forward in terms of budget and industry clout. Adapted from the 1957 novel by Alistair MacLean, *The Guns of Navarone* was etched in decidedly anti-war shades, which did not instantly endear it to postwar British audiences. Forty years on, the film is rightly considered a classic, prized for the ensemble performances of Gregory Peck, David Niven, Irene Pappas and Anthony Quinn; it remains Thompson's favourite piece.

The following year he directed two distinctly dissimilar projects. Yul Brynner was the star of the Ukraine-set costume epic *Taras Bulba* (based on the short story by Gogol), as a fierce sixteenth-century Cossack chieftain whose hatred of Poles is put to the test when his son (Tony Curtis) falls in love with a Polish noblewoman. Handsomely lensed by Joseph P. MacDonald on location in Argentina, *Taras Bulba* was dressed down by critics for being overblown and unconvincing and is rarely discussed today unless for its superior score by Franz Waxman. More successful was the smaller scale but undeniably powerful *Cape Fear*, an adaptation of the John D. MacDonald novel 'The Executioners', whose creeping aura of southern gothic informed the deceptively simple scenario of a habitual criminal (Robert Mitchum) taking his revenge on the lawyer (Gregory Peck) who had him sent down. Photographed in black and white by Academy Award-winning cinematographer Sam Leavitt – with Savannah, Georgia, doubling for the actual Cape Fear, North Carolina – and scored by frequent Alfred Hitchcock collaborator Bernard Herrmann, *Cape Fear* was Thompson's first American film and remains his last truly great work.

None of Thompson's work throughout the remainder of the decade was distinguished, and most bore the indelible stamp of contractual obligation for director and stars. Yul Brynner re-teamed with Thompson for the Mexico-lensed historical actioner *Kings of the Sun* (1963), as a Native American chief who clashes with a tribe of migrating Mayans (led by dancer-turned-actor George Chakiris). *What a Way to Go!* (1964) marked Thompson's return to comedy, with a Betty Comden-Adolph Green script about a luckless small-town girl (Shirley MacLaine) whose string of successful husbands (Dick Van Dyke, Paul Newman, Robert Mitchum, Gene Kelly) leave her a widow four times over but wealthy beyond imagining. Shot in CinemaScope and teaming with celebrity cameos, *What a Way to Go!* is typical of its time and largely succeeds in giving its audience decent entertainment The same cannot be said for Thompson's subsequent comedy, *John Goldfarb, Please Come Home* (1965), which reunited the director with Shirley MacLaine. She stars as a magazine photographer going undercover inside the harem of an Arabian potentate (Peter Ustinov), who eventually joins forces with a downed American fighter pilot (Richard Crenna) to help the king's football team defeat Notre Dame. William Peter Blatty provided the jokey screenplay, which resorts to facetious character names to telegraph personality quirks. Telly Savalas appears briefly as a harem recruiter.

Returning to serious subjects, Thompson directed the post-war suspense melodrama *Return from the Ashes* (1965), which starred Ingrid Thulin as the scarred survivor of a German concentration camp who finds herself embroiled in a love and money triangle with stepdaughter Samantha Eggar and former lover Maximilian Schell. Plastic surgery, uncertain loyalties, greed and murder are the plot points for an unlikely story that is ultimately sold on the strength of its ensemble cast, Christopher Challis' searing black and white photography and the script by Julius J. Epstein. *Eye of the Devil* (1967) told the even more improbable story of an ill-starred French aristocrat (David Niven) who must sacrifice his life for the good of the vineyards that encircle his ancestral chateau. Niven brings the right note of sadness to his role as the altruistic Marquis de Bellac and Deborah Kerr is appropriately frantic as his disbelieving wife. Thompson's cast benefits from support turns by Donald Pleasence, Emlyn Williams, David Hemmings and American model-turned-actress Sharon Tate. Dismissed as ponderous, even by aficionados of the unusual, *Eye of the Devil* was perhaps hurt in the marketplace by its utter sobriety and cold black and white photography, but the film is better than its miserable reputation and is worthy of reassessment.

The re-teaming of Thompson with star Gregory Peck and producer-screenwriter Carl Foreman for *Mackenna's Gold* (1969) was likely a bid by Columbia Studios to recapture the scale and grandeur of *The Guns of Navarone*, but the results were at best middling. 1874 Arizona is the setting for this western adventure concerned with the struggle over a fortune in hidden Apache gold. Shot by Joseph MacDonald in 70mm Super Panavision (although not always exhibited with this process), *Mackenna's Gold* boasted another stellar cast (Omar Sharif, Lee J. Cobb, Raymond Massey, Edward G. Robinson, Eli Wallach) and an invigorating score by jazz musician Quincy Jones. Still, it came nowhere near the success of the earlier collaborations between Thompson and Peck. *Before Winter Comes* (1969) brought David Niven and Thompson back in their third and final collaboration, with a bittersweet comedy of manners involving a post-war Austrian internment camp whose conscientious British commandant (Niven) clashes with a Russian army deserter played by Topol. For *The Chairman* (1969), Thompson was brought together one final time with Gregory Peck, who starred as a Nobel Prize-winning American scientist sent into Communist China to obtain the formula for a synthetic agricultural enzyme that would enable the holder to corner the world market. *Country Dance* (1970) starred Peter O'Toole as an intemperate Scottish lord with incestuous yearnings for sister Susannah York; his performance anticipates his more outrageous turn as the troubled heir apparent of Peter Medak's *The Ruling Class* (1972).

Although Thompson and producer Arthur P. Jacobs had bought the rights to the French novel that would ultimately become *Planet of the Apes* (1968), Thompson had been contractually obligated to finish another film when 20th Century Fox finally gave the green light for the big-budget science fiction project. It was eventually directed by Franklin J. Schaffner. Four years (and two successful sequels) later, Fox brought Thompson on board to direct the final two films in the profitable but progressively cheap franchise. For its cost-cutting use of Los Angeles' Studio City as a backdrop for a story of a simian rebellion in Earth's near future, *Conquest of the Planet of the Apes* (1972) remains a thrilling and disturbing exercise. Toned down by the studio, who feared its stridently pro-ape stance would encourage Watts-style urban riots, *Conquest of the Planet of the Apes* is still a persuasive thriller thirty years on. Directed more at the matinee audience, *Battle for the Planet of the Apes* (1973) is at once charming and dumb but never comes close to achieving the apocalyptic stature promised in its advertising. More expensive and satisfying was Thompson's musical adaptation, *Huckleberry Finn* (1974), which featured the songs of Richard and Robert Sherman.

The Reincarnation of Peter Proud (1975) was a supernatural thriller produced in the wake of the success of The Exorcist (1973), but failed to do for past-life experience what William Friedkin's landmark shocker had done for demonic possession.

With St. Ives (1976), Thompson began a multi-film collaboration with the action star Charles Bronson. Although none of their ten films are especially noteworthy, all are passable thrillers that make the most of their 'B' film status. Cast against type in St. Ives, Bronson is a violence-hating writer who becomes a patsy for a clutch of affluent evil-doers led by John Houseman. The ageing action star donned buckskins and eye shades to play a syphilitic Wild Bill Hickok for the Dino DeLaurentis-backed The White Buffalo (1977), which marked a rare later big screen appearance for lady Kim Novak. Caboblanco (1980) was a South American-set retooling of Casablanca, with Bronson cast as a dive bar permitee caught between Nazis and those who oppose them.

More typical Bronson fare followed with the actor playing a variety of roles: a Dirty Harry-style enforcer in the urban serial-killer thriller 10 to Midnight (1983); an isolationist mercenary hired to bring down a Joseph Mengele-type British doctor in Latin America in The Evil that Men Do (1984); a detective framed for murder and forced to run from his fellow officers in Murphy's Law (1986); the perambulating avenger Paul Kersey in the Los Angeles-set Death Wish 4: The Crackdown (1987); a reporter caught between warring religious sects in Messenger of Death (1988); and yet another cop in Kinjite: Forbidden Subjects (1989), who opposes an oily pimp and helps a Japanese businessman track down his missing daughter.

Between projects with Bronson, Thompson turned his hand to half-a-dozen disparate projects. He was reunited with Guns of Navarone star Anthony Quinn for two films towards the end of the decade: the thinly veiled Aristotle Onassis biopic The Greek Tycoon (1978); and the World War Two escape film The Passage (1979), in which Quinn played a Basque mountain guide shepherding mathematician James Mason and family over the Pyrenees with the Third Reich in hot pursuit.

Cashing in on the success of Sean Cunningham's teens-in-peril film Friday the 13th (1980) and its first sequel, Thompson took the reins on the gruesome, Canadian body-count horror Happy Birthday to Me (1981), starring television ingenue Melissa Sue Anderson as the head of a class of rapidly diminishing high school seniors. Rock Hudson turned in his last big screen performance for Thompson in The Ambassador (1984), a loose adaptation of a novel by Elmore Leonard, in which a cuckolded American diplomat finds himself caught up in the Israeli-Palestinian conflict. King Solomon's Mines (1985) was an unsuccessful bid to introduce H. Rider Haggard's Victorian-era adventurer Allan Quatermain into the Indiana Jones era, and the film is little remembered or discussed now apart from its casting of a pre-stardom Sharon Stone. Somewhat similar in style was the contemporary actioner Firewalker (1986), a more light-hearted vehicle for stone-faced martial arts star Chuck Norris.

Although Thompson stopped directing feature films in 1989, he continues to remain active in the industry as a producer and is enjoying his retirement giving interviews and providing audio commentaries for his films on DVD. **RHS**

Jamie THRAVES

The Low Down (2000) Born in Dagenham, UK, in 1969, Jamie Thraves studied at the Royal College of Art in London. While there, he won Best Student Film at the 1993 Rimini Festival for *Scratch*, a short he had written and directed in 1991. He went on to direct a commercial for cinema, the video for Radiohead's single 'Just', and several shorts, the most prominent of which was *I Just Want to Kiss You* (1998), the story of a young Londoner, Frank (Martin Freeman), and his thieving best friend. The black and white film had a loose-limbed, improvised feel and non-naturalistic flourishes. It won Best Drama at the British Short Film Festival, and a Fox Searchlight Award for Best Short at the Edinburgh Film Festival.

Thraves has cited the work of Yasujiro Ozu and various American directors of the 1970s amongst his influences. In his debut feature, *The Low Down* (2000), a film that explores the theme of friendship in the face of disappointment, it is Ozu's influence that is the most detectable. It focuses on episodes in the life of Frank (Aidan Gillen), an Irish man living below his means in a run-down area of north London. His brief relationship with estate agent Ruby (Kate Ashfield) provides an opportunity to escape the comfort-trap into which his twenty-something life has sunk. The manner in which Frank toys with Ruby sometimes carries a latent menace, while his job as a television props man provides some gently surreal images (a giant head; a pink tree made of hands). Despite working from a script, the actors improvised their characters in a pre-shoot workshop – both amateurs and professionals alike provide remarkable performances. Thraves, meanwhile, proved his ability to examine the minutiae of human behaviour without becoming trivial. He also demonstrated a skill for capturing the rhythms of London speech – often provided on a non-synchronous track – only occasionally straying into repetition and longeurs. **KP**

Paul TICKELL

Once in training for the Catholic priesthood, Paul Tickell, born in Carlisle, UK, in 1949, decided instead to pursue a career as a journalist and television documentarian, directing his first feature, *Crush Proof*, in 1998. Building on the success of the BAFTA award-winning short film *Zinky Boys Go Underground* (1994), a tale of marginalised Russian veterans who delve into the volatile St. Petersburg black market, the Irish-set *Crush Proof* garnered some excellent reviews for the director.

Crush Proof (1998)
Christie Malry's Own Double-Entry (2000)

The drama centres on teenaged malcontent Neal (a powerful, instinctual performance from Darren Healy) and his attempts to pick up the threads of his life after a prison stretch. The film's determination to find a raw beauty in life at its most quotidian, or even in moments of violence, situates Tickell within the same artistic parameters as Shane Meadows and Lynne Ramsay (although little in *Crush Proof* is as elegantly presented as Ramsay's *Ratcatcher* (1999)). Essentially attempting to combine the naturalism of Ken Loach, the defamiliarising shock effects of Jean-Luc Godard, and the tarnished romanticism of John Ford or Anthony Mann, the film aims high and sporadically achieves this unlikely synthesis. The collapse of Neal's emotional world, hastened by his own anti-social tendencies (which are captured in an early scene of prison violence, rendered via a series of jump-cuts), is played out against a backdrop of Dublin housing estates, explicitly modelled on the western landscapes of Ford. Disaffected teenage gang members roam around these urban wastelands on horseback, and it is clear that Tickell is attempting to borrow some of the mythical weight of the western (with its tradition of psychologically-split protagonists) for his narrative. However, poor dialogue and a rather hackneyed vision of gang life bring the film's more lyrical aspirations back down to earth.

Neal's emotional side is brought out in his interaction with his young sister, although his desire to see his baby son is frustrated by his inability to keep his anger in check, articulating the vicious circle that his life has become.

The film has a problem with the representation of its female characters, who are given little independent existence save for the purpose of eluding or frustrating Neal in various ways. Although Tickell may be resolutely rejecting the idea that complicated lives can be resolved for the sake of narrative closure, the obscure ending is still unsatisfactory. Hardly a smooth ride for the viewer, *Crush Proof* is not an obvious career choice for Tickell, but there is enough raw promise in the film to make observation of his future work necessary.

A second feature, *Christie Malry's Own Double-Entry* (2000), starring Nick Moran and Neil Stuke, had yet to receive a release in the UK at the time of writing. **MF**

Michael TUCHNER

Born in 1934 in Berlin, Michael Tuchner grew up in England. Although he has directed several films, his strengths are more evident in television projects where his best work is both sensitive and involving.

Villain (1971)
Fear is the Key (1972)
Mr. Quilp (1975)
The Likely Lads (1976)
Trenchcoat (1983)
Wilt (1989)
The Rainbow Warrior (1992)

Trained by the BBC, he initially joined the programme 'Tonight' as an editor, becoming an associate producer and then a director. His subsequent programmes include 'Whicker's World', 'The Wednesday Play' and 'Play for Today'. One production of the latter, 'Barmitzvah Boy' (1976), written by Jack Rosenthal, was particularly well received.

Often accused in his feature work of obfuscation and uneven direction, he berates the lack of good screenwriters in the UK.

Happy for a while working on quality programmes, he still craved an opportunity to do more features. His first, *Villain* (1971), like *Get Carter*, which was released in the same year, was a strikingly seedy depiction of London intended as a demythologisation of the gangster movie. Richard Burton plays a sadistic homosexual gang boss with a mother fixation and useful contacts in high places, reminiscent of the Krays. Unlike *Get Carter*, however, it failed to convince most critics and audiences avoided it. Tuchner later described both *Villain* and his following feature, *Fear is the Key* (1972), as 'pieces of mindless violence'. *Fear is the Key* is an adaptation of the Alistair MacLean novel of the same name; though well paced, suspenseful and slick, it is ultimately confusing and unsatisfying. His next attempt, *Mr. Quilp* (1975), is a bizarre musical version of the Dickens' novel 'The Old Curiousity Shop' sponsored by Readers Digest which could only really be enjoyed by Anthony Newley fans. Released at an unpopular time for the genre, it further suffered from perfunctory direction. *The Likely Lads* (1976), an attempt by Dick Clement and Ian Le Frenais to open out their popular television series to feature length, is let down by flat direction.

Although he had no plans to go to Hollywood, in 1978 Tuchner was offered a promising television movie, *Summer of My German Soldier*, a tender but uncompromising story along the lines of *Whistle Down the Wind* (1961) about a Jewish girl who befriends and falls for a Nazi POW. It premiered as Movie of the Week and Tuchner became, as he says, 'the hottest director in Hollywood ... for about 15 seconds'. In the heat that followed, he made another television movie, *Haywire* (1980), and then *Parole* (1982). As his popularity waned he became disillusioned with Hollywood, stating 'it's tricky because it operates on optimism ... In the UK there's a more long-term view'.

He returned to the UK, however, to find projects ever more evasive. He made a well-received television version of 'The Hunchback of Notre Dame' before his next feature, *Trenchcoat* (1983), a Disney comedy thriller with Margot Kidder that was a forced and failed attempt by the studio to branch out. A period of television movies and dramas followed, interspersed with the uninvolving *Rainbow Warrior* (1992), the true story of the investigation of the terrorist act that sunk the Greenpeace vessel, and the painful comedy *Wilt* (1989), based on the best-selling Tom Sharpe novel. Despite the latter's slating, with Tuchner's direction described as pedestrian and poorly paced, he has declared that he would like to concentrate more on comedy.

Complaining about the concentration on words in Britain's screenwriter culture, he has said: 'If the words are funny, then the film must be the same. Not true of course. It's not easy to mess up a very good script, but even if you make a good job of filming a bad script it will always show ... the director so often has to fill in the gaps ... so many writers don't visualise'. However, the scripts for *Fear is the Key* and *The Likely Lads* were generally considered to be good, even if the latter was made on a ridiculously tight schedule. His most recent film, *Back to the Secret Garden*, starring Joan Plowright, was made for television in 2000. **FG**

Anand TUCKER

Born in Bangkok, Thailand, in 1963, Anand Tucker's film debut, *Saint-Ex* (1997), is self-described as a 'work of imagination'. Poetic and surreal, it is freely inspired by the life of the writer of 'The Little Prince', Antoine de Saint-Exupéry. Written by regular collaborator Frank Cottrell Boyce, the film is not a standard screen biography; instead, the narrative is interspersed with interviews of real people who knew the famed aviator and author. It has a distinct labour-of-love feel to it, and Tucker has invested the proceedings with a magical and whimsical touch. He elicits strong performances from his eclectic cast (notably Wim Wender's favourite Bruno Ganz as Antoine, and Miranda Richardson as the spirited and strong-minded love of his life) and it is a shame that the film was not granted a theatrical release in Britain.

Hilary and Jackie (1998) was released to great critical reception, due mainly to its *Amadeus*-style dissection of a musical genius and a keen sense of a very specific Britishness that avoids parody or preachiness. Emily Watson plays gifted cellist

Jacqueline du Pré with just the right amount of arrogance and brittle self-esteem, and watching her descent into the ravages of multiple sclerosis is a harrowing, yet ultimately uplifting, experience. Rachel Griffiths is also good as du Pré's sister, Hilary, on whose memoirs the film is based. Although Boyce's script occasionally airbrushes out important details (the timescale, for instance, is annoyingly foggy), the film makes an interesting attempt to come to a definition of what it is to be a genius. The direction is often a little self-consciously inventive – there are several 360-degree pans and sweeps – but Tucker displays a deft touch in his portrayal of the sisters' relationship. Almost symbiotic in their ability to feel each other's pain, he invests everyday objects (the cello and the country cottage) with a latent symbolism that offers an oblique comment on the siblings' own lives. Perhaps Tucker's greatest achievement is making a film that is as much about the suppressed emotions in an emotionally bereft English middle-class family as it is about music.   **BM**

U

Paul UNWIN

Born in 1957, English writer and director Paul Unwin might be more familiar as *The American* (1998) the co-creator of the hit BBC drama series 'Casualty'. After such a successful start, he continued his television career with the period medical drama 'Bramwell' and the precursor to *The Full Monty*, 'The Bare Necessities'. His first cinematic offering was a short film. Only 12-minutes long, *Syrup* (1993), a comedy concerning a man whose life changes when he gets a hair piece, won the deuxième prix for shorts at the 1994 Cannes Film Festival.

His feature-length debut, *The American* (1998), the BBC film adaptation of the Henry James novel, returned to the realms of the costume drama. With Matthew Modine cutting a striking figure as James' all-American hero, juxtaposed with Diana Rigg's scorned and brooding arch villain, this is a fantastically vivid and concisely portrayed story of the archetypal cultural outsider. Theatrical in style and composition – reminiscent, perhaps, of Unwin's days as the Artistic Director of the Bristol Old Vic Theatre – and complete with scarlet proscenium-esque velvet drapes and dramatic lighting, the mise-en-scène often resembles a Baroque painting in its sumptuous precision. Unwin has a remarkable sense of the relevant; it is in this that he succeeds where other literary dramatisations have failed. Instead of becoming woefully bogged down by the author's self-indulgent habit of including the mundane, Unwin steps, lightfooted, from one memorable image to another. Sincere yet not overly serious, it is clear that he enjoys his role as a storyteller. **BPr**

Stuart URBAN

Stuart Urban was born in 1959. His short film, *The Virus of War* (1972), took him *Preaching to the Perverted* to Cannes at the age of thirteen, making him the youngest entrant in the festival's (1997) history. He subsequently began a successful career in television. His satire on the Falklands conflict, *An Ungentlemanly Act* (1992), won him a British Academy Award for Best Single Drama. *Deadly Voyage* (1996), scripted by Urban and based on an actual massacre of stowaways aboard a Ukrainian ship, won the Silver Nymph for Best

Script at the Monte Carlo Television Festival. Given these credentials, Urban's feature debut is disappointing. *Preaching to the Perverted* (1997), which he wrote, produced and directed, belongs to a long tradition of British sex cinema that is neither sexy nor cinematic. The film refers to and is inspired by a 1980s court case centring on sado-masochism between consenting men. It follows the young, naïve Peter (Christien Anholt), who goes undercover at the notorious S&M club, the House of Thwax, in order to provide Christian moralisers with a victim of actual bodily harm and hence a basis for litigation. As soon as Peter is ensconced, however, he falls in love with the club's celibate hostess, Tanya Cheex (Guinevere Turner), and begins to go native.

Preaching to the Perverted was banned in Ireland, but caused little fuss in the UK. Despite defending self-harm, the film is often flippant when dealing with sex (fellatio causes crossed eyes), and attempts to expose anyone opposed to S&M as repressed hypocrites. Tanya's domination fetish is revealed to be merely symptomatic of fear of commitment to a 'vanilla' lifestyle; when last seen, she is raising a child with Peter, who has become her manager.

Urban's most recent film, *Revelation*, an occult fantasy starring Terence Stamp, has not yet received a theatrical release.   **KP**

V

Colm VILLA

Following a career in British television Colm Villa wrote, directed and edited his first low- Open Asylum (1982)
budget thriller, *Open Asylum*, in 1982. Set in Northern Ireland in the 1970s, it tells Sunset Heights (1998)
the story of Tom Bradley (Francis McMenamin), a young man who is unfairly blamed
by the media for a terrorist bombing he did not commit. Villa also wrote and directed
Paradiso (1983), the tale of a young woman whose life is irrevocably changed when her
father, the local harbour-master, comes under investigation for fraud. *Paradiso* was shot
on location in Derry and Donegal on 16mm. In 1986 Villa co-wrote, co-produced and
directed another 16mm short, *Cuban Breeze*, about an Irishman, Vincent Coke (Patrick
David Byrne), facing the death penalty in a Florida jail. After faking his own execution,
Vincent escapes and finds salvation on a beach in Honduras.

Villa's most ambitious feature to date was co-directed with Stephen Maloney and
Mark Ward. *Sunset Heights* (1998) is set in the city of Derry, sometime in the near
future. Following the murder of his son, Luke Bradley (Toby Stephens) gets entangled
with two rival gangs (thinly-disguised ciphers for republican and loyalist paramilitaries).
The gangs join forces to find the killer, who is eventually tried and executed on an ancient
druidic site. Their uneasy truce is broken, however, when another child goes missing and
Luke has to directly confront the spectre of violence before he can redeem the city.

In a macabre coincidence, *Sunset Heights* had its premiere at the Galway Film
Fleadh in July 1998, on the same night that three children were burned to death in a
sectarian attack in Northern Ireland. Despite his obvious commitment to dramatising the
Northern Irish conflict in a low-budget thriller format, Villa's allegories of violence suffer
from poor production values and rather melodramatic scripting. As critic Martin McLoone
has noted, *Sunset Heights* 'offers some interestingly different iconography and settings,
and evokes an almost pagan atmosphere of ghostly apparitions and Halloween spooki-
ness'. In doing so, however, it ends up promoting a familiar image of a Northern Ireland
caught in a cycle of aimless violence of its own making, devoid of political or historical
content. Forthcoming projects include *The Saint and the Non-believers* and *The Wind
that Shakes the Barley*.   **KHo**

Rupert WAINWRIGHT

The feature films of English-born music-video director Rupert Wainwright are made using Blank Check (1994)
many of the tricks of the video form. That all three are tremendously diverse demon- The Sadness of Sex (1995)
strates the versatility of video techniques, as well as Wainwright's own talent – from Stigmata (1999)
the children's fantasy *Blank Check* (1994), to the mental wandering of a poet in *The
Sadness of Sex* (1995), and finally to the religious apocalypse in *Stigmata* (1999).

A better-than-average childrens' film, with a comparatively complex plot, the Disney-
produced *Blank Check* is the story of Preston (Brian Bonsall), a young boy who is given
the eponymous document when his bicycle is run over by a convicted thief (Miguel
Ferrer) who is in the process of laundering a million dollars cash with a complicit bank
manager (Michael Lerner). Preston coincidentally cashes the cheque for a million dollars,
causing a mix-up for the bank manager who confuses the boy for the intended pick-up
man (Tone Loc). Preston then proceeds to live the high-life, pursued by the three criminals. Virtually a paean to consumerism, Wainwright manages to infuse *Blank Check*
with a personal style that elevates the usual sentimental Disney dross. The camera tilts
and quick editing, as well as an interesting noirish opening and fetishisation of television
monitors and video games, betray Wainwright's roots. He imbues the film with efficiency
and urgency, ensuring that the viewer never loses interest.

The Sadness of Sex is an experimental collaboration with spoken-word performer
Barry Yourgrau, which consists of 15 segments illustrating stories of love and sex that
the actor delivers while on stage. Influenced by Oliver Stone's *JFK* (1991) and *Natural
Born Killers* (1994), Wainwright uses multiple film stocks and other tricks, including
some computer and stop-motion animation, to give the film a glossy sheen despite a
budget of less than a million dollars.

Stigmata, Wainwright's most recent film, is tailor-made for his hyperkinetic style.
A collage of quick cuts, tilted camera, circular pans, zooms and special effects, it is
the story of a young Pittsburgh woman (Patricia Arquette) who becomes stigmatic after
receiving the gift of a South American rosary. At the time of its release the film was
attacked for its criticism of the Catholic Church. It does indeed take a stand against the

Church, but more its institutionalism than its Christian faith. While it has the potential to interestingly provoke, *Stigmata*'s overbearing and self-conscious style – continuous rain, simulated flames and doves flying in slow motion – detracts from its value. The film is essentially an elongated music video with an inflated narrative. The industrial score by The Smashing Pumpkins' Billy Corgan further enhances this impression.   **DH**

Peter WALKER

Born in Brighton, UK, in 1939, Peter Walker directed 16 films between 1967 and 1983, producing and financing all but one of them. As a low-budget auteur, he is perhaps Britain's closest equivalent to America's Roger Corman and Russ Meyer, possessing the talent to make mainstream movies but the desire to remain independent and offer mordant commentaries from the sidelines. Not all of his movies are particularly distinguished, but the best – the horror films he made in the middle of his career – are extraordinary explorations of madness, obsession and vindictive violence.

After a difficult childhood spent in orphanages, foster homes and Catholic schools, Walker came to film directing via unsatisfactory careers in acting and stand-up comedy, a technical apprenticeship at Brighton Studios and a youth spent enthralled by film noir. Returning from a working visit to the United States, he set up a successful business making and distributing 8mm 'glamour' films before ploughing the profits into a series of sex comedies and thrillers including *School for Sex* (1969), *Man of Violence* (1970), and *Die Screaming, Marianne* (1971), and began to experiment with 3-D in *Four Dimensions of Greta* (1972). He initially presented youthful permissiveness as a spectacle for an older male audience, but went on to depict the new libertarian lifestyles in movies made specially for the 18–25 year old audience.

In 1972, however, Walker's cinema took a change of direction when he commissioned the patrician director and screenwriter Alfred Shaughnessy to write a whodunnit about serial murder in an isolated theatrical setting. The narrative structure of Shaughnessy's script may have had more than a whiff of Agatha Christie, but there all similarities with genteel English crime fiction ended. The luridly-titled *The Flesh and Blood Show* (1972), with its gloomy mise-en-scène and gruesome Grand Guignol flourishes, became a psychiatric couch for the obsessions of its creators. In the process it sardonically laid bare the philosophy and mechanics of exploitation film-making and tapped the vein of youthful discontent with the established order. He went on to make six more horror films over the next decade before, disillusioned with the parlous state of the film business in the early 1980s, he turned to property dealing and the exhibition side of cinema. It is on the three gothic chillers that Walker made immediately after *The Flesh and Blood Show*, however, that his reputation as a significant figure in British horror cinema rests. These films – *House of Whipcord* (1974), *Frightmare* (1974) and *House of Mortal Sin* (1975) – form something of a missing link between the Italian gialli and the American stalk-and-slash teenpics. Their main difference though, lies in their allegorical power and the richness of their sub-textual life.

Walker is neither a great visual stylist nor an innovator of cinematic form. He is a pragmatist rather than a visionary, and thinks of himself as a conservative rather than a radical – but he is proof nevertheless that mischief and transgression are not the sole preserves of the avant-garde. Like Roger Corman, Walker is a director who is able to combine a feeling for past cinema with a keen sense of current controversy. This enabled the best of his 1970s output to capture an essence of the period and, almost unconsciously, to encode key cultural issues and attitudes together with the residues of his own biography into the mythic structures of the gothic. His skill is not so much in thesis but in synthesis – the drawing together of the diverse strands linking cinema to society at a passing historical moment.

In the 1970s Walker was British cinema's premier exponent of 'paranoid' horror, an anti-authoritarian and nihilistic treatment of the genre perhaps first introduced by Romero's *Night of the Living Dead* (1968). Rather than clarifying the boundaries between moral opposites, 'paranoid' narratives obscure them, clouding the distinctions betweenthe conscious and unconscious mind, normal and abnormal sexuality, sanity and insanity, health and disease. At the same time, faith in the efficacy and legitimacy of established social authority is undermined, leaving an audience in a general state of doubt and unease.

Paranoid horror indexed the anxieties created by the conflict between a reactionary establishment and libertarian youth, and Walker negotiated this conflict as a kind of cultural carpetbagger, taking full advantage of the ensuing disruption of normative expectations. A self-made man with a strong sense of independence and a certain amount of cultural detachment, he turned a cynical eye on the social upheavals of his age. The results were pessimistic and morally ambivalent but with a leavening sense of camp irony developed through his long association with the theatrical profession. His films of the 1970s reflect a widespread sense of cultural crisis and disunity and dramatise the moral backlash evidenced in the return of the Conservative government and the evangelical Puritanism of Britain's Festival of Light movement. They obsessively refer to the threat posed to the young by a vindictive and morally-bankrupt older order and their repressive institutions, but far from being tracts advocating free love and the counterculture, they almost gleefully depict their age as one of moral dissolution in which hypocrisy is challenged by a hedonism that is only slightly less ethically repellent. Walker delights in creating mischievously shocking entertainments that marry contemporary discourses of liberty and authority with transgressive sequences of visceral violence.

Conceived by Shaughnessy and Walker with a script by the young cineaste David McGillivray, *House of Whipcord* has a retired judge and disgraced prison governor setting up their own private correctional institution for wanton women, and unilaterally bringing back flogging and hanging. As an allegory of the moral backlash against 1960s permissiveness, the film is powerfully suggestive. It is also wonderfully evocative of what Raymond Durgnat has called the 'punitive streak' in British Puritanism, relating sadism to family hypocrisy and dysfunction. Walker remains of the opinion that 'there are very few "happy families"', and the one depicted in the McGillivray-scripted *Frightmare* is very disturbed indeed. Sardonically dubbed 'an everyday story of countryfolk' in its publicity, *Frightmare* draws on the story of Hansel and Gretel to tell a tale of hereditary madness and cannibalism in rural Surrey. Prematurely released from a mental hospital where she has been confined for 15 years, monstrous matriarch Dorothy Yates (Sheila Keith) lures young victims to her country cottage where she extracts their brain matter with a power drill. In the film's chilling final scene, Dorothy's ineffectual husband (Rupert Davies) watches in horror as his wife (the ultimate wicked stepmother) and their delinquent daughter turn murderously on his older daughter. The film is both a sly satire on the pretensions and failings of the psychiatric profession and a ferocious attack on the beatification of motherhood and our faith in the essential goodness of family life.

Just as a mother preys on her family in *Frightmare*, another symbol of love and security, a Catholic priest, preys on his flock in Walker and McGillivray's *House of Mortal Sin*. Father Meldrum (Anthony Sharp) is a pillar of the community who has been warped and cracked by maternal control and sexual denial. 'I was put on this earth to combat sin, and I shall use every available means to do so,' he declares as he sets about his parishioners, blasphemously turning the paraphernalia and sacraments of his profession into murder weapons. Although its message is obscured by gratuitously offensive guignol and softened by camp, the film clearly portrays Meldrum as a symbolic representative of a malign institution. Moreover, his freedom to continue his killing spree at the end of the film suggests that the system which produced him remains a threat to individual and social well-being. The threat will apparently endure as long as 'mothers' and 'fathers' (in both their familial and ecclesiastical forms) are allowed to control the minds and bodies of their children. As a deserted child and lapsed Catholic, Walker's cynicism about family and church is both bitter and personal.

In synthesising emerging themes of generational conflict, family monstrosity, Sadean spectacle, camp excess and paranoia, Walker was fully aware that his 'terror' pictures were taking the British gothic horror film in a revisionist direction. Whereas the Hammer horror tradition locates the action in a mythic (usually nineteenth century) past, Walker's shockers are determinedly contemporary in their settings. The resulting sense of immediacy helped to give his films their primarily subjective appeal. Terror is what we feel when we ourselves are in danger, whereas horror is an emotion we might experience at the plight of others. Hammer's classical style creates interested voyeurs, but Walker strives for a greater sense of involvement and more opportunities for audience members to identify with the protagonists. Eschewing the exoticism of Hammer, Walker tries to create an illusion of naturalness within the fantastic, of real people in unreal situations.

In the classical tradition of Hammer we are generally asked to empathise with demure and naïve beauties and to put our trust in a wise and heroic father figure with a belief in a judicious combination of Christian faith and scientific rationality. In Walker's disturbing tales, this reassuring world is turned upside down. His female protagonists are anything but virginal and his father figures are not to be trusted. His male protagonists are generally ineffectual and possess no more special qualities than the average viewer. Walker's world may be free of supernatural threat, but it is a world without reassurance. The threat in his movies results from the way in which social life is organised and regulated, particularly through the family, the Church, the medical profession and the legal system. At the same time, danger lies not in the free expression of sexual desire, but in its repression. This makes these films 'progressive' in Robin Wood's terms, in spite of their director's self-proclaimed reactionary disposition. Where the Hammer tradition so often offered moral lessons, Walker left unease, disquiet and a sardonic commentary on a legacy of corruption that continues to recommend him to cynical audiences today.

His films draw heavily on gothic elements – the persecuted and the fatal woman, and the sense of menace, isolation and despair – but reconstitute them in imaginative and contemporary ways. The brooding atmosphere of menace, isolation and despair which often characterises Walker's films is pure gothic, as are the ways in which the films employ cruel and violent spectacles to horrify their audiences. Walker's use of the gothic tradition's 'persecuted woman' is particularly evident in *House of Whipcord* and *House of Mortal Sin*, but his 'fatal woman' differs strikingly from the classical femme fatale, the eroticised woman who corrupts through her sexuality. Walker's dangerous dames are more likely to be de-eroticised crones. They relate to an even older literary source, the folk tale, with its witches, bad mothers and evil queens. Similarly, his villains derive their destructive power not from their sexual seductiveness and alluring cruelty, like Dracula, but from their repressed desires and their social positions of trust and respect. In Walker's modern gothic they are privileged professional men who replace the decadent aristocrats of the classical tradition.

This contemporising of the traditional is again evident in the way in which the key setting of gothic drama and its most potent signifier, the castle, is re-configured more modestly as 'the house'. Its central place in Walker's cinema is confirmed by its presence in the titles of three of his terror pictures, and its prominence in different institutional guises (school, theatre, prison) throughout his cinema. Just as in classical gothic literature, Walker's antagonists are creatures of a building with a malevolent aura, the 'Terrible House'. All Walker's houses are sites of authority, and symbolically represent continuity with the past. They are the repositories of memory and the conduits through which malign atavistic influences flow, as they are in classical gothic stories which are permeated by ideas of fate and destiny. In Walker's films, this concern with fate is all that remains of the gothic tradition's fascination with the supernatural. The rest has been lost to the same cynical rationalism that made the romantic hero obsolete in his cinema.

All the elements of Walker's terror films came into prime alignment between 1973 and 1975. By the time he came to make *Schizo* (1976), he was beginning to struggle to hold them in place. *Schizo* is the story of a young wife and her sinister middle-aged stalker. Its somewhat ill-disguised twist on the conventional stalk-and-slash narrative is that the potential victim (an undiagnosed sufferer from multiple personality disorder) turns out to be the slasher. The killings are as bloody as ever, and there is the same lack of retribution for their perpetrator, but the oppositional politics of earlier films have become muted in a conscious attempt by the director to broaden the appeal of his work.

With the appearance of *The Comeback* (1978), the direction which Walker's cinema was taking became clearer. David McGillivray was replaced as scriptwriter by an earlier collaborator, Murray Smith, and a transatlantic market was directly targeted by the casting of popular American singer Jack Jones as the film's protagonist. *The Comeback* contains Walker's most accomplished exercises in suspense, but the film's tongue is more firmly in its cheek than ever before. Smith's script was conceived as a pastiche of the psycho-chillers that Jimmy Sangster wrote for Hammer in the 1960s; his dialogue punctures any of the film's pretensions to pure terror with sly touches of macabre humour. Twenty years before *Scream* (1997) Walker happily chances his arm at genre parody and even lampoons his own themes when the psychos are revealed as a puritanical old couple whose daughter had been driven to suicide by unrequited passion for Jones.

By Walker's final film, *House of the Long Shadows* (1983), camp parody and pastiche have become ends in themselves, thoroughly predominating over all the other themes which his mid-1970s pictures had so artfully integrated. Supplied by Cannon Films with a dream cast of horror genre greats – Vincent Price, Peter Cushing, Christopher Lee and John Carradine – together for the first and only time, Walker realised that a new generation of cinemagoers would struggle to accept them in straight roles and so decided to play for laughs. Michael Armstrong fashioned a script of wit and substance, playing with ideas about genre, performance and dramatic truth, much as Shaughnessy had done in *The Flesh and Blood Show*. It was a fitting elegy for both a version of gothic melodrama that faded away in the 1970s, and for Walker's own career as an astringent genre revisionist.   **SC**

Rob WALKER

Born in Richmond, UK, Rob Walker began his career directing television documentary *Circus* (2000) and plays. His work, which has been predominantly within this area, includes Howard Brenton's series 'Dead Head' in 1985, directing duties on various television series such as 'Lovejoy', adaptations of Ruth Rendell novels and, more recently, the popular drama 'Dangerfield'. He wrote the screenplay for Vadim Jean's critically lambasted *Beyond Bedlam* (1994) and turned to feature directing with *Circus* (2000).

A contribution to the recent spate of British gangster movies, including Paul McGuigan's audacious *Gangster No 1* (2000), the lamentable *Love, Honour and Obey* (Dominic Anciano and Ray Burdis, (2000), and Guy Ritchie's *Lock, Stock and Two Smoking Barrels* (1998) and *Snatch* (2000), *Circus* recalls the great *Brighton Rock* (1947) in its setting but little else. A typical rise and fall gangster plot, involving blackmail scams and double-crossing, the film is tricksy and irritating rather than complex and ingenious. Characters die and are mysteriously resurrected, or simply vanish with no narrative explanation. The casting of C-list British comedians and celebrities in 'straight' roles backfires with the dubious involvement of Brian Conley and Christopher Biggins as two gangster heavies.

Attempts to invest the film with originality come via the laboured quirks of some of the characters: Eddie Izzard bathes nude near Brighton Pier and Conley chews off a victim's ear. The latter, which references Quentin Tarantino's *Reservoir Dogs* (1992), is only one amongst many such sub-standard steals. A finale that defies belief, and a tone that undermines any possible tension, make for a film which may well find itself becoming a cult addition to a great British trend, rather than a classic addition to the genre.   **JD**

Anthony WALLER

Born of British nationality in Lebanon in 1959, Anthony Waller attended school in Beirut *Mute Witness* (1994) and the UK. In 1978 he was the youngest student ever to have been admitted to Britain's *An American Werewolf in Paris* National Film School. In 1981 his short *When the Rain Stops* won first prize for a work (1997) of fiction at the first European Student Film Competition, and he also received the annual *The Guilty* (1999) Shakespeare Scholarship to study film in Germany. After a year at the Munich Film and TV School, he started work in German television as a vision mixer and editor. He has directed and edited a number of music videos and movie trailers and, since the mid-1980s, over a hundred commercials (for IBM, Camel, Super Nintendo and others). In 1991 he was awarded the Gold Medal at the New York Advertising Film Festival and in 1989 he compiled the erotic feature *Als die Liebe laufen lernte–2. Teil*.

Mute Witness (1994), which he wrote, directed and produced, is a complex thriller about a mute special-effects make-up artist who witnesses a brutal murder and is drawn into the snuff-movie demi-monde and criminal underworld of the former Soviet Union.

Originally set in Chicago, it was rewritten and relocated to take advantage of the possibility of shooting in Russia (Alec Guinness' scenes were shot in Germany in 1985) and consequently its bilingual cast sometimes struggle with poor dialogue. Occasionally a little too self-conscious, stylistically and in its repeated narrative rug-pulling, it is well-staged and beautifully shot. Playing almost in real-time, it is replete with allusions to Alfred Hitchcock and Dario Argento.

Waller went on to direct *An American Werewolf in Paris* (1997), a belated and sophomoric sequel of sorts to the quintessential, modern horror-comedy movie *An American Werewolf in London* (1981). Frequently unconvincing CGI effects replace the groundbreaking physical effects of the original, and filming in Amsterdam and Luxembourg prevent Paris from being as essential to the movie as London was to Landis'. A well-shot opening sequence, again alluding to Hitchcock and Argento, gives way to direction and camerawork that is as pedestrian as the humourless rock soundtrack. The camera is at its best when it is mobile, but too many shots and sequences look as if they have been taken verbatim from adverts.

Subsequently, Waller directed *The Guilty* (1999), a thriller about a young lawyer accused of assaulting his assistant, and executive produced *The Little Vampire* (2000), an adaptation of Angela Sommer-Bodenburg's novel.					**MB**

Tom WALLER

Monk Dawson (1998) Tom Waller was born in 1974, in Bangkok, Thailand, and studied at the Northern Film School in Leeds. Fresh from graduation, aged 22, he scoured the *Sunday Times* 500 rich list in order to find funding. He secured £80,000, and immediately began producing a feature. *Monk Dawson* (1998) is based on the 1969 novel by Piers Paul Read, who attended the same Catholic school as Waller – Ampleforth College. It spans 1954 to 1991, and tells the story of Dawson (John Michie), a young idealistic monk who is defrocked for aiding an unwed mother and sent to swanky Chelsea. He falls in love with a rich socialite widow, Jenny (Paula Hamilton), and marries the wrong woman when she turns him down in favour of his best friend, Bobby (Benedict Taylor). Dawson eventually returns to the priesthood after his wife's suicide, unaware that Jenny is carrying his baby.

Polished without being innovative, *Monk Dawson* is more impressive as a logistical achievement than as a formal one. It was shot on 26 locations around the British Isles, and Waller acquired a full score by hiring a 35-piece orchestra in Romania. The plot is unusual enough to maintain interest, and despite being provided with ample opportunity for sensation, Waller remains unexploitative. The film is not well served by its minor players, although the central trio of actors is strong; Paula Hamilton (best known for appearing in a Volkswagen commercial) acquits herself particularly well.

Monk Dawson was shown at the Sochi International Film Festival in Russia, as well as festivals in Leeds, Bangkok and Las Vegas. In the US, the film went straight to television. It was followed by *Eviction* (1999) a 35mm short about Irish tenant farmers, set in the nineteenth century. Waller's next feature, *The Butterfly Man*, is due for release in 2001.					**KP**

Kieron J. WALSH

When Brendan Met Trudy Following the success of his fresh, imaginative and anarchic Royal College of Art gradu-
(2000) ation film, *Bossanova Blues* (1991), a multi-award winner – including a Golden Square Award for Best Graduation Film and BBC Drama Award at BP Expo – Irish-born Kieron J. Walsh made the transition into the lucrative commercials market. Once there, he brought a playful visual style to the medium that has served him well in his subsequent directorial career.

Work in television, on programmes such as the wildly popular and irreverent 1998 series 'The Young Person's Guide to Becoming a Rock Star' – in which Walsh also appeared – brought further acclaim and the inevitable opportunity to direct a feature two years later. *When Brendan Met Trudy* (2000) was the first original film script from celebrated novelist Roddy Doyle, whose books, including 'The Van' and

'The Commitments', had successfully survived the transfer to the big screen in the hands of British directors Alan Parker and Stephen Frears. Walsh became the first Irish director to helm a Doyle project.

The simple story of Brendan (Peter McDonald), a teacher, classic movie buff, baritone and loner who has lost touch with the world, his fortunes enjoy a turn for the better when he meets Trudy (Flora Montgomery), a feisty, fiery blond whose rejection of all black and white films initially threatens to prove an obstacle for the blossoming relationship. An easy-going romantic comedy (the two leads seem particularly well-matched), the film is also an engaging love story with the cinema, peppered with enjoyable visual and verbal references as such venerable classics as *Sunset Boulevard* (1950) and *A Bout de Souffle* (1960). The background mise-en-scène offers numerous comments on both the film we are watching and the medium itself, much like Wim Wenders' *Kings of the Road* (1976); *When Brendan Met Trudy* is ultimately a timely elegy to the demise of repertory cinema.

Walsh has recently completed *Rough for the Theatre 1* (2000), his idiosyncratic entry to the 'Beckett on Film' series. **JWo**

Matthew WARCHUS

Matthew Warchus' theatre productions – ranging from 'Hamlet' for the Royal Shakespeare Company to 'Death of a Salesman' for the West Yorkshire Playhouse, via opera for Opera North and the Welsh National Opera company – earned him awards and a reputation as one of the wunderkinds of British theatre. This is a reputation he shared with Sam Mendes and Stephen Daldry, both of whom have moved into film directing.

Simpatico (1999)

Thus it seems logical that Warchus, who trained in drama and music at Bristol University, should follow them. His film debut is the starry but under-distributed *Simpatico* (1999), which he co-wrote from Sam Shepard's play and also co-produced. A comedy drama, it is the story of Vinnie and Lyle (Nick Nolte and Jeff Bridges), former best friends who are now enemies. Attempts at settling scores and a blackmail plot enable the film to evoke the themes of loyalty, betrayal and sexual intensity common to Shepard's work. Warchus directs with varying success. The film's roots as a play remain evident although he attempts to open the action up for the screen, not least with some mobile camera work. He utilises tight close-ups, theatrical monologues and flashbacks, all of which emphasise the noirish qualities of the work. Strong performances and parallels with the Shepard-scripted *Paris, Texas* (1984) provide interest. Overall, however, the film lacks the depth and intensity of Shepard's and Warchus' previous work. **JD**

Deborah WARNER

Before making her feature debut with *The Last September* in 1999, Deborah Warner worked in theatre and television. In 1993 she directed the television production 'Hedda Gabler', an adaptation of Ibsen's play, and in 1997 a version of Shakespeare's 'Richard II', starring Fiona Shaw. Shaw also appeared in Warner's 1995 short *The Waste Land*, based on the T.S. Eliot poem. *The Last September* is also a literary adaptation, based on a novel by Elizabeth Bowen. Set in 1920 during Anglo-Irish troubles, the film is set in Co. Cork, where Bowen herself grew up in Bowen's Court, a country house owned by her family during this period. Estate owners Sir Richard Naylor (Michael Gambon) and Lady Myra (Maggie Smith) attempt to preside over their manor and guests whilst the tide of Irish Republicanism rises around them. Noticing her niece Lois' (Keeley Hawes') growing affection for Gerald Colthurst (David Tennant), a British captain, Lady Myra becomes increasingly concerned; she is unaware that Lois is also hiding wanted Irish killer Connolly (Gary Lydon) on the estate.

The Last September (1999)

Shot by Slavomir Idziak, cinematographer to Krzysztof Kieslowski, *The Last September* contains beautiful imagery, with much attention paid to the detailing of the country house. Despite some fine performances from Smith and Gambon, however, the characters are generally underdeveloped and uninspiring. The pace of the film is deliberate to convey the sense of impending doom, but ultimately feels a little too leaden. Warner continues to work in the theatre. **LB**

Simon WEST

With a professed love of David Lean and Stanley Kubrick, one a true-blue Brit and one an adopted son, it is a shame that fellow countryman Simon West has eschewed his heroes' flair and depth for a trademark shallow visual style. Born in London in 1961, West directed several well-known television commercials, including the Budweiser frog advert, and music videos, before he started his feature-film career. This is evident in his debut, *Con Air* (1997), for the dialogue, when it can be heard, is witty. As a graduate of the Jerry Bruckheimer school of cinema (loud and then louder still, as in *Beverly Hills Cop* (1984), *Days of Thunder* (1990) and *Crimson Tide* (1995)), the film centres on Nicolas Cage as a tough parolee who joins forces with the police when his plane is hijacked by a group of master criminals led by John Malkovich. With an eclectic cast (including established character actors John Cusack, Steve Buscemi and Ving Rhames) and thumping visuals, the film may fail on basic levels of cohesion and believability, but provides the audience with a sensory trip that ups the ante on every previous film in this genre. Indeed, Bruckheimer is arguably the auteur here – *Con Air* mixes the dogged earnestness of his earlier 1980s films with a knowing, self-reflexive humour typical of post-*Pulp Fiction* (1994) visceral cinema. The film seems to revel in its own absurdities and does little to deny it, inviting us to buy into such hyperkineticism with lines like: 'Somehow they managed to get every creep and freak in the universe on this one plane'.

At least his next feature, *The General's Daughter* (1999), allows women to share some screen time with West's testosterone-charged misogynists. CID officials, played by John Travolta and Madeleine Stowe, investigate the murder of a war hero's daughter. Predictably, the investigation runs up against all manner of obstruction, suspicion and closed ranks. It is a well-made thriller that allows the audience to pause for breath, but the death of Elizabeth Campbell is so gruesomely framed that the film is tinged with an unwarranted sordidness and voyeurism. Admittedly, West's visual flair creates a gloomy gothic feel, which is similar to film noir in its use of light and shadow, while he again proves adept at choreographing verbal sparring. With a little help from Oscar®-winning writer William Goldman, he films the conversation between Travolta and James Woods as part sex scene and part title fight.

Lara Croft: Tomb Raider (2001), starring Angelina Jolie as the eponymous computer game heroine, has proved to be West's biggest commercial earner to date ($120 million and rising). The film is a hybrid of *Indiana Jones* and the classic 'shoot-em-up', laced with a strong feminist undercurrent. West's affinity with the film is clear – he rejected the chance to direct *Erin Brockovich* (2000) – and he treats the narrative with a stolid earnestness that avoids tongue-in-cheek humour, paying due reverence to the game's original aesthetic. Full of swooping tracking shots, balletic gunfights and CGI visuals, *Tomb Raider*'s charged story almost eclipses its generic deficiencies, but it lacks the kind of characterisation and intricate plot that made *Raiders of the Lost Ark* (1981) such a success. Still, a slick action adventure, featuring some astute casting, *Tomb Raider* proves a competent addition to West's portfolio. What the film lacks in consistency is tempered somewhat by its joyful laddishness.

West in currently in pre-production on a big-screen adaptation of the 1960s cult television series 'The Prisoner'. **BM**

Richard WILLIAMS

With a career spanning over forty years and some two hundred and fifty international awards, Richard Williams is an animator whose vision and substance is rivaled by few in the film-making industry. Working in virtually every production aspect of the animation process and almost every medium, he continues to pass his expertise to future animators. After spending his early years in Canada and Spain, Williams moved to England where he began work on the short film *The Little Island* (1958). The film won a BAFTA for Best Animated Film and quickly cemented his reputation as one of the top animators in the world. He then directed the short film *Love ME! Love ME! Love ME!* (1961), beginning to work, as he would continue to do, on several projects at once.

Aside from directing, he works in various other animation capacities, on commercials, television programmes and other people's films. He has thrived as a titles designer, for instance, on films such as *What's New Pussycat?* (1965), *A Funny Thing Happened on the Way to the Forum* (1966) and *Casino Royale* (1967).

In the 1970s, Williams continued to work on various different projects, earning his first American Academy Award for the adaptation *A Christmas Carol* (1972). He also worked on *The Pink Panther Strikes Again* (1976) as director of the animated titles, and directed *Raggedy Ann and Andy* (1977), which he resurrected when the original film-maker, his friend Abe Levitow, was unable to complete the project. Entering the 1980s, Williams worked on the animated television special *Ziggy's Gift* (1981) which won him an Emmy Award, and continued to make commercials.

Robert Zemeckis' *Who Framed Roger Rabbit* (1988), on which Williams worked as animation director, is his biggest achievement to date. His unique vision brought animated characters out of the cartoon world and into the 'real' world. Seamlessly blending live action and animation, it garnered Williams another two Academy Awards. He is also credited with starting the second golden age of animation with the film.

With *Roger Rabbit's* success, Williams attempted to finish a project that had started some twenty years earlier, *Arabian Nights* (1995). It went through several transformations during the years leading up to its release and has been widely heralded as the film that American animation killed; it was taken out of Williams' hands in 1994 and re-edited as a musical to cash in on the success of Disney's *Aladdin* (1992). Williams' vision of this film was to 'relearn the craft' but unfortunately he was never given the chance; the existence of his famous 'workprint' is a legend to most serious animation fans.

Williams is currently living in Canada and working on an undisclosed project. Careful not to have another film stolen from him, he has released no information.   **JM**

Nick WILLING

Based on the true story of the Cottingley Fairies – when photographs of fairies taken by two young girls in 1917 were discovered to be fakes – as its basis, *Photographing Fairies* (1997) is refreshingly free from cynicism. However, this desire to explore the implications of such a miraculous event proves at times to be the film's downfall; sometimes the essence Nick Willing creates in his own screenplay, he struggles to bring to fruition as a director. His style is generally confident and strong, affording his audience much pleasure through satisfying narrative closure, guiding the film cyclically from tragic beginning to its unfortunate, poignant end.

Photographing Fairies (1997)

Willing successfully establishes and sustains an unnerving sense of displacement – in part through the haunted performance of his leading man (Toby Stephens) and also in his use of accelerated footage, slow-motion and rewound images (perfectly executed by cinematographer John de Borman). This effectively lends itself to the overall impression of a drug-induced fairytale for adults; Willing employed similar techniques in his 1999 all-star-cast television adaptation, *Alice in Wonderland*.

Perhaps Willing's strongest asset is his evident adherence to the maxim that less is more and his shortest scenes are the most striking. We are shown less than two minutes of Castle's (Stephens') experience of World War One and the effect of its length is as powerful as it is comic. The most memorable image of the entire film is simply a hangman's scaffold covered with a gentle layer of snow. Though the pace drops on occasion, and the film borders on self-indulgence, it is intelligent and well-crafted.

Willing is currently in production with *Doctor Sleep*, a pyschological thriller. Goran Visnjic – Dr Kovac in 'ER' – plays a hypnotherapist with psychic powers who is drawn into helping the police track down a serial killer.   **BPr**

Nigel WINGROVE

It might be said that Nigel Wingrove represents a one-man renaissance for the long moribund British exploitation industry. Initially establishing himself as a graphic designer in the mid-1980s, he courted controversy in 1989 with his short film *Visions of Ecstacy*, an erotic interpretation of the sexual imaginings of the sixteenth-century Carmelite nun, St. Theresa of Avila. The film became embroiled in a long-running legal battle, breaking a

Sacred Flesh (2000)

British blasphemy law that dates back to the Middle Ages. After failing to win an appeal in the European Courts, it remains banned in its country of origin to this day. Undeterred, Wingrove embarked upon an alternative career as a video distribution mogul, using his Redemption and Jezebel labels to make a whole range of neglected European horror and sleaze titles available to the British public, much of it for the first time.

His sole feature film to date also demonstrates his ongoing interest in the sacred and the profane. *Sacred Flesh* (2000) blends religious iconography with almost hardcore sexual imagery, reviving a tradition of European 'naughty nun' films. However, this is a deliriously daft film, torn between satisfying its own brand of liberal, sexual philosophising and catering to the lad-mag brigade to whom it would obviously appeal. The narrative is little more than an excuse to stitch together a series of sexual encounters; in a medieval convent, Sister Elizabeth (Sally Tremaine), tormented by visions of a mocking Mary Magdalene (Kristina Bill), describes the confessions of various nuns while struggling with her own repressed longings. Shot on digital video, the film makes good use of its obviously limited resources and is often reminiscent of the dense visual detailing of Peter Greenaway (elaborate costuming, the use of text) and Ken Russell (sexualised crucifixion imagery). While flirting with an avant-garde style and structure, it intersperses its sexual (mostly lesbian) shenanigans with heavy-handed verbalisations of the main thematic concerns. As a result there is some wicked pleasure to be had in seeing bad actors deliver lines like 'isn't your reality a kind of pious paradise, where rank hypocrisy and ecclesiastical dogma fuse in a kind of perverse display of gratuitous abstinence?' That said, there is an unabashed energy to the film, its utter shamelessness encapsulated by the recurring detail of nominally chaste nuns, almost all seemingly equipped with full make-up, fresh manicures, sun tan lines, waxed pudenda and surgically enhanced breasts.

Ultimately, the film might have done better to acknowledge more overtly its juggling act between serious sexual diatribe and full on fumble fest – there is a solemn joylessness to the sex scenes that sits uncomfortably alongside the stated need for the unleashing of Christian repression. For all of its contempt for the Church's sexual dogma, it seems content to allow its orgasmic nuns to find no personal realisation beyond that of self loathing, a suggestion borne out by Sister Elizabeth's climactic self-mutilation.   **NJ**

Michael WINNER

Michael Winner is a strange character in British film-making. A well-known and very public figure, widely disliked for his provocative and oft-expressed moral and political values, he has proved to be a prolific director, having made over twenty films in a forty-year career. Few filmgoers, however, could name more than a handful of his films, and beyond the ubiquitous *Death Wish* series and the more recent well-publicised flops, they have largely sunk without trace, little remembered or admired. A director with an unerring capacity for imitation and a keen eye for the prevailing genre zeitgeist, Winner's style is essentially indistinct, the slick and competent treatment of subject that denotes a director who is technically proficient, commercially professional and depressingly cynical. Although Winner has made sporadic forays into comedy, the majority of his films are violent, gory exploitation and genre works which coolly cash in on the cultural climate. Psychological thrillers, bloody westerns or urban dramas, they are passable but unimaginative derivations of the groundbreaking films of the period, the second-class carriages of the endless Hollywood bandwagon. The Winner hero, frequently an ordinary man forced by circumstance into violent retribution, is best exemplified by his long-standing partnership with Charles Bronson, an actor whose well-practised air of brooding menace and stock expressions are the ideal vehicles for Winner's targeted, soulless brand of film-making. A survivor, an opportunist, a chameleon-like adapter of style, certainly, but also the ultimate director-for-hire.

Born in 1935 in London, Winner had already worked as a film critic and entertainment columnist by the time he attended Cambridge to study law. He began making television films in the mid-1950s for the BBC, and moved into the British motion picture industry in the early 1960s. His work during this early period, located in Britain and reined in by the need to appeal to a British audience, is eminently more enjoyable than that produced later in Hollywood where the 1970s exploitation trends and bigger budgets steered him towards different and less palatable modes of storytelling. Following little-seen early works *Shoot to Kill* (1960), *Old Mac* (1961), *Some Like it Cool* (1961) and *Murder on the Campus* (1962), which received scant attention, Winner made an early mark with *Play It Cool* (1962), a star vehicle for British pop acts including wannabe-Elvis Billy Fury, Helen Shapiro and Bobby Vee. A musical comedy, and an early example of the pop music film of which the 1960s produced many, it sets up a screwball comic style which Winner would sporadically explore. The approach continued in *The Cool Mikado* (1962), an update of the Gilbert and Sullivan operetta 'The Mikado', using various name comedians, including Frankie Howerd and Tommy Cooper, and *You Must Be Joking!* (1965), another franchise comedy starring Terry-Thomas, Bernard Cribbins and Denholm Elliott. Filmed succinctly and competently on location, the films demonstrate Winner's ability to imitate and conform to the demands of genre film-making; audiences knew what to expect from these types of films, and Winner apparently knew how to deliver them. *The System* (1966) and *The Jokers* (1966), while never groundbreaking, show more flair and touch. The former, the story of an eponymous 'system' for getting girls in a washed-out South Coast seaside town, is suitably sleazy, filmed with a bleak, bleached feel by Nic Roeg, and enlivened by a neat twist as the system backfires on main man Oliver Reed. Reed proved a regular lead in Winner's subsequent British films; the burly, engaging screen presence, heavy on mood and attitude, which would later transmute into Charles Bronson in Winner's American films minus Reed's appreciable acting skills. He shares the lead with Michael Crawford in *The Jokers* (1966), one of Winner's most appealing films. With a bright comedy scripted by celebrated writing team Dick Clement and Ian La Frenais, it is set in swinging London and focuses on two brothers who plan to steal the crown jewels as a practical joke that will act as a wake-up call to the establishment. Swift, smart and funny, with a sharp eye for the idle pastimes of young moneyed men in a Britain struggling with class-riven society, and a keen sense of period detail, the film blends action, screwball and double-cross with an admirably light touch which Winner seldom displays elsewhere. *Hannibal Brooks* (1969), again scripted by Clement and La Frenais, is an odd attempt at mixing slapstick and war movie, in which British POW Reed escapes over the Alps astride an elephant; a daft, enjoyable mix of action and comedy.

Winner displays another side to his direction with the more serious dramas he produced alongside his comedies. The trend of kitchen-sink social comment and realist drama, set in motion by the 'angry young men' of British theatre and film-makers like Tony Richardson, was not missed by Winner. He produced a number of films in this earnest, forthright style: *West 11* (1963), a dingy urban story in which a down-and-out young London hobo is offered £10,000 to commit a murder, and *I'll Never Forget What's 'is name* (1967), a heavy-handed contrast of aspiration and necessity, in which a young advertising executive gives up his career to work for a small literary magazine, but is ultimately forced to rejoin the grind. The tragi-comic approach, the exploration of corruption and purity, of duty and dream, of freedom and liberation, are all very voguish but undistinguished examples of 1960s style. *The Games* (1970), a sports drama following four runners preparing for the 1970 Rome Olympics, is perhaps Winner's most enjoyable film of this type, contrasting various national characteristics and showing an admirable touch with tense action and climactic finale, especially with the culminating emotive race.

Winner's ability to adapt to the demands of subject, to deliver on time, under budget and to the letter, all made for a professional, employable and very commercial practitioner, a competent director of action, drama and comedy. His style was patently dictated by the marketplace and the intended audience rather than any personal vision. In 1970s Hollywood, with an industry increasingly reliant on genre flicks and sure things in the wake of the wild unpredictability of the Brat Generation, this kind of solidly reliable, malleable talent was just what the drive-in ordered. Winner was thus to make a lucrative continental switch.

The shift in focus as well as geography is evident from the outset. Where Winner had produced passable and mostly entertaining fare during his British career; modest and undemanding films shot through with a rather British comic sense and interest in

Won Ton Ton, the Dog Who Saved Hollywood (1976)
The Sentinel (1977)
The Big Sleep (1978)
Firepower (1979)
Death Wish II (1982)
The Wicked Lady (1983)
Scream for Help (1984)
Death Wish 3 (1985)
Dirty Weekend (1987)
Appointment with Death (1988)
A Chorus of Disapproval (1988)
Bullseye! (1990)
Parting Shots (1998)

drama, the 1970s saw a steady move into the territory of exploitation. As violence and sex became more prevalent in Winner's films, the comic and dramatic impetus dwindled; cheap thrills, cheap action and even cheaper morals steadily became the overriding forces of his work. Shooting almost entirely on location, using few set-ups and rehearsals, and stripping narrative and camerawork down to the barest bones, Winner was able to consistently deliver low-budget, economical genre thrillers targeted at specific crowds: cheaply made, neatly packaged and swiftly sold.

The two westerns he produced at the outset of his Hollywood career, though violent and gory and very obviously influenced by Sergio Leone and Sam Peckinpah, are passable attempts at the genre. *Lawman* (1971) is a well photographed chase western in which Burt Lancaster (another ideal Winner square-jawed hero) pursues a gang of gunmen who accidentally killed an old man. *Chato's Land* (1971) is a hyper-violent fugitive western in which an Apache half-breed (a faintly ridiculous Bronson in his first Winner role) kills a man in self-defence following the rape of his wife and is forced to go on the run from the law. Both films closely mirror later themes; the muddled moral ground of violent defence and the sanctity of the Second Amendment (the 'right to bear arms') to the American character, the pursuit of justice and retribution, and the mentality of vigilantism. These are themes on which Winner would found the majority of his films throughout the decade, and which demonstrate his increasingly righteous right-wing attitude. A host of Winner's films explore these ideas in different ways, but with an increasingly uniform visual style and approach. They are glossy, slick and sanitised, laced with what critics have called 'technological violence', purely and simply placed to thrill, excite and incite, the orgasmic pay-off to the gaudy cinema of cheap stimulation. There is *The Mechanic* (1972), in which Bronson stars as a hitman who makes his assassinations look like accidents, *Scorpio* (1973), a cat-and-mouse thriller between two CIA agents trying to kill each other, *Stone Killer* (1973), featuring Bronson as a lone cop pursuing the mafia, and *Firepower* (1979), another bangs-and-bucks thriller involving a drugs racket and a global chase of killers. All are almost interchangeable narratively and visually, directed in an identikit style, throwing in the requisite explosions, shootouts, car chases, stand-offs and cardboard characters. It is throwaway, plastic-wrapped filmmaking of a kind that becomes tiresome and indigestible after only a few bites.

Most notable of these exploitation thrillers is of course the *Death Wish* series, for which Winner is still mostly remembered. The controversial original *Death Wish* (1974) sets the template. Paul Kersey, a successful architect and 'bleeding-heart liberal' seduced by the supposed civilising effects of urban life in New York, is soon overtly confronted by the consequences of his left-wing outlook when his wife is raped and murdered and his daughter brain-damaged by a gang of listless, bored young thugs (led by a very young and gawky Jeff Goldblum in his film debut). Following a business trip to the (wild) west, various heavy-handed visual allusions to cowboys and gunslingers and a visit to a gun range, Kersey returns to New York as an urban vigilante cowboy, courting muggers that he then blows away without conscience. The drop in crime rate and resurgence in community spirit the vigilante causes make Winner's sympathies all too plain. The attempt to portray Kersey as a modern-day avenging angel, a gunslinger mopping up the lowlifes to keep the town safe, is indicative of Winner's deliberately provocative style and bludgeoning treatment. Despite its slick filming in the relocated frontier of New York, *Death Wish*, like almost all Winner's American films, is totally lacking in charm or persuasiveness and makes for lifeless, trashy and simplistic viewing. That said, it is not quite as dull as the sequels that pointlessly repeat the formula, two of which Winner directed.

Just as vapid are the psychological horrors Winner directed in the 1970s. *The Nightcomers* (1972), a truly sleazy sado-masochistic tale which purports to explain the origins of the ghosts in Henry James' 'The Turn of the Screw', displays an almost complete lack of originality or interest, resorting to a variety of clichéd images and symbols for its thrills. *The Sentinel* (1977) is an even more shameless rip-off of celebrated horrors including *Rosemary's Baby* (1968) and *The Exorcist* (1973), in which a young woman in a block of apartments discovers hers to be the gateway to hell; it revels in its variety of imitated styles and the mannerisms of more imaginative directors. Worst of all is the dreadful star showcase *Won Ton Ton, the Dog Who Saved Hollywood* (1976), which woefully attempts to exploit a multitude of star cameos to cover the film's total lack of amusing jokes or situations. If this is the evidence of Winner's ability to direct different styles of material, it is unsurprising that he preferred to stick with the bland interchangability of his tough-guy thrillers.

When the exploitation trend began to segue into the straight-to-video market of the 1980s, the commercial returns and demand for Winner's kinds of film markedly dropped. He returned to madcap comedy with *The Wicked Lady* (1983), a dire, clichéd romp through Restoration history and a remake of a Gainsborough original, all big bosoms, maypoles and smutty innuendo. Its sole interest is the women's whip-fight that Winner fought to keep following threats of censorship. Similarly uninspired are *Scream for Help* (1984), a leaden comedy involving a girl who discovers a convoluted murderous plot headed by her father, and *Dirty Weekend* (1987), in which Winner 'amusingly' covers the female flipside to *Death Wish* with a proto-feminist avenger who dispatches various male chauvinists using her feminine wiles and assorted tools including a polythene bag, a car, a knife and a hammer. Following a passable tongue-in-cheek Agatha Christie adaptation, *Appointment with Death* (1988), an appalling version of Alan Ayckbourn's *A Chorus of Disapproval* (1988), and *Bullseye!* (1990), a pitiful comedy centring on two con-men who are mistaken for nuclear scientists, Winner understandably took an eight-year hiatus.

He returned to spectacular form, however, with *Parting Shots* (1998) – *Death Wish* reworked as a comedy – in which a photographer is told he has six weeks to live and decides to dispatch all the people who have humiliated him. Blessed with another embarrassed roll-call of stars, more clunking dialogue and feckless direction, and an almost total lack of imagination, the film makes a bold challenge for the hotly contested mantle of worst British film ever made. The result truly has to be seen to be believed, the ludicrous culmination of a career that seems to have been in artistic freefall since his migration to Hollywood.

Quite why such star names continue to work with Winner is a mystery; even more inexplicable is the fact that he continues to be able to finance his particular brand of derivative, uninspired and largely repellent film-making. Dominated by a cynical, magpie mind, Winner's films show a peculiarly nihilistic approach to his profession that has constantly teetered on the edge of self-destruction. **OB**

Terry WINSOR

A student of the National Film and Television School, Terry Winsor's first feature, *Party Party* (1983), was developed with the co-writer and original star of his graduate short film, Daniel Peacock, who later found fame as part of 'The Comic Strip Presents...' team. The film unleashed a cast of British hopefuls, including Perry Fenwick, Gary Olsen, Karl Howman and Caroline Quentin, in a film set at a teen New Year's Eve party, which takes place while the unwitting parents are at a vicarage dance. Featuring Elvis Costello, Squeeze and Bananarama on its soundtrack, it charts the typical attempts of clumsy teenage geeks to 'see the new year in with a bang'. With much of its humour deriving from the characters, it is a pity they are reduced to stereotypes: the funny vicar; the nubile babe; the geek; and the thug who threatens the already vulnerable host. The film even dares to bring in stock comedy police officers, and confirms our expectations by using their handcuffs and truncheons for 'comic effect'.

Not without its funny moments, the film still relies too much on the mugging and strutting of its performers, who often fail to develop characters beyond their allotted types. Although perceptive on some aspects of the teenage party, Winsor steers clear of any controversy, avoiding attempts to articulate the more experimental side of teenage nature. The overall effect is of a promising premise that flounders under the weight of its own obviousness and repetition.

Continuing to mine the teen milieu with his next feature, Winsor eventually took his name off of *Morgan Stewart's Coming Home* (1987) and directing duties were taken over by Paul Aaron, rendering the film An Alan Smithee Production. Following a short film, Winsor made *Cresta Run* (1990) unreleased in the UK, in which a DJ conducts a contest among his teen listeners: babes are selected to ride a trolley car to Pleasure

Beach, followed by hapless teen boys who compete for them by chasing the car. The winner, of course, gets the girl. Again co-scripted with Daniel Peacock, the film fails to capitalise on the DJ character, denying him the kind of dialogue that could elevate the film onto a more satirical plane. As with *Party Party*, Winsor displays a competent grasp of visuals by utilising an interesting colour palette, but the film ultimately runs out of steam.

After a stint directing television programs such as 'The Magician' and 'The Great Kandinsky', plus a series of the drama 'Thief Takers', Winsor recently returned with his latest feature. *Essex Boys* (2000) takes as its starting point the real-life murder of three criminals found dead in a car in an Essex lane. Thereafter, it becomes fiction, with a convoluted plot in which the typical rise-and-fall narrative of the gangster movie is played out against double-crossings and confused relationships. A good cast, including Sean Bean's refreshingly unsympathetic gangster, and Alex Kingston's Essex Girl moll, lend the film one of its strengths, as does its grim setting among the Essex marshes and flatlands. Although Winsor directs with some degree of power and passion for his subject, he cannot illuminate his scenario; the film is effectively another British gangster film that aims higher than such a traditional story and narrative style is able reach.　　**JD**

Michael WINTERBOTTOM

Butterfly Kiss (1995)
Jude (1996)
Welcome to Sarajevo (1997)
I Want You (1998)
Wonderland (1999)
The Claim (2000)

Born in Lancashire, UK, in 1961, Michael Winterbottom studied English at Oxford and film at Bristol. He emerged from, and continues to work intermittently in, television. His feature-length television dramas, some of them given limited or theatrical releases, include *Love Lies Bleeding* (1994), which explores the psychology of an IRA prisoner on temporary release, *Go Now* (1995), where Robert Carlyle's construction worker confronts the onset of multiple sclerosis, and the relationship drama, *With or Without You* (1999). Winterbottom's theatrical features aspire to higher cultural status. European auteurs, Ingmar Bergman especially, are unashamedly cited as reference points in interviews and in the films themselves. A liking for films in which 'it's all about you having to work it out, rather than having it spelt out for you', is evident in his cinema.

Butterfly Kiss (1995), *I Want You* (1998) and *Wonderland* (1999), in particular, consist of loosely-connected episodes, with links between them only gradually falling into place. Stark landscapes evoking an atmosphere of metaphysical bleakness predominate. Shock techniques, diverse stylistic experiments, and modish soundtracks counterbalance, or sometimes sit uneasily with, these more contemplative elements. This attempt to synthesise concerns associated with high culture and auteur cinema with an appeal to more contemporary sensibilities has yet to be rewarded with commercial success.

Winterbottom's first feature, *Butterfly Kiss*, immediately grabs attention, opening with one of several random murders by a tattooed, body-pierced drifter searching the roads of Northern England for the 'Biblical Judith'. She and her accomplice are enclosed throughout the film within repetitive, colourless motorways, service stations and car parks. A soundtrack featuring melancholic songs by The Cranberries lends pathos to their relationship. *Butterfly Kiss* is an astute hybrid: a British road movie that taps into the fascination with cinematic serial killers and, more problematically, murderous queers. Winterbottom's subsequent films similarly rework elements from a range of recent generic cycles.

A thematic consistency across Winterbottom's collaborations with various scriptwriters is an emphasis upon endangered, traumatised children. His next project, *Jude* (1996), an adaptation of a Thomas Hardy novel, was aptly described by scriptwriter Hossein Amini as an attempt to 'destroy the heritage film from within'. *Jude* rarely lingers on the visual pleasure of landscapes, buildings, or beautiful costumes. Instead, the narrative drives forward with a restlessness that is unusual in this type of film. The sudden discovery of the protagonists' dead children in their cramped accommodation is powerfully rendered.

Suffering (and often the death) of humans and animals recurs frequently in Winterbottom's films. *Welcome to Sarajevo* (1997) pushes this further; too far for some viewers. Based upon ITN journalist Michael Nicholson's experiences, the narrative centres around a young girl's 'rescue' from Sarajevo, indicting Western reluctance to do more for children caught in the conflict. It is indebted to Oliver Stone's frenetic style in his 'journalist-under-fire' film *Salvador* (1986), as well as the audacious mixture of film and video formats in *Natural Born Killers* (1994). Partly shot on location, it controversially incorporates archive news footage of civilians killed or wounded in the war.

In *I Want You* a silent young boy obsessively spies on and listens to a series of increasingly disturbing events, including attempted rape and murder. Linked to this is a recurring motif of the boy gazing intently at stones and fossils on the beach, perhaps suggesting his (and the male spectator's) emotional petrification. The film is a low-key, neo-noir erotic thriller which makes explicit stylistic nods to Alfred Hitchcock's *Marnie* (1964) and Orson Welles' *The Lady from Shanghai* (1948). Slavomir Idziak's cinematography represents Hastings as a coastal resort characterised by faded, garish colours. It becomes a place as desolate in its own way as cinematographer Alwin Kuchler's representation of the purpose-built pioneer town of Kingdom Come in *The Claim* (2000).

Wonderland is another radical shift of genre. A distinctive variant on the slew of late 1990s London films, it remains constant to the concern with oppressive environments and endangered, traumatised children. Less charmingly enthralled to the fantasy of comfortably affluent, middle-class metropolitan life than *Notting Hill* (1999) or *Sliding Doors* (1998), it is designed for wider appeal than Patrick Keiller's uncompromisingly intellectual *London* (1994). A compelling strand within its various mini-narratives of mundane, disconnected city lives involves the abrupt mugging of a small boy lost during a fireworks display.

Stop-frame sequences, Sean Bobbitt's hand-held Super-16 images of real Londoners, and editor Trevor Waite's jump cuts combine with Michael Nyman's strangely uplifting score to make *Wonderland* Winterbottom's most experimental film to date. Here, London is both exhilarating and anomic. The ending, in which lovelorn Nadia (Gina McKee) takes her first steps towards a new relationship, has attracted criticism as a forced concession to populist appeal. An alternative explanation is that this is the clearest example of a fragile thread of optimism running throughout Winterbottom's work. Arguably, all of the films hang on to the humanist notion that unlikely relationships formed in adversity are the only bulwark against an otherwise threatening world.

The Claim, scripted by regular collaborator Frank Cottrell Boyce, translates Thomas Hardy's 'The Mayor of Casterbridge' to a freezing nineteenth-century gold-rush town in Sierra Nevada. It combines western iconography with an emphasis on the strangeness of the past. Reminiscent of Bergman, the elliptical narrative is studded with brooding images of the mayor (Peter Mullan) and the wife and daughter he sold for a claim. Majestic shots of snow falling down a mountain, and the deserted, burning town at the end, provide austere spectacle on a larger scale than in Winterbottom's earlier work. The mayor achieves a reconciliation of sorts with his wife but, after she dies, his daughter abandons him. She leaves with the surveyor who condemns his town to oblivion by routing a railway away from, rather than through, it.

Winterbottom's tally of one completed feature per year since the mid-1990s makes him one Britain's most prolific directors. His latest project is another collaboration with Frank Cottrell Boyce, which maintains his reputation for an eclectic choice of subject matter. *24 Hour Party People*, centred around the exploits of cultural entrepreneur Tony Wilson, charts the Manchester music scene from the mid-1970s to the early 1990s. **MSt**

Peter WOLLEN

Peter Wollen's interest in film-making appears to have arisen out of his commitment to film theory, in particular avant-garde cinema, feminist and structuralist theory. An academic and writer, he is responsible for some seminal film studies texts, including 'Signs and Meanings in the Cinema' (1969) and the film journals *Framework* and *Screen*. He also contributed to the screenplay of Michelangelo Antonioni's *The Passenger* (1975).

His relationship with fellow academic and writer Laura Mulvey, author of one of the most central and enduring feminist film theory pieces, 'Visual Pleasure and Narrative Cinema', led to their collaboration on a series of features and short films. Each

Penthesilea: Queen of the Amazons (1974)
Riddles of the Sphinx (1977)
Crystal Gazing (1982)
Friendship's Death (1987)

interrogates traditional film-making forms and deals with theoretical aspects of the cinema. Wollen has talked of 'the problems [of finding] a way of working with narrative ... not to be caught between a complete refusal of narrative and a complete acceptance of it'.

They made their first project, *Penthesilea: Queen of the Amazons*, in 1974. Divided into five sections, each preceded by a quote from the likes of Jacques Lacan, Sigmund Freud and Stephan Mallarme, the film deals with various considerations of the iconography of woman as warrior. In it, Wollen delivers a lecture on the myth of Penthesilea whilst moving about a living room and adjoining terrace, followed by the camera, which at times focuses in on his lecture notes left lying around the room. His interest in formalism is evident in the structure of the film, and in the inclusion of four television screens presenting sections, occasionally isolated by the film camera.

This interest in the forms of cinema was developed in their next film, *Riddles of the Sphinx* (1977). Similarly demonstrating anti-traditional narrative forms, it is divided into seven numbered chapters with titles including '2: Laura Talking' in which Mulvey explains the purpose and content of the film. It conveys an avant-garde interest in that which is ignored or repressed in patriarchal society, focusing on the forgotten element of the Oedipus story: the (female) Sphinx who sits outside of the city, challenging its culture and values. One chapter, 'Louise's Story Told in Thirteen Shots', further demonstrates the film's formal concerns, as do the slow 360-degree pans from left to right and back again. This film is widely considered to be their most successful attempt to marry experimentations in both form and content.

Between the shorts, *Amy!* (1980), in which Amy Johnson's exploits are analysed within a women's group who discuss heroic images of females, and *Frida Kahlo and Tina Modotti* (1983), Wollen and Mulvey made *Crystal Gazing* (1982). Unlike the formal austerity of their previous films, this employs a more conventional narrative device, interweaving the lives of four central characters: a rock musician (Lora Logic), a science-fiction illustrator (Gavin Richards), a PhD student (Jeff Rawle) and a satellite-photography analyst (Mary Maddox). Here, Wollen and Mulvey's concern with historical figures is supplanted by a more contemporary relevance: set against the background of Margaret Thatcher's Britain, events are shadowed by their historical and geographical background. Despite the references to a more traditional structure, the film still utilises Wollen's and Mulvey's anti-conventional techniques: framing quotations; emphasis of sound over image to the point of confusion; repeated pans which link characters; and a self-consciousness that belies the film's theoretical roots.

Wollen's most recent feature film, *Friendship's Death* (1987), was inspired by his time as a journalist in Amman. Set during Black September in 1970, the film is about the meeting of a war correspondent with an extra-terrestrial. Bill Paterson plays Sullivan, the journalist, who saves a mysterious woman (Tilda Swinton) from the PLO only to find that she is a robot on a mission from another galaxy. Although less formally unconventional than his work with Mulvey, the film still attempts a theoretical basis in its story, interweaving Palestinians' issues with observations on the relationship between man and machine. Making extensive use of post-production special effects, it heralds a move away from Wollen's more hardcore avant-garde concerns.

More television writing and directing, both in the UK and Europe, include 'The Bad Sister', based on Emma Tennant's novel about the illegitimate daughter of a Scottish landowner, and work for Channel 4's 'Rear Window' strand. Wollen has returned to full-time lecturing in the US, where he is considered one of the foremost figures in film theory and academia.   **JD**

Jason WOOD
See **Eileen ANIPARE**

Y

David YATES

With screens both large and small already awash with period drama and the inescapable The Tichborne Claimant adaptations of Dickens, Austen and every other Victorian author in the Empire, David (1998) Yates' debut feature has its work cut out to make an impression. *The Tichborne Claimant* (1998) is based on a celebrated true story, one that captured a multitude of headlines as well as the imagination of the Victorian public. The Tichborne fortune remains unclaimed due to a lack of established heirs; manservant Bogle travels to Australia to investigate claims that missing son Sir Roger is still alive, hatching a fraudulent plot to secure the estate by schooling a drunken butcher, Thomas Castro, to imitate the absent heir. Cultures clash, and Yates sets out to show the folly of inheritance and the corruption of the class-based society. The *My Fair Lady* premise is promising enough, with plenty of comic potential as the boorish Castro attempts to pass himself off as blueblood born, learning to dance, discuss art and eat at the table.

Yates' direction is competent but never incendiary, weighed down by the flashback framework of Bogle recalling events from the gloom of the workhouse, while the satire is never quite fluent enough to be really funny and events move too swiftly to allow true depth of character to shine through. His use of the various stock Victorian characters – pompous aristocrats, Machiavellian lawyers, eccentric *vielles femmes* – shows a keen eye for era and setting, but the film lacks the subtle touches of grotesque and burlesque that distinguish the best period satires.

The culminating trial scene, in which Tichborne/Castro is brought down by the Machiavellian manoeuvering of jealous relatives and unscrupulous judges, is the film's best moment. Marketed as a proletarian hero struggling against the corrupted upper classes to fund his legal expenses, Tichborne is ultimately shown as a victim of exploitation by English society at large, an innocent who refuses to conform to the exclusive rules of either class. Meanwhile, the real mystery – whether Castro may in fact be the estranged Tichborne – is not given the narrative weight it deserves.

As a director of period drama, Yates has made a convincing case; as a director of state-of-the-age satire, the jury is still out. **OB**

Peter YATES

Peter Yates' modus operandi, like other successful yet slightly anonymous British directors in Hollywood (such as Mick Jackson and Roger Spottiswoode), is based on turning out proficient, relatively unambitious pictures in a variety of genres. Yates' longevity – three decades in the upper echelons of the industry – no doubt owes much to his adaptability. When entrusted with a star vehicle or big-budget release he can turn on the style and score at the box office (*Bullitt* (1968), *The Deep* (1977)). Conversely, as he proved with the coming-of-age tale *Breaking Away* (1979), he can work on a more intimate scale too, fashioning a wistful sleeper-hit tailored to the exact mood of the US film-going public. Although a reliable director with a string of solid mainstream successes to his name, he is no auteur, yet a certain thematic consistency can be identified throughout his work.

Yates was born in Aldershot, UK, in 1929, and educated at the Royal Academy of Dramatic Art. As he rose from dubbing assistant to assistant director on films such as Tony Richardson's *A Taste of Honey* (1961), he indicated where his talents lay in television work on action series' such as 'The Saint' and 'Danger Man'. Considering the substantial US success that was to come, Yates' emergence as a features director with the rather parochial *Summer Holiday* (1963), a vehicle for anodyne pop singer Cliff Richard, seems rather unlikely now. His effective handling of the action sequences in *Robbery* (1967), starring Stanley Baker, led to an invite to go to Hollywood and helm the Steve McQueen cop thriller *Bullitt*. Establishing a pattern that would frequently recur in his career, Yates makes the most of a dull plot, giving cinema one of the all-time great car chase sequences, manufacturing McQueen's most iconic image outside of *The Great Escape* (1963). The enduring appeal of the film's late-1960s stylings, automobile fetishisation, and the cultural currency of McQueen were reflected in the adoption of key scenes from *Bullitt* for a 1990s Ford advertising campaign.

After experimenting with free-love relationship angst in the Dustin Hoffman-starring *John and Mary* (1969), Yates handled more big stars and action set pieces in the heist caper *The Hot Rock* (1972) and the World War Two adventure *Murphy's War* (1971). He then returned to the crime and ethics milieu familiar from *Bullitt* in *The Friends of Eddie Coyle* (1973). Robert Mitchum's protagonist, however, is on the other side of the law from McQueen's Bullitt, and the star turns in one of his late, great performances in a role that prefigures his world-weary cop in Sidney Pollack's *The Yakuza* (1975).

In 1974 Yates' made an unsuccessful move outside the sphere of the action-crime movie in the misfiring farce *For Pete's Sake*, starring Barbra Streisand. Charged with following Universal's massive shark success *Jaws* (1975), he directed *The Deep*, an adaptation of Peter Benchley's novel. Far from Yates' best work, the film delivered on Columbia's investment but little else; the only common ground it shares with Spielberg's masterful suspense is the casting of a waning Robert Shaw. Wisely shifting away from the large canvas of *The Deep*, he then made a small but perfectly observed adolescent comedy-drama, *Breaking Away*, arguably his finest film. Featuring Dennis Quaid and Daniel Stern, the story centres on four teenagers in the college town of Bloomington, Indiana. Although the problems they face – lack of parental understanding, unemployment, a sense of blue-collar inferiority to college kids – are stock devices of many a teen movie, the film is rooted in a level of social observation that lends a balancing depth to its sometimes wistful tone. Nicknamed 'cutters' by the local students, after the stonecutting industry that the town was built around, the youths' ambiguous attitude to the future is summed up by the hero Dave, a promising cyclist who tries to escape his oppressive identification with a declining town by styling himself as an Italian. This leads to some effective comic scenes as his patriotic father at first resists, then succumbs to, the pervasive influence of Dave's eating habits and love of Italian opera. Dennis Quaid's bitter, inarticulate ex-quarterback, saddled with a policeman brother and a chip on his shoulder about the town's reliance on the campus dollar, stands out. So too does Daniel Stern in the first of a series of roles in films such as *Diner* (1982) and *City Slickers* (1991) that explore the emotional journeys undertaken in the name of male bonding.

A cycle race between the 'cutters' and the college boys becomes the vehicle for regenerating these wasting lives and the pride of the town, although chase specialist Yates clearly relishes the logistics of staging the race for the camera. Peter Bogdanovich's

The Last Picture Show (1971), which also highlights the frustrations of youth in a declining small-town setting, is a reference point for the film. However, where Bogdanovich opts for the monochrome gravitas of Liberty Valance-era John Ford, the preoccupation with the world of work displayed in Breaking Away's scenes of stonecutting and the menial jobs taken by the protagonists aligns Yates' film with the spirit of Howard Hawks. A moving and accomplished picture that marries light comedy with an unobtrusive subtext concerning the erosion of the manufacturing base, Breaking Away earned Yates a Best Director nomination from the Academy, and won an Oscar® for writer Steve Tesich. Yates' and Tesich's next collaboration was not so fruitful; Eyewitness (1981) is a dreary and often confusing thriller. William Hurt stars as a janitor who discovers the corpse of an Asian businessman in his building and uses his involvement in the case to ingratiate himself with a television reporter (Sigourney Weaver) for whom he has harboured an obsessive crush. The class conflict so sensitively rendered in Breaking Away, comes to the fore again in the identification of Hurt and buddy James Woods as Vietnam vets who have returned from the war only to be excluded from the economic success story of 1980s big business. Christopher Plummer appears as Weaver's lover, the shadowy Jewish activist who organises the safe passage of politically compromised Russian Jews to the West. However, the racial subtext suggested by Woods' fear and distrust of Asians, Plummer's crusade for his compatriots and the African-American cop assigned to the case, Black (an early role for Morgan Freeman), never comes together. The thin thriller plot is too insubstantial to support such concerns. Some nice touches – the camera subtly adopting a CCTV angle as it observes Hurt and a jokey reference to the similarly-themed Chinatown (1974) – fail to relieve the leaden tone.

Although Tesich furnished Breaking Away with a fresh homespun voice, his dialogue in Eyewitness fails to ring true, and the contrivances of the plot and the obviousness of the character conflict betray a genre exercise that tries too hard. Ultimately not neurotic enough to stand alongside the great paranoid thrillers of the 1970s, nor as giddily self-reflexive as Brian De Palma's superior Blow Out, released in the same year, it is a formulaic waste of performing, writing and directing talent. Tesich and Yates collaborated once more, on the 1985 drama Eleni.

As if to prove the Jekyll and Hyde nature of his talent, in 1983 Yates produced two films of wildly differing quality. The Dresser, an adaptation of Ronald Harwood's theatrical two-hander, is a character-led piece in the tradition of Breaking Away. Albert Finney and Tom Courtenay, in a pair of excellent performances, portray the Shakespearean actor-manager of a British travelling company and his long-suffering valet. Yates sketches out the mood of wartime northern England in a few brief scenes outside the theatre, but the dressing room, regarded with an almost religious aura of ritual and sanctity, is where the shifting power dynamic and obvious love between the two is examined. The Dresser touches upon the same issues of class and family evoked in Breaking Away, although the social contexts of each could not be more different. Yates handles both the intimate moments between Finney and Courtenay and the broadly comic backstage antics of the overstretched company with confidence and sensitivity (earning another Best Director Oscar® nomination for his trouble). Yates' other 1983 offering, Krull, showcases the director in lacklustre action mode. It is a redundant genre entry along the lines of Eyewitness, a big-budget attempt to siphon off a little of the science-fiction fantasy success enjoyed in the same year by George Lucas' Return of the Jedi, and adds little of note to Yates' oeuvre. By the mid-1980s, Yates was well established as a reliable handler of off-the-peg studio assignments, more often than not in the thriller genre. The House on Carroll Street (1988) and An Innocent Man (1989) have little to recommend them. Suspect (1987), however, stands out as a well-crafted legal thriller with an admirable (if occasionally simplified) intention to highlight the interconnected power relations across the varying strata of Washington DC society, from Circuit Court judges and political lobbyists to homeless itinerants. The film also provided an unusually substantial role for Cher. Yates' most recent cinema release, Run of the Country (1995), reunited him with Albert Finney in an Irish family drama based on a novel by Shane Connaughton. The sheer diversity present in Yates' work speaks more for his ability and film-making-intelligence than the mainstream successes he will probably be remembered for. He deserves a reputation as an interesting and capable director. **MF**

Robert YOUNG

Robert Young has directed a bewildering array of projects from shorts, adverts and television shows, to features. After shooting a number of short films he made his feature debut, *Vampire Circus* (1972), for Hammer films. A strikingly odd addition to the vampire cycle Hammer began with Terence Fisher's *Dracula* (1958), it remains one of his best works. The Circus of Nights comes to a plague-ridden Transylvanian town and after a series of blood-drained bodies are found, they are revealed to be vampires. Although silly, the film is unusual and delivers plenty on the soft-core sex and gore front. One of its more memorable ideas comes in the form of vampires that can transform themselves into panthers and tigers. Robert Tayman is a weak villain, however, and Christopher Lee is sorely missed.

Romance with a Double Bass (1974) was the first collaboration between Young and John Cleese. Adapted from an Anton Chekov short story, this is an off-beat, gentle comedy co-written by Cleese and his then wife, Connie Booth, with Bill Owen. Diverting enough, it features a cast of excellent British character actors including Graham Crowden and Freddie Jones.

Young followed with the dubious sex romp, *Keep It Up Downstairs* (1976). A talented (but clearly desperate) cast, including Diana Dors, Willie Rushton and the former child star Jack Wild, flounder in this tale of the aristocratic Cockshute family and the soft-porn carryings-on in Cockshute Manor. This is a lame rehash of stage farces, saucy-postcard humour and jokes too corny for a *Carry On* movie.

The Jackie Collins adaptation, *The World Is Full of Married Men* (1979) was a slight improvement. Made after the shoddy but amusing Collins adaptations *The Stud* (Quentin Masters, 1978) and *The Bitch* (Gerry O'Hara, 1979), starring her sister, Joan, Young's film is less sexy and stars the less iconic duo of Carroll Baker and Paul Nicholas. The cod-feminist plot is concerned with wronged wife, Linda Cooper, who, tired of her husband's infidelity, has a whirlwind romance with Gem Gemini (Paul Nicholas). This is extremely unconvincing as a feminist tale and not lurid enough to be fun; the uncharismatic leads do not help. Particularly annoying is the way in which the story is presented as a morality lesson.

Young directed for television in the 1980s, including episodes of 'Bergerac' and 'Robin of Sherwood', and an enjoyable episode of 'Hammer House of Horror' about a voodoo doll. In the 1990s he directed the US television movie *Ruby Ridge: An American Tragedy* (1996) and an adaptation of 'Jane Eyre' in Britain. The high point of his small-screen work is his work on Alan Bleasdale's ambitious mini-series about dirty politics, 'GBH'.

Splitting Heirs (1993) is a painful would-be-Ealing comedy about the wrangling over an inheritance. Any pretence at credibility is diminished with the casting of well-preserved Barbara Hershey as the mother of a visibly older Eric Idle. Idle must take much of the blame as co-writer and executive producer; the presence of his former Monty Python colleague John Cleese only serves to remind the viewer that this is a far cry from Terry Jones' *The Life of Brian* (1979).

Young went on to direct the 'semi-sequel' to the impressive (and very successful) British comedy *A Fish Called Wanda* (1988). *Fierce Creatures* (1997) reunited the stars of the earlier film (John Cleese, Jamie Lee Curtis, Kevin Kline and Michael Palin) in a bland story about a small zoo taken over by a commercially minded American company who stock it with the eponymous beasts. The film did bad business, due, in part, to the fact that the Australian director Fred Schepisi (*A Cry in the Dark* (1985), *Six Degrees of Separation* (1995)) was brought in to re-shoot scenes in a vain attempt to 'rescue' the film resulting in a finished product lacking in coherence.

Captain Jack (1998) is based on a script by the acclaimed playwright Jack Rosenthal and stars Bob Hoskins as a sailor who assembles a motley crew to follow in the sea-faring footsteps of his hero, eighteenth-century explorer Captain Scoresby. As they sail from Whitby to the Arctic Circle, pursued by the authorities, they have to learn to work together. This is passable enough, if a little predictable and twee. There are some familiar faces in the cast – Sadie Frost, Anna Massey and Maureen Lipman – but Young's direction is anonymous. **IC**

Filmography

A

Abominable Snowman of the Himalayas, The
(Val Guest, 1957)

About Adam (Gerry Stembridge, 2000)

Absolute Beginners (Julien Temple, 1986)

Accelerator (Vinny Murphy, 1999)

Accident (Joseph Losey, 1967)

Accidental Hero (Stephen Frears, 1992)

Aces High (Jack Gold, 1976)

Acid House, The (Paul McGuigan, 1998)

Across the Bridge (Ken Annakin, 1957)

Act of Murder (Alan Bridges, 1965)

Admirable Crichton, The (Lewis Gilbert, 1957)

Adventurers, The (Lewis Gilbert, 1970)

Adventures of Baron von Munchausen, The
(Terry Gilliam, 1988)

Adventures of Pinocchio (Steve Barron, 1996)

Afraid of the Dark (Mark Peploe, 1991)

Against the Wind (Charles Crichton, 1948)

Agatha (Michael Apted, 1979)

Age of Innocence (Alan Bridges, 1977)

Ailsa (Paddy Breathnach, 1994)

Air America (Roger Spottiswoode, 1990)

Albert R.N. (Lewis Gilbert, 1953)

Alfie (Lewis Gilbert, 1966)

Alfred the Great (Clive Donner, 1969)

Alien (Ridley Scott, 1979)

Alive and Kicking (Nancy Meckler, 1996)

All for Love (Harry Hook, 1997)

All Soul's Day (Alan Gilsenan, 1997)

All the Little Animals (Jeremy Thomas, 1998)

All the Right Noises (Gerry O'Hara, 1969)

All Things Bright and Beautiful (Barry Devlin, 1994)

Alligator Named Daisy (J. Lee Thompson, 1955)

Altered States (Ken Russell, 1980)

Always (Henry Jaglom, 1985)

Amazing Grace and Chuck (Mike Newell, 1987)

Ambassador, The (1984)

American Beauty (Sam Mendes, 1999)

American History X (Tony Kaye, 1998)

American, The (Paul Unwin, 1998)

Among Giants (Sam Miller, 1998)

Amsterdam Affair (Gerry O'Hara, 1968)

Amy! (Laura Mulvey, 1979)

Amy Foster (Beeban Kidron, 1997)

An American Werewolf in Paris (Anthony Waller, 1997)

An Awfully Big Adventure (Mike Newell, 1994)

Anchoress, The (Chris Newby, 1993)

...And Now the Screaming Starts (Roy Ward Baker, 1973)

And the Band Played On (Roger Spottiswoode, 1993)

An Englishman Abroad (John Schlesinger, 1983)

Angel (Neil Jordan, 1982)

Angela's Ashes (Alan Parker, 1999)

Angel Heart (Alan Parker, 1987)

Angelic Conversation, The (Derek Jarman, 1985)

An Ideal Husband (William Cartlidge, 1998)

An Ideal Husband (Oliver Parker, 1999)

An Innocent Man (Peter Yates, 1989)

An Inspector Calls (Guy Hamilton, 1954)

Anna Karenina (Bernard Rose, 1997)

Anne Devlin (Pat Murphy, 1984)

Anniversary, The (Roy Ward Baker, 1968)

Another Country (Marek Kanievska, 1984)

Another Shore (Charles Crichton, 1948)

Another Time, Another Place (Michael Radford, 1983)

Antitrust (Peter Howitt, 2001)

Antonia and Jane (Beeban Kidron, 1991)

An Unsuitable Job for a Woman (Chris Petit, 1981)

Appaloosa, The (Sidney J. Furie, 1966)

Appointment with Death (Michael Winner, 1988)

Arabian Nights (Richard Williams, 1995)

Argument, The (Donald Cammell, 1999)

Aria (Charles Sturridge, segment, 1987)

Aria (Don Boyd, segment, 1987)

Aria (Franc Roddam, segment, 1987)

Aria (Julien Temple, segment, 1987)

Aria (Nicolas Roeg, segment, 1987)

As Long as They're Happy (J. Lee Thompson, 1955)

Assassination of Trotsky, The (Joseph Losey, 1972)

Assignment K (Val Guest, 1968)

Asylum (Roy Ward Baker, 1972)

As You Like It (Christine Edzard, 1992)

At the Cinema Palace: Liam O'Leary (Donald Taylor Black, 1983)

At the Max (Julien Temple, 1991)

Autobiography of a Princess (James Ivory, 1975)

Au Pair Girls (Val Guest, 1972)

Awakening, The (Mike Newell, 1980)

B

Babyfever (Henry Jaglom, 1994)

Babymother (Julian Henriques, 1998)

Baby of Macon, The (Peter Greenaway, 1993)

Bachelor, The (Gary Sinyor, 1999)

Backbeat (Iain Softley, 1993)

Bad Behaviour (Les Blair, 1993)

Bad Blood (Mike Newell, 1981)

Bad Timing (Nicolas Roeg, 1980)

Ballad of the Sad Café, The (Simon Callow, 1991)

Bandit Queen (Shekhar Kapur, 1994)

Bank Robber (Nick Mead, 1993)

Banner in the Sky (Ken Annakin, 1959)

Barry Lyndon (Stanley Kubrick, 1975)

Battlefield Earth (Roger Christian, 2000)

Battle for the Planet of the Apes (J. Lee Thompson, 1973)

Battle of Britain (Guy Hamilton, 1969)

Battle of the Bulge (Ken Annakin, 1965)

Battle of the Sexes, The (Charles Crichton, 1960)

Beach, The (Danny Boyle, 2000)

Bean (Mel Smith, 1997)

Bear Island (Don Sharp, 1979)

Beautiful Creatures (Bill Eagles, 2000)

Beautiful Mistake (Marc Evans, 2000)

Beautiful People (Jasmin Dizdar, 1999)

Beautiful Thing (Hettie MacDonald, 1996)

Beauty Jungle, The (Val Guest, 1964)

Bed Sitting Room, The (Richard Lester, 1969)

Bees in Paradise (Val Guest, 1944)

Before Winter Comes (J. Lee Thompson, 1969)

Being Human (Bill Forsyth, 1993)

Believers, The (John Schlesinger, 1987)

Belles of St. Trinian's, The (Frank Launder, 1954)

Belly of an Architect, The (Peter Greenaway, 1987)

Bent (Sean Mathias, 1996)

Best (Mary McGuckian, 2000)

Best Laid Plans (Mike Barker, 1999)

Best of Enemies, The (Guy Hamilton, 1961)

Best of Times, The (Roger Spottiswoode, 1986)

Better Late Than Never (Bryan Forbes, 1982)

Beverly Hills Cop II (Tony Scott, 1987)

Beyond Bedlam (Vadim Jean, 1993)

Beyond Rangoon (John Boorman, 1995)

Bhaji on the Beach (Gurinder Chadha, 1993)

Biddy (Christine Edzard, 1983)

Biggest Bundle of Them All, The (Ken Annakin, 1968)

Big Man, The (David Leland, 1990)

Big Night, The (Joseph Losey, 1951)

Big Sleep, The (Michael Winner, 1978)

Big Swap, The (Niall Johnson, 1998)

Big Tease, The (Kevin Allen, 1999)

Bill and Ted's Bogus Journey (Peter Hewitt, 1991)

Billion Dollar Brain (Ken Russell, 1967)

Billy Elliot (Stephen Daldry, 2000)

Billy Liar! (John Schlesinger, 1963)

Billy the Kid and the Green Baize Vampire (Alan Clarke

Bird on a Wire (Tony Palmer, 1972)

Birdy (Alan Parker, 1984)

Birthday Girl (Jez Butterworth, 2000)

Bishop's Story, The (Bob Quinn, 1995)

Bitch, The (Gerry O'Hara, 1979)

Black Jack (Ken Loach, 1979)

Black Rain (Ridley Scott, 1989)

Black Rainbow (Mike Hodges, 1989)

Blade Runner (Ridley Scott, 1982)

Blade Runner – The Director's Cut (Ridley Scott, 1991)

Blame it on the Bellboy (Mark Herman, 1992)

Blank Check (Rupert Wainwright, 1994)

Bleak Moments (Mike Leigh, 1971)

Blind Date (Joseph Losey, 1959)

Blind Justice (Richard Spence, 1994)

Blink (Michael Apted, 1994)

Bliss of Mrs Blossom, The (Joseph McGrath, 1968)

Blithe Spirit (David Lean, 1945)

Blonde Fist (Frank Clarke, 1991)

Blow Dry (Paddy Breathnach, 2001)

Blue (Derek Jarman, 1993)

Blue Lagoon, The (Frank Launder, 1949)

Blue Murder at St. Trinian's (Frank Launder, 1957)

Blue Sky (Tony Richardson, 1994)

B Monkey (Michael Radford, 1998)

Body Contact (Bernard Rose, 1987)

Body Said No!, The (Val Guest, 1950)

Bofors Gun, The (Jack Gold, 1968)

Bombay Talkie (James Ivory, 1970)

Bones (Jim Goddard, 1984)

Boom (Joseph Losey, 1968)

Border, The (Tony Richardson, 1982)

Born Romantic (David Kane, 2000)

Borrowers, The (Peter Hewitt, 1997)

Bostonians, The (James Ivory, 1984)

Boxer, The (Jim Sheridan, 1997)

Boy Friend, The (Ken Russell, 1971)

Boy from Mercury, The (Martin Duffy, 1996)

Boys in Blue, The (Val Guest, 1982)

Boys in Company C, The (Sidney J. Furie, 1978)

Boys, The (Sidney J. Furie, 1962)

Boy Who Stole a Million, The (Charles Crichton, 1960)

Boy with Green Hair, The (Joseph Losey, 1948)

Brassed Off (Mark Herman, 1996)

Brazil (Terry Gilliam, 1985)

Bread and Roses (Ken Loach, 2000)

Breaking Away (Peter Yates, 1979)

Breaking Glass (Brian Gibson, 1980)

Breaking In (Bill Forsyth, 1989)

Break in the Circle (Val Guest, 1955)

Bridal Path, The (Frank Launder, 1959)

Bride, The (Franc Roddam, 1985)

Brides of Fu Manchu, The (Don Sharp, 1966)

Bridge on the River Kwai, The (David Lean, 1957)

Bridge Too Far, A (Richard Attenborough, 1977)

Bridge, The (Sydney McCartney, 1992)

Bridget Jones's Diary (Sharon Maguire, 2001)

Brief Encounter (David Lean, 1945)

Brief History of Errol Morris, A (Kevin MacDonald, 2000)

Bring on the Night (Michael Apted, 1985)

Britannia Hospital (Lindsay Anderson, 1982)

Broken Journey (Ken Annakin, 1948)

Brothers (Martin Dunkerton, 2000)

Brothers in Trouble (Udayan Prasad, 1996)

Browning Version, The (Mike Figgis, 1994)

Brute, The (Gerry O'Hara, 1977)

Bugsy Malone (Alan Parker, 1976)

Bullet (Julien Temple, 1995)

Bullitt (Peter Yates, 1968)

Bumblebee Flies Anyway, The (Martin Duffy, 1998)

Burning Secret (Andrew Birkin, 1988)

Butch and Sundance: The Early Days (Richard Lester, 1979)

Butcher Boy, The (Neil Jordan, 1997)

Butterfly Kiss (Michael Winterbottom, 1995)

C

Caboblanco (J. Lee Thompson, 1980)

Cal (Pat O'Connor, 1984)

Callan (Don Sharp, 1974)

Call of the Wild (Ken Annakin, 1972)

Camp on Blood Island, The (Val Guest, 1958)

Candyman (Bernard Rose, 1992)

Can She Bake a Cherry Pie? (Henry Jaglom, 1983)

Caoineadh Airt Uí Laoire/Lament for Art O'Leary
    (Bob Quinn, 1975)

Cape Fear (J. Lee Thompson, 1962)

Captain Boycott (Frank Launder, 1947)

Captain Corelli's Mandolin (John Madden, 2001)

Captain Jack (Robert Young, 1998)

Caravaggio (Derek Jarman, 1986)

Card, The (Ronald Neame, 1952)

Career Girls (Mike Leigh, 1997)

Caretaker, The (Clive Donner, 1964)

Carla's Song (Ken Loach, 1996)

Carrington (Christopher Hampton, 1995)

Carry on, Admiral (Val Guest, 1957)

Carve Her Name With Pride (Lewis Gilbert, 1958)

Casino Royale (Val Guest, Joseph McGrath et al, 1967)

Cast a Dark Shadow (Lewis Gilbert, 1955)

Castaway (Nicolas Roeg, 1987)

Catch Us If You Can (John Boorman, 1965)

Cement Garden, The (Andrew Birkin, 1993)

Center Stage (Nicholas Hytner, 2000)

Chain, The (Jack Gold, 1985)

Chairman, The (J. Lee Thompson, 1969)

Chalk Garden, The (Ronald Neame, 1964)

Champions (John Irvin, 1983)

Changeling, The (Peter Medak, 1980)

Chaplin (Richard Attenborough, 1992)

Charge of the Light Brigade, The (Tony Richardson, 1968)

Chariots of Fire (Hugh Hudson, 1981)

Charley Moon (Guy Hamilton, 1956)

Charlie Chan and the Curse of the Dragon Queen
    (Clive Donner, 1981)

Chato's Land (Michael Winner, 1971)

Cheaper to Keep Her (Ken Annakin, 1980)

Checking Out (David Leland, 1989)

Chicago Joe and the Showgirl (Bernard Rose, 1990)

Chicken Run (Nick Park, 2000)

Children, The (Tony Palmer, 1990)

Chinese Boxes (Chris Petit, 1984)

Chorus Line, A (Richard Attenborough, 1985)

Christie Malry's Own Double-Entry (Paul Tickell, 2000)

Christmas Carol, A (Richard Williams, 1972)

Christopher Columbus: The Discovery (John Glen, 1992)

Circle of Friends (Pat O'Connor, 1995)

Circus (Rob Walker, 2000)

City of Industry (John Irvin, 1997)

City of Joy (Roland Joffé, 1992)

Claim, The (Michael Winterbottom, 2000)

Clandestine Marriage, The (Christopher Miles, 1999)

Clash of the Titans (Desmond Davis, 1981)

Class Action (Michael Apted, 1991)

Climb Up the Wall (Michael Winner, 1957)

Clock Strikes Eight, The (Michael Winner, 1957)

Clockwork Mice (Vadim Jean, 1995)

Clockwork Orange, A (Stanley Kubrick, 1971)

Close My Eyes (Stephen Poliakoff, 1991)

Closer You Get, The (Aileen Ritchie, 2000)

Close Shave, A (Nick Park, 1995)

Clue (Jonathan Lynn, 1985)

Coal Miner's Daughter (Michael Apted, 1980)

Cold Comfort Farm (John Schlesinger, 1995)

Cold Heaven (Nicolas Roeg, 1992)

Colditz Story, The (Guy Hamilton, 1955)

Collectors, The (Sidney J. Furie, 1999)

Comeback, The (Peter Walker, 1978)

Come See the Paradise (Alan Parker, 1990)

Comfort and Joy (Bill Forsyth, 1984)

Commitments, The (Alan Parker, 1991)

Company of Wolves, The (Neil Jordan, 1984)

Complicity (Gavin Millar, 2000)

Comrades (Bill Douglas, 1987)

Con Air (Simon West, 1997)

Coneheads (Steve Barron, 1993)

Confessions of a Window Cleaner (Val Guest, 1974)

Conquest (Piers Haggard, 1998)

Conquest of the Planet of the Apes (J. Lee Thompson,

Continental Divide (Michael Apted, 1981)

Cook, the Thief, His Wife & Her Lover, The
    (Peter Greenaway, 1989)

Cool it Carol (Peter Walker, 1970)

Cool Mikado, The (Michael Winner, 1962)

Cool Sound From Hell (Sidney J. Furie, 1959)

Copycat (Jon Amiel, 1995)

Cord (Sidney J. Furie, 1999)

Cosh Boy (Lewis Gilbert, 1953)

Cotton Mary (Ismail Merchant, 1999)

Country Dance (J. Lee Thompson, 1970)

Craze (Freddie Francis, 1973)

Creature Comforts (Nick Park, 1990)

Creeping Flesh, The (Freddie Francis, 1973)

Cresta Run (Terry Winsor, 1990)

Crimes of Passion (Ken Russell, 1984)

Criminal, The (Joseph Losey, 1960)

Criminal, The (Julian Simpson, 2000)

Crimson Tide (Tony Scott, 1995)

CrissCross (Chris Menges, 1992)

Critical Condition (Michael Apted, 1987)

Crooks Anonymous (Ken Annakin, 1963)

Croupier (Mike Hodges, 1997)

Crow: Salvation, The (Bharat Nalluri, 2000)

Crucible, The (Nicholas Hytner, 1996)

Crush Proof (Paul Tickell, 1998)

Cry Freedom (Richard Attenborough, 1987)

Cry from the Streets, A (Lewis Gilbert, 1958)

Crying Game, The (Neil Jordan, 1992)

Crystal Gazing (Laura Mulvey and Peter Wollen, 1982)

Cuba (Richard Lester, 1979)

Curse of the Fly (Don Sharp, 1965)

D

Damned, The (Joseph Losey, 1963)

Dance Hall (Charles Crichton, 1950)

Dance Little Lady (Val Guest, 1955)

Dance with a Stranger (Mike Newell, 1985)

Dancing at Lughnasa (Pat O'Connor, 1998)

Dancing at the Blue Iguana (Michael Radford, 2000)

Dangerous Age, A (Sidney J. Furie, 1958)

Dangerous Davies – The Last Detective (Val Guest, 1980)

Dangerous Liaisons (Stephen Frears, 1988)

Danny, the Champion of the World (Gavin Millar, 1989)

Darker Side of Black, The (Isaac Julien, 1993)

Darkest Light, The (Simon Beaufoy and
    Bille Eltringham, 1999)

Darling (John Schlesinger, 1965)

Dark Places (Don Sharp, 1974)

Dark Tower, The (Freddie Francis, 1989)

Day in the Death of Joe Egg, A (Peter Medak, 1972)

Day of the Locust, The (John Schlesinger, 1975)

Days of Thunder (Tony Scott, 1990)

Day the Earth Caught Fire, The (Val Guest, 1961)

Dead Again (Kenneth Branagh, 1991)

Dead Babies (William Marsh, 2000)

Dead Cert (Tony Richardson, 1974)

Deadfall (Bryan Forbes, 1968)

Deadly Advice (Mandie Fletcher, 1994)

Deadly Bees, The (Freddie Francis, 1966)

Dead of Night (Charles Crichton et al, 1945)

Dead TV (Chris Petit, 1999)

Dear Boy: The Story of Micháel MacLiammóir
    (Donald Taylor Black, 1999)

Death and the Compass (Alex Cox, 1996)

Death Wish (Michael Winner, 1974)

Death Wish 3 (Michael Winner, 1985)

Death Wish II (Michael Winner, 1982)

Death Wish 4: The Crackdown (J. Lee Thompson, 1987)

Debt Collector, The (Anthony Neilson, 1999)

Decadence (Steven Berkoff, 1994)

December Bride (Thaddeus O'Sullivan, 1990)

Deep, The (Peter Yates, 1977)

Déjà Vu (Henry Jaglom, 1997)

Delicate Balance, A (Tony Richardson, 1973)

Deliverance (John Boorman, 1972)

Demon Seed (Donald Cammell, 1977)

Designated Mourner, The (David Hare, 1997)

Devil's Chimney, The (Sandra Goldbacher, 1999)

Devil's Disciple, The (Guy Hamilton, 1959)

Devil's Pale Moonlit Kiss (Roger Spottiswoode, 2000)

Devils, The (Ken Russell, 1971)

Devil-Ship Pirates, The (Don Sharp, 1964)

Diamonds Are Forever (Guy Hamilton, 1971)

Diamond Skulls (Nick Broomfield, 1989)

Die Screaming, Marianne (Peter Walker, 1971)

Different for Girls (Richard Spence, 1996)

Digby, the Biggest Dog in the World (Joseph McGrath, 1973)

Dilapidated Dwelling, The (Patrick Keiller, 2000)

Dirt (David Evans, 1999)

Dirty Weekend (Michael Winner, 1987)

Disappearance of Finbar, The (Sue Clayton, 1996)

Distant Voices, Still Lives (Terence Davies, 1988)

Distinguished Gentleman, The (Jonathan Lynn, 1992)

Divided Heart, The (Charles Crichton, 1954)

Divorcing Jack (David Caffrey, 1998)

Doc Hollywood (Michael Caton-Jones, 1991)

Doctor and the Devils, The (Freddie Francis, 1985)

Doctor Blood's Coffin (Sidney J. Furie, 1961)

Doctor Zhivago (David Lean, 1965)

Dogs of War, The (John Irvin, 1980)

Doll's House, A (Joseph Losey, 1973)

Donald Cammell: The Ultimate Performance
    (Kevin MacDonald, 1998)

Donnie Brasco (Mike Newell, 1997)

Don Giovanni (Joseph Losey, 1979)

Don't Bother to Knock (Roy Ward Baker, 1952)

Don't Go Breaking My Heart (Willi Patterson, 1998)

Don't Look Now (Nicolas Roeg, 1973)

Don't Tell Her it's Me (Malcolm Mowbray, 1990)
Double Confession (Ken Annakin, 1950)
Down the Corner (Joe Comerford, 1977)
Downtime (Bharat Nalluri, 1997)
Dracula Has Risen from the Grave (Freddie Francis, 1968)
Draughtsman's Contract, The (Peter Greenaway, 1982)
Dreamchild (Gavin Millar, 1985)
Dreaming of Joseph Lees (Eric Styles, 1999)
Dresser, The (Peter Yates, 1983)
Driftwood (Ronan O'Leary, 1996)
Drinking Crude (Owen McPolin, 1997)
Driving Me Crazy (Nick Broomfield, 1988)
Dr Jekyll and Sister Hyde (Roy Ward Baker, 1971)
Drowning by Numbers (Peter Greenaway, 1988)
Dr Strangelove: or, How I Learned to Stop Worrying
      and Love the Bomb (Stanley Kubrick, 1964)
Dr. Terror's House of Horrors (Freddie Francis, 1965)
Duellists, The (Ridley Scott, 1977)
During One Night (Sidney J. Furie, 1961)
Dust Devil (Richard Stanley, 1992)
D.W. Griffith: Father of Film (Kevin Brownlow, 1993)

E

Earth Girls are Easy (Julien Temple, 1989)
East Is East (Damien O'Donnell, 1999)
East of Elephant Rock (Don Boyd, 1977)
Eating (Henry Jaglom, 1990)
Eat the Rich (Peter Richardson, 1987)
Educating Rita (Lewis Gilbert, 1983)
Edward II (Derek Jarman, 1991)
8 1/2 Women (Peter Greenaway, 1999)
80,000 Suspects (Val Guest, 1963)
Electric Dreams (Steve Barron, 1984)
Eleni (Peter Yates, 1985)
Elephant Gun (Ken Annakin, 1958)
Elephant Juice (Sam Miller, 1999)
Elizabeth (Shekhar Kapur, 1998)
El Patrullero/Highway Patrolman (Alex Cox, 1992)
Emerald Forest, The (John Boorman, 1985)
Emergency Call (Lewis Gilbert, 1952)
Eminent Domain (John Irvin, 1991)
Empire State (Ron Peck, 1987)

Enchanted April (Mike Newell, 1992)
End of the Affair, The (Neil Jordan, 1999)
Enemy of the State (Tony Scott, 1998)
England Made Me (Peter Duffell, 1973)
England, My England (Tony Palmer, 1995)
English Patient, The (Anthony Minghella, 1996)
Enigma (Michael Apted, 2001)
Entertainer, The (Tony Richardson, 1960)
Entity, The (Sidney J. Furie, 1981)
Entrapment (Jon Amiel, 1999)
Erik the Viking (Terry Jones, 1989)
Escape from Zahrain (Ronald Neame, 1962)
Essex Boys (Terry Winsor, 2000)
Ethan Frome (John Madden, 1993)
Eureka (Nicolas Roeg, 1982)
Europeans, The (James Ivory, 1979)
Eva (Joseph Losey, 1963)
Event Horizon (Paul Anderson, 1997)
Everybody Wins (Karel Reisz, 1990)
Evil of Frankenstein, The (Freddie Francis, 1964)
Evil that Men Do, The (J. Lee Thompson, 1984)
Evil Under the Sun (Guy Hamilton, 1982)
Evita (Alan Parker, 1996)
Excalibur (John Boorman, 1981)
Executive Decision (Stuart Baird, 1996)
Exorcist II: The Heretic (John Boorman, 1977)
Exposé (James Kenelm Clarke, 1975)
Expresso Bongo (Val Guest, 1960)
Extreme Measures (Michael Apted, 1996)
Eye for an Eye (John Schlesinger, 1996)
Eye Hears, The Ear Sees, The (Gavin Millar, 1970)
Eye of the Devil (J. Lee Thompson, 1967)
Eyes Wide Shut (Stanley Kubrick, 1999)
Fyewitness (Peter Yates, 1981)

F

Face (Antonia Bird, 1997)
Face of Fu Manchu, The (Don Sharp, 1965)
FairyTale: A True Story (Charles Sturridge, 1997)
Falcon and the Snowman, The (John Schlesinger, 1984)
Falconer, The (Chris Petit and Iain Sinclair, 1998)
Fall of the House of Usher, The (Ken Russell, 2001)

Falls, The (Peter Greenaway, 1980)

Fame (Alan Parker, 1980)

Family Life (Ken Loach, 1971)

Fan, The (Tony Scott, 1996)

Fanny Hill (Gerry O'Hara, 1983)

Fantasist, The (Robin Hardy, 1986)

Far From the Madding Crowd (John Schlesinger, 1967)

Fast Food (Stewart Sugg, 1998)

Fast Lady, The (Ken Annakin, 1962)

Fatal Attraction (Adrian Lyne, 1987)

Fatherland (Ken Loach, 1986)

Fat Man and Little Boy (Roland Joffé, 1989)

Fear and Desire (Stanley Kubrick, 1953)

Fear and Loathing in Las Vegas (Terry Gilliam, 1998)

Fear is the Key (Michael Tuchner, 1972)

Feast at Midnight, A (Justin Hardy, 1994)

Ferry to Hong Kong (Lewis Gilbert, 1959)

Fetishes (Nick Broomfield, 1996)

Fever Pitch (David Evans, 1997)

Field, The (Jim Sheridan, 1990)

Fiendish Plot of Dr Fu Manchu, The
    (Piers Haggard, 1980)

Fierce Creatures (Robert Young, 1997)

Fifth Musketeer, The (Ken Annakin, 1979)

Fifth Province, The (Frank Stapleton, 1999)

Figures in a Landscape (Joseph Losey, 1970)

Filth and the Fury, The (Julien Temple, 2000)

Final Cut (Dominic Anciano and Ray Burdis, 1999)

Final Cut, The (Roger Christian, 1995)

Finders Keepers (Richard Lester, 1984)

Firepower (Michael Winner, 1979)

Fire Princess (Alan Bridges, 1990)

Firewalker (1986)

Firstborn (Michael Apted, 1984)

First Monday in October (Ronald Neame, 1981)

Fish Called Wanda, A (Charles Crichton, 1988)

Fisher King, The (Terry Gilliam, 1991)

Flame in the Streets (Roy Ward Baker, 1961)

Flash Gordon (Mike Hodges, 1980)

Flashdance (Adrian Lyne, 1983)

Flesh and Blood Show, The (Peter Walker, 1972)

Flick (Fintan Connolly, 2000)

Flight to Berlin/Fluchtpunkt Berlin (Chris Petit, 1983)

Floods of Fear (Charles Crichton, 1959)

Following (Christopher Nolan, 1998)

Folly to Be Wise (Frank Launder, 1953)

Food of Love (Stephen Poliakoff, 1997)

Fool, The (Christine Edzard, 1990)

Fools of Fortune (Pat O'Connor, 1990)

For Better, For Worse (J. Lee Thompson, 1954)

Force Ten From Navarone (Guy Hamilton, 1978)

Foreign Body (Ronald Neame, 1986)

Formulas for Seduction: The Cinema of Atom Egoyan
    (Eileen Anipare and Jason Wood, 1999)

For Pete's Sake (Peter Yates, 1974)

For Those in Peril (Charles Crichton, 1944)

For Your Eyes Only (John Glen, 1981)

Four Dimensions of Greta (Peter Walker, 1972)

Four Musketeers, The (Richard Lester, 1974)

1492: Conquest of Paradise (Ridley Scott, 1992)

Fourth Protocol, The (John MacKenzie, 1987)

Four Weddings and a Funeral (Mike Newell, 1993)

Foxes (Adrian Lyne, 1980)

Fragments of Isabella (Ronan O'Leary, 1989)

Frankenstein (Kenneth Branagh, 1994)

Frankie Starlight (Michael Lindsay-Hogg, 1995)

Frantz Fanon: Black Skin, White Mask
    (Isaac Julien, 1995)

Freefall (John Irvin, 1994)

French Dressing (Ken Russell, 1963)

French Lieutenant's Woman, The (Karel Reisz, 1981)

Friends (Lewis Gilbert, 1971)

Friendship's Death (Peter Wollen, 1987)

Friends of Eddie Coyle, The (Peter Yates, 1973)

Frightmare (Peter Walker, 1974)

Frog Prince, The (Brian Gilbert, 1984)

Full Metal Jacket (Stanley Kubrick, 1987)

Full Monty, The (Peter Cattaneo, 1997)

Full Treatment, The (Val Guest, 1961)

Funeral in Berlin (Guy Hamilton, 1966)

Funny Bones (Peter Chelsom, 1995)

Funny Money (James Kenelm Clarke, 1982)

Funny Thing Happened On the Way to the Forum, A
    (Richard Lester, 1966)

Further Up the Creek (Val Guest, 1958)

G

Gable and Lombard (Sidney J. Furie, 1976)

Galileo (Joseph Losey, 1975)

Gallivant (Andrew Kötting, 1997)

Gambit (Ronald Neame, 1966)

Gambler, The (Karel Reisz, 1974)

Game for Three Losers (Gerry O'Hara, 1964)

Games, The (Michael Winner, 1970)

Gandhi (Richard Attenborough, 1982)

Gangster No. 1 (Paul McGuigan, 2000)

Garden, The (Derek Jarman, 1990)

General, The (John Boorman, 1998)

General's Daughter, The (Simon West, 1999)

Genghis Cohn (Elijah Moshinsky, 1993)

Geordie (Frank Launder, 1955)

Get Back (Richard Lester, 1991)

Get Carter (Mike Hodges, 1971)

Ghost in the Noonday Sun (Peter Medak, 1973)

Ghost of Greville Lodge, The (Niall Johnson, 2000)

Ghost Story (John Irvin, 1981)

Ghoul, The (Freddie Francis, 1975)

G.I. Jane (Ridley Scott, 1997)

Girls Come First (Joseph McGrath, 1975)

Girls' Night (Nick Hurran, 1998)

Girl with Brains in Her Feet, The (Robert Bangura, 1997)

Girl with Green Eyes (Desmond Davis, 1964)

Give Us the Moon (Val Guest, 1943)

Glad All Over (Tony Palmer, 1971)

Gladiator (Ridley Scott, 2000)

Glitterbug (Derek Jarman, 1994)

Go-Between, The (Joseph Losey, 1971)

Gold Diggers, The (Sally Potter, 1983)

Golden Bowl, The (James Ivory, 2000)

Golden Gate (John Madden, 1994)

Golden Salamander, The (Ronald Neame, 1950)

Goldfinger (Guy Hamilton, 1964)

Gold in the Streets (Elizabeth Gill, 1996)

Good Companions, The (J. Lee Thompson, 1957)

Good Die Young, The (Lewis Gilbert, 1954)

Good Father, The (Mike Newell, 1987)

Goodbye Lover (Roland Joffé, 1999)

Gorillas in the Mist (Michael Apted, 1988)

Gorky Park (Michael Apted, 1983)

Gothic (Ken Russell, 1986)

Got it Made (James Kenelm Clarke, 1974)

Governess, The (Sandra Goldbacher, 1998)

Grand Day Out, A (Nick Park, 1992)

Grass Arena, The (Gillies Mackinnon, 1991)

Great Expectations (David Lean, 1946)

Great Gatsby (Jack Clayton, 1974)

Great McGonagall, The (Joseph McGrath, 1974)

Great Rock 'n' Roll Swindle, The (Julien Temple, 1979)

Great St. Trinian's Train Robbery, The (Frank Launder, 1

Greedy (Jonathan Lynn, 1994)

Greek Tycoon, The (J. Lee Thompson, 1978)

Greengage Summer, The (Lewis Gilbert, 1961)

Gregory's Girl (Bill Forsyth, 1981)

Gregory's Two Girls (Bill Forsyth, 1999)

Grey Owl (Richard Attenborough, 1999)

Greystoke: The Legend of Tarzan, Lord of the Apes
    (Hugh Hudson, 1984)

Grifters, The (Stephen Frears, 1990)

Guest House Paradiso (Adrian Edmondson, 1999)

Guiltrip (Gerry Stembridge, 1996)

Guilty, The (Anthony Waller, 1999)

Gumshoe (Stephen Frears, 1972)

Guns of Navarone, The (J. Lee Thompson, 1961)

Guru, The (James Ivory, 1969)

Guy (Michael Lindsay-Hogg, 1996)

Gypsy and the Gentleman, The (Joseph Losey, 1958)

H

Hackers (Iain Softley, 1995)

Hamburger Hill (John Irvin, 1987)

Hamlet (Kenneth Branagh, 1996)

Hamlet (Tony Richardson, 1969)

Handful of Dust, A (Charles Sturridge, 1988)

Handgun (Tony Garnett, 1982)

Handsworth Songs (John Akomfrah, 1986)

Hannibal (Ridley Scott, 2001)

Hannibal Brooks (Michael Winner, 1969)

Happiest Days of Your Life, The (Frank Launder, 1950)

Happy Birthday to Me (J. Lee Thompson, 1981)

Hard Day's Night, A (Richard Lester, 1964)

Hardcore (James Kenelm Clarke, 1977)

Hard Men (J.K. Amalou, 1997)

Hardware (Richard Stanley, 1990)

Haunted (Lewis Gilbert, 1995)

Hawk, The (David Hayman, 1993)

Hawk the Slayer (Terry Marcel, 1980)

Hear My Song (Peter Chelsom, 1991)

Heart of a Child (Clive Donner, 1958)

Heat and Dust (James Ivory, 1982)

Hedda (Trevor Nunn, 1975)

Hell in the Pacific (John Boorman, 1968)

Hell is a City (Val Guest, 1960)

Hellions, The (Ken Annakin, 1961)

Hellraiser (Clive Barker, 1987)

Help! (Richard Lester, 1965)

Hennessy (Don Sharp, 1975)

Henry V (Kenneth Branagh, 1989)

Henry VIII and His Six Wives (Waris Hussein, 1973)

Here We Go Round the Mulberry Bush (Clive Donner, 1968)

He Who Rides a Tiger (Charles Crichton, 1966)

Hidden Agenda (Ken Loach, 1990)

Hideous Kinky (Gillies Mackinnon, 1998)

High Boot Benny (Joe Comerford, 1993)

High Fidelity (Stephen Frears, 2000)

High Heels and Low Lifes (Mel Smith, 2001)

High Hopes (Mike Leigh, 1988)

Highly Dangerous (Roy Ward Baker, 1950)

High Spirits (Neil Jordan, 1988)

Hilary and Jackie (Anand Tucker, 1998)

Hi-Lo Country, The (Stephen Frears, 1998)

Hireling, The (Alan Bridges, 1973)

Hit! (Sidney J. Furie, 1973)

Hit, The (Stephen Frears, 1984)

HMS Defiant (Lewis Gilbert, 1962)

Hobson's Choice (David Lean, 1954)

Hole, The (Nick Hamm, 2001)

Holiday Camp (Ken Annakin, 1948)

Hollow Point (Sidney J. Furie, 1995)

Home Before Midnight (Peter Walker, 1979)

Homecoming, The (Peter Hall, 1973)

Honest (David A. Stewart, 2000)

Honky Tonk Freeway (John Schlesinger, 1981)

Honorary Consul, The (John MacKenzie, 1983)

Hookers, Hustlers, Pimps, and their Johns
    (Beeban Kidron, 1993)

Hope and Glory (John Boorman, 1987)

Hopscotch (Ronald Neame, 1980)

Horse's Mouth, The (Ronald Neame, 1958)

Hotel New Hampshire, The (Tony Richardson, 1984)

Hotel Paradise (Nicolas Roeg, 1995)

Hotel Sahara (Ken Annakin, 1951)

Hotel Splendide (Terence Gross, 2000)

Hot Rock, The (Peter Yates, 1972)

Hour of the Pig, The (Leslie Megahy, 1993)

Householder, The (James Ivory, 1963)

House in the Square, The (Roy Ward Baker, 1951)

Housekeeping (Bill Forsyth, 1987)

House of America (Marc Evans, 1997)

House of Angelo, The (Jim Goddard, 1997)

House of Mirth, The (Terence Davies, 2000)

House of Mortal Sin (Peter Walker, 1975)

House of the Long Shadows (Peter Walker, 1983)

House of Whipcord (Peter Walker, 1974)

House on Carroll Street, The (Peter Yates, 1988)

House that Dripped Blood, The (Peter Duffell, 1970)

Howard Hawks: American Artist (Kevin MacDonald, 1996)

Howard's End (James Ivory, 1992)

How I Won the War (Richard Lester, 1967)

How to Get Ahead in Advertising (Bruce Robinson, 1989)

Huckleberry Finn (J. Lee Thompson, 1974)

Hue and Cry (Charles Crichton, 1947)

Huggets Abroad (Ken Annakin, 1949)

Human Traffic (Justin Kerrigan, 1999)

Hunger, The (Tony Scott, 1983)

Hunted (Charles Crichton, 1952)

Hush-A-Bye Baby (Margo Harkin, 1990)

Hysteria (Freddie Francis, 1964)

I

I Aim at the Stars (J. Lee Thompson, 1959)

I Can't ... I Can't (Piers Haggard, 1969)

Ice Cold in Alex (J. Lee Thompson, 1958)

I Could Go on Singing (Ronald Neame, 1963)

I Could Read the Sky (Nichola Bruce, 1999)

I Dreamed of Africa (Hugh Hudson, 2000)

I Dreamt I Woke Up (John Boorman, 1991)

If... (Lindsay Anderson, 1968)

I Like Birds (Peter Walker, 1967)

I'll Be Your Sweetheart (Val Guest, 1945)

I'll Never Forget What's 'is Name (Michael Winner, 1967)

Il Postino (Michael Radford, 1994)

Immortal Beloved (Bernard Rose, 1994)

I'm Not Feeling Myself Tonight (Joseph McGrath, 1976)

In Celebration (Lindsay Anderson, 1975)

Incident at Oglala (Michael Apted, 1992)

In Custody (Ismail Merchant, 1993)

Indecent Proposal (Adrian Lyne, 1993)

In Dreams (Neil Jordan, 1998)

Inferno (Roy Ward Baker, 1953)

Informers, The (Ken Annakin, 1965)

In Her Defense (Sidney J. Furie, 1998)

In Love and War (Richard Attenborough, 1996)

Innocent Sleep, The (Scott Michell, 1996)

Innocent, The (John MacKenzie, 1985)

Innocent, The (John Schlesinger, 1993)

Innocents, The (Jack Clayton, 1961)

Inside Out (Peter Duffell, 1975)

Insignificance (Nicolas Roeg, 1985)

Inspirations (Michael Apted, 1997)

Institute Benjamenta (Stephen and Timothy Quay, 1995)

Internal Affairs (Mike Figgis, 1990)

International Velvet (Bryan Forbes, 1978)

Interview with the Vampire (Neil Jordan, 1994)

In the Bleak Midwinter (Kenneth Branagh, 1995)

In the Name of the Father (Jim Sheridan, 1993)

Intimate Reflections (Don Boyd, 1974)

Intimate Stranger, The (Joseph Losey, 1956)

Into the West (Mike Newell, 1992)

Intrepid Mr. Twigg, The (Freddie Francis, 1968)

Intruder, The (Guy Hamilton, 1954)

Invasion (Alan Bridges, 1966)

Inventing the Abbotts (Pat O'Connor, 1997)

In Which We Serve (David Lean, 1942)

Ipcress File, The (Sidney J. Furie, 1965)

Irish Cinema: Ourselves Alone? (Donald Taylor Black, 1995)

Iron Eagle (Sidney J. Furie, 1986)

Iron Eagle IV (Sidney J. Furie, 1995)

Iron Eagle III: Aces (John Glen, 1992)

Iron Eagle II (Sidney J. Furie, 1988)

Isadora (Karel Reisz, 1968)

I See a Dark Stranger (Frank Launder, 1946)

Is That All There Is? (Lindsay Anderson, 1993)

I Still Know What You Did Last Summer
(Danny Cannon, 1998)

It Happened Here (Kevin Brownlow, 1966)

It's All Happening (Don Sharp, 1963)

It's a Wonderful World (Val Guest, 1956)

It's Trad, Dad! (Richard Lester, 1962)

I Want You (Michael Winterbottom, 1998)

I Was Happy Here (Desmond Davis, 1966)

I Went Down (Paddy Breathnach, 1997)

Ivansxtc (Bernard Rose, 2000)

J

Jabberwocky (Terry Gilliam, 1977)

Jackal, The (Michael Caton-Jones, 1997)

Jacob's Ladder (Adrian Lyne, 1990)

Jacqueline (Roy Ward Baker, 1956)

James Gang, The (Mike Barker, 1997)

Jane and the Lost City (Terry Marcel, 1987)

Jane Austen in Manhattan (James Ivory, 1980)

Janice Beard: 45 wpm (Clare Kilner, 1999)

January Man, The (Pat O'Connor, 1989)

Jefferson in Paris (James Ivory, 1995)

Jeffrey (Christopher Ashley, 1995)

Jennifer 8 (Bruce Robinson, 1992)

Jigsaw (Val Guest, 1962)

Joey Boy (Frank Launder, 1965)

John and Mary (Peter Yates, 1969)

John Goldfarb, Please Come Home (J. Lee Thompson, 1

Johnny on the Run (Lewis Gilbert, 1953)

Jokers, The (Michael Winner, 1966)

Joseph Andrews (Tony Richardson, 1977)

Jubilee (Derek Jarman, 1978)

Jude (Michael Winterbottom, 1996)

Judge Dredd (Danny Cannon, 1995)

Juggernaut (Richard Lester, 1974)

Jump the Gun (Les Blair, 1996)

Juror, The (Brian Gibson, 1996)

Just In Time (John Carney and Tom Hall, 1998)

Just William's Luck (Val Guest, 1948)

K

Keep It Up Downstairs (Robert Young, 1976)
Keep the Aspidistra Flying (Robert Bierman, 1997)
Kes (Ken Loach, 1969)
Kevin and Perry Go Large (Ed Bye, 2000)
Kevin of the North (Bob Spiers, 2001)
Killer Force (Val Guest, 1975)
Killer's Kiss (Stanley Kubrick, 1955)
Killing Dad (Michael Austin, 1989)
Killing Fields, The (Roland Joffé, 1984)
Killing Time (Bharat Nalluri, 1998)
Killing, The (Stanley Kubrick, 1956)
Kind of Hush, A (Brian Stirner, 1997)
Kind of Loving, A (John Schlesinger, 1962)
King and Country (Joseph Losey, 1964)
King of the Wind (Peter Duffell, 1989)
King Rat (Bryan Forbes, 1965)
Kings of the Sun (J. Lee Thompson, 1963)
King Solomon's Mines (J. Lee Thomspon, 1985)
Kinjite: Forbidden Subjects (J. Lee Thompson, 1989)
Kiss Before Dying, A (James Dearden, 1991)
Kiss of the Vampire (Don Sharp, 1963)
Kitchen Toto, The (Harry Hook, 1987)
Kleptomania (Don Boyd, 1995)
Knack ... and how to get it, The (Richard Lester, 1965)
Korea (Cathal Black, 1995)
Krays, The (Peter Medak, 1990)
Krull (Peter Yates, 1983)
K2 (Franc Roddam, 1991)
Kurosawa: The Last Emperor (Alex Cox, 1999)
Kurt and Courtney (Nick Broomfield, 1998)

L

Ladybird, Ladybird (Ken Loach, 1994)
Ladybugs (Sidney I. Furie, 1992)
Lady Godiva Rides Again (Frank Launder, 1951)
Lady Jane (Trevor Nunn, 1986)
Lady Sings the Blues (Sidney J. Furie, 1972)
Lair of the White Worm, The (Ken Russell, 1988)

Land and Freedom (Ken Loach, 1995)
Landfall (Ken Annakin, 1949)
Land Girls (David Leland, 1998)
Land of Fury (Ken Annakin, 1954)
Lara Croft: Tomb Raider (Simon West, 2001)
Last Angel of History, The (John Akomfrah, 1995)
Last Boy Scout, The (Tony Scott, 1991)
Last Bus Home, The (Johnny Gogan, 1997)
Last of England, The (Derek Jarman, 1987)
Last of His Tribe, The (Harry Hook, 1992)
Last of the Finest, The (John MacKenzie, 1990)
Last of the High Kings, The (David Keating, 1996)
Last Resort, The (Pawel Pawlikowski, 2000)
Last Seduction II, The (Terry Marcel, 1999)
Last September, The (Deborah Warner, 1999)
Last Summer in the Hamptons (Henry Jaglom, 1995)
Late Night Shopping (Saul Metzstein, 2001)
Laughterhouse (Richard Eyre, 1984)
Laughter in the Dark (Tony Richardson, 1969)
Lavender Hill Mob, The (Charles Crichton, 1951)
Law and Disorder (Charles Crichton, 1958)
Lawless, The (Joseph Losey, 1950)
Lawman (Michael Winner, 1971)
Lawrence of Arabia (David Lean, 1962)
Lawyer, The (Sidney J. Furie, 1970)
Leather Boys, The (Sidney J. Furie, 1963)
Leaving Las Vegas (Mike Figgis, 1995)
Legend (Ridley Scott, 1985)
Legend of the Seven Golden Vampires, The
  (Roy Ward Baker, 1974)
Legend of the Werewolf (Freddie Francis, 1975)
Leon the Pig Farmer (Vadim Jean and Gary Sinyor, 1992)
Leopard in the Snow (Gerry O'Hara, 1978)
Leo the Last (John Boorman, 1970)
Les Routes du Sud (Joseph Losey, 1978)
Less Than Zero (Marek Kanievska, 1987)
Let Him Have It (Peter Medak, 1991)
Let It Be (Michael Lindsay-Hogg, 1970)
Let's Get Laid (James Kenelm Clarke, 1977)
Letter to Brezhnev (Chris Bernard, 1985)
Letters from the East (Andrew Grieve, 1995)
Letters to an Unknown Lover/Les Louves (Peter Duffell, 1985)
Liam (Stephen Frears, 2000)

Licence to Kill (John Glen, 1989)

Liebestraum (Mike Figgis, 1991)

Life is a Circus (Val Guest, 1958)

Life is Sweet (Mike Leigh, 1990)

Life Less Ordinary, A (Danny Boyle, 1997)

Life of Stuff, The (Simon Donald, 1998)

Life with the Lyons (Val Guest, 1954)

Lighthouse, The (Simon Hunter, 1999)

Light Up the Sky (Lewis Gilbert, 1960)

Likely Lads, The (Michael Tuchner, 1976)

Lily Tomlin (Nick Broomfield, 1986)

Lion's Mouth (Ken Russell, 2000)

Lisztomania (Ken Russell, 1975)

Little Ballerina (Lewis Gilbert, 1947)

Little Bit of Lippy, A (Chris Bernard, 1992)

Little Dorrit (Christine Edzard, 1987)

Little Fauss and Big Halsy (Sidney J. Furie, 1970)

Little Voice (Mark Herman, 1998)

Live and Let Die (Guy Hamilton, 1973)

Living Daylights, The (John Glen, 1987)

Local Hero (Bill Forsyth, 1983)

Lock, Stock and Two Smoking Barrels (Guy Ritchie, 1998)

Lolita (Stanley Kubrick, 1962)

Lolita (Adrian Lyne, 1997)

London (Patrick Keiller, 1994)

London Kills Me (Hanif Kureishi, 1991)

London Labyrinth (Chris Petit, 1993)

Loneliness of the Long Distance Runner, The
(Tony Richardson, 1962)

Lonely Passion of Judith Hearne, The (Jack Clayton, 1987)

Long Day Closes, The (Terence Davies, 1992)

Long Duel, The (Ken Annakin, 1967)

Longest Day, The (Ken Annakin et al, 1962)

Long Good Friday, The (John MacKenzie, 1979)

Look Back In Anger (Tony Richardson, 1959)

Look Back in Anger (Lindsay Anderson, 1980)

Looking for Langston (Isaac Julien, 1988)

Looks and Smiles (Ken Loach, 1981)

Loop (Alan Niblo, 1997)

Loose Connections (Richard Eyre, 1983)

Lorca and the Outlaws (Roger Christian, 1985)

Lord of Illusions (Clive Barker, 1995)

Lord of the Flies (Harry Hook, 1990)

Lords of Discipline, The (Franc Roddam, 1982)

Loser Takes All (Ken Annakin, 1956)

Loss of Sexual Innocence, The (Mike Figgis, 1999)

Lost Angels (Hugh Hudson, 1989)

Lost Son, The (Chris Menges, 1999)

Love and Death on Long Island (Richard Kwietniowski,

Love and Rage (Cathal Black, 1998)

Love Divided, A (Sydney McCartney, 1999)

Love, Honour and Obey (Dominic Anciano and
Ray Burdis, 2000)

Love is the Devil (John Maybury, 1998)

Love Lottery, The (Charles Crichton, 1954)

Love's Labour's Lost (Kenneth Branagh, 2000)

Loved One, The (Tony Richardson, 1965)

Loved Up (Peter Cattaneo, 1995)

Low Down, The (Jamie Thraves, 2000)

L-Shaped Room, The (Bryan Forbes, 1962)

Lucia (Don Boyd, 1998)

Luv (Clive Donner, 1967)

Lyons in Paris, The (Val Guest, 1955)

M

M (Joseph Losey, 1951)

Mackenna's Gold (J. Lee Thompson, 1969)

Mad About Mambo (John Forte, 2000)

Madagascar Skin (Chris Newby, 1995)

Madame Sousatzka (John Schlesinger, 1988)

Mad Cows (Sara Sugarman, 1998)

Mad Dogs and Englishmen (Henry Cole, 1995)

Made (John MacKenzie, 1972)

Madeleine (David Lean, 1949)

Mademoiselle (Tony Richardson, 1966)

Mad Love (Antonia Bird, 1995)

Madness of King George, The (Nicholas Hytner, 1994)

Madwoman of Chaillot, The (Bryan Forbes, 1969)

Maeve (Pat Murphy, 1981)

Magic (Richard Attenborough, 1978)

Magic Balloon, The (Ronald Neame, 1990)

Magic Christian, The (Joseph McGrath, 1970)

Mahler (Ken Russell, 1974)

Maids, The (Christopher Miles, 1974)

Man Could Get Killed, A (Ronald Neame, 1966)

Man Friday (Jack Gold, 1975)

Man in the Iron Mask, The (Mike Newell, 1976)

Man in the Middle (Guy Hamilton, 1964)

Man in the Sky, The (Charles Crichton, 1956)

Man of Violence (Peter Walker, 1970)

Man Who Cried, The (Sally Potter, 2000)

Man Who Fell to Earth, The (Nicolas Roeg, 1976)

Man Who Knew Too Little, The (Jon Amiel, 1997)

Man Who Never Was, The (Ronald Neame, 1956)

Man With a Gun (Michael Winner, 1958)

Man with the Golden Gun, The (Guy Hamilton, 1974)

Marathon Man (John Schlesinger, 1976)

Maroc 7 (Gerry O'Hara, 1967)

Martha Meet Frank, Daniel and Laurence (Nick Hamm, 1998)

Martin Luther King – Days of Hope (John Akomfrah, 1997)

Mary Reilly (Stephen Frears, 1996)

Masoom (Shekhar Kapur, 1983)

Masterminds (Roger Christian, 1997)

Match, The (Mick Davis, 1999)

Maurice (James Ivory, 1987)

Me & Issac Newton (Michael Apted, 1999)

Mechanic, The (Michael Winner, 1972)

Medusa Touch, The (Jack Gold, 1978)

Melody (Waris Hussein, 1971)

Memento (Christopher Nolan, 2000)

Memphis Belle (Michael Caton-Jones, 1990)

Men of Sherwood Forest (Val Guest, 1954)

Men's Club, The (Peter Medak, 1986)

Mesmer (Roger Spottiswoode, 1994)

Messenger of Death (J. Lee Thompson, 1988)

Meteor (Ronald Neame, 1979)

Michael Collins (Neil Jordan, 1996)

Midnight Cowboy (John Schlesinger, 1969)

Midnight Express (Alan Parker, 1978)

Midsummer Night's Dream, A (Peter Hall, 1968)

Midsummer Night's Dream, A (Adrian Noble, 1996)

Mighty, The (Peter Chelsom, 1998)

Million Pound Note, The (Ronald Neame, 1953)

Millions Like Us (Frank Launder, 1943)

Miracle, The (Neil Jordan, 1991)

Miranda (Ken Annakin, 1948)

Mirror Crack'd, The (Guy Hamilton, 1980)

Misadventures of Margaret, The (Brian Skeet, 1998)

Mission, The (Roland Joffé, 1986)

Mississippi Burning (Alan Parker, 1988)

Miss Julie (Mike Figgis, 1999)

Miss London Ltd. (Val Guest, 1943)

Miss Pilgrim's Progress (Val Guest, 1950)

Mister Moses (Ronald Neame, 1965)

Modesty Blaise (Joseph Losey, 1966)

Mojo (Jez Butterworth, 1997)

Mona Lisa (Neil Jordan, 1986)

Monk Dawson (Tom Waller, 1998)

Monster Club, The (Roy Ward Baker, 1980)

Monster in a Box (Nick Broomfield, 1991)

Month by the Lake, A (John Irvin, 1995)

Month in the Country, A (Pat O'Connor, 1987)

Monty Python and the Holy Grail (Terry Gilliam and
    Terry Jones, 1975)

Monty Python's Life of Brian (Terry Jones, 1979)

Monty Python's The Meaning of Life (Terry Gilliam and
    Terry Jones, 1983)

Moon Zero Two (Roy Ward Baker, 1969)

Moonraker (Lewis Gilbert, 1979)

Morgan: A Suitable Case for Treatment (Karel Reisz, 1966)

Morning Departure (Roy Ward Baker, 1950)

Morons from Outer Space (Mike Hodges, 1985)

Mortal Kombat (Paul Anderson, 1995)

Mother, Jugs and Speed (Peter Yates, 1976)

Moving the Mountain (Michael Apted, 1994)

Mr. and Mrs. Bridge (James Ivory, 1990)

Mr. Drake's Duck (Val Guest, 1951)

Mr. India (Shekhar Kapur, 1987)

Mr Jones (Mike Figgis, 1993)

Mr. Klein (Joseph Losey, 1976)

Mr Know All (Ken Annakin, 1950)

Mr. Quilp (Michael Tuchner, 1975)

Mrs Brown (John Madden, 1997)

Mr Wonderful (Anthony Minghella, 1993)

Much Ado About Nothing (Kenneth Branagh, 1993)

Mummy Lives, The (Gerry O'Hara, 1993)

Mumsy, Nanny, Sonny, and Girly (Freddie Francis, 1969)

Murder at the Mardi Gras (Ken Annakin, 1977)

Murder at the Windmill (Val Guest, 1949)

Murder on the Campus (Michael Winner, 1962)

Murder Without Crime (J. Lee Thompson, 1950)

Murphy's War (Peter Yates, 1971)

Murphy's Law (J. Lee Thompson, 1986)

Music Lovers, The (Ken Russell, 1971)

Mute Witness (Anthony Waller, 1994)

My Ain Folk (Bill Douglas, 1973)

My Beautiful Laundrette (Stephen Frears, 1985)

My Childhood (Bill Douglas, 1972)

My Cousin Vinny (Jonathan Lynn, 1992)

My Left Foot (Jim Sheridan, 1989)

My Life So Far (Hugh Hudson, 1998)

My Name is Joe (Ken Loach, 1998)

My Son the Fanatic (Udayan Prasad, 1997)

Mystery of Edwin Drood, The (Timothy Forder, 1993)

My Way Home (Bill Douglas, 1978)

N

Naked (Mike Leigh, 1993)

Naked Face, The (Bryan Forbes, 1985)

Naked Runner, The (Sidney J. Furie, 1967)

Nasty Habits (Michael Lindsay-Hogg, 1977)

Nasty Neighbours (Debbie Isitt, 1999)

National Health, The (Jack Gold, 1973)

National Lampoon Goes to the Movies
    (Henry Jaglom, 1981)

Near Room, The (David Hayman, 1996)

Ned Kelly (Tony Richardson, 1970)

Negatives (Peter Medak, 1968)

Nell (Michael Apted, 1994)

Neon Bible, The (Terence Davies, 1995)

Never Talk to Strangers (Peter Hall, 1995)

New Adventures of Pippi Longstocking, The
    (Ken Annakin, 1988)

New World Disorder (Richard Spence, 1999)

New Year's Day (Henry Jaglom, 1989)

Next Best Thing, The (John Schlesinger, 2000)

Next of Kin (John Irvin, 1989)

Nice Girl Like Me, A (Desmond Davis, 1969)

Night Must Fall (Karel Reisz, 1964)

Night to Remember, A (Roy Ward Baker, 1958)

Night Train (John Lynch, 1998)

Night Train to Murder (Joseph McGrath, 1983)

Night Without Sleep (Roy Ward Baker, 1952)

Nightbreed (Clive Barker, 1990)

Nightcomers, The (Michael Winner, 1972)

Nighthawks (Ron Peck, 1978)

Nightmare (Freddie Francis, 1963)

Nil by Mouth (Gary Oldman, 1997)

9 1/2 Weeks (Adrian Lyne, 1985)

Nine Lives of Tomas Katz, The (Ben Hopkins, 2000)

1984 (Michael Radford, 1984)

No Child of Mine (Peter Kosminsky, 1997)

No Trees in the Street (J. Lee Thompson, 1958)

Nora (Pat Murphy, 2000)

North West Frontier (J. Lee Thompson, 1958)

Nostradamus (Roger Christian, 1994)

Not Quite Jerusalem (Lewis Gilbert, 1984)

Not Without My Daughter (Brian Gilbert, 1991)

Nothing But the Best (Clive Donner, 1964)

Nothing Personal (Thaddeus O'Sullivan, 1995)

Notting Hill (Roger Michell, 1999)

November Afternoon (John Carney and Tom Hall, 1997)

Nude Bomb, The (Clive Donner, 1980)

Number One (Les Blair, 1984)

Nuns on the Run (Jonathan Lynn, 1990)

Nutcracker, The (Christine Edzard, 1997)

O

Object of Beauty, The (Michael Lindsay-Hogg, 1991)

Object of My Affection, The (Nicholas Hytner, 1998)

October Man, The (Roy Ward Baker, 1947)

Octopussy (John Glen, 1983)

Odd Job, The (Peter Medak, 1978)

Odessa File, The (Ronald Neame, 1974)

Off the Beaten Track (Jaap Mees, 2000)

Of Human Bondage (Bryan Forbes, 1964)

Oh! What a Lovely War! (Richard Attenborough, 1969)

Old Mac (Michael Winner, 1961)

Oliver Twist (David Lean, 1948)

O Lucky Man! (Lindsay Anderson, 1973)

On the Black Hill (Andrew Grieve, 1987)

One Brief Summer (John MacKenzie, 1969)

Once a Sinner (Lewis Gilbert, 1950)

One Day in September (Kevin MacDonald, 1999)

Onegin (Martha Fiennes, 1999)

One More Kiss (Vadim Jean, 1999)

One Night Stand (Mike Figgis, 1997)

One That Got Away, The (Roy Ward Baker, 1957)

One Way Pendulum (Peter Yates, 1965)

Open Asylum (Colm Villa, 1982)

Operation Daybreak (Lewis Gilbert, 1975)

Ordeal by Innocence (Desmond Davis, 1984)

Ordinary Decent Criminal (Thaddeus O'Sullivan, 2000)

Orlando (Sally Potter, 1992)

Orphans (Peter Mullan, 1997)

Othello (Oliver Parker, 1995)

Our Boy (David Evans, 1997)

Our Man in Marrakesh (Don Sharp, 1966)

Our Mother's House (Jack Clayton, 1967)

Out Cold (Malcolm Mowbray, 1989)

Out of Season (Alan Bridges, 1975)

Outpost in Malaya (Ken Annakin, 1952)

P

Pacific Heights (John Schlesinger, 1990)

Painted Boats (Charles Crichton, 1945)

Pandaemonium (Julien Temple, 2000)

Paperhouse (Bernard Rose, 1988)

Paper Orchid (Roy Ward Baker, 1949)

Paper Tiger (Ken Annakin, 1976)

Paranoiac (Freddie Francis, 1963)

Paris by Night (David Hare, 1988)

Party Party (Terry Winsor, 1983)

Party's Over, The (Guy Hamilton, 1966)

Pascali's Island (James Dearden, 1988)

Passage Home (Roy Ward Baker, 1955)

Passage to India, A (David Lean, 1984)

Passage, The (J. Lee Thompson, 1979)

Passionate Friends, The (David Lean, 1948)

Passion of Darkly Noon, The (Philip Ridley, 1995)

Passion of Remembrance, The (Isaac Julien, 1986)

Paths of Glory (Stanley Kubrick, 1957)

Paul and Michelle (Lewis Gilbert, 1974)

Peaches (Nick Grosso, 2000)

Penny Princess (Val Guest, 1952)

Penthesilea: Queen of the Amazons (Laura Mulvey and Peter Wollen, 1974)

Perfect Friday (Peter Hall, 1970)

Performance (Donald Cammell and Nicolas Roeg, 1970)

Personal Services (Terry Jones, 1987)

Peter's Friends (Kenneth Branagh, 1992)

Pete's Meteor (Joe O'Byrne, 1998)

Petulia (Richard Lester, 1968)

Photographing Fairies (Nick Willing, 1997)

Pigs (Cathal Black, 1984)

Pillow Book, The (Peter Greenaway, 1995)

Pink Floyd: The Wall (Alan Parker, 1982)

Pirate Movie, The (Ken Annakin, 1982)

Pirate, The (Ken Annakin, 1978)

Planter's Wife, The (Ken Annakin, 1952)

Play It Cool (Michael Winner, 1962)

Playboys, The (Gillies Mackinnon, 1992)

Pleasure Girls, The (Gerry O'Hara, 1965)

Ploughman's Lunch, The (Richard Eyre, 1983)

Plunkett and Macleane (Jake Scott, 1999)

Point Blank (John Boorman, 1967)

Poitin (Bob Quinn, 1979)

Poltergeist 2: The Other Side (Brian Gibson, 1986)

Pontiac Moon (Peter Medak, 1994)

Poor Cow (Ken Loach, 1968)

Pope Must Die, The (Peter Richardson, 1991)

Poseidon Adventure, The (Ronald Neame, 1972)

Possession of Joel Delaney, The (Waris Hussein, 1972)

Prague (Ian Sellar, 1992)

Prayer for the Dying, A (Mike Hodges, 1987)

Preaching to the Perverted (Stuart Urban, 1997)

Prick Up Your Ears (Stephen Frears, 1987)

Priest (Antonia Bird, 1994)

Priest of Love (Christopher Miles, 1981)

Prime of Miss Jean Brodie, The (Ronald Neame, 1969)

Princess Caraboo (Michael Austin, 1994)

Prisoners of the Lost Universe (Terry Marcel, 1983)

Private Function, A (Malcolm Mowbray, 1985)

Project: Assassin (Andy Hurst, 1997)

Proprietor, The (Ismail Merchant, 1996)

Prospero's Books (Peter Greenaway, 1991)

Prostitute (Tony Garnett, 1980)

Prowler, The (Joseph Losey, 1951)

Prudence and the Pill (Ronald Neame, 1968)

Psychomania (Don Sharp, 1971)

Psychopath, The (Freddie Francis, 1966)
Pulp (Mike Hodges, 1972)
Pumpkin Eater, The (Jack Clayton, 1964)
Puppet Masters, The (Stuart Orme, 1994)
Pure Hell of St. Trinian's, The (Frank Launder, 1961)
Purely Belter (Mark Herman, 2000)
Purple Hearts (Sidney J. Furie, 1984)
Pursuit of D B Cooper, The (Roger Spottiswoode, 1981)
Pushing Tin (Mike Newell, 1999)

Q

Quackser Fortune Has a Cousin in the Bronx
     (Waris Hussein, 1970)
Quadrophenia (Franc Roddam, 1979)
Quartet (James Ivory, 1981)
Quartet (Ken Annakin, segment, 1949)
Quatermass and the Pit (Roy Ward Baker, 1967)
Quatermass II (Val Guest, 1957)
Quatermass Xperiment, The (Val Guest, 1955)
Queen of Hearts (Jon Amiel, 1989)
Question of Attribution, A (John Schlesinger, 1992)

R

Radioland Murders (Mel Smith, 1994)
Radio On (Chris Petit, 1979)
Radio On (remix) (Chris Petit, 1998)
Raggedy Ann and Andy (Richard Williams, 1978)
Raggedy Rawney, The (Bob Hoskins, 1988)
Raging Moon, The (Bryan Forbes, 1971)
Rainbow (Bob Hoskins, 1995)
Rainbow, The (Ken Russell, 1988)
Rainbow Warrior, The (Michael Tuchner, 1992)
Raining Stones (Ken Loach, 1993)
Rancid Aluminium (Edward Thomas, 2000)
Rasputin the Mad Monk (Don Sharp, 1966)
Rat (Steve Barron, 2000)
Ratcatcher (Lynne Ramsay, 1999)
Ravenous (Antonia Bird, 1999)
Raw Deal (John Irvin, 1986)
Reach for the Sky (Lewis Gilbert, 1956)
Real Howard Spitz, The (Vadim Jean, 1998)

Reckoning, The (Jack Gold, 1969)
Reefer and the Model (Joe Comerford, 1988)
Reflecting Skin, The (Philip Ridley, 1990)
Regeneration (Gillies Mackinnon, 1997)
Reincarnation of Peter Proud, The (J. Lee Thompson, 1⁹
Relative Values (Eric Styles, 2000)
Remains of the Day, The (James Ivory, 1993)
Remember Me? (Nick Hurran, 1997)
Remo Williams: Unarmed and Dangerous
     (Guy Hamilton, 1985)
Repo Man (Alex Cox, 1984)
Resurrected (Paul Greengrass, 1989)
Resurrection Man (Marc Evans, 1998)
Return from the Ashes (J. Lee Thompson, 1965)
Return of the Musketeers, The (Richard Lester, 1989)
Return of the Soldier, The (Alan Bridges, 1982)
Revenge (Tony Scott, 1990)
Revengers' Comedies, The (Malcolm Mowbray, 1998)
Revolution (Hugh Hudson, 1985)
Riddles of the Sphinx (Laura Mulvey and Peter Wollen, 1
Riff-Raff (Ken Loach, 1991)
Ringer, The (Guy Hamilton, 1953)
Rising Damp (Joseph McGrath, 1980)
Rita, Sue and Bob Too (Alan Clarke, 1987)
Ritz, The (Richard Lester, 1976)
Road to God Knows Where, The (Alan Gilsenan, 1989)
Road to Wellville, The (Alan Parker, 1994)
Rob Roy (Michael Caton-Jones, 1995)
Robbery (Peter Yates, 1967)
Robin and Marian (Richard Lester, 1976)
Robinson in Space (Patrick Keiller, 1997)
Rocket to the Moon (Don Sharp, 1967)
Rogue Trader (James Dearden, 1999)
Rolling Stones Rock and Roll Circus
     (Michael Lindsay-Hogg, 1996)
Romance with a Double Bass (Robert Young, 1974)
Romantic Englishwoman, The (Joseph Losey, 1975)
Romeo is Bleeding (Peter Medak, 1993)
Room at the Top (Jack Clayton, 1959)
Room for Romeo Brass, A (Shane Meadows, 1999)
Roommates (Peter Yates, 1995)
Room with a View, A (James Ivory, 1986)
Roseland (James Ivory, 1977)

Royal Flash (Richard Lester, 1975)

Ruby (John MacKenzie, 1992)

Ruling Class, The (Peter Medak, 1972)

Runaway Bus, The (Val Guest, 1954)

Runners (Charles Sturridge, 1983)

Run of the Country (Peter Yates, 1995)

Ryan's Daughter (David Lean, 1970)

S

Sacred Flesh (Nigel Wingrove, 2000)

Sadness of Sex, The (Rupert Wainwright, 1995)

Safe Place, A (Henry Jaglom, 1971)

Sailor from Gibralter, The (Tony Richardson, 1967)

Sailor's Return, The (Jack Gold, 1978)

Saint-Ex (Anand Tucker, 1997)

Salomé's Last Dance (Ken Russell, 1988)

Salt on Our Skin (Andrew Birkin, 1992)

Saltwater (Conor McPherson, 2000)

Sammy and Rosie Get Laid (Stephen Frears, 1987)

Satan's Skin (Piers Haggard, 1971)

Saturday Night and Sunday Morning (Karel Reisz, 1960)

Savage Hearts (Mark Ezra, 1995)

Savage Messiah (Ken Russell, 1972)

Savages (James Ivory, 1972)

Saving Grace (Nigel Cole, 2000)

Scandal (Michael Caton-Jones, 1989)

Scarlet Letter, The (Roland Joffé, 1995)

Scarlet Thread, The (Lewis Gilbert, 1951)

Scars of Dracula (Roy Ward Baker, 1970)

Scent of Fear (Val Guest, 1985)

Schizo (Peter Walker, 1976)

School For Sex (Peter Walker, 1969)

Scorpio (Michael Winner, 1973)

Scream for Help (Michael Winner, 1984)

Scrooge (Ronald Neame, 1970)

Scum (Alan Clarke, 1979)

Sea Shall Not Have Them, The (Lewis Gilbert, 1954)

Seance on a Wet Afternoon (Bryan Forbes, 1964)

Sebastiane (Derek Jarman, 1976)

Second Best (Chris Menges, 1994)

Secret Agent, The (Christopher Hampton, 1996)

Secret Ceremony (Joseph Losey, 1968)

Secret Laughter of Women, The (Peter Schwabach, 1998)

Secret Place, The (Clive Donner, 1957)

Secret Policeman's Ball, The (Julien Temple, 1979)

Secret Policeman's Other Ball, The (Julien Temple, 1982)

Secret Rapture, The (Howard Davies, 1993)

Secrets (Gavin Millar, 1983)

Secrets and Lies (Mike Leigh, 1996)

Seekers, The (Ken Annakin, 1954)

Sender, The (Roger Christian, 1982)

Sense of Freedom, A (John MacKenzie, 1979)

Sentinel, The (Michael Winner, 1977)

Separate Tables (John Schlesinger, 1983)

Servant, The (Joseph Losey, 1963)

Seven Nights in Japan (Lewis Gilbert, 1976)

Seven Songs for Malcolm X (John Akomfrah, 1993)

7th Dawn, The (Lewis Gilbert, 1964)

Seventh Sin, The (Ronald Neame, 1957)

Sexy Beast (Jonathan Glazer, 2000)

Sgt. Bilko (Jonathan Lynn, 1996)

Shadowlands (Richard Attenborough, 1993)

Shadow of the Earth (Chris Bernard, 1987)

Shakespeare in Love (John Madden, 1998)

Shakespeare Wallah (James Ivory, 1965)

Shallow Grave (Danny Boyle, 1994)

Shanghai Surprise (Jim Goddard, 1986)

Sharma and Beyond (Brian Gilbert, 1986)

Sheila Levine is Dead and Living in New York
     (Sidney J. Furie, 1975)

She's Been Away (Peter Hall, 1989)

Shillingsbury Blowers, The (Val Guest, 1980)

Shining, The (Stanley Kubrick, 1980)

Shirley Valentine (Lewis Gilbert, 1989)

Shoot the Moon (Alan Parker, 1982)

Shoot to Kill (Michael Winner, 1960)

Shoot to Kill (Roger Spottiswoode, 1988)

Shooting Fish (Stefan Schwartz, 1997)

Shooting Party, The (Alan Bridges, 1984)

Shooting Stars (Chris Bernard, 1991)

Shopping (Paul Anderson, 1994)

Short Film About Decalogue: An Interview with Krzysztof
     Kieslowski, A (Eileen Anipare and Jason Wood, 1996)

Sid and Nancy (Alex Cox, 1986)

Silent Scream (David Hayman, 1990)

Simon Magus (Ben Hopkins, 1999)

Simpatico (Matthew Warchus, 1999)

Simple Twist of Fate, A (Gillies Mackinnon, 1994)

Singer Not the Song, The (Roy Ward Baker, 1961)

Singing Lesson, The (Lindsay Anderson, 1967)

Sink the Bismarck (Lewis Gilbert, 1960)

Sister, My Sister (Nancy Meckler, 1994)

Sitting Ducks (Henry Jaglom, 1980)

6th Day, The (Roger Spottiswoode, 2000)

Sixth Happiness, The (Waris Hussein, 1997)

Skull, The (Freddie Francis, 1965)

Slab Boys, The (John Byrne, 1997)

Slaves of New York (James Ivory, 1989)

Sleeping Tiger, The (Joseph Losey, 1954)

Sliding Doors (Peter Howitt, 1998)

Slipper and the Rose, The (Bryan Forbes, 1976)

Small Faces (Gillies Mackinnon, 1996)

Smalltime (Shane Meadows, 1996)

Small Time Obsession (Poitr Szkopiak, 2000)

Smashing Time (Desmond Davis, 1967)

Snake Woman, The (Sidney J. Furie, 1961)

Snakes and Ladders (Trish McAdam, 1996)

Snapper, The (Stephen Frears, 1993)

Snatch (Guy Ritchie, 2000)

Soft Top Hard Shoulder (Stefan Schwartz,1992)

Soldier (Paul Anderson, 1998)

Soldier's Daughter Never Cries, A (James Ivory, 1998)

Solitaire for Two (Gary Sinyor, 1995)

Solomon and Gaenor (Paul Morrisson, 1999)

Some Like It Cool (Michael Winner, 1961)

Someone to Love (Henry Jaglom, 1987)

Someone to Watch Over Me (Ridley Scott, 1987)

Some People (Clive Donner, 1962)

Something Wicked This Way Comes (Jack Clayton, 1983)

Some Voices (Simon Cellan Jones, 2000)

Sommersby (Jon Amiel, 1993)

Son of Dracula (Freddie Francis, 1974)

Sound Barrier, The (David Lean, 1952)

Sound of Murder, The (Michael Lindsay-Hogg, 1982)

Soursweet (Mike Newell, 1988)

Space Movie, The (Tony Palmer, 1979)

Spartacus (Stanley Kubrick, 1960)

Speaks Like a Child (John Akomfrah, 1998)

Species II (Peter Medak, 1998)

Spice World (Bob Spiers, 1997)

Splitting Heirs (Robert Young, 1993)

Spy Who Loved Me, The (Lewis Gilbert, 1977)

Squeeze, The (Michael Apted, 1977)

Staggered (Martin Clunes, 1994)

Stardust (Michael Apted, 1974)

Stars and Bars (Pat O'Connor, 1988)

Stealing Heaven (Clive Donner, 1988)

Steaming (Joseph Losey, 1985)

Stella Does Tricks (Coky Giedroyc, 1996)

Stepford Wives, The (Bryan Forbes, 1975)

Stepping Out (Lewis Gilbert, 1991)

Stiff Upper Lips (Gary Sinyor, 1998)

Stigmata (Rupert Wainwright, 1999)

Still Crazy (Brian Gibson, 1998)

St. Ives (J. Lee Thompson, 1976)

Stone Killer, The (Michael Winner, 1973)

Stop! or My Mom Will Shoot (Roger Spottiswoode, 1992

Stories from a Flying Trunk (Christine Edzard, 1979)

Stormy Monday (Mike Figgis, 1988)

Story of Robin Hood and His Merrie Men, The
    (Ken Annakin, 1952)

Stowaway Girl (Guy Hamilton, 1957)

Straight to Hell (Alex Cox, 1987)

Strange Case of the End of Civilisation as We Know
(Joseph McGrath, 1977)

Stranger on the Prowl (Joseph Losey, 1952)

Strapless (David Hare, 1989)

Stringer, The (Pawel Pawlikowski, 1997)

Strip Jack Naked (Ron Peck, 1991)

Strip Poker (Peter Walker, 1968)

Strong Language (Simon Rumley, 1998)

Summer Holiday (Peter Yates, 1963)

Summer Story, A (Piers Haggard, 1988)

Summertime (David Lean, 1955)

Sunday Bloody Sunday (John Schlesinger, 1971)

Sunday Lovers (Bryan Forbes, 1980)

Sunset Heights (Colm Villa, 1998)

Supergrass, The (Peter Richardson, 1985)

Superman IV: The Quest for Peace (Sidney J. Furie, 198

Superman III (Richard Lester, 1983)

Superman II (Richard Lester, 1980)

Surveillance (Chris Petit, 1993)

Surviving Picasso (James Ivory, 1996)

Suspect (Peter Yates, 1987)

Swann (Anna Benson Gyles, 1996)

Sweet Dreams (Karel Reisz, 1985)

Sweet November (Pat O'Connor, 2001)

Sweety Barrett (Stephen Bradley, 1998)

Swing (Nick Mead, 1999)

Swiss Family Robinson (Ken Annakin, 1960)

Sword and The Rose, The (Ken Annakin, 1953)

System, The (Michael Winner, 1966)

T

Tailor of Panama, The (John Boorman, 2001)

Take My Life (Ronald Neame, 1947)

Taking of Beverly Hills, The (Sidney J. Furie, 1992)

Talented Mr Ripley, The (Anthony Minghella, 1999)

Tales from the Crypt (Freddie Francis, 1972)

Tales that Witness Madness (Freddie Francis, 1973)

Talk of Angels (Nick Hamm, 1998)

Tall Guy, The (Mel Smith, 1989)

Tango Lesson, The (Sally Potter, 1997)

Taras Bulba (J. Lee Thompson, 1962)

Taste of Excitement (Don Sharp, 1969)

Taste of Honey, A (Tony Richardson, 1961)

Teenage Mutant Ninja Turtles (Steve Barron, 1990)

Tempest, The (Derek Jarman, 1979)

10 to Midnight (J. Lee Thompson, 1983)

Terence Davies Trilogy, The (Terence Davies, 1984)

Terminal Man, The (Mike Hodges, 1974)

Territories (Isaac Julien, 1985)

Terror Train (Roger Spottiswoode, 1980)

Testament (John Akomfrah, 1988)

Testimony (Tony Palmer, 1988)

Testimony of Taliesin Jones, The (Martin Duffy, 2000)

That Darn Cat (Bob Spiers, 1997)

That Kind of Girl (Gerry O'Hara, 1963)

That Lucky Touch (Christopher Miles, 1975)

That Sinking Feeling (Bill Forsyth, 1979)

Thelma and Louise (Ridley Scott, 1991)

Theory of Flight, The (Paul Greengrass, 1998)

There Goes the Bride (Terry Marcel, 1979)

There is Another Sun (Lewis Gilbert, 1951)

They Came from Beyond Space (Freddie Francis, 1967)

They Can't Hang Me (Val Guest, 1955)

Thief of Baghdad, The (Clive Donner, 1978)

Third Man on the Mountain (Ken Annakin, 1959)

Third Secret, The (Charles Crichton, 1964)

Thirty is a Dangerous Age, Cynthia (Joseph McGrath, 1967)

Thirty-Nine Steps, The (Don Sharp, 1978)

This Boy's Life (Michael Caton-Jones, 1993)

This Happy Breed (David Lean, 1944)

This Is My Father (Paul Quinn, 1998)

This Is the Sea (Mary McGuckian, 1998)

This Sporting Life (Lindsay Anderson, 1963)

This Year's Love (David Kane, 1999)

Those Daring Young Men in Their Jaunty Jalopies
    (Ken Annakin, 1969)

Those Magnificent Men in Their Flying Machines
    (Ken Annakin, 1965)

Three Businessmen (Alex Cox, 1998)

Three Into Two Won't Go (Peter Hall, 1969)

Three Men in a Boat (Ken Annakin, 1956)

Three Musketeers, The (Richard Lester, 1973)

Three on a Spree (Sidney J. Furie, 1961)

Thriller (Sally Potter, 1979)

Thunderheart (Michael Apted, 1992)

Tichborne Claimant, The (David Yates, 1998)

Tiffany Jones (Peter Walker, 1973)

Tiger Bay (J. Lee Thompson, 1959)

Tiger in the Smoke (Roy Ward Baker, 1956)

Time Bandits (Terry Gilliam, 1981)

Time Code (Mike Figgis, 2000)

Time for Loving, A (Christopher Miles, 1971)

Time Gentlemen Please! (Lewis Gilbert, 1952)

Time Will Tell (Declan Lowney, 1991)

Time Without Pity (Joseph Losey, 1956)

Titanic Town (Roger Michell, 1998)

Titfield Thunderbolt, The (Charles Crichton, 1953)

Tom and Huck (Peter Hewitt, 1995)

Tom and Viv (Brian Gilbert, 1994)

Tom Jones (Tony Richardson, 1963)

Tommy (Ken Russell, 1975)

Tomorrow Never Dies (Roger Spottiswoode, 1997)

Toomorrow (Val Guest, 1970)

Top Gun (Tony Scott, 1986)

Top of the World (Sidney J. Furie, 1997)

Topsy-Turvy (1999) (Mike Leigh, 1999)

Torture Garden (Freddie Francis, 1967)

Touch of Larceny, A (Guy Hamilton, 1959)

Touch of Love, A (Waris Hussein, 1969)

Town and Country (Peter Chelsom, 2001)

To Wong Foo, Thanks For Everything! Julie Newmar
  (Beeban Kidron, 1995)

Tracks (Henry Jaglom, 1976)

Track 29 (Nicolas Roeg, 1988)

Train of Events (Charles Crichton, segment, 1949)

Trainspotting (Danny Boyle, 1996)

Traitor's Gate (Freddie Francis, 1964)

Traveller (Joe Comerford, 1981)

Trenchcoat (Michael Tuchner, 1983)

Trench, The (William Boyd, 1999)

Trial and Error (Jonathan Lynn, 1997)

Trio (Ken Annakin, 1950)

Tripwire (Sidney J. Furie, 1999)

Trog (Freddie Francis, 1970)

Trojan Eddie (Gillies Mackinnon, 1996)

Trouble and Desire: An Interview with Hal Hartley
  (Eileen Anipare and Jason Wood, 1997)

True Romance (Tony Scott, 1993)

Truite, La (Joseph Losey, 1982)

Truly, Madly, Deeply (Anthony Minghella, 1991)

Truth Game, The (Simon Rumley, 2000)

Try This One for Size (Guy Hamilton, 1989)

Tune in Tomorrow/Aunt Julia and the Scriptwriter
  (Jon Amiel, 1990)

Tunes of Glory (Ronald Neame, 1960)

Turner and Hooch (Roger Spottiswoode, 1989)

Turtle Diary (John Irvin, 1985)

Twelfth Night (Trevor Nunn, 1996)

12 Days in July (Margo Harkin, 1997)

Twelve Monkeys (Terry Gilliam, 1995)

24 Hours in London (Alexander Finbow, 2000)

Twentyfourseven (Shane Meadows, 1997)

Twenty-One (Don Boyd, 1991)

Twin Town (Kevin Allen, 1997)

Two and Two Make Six (Freddie Francis, 1962)

2by4 (Jimmy Smallhorne, 1998)

Two Deaths (Nicolas Roeg, 1995)

200 Motels (Tony Palmer, visuals, 1971)

Two Left Feet (Roy Ward Baker, 1963)

Two Nudes Bathing (John Boorman, 1995)

2001: A Space Odyssey (Stanley Kubrick, 1968)

Two Thousand Women (Frank Launder, 1944)

U

Uncle, The (Desmond Davis, 1965)

Under Fire (Roger Spottiswoode, 1983)

Underground (Paul Spurrier, 1998)

Under One Roof (Lewis Gilbert, 1947)

Under the Skin (Carine Adler, 1997)

Underworld (Roger Christian, 1997)

Unman, Wittering and Zigo (John MacKenzie, 1971)

Up 'n' Under (John Godber, 1998)

Up the Creek (Val Guest, 1958)

Urban Ghost Story (Genevieve Jolliffe, 1998)

Used People (Beeban Kidron, 1992)

US Marshals (Stuart Baird, 1998)

V

Valiant, The (Roy Ward Baker, 1962)

Value for Money (Ken Annakin, 1955)

Vampira (Clive Donner, 1974)

Vampire Circus (Robert Young, 1972)

Vampire Happening (Freddie Francis, 1971)

Vampire Lovers, The (Roy Ward Baker, 1970)

Vampire's Kiss (Robert Bierman, 1989)

Van, The (Stephen Frears, 1996)

Vatel (Roland Joffé, 2000)

Vault of Horror (Roy Ward Baker, 1973)

Vengeance (Freddie Francis, 1962)

Venice/Venice (Henry Jaglom, 1992)

Venom (Piers Haggard, 1982)

Venus Peter (Ian Sellar, 1989)

Very Annie Mary (Sara Sugarman, 2001)

Very Important Person, A (Ken Annakin, 1961)

Vice Versa (Brian Gilbert, 1988)

Victory (Mark Peploe, 1995)

View to a Kill, A (John Glen, 1985)

Vigo – A Passion for Life (Julien Temple, 1999)

Villain (Michael Tuchner, 1971)

Violent Enemy, The (Don Sharp, 1968)

Virgin and The Gypsy, The (Christopher Miles, 1970)

Virtual Sexuality (Nick Hurran, 1999)

Visions of Eight (John Schlesinger, segment, 1973)

Vote for Huggett (Ken Annakin, 1949)

W

Waiting for Godot (Michael Lindsay-Hogg, 2001)

Waking Ned (Kirk Jones, 1998)

Walkabout (Nicolas Roeg, 1971)

Walker (Alex Cox, 1987)

War Party (Franc Roddam, 1989)

War Requiem (Derek Jarman, 1989)

War Zone, The (Tim Roth, 1999)

We Are the Lambeth Boys (Karel Reisz, 1958)

Weak and the Wicked, The (J. Lee Thompson, 1953)

Weaker Sex, The (Roy Ward Baker, 1948)

Weapon, The (Val Guest, 1957)

Weekend, The (Brian Skeet, 1999)

Welcome to Sarajevo (Michael Winterbottom, 1997)

We're No Angels (Neil Jordan, 1989)

West 11 (Michael Winner, 1963)

Wetherby (David Hare, 1985)

Whales of August, The (Lindsay Anderson, 1987)

What a Way to Go! (J. Lee Thompson, 1964)

Whatever Happened to Harold Smith? (Peter Hewitt, 1999)

What's Cooking? (Gurinder Chadha, 2000)

What's Love Got to Do With It (Brian Gibson, 1993)

What's New Pussycat (Clive Donner, 1965)

What Waits Below (Don Sharp, 1984)

What Where? (Damien O'Donnell, 2000)

When Brendan Met Trudy (Kieron J. Walsh, 2000)

When Dinosaurs Ruled the Earth (Val Guest, 1970)

When Saturday Comes (Maria Giese, 1996)

When the Sky Falls (John MacKenzie, 1999)

Where Angels Fear to Tread (Charles Sturridge, 1991)

Where the Heart Is (John Boorman, 1990)

Where the Money Is (Marek Kanievska, 2000)

Where the Spies Are (Val Guest, 1965)

Whisperers, The (Bryan Forbes, 1966)

Whistle Down the Wind (Bryan Forbes, 1961)

White Angel (Chris Jones, 1993)

White Buffalo, The (J. Lee Thompson, 1977)

White Bus, The (Lindsay Anderson, 1966)

White Mischief (Michael Radford, 1987)

White of the Eye (Donald Cammell, 1987)

White Squall (Ridley Scott, 1996)

Who? (Jack Gold, 1974)

Whole Nine Yards, The (Jonathan Lynn, 2000)

Who'll Stop the Rain (Karel Reisz, 1978)

Who Needs a Heart (John Akomfrah, 1991)

Whore (Ken Russell, 1991)

Why Not Stay for Breakfast? (Terry Marcel, 1979)

Wicked Lady, The (Michael Winner, 1983)

Wicker Man, The (Robin Hardy, 1973)

Widow's Peak (John Irvin, 1994)

Wild About Harry (Declan Lowney, 2000)

Wildcats of St. Trinian's, The (Frank Launder, 1980)

Wilde (Brian Gilbert, 1997)

Wild Party, The (James Ivory, 1975)

Wild Side (Donald Cammell, 2000)

Wild West (David Attwood, 1992)

William at the Circus (Val Guest, 1948)

Wilt (Michael Tuchner, 1989)

Wind in the Willows, The (Terry Jones, 1996)

Windom's Way (Ronald Neame, 1958)

Wings of the Dove, The (Iain Softley, 1997)

Winstanley (Kevin Brownlow, 1975)

Winter Guest, The (Alan Rickman, 1997)

Wish You Were Here (David Leland, 1987)

Wish You Were There (Lindsay Anderson, 1985)

Witchcraft (Don Sharp, 1964)

Witches, The (Nicolas Roeg, 1990)

Withnail and I (Bruce Robinson, 1987)

Wittgenstein (Derek Jarman, 1993)

Wolves of Willoughby Chase, The (Stuart Orme, 1988)

Woman in a Dressing Gown (J. Lee Thompson, 1957)

Women in Love (Ken Russell, 1969)

Women Talking Dirty (Coky Giedroyc, 1999)

Won Ton Ton, the Dog Who Saved Hollywood
(Michael Winner, 1976)

Wonderful Life (Sidney J. Furie, 1964)

Wonderland (Michael Winterbottom, 1999)

Words Upon the Window Pane (Mary McGuckian, 1994)

Work Is a Four Letter Word (Peter Hall, 1967)

World Apart, A (Chris Menges, 1988)

World Is Full of Married Men, The (Robert Young, 1979)

World is Not Enough, The (Michael Apted, 1999)

Wrong Box, The (Bryan Forbes, 1966)

Wrong Trousers, The (Nick Park, 1993)

Wuthering Heights (Peter Kosminsky, 1992)

Y

Yanks (John Schlesinger, 1979)

Year of the Comet (Peter Yates, 1992)

Yellow Balloon, The (J. Lee Thompson, 1953)

Yesterday's Enemy (Val Guest, 1959)

Yield to the Night (J. Lee Thompson, 1956)

Ymadawiad Arthur/Arthur's Departure (Marc Evans, 1994)

You Know What Sailors Are (Ken Annakin, 1954)

You, Me, and Marley (Richard Spence, 1992)

You Must Be Joking! (Michael Winner, 1965)

You Only Live Twice (Lewis Gilbert, 1967)

You're Dead (Andy Hurst, 1998)

Young Americans (Danny Cannon, 1993)

Young Ones, The (Sidney J. Furie, 1961)

Young Poisoner's Handbook, The (Benjamin Ross, 1995)

Young Soul Rebels (Isaac Julien, 1991)

Young Winston (Richard Attenborough, 1972)

Z

Zardoz (John Boorman, 1974)

Zed & Two Noughts, A (Peter Greenaway, 1985)

Zorro, the Gay Blade (Peter Medak, 1981)

THE WALLFLOWER CRITICAL GUIDE TO CONTEMPORARY NORTH AMERICAN DIRECTORS

Edited by Yoram Allon, Del Cullen and Hannah Patterson
Introduction by Nick James, Editor of *Sight and Sound*

The Wallflower Critical Guide to Contemporary North American Directors encompasses the careers of over 500 directors working in the United States and Canada today. In comprehensively covering a wide range of film-makers – from established luminaries such as Steven Spielberg, Martin Scorsese, James Cameron and Kathryn Bigelow, through independent mavericks like Quentin Tarantino, Hal Hartley, Jim Jarmusch and the Coen brothers, to innovative emerging talents including Spike Jonze, Todd Solondz, Kimberly Peirce, and David O. Russell – the evolving landscape of contemporary film-making is brought into sharp focus. For each director, the volume provides brief biographical material, a complete filmography, and critical analysis of indivdual works.

2000   548 pages   1-903364-09-4 £17.99 pbk
1-903364-10-8 £50.00 hbk

"Must buy. Threatens to become indispensable … the prose is clear and accessible."
Empire

"An excellent launch to the series and a real bargain for the quality … the judgements are informative, perceptive, and on the mark. Highly recommended for all film studies collections."
Library Journal

"Offers an extremely useful, incisive and lucid account of an extraordinary range of modern American film-makers."
Geoff Andrew, *Time Out*

"The entries are up-to-date, lively and informed: the *critical guide* promises to be an indispensible resource for all who love American cinema."
Professor Richard Allen, New York University

Yoram Allon is editorial director of Wallflower Press. Del Cullen is chief editor of Wallflower Press and is a novelist and screenwriter. Hannah Patterson is series editor of the *Wallflower Critical Guides* and a freelance film critic.

Further volumes in the series: *Contemporary Continental European Film Directors* and *Contemporary World Cinema Directors*

SHORT CUTS

The SHORT CUTS series is a comprehensive library of introductory texts covering the full spectrum of Film Studies, including genres, critical concepts, film histories/movements, and film technologies.

With concise discussion of contemporary issues within historical and cultural context and the extensive use of illustrative case studies, this list of study guides is perfectly suited to building an individually-styled library for all students and enthusiasts of cinema and popular culture.

The series will grow to over forty titles; listed here are the first waves of this ambitious attempt to systematically treat all the major areas of undergraduate Film Studies.

"Tailor-made for a modular approach to film studies ... an indispensable tool for both lecturers and students."

Professor Paul Willeman, University of Ulster

November 2001

128 pages

1-903364-18-3

£11.99 pbk

COSTUME AND CINEMA
Dress Codes in Popular Film

Sarah Street

Costume and Cinema presents an overview of the literature on film costume, together with a series of detailed case studies which highlight how costume is a key signifier in film texts. Sarah Street demonstrates how costume relates in fundamental ways to the study of film narrative and mise-en-scène, in some cases constituting a language of its own. In particular the book foregrounds the related issues of adaptation and embodiment in a variety of different genres and films including *The Talented Mr Ripley, Desperately Seeking Susan, Titanic* and *The Matrix*.

Sarah Street is Reader in Screen Studies at the University of Bristol, UK. She has written widely on many aspects British cinema.

"A valuable addition to the growing literature on film and costume ... engagingly written, offering a lucid introduction to the field."

Stella Bruzzi, Royal Holloway College, University of London

PSYCHOANALYSIS AND CINEMA
The Play of Shadows

Vicky Lebeau

Psychoanalysis and Cinema examines the long and uneven history of developments in modern art, science and technology that brought pychoanalysis and the cinema together towards the end of the nineteenth century. Vicky Lebeau explores the subsequent encounters between the two: the seductions of psychoanalysis and cinema as converging, though distinct, ways of talking about dream and desire, image and illusion, shock and sexuality. Beginning with Freud's encounter with the spectacle of hysteria on display in fin-de-siècle Paris, this study offers a detailed reading of the texts and concepts which generated the field of psychoanalytic film theory.

November 2001
144 pages
1-903364-19-1
£11.99 pbk

Vicky Lebeau is Senior Lecturer in English at the University of Sussex, UK. She has published widely on the topics of psychoanalysis and visual culture.

"A very lucid and subtle exploration of the reception of Freud's theories and their relation to psychoanalysis's contemporary developments – cinema and modernism. One of the best introductions to psychoanalytic film theory available."

Elizabeth Cowie, University of Kent

NEW CHINESE CINEMA
Challenging Representations

Sheila Cornelius with Ian Haydn Smith

New Chinese Cinema examines the 'search for roots' films that emerged from China in the aftermath of the Cultural Revolution. Sheila Cornelius contextualises the films of the so-called Fifth Generation directors who came to prominence in the 1980s and 1990s such as Chen Kaige, Zhang Yimou and Tian Zhuangzhuan. Including close analysis of such pivotal films as *Farewell My Concubine*, *Raise the Red Lantern* and *The Blue Kite*, the book also examines the rise of contemporary Sixth Generation underground directors whose themes embrace the disaffection of urban youth.

December 2001
144 pages
1-903364-13-2
£11.99 pbk

Sheila Cornelius is Visiting Lecturer in Chinese Cinema at Morley College, London. Ian Haydn Smith is a freelance film critic, and the author of *The Cinema of Ang Lee* (Wallflower Press, 2002).

"Very thorough in its coverage of the historical and cultural background to New Chinese Cinema ... clearly written and appropriately targeted at an undergraduate audience."

Leon Hunt, Brunel University

MISE-EN-SCÈNE
Film Style and Interpretation

John Gibbs

Mise-en-scène explores and elucidates constructions of this fundamental concept in thinking about film. In uncovering the history of mise-en-scène within film criticism, and through the detailed exploration of scenes from films as *Imitation of Life* and *Lone Star*, John Gibbs makes the case for the importance of a sensitive understanding of film style, and provides an introduction to the skills of close reading. This book thus celebrates film-making and film criticism alive to the creative possibilities of visual style.

John Gibbs is Lecturer in Film and Television Studies at The London Institute, UK.

December 2001
128 pages
1-903364-06-X
£11.99 pbk

"An immensely readable and sophisticated account of a topic of central importance to the serious study of films."

Deborah Thomas, University of Sunderland

SCENARIO
The Craft of Screenwriting

Tudor Gates

Scenario presents a system of logical analysis of the basic structures of successful screenplays, from initial plot-lines to realised scripts. All the essential building blocks are discussed in depth: the need for a strong premise; the roles of protagonist and antagonist; the orchestration of plot, characters and dialogue leading to a clear resolution. Written by a highly-experienced and successful screenwriter, this is a book which not only instructs first-time writers how to go about their work but also serves as a valuable check-list for established authors, and for actors, directors and teachers, in their task of deconstructing and assessing the value of the material placed before them.

Tudor Gates has written, directed and produced numerous teleplays, theatre plays, and feature films (including *Barbarella*). He has also served as Chairman of the National Film Development Fund and the Joint Board for Film Industry Training.

February 2002
144 pages
1-903364-26-4
£11.99 pbk

"This is an immensely readable introduction to the craft of screenwriting and is very helpful for budding screenwriters."

Alby James, Northern Film School

ANIMATION
Genre and Authorship

Paul Wells

Animation: Genre and Authorship is an introductory study which seeks to explore the distinctive language of animation, its production processes, and the particular questions about who makes it, under what conditions and with what purpose. Arguably, animation provides the greatest opportunity for distinctive models of 'auteurism' and revises generic categories. This is the first study to look specifically at these issues, and to challenge the prominence of live action movie-making as the first form of contemporary cinema and visual culture.

Professor Paul Wells is Head of the Media Portfolio at the University of Teesside, UK. He has published *The Horror Genre: From Beelzebub to Blair Witch* (Wallflower Press, 2000).

February 2002
144 pages
1-903364-20-8
£11.99 pbk

BRITISH SOCIAL REALISM
From Documentary to Brit Grit

Samantha Lay

British Social Realism details and explores the rich tradition of social realism in British cinema from its beginnings in the documentary movement of the 1930s to its more stylistically eclectic and generically-hybrid contemporary forms. Samantha Lay examines the movements, moments and cycles of British social realist texts through a detailed consideration of practice, politics, form, style and content, using case studies of key texts including *Listen To Britain, Saturday Night and Sunday Morning, Letter To Brezhnev*, and *Nil By Mouth*. The book considers the challenges for social realist film practice and production in Britain, now and in the future.

Samantha Lay is Lecturer in Film and Media Studies at West Herts College, UK.

May 2002
144 pages
1-903364-41-8
£11.99 pbk

WOMEN'S CINEMA
The Contested Screen

Alison Butler

W*omen's Cinema* provides an introduction to critical debate around women's film-making and relates those debates to a variety of cinematic practices. Taking her cue from the ground-breaking theories of Claire Johnston and the critical tradition she inspired Alison Butler argues that women's cinema is a minor cinema which exists inside other cinemas, inflecting and contesting the codes and systems of the major cinematic traditions from within. Using canonical directors and less established names as examples, ranging from Chantal Akerman to Moufida Tlatli, the book argues that women's cinema is unified in spite of its diversity by the ways in which it reworks cinematic conventions.

Alison Butler is Lecturer in Film Studies at the University of Reading, UK.

May 2001
144 pages
1-903364-27-2
£11.99 pbk

THE WESTERN GENRE
From Lordsburg to Big Whiskey

John Saunders

T*he Western Genre* offers close readings of the definitive American film movement as represented by such leading exponents as John Ford, Howard Hawks and Sam Peckinpah. In his consideration of such iconic motifs as the Outlaw Hero and the Lone Rider, John Saunders traces the development of perennial aspects of the genre, its continuity and, importantly, its change. Representations of morality and masculinity are also foregrounded in consideration of the genre's major stars John Wayne and Clint Eastwood, and the book includes a number of detailed analyses of such landmark films as *Shane, Rio Bravo, The Wild Bunch* and *Unforgiven.*

John Saunders is Senior Lecturer in film and literature at the University of Newcastle, UK.

2001
144 pages
1-903364-12-4
£11.99 pbk

"A clear exposition of the major thematic currents of the genre providing attentive and illuminating reading of major examples."

Ed Buscombe, Editor of the *BFI Companion to the Western*

DISASTER MOVIES
The Cinema of Catastrophe

Stephen Keane

Disaster Movies provides a comprehensive introduction to the history and development of the disaster genre. From 1950s sci-fi B-movies to high concept 1990s millennial movies, Stephen Keane looks at the ways in which the representation of disaster and its aftermath are borne out of both contextual considerations and the increasing commercial demands of contemporary Hollywood. Through detailed analyses of such films as *Airport, The Poseidon Adventure, Independence Day* and *Titanic*, the book explores the continual reworking of this, to-date, undervalued genre.

2001
144 pages
1-903364-05-1
£11.99 pbk

Stephen Keane is Lecturer in Film at Bretton Hall College, University of Leeds, UK.

"Providing detailed consideration of key movies within their social and cultural context, this concise introduction serves its purpose well and should prove a useful teaching tool."

Nick Roddick

READING HOLLYWOOD
Spaces and Meanings in American Film

Deborah Thomas

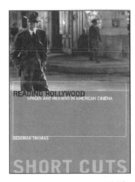

Reading Hollywood examines the treatment of space and narrative in a selection of classic films including *My Darling Clementine, Its a Wonderful Life* and *Vertigo*. Deborah Thomas employs a variety of arguments in exploring the reading of space and its meaning in Hollywood cinema, and film generally. Topics covered include the importance of space in defining genre (such as the necessity of an urban landscape for a gangster film to be a gangster film); the ambiguity of offscreen space and spectatorship (how an audience reads an unseen but inferred setting) and the use of spatially disruptive cinematic techniques such as flashback to construct meaning.

2001
144 pages
1-903364-01-9
£11.99 pbk

Deborah Thomas is Reader in Film Studies at the University of Sunderland, UK, and a member of the editorial board of *Movie*.

"Amongst the finest introductions to Hollywood in particular and film studies in general ... subtler, more complex, yet more readable than most of its rivals, many of which it will displace."

Professor Robin Wood

2000

144 pages

1·903364·04·3

£11.99 pbk

EARLY SOVIET CINEMA
Innovation, Ideology and Propaganda

David Gillespie

*E*arly Soviet Cinema examines the aesthetics of Soviet cinema during its golden age of the 1920s, against a background of cultural ferment and the construction of a new socialist society. Separate chapters are devoted to the work of Sergei Eisenstein, Lev Kuleshov Vsevolod Pudovkin, Dziga Vertov and Alexander Dovzhenko. David Gillespie places primary focus on the text, with analysis concentrating on the artistic qualities, rather than the political implications, of each film.

David Gillespie teaches Russian Language and Culture at the University of Bath, UK.

"An excellent book ... lively and informative. It fills a significant gap and deserves to be on reading lists wherever courses on Soviet cinema are run."

Graham Roberts, University of Surrey

2000

144 pages

1·903364·03·5

£11.99 pbk

SCIENCE FICTION CINEMA
From Outerspace to Cyberspace

Geoff King and Tanya Krzywinska

*F*rom lurid comic-book blockbusters to dark dystopian visions, science fiction is seen as both a powerful cultural barometer of our times and the product of particular industrial and commercial frameworks. The authors outline the major themes of the genre and explore issues such as the meaning of special effects and the influence of science fiction cinema on the entertainment media of the digital age. The book concludes with an extensive case-study of *Star Wars Episode I: The Phantom Menace*.

Both authors lecture in Film and Television Studies at Brunel University, London. Geoff King has written on contemporary Hollywood cinema and cultural studies. Tanya Krzywinska has written on explicit sex films and the cinema of the occult.

"The best overview of English-language science-fiction cinema published to date ... thorough, clearly written and full of excellent examples. Highly recommended."

Steve Neale, Sheffield Hallam University

THE STAR SYSTEM
Hollywood's Production of Popular Identities

Paul McDonald

The Star System looks at the development and changing organisation of the star system in the American film industry. Tracing the popularity of star performers from the early 'cinema of attractions' to the internet universe, Paul McDonald explores the ways in which Hollywood has made and sold its stars. Through focusing on particular historical periods, the key conditions influencing the star system in silent cinema, the studio era and the New Hollywood are discussed and illustrated by cases studies of Mary Pickford, Bette Davis, James Cagney, Julia Roberts, Tom Cruise, and Will Smith.

2000
144 pages
1-903364-02-7
£11.99 pbk

Paul McDonald is Senior Lecturer in Film and Television Studies at the University of Surrey, Roehampton, UK.

> "A very good introduction to the topic filling an existing gap in the needs of teachers and students of the subject."
>
> Roberta Pearson, University of Wales, Cardiff

THE HORROR GENRE
From Beelzebub to Blair Witch

Paul Wells

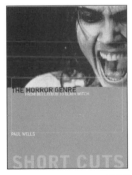

The Horror Genre is a comprehensive introduction to the history and key themes of the genre. The main issues and debates raised by horror, and the approaches and theories that have been applied to horror texts are all featured. In addressing the evolution of the horror film in social and historical context, Paul Wells explores how it has reflected and commented upon particular historical periods, and asks how it may respond to the new millennium by citing recent innovations in the genres development, such as the urban myth narrative underpinning *Candyman* and *The Blair Witch Project*.

2000
144 pages
1-903364-00-0
£11.99 pbk

Paul Wells is Head of the Media Portfolio at the University of Teesside, UK. He is the author of *Animation: Genre and Authorship* (Wallflower Press, 2002)

> "A valuable contribution to the body of teaching texts available ... a book for all undergraduates starting on the subject."
>
> Linda Ruth Williams, University of Southampton

DIRECTORS' CUTS

The DIRECTORS' CUTS series, parallel to the SHORT CUTS series, focuses on the work of many of the most significant contemporary international film-makers.

THE CINEMA OF EMIR KUSTURICA
Notes from the Underground

Goran Gocic

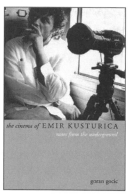

The Cinema of Emir Kusturica is the first book on the Sarajevan film-maker to be published in English. With seven highly acclaimed films to his credit, Kusturica is already established as one of the most important of contemporary film-makers, with each of his films winning prizes at the major festivals around the world. His films include *Underground, Arizona Dream, Black Cat, White Cat*, and most recently, *Super 8 Stories*. This ground-breaking study delves into diverse facets of Kusturicas work, much of which is passionately dedicated to the marginal and the outcast.

October 2001
192 pages
1-903364-14-0 £13.99 pbk
1-903364-16-7 £42.50 hbk

"This is a comprehensive and fascinating study of one of Europe's most important film directors. A sharp and perceptive monograph and long overdue as far as English-language film criticism is concerned: this is a must read."

John Orr, Edinburgh University

THE CINEMA OF KEN LOACH
Art in the Service of the People

Jacob Leigh

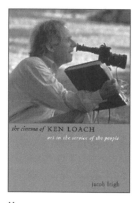

The Cinema of Ken Loach examines the linking of art and politics that distinguishes the work of this leading British film director. Loach's films manifest recurrent themes over a long period of working with various collaborators, yet his handling of those themes changes throughout his career. This book examines those changes as a way of reaching an understanding of Loach's style and meaning. It evaluates how Loach incorporates his political beliefs and those of his writers into his work. Each of the six chapters explores changes in his style by interpreting one or two of his works. The book augments the thematic interpretation with contextual information gleaned from original archive research and includes new interviews.

May 2002
192 pages
1-903364-31-0 £13.99 pbk
1-903364-32-9 £42.50 hbk

Jacob Leigh is Lecturer in Film Studies at Royal Holloway, University of London.

THE CINEMA OF WIM WENDERS
The Celluloid Highway

Alexander Graf

The Cinema of Wim Wenders is a new study of the films of this prominent German director, and penetrates the seductive sounds and images for which he is best known. The book analyses the individual films in the context of a preoccupation central to all of Wenders' work and writings: why modern cinema – a recording art, solely composed of sounds and images – has so naturally developed into a primarily narrative medium, a domain traditionally associated with words and sentences? With its greater emphasis on analysing the films themselves, this book identifies and critically elucidates Wenders' chief artistic motivation: that the act of seeing can constitute a creative act in its own right.

Alexander Graf lives in Berlin and works in film production. He has published widely on many aspects of European cinema.

May 2002
192 pages
1-903364-29-9 £13.99 pbk
1-903364-30-2 £42.50 hbk

THE CINEMA OF ROBERT LEPAGE
The Poetics of Memory

Aleksandar Dundjerovich

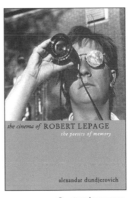

The Cinema of Robert Lepage is the first critical study of one of the most striking artists of Quebecois and Canadian independent filmmaking. The work examines Lepage's creative method of film-making in their cultural and social context and argues that his work cannot be seen separately from his artistic opus as a total author and multidisciplinary artist. Further this study demonstrates that like Jean Cocteau, Mike Leigh, and Alain Resnais, Lepage is a multi-faceted artist who works with a group of actors on very personal themes, building his films during months or years of a perpetual rehearsal process; thus it challenges the notions that Lepage be considered only in the terms of Quebecois film tradition

Aleksandar Dundjerovich is Lecturer in Theatre Studies and Multidisciplinary Performance at Liverpool Hope, University of Liverpool. He is also a professional theatre director who has staged numerous productions in Yugoslavia, the United Kingdom, Colombia and North America.

September 2002
192 pages
1-903364-33-7 £13.99 pbk
1-903364-34-5 £42.50 hbk